BIOGRAPHICAL MEMOIRS OF
FELLOWS OF THE BRITISH ACADEMY
XVI

Biographical Memoirs of Fellows of the British Academy
XVI

Published for THE BRITISH ACADEMY
by OXFORD UNIVERSITY PRESS

Oxford University Press, Great Clarendon Street, Oxford OX2 6DP

Articles © The British Academy, 2017
Database right The British Academy (maker)

First edition published 2017

These articles are licensed under a Creative Commons
Attribution-NonCommercial-NoDerivs 3.0 Unported License.
Enquiries concerning reproduction outside the scope of the above
should be sent to the Publications Department,
The British Academy, 10–11 Carlton House Terrace, London SW1Y 5AH,
or by email to pubs@britac.ac.uk

You must not circulate this book in any other binding or cover
and you must impose this same condition on any acquirer

British Library Cataloguing in Publication Data
Data available

Library of Congress Cataloging in Publication Data
Data available

ISBN 978-0-19-726622-9

Typeset by New Leaf Design, Scarborough, North Yorkshire
Printed in Great Britain by
Antony Rowe, Chippenham, Wiltshire

The Academy is grateful to Professor Ron Johnston, FBA
for his editorial work on this volume

This print publication reproduces articles that have been published on the British Academy website as open access PDF files. More information is available at www.britishacademy.ac.uk/memoirs

Articles published online may include colour versions of the portraits of Fellows and additional illustrations not printed here.

Contents

Ernst Badian W. V. HARRIS	3
Philip Walter Edwards GORDON CAMPBELL	21
Alan Geoffrey Hill STEPHEN GILL	43
Glyn William Humphreys JOHN DUNCAN	55
Oliver Nicholas Millar CHRISTOPHER WHITE	67
Marilyn Speers Butler NIGEL LEASK	85
Beatrice Eileen de Cardi HARRIET CRAWFORD	109
Paul Langford PAUL SLACK	121
Geoffrey Neil Leech GREG MYERS	147
Claus Adolf Moser DAVID BARTHOLOMEW	171
John David Yeadon Peel RICHARD FARDON	191
John Tiley CHANTAL STEBBINGS	219
Christopher Nugent Lawrence Brooke DAVID ABULAFIA, DAVID LUSCOMBE & HENRY MAYR-HARTING	239

Michael John Mustill STEWART BOYD	281
Robert Brian Tate BARRY TAYLOR & ALEJANDRO COROLEU	303
Tony James Wilkinson JOHN BINTLIFF	325
Stroud Francis Charles Milsom JOHN BAKER	333
David Russell Harris STEPHEN SHENNAN & HUGH CLOUT	363
Michael John Artis CHARLES GOODHART & MERVYN LEWIS	389
John Adney Emerton H. G. M. WILLIAMSON	417
Margaret Joy Gelling O. J. PADEL	443
John Rankine Goody CHRIS HANN	457
Frank Horace Hahn DAVID NEWBERY	485
Asa Briggs PAT THANE	529

ERNST BADIAN

Ernst Badian
1925–2011

THE ANCIENT HISTORIAN ERNST BADIAN was born in Vienna on 8 August 1925 to Josef Badian, a bank employee, and Salka née Horinger, and he died after a fall at his home in Quincy, Massachusetts, on 1 February 2011. He was an only child. The family was Jewish but not Zionist, and not strongly religious. Ernst became more observant in his later years, and received a Jewish funeral.

He witnessed his father being maltreated by Nazis on the occasion of the *Reichskristallnacht* in November 1938; Josef was imprisoned for a time at Dachau. Later, so it appears, two of Ernst's grandparents perished in the Holocaust, a fact that almost no professional colleague, I believe, ever heard of from Badian himself. Thanks in part, however, to the help of the young Karl Popper, who had moved to New Zealand from Vienna in 1937, Josef Badian and his family had by then migrated to New Zealand too, leaving through Genoa in April 1939.[1] This was the first of Ernst's two great strokes of good fortune.

His Viennese schooling evidently served Badian very well. In spite of knowing little English at first, he so much excelled at Christchurch Boys' High School that he earned a scholarship to Canterbury University College at the age of fifteen. There he took a BA in Classics (1944) and MAs in French and Latin (1945, 1946). After a year's teaching at Victoria University in Wellington he moved to Oxford (University College), where

---

[1] K. R. Popper, *Unended Quest: an Intellectual Autobiography* (La Salle, IL, 1976), p. 111, recalled that 'a committee in Christchurch was constituted to obtain permits for refugees to enter New Zealand; and some were rescued from concentration camps and from prison thanks to the energy of Dr. R. M. Campbell, of the New Zealand High Commission in London'.

he was tutored in ancient history by George Cawkwell—another New Zealander, as it happens—and completed Greats in two years, appearing in the first class in the honours list of 1950; he had also won the Chancellor's Prize for Latin Prose. The British School at Rome awarded him a scholarship for 1950–2.

In January 1950 Badian married Nathlie Ann Wimsett of Wellington, whom he had met at Canterbury some five years earlier; his second great stroke of good fortune. She was a Classics graduate and an accomplished violinist, who later earned a doctorate in special education and child psychology and had a fruitful career, including research, as a child psychologist. Together Ernst and Nathlie had two children, Hugh (b. 1953) and Rosemary (b. 1958); there are now seven grandchildren and twelve great-grandchildren.

*****

What led Badian into ancient and specifically Greek and Roman history is scarcely to be guessed, though a number of his experiences may have caused him to reflect about the construction and the durability or otherwise of empires. His school friend E. A. Judge, later a professor at Macquarie University, recalls the influence of L. G. Pocock, Professor of Classics at Canterbury and a specialist in the late Republic. Cawkwell's vigorous personality must also have had a considerable influence.

Clearly a third New Zealand scholar, Ronald Syme, who had become Camden Professor of Ancient History at Oxford in 1949, was a powerful inspiration; he suggested the subject of Badian's doctoral thesis and supervised it. Both Syme and Badian sought to unearth the power structures of Rome rather than meditate on its constitutional structure, and in consequence they both pursued lines of prosopographical research that had been opened up a generation earlier by Friedrich Münzer and a whole group of other German scholars.

By contrast, the British School at Rome, then directed by John Ward-Perkins, seems not to have had much impact on Badian. One of his first articles,[2] 'Notes on Roman Policy in Illyria (230–201 BC)', appeared in the

---

[2] There is no full bibliography in print, but see C. G. Thomas (ed.), *The Legacy of Ernst Badian* (Erie, PA, 2013), pp. 79–99, which, however, omits reviews, including the seven substantial essays that Badian contributed to the *New York Review of Books* between 1974 and 1982. Quite apart from the *NYRB*, some of the reviews that are omitted are variously interesting, for example the withering critique of J. Carcopino, *Profils des conquérants*, in *Journal of Roman Studies*, 53 (1963), 181, in which he noticeably declines to mention that scholar's Vichy past. It is to be hoped that one of his former students will publish a full bibliography.

1952 volume of the school's *Papers*, but Badian neither then nor later showed any interest in Roman material culture or Ward-Perkins' ways of studying it. It is striking that when he came to publish his doctoral thesis, under the title *Foreign Clientelae, 264–70 BC* (Oxford, 1958), he wrote that 'this book is above all an Oxford work: almost every idea in it was formed in Oxford and almost every word in it was written there',[3] even though he had spent two of his six years of thesis preparation in Rome, followed by two years at the University of Sheffield (1952–4) as an assistant lecturer and then by two more years at Durham, where he served as a lecturer from 1954 to 1965.

Foreign Clientelae was a highly impressive work for a young scholar. Its title gives little idea of its sweep, or of its ambitious attempt to link the structure of Rome's 'foreign policy' to the structures of internal politics. Self-confident and well informed, it rapidly became obligatory reading for all Roman historians. It maintained an overarching thesis of considerable interest, to the effect that Roman senators imagined Rome's relationship with other states on the pattern of a Roman patron's relationship with his *clientes*. This was an attempt to 'throw some light on the importance for Roman history of a specifically Roman category of thought' (p. 14).[4] What seems questionable about the book in retrospect is that it provides an incoherent account of the attitude of the Roman senatorial class towards territorial expansion—sometimes they engage in 'conscious imperialism', more often they showed 'no desire for expansion'. But it contained so much else, and its account of Roman politics from the Gracchi to Sulla was regarded for some years as the best available.

This dissonance about imperialism can be understood from its context. The historiography of Roman republican imperialism that prevailed in Britain in the 1950s was chiefly the work of M. Holleaux, H. H. Scullard and A. N. Sherwin-White, which sometimes reached hallucinatory levels of exculpation. And these were of course the years when the British Empire was rapidly disintegrating (Suez, 1956; 'the wind of change', 1960). What was surprising about the Roman imperialism of *Foreign Clientelae* was not that it so often softened Roman actions (the military conquest of peninsular Italy produced a 'protectorate', and so on) but that its author occasionally saw through the then-conventional tale.

---

[3] E. Badian, *Foreign Clientelae* (Oxford, 1958), p. viii. The oddity of this assertion is heightened by the fact that the book was dedicated, with gratitude, to G. F. Tibiletti and to the author's 'other Italian friends and colleagues'.

[4] This thesis was effectively criticised by J. Bleicken in a review in *Der Gnomon*, 36 (1964), 176–87, in which, however, he recognised the book's many merits.

Badian's other most notable scholarly achievement in these years was the first—and most important—of his many articles about Alexander of Macedon, 'Alexander the Great and the unity of mankind'.[5] (It was, incidentally, a salutary doctrine of Badian's that a historian of the classical world should eventually work on both Greek and Roman history.) In twenty pages he overturned a central claim of the chief anglophone authority of the time on Alexander, Sir W. W. Tarn,[6] according to whom Alexander hoped and planned that the numerous peoples he had conquered would become 'partners in the realm rather than subjects'. It would not be an exaggeration to say that this article of Badian's was the beginning of the end of the idealised Alexander who had beguiled many others besides Tarn; it helped to establish the ultra-violent, brutal and paranoid Alexander who is now familiar to all interested scholars.

Badian continued to work on topics connected with Alexander: his posthumous *Collected Papers on Alexander the Great* (London, 2012), which was his other big book besides *Foreign Clientelae*, contained twenty-seven items, while omitting a number of others. He is thought by some to have aimed at a large-scale work about the Macedonian conqueror, who was certainly a lifelong obsession, but he told his friends, by 1971 at least, that he had no such intention. The nearest thing to a synthesis is his admirably realistic chapter 'Alexander in Iran' in *The Cambridge History of Iran*, written in the early 1970s though not published until 1985.[7] Even though he more or less detested most other people's attempts at big books about Alexander, in particular Robin Lane Fox's *Alexander the Great* (London, 1973), they did not provoke him to write one of his own. There is more to say about this.

Meanwhile, there had been both difficulties and recognition. In 1962–3 Badian was convinced that his health was seriously compromised. The nature of this illness is obscure, and doctors could never apparently diagnose anything specific, but nonetheless Badian's friends took the matter seriously and P. A. Brunt suggested the publication of a volume of his *opera minora*, which came out as *Studies in Greek and Roman History*

---

[5] E. Badian, 'Alexander the Great and the unity of mankind', *Historia*, 7 (1958), 425–44, reprinted in his *Collected Papers on Alexander the Great* (London, 2012). He also assailed Tarn in 'The eunuch Bagoas: a study in method', *Classical Quarterly*, 8 (1958), 144–57 (reprinted in *Collected Papers*), while characterising Tarn's major book as a 'masterly work'.

[6] Tarn died at the age of eighty-eight, a few months before Badian's article was published.

[7] E. Badian, 'Alexander in Iran', in I. Gershevitch (ed.), *The Cambridge History of Iran*, vol. 2 (Cambridge, 1985), pp. 420–501, was not included in *Collected Papers*. The chapter extends far beyond Iran in the narrow sense. It also benefited from the author's tour of Iran and Afghanistan in the winter of 1971–2.

(Oxford, 1964). Quite unusual for a scholar of thirty-nine! The following year, while still a lecturer at Durham, he was elected to the Academy—one of the youngest Fellows in many a season (even Ronald Syme had been a year older when he was elected)—and was appointed to the Chair of Ancient History at Leeds.

In 1965 Badian went to South Africa to lecture, and to explore local conditions. The great majority of educated Britons believed by that date that they knew quite enough about apartheid without inspecting its operations at first hand, but a visit was not of course an endorsement (the ancient historian Russell Meiggs also intended to visit that year, though ill health prevented him). All the signs, however, say that Badian was opposed to any dramatic improvement in the rights of the country's black inhabitants. The year 1965 was also that of a much contested political event—the unilateral declaration of independence (UDI) by the white settlers in Southern Rhodesia (Zimbabwe). Britain was unwilling to grant independence without a plan that would lead to majority rule. Some of Badian's new colleagues at Leeds were surprised—surprisingly—to see a poster on his office door that read 'Recognize Rhodesia Now!'.

It was in Pretoria in 1965 that Badian gave the lectures that became his brief book *Roman Imperialism in the Late Republic* (Oxford, first edition, 1967; revised edition, 1968). I may not be thought the ideal person to comment on that production because it struck me from the first as superficial and doctrinaire, with the consequence that I attempted to negate some of its central contentions—including its claim that the Roman imperialists of the second century BC had no 'economic motives'—first in an article and later in more detail in several chapters of a book. *Roman Imperialism* contains in fact a fair amount of good sense, and much of the time it represents a further very definite retreat from the doctrines of Holleaux, Scullard and Sherwin-White. But there was too much half-voluntary misuse of language, as when the author conspicuously maintains, with no good evidence, that the mid-republican Senate regularly 'reject[ed] opportunities for the extension of power' (p. 1: what he meant was that it declined opportunities for outright annexation, opportunities that in my view are mostly modern illusions). But now he was certainly much more inclined to see ruthless warmongering for what it was, especially when it was the work of his second—and arguably more complex—bête noire, Julius Caesar, who was in his opinion 'the greatest brigand of them all'.

Then there was Badian's phobia of the moderate left, not to mention the far left, which comes out in a somewhat absurd way when he speaks in this book of other scholars of the time as 'a generation nourished on Marx': there was of course, as of 1968, no such generation of ancient historians anywhere in the English-speaking world. And Badian's anti-Marxist vehemence prevented him from seeing that economic motives quite different in kind from those whose existence he attempted to disprove were real and important forces in republican Rome. It also led to the radically limiting, yet carefully hedged, final sentence of the book: 'The study of the Roman Republic—and that of the Empire to a considerable degree—is basically the study, not of its economic development, or of its masses, or even of great individuals: it is chiefly the study of its ruling class.' This was inherited from Ronald Syme, and apparently it was a comforting vision. It accompanied his obsessive idea that reformers of all kinds were misguided and extremely dangerous. From Tiberius Gracchus through Sulla (some reformer!) to Julius Caesar and Lyndon Johnson, they did nothing but harm.

The Badians had first visited the United States in 1960 or 1961 and had found it to their liking. The offer of a professorship at the State University of New York at Buffalo in 1969 was accepted with alacrity, partly it seems because of the existence in Buffalo of a school that the Badians thought suitable for their gifted daughter Rosemary. Badian's friends were surprised that he agreed to live so far from a first-rate library, but it was a short stay: two years later, thanks in good part to Glen Bowersock and Bernard Bailyn, he was invited to move to the Harvard History Department, where he stayed until his retirement, as John Moors Cabot Professor of History, in 1998. (Early in his Harvard period he was also given a courtesy appointment in the Classics Department, which he found more congenial.) There he trained a number of ancient history scholars, but not as many as might have been expected; his own view was that he was more demanding than the professors in other places such as Columbia and Yale, and he may have been right.

Throughout the rest of his career Badian complained about Harvard, and he would probably have moved to Cornell in 1974 if Cornell had agreed to find a position for Nathlie. In the mid-1970s he apparently thought of returning to Buffalo. Eventually he came to blame Harvard for what he perceived, by 1986 at the latest, as his 'ruin' as a scholar.[8] Yet it remains unclear why he so much professed to hate the place. Was it simply because in a large group of other established scholars who gave no primacy

---

[8] 'Harvard, which I detest and which has ruined me as a scholar' (letter to Charles Garton, 4 January 1986).

to the Greeks and Romans he inevitably counted for less than he had at Leeds and Buffalo? There were indeed objective frustrations, but outsiders found it hard to believe that Harvard was any more annoying—or less stimulating—than any other sharp-edged first-rank American university. An excellent library, outstanding students, ample secretarial help, no huge administrative burden, plenty of interesting visitors—this combination never staunched his unceasing complaints.

The 1970s were full of projects, some of which turned out well, others less so. Lectures delivered at the University of Otago resulted in another fairly short book *Publicans and Sinners: Private Enterprise in the Service of the Roman Republic*,[9] in which the political message indicated by the subtitle interferes to no more than a moderate degree with his scholarly history of the republican *publicani*.

Badian was himself a man of enterprise in this period. He played a very important role in bringing into being North America's Association of Ancient Historians, organising the meeting at Harvard in 1974 at which it was formally constituted after a period of informal meetings. He was never its president and it passed into other hands. The Association is alive and well.

But he began to spend too much time on editorial projects that did not allow him to develop much as a historian. In the late 1960s he began a prolonged attempt to publish in translation a collection of the *kleine Schriften* of Friedrich Münzer, which was at best a quixotic enterprise. Much hard work was compounded by the decision to list all Münzer's prosopographical contributions to Pauly-Wissowa's monumental encyclopedia, which are said to number more than 5,000. The book was eventually completed but no one would publish it.[10] Then, starting in 1973, Badian also undertook the republication of the extensive minor works of Ronald Syme, a worthwhile project that led in the end to a permanent cooling of the relationship between the older man and the younger. The problem was ostensibly the index of persons, necessarily quite a long one in the work of a prosopographical scholar. It did not help that Badian employed someone else to do the work, or that he took it upon himself to bring Syme's footnotes up to date (nowadays this would be regarded as the author's job). The Clarendon Press waited more than six years for this

---

[9] E. Badian, *Publicans and Sinners: Private Enterprise in the Service of the Roman Republic* (Oxford, 1972).
[10] Eventually Münzer's collected papers were edited, in the original, by M. Haake and A. C. Harders (eds.), *Kleine Schriften: Friedrich Münzer* (Stuttgart, 2012).

index, and finally printed the first two volumes of *Roman Papers* without it.[11] A. R. Birley fortunately became the editor of the remaining volumes, and in twenty months completed Volume III with a detailed index of all the first three volumes. The project had consumed a huge amount of Badian's time, not to mention the goodwill of Syme and others.

Starting in 1976, supported by a small but distinguished editorial board, he began to publish the *American Journal of Ancient History* (*AJAH*). This he continued to manage for many years. At first it was reasonably successful, and it seemed to disprove the opinion of those who supposed that there was no need of a new journal of this description. It was after all true and regrettable that there was no journal devoted to ancient history in the English-speaking world, while such journals existed in France, Germany and Italy. The ill effects of this lack live on. After about five years, however, Badian's journal began to fall behind its calendar date, and then it fell far behind—the 1984 issues came out in 1990 and so on. The number of publishable submissions declined. The contrast with the later history of the successful *Journal of Roman Archaeology* is instructive. Such an enterprise probably has to have real institutional support, which the *AJAH* never had. And the ideal editor of a new journal needs to be a person of tact, capable of dealing effectively with printers as well as professors; it probably helps if he or she is not associated with extreme or dogmatic views of any kind. And in modern times few scholars have edited journals for long periods and simultaneously brought large research projects to fruition: everyone knows that it is a hugely time-consuming activity. (John Ward-Perkins, as it happens, was one of those who managed both challenges at once for a long period.) Badian's *AJAH* eventually ceased publication after fifteen volumes, a sad conclusion which, however, allowed him much more time for his own work.

Also in 1976 Badian gave the Sather Lectures at Berkeley, a noteworthy honour that usually leads to a book published by the University of California Press. Badian wanted to lecture about Roman provincial administration but also wanted to publish his book on that subject with another publisher. Finding that he could not escape his obligation to the California Press, he decided at the last minute to lecture at Berkeley on 'The Freedom of the Greeks', a huge and difficult topic. A similar subject had previously frustrated Arnaldo Momigliano, and, sure enough, Badian never succeeded in turning his six lectures into a book (by the mid-1990s

---

[11] Ronald Syme, *Roman Papers I–II* (ed. E. Badian) (Oxford, 1979).

the project was no longer even mentioned). The provincial administration book was never completed either.

The history of scholarship also attracted Badian's attention in the late 1970s. If there was a large project involved I have not been able to discover it, but a good deal of work went into studying both Gibbon and Barthold Georg Niebuhr. The work on Gibbon resulted in two solid articles, both well informed and interestingly free from the customary adulation.[12]

That there was indeed a certain scholarly trailing off would be hard to deny. Caution is necessary, since it is after all every scholar's right to decide what to work on, and many of us have had the experience of being told by wiser persons that we were studying the wrong thing, only to be more or less vindicated later. Badian regularly produced sixty or seventy pages of learned articles every year for many years, but intellectually he ran into the doldrums—as he seems to have felt himself. His not completing the larger projects that he started (the Martin Lectures that he delivered at Oberlin in 1979 on the subject of Demosthenes went unpublished like the Sather Lectures, and in this case the topic seemed quite manageable) was an unhealthy sign. By the early 1980s his work consisted mostly of minor questions, expertly handled—and he clearly knew that.

Some have suggested that this trailing off was due to perfectionism, others that it was simply the consequence of spending too much time on the *AJAH* and on helping other scholars with their manuscripts. And it is true that very many young scholars who were not even Badian's pupils benefited considerably from his detailed critiques (he expected gratitude, not unreasonably). He really went to extraordinary lengths in this respect, and he was repaid with a sizeable Festschrift in 1996.[13] But neither perfectionism nor voluntary distraction is a wholly satisfying explanation. Perhaps fortune had been a little too kind a little too quickly, but that does not provide a neat psychological explanation. Badian was not in any case one of those Britons who were elected to Oxbridge fellowships on the basis of promise rather than achievement.[14]

Badian did not take any part in the opening up of ancient history that gathered strength in the late 1960s and early 1970s under the initial impact

---

[12] E. Badian, 'Gibbon on War', in P. Ducrey (ed.), *Gibbon et Rome à la lumière de l'historiographie moderne* (Geneva, 1977), pp. 103–10; E. Badian, 'Imposing Gibbon', *New York Review of Books* (13 October 1977).

[13] R. W. Wallace and E. M. Harris (eds.), *Transitions to Empire: Essays in Greco-Roman History, 360–146 B.C., in Honor of E. Badian* (Norman, OK, 1996).

[14] In fact he was passed over at Magdalen in 1958 in favour of a scholar who turned out to be something of a disappointment.

of scholars as diverse as Peter Brunt, Moses Finley, Keith Hopkins and Peter Brown. A vast expansion in the subject matter of the ancient historian made demographic and economic history, social history and slavery, gender history and sexuality, ethnicity and identity history and visual commemoration into topics as worthy of a scholar's attention as politics and warfare—topics which were themselves beginning to be looked at in new ways—if not more so. Badian expressed interest in Keith Hopkins' work on slavery and on demography and added a demographic detail of his own, but such work provoked no emulation.[15]

The scholar whom Badian denounced most violently in the 1970s and 1980s, to anyone who would listen, was Peter Brunt (the latter's kindness during Badian's illness prevented this viewpoint from appearing in print), for the fairly obvious though not explicit reason that it was Brunt who, more than anyone, brought to an end the obsession of anglophone Romanists with prosopography, and by means of articles and his book *Italian Manpower 225B.C.–A.D.14* (Oxford, 1971) showed the way to a new and broader history of the Roman Republic. The resentment was no doubt all the greater because in 1971 Brunt was elected to the Camden chair in succession to Syme. This is not a simple matter, for Badian was not entirely opposed to the new social history, as his relatively tolerant attitude towards the work of Hopkins demonstrates (it probably helped that the latter was considerably younger). In my view Badian was much impeded by the notion that the boundaries between fields were very hard to cross, so that sociology and anthropology, for example, were far away indeed from Greek and Roman history. This was an attitude that was fairly widespread in American Classics departments, and even in History departments, in the 1970s.

In this intellectually conservative context it is intriguing to reread Badian's lengthy review of Geoffrey de Ste. Croix's well-known Marxist summa *The Class Struggle in the Ancient Greek World* (1981).[16] The review appears to be the work of an 'admiring dissident', in the words of Robert Parker. It predicted that 'the writing of ancient history, at least in English, will never be quite the same again', not a particularly fortunate prophecy. The reviewer claimed to recognise de Ste. Croix for what he in fact was, a

---

[15] Compare his long review of Hopkins' *Conquerors and Slaves* in E. Badian, 'Figuring out Roman slavery', *Journal of Roman Studies*, 72 (1982), 164–9; 'mixed', as its author says. The pertinent detail concerns the likely sex ratio in a frontier or colonial population.
[16] E. Badian, 'Marx in the Agora', *New York Review of Books* (2 December 1982). For Robert Parker's comments see R. Parker, 'Geoffrey Ernest Maurice de Ste. Croix, 1910–2000', *Proceedings of the British Academy*, 111 (2001), pp. 473–4.

man of profound learning and integrity; and no reader, he said, could fail to feel the latter's passionate hatred of injustice. What is discordant about this is that anyone minimally acquainted with Badian knew—and his private letters confirm—that he violently disapproved of de Ste. Croix's scholarship and politics alike. The best interpretation seems to be that Badian thought that if he seemed to dilute his hostility towards *The Class Struggle* his disagreement would be all the more effective; he may also have thought that if he could disprove the central contentions of the most scholarly of all Marxist historians of antiquity—a title that de Ste. Croix certainly deserved as far as the English-speaking world was concerned—he would have no need to bother with the rest.

But why did Badian consider that he had been 'ruined' as a scholar by the mid-1980s? He continued to produce learned articles in his old manner. Was it simply because so many years had passed since the publication of his last book and no book of his was anywhere near completion? Some people thought that such an abrasive critic should have the nerve to set out his own views for others to assess. It should have been easy for him to finish his book on Demosthenes. I suppose that Badian very much wanted to be at the centre of attention within his own *Gebiet*. But the centre was steadily moving away from him, and he was too informed and too acute to be unaware of the fact. Blaming others (Harvard in particular) made it all the more difficult to get away from the critical mode and return to the constructive mode.

Not that he was ever anything less than a hard worker. Being always concerned that inexpert readers would have precise facts at their disposal, he reserved time for works of reference, and in particular for the *Oxford Classical Dictionary*. The huge improvement in the latter between its second edition (1970) and its fourth (2011) was as much due to him as to anyone else except the actual editors of the third and fourth editions. The recent proliferation of inaccurate works of reference makes this work all the more valuable.

Two more collections of previously published essays were to come: *From Plataea to Potidaea: Studies in the History and Historiography of the Pentecontaetia* (Baltimore, MD, and London, 1993), and the posthumous book about Alexander. *From Plataea to Potidaea* was Badian's considered contribution to the modern refighting of the Peloponnesian War (or more accurately to the assigning of war guilt). Left-leaning historians such as de Ste. Croix have always tended to blame authoritarian Sparta for the outbreak of the war, making ample use of Thucydides. That was not Badian's view. But Thucydides' reputation as a disinterested objective historian had long been in trouble, thanks to de Ste. Croix himself, to Robert Connor, Virginia Hunter and others. Badian brought his full battery of critical artillery into this battle. He critiqued the arguments of others with gusto, but he could not write the history of the Athenian Empire. Philip Stadter's judgement of this book was precise: 'B.'s prosecutorial rhetoric creates a Thucydides who is in the end a very simple writer, deceptive and artistic (a negative word), but easily caught out by the perceptive reader. Not everyone has [found] or will find him so transparent.'[17]

Another paradox concerns the Austrian scholar Fritz Schachermeyr (1895–1987), who was best known to scholars for his writings about Alexander of Macedon, especially his book of 1949, which attempts, not very successfully, to avoid the sort of hero worship that Badian later deplored. Schachermeyr was a productive scholar in his day but Badian was undoubtedly unique in thinking that he was 'one of the towering figures in our discipline in this century, who need not fear comparison with any other who might be named'.[18] What was always known about Schachermeyr, however, was his fervent support for Nazism: he was quite openly an energetic member of Hitler's ideological army. How we should treat the scholarly work of people who were complicit in the Nazi regime and in the Holocaust is of course a familiar question. Many would presumably say that we should take the work of such scholars for what it is worth, ignoring their political and moral acts. But it is another matter entirely to go out of one's way to commemorate and heroise such an individual.[19] Badian in fact befriended Schachermeyr in 1975.[20] He wrote to Peter Brunt that Schachermeyr had been 'the historical theoretician of the [Nazi] movement'; 'one cannot forget ... but one ought to forgive'.[21] It

---

[17] P. A. Stadter, 'Badian on Thucydides', *Classical Review*, 44 (1994), 338.

[18] 'Editor's Introduction', *American Journal of Ancient History*, 13 (1988) [1996], 1. A. B. Bosworth's sober assessment, in the same volume, of Schachermeyr's work on Alexander does nothing to justify Badian's assessment. The point of departure for any study of Schachermeyr is the massive biography by M. Pesditschek, *Barbar, Kreter, Arier: Leben und Werk des Althistorikers Fritz Schachermeyr* (Saarbrücken, 2009); cf. M. Willing, 'Konsequente "geistige Durchordnung". Fritz Schachermeyr, der Nationalsozialismus und die alte Geschichte', *Das Altertum*, 58 (2013), 201–36.

[19] It is to be regretted that Badian printed in the *AJAH* a thoroughly bowdlerised version of Schachermeyr's bibliography (see Willing, 'Konsequente', 227; and G. Dobesch, 'Schriftenverzeichnis', *American Journal of Ancient History*, 13 (1988), 79–91).

[20] On their first meeting Badian found Schachermeyr 'a delightful Austrian gentleman... It is impossible not to forgive him his murky past and to be very fond of him' (to Zvi Yavetz, 9 September 1975).

[21] To Peter Brunt, 15 February 1979. It is evident from Badian's paper 'Some recent interpretations of Alexander', *Entretiens* [de la Fondation Hardt] *sur l'antiquité classique*, 22 (1976), 279–303,

remains very difficult to explain his heroisation of Schachermeyr in a satisfactory fashion. He repeatedly referred to him as a 'genius', without explanation, incidentally setting him above Syme.²²

It is evident that in his old age Badian felt some nostalgia for Austria, and in 1999 he accepted the Österreichische Ehrenkreuz für Wissenschaft und Kunst (as did Antony Raubitschek and Erich Gruen). This nostalgia may have dimmed his perception of the Austrian scholar's disgraceful record. It is also clear from Badian's correspondence that by 1987 his paranoia about Marxists had reached the point that he was willing to find allies anywhere.²³ But that does not resolve the strangeness.

Schachermeyr takes us back to Alexander, who inspired all of Badian's better work in his old age. The liveliest of these essays is probably 'Conspiracies' (2000), where he puts the various conspiracies by and against Alexander into a broader historical context and makes use of his lengthy experience with the sources (while also finding I. F. Stone guilty of 'treason').²⁴ But the central problem of Alexander studies, as Badian often stated, is precisely the weakness of the sources, which make any kind of psychological analysis hypothetical. Yet no modern book about that extraordinary figure can possibly do without a certain minimum of psychological analysis, and it is scarcely sufficient to conclude that he was 'a mystic in his ultimate motivation'.²⁵

*****

Badian always had a circle of devoted academic friends, some of whom treated him as a rather fearsome kind of mascot, instantly recognisable by his small stature and his self-consciously Trotsky-like beard. But many scholars of various nationalities who encountered him found him ill-mannered and inconsiderate (anecdotes proliferated). He would help the young, but there were not many contemporaries or rivals with whom he succeeded in remaining on amicable terms. It is not the role of a British

---

esp. 282–6, that he took Schachermeyr's disowning of his racial views at the end of the Second World War in the most naïve possible way.

[22] To Konrad Kinzl, 11 January 1988.

[23] 'Some historian in a very distant future will no doubt [illegible] the penetration of American universities by Marxism and the collaboration of academics with a (future) Marxist regime here. There are some very interesting articles in some of the right-wing magazines I occasionally read, with ample documentation' (to Gerhard Wirth, 3 February 1987).

[24] E. Badian, 'Conspiracies', in A. B. Bosworth and E. J. Bayham (eds.), *Alexander the Great in Fact and Fiction* (Oxford, 2000), pp. 50–95, reprinted in *Collected Papers*, pp. 420–56.

[25] Badian, 'Alexander in Iran', p. 473.

Academy memoirist to issue judgements about the subject's personality, especially when the memoirist was not an intimate acquaintance of the person being commemorated. But it should be said that Badian's virtues and vices both made his life more difficult. He spent a generous and inordinate amount of time advising others, quite apart from his professorial responsibilities, both about their manuscripts and their lives, but in the end it was to the detriment of his own work.

By the time he was thirty-two, Ernst Badian had written two of the most important ancient historical works of the 1950s (*Foreign Clientelae* and 'Alexander the Great and the unity of mankind'), but although he continued to be a consistently productive and precise scholar into his old age he never equalled those achievements again, which was and is a cause of some surprise. He helped to create important new frameworks for the discipline of ancient history in the United States, first as co-founder of the Association of Ancient Historians, a little latter as founder and first editor of the *American Journal of Ancient History* (1976), yet—somewhat paradoxically— his relationships with his colleagues were often unusually difficult.

Ernst Badian did not in truth fulfil all his potential as a scholar. He continued to publish, but did not complete major projects that arose out of his early work, nor did he, over a period of forty more years of active scholarly life, branch out into any of the more or less adventurous directions that ancient history had begun to explore. Even within his existing expertise one might have hoped for so much more. Yet he was an exceptionally hard-working scholar, with a remarkable knowledge of Roman republican institutions and an unrivalled knowledge of Alexander of Macedon.

The most marked of his eccentricities was his passion for parrots, part of a larger interest in the animal kingdom which, according to Carol Thomas, led him to many a zoo. At one point there were as many as seven parrots in residence; whether their claws were as sharp as their master's is not recorded.

Ernst Badian was elected a Fellow of the American Academy of Arts and Sciences in 1974, he was a Member of the Institute for Advanced Study in 1980–1 and 1992–3, he was awarded a Guggenheim Fellowship in 1984, and he was a Fellow at the National Humanities Center in 1988–9.

W. V. HARRIS
Fellow of the Academy

Note. I am deeply indebted to Dr Nathlie Badian for answering my numerous questions. Professor Corey Brennan (Rutgers University), Ernst Badian's literary executor, generously gave me access to both his own memories of Badian and the voluminous archive of letters written by Badian that are now in his possession. In addition I am very grateful indeed for information provided by Anthony Birley, Glen Bowersock, Stanley Burstein, Erich Gruen, Judith Hallett, James Hankins, Simon Hornblower, Christopher Jones, E. A. Judge, Jerzy Linderski, Richard Thomas, Robert Wallace and Peter Wiseman, and for editorial suggestions made by Christopher Carey. But all judgemental statements are strictly my own.

PHILIP WALTER EDWARDS

Philip Walter Edwards
1923–2015

PHILIP EDWARDS WAS BORN ON 7 February 1923 in Barrow-in-Furness. His father's family came from North Wales, his mother's from Cheshire. His father's family were not well off, but they were 'church' rather than 'chapel' and strong supporters of the Conservative Party. After distinguished service in the First World War (when he won the Military Cross), Philip's father decided to make politics his profession, and became a Conservative Party agent, initially in the north-west of England. He was promoted frequently, and so moved regularly. Philip was born during a short sojourn in Barrow. In the late 1920s, when young Philip was living with his parents in Bristol, Neville Chamberlain recruited Philip's father to run the Conservative Party in Birmingham. By this time Philip's father was moving in distinguished circles, but struggled on a modest income to maintain his social position, which entailed private schools for a large family, a car and an enormous wardrobe.

In 1934 Philip passed the entrance examination to secure admission to King Edward VI High School in Birmingham. As his early education had equipped him with a competence in Latin, French and algebra, Philip initially felt superior to the state-school boys who had won free places and had to learn these subjects from scratch. In Philip's own account, he insists that the state-school boys quickly overtook him in every subject except English and every sport except rugby, and that the experience was a lesson in humility. In the School Certificate Examination (taken at the age of sixteen), Philip failed the arithmetic examination.

Philip's father was expecting him to leave school at sixteen and become a useful citizen. Philip's uncertainty about what that might entail persuaded his father to allow him to stay on for the Upper Sixth year. This was, however, the summer of 1939, and when war was declared Philip took the decision to leave school. He had become very political, but with convictions that had nothing in common with his father's, and he was idealistically committed to taking part in the war against Fascism. In the event, none of the services wanted to enlist a boy of sixteen and a half, and no bombs fell. One of Philip's friends had declined a place at Oxford and instead entered Birmingham University in order to make a start on a degree course before being called up. The modest financial circumstances of Philip's family meant that Oxford was beyond his financial reach, so late in the term his father gave him permission to follow his friend to Birmingham University. He was admitted, under age, by a registrar who was a family friend, and who did not expect urban universities to survive beyond Christmas. As an undergraduate Philip attended the lectures of A. M. D. Hughes, who retired as Philip arrived but continued to teach. Hughes' lecturing style was oratorical and old-fashioned, redolent of the Welsh preaching tradition. Philip's lecturing style seems to have been moulded by the experience of listening to Hughes. Sixty years later Philip was able to acknowledge his debt to Hughes when he gave the third of the A. M. D. Hughes Memorial Lectures in 2003.

At the end of his course Philip was granted a viva, but was not awarded a first. There was, however, a consolation prize: one of the examiners, Ernest de Sélincourt, was sufficiently impressed with the work of nineteen-year-old Philip that he secured for him a postgraduate scholarship. In Philip's mature assessment, he owed his entire academic career to that act of professorial patronage.

Philip deferred his scholarship until the end of hostilities, and after a brief period on Cadbury's assembly lines joined the Royal Navy. He served for three years, latterly as sub-lieutenant (the equivalent of lieutenant in the Army) in the Royal Naval Volunteer Reserve on the aircraft carrier HMS *Victorious*. Philip was present for the final onslaught on Japan, and after the two atomic bombs were dropped his ship sailed to Sydney. There he collected a letter from the Birmingham registrar, who explained that he was investigating the possibility of early demobilisation under class B, a class of 'key men' who had worked in pre-war civilian occupations that were deemed vital to construction. Class B was meant to bring men in occupations such as mining, civil engineering and the police service home ahead of the rest of their release group. The registrar's ploy was successful, and by the end of September Philip was back in Birmingham, the proud possessor of an order that declared that he was being released from the Royal Navy for work of 'urgent national reconstruction' as 'an Arts student'.

Philip had cherished a plan to write about the tragic sense in Chaucer under Helen Gardner, who taught him as an undergraduate, but she left for Oxford in 1941 and Philip's interest was not encouraged by her successor. He therefore decided to work on the seventeenth century under the supervision of Allardyce Nicoll, who had just returned to England after twelve years in America. This was an MA by research, and Philip chose to work on the courtier and intellectual Sir Kenelm Digby. At the end of the year Philip's recently demobbed seniors and contemporaries, many of whom would never have contemplated higher education before the war, took the opportunity of FETS (the Further Education and Training Scheme) to enrol at Britain's universities. Extra lecturers were urgently needed, and Allardyce Nicoll asked Philip to apply for an Assistant Lectureship in the Department of English. In the event the job went to another candidate, so Philip reluctantly accepted a post at Saltley Training College in Birmingham. Before he could take up this post, Nicoll effected a rescue and conjured up a second post in his department. In October 1946 Philip was appointed, without interview, as a probationary Assistant Lecturer in English at Birmingham on a salary of £400 a year.

Philip later described his first year of teaching as exhilarating, but it was full of challenges. The heating arrangements were wholly inadequate to deal with the bitter winter of 1946–7, and Philip routinely took tutorials wearing his naval greatcoat. He was for the most part younger than his students, many of whom had served for five or six years, as opposed to Philip's three. Philip found himself acting as an untrained counsellor to men who had been scarred by war or by the return to civilian life, and he struggled to deal with the depth of their problems. He was dismayed when one of his best students, with a fine war record, crumbled during his first examination, left the room in distress, walked to New Street Station and put his head on the line. The attentive compassion that characterised Philip's dealings with distressed students throughout his career was formed in the crucible of his experience of teaching veterans.

Philip's salary was sufficient to enable his marriage to Hazel Valentine, the youngest daughter of C. W. Valentine, Professor of Education, a well-known child psychologist. Philip's best man was Michael McCrum, who had been a shipmate on HMS *Victorious* and was at the time reading Classics at Cambridge; he later went on to become Headmaster of Eton and Master of Corpus Christi, Cambridge. In July 1947 Philip and Hazel set up house in the damp basement of a house called Highfield in Selly

Park Road. The flat had no lavatory, so the newlyweds had to share facilities with the owners, Philip Sargent Florence, Professor of Commerce at Birmingham, and his American wife, the campaigner Lella Secor Florence.

Philip, who had a lifelong allegiance to particular houses, was enormously pleased to be living in a house with strong literary and political associations, and the experience marked him forever. The Florences had made Highfield the epicentre of Birmingham culture in the 1930s, and rented flats in the house to colleagues at the university. Louis MacNeice had lived in the flat above the coach house for six years, and wrote about Highfield in his autobiography.[1] William Empson lived in the house after he was banished from Cambridge. There were many literary gatherings at the house, accounts of which survive in an appendix to Barbara Moench Florence's edition of her mother's letters.[2] Regular visitors included the poets W. H. Auden and Henry Reed, the novelists Walter Allen, Walter Brierley and John Hampson, the architectural historian Nikolaus Pevsner, and the playwrights Reggie Smith and Leslie Halward. Walter Allen declared that 'most English left-wing intellectuals and American intellectuals visiting Britain must have passed through Highfield between 1930 and 1950'.[3] House guests included Ernest Bevin, Walter Gropius, Julian Huxley and Margaret Mead. In 1982, David Lodge, who was Philip's successor at Birmingham, made a television documentary about the literary culture of Highfield. The academic culture of the English Department at Birmingham was sturdily historical, but the experience of Highfield opened a new world to Philip, and left him with an educated passion for contemporary writing, especially poetry.

The summer of 1947 also inaugurated Philip's long association with Stratford. He and Hazel spent part of the summer near Malvern, in a small toll-cottage that belonged to Allardyce and Josephine Nicoll, who lived nearby. Philip was working on *Pericles*, trying to establish what light the poor quality of the text might shed on the question of authorship; at that time this was a wonderfully untilled field. Nicoll regularly drove Philip over to Stratford, where they would have long and memorable discussions about the future shape of Shakespeare studies. Their

---

[1] L. MacNeice, *The Strings are False: an Unfinished Autobiography* (London, 1965).
[2] 'Afterword' to B. M. Florence (ed.), *Lella Secor: a Diary in Letters, 1915–1922* (New York, 1978), pp. 267–73.
[3] W. Allen, *As I Walked Down New Grub Street: Memories of a Writing Life* (London and Chicago, 1981).

interlocutors included people at the theatre (notably Barry Jackson, the new director), the Birthplace Trust (Levi Fox) and the British Council. Barry Jackson had brought Paul Scofield from the Birmingham Rep to play the title role in a new production of *Pericles*. It was a truncated version, directed by Nugent Monck, but it was a timely and unprecedented opportunity to see the play being acted, and for Philip it was an unexpectedly moving experience.

The other formative event of that golden summer was the Shakespeare Conference at Mason Croft, then the home of the British Council (and, since 1951, the Shakespeare Institute). Ever alert to the literary dimensions of houses, Philip noted that it had previously been the home of Marie Corelli. The conference was described as the second, but the first had been a very small private affair at which plans had been laid for a wider international conference and the launching of the journal that became *Shakespeare Survey*, the most important journal in the subject. Philip was deeply involved with the planning and running of this 1947 conference, and relished the privilege of meeting luminaries such as F. P. Wilson, Una Ellis-Fermor, E. M. W. Tillyard, J. Dover Wilson, D. J. Gordon, R. C. Bald, Alfred Harbage, George Rylands and Peter Alexander, all of whom he later came to know well. The Secretary of the conference was Allardyce Nicoll, who exercised his authority by securing a slot for Philip at the next conference (1948), where he gave a short paper outlining the conclusions of his research on *Pericles*.

Back at Edmund Street in central Birmingham, the city centre site of the Faculties of Arts and Law (yet to be reunited with the main campus at Edgbaston), the department had new recruits, including Geoffrey Shepherd, Derek Brewer, Eric Stanley and Joan Smethurst (later Rees). When the Shakespeare Institute got under way at Stratford, the new Fellows included Reg Foakes (who had been an undergraduate with Philip at the start of the war), Ernst Honigmann and John Russell Brown. Every one of these colleagues went on to distinguished careers, and Philip was quick to acknowledge his debt to them.

Allardyce Nicoll's patronage continued apace, and Philip was enrolled as the Secretary of both *Shakespeare Survey* and the newly instituted Shakespeare Conference. Much to Philip's confused gratification, Nicoll offered him a Fellowship at the Institute with senior lecturer status. It was an incredible offer for such an untried scholar and, incredibly, Philip refused it, explaining as best he could that he did not want to become a professional Shakespearean, but rather wanted to remain as a university teacher of English literature.

In September 1950 Philip endured the greatest sorrow of his life. His wife Hazel, who had a congenital heart defect, collapsed and died after climbing many flights of stairs to visit Philip in his room at the top of the building. She was twenty-five years old. Philip had already been hard hit by the premature death of his father, aged fifty-nine, a few months earlier. Philip somehow carried on. At about this time Cyprian Blagden of Longman walked into his Edmund Street room and asked whether he had a book in mind for a series on English writers. Philip had been delivering a course of lectures on Elizabethan poetry and, rifling through his mental filing cards, remembered that he had spoken with enthusiasm about Sir Walter Ralegh, whose verse at that time was little regarded. Off the cuff he suggested Ralegh, and Blagden liked the idea.

In 1953 *Sir Walter Ralegh* was published.[4] It begins with the disarming observation that 'there are already too many books about Sir Walter Ralegh', which leads to a modest assertion that the distinctive feature of this book is its attention to Ralegh's intellectual and literary treatments. After an oddly solemn discussion of how 'Ralegh' should be pronounced, the book becomes a humane survey of Ralegh's works from Philip's chosen perspective. The high point of the book is the long discussion of *The Ocean to Cynthia*. In terms of Philip's life, the most significant aspect of the book is its analysis of Ralegh's accounts of his voyages. This was a subject to which he was to return in the final decades of his life.

Sir Walter Ralegh was Philip's first book, and it remains a useful account. Its importance, however, is modest by comparison to his long article on *Pericles* in *Shakespeare Survey*. 'An approach to the problem of *Pericles*' not only established Philip as a serious scholar, but also proved to be a seminal piece in the history of author attribution.[5] Some sixty-five years after its publication, Philip's painstaking account of two reporters reconstructing the text from memory, and three compositors setting the type, still commands wide assent, and is the starting point of any discussion of the text of the play. He is also alert to the implications of his findings for the question of the authorship of the play. He concludes that:

> The problem that has to be solved is whether the different aptitudes of the two reporters are the *sole* cause of the difference in literary value between the two halves of the play; whether, in fact, the original play of *Pericles* was all of one standard, all by one author, and that the first reporter, in his crude attempts to

---

[4] P. Edwards, *Sir Walter Ralegh* (London, New York and Toronto, 1953).
[5] P. Edwards, 'An approach to the problem of *Pericles*', *Shakespeare Survey*, 5 (1952), 25–49.

rebuild a verse structure and in his reliance on a palpably defective memory, has perverted language such as is found in the later acts.⁶

In this conclusion lay the seeds of the debate about Shakespeare's collaboration that has extended up to the present. Philip's tentative conclusion that Shakespeare may well have been the sole author is no longer received wisdom, but that shift in the academic consensus does not detract from the analytical power of the article.

Philip's only regret with respect to his work on *Pericles* was that he was never able to prepare a scholarly edition of the play. He enjoyed excellent relations with the general editors of the Arden Shakespeare, which was then the best scholarly series of Shakespeare's plays, and he was always puzzled that he was never asked to edit *Pericles* or any other play in that distinguished series. In the case of *Pericles*, the choice of editor was in the gift of Una Ellis-Fermor, who chose to commission a former doctoral student. F. D. Hoeniger produced a satisfactory edition, and in his account of the text acknowledged that 'much of what follows is indebted to his [Philip Edwards'] article'. Philip eventually published the New Penguin *Pericles*,⁷ into which he packed some brilliant observations, but the constraints of that series did not allow him the space to pursue his interest in the text and authorship of the play.

In May 1952 Philip was married to Sheila Wilkes, who, some years earlier, had been in one of his first-year classes. At the time of their marriage, Sheila was working as an administrative assistant in the Extra-Mural Department. They were to be happily married for sixty-three years, until Philip died. Two years after their marriage Philip was awarded a Commonwealth Fund Fellowship (later called Harkness Fellowships) for a year's study in the United States. These were originally fellowships for young graduates, mostly from Oxford and Cambridge, but the Trustees had recently decided to spread their net more widely, and to recruit one or two of what would now be called 'early career scholars'. Philip chose to go to Harvard, where he wanted to work with Douglas Bush. He planned to expand his MA work on Sir Kenelm Digby into a broader consideration of the literary and intellectual circles in the court of Charles I.

Philip and Sheila sailed to America with their one-year-old son Matthew, and Philip was soon absorbed into the intellectual life of the Harvard department. Eminent scholars such as Douglas Bush, Alfred Harbage and Harry Levin were all kind to him, and Philip revelled in the

⁶ Ibid., p. 45.
⁷ W. Shakespeare, *Pericles: Prince of Tyre*, ed. P. Edwards (Harmondsworth, 1976).

vast resources of the Houghton Library, making copious notes arising out of his work on literary manuscripts. By the end of the year he had amassed a large pile of notes, but not developed any sense of where this material might lead. This frustration was compounded by a second challenge, which was that it was a condition of the Fellowship that the Fellow undertake a grand tour of America for a minimum of two months. Philip and Sheila had to travel with a toddler in a 1950 Studebaker, which Philip had bought as a joke because of its bullet nose. The car constantly broke down, and a disproportionate amount of Philip's scholarship stipend had to be spent keeping it on the road. Nonetheless, they drove relentlessly on, and Philip was able to visit scholars for whom he had huge respect, including Fredson Bowers in Virginia, George Reynolds in Boulder, M. H. Abrams in Cornell and R. C. Bald in Chicago.

In the summer of 1955 Philip and Sheila returned to Birmingham. They were to remain in the British Isles, but their affection for America never dimmed. On arrival in the department, Philip found an invitation from Clifford Leech to edit Thomas Kyd's *The Spanish Tragedy* for a new series of editions of the plays of Shakespeare's contemporaries, later to be called the Revels Plays. Philip jumped at the opportunity, set aside (forever) the notes of his year in Harvard, and plunged into work on an edition which he always held in special affection. The edition was published in 1959,[8] and was in many ways the first scholarly edition of the play. Philip's work on *Pericles* had endowed him with a formidable ability to deal with complex textual issues and fraught questions of authorship and dating, and the scrupulous thoroughness of Philip's treatment of these issues contributed both to the standard of scholarly editing of Elizabethan plays by authors other than Shakespeare and to the emerging sense of *The Spanish Tragedy* as a play with intrinsic worth rather than a feeble foreshadowing of Shakespeare. Philip was later to return to Kyd with a short monograph called *Thomas Kyd and Early Elizabethan Tragedy* (1966),[9] in which he set the play in its proper context rather than reducing it to a preface to Shakespeare.

In 1956, while he was still at work on *The Spanish Tragedy*, Philip was approached by Dan Davin of Oxford University Press, asking him if he would be interested in completing the Clarendon Press edition of Massinger's plays, left unfinished by A. K. McIlwraith at his death. Philip hesitated, and as he asked around he quickly discovered that he had not

---

[8] T. Kyd, *The Spanish Tragedy*, ed. P. Edwards (London, 1959).
[9] P. Edwards, *Thomas Kyd and Early Elizabethan Tragedy* (London, 1966).

been the first to be approached. His colleague John Russell Brown told him enigmatically that he had turned it down 'on moral grounds'; Philip never worked out what Brown meant, but there is a sense in which his own decision to accept was based on moral grounds. At this stage in his career Philip was deeply suspicious of literary criticism built on sandy foundations. Good editions, on the other hand, with sound texts, considered judgements of textual variants, proper introductions and full annotation, were the rocks on which all professional work, including literary criticism, must be built.

When the pantechnicon arrived with decades of McIlwraith's work in several tea-chests, Philip wished that he had not accepted the commission. *The Spanish Tragedy* was completed, so Philip embarked on what proved to be more than a decade of laborious work on his own. He subsequently enlisted Colin Gibson of Otago University as an enthusiastic co-editor; Philip had examined his doctoral dissertation edition of *The Roman Actor*, so he knew that he was acquiring serious competence as well as an injection of energy. McIlwraith had been a good scholar but, as they were later to admit in their preface, Philip and Colin sometimes thought 'as they puzzled their way through manuscripts and photostats thirty to forty years old that it would be quicker to edit Massinger *ab initio*'. In the event, the publication of the five-volume edition in 1976 was a triumph,[10] and it was rightly praised as a major work of scholarship.

For some time Philip had had a growing conviction that he should move on from Birmingham, not because of any disaffection but because he felt that he had been there too long—as undergraduate, postgraduate, lecturer and (since 1958) senior lecturer. As the entry points in the profession were almost all at lecturer and professor level, he began to wonder whether he stood any chance of securing a chair. He decided that it would be advantageous to have a doctorate, and so in 1960 supplicated as a member of staff on the basis of his publications; the examiners were free to recommend any degree, and sensibly awarded a PhD.

Philip's first attempt to secure a chair was at Bangor, but he did not succeed. In January 1960 his close friend Donald Dudley (later Professor of Latin) told Philip that he had noticed an advertisement for the Chair of English Literature at Trinity College, Dublin (TCD), and urged him to apply. Philip had never been to Ireland, and the account of the TCD syllabus that he found in the library was utterly bewildering. Nonetheless, it seemed an exciting possibility, and he submitted an application. He did

---

[10] P. Edwards and C. Gibson (eds.), *The Plays and Poems of Philip Massinger*, 5 vols. (Oxford, 1976).

so thinking that he would not be offered the post, because the obvious candidate was Donald Davie, who was *in situ*. What Philip did not know was that Davie had decided to leave TCD for Cambridge, and that he had no interest in a post that involved administration.

Philip was interviewed on a cold winter's day in Dublin. The external assessor was the Shakespearean Geoffrey Bullough, and Philip was always confident that it was Bullough's advocacy that led to him being appointed. He subsequently learned that his candidacy had the strong backing of a group of college officers (Professors of Latin and Modern History) who thought that Philip could invigorate what they saw as a rather comatose department. He also discovered that other colleagues looked askance at the appointment of a young Englishman who knew nothing of Ireland or TCD and had not attended either of what were regarded as England's two universities.

Philip saw the six years that he and Sheila spent in Ireland as the most important experience of their lives. The conferring of an MA *jure officii* and election to a College Fellowship were formalities, but Philip always felt proud of them. The post was extraordinarily challenging. Innovation was particularly difficult because the college's funding was utterly inadequate. Provision for English was also inadequate. English literature was only available to the four-year honours students as part of a joint degree with another language, such as French or Latin. Philip regarded joint degrees as a strength rather than a weakness, but much regretted that, in a university with a great tradition in medieval studies, the effect of the joint degree structure was that important areas of English literature, especially Old and Middle English, were not part of the syllabus. When the demand arose for medieval English from candidates for Scholarship who were seeking extra subjects, teachers were drafted in from outside the college (notably Father Thomas Dunning from University College Dublin – UCD). Philip therefore instituted the 'sole English' curriculum, and hired Joseph Pheifer from UCD to teach Old English. The new syllabus was a runaway success, and Philip was embarrassed that it drained so many students away from joint honours courses. The first Scholar in 'sole English' was John Kelly, who was later to become a distinguished student of Yeats.

Staffing was a nightmare. Philip was fond of saying that the English Department consisted of two men and a boy, and that he was the boy. A great deal of the teaching was done by part-time assistants, some of whom were very distinguished (notably A. J. 'Con' Leventhal, the friend of Samuel Beckett), but could not participate fully in the life of the department. Philip learned a great deal by having to lecture in areas with which he was unfamiliar. He always enjoyed teaching students who had just arrived at university, and so taught a course on the history of English criticism to first-year students. What was completely revolutionary was Philip's practice of including discussion periods within his lectures, canvassing student views and promoting discussion as part of the learning process. Here was a professor who positively wanted students to talk rather than just listen.

Reflecting on the syllabus, Philip was astonished by the lack of attention to Irish literature, and found himself, an imported Englishman, instituting regular courses in Irish literature in an Irish university. He managed to create a junior lectureship for his student Brendan Kennelly, who was already a fine poet—and an Irish Catholic—to assist in establishing Irish literature on a wider and more secure footing. He was also able to create a part-time post for the short-story writer Frank O'Connor, whose weekly lectures on Irish literature attracted large audiences. Philip was immensely proud of this appointment, and wrote about O'Connor's contribution to the department in a book of tributes.[11]

The appointment of Irish writers to teaching posts reflected Philip's conviction, shaped by his experience of Highfield, that the study of literature extended up to the present and that writers could afford insights that were denied to antiquarian academics. He also became a passionate advocate of Ireland's literary tradition, and for the rest of his professional life always taught courses on Irish literature. Visitors to his personal library later in life would be shown his Irish holdings, notably a magnificent collection of early editions of George Moore, of whose works Philip had a capacious command.

Early in 1964 Philip received an invitation from G. B. Harrison to spend the next academic year as a Visiting Professor at the University of Michigan in Ann Arbor. Philip had a great deal of respect for Harrison and his scholarship, and was aware that the emotional depth of Harrison's writing about loss in Shakespeare's tragedies was grounded in the loss of two sons during the Second World War. Philip accepted immediately, but when he and Sheila met Harrison in London to discuss arrangements for the visit, he was discomfited to discover that he was being asked as a trial run for replacing Harrison. Philip and Sheila loved the United States, but at that point they had no wish to leave Ireland, nor to make a permanent

---

[11] P. Edwards, 'Frank O'Connor at Trinity', in M. Sheehy (ed.), *Michael/Frank: Studies on Frank O'Connor with a Bibliography of his Writing* (Dublin, 1969), pp. 120–36.

home in America. The whole family went nonetheless, and they had a fine year. Philip's colleagues included Edward Engelberg, whose knowledge of Yeats prompted him to read the whole of Yeats during his time in Ann Arbor. Philip had to give a year-long Shakespeare course, and his rereading of the whole of Shakespeare laid the foundations for *Shakespeare and the Confines of Art*,[12] which presents Shakespeare as a conscious creator of an art form that can set human experience within its confines.

Shakespeare and the Confines of Art is in many respects the most personal of Philip's books, in that it sees in Shakespeare a craftsman who battles against his own scepticism about the ability of his craft to achieve its aims. On one level the book is a series of insightful readings of the Sonnets and a selection of the plays; on another level it is a reflection of the constant need felt by Philip to justify both the utility and the capability of his own work as a scholar and teacher. Academics from very comfortable backgrounds sometimes seem content to feel that they are saying something significant to their readers; Philip was a modest man from a modest background, and never lost the anxiety that his work might not be worthwhile.

That anxiety may be one reason why Philip never deserted his research, even when he was teaching or discharging senior managerial responsibilities. He lacked sympathy for colleagues who complained that they had no time for research when they were teaching. Philip's capacious appetite for research meant that he always created research time while teaching, and research questions never left his mind. Later in his career, when he was editing *Hamlet*, he walked to lunch with a colleague after a long morning of teaching, and confessed that he sometimes woke up in the morning quivering with excitement about whether he would decide for 'solid flesh' or 'sullied flesh'. That boyish enthusiasm for literature, for textual scholarship and for teaching stayed with Philip throughout his career.

In the course of the year in America Philip's determination to stay in Ireland was gradually sapped by enquiries about his willingness to take posts elsewhere. Clifford Leech offered him a post at University of Toronto, and Hazard Adams offered him a well-paid post at the new university at Irvine in California. There were also invitations to join one of the new universities being created in England in the wake of the Robbins Report, and to join Frank Kermode as the second chair at Manchester. In the event, the decisive figure was Donald Davie, whom Philip regarded as the architect of the rest of his career (and whose memoir he was later to

---

[12] P. Edwards, *Shakespeare and the Confines of Art* (London, 1968).

write for the British Academy).[13] At TCD Philip had been consulted by Albert Sloman, who was planning the new University of Essex, about the suitability of Donald Davie as Essex's inaugural Professor of Literature, and Philip was enthusiastic. Donald and Doreen had become fast friends of Philip and Sheila, and Philip was proud to have played a small role in Davie's career.

Soon the favour was reciprocated. Davie came to Ann Arbor to deliver a prestigious lecture, and pressed Philip to join him at Essex. Davie's argument was that he had agreed to the very experimental comparative syllabus that Sloman was instituting at Essex, but he wanted to ensure that the core canon of English literature was not neglected, and saw the appointment of Philip, as a Shakespearean, as a kind of conservationist insurance. He was lavish in his description of what Philip could expect with regard to the freedom to plan courses and appoint staff. After Davie left, Philip and Sheila talked about the matter at great length. They had always assumed that they would eventually return to England, and Essex was an appealing prospect. They agreed that they would go to Colchester early in autumn to look around and have a talk with Albert Sloman.

Having resolved on a plan of action, Philip got on with his work in America. He spent the spring of 1965 at the Huntington Library, working on Massinger and his Shakespeare book. Sheila and the boys came to California to join Philip, and the family embarked on a protracted holiday that began in Sequoia National Park and ended in Vermont. This experience rounded off a fine year, and Philip returned to Ireland looking forward to his impending visit to Essex.

The visit went all too well. The weather was beautiful, and the countryside of the Essex–Suffolk borders was breathtaking. While Philip was getting to know people at the university, Sheila found some attractive houses for sale, including Twentymans, the house that they eventually bought in Brightlingsea. By November it was all settled, and Philip agreed to start work in October 1966. Departure from Dublin was protracted and difficult. Philip was reluctant to leave, friends were telling him that going to Essex was a big mistake, and the challenge of finding someone to replace him at TCD after Denis Donoghue and John Holloway both lost interest left Philip feeling that he was deserting the ship. There were also practical difficulties, which reached their zenith when a bank strike in Ireland meant that Philip could not make a down payment on Twentymans.

---

[13] P. Edwards, 'Donald Alfred Davie, 1922–1995', *Proceedings of the British Academy*, 94 (1997), pp. 391–412.

Philip published a letter in the *Irish Times* setting out his plight. He then received an anonymous telephone call inviting him to come to the back door of the bank, where he was given a sackful of banknotes. Philip and Sheila had to stuff the banknotes into envelopes for posting to the Essex solicitor who was handling the purchase.

The initial experience of Essex was a delight. Philip and Sheila loved Twentymans and its large garden, enjoyed exploring Suffolk, and made many friends outside as well as inside the university. Philip also relished the easy access to London, both for theatres and the British Museum. The university, however, was a huge disappointment, utterly alien to Philip's values. Contrary to what he had been led to expect, he found himself in a straitjacket with respect to teaching and appointments. In the wake of the destructive student rebellion of May 1968, founding professors began to leave in large numbers. To Philip's distress, their numbers included Donald Davie, his friend and ally, who suddenly departed for Stanford to succeed Ivor Winters. Philip was left as head of department administering a system in which he had no faith. His attempts to modify the arrangements were denigrated by some of his colleagues as a betrayal of founding principles, and even students turned against him: Philip never forgot being mocked and berated by angry students as he was pushing a pram holding his young daughter Kate.

Philip realised that the move to Essex had been a mistake, but he was determined to make a decent fist of it, and to outsiders he could be defensive of the Essex experiment. In the course of a Visiting Fellowship at All Souls, he endured the sneers and voiced contempt for Essex of Max Beloff and A. L. Rowse. The latter's repeated dismissal of Essex as 'third-rate' irritated Philip immensely, and he insisted that whatever its shortcomings, Essex was never third-rate. He declared that with senior colleagues such as Alasdair Macintyre, Tony Atkinson, Joseph Rykwert, Jean Blondel and Anthony King, intellectual life could never be dull.

There were many opportunities to leave, the first of which came from TCD, when Philip was invited to join the panel at the annual meeting of the 'Hist' (the College Historical Society). He was startled to be asked by the Provost, A. J. McConnell, to stay at the Provost's House. Late in the evening, over a large tumbler of whisky, McConnell invited Philip to return to his old position. Philip was utterly miserable: there was nothing for which he wished more, as he missed Trinity acutely, but he felt that he could not accept. In the event, Philip endured Essex for eight years, all the while resisting overtures from other universities.

Despite the unhappiness, the Essex years were immensely productive. Philip and Colin Gibson brought the Massinger edition close to completion, and Philip did a great deal of research and writing. He also assumed a series of demanding administrative roles. He was the university's first Public Orator, and was particularly proud to have been able to deliver the oration for Harold Wilson, who was then Prime Minister. The student troubles of 1968 took a dreadful toll on student recruitment, as parents and schools were uneasy about recommending Essex. Albert Sloman asked Philip to become his first Dean of Admissions, hoping that Philip's charm might influence schools that had given up on Essex to send students once more. The schools that he visited included Eton, where he stayed with his old shipmate Michael McCrum. Any hope that the visit might have been worthwhile was crushed when he returned to Essex; rebellion had broken out again, and he discovered that the students were being rallied into action over the Tannoy by an undergraduate who was an Old Etonian.

In the autumn of 1969 Philip and Sheila (and three of their four children) moved to Williamstown, Massachusetts. Philip much enjoyed teaching at Williams College, which offered very small classes, polite and hard-working students, and friendly and stimulating colleagues. It was a timely period of respite from the tensions of Essex, where Philip battled on. Ever alert to the importance of having contemporary writers undertake some teaching, Philip managed to persuade Robert Lowell to come to Essex for two years as a visiting professor. Philip relished Lowell's company, and took particular pleasure in discussing English Renaissance poetry with him.

The Essex years were for the most part a dreadful experience, but Philip did not regard the disaster as unmitigated. He loved his house, he enjoyed the area and, as ever, had a wide circle of friends. When, however, Kenneth Muir sounded him out in 1973 about succeeding him as King Alfred Professor at Liverpool, Philip responded very positively. Muir had built up a fine department, and Philip was far more sympathetic to its ethos than to that of Essex. He shared with Sheila, however, a reluctance to leave Twentymans and friends and countryside for the urban horrors of Merseyside, an area that has now been imaginatively regenerated but was, when Philip (and I) arrived in 1974, a very unattractive place. These reservations were exacerbated by the strains of a move that Philip described as singularly difficult, protracted and expensive. His negotiations over salary failed, the university only covered partial removal expenses and it took some time to recover his financial equilibrium.

Philip and Sheila bought a fine house on the Wirral and settled in contentedly. They were to stay in Liverpool for sixteen years, and both enjoyed the experience. Philip noted with pleasure that his students were studious, his colleagues collegial and the department was not cloven by the theory wars (as many were). He delighted in the friendship of many in the department, which suited his temperament admirably. He was a wonderfully benign head of department, but quietly insisted that standards be maintained. On one occasion those teaching a drama course, including myself, went to his room to propose a revision of the course in which English drama would be interspersed with the study of plays by writers such as Molière, Ibsen, Chekhov and Brecht. Philip responded warmly, and stipulated two conditions: one was that the colleague lecturing on the play would be familiar with the text in the original language (Nicholas Grene had Russian and I could bluff my way through Norwegian), and the other was that any joint honours students in seminars (English could be combined with French or German or Russian) would be asked to read the plays in the original language. We left the room pleased that our initiative had been taken seriously, and the course ran successfully for many years.

Provision for study leave was sufficient for Philip to make progress on books such as *Threshold of a Nation*,[14] and his edition of *Hamlet* for the New Cambridge Shakespeare,[15] at the Huntington, New College, Oxford and Otago University. He also became a Visiting Professor at the International Christian University in Tokyo. *Threshold of a Nation* proposed a fruitful analogy between the drama of Elizabethan and Jacobean England, which heralded what Philip saw as the birth of the modern nation, and the drama of late nineteenth- and early twentieth-century Ireland, which played a significant role in the emergence and identity of an independent Ireland. The edition of *Hamlet* afforded Philip an opportunity long denied him—to prepare a scholarly edition of a major Shakespeare play. Philip relished the theatrical dimension that is a central feature of the New Cambridge Shakespeare. He had little enthusiasm for the idea of the text as a document to be read and performed in the reader's head, so his careful account of textual history and his deft summary of the vast critical tradition is complemented by an insistence that the text is a theatrical document that only comes to life when the play is realised in a stage performance.

---

[14] P. Edwards, *Threshold of a Nation: a Study in English and Irish Drama* (Cambridge, 1979).
[15] W. Shakespeare, *Hamlet, Prince of Denmark*, ed. P. Edwards (Cambridge, 1985).

At Liverpool Philip declined the position of Dean, but accepted the office of Pro-Vice-Chancellor, partly in the hope that the extra £2,000 a year would help the family to support their son Richard in drama school. The latter part of his tenure as PVC was rendered a misery by the need to impose the cuts imposed on the universities by Margaret Thatcher in 1981, and Philip was pleased to be able to return to his department at the end of his stint. He finished his book on *Shakespeare: a Writer's Progress*,[16] plunged into research on voyaging in Early Modern England and happily assumed a full teaching load. In 1986 he was elected to the British Academy, and took enormous pleasure in this honour.

In his last years at Liverpool Philip was suffering from cataracts in both eyes, and received what he later regarded as poor advice from a private consultant to delay seeking treatment. He was happy to accept an invitation to act as an external examiner at Oxford, but the usual challenges of reading handwritten scripts were compounded by the advent of word processing, because many candidates saved money by printing their dissertations in draft mode, and Philip struggled with the pale inking. He was also dispirited by the reception of his book *Last Voyages: Cavendish, Hudson, Ralegh*,[17] which was widely ignored except by specialists who resented the cheek of an intruder. He later wrote that 'I never convinced my own tribe of the worth of what I was doing, nor the "experts" of my right to be in their field.'

Such experiences wholly reconciled Philip to the prospect of retirement in 1990; he was also buoyed by the thought that, for the first time, his library would be consolidated under one roof. He and Sheila had bought a retirement home in Kendal, and Philip resolved to give up academic work altogether. In the event, Kendal revivified his spirits, and he soon returned to academic work with renewed energy. He defiantly decided to continue his work on early voyages, and in the years that followed published *The Story of the Voyage: Sea Narratives in Eighteenth-Century England* (1994),[18] *Sea-Mark: the Metaphorical Voyage, Spenser to Milton* (1997),[19] and the Penguin edition of *The Journals of Captain Cook*.[20] He also engaged with characteristic energy in the life of his community: he

---

[16] P. Edwards, *Shakespeare: a Writer's Progress* (Oxford, 1986).
[17] P. Edwards, *Last Voyages: Cavendish, Hudson, Ralegh* (Oxford, 1988).
[18] P. Edwards, *The Story of the Voyage: Sea Narratives in Eighteenth-Century England* (Cambridge, 1994).
[19] P. Edwards, *Sea-Mark: the Metaphorical Voyage, Spenser to Milton* (Liverpool, 1997).
[20] P. Edwards (ed.), *The Journals of Captain Cook* (London, 1999).

lectured at the local arts centre, started a poetry group and supported local causes, such as stopping quarry lorries from driving through Kendal. He was also an active opponent of the UK's involvement in the war in Iraq.

Philip's last book, called *Pilgrimage and Literary Tradition*, was published in 2005.[21] Books on pilgrimage tend to end with the Reformation. Philip chose to make the Reformation his starting point, and to consider how pilgrimage lived on as a literary motif in the work of writers such as Shakespeare, Conrad, Eliot, Yeats and Heaney, none of whom is normally associated with pilgrimage. The book is chiefly remarkable for its account of *Hamlet*, in which Philip discerns a tragic version of pilgrimage that may have its origins in the ancient literature of Ireland. This book did not receive the wide notice that it merited, but one strand of his research for the book received national newspaper coverage when Philip first announced it in 2003.[22] T. S. Eliot's seventy-nine-word poem 'Usk' contains an allusion to 'the white hart behind the white well'. Philip visited Llangybi (Usk), and there found a pub called the White Hart Inn. He soon discovered that behind the pub lay the ruins of a whitewashed beehive well that had once been a place of pilgrimage. He had solved the riddle of the lines.

Philip's writing career ended with *Pilgrimage and Literary Tradition*. Thereafter he carried on gardening as long as he could, and kept up the practice of correspondence. He always addressed his letters by hand, and his lifelong interest in calligraphy ensured that recipients took pleasure in his letters even before opening them.

Philip Edwards died on 27 November 2015. He is survived by his wife Sheila, by their children Matthew, Stephen, Charles and Kate, by their eight grandchildren and by one great-grandson. Philip lives on in their memories, and in those of the many people who enjoyed his infectious delight in literature and the warm embrace of his friendship.

GORDON CAMPBELL
Fellow of the Academy

---

[21] P. Edwards, *Pilgrimage and Literary Tradition* (Cambridge, 2005).
[22] See for example J. Ezard, 'TS Eliot scholar finds answer to pub poet's riddle', *The Guardian* (6 August 2003), http://www.theguardian.com/uk/2003/aug/06/highereducation.books (accessed 9 December 2016).

Note. Philip Edwards deposited two accounts of his life with the British Academy, in 1988 and 2000. There are of course variants and second thoughts of a type that Philip associated with the texts of Shakespeare's plays. I have also drawn on the memories (and incorporated the corrections) of Matthew Edwards (on behalf of Philip's family), Neville Davies and Nicholas Grene, all of whom kindly read a preliminary draft of this memoir.

ALAN GEOFFREY HILL

Alan Geoffrey Hill
1931–2015

ALAN GEOFFREY HILL WAS born on 12 December 1931 to a comfortably off family in London. He attended Dulwich College, was an undergraduate at St Andrews and a postgraduate at Merton College, Oxford. In 1960 he married Margaret Rutherford and three children followed this, 'the happiest decision of my life'. In 1994 Hill, now Professor of English at Royal Holloway, was elected Fellow of the British Academy (FBA)—'the greatest honour I have ever received'. Shortly afterwards he retired and moved to Malvern, where, after a long illness of intermittent periods of severity, he died on 14 April 2015.

My first meeting with Alan was in the late 1960s, when I was just starting out in Edinburgh University and he was already a Senior Lecturer in Dundee. As members of the Wordsworth Trust we continued to meet over many years, both regularly in the formal meetings of the Trust and more occasionally at convivial Wordsworthian events, so that I got to know him quite well. Or rather, I thought I did. It is a mark of Alan's sober character that he never, at least in my hearing, advertised himself or paraded his honours, and it is only from the autobiographical memorandum which he deposited with the Academy that I have become aware of many aspects of his interests and achievements. He was profoundly engaged with orchestral music and opera, an enjoyment which he declares he owed to early encouragement from his father. Drama and film were lifelong interests. He acknowledges very gratefully the immersion in the classics he received in his old-fashioned prep school and later at Dulwich, a grounding which was of enormous value in the kind of literary study he was to embrace. His love of the English countryside and in particular of its church heritage, what he termed his 'ecclesiology', is traced right back to childhood, to time spent in a Sussex cottage his father had acquired 'as a bolt-hole'. But he was also widely travelled in Europe. His autobiographical memorandum touches repeatedly on his pleasure in exploring and learning from Greece, Italy and the Mediterranean more widely, 'before the days of tarmac roads and tourism in the South'.

What emerges also from the autobiographical reminiscences is Alan's capacity for friendship. Recollection of each stage of his life is accompanied by a roll-call of people whose friendship he valued or whose influence he gratefully acknowledged. Almost without exception Alan's comments on a new acquaintance are warmly positive. In all the years I knew him I never heard him be less than generous to colleagues, even when in his later career university politics were challenging and disappointment not unknown.

This capacity for appreciating and valuing the capacities of other people is strikingly revealed in his account of a year (1948–9) spent in a sanatorium at Ventnor, Isle of Wight, where the schoolboy had been sent to recover from pleurisy and residual tuberculosis. Ventnor was 'a liberating experience', partly because of the wide cross-section of people he met there—mostly ex-servicemen, a brigadier, a dentist, a bus driver, some adherents of curious fringe political groups and a few cranks. Alan recalls that among the inmates of the sanatorium was one of the most intelligent people he ever met, a man who ran a winkle stall in Portsmouth Market and who completed the Ximenes crossword in *The Observer* in about ten minutes.

The stay in Ventnor was also important in that it marked a change in Alan's intellectual direction. He ended the year impatient with the confines of school and determined to read English at university. He failed to get into Oxford, but this setback was in fact a blessing. A place at St Andrews was offered and accepted, and so began Alan's 'Scottish experience'; as he termed it, 'one of the most formative of [his] life'. Alan made many enduring friendships at St Andrews, and he revelled in the intellectual possibilities the university offered. Continuing with Latin, Greek Literature and Ancient History for a further year, he was able to take Philosophy courses for two years as part of the four-year course. He records that he 'was left with a lasting admiration for the Scottish University system and a suspicion of over-specialisation'. From the present-day perspective, it is striking that he also notes that of the ten papers examined in finals in the English school, three were not covered by teaching. Students were expected to 'get them up' out of term. Freedom of this sort allowed Alan to explore the Victorian sages—Carlyle, Arnold, Ruskin, Morris—and to develop an already active interest in Newman and the Oxford Movement. The autobiographical memorandum affords a rather touching glimpse of the young Hill reading Newman's *Apologia* and *Tract XC* 'in the Cathedral grounds on a warm spring afternoon'.

These interests determined the next stage of Alan's career. Supported by a Carnegie Trust Research Scholarship he went to Oxford—Merton College—and worked for a BLitt—doctoral research status at that time being granted only to a very few 'except as a grudging concession to Americans'. Though Oxford had been the taproot of the High Church revival, it had little time for study of allied intellectual movements within literature and Alan found himself regarded as somewhat eccentric for pursuing the literature of the Catholic Revival. His taste for the art of the Gothic Revival was thought almost laughable. As many others have testified, supervision of graduates in Oxford in the late 1950s was often somewhat less than diligent. Although he records encounters with many of the fabled Oxford names, and singles out Humphry House as someone who did help by encouragement, it is clear that Alan's research was largely self-directed. The resultant thesis—*Some Social and Historical Points of View in Nineteenth Century Literature in Relation to the Catholic Revival*—was ambitious, encompassing Scott, Cobbett, Southey, Kenelm Digby, Pugin, Tractarian novels, 'Young England' and Disraeli, Carlyle and Kingsley, with the Wordsworth of *The Excursion* and *Ecclesiastical Sketches* as an important background presence. It was successfully presented to examiners Hugo Dyson and John Sparrow in 1957.

After a year of precarious existence as a part-time college tutor, Alan's career proper began with a lectureship at the University of Exeter. Professionally challenged by the demands of the courses he was required to design and deliver, Alan, by his own account, also felt enlarged by them and by some of the colleagues he shared them with. Reviewing new work on the novel gave impetus to his own interest in genre study, leading many years later to a well-regarded lecture tour for the British Academy on 'Shakespeare and the Novel'. It was in Exeter that he met and married Margaret Rutherford, herself a graduate of St Andrews in French and Spanish, and here their first child was born.

A return to St Andrews in 1963, however, was not to be resisted and now the focus of Alan's life's work became clear. He enjoyed the wider teaching opportunities on offer—Chaucer and seventeenth-century as well as more modern literature—but in research Wordsworth came to the fore. Envisaging a study defined as 'Wordsworth and the Church Tradition:

Form and Spirit in the Poetry of William Wordsworth', Alan spent a lot of time at the library of the Wordsworth Trust at Grasmere and in archives in Carlisle and Kendal. He became editor of the multi-volume Oxford University Press edition of the *Letters of William and Dorothy Wordsworth* and a member of the Wordsworth Trust. Living 'in one of the most venerable historic cities in the British Isles and among the ruins of past greatness' was a privilege, one which directly fed into the study of a poet who was fascinated by the significance of ecclesiastical ruins and by the Scottish past.

Alan's next move, though, embraced the future rather more than the past. In 1968 Dundee University, having recently established its independence, offered him a Senior Lectureship with responsibility for running the department and, it was hoped, establishing a School of Literature. Though this latter was not realised, Alan did introduce courses in American Studies and Scottish Literature and was gratified that his was one of the first universities to appoint a Fellow in Creative Writing.

North America played a large part in Alan's life in the next few years. A tour of New England and Thoreau territory; study of religious sects as well as the American Episcopal tradition; archival study in the magnificent Wordsworth collection at Cornell University—all contributed greatly to Alan's understanding of the later Wordsworth's religious affiliations. This westward tendency also prepared the way for a year, 1973-4, as Visiting Professor at the University of Saskatchewan at Saskatoon and to further exploration in American archives. In later years Alan was to enjoy notable success on lecture visits to the University of Arizona at Tucson and the University of Toronto. Twenty years later, after retirement, Alan's ability through profound historical awareness to generate links between his various interests in language and the visual arts ensured that he remained in demand as a visiting lecturer in the USA, Canada, Malta and Italy. He dutifully served as external examiner at the new University of Buckingham and much further afield in Singapore. In short, he was an academic with a real sense of what he owed to his profession.

When offered the Chair of English at Royal Holloway College in 1980, in succession to Francis Berry, Alan had no hesitation in embracing a move to what he described as 'very much my kind of place'. The Picture Gallery, the splendid buildings, the proximity to London, the opportunity to create courses in the mould he had always favoured—all invited. And Alan did inaugurate a much-needed course in Introduction to Literary Studies, a Classical Heritage course and the Centre for the Study of Victorian Art to develop the potential of the Picture Gallery for research and teaching. But it was not overall a happy time, nor one that need be dwelt on here. Within a few months of Alan's arrival, the merger with Bedford College was effected with, in his view, too little thought in too little time. Alternating headships generated much stress; a few members of staff from both sides were reluctant to see the merger experiment work; temporary overcrowding became intolerable. It was with relief that Alan took slightly early retirement in 1994, when he and Margaret moved to a house in the Malvern Hills.

In retirement Alan was elected to a Fellowship at the Institute for Advanced Research in the Humanities at Birmingham University, and he valued the facilities offered and the resources available at the Barber Institute and the Birmingham Oratory Library. He gave lectures and seminars at the university, while continuing research and writing. From the beginning of his career Alan's interests in literature had been wide, but he wrote and lectured mostly on nineteenth- and early twentieth-century figures. Hopkins, Ruskin, Swinburne, Scott, Arnold, Clough, Gissing and many other Victorian heavyweights appear in his earliest publications but eventually two topics came to the fore—Wordsworth and his circle, and Newman and his. What fostered both these concerns was Alan's abiding interest in religion and literature.

With his own classical grounding, his interest in the history of ideas and not least his love of Oxford, the Anglo-Catholic literary-historical scholar clearly had a deep sympathy for, perhaps even a sense of kinship with, John Henry Newman, and was to play a significant part in the revival of interest in him in the later twentieth century. Alan's edition of Newman's novel *Loss and Gain* (Oxford, 1986) was a landmark. Published in 1848, just three years after Newman's own reception into the Roman Church had brought the first phase of the Oxford Movement to an anguished close, *Loss and Gain*, subtitled *The Story of a Convert*, might be supposed to have little more interest now than as an historical *roman à clef*. What Alan does so deftly in his introduction is show what an impoverished reading of the novel this would be. Fully aware of the historical contingencies that motivated the production of this story at this time, and which determine its polemical charge, the editor acknowledges that 'Newman himself was deeply implicated in his fiction, and brought a profounder *personal* response to the discussion of issues which might otherwise seem uncongenial or irrelevant' (p. xix). But what he also insists on is the imaginative generosity of the novelist who dramatises with great sympathy and persuasiveness troubled young men taking up theological positions which he had himself relinquished. It is Newman's literary gifts that are emphasised, his sense of the possibilities of the novel as a form which could 'appeal as much to the heart and imagination as to the head' (p. xii), an emphasis that was returned to in a fine essay in *Newman after a Hundred Years*, a collection of essays co-edited (Oxford, 1990) by Alan and Ian Ker. In his contribution, 'Originality and realism in Newman's novels', Alan explored the effect on the novel of Newman's 'penchant for racy language'. Copious examples of linguistic oddities demonstrate just how attentive Newman was to details of usage in establishing the novel's differing scenes and dramatis personae. It is a fine, original essay which suggested possibilities for understanding the linguistic texture of nineteenth-century novels more widely.

Alan's greatest achievement, and his most significant contribution to historical research into the nineteenth century, is his body of work on William and Dorothy Wordsworth, their wide circle of acquaintance, and the line of ecclesiastics and educationalists who constituted the distinguished Wordsworth family dynasty. In a series of articles Alan presented entirely new research on the poet's American friends (this a very influential piece), on his educational theories, on Wordsworth and Pagan Gods, on his reception in Germany, on the last phase of the relationship between Wordsworth and Francis Jeffrey, and on many other biographical and literary-historical topics. Every one of these articles adds to our knowledge of Wordsworth and the historical circumstances which enabled his writings in prose and verse to become an important cultural force.

The 1986 British Academy Warton Lecture on English Poetry, 'Wordsworth's "Grand Design"', deserves particular notice (published in *Proceedings of the British Academy*, 72, 1986, 187–204). In 1798 Wordsworth let it be known amongst a few friends that he had the ambition of writing a poem with the object of giving 'pictures of Nature, Man, and Society', adding, with the confidence of youth, 'Indeed, I know not any thing which will not come within the scope of my plan' (6 March 1798). It was to be called *The Recluse*. As the years passed, nothing seemed to have come of this work, but in 1814 Wordsworth gave, as it were, a substantial work-in-progress report by publishing a long blank verse poem, *The Excursion*, which, readers were informed in a Preface, was but part of the still-ongoing larger whole, *The Recluse*. After that, however, apparently nothing. Wordsworth grew tetchy in old age at people who kept asking after progress on *The Recluse*, and the posthumous critical and biographical consensus has been that the poet failed in the great task he had set himself, that *The Excursion* was at best only a partial success, and that the appearance of it in 1814 actually marked the beginning of such a marked decline in the quality of Wordsworth's poetry that almost everything he wrote after 1815 could be disregarded. It is a consensus challenged on every front in Alan's consideration of Wordsworth's grand design. Beginning with the proposition that it is more profitable to look at what was achieved rather than lamenting what was not, Alan suggests that much of Wordsworth's later poetry consists of what might be called '*Recluse* materials', and that it constitutes a coherent body of work from a poet with a profound understanding of the nature of religious faith and its place in human life and with, in particular, a growing interest in the history of the Christian Church.

Alan's sympathetic reading of *The Excursion* and of *Ecclesiastical Sketches*—this latter pretty well unique in Wordsworthian scholarship at the time—has been very important in shaping the move towards a better appreciation of Wordsworth's later poetry. His telling use of historical detail has been a model, but in its range and depth also a warning against casual contextualisation; the subtlety of his exploration of the poet's attitude to religious faith and its relation to literature is inspiring but also quite properly daunting. Alan's greatest contribution to literary-historical scholarship in the Romantic period, however, was the multi-volume edition of *The Letters of William and Dorothy Wordsworth* (Oxford, 1970–88; supplementary volume 1993). It is unquestionably a magnificent achievement.

The Wordsworth family letters had been edited by the indefatigable Wordsworthian William Angus Knight at the end of the nineteenth century. His pioneering work was built on by Ernest de Sélincourt, another enormously diligent scholar, who assembled a great deal of fresh material for six volumes for the Clarendon Press from 1935 onwards. By the 1960s, however, it was clear that further editorial work was called for. A revised volume covering 'The Early Years: 1787–1805' appeared in 1967, edited by Chester L. Shaver. A second volume, for 1806–11, appeared two years later under the editorship of Wordsworth's biographer, Mary Moorman, who mentioned in the Preface the help she had received in the later stages of her work from Alan Hill. The title page of the second part of this 'Middle Years' volume, which was published in 1970, properly acknowledged that it was the work of Moorman and Hill and from then on, to the completion of the series in eight volumes in 1993, the editorial labours were Alan's alone.

These were immense. Working before the era of databases and union catalogues online he brought into view hundreds of new letters. In the Acknowledgements pages of each volume Alan thanked with characteristic scrupulousness everyone who had helped him in his quest, but he was the coordinator and commentator. The copious annotation to each volume cannot be over-praised. It supplies a context for the correspondence, makes links between letters and, most usefully of all, it identifies recipients, not all of whom are well known. Wordsworth was dutiful in maintaining correspondence with figures who are now quite obscure, and to produce the notes which bring them to life must have demanded so many hours of dull detective work that one cannot but be grateful for Alan's resourcefulness and assiduity. Knowing that as a grateful end-user I would have some appreciation of what was involved, Alan once told me that he actually enjoyed this jigsaw work amongst the obscure dead; that the rewards were small but very satisfying.

What emerged very strikingly from the later volumes of the letters was the extent of Wordsworth's engagement with churchmen and with ecclesiastical concerns; what was demonstrated from the accompanying detailed annotation was just how fitted Alan was to write the much-needed study of Wordsworth and the Church. That Wordsworth moved increasingly in Anglican circles was not news—his brother, son and nephew were all ecclesiastics—and he corresponded with leading churchmen of the day. Scholars had explored to some extent the relation between many of his later poems and important movements within the Church, and the poet's growing reputation over the last thirty years of his life as a not-too-specific spiritual guide had been acknowledged in literary-cultural histories. But no one had yet explored Wordsworth's ecclesiological imagination with the care that the subject demanded, not least because of what would be required of the scholar who attempted it. Wordsworth read widely in Church history; he was particularly interested in the monastic life; he thought deeply about the interdependence of personal faith and the institutional forms of religion as they had evolved in differing societies over the centuries; he was much occupied—often anxiously—with contemporary developments in the Church; he had strong views about the relative importance of religious faith and writing about religion. In the 1986 Warton Lecture Alan wrote with brilliant, highly suggestive economy about Wordsworth as didactic poet and declared, 'No purely literary approach can do justice to Wordsworth's significance here, and another occasion must be found for following his influence through the conflicts of the nineteenth century to the modern ecumenical movement.' His monograph for the Tennyson Society ten years later, *Tennyson, Wordsworth and the 'Forms' of Religion* (Lincoln, 1997), demonstrated his ongoing engagement with this fundamental aspect of the poet and seemed to promise that the book we all knew Alan was best placed to write would appear. But illness prevented what would have been the culmination of a career devoted to literature and the literature of religion, and I have no doubt that the disappointment was felt as deeply by Alan as it was by his many admirers.

Alan Hill was a fine scholar, whose work added greatly to knowledge and understanding of the literary and religious culture of the nineteenth century. Much of his editorial labour was unglamorous, but, though he would have been the last person to trumpet this claim, it underpinned the scholarship of a generation of Romanticists and will continue to do so for the foreseeable future.

STEPHEN GILL
Lincoln College, Oxford

GLYN WILLIAM HUMPHREYS

Glyn William Humphreys
1954–2016

GLYN HUMPHREYS WAS A distinguished and influential figure in British neuropsychology and cognitive science. Born on 28 December 1954, Glyn was brought up in Aughton, West Lancashire. The family was academic, with Glyn's father working as a Lecturer in Building Management at Liverpool University; after primary school, Glyn won a scholarship to Merchant Taylors' Boys' School in Crosby. From his earliest years, Glyn was a person who jumped into life's opportunities, with a flair for organisation and for inspiring and including those around him. He was keen on all kinds of competitive sport, from beach games during the traditional family holidays in North Wales to the cricket matches that he continued to organise well into his fifties, and was a lifelong undeterred enthusiast for the triumphs and more frequent woes of Everton FC. An amateur guitarist and recorder player, in his adolescence he was the one to organise long jam sessions at the family home, and forty years later, now working long hours in his academic career, was still playing the recorder and organising the neighbourhood choir in Birmingham. Always ready for a challenge, to seize an opportunity, and to encourage and inspire others, Glyn became a mainstay of his discipline in the UK and abroad, with a staggering record of research productivity, influence and professional service.

In the early 1970s, psychology was still an unusual choice of degree topic. In his teens, Glyn had joined friends to volunteer on Sundays for work in a hospice for young children with psychological problems, as well as working at the Camphill Community for people with learning disabilities on the North York Moors. Perhaps influenced by these experiences,

Glyn elected to study psychology at the University of Bristol, where he obtained a First as an undergraduate, then continued into his PhD.

Along with attention and consciousness, one early interest was the perception of letters and words. Before the introduction of laboratory computers, a key piece of equipment was the tachistoscope, allowing extremely precise control over stimulus presentation and timing. To use a tachistoscope, dozens or hundreds of stimulus cards had to be prepared by hand; on each trial, selected cards were slotted into the machine which then revealed them to the subject in a controlled order and for controlled times. With another student in Bristol, Lindsay Evett, Glyn developed a tachistoscopic procedure for examining how letter identities combine to determine word recognition. In this 'four field' procedure, each trial began with a nonsense stimulus used as a 'mask', followed by a brief letter string or 'prime', a brief word which the subjects were to identify if they could, and finally the mask again. Under these circumstances subjects were largely unaware of the prime but, still, the word was identified better if the prime shared some of its letters. This happened even when prime and target were in different cases, with little visual similarity between them, and especially when prime and target letters were in the same positions *relative to string ends*. Carried out in the early days of cognitive psychology, these experiments remain intriguing for the light they cast on abstract letter coding, word reading and consciousness.

With this strong academic start behind him, and interests already in perception, attention and consciousness, Glyn moved to London in 1979 to take up his first academic job at Birkbeck College. At Bristol Glyn had already married his first wife, Pauline, but the marriage had not lasted. In London in 1981, Glyn met Jane Riddoch, a young clinical neuropsychologist then studying for her PhD. Among the most striking cognitive disorders that can follow damage to one side of the brain, usually a stroke in the right hemisphere, is a tendency to ignore or neglect the opposite side of space. Such unilateral neglect can cause a patient to ignore somebody speaking on their left side, to leave one side of their face unshaven or without make-up, to draw just half-objects from memory. When Jane introduced Glyn to some of her patients, he was immediately fascinated, and from this point on their private and research lives were intertwined. They were married in 1984, raising two young sons from Jane's previous marriage, Iain and Alec, and their daughter Katie. At the same time they became lifetime collaborators, with new ideas constantly sparked by the many kinds of neuropsychological patients daily encountered in the clinic. Over the next thirty-five years, Glyn's work involved many different people using many different methods, but the core was neuropsychology and his work with Jane.

In one of their first projects together, they began their lifetime interest in object recognition, and also a lifetime friendship with 'patient HJA'. Though, like many neglect patients, HJA had suffered a stroke, the effects of this stroke were restricted to the rear part of the brain, the occipital lobes, with their core role in vision. He was left not with neglect but with agnosia, a severe disturbance in the ability to recognise visually presented objects such as a guitar or an owl. Since the nineteenth century, agnosias had traditionally been divided into two forms, 'apperceptive', or a disturbance in constructing the visual percept, and 'associative', or inability to attach meaning to the shape that was seen. An apperceptive agnosic, for example, might be unable even to copy a drawing, while an associative agnosic would copy well but still be unable to say what object had been drawn. HJA, however, fitted neither of these categories perfectly. His knowledge of object shapes in itself was good, as he could draw well from memory. His copying was also good. His core problem appeared to be dealing with the separate parts of an object and integrating them into an organised whole, a deficit Jane and Glyn called 'integrative agnosia'. For example, quite unlike a person with normal vision, HJA recognised silhouettes of objects better than objects with fully drawn details, as if the details themselves created confusion. Over the next twenty-six years before HJA died, Glyn and Jane published over thirty papers and two books based on his impaired and preserved visual abilities. Becoming firm friends with their patient and his wife, they would travel monthly to Guildford to test him at his home, fitting the more strenuous testing into the mornings before the large sherry that HJA enjoyed before lunch. For Glyn and Jane, this work launched a lifelong research interest, pursued using many different approaches, in the component processes and stages by which the visual system transforms the image on the retina into perceived objects and their relations. HJA also became one of the few neuropsychological patients to be followed over decades, bringing new insights into long-term visual representations. As the years went by, for example, his ability to draw objects from memory gradually degraded, as if details were progressively lost now that new examples were no longer being recognised.

A second of Glyn's lifetime interests was visual attention, studied partly in patients with unilateral neglect, but also with many other techniques and approaches. Perhaps typically, my own work with Glyn began with a talk he delivered in Cambridge in the mid-1980s and a subsequent trip to the nearest pub to discuss his results. At this time, Anne Treisman had just published her massively influential and important feature integration theory of visual attention. According to feature integration theory, elementary visual features such as colour, motion or size were perceived in parallel across the visual field. Serial attention to one object after another was needed to integrate these features into the correct conjunctions, ensuring, for example, that a pink O and green X were not perceived as a green O and pink X. One case of feature integration was supposed to be the organisation of shape parts into the correct spatial wholes—for example, the combination of horizontal and vertical letter strokes to form an L versus a T—but Glyn's data showed something wrong with this story because sometimes people could find a target T in a field of non-targets without serial processing, even though the non-targets were made up of just the same strokes (e.g. Ts rotated by 90 degrees). Glyn just had the knack of running interesting experiments and, with the help of a few beers, we decided that the critical factor was his use of a homogeneous non-target field, with the target standing out against the repeated, identical non-targets. With the help of a couple of years' further experiments, we moved to a new view of visual search, one based on competition between the elements of a visual display, with the target matching the needs of the task and hence competing strongly for attention, and grouped or similar non-targets supporting one another's rejection. Over the next ten years, Glyn and I worked to develop this competitive model and apply it to underlying brain functions. Competition, for example, proved a useful approach to understanding attentional impairments after brain damage, including the apparent disappearance of a stimulus on the side opposite to a brain lesion when it was accompanied by a second stimulus on the good or undamaged side. Visual search and feature integration remained mainstays of Glyn's work for the rest of his career. With Derrick Watson, for example, in the 1990s Glyn designed a new kind of visual search experiment, revealing some elements of the display before others and showing sustained, active inhibition of these early non-targets. In a paper published in 2013, Glyn and Jane returned to feature integration theory, using visual search to show hard-wired brain coding of familiar feature conjunctions, such as a red tomato or yellow corn.

Beyond visual search, Glyn used many other methods to study attention and its impairments. Much of this work developed his early interest in unilateral neglect, and its many fascinating variations. Sometimes, for example, a patient might ignore everything drawn on the left half of a sheet of paper, but in other cases it is the left half of each object that is ignored, even the left half of an object drawn on the right side of the sheet. In early work with Jane, Glyn showed the dissociation between these two forms of neglect, and later with Pia Rotshtein worked on the different kinds of brain lesion involved. Linking to our early work on visual search, much of this neglect work also addressed the effects of similarity and grouping; often, an object that is ignored when it occurs in isolation on the left can be rescued if strong perceptual cues group it to a second object on the right. Grouping also became a core theme in work with a second patient who became a lifetime friend, the simultanagnosic GK. In unilateral neglect, one side of the brain is damaged and information on the opposite side of space is ignored, reflecting each hemisphere's largely contralateral representation of space. In simultanagnosia, there are lesions to both sides, and the result is an extraordinary tendency to see only one small part of the visual field at once, leaving everything else apparently invisible. Glyn and Jane began work with GK while still in London, after he was referred to them by a student on Glyn's neuropsychology Masters course. His impairments were so major that he was registered legally blind, walked with a cane and had at one stage been transferred to a blind rehabilitation centre. GK, however, was not blind, just massively simultanagnosic, and over more than twenty years of work with him, Glyn and Jane documented just what it was that he could and could not see. For example, if GK was shown two outline squares, one more perceptually intact than the other, he would see just the more intact shape and deny that the other was present. When the competing, better shape was removed, however, now GK could see the remaining square perfectly well!

Beyond neuropsychology, Glyn was always alive to new ways of understanding attentional functions and limits. In the 1980s, there was an explosion of interest in understanding cognition through connectionist models, and with Hermann Müller Glyn soon developed his own connectionist model of visual search, based on a process of grouping together parts of the visual field with shared properties, then rejecting whole regions as a single chunk. A second major connectionist model, published with Dietmar Heinke in 2003, addressed roles of objects and space in neglect. Another complement to neuropsychology was transcranial magnetic stimulation or TMS, using magnetic pulses delivered over the scalp to reduce activity in the underlying brain tissue temporarily. In a long collaboration with Carmel Mevorach, Glyn used TMS to overturn conventional thinking about the complementary roles of left and right parietal context in attentional selection. Often, it has been thought that the right hemisphere directs attention to more global, large-scale aspects of the visual input, while the left hemisphere directs attention to local detail. Often, however, it is the global aspects of a display that are more physically salient, and using TMS Glyn and Carmel found that salience is crucial. Their evidence suggests that, instead of adjudicating between global versus local, the right hemisphere permits a natural bias to whatever is most salient, while the left overcomes this to allow focus on something less salient but more important.

Though attention and vision were core topics for Glyn, there was always much besides. With Jane he shared a lifetime interest in action, including the impairments in reaching, grasping and goal-directed action planning that can follow damage to parietal and frontal lobes, and the way attention is influenced by visual prompts to action, such as the orientation of a handle. Beyond simple reaching and grasping, they went on to show how attention depends on perceived functional relations between two objects. For example, a patient who has trouble seeing both of two objects in a brief display, such as a cup and a jug, may suddenly do much better when these are positioned to suggest their usual functional interaction (the jug pouring into the cup). Glyn's interest in vision fed into a further interest in the neuropsychology of semantics, and the intriguing finding of patients whose knowledge of some objects, for example living things, is impaired while knowledge of other categories is preserved. Glyn believed that knowledge is organised at many levels, from visual features to many kinds of associations, that different aspects of knowledge interact as meaning is retrieved, and that impairments—for example, in knowledge of visual features—will selectively affect some object categories more than others. Towards the end of his career, with Pia Rotshtein, Glyn developed an interest in social cognition, and in particular the concepts of self versus other. The experiments had all Glyn's usual ingenuity and surprise value. Participants first learned associations between geometrical shapes and one of three personal labels—self, friend, stranger—and then in a series of trials had to decide whether shape–label pairs were consistent with the previously learned association. Though shapes and their labels were arbitrary, and without real meaning outside the context of the experiment, still people showed a strong focus on the self, with much faster decisions for 'self' pairs.

Towards the end of his career, too, Glyn and Jane turned increasingly to the clinical application of neuropsychological knowledge. For them, work with patients had always meant personal commitment, from lifetime friendships with HJA and GK to regular events organised for the many patients and carers that Glyn, Jane and their groups worked with, stimulating interest in research and feeding back its implications for the patients' lives. In 2014 they published the BCoS (Birmingham Cognitive Screen), a comprehensive screen for common neuropsychological impairments, and began actively promoting its use within the NHS and internationally. This was followed by a shorter version, the OCS (Oxford Cognitive Screen), which Glyn dreamt would become internationally accepted as the standard tool for stroke assessment, and which already is used in more than a dozen countries worldwide. With Tom Manly, Glyn, at the time of his death, was working on a tablet-based version, aiming to remove the burden of paper tests from busy clinical neuropsychologists and occupational therapists.

Glyn's commitment and productivity were simply awe-inspiring. Over a career approaching forty years, he published over 650 research articles, along with eighteen authored or edited books, and held over eighty research grants. At the age of just thirty-four, he took up his first head of department post at Birkbeck, soon afterwards moving to become head of department at the University of Birmingham, where he remained for over twenty years. Under his stewardship, Birmingham built up one of the country's premier psychology departments, with state-of-the-art facilities and world-leading staff. In 2011, Glyn moved to lead the UK's top department at the University of Oxford. He had unswerving commitment to the discipline, founding a new journal, *Visual Cognition*, and later serving as the first non-US editor of his field's premier empirical journal, the *Journal of Experimental Psychology: Human Perception and Performance*. At the same time he poured effort into committee and consultation work, serving in 2014 as Chair of the Research Excellence Framework panel for Psychology, Neuroscience and Psychiatry, from 2002 to 2004 as President of the Experimental Psychology Society, and from 2012 to 2014 as President of the British Neuropsychology Society.

As their ideas became established, and their students and post-docs moved to set up their own laboratories, Glyn and Jane also took their family to visiting positions around the world—the University of Waterloo with Derek Besner in 1983 (a long daily commute with the boys listening to Glyn's self-recorded *Star Wars* tapes); the Montreal Neurological Institute with Andrew Kertesz in 1988; Paris in 1992 to begin a long-term collaboration with Muriel Boucart; Bologna with Elisabetta Ladavas in 1997; Leipzig in 1998 with Glyn's former post-doc Hermann Müller; the Salk Institute in 1998 to discuss feature integration theory with Francis

Crick; Melbourne in 1999 with Umberto Castiello; Peking in 1997 and again in 2005–8 with Lin Chen (equipment kept under draperies to protect from sandstorms); Granada in 2009 and 2011 (police escort to their accommodation in the Albaicín); and Hong Kong in 2013–16 to work with Brendan Weekes developing Cantonese and Mandarin versions of their cognitive screen.

Glyn's influence was recognised in a lifetime of awards in the UK and overseas—including the Spearman Medal from the British Psychology Society in 1986; Leibniz Lecturer at the University of Leipzig along with the Humboldt Research Award in 1998; British Psychological Society President's Award in 1999; Honorary Member of the Belgian Experimental Psychology Society in 2002; Special Professor at the Chinese Academy of Science in 2011; Distinguished Professor at the University of Hong Kong in 2013–16; Broadbent Lecturer of the European Society for Cognitive Psychology in 2013; and British Psychological Society's Lifetime Achievement Award in 2015. He was elected Fellow of the British Academy in 2009. A sense of his research contribution is given by his book *Attention, Perception and Action: Selected Works of Glyn Humphreys* (London, 2016), which brings together some of his most influential works published between 1987 and 2014.

Though their work programme was ferocious—typically, Glyn and Jane worked together until ten o'clock, paused to watch the news and then returned to their laptops—they remained equally uncompromising in the time devoted to personal and family lives. Running, swimming, cricket, music, family holidays, children, grandchildren all received the same attention; visiting their home, it was not rare to find Glyn running out to buy food, Jane placing a painting or new piece of furniture, and several grandchildren playing in the kitchen. Somehow, too, there was a striking air of calm, and always time to add one more professional or family demand into the mix.

Both literally and metaphorically, Glyn never stopped running and, sadly but appropriately, on 14 January 2016 he died of a heart attack while out running in Hong Kong. With his death, cognitive neuroscience lost one of its most active, productive and broadly influential figures. Within a few days, messages flooded onto his memorial website from around the world, filled with the gratitude of the countless young scientists he had encouraged and inspired. These messages paint a picture of a true gentleman, always racing between commitments but always with time for the people who needed him, with unswerving focus on what needed to be done coupled to a modest, gentle manner and characteristic twinkling eyes. There are few areas of our discipline that were not influenced by his energy and ideas; he helped to shape a generation, and will be affectionately and admiringly remembered.

JOHN DUNCAN
Fellow of the Academy

OLIVER NICHOLAS MILLAR

© *National Portrait Gallery, London*

Oliver Nicholas Millar
1923–2007

SIR OLIVER MILLAR DEVOTED his career to serving as the first full-time curator of the approximately seven thousand pictures belonging to the Royal Collection, one of the greatest assemblies still in private hands.[1] Over the span of forty-one years in office, he achieved a remarkable double achievement of curation and scholarship, which has placed the Royal Collection virtually on a par with the best run museums in the country. As the editor of *The Burlington Magazine* wrote on the occasion of his retirement: 'What he has achieved at the Royal Collection will stand as a monument to a most distinguished Surveyorship.' At the same time Millar was also a celebrated scholar with an international reputation, who was for many years the doyen of Van Dyck studies.

He was born at Standon, Ware, Hertfordshire, on 26 April 1923, the elder son of Gerald Arthur Millar (1895–1975), publisher, writer and cousin of Daphne du Maurier, and of his wife Ruth (1900–71). He was educated at Rugby. Although his lifelong interest in royal iconography, illustrated by his growing collection of postcards of kings and queens, had already begun at his preparatory school, he was, as Sir John Guinness, a later pupil at the school, wrote:

> partly inspired by a master at Rugby and housemaster of Kilbracken House called Harold Jennings, a.k.a., Squid Jennings. He taught history to 15/16 year olds and also classics. He was very keen on the lives and quirks of individual

---

[1] The British Academy is exceedingly grateful to Sir Christopher White for agreeing to take over responsibility for writing this Memoir because the original memorialist was unable to complete the task.

historical figures and had no time for economic history, e.g. the history of the cloth trade in fifteenth-century England. If he was talking about the reign of James I, he would pin up on his blackboard reproductions of portraits of the main people involved from his immense collection of photographs, reproductions and engravings of historical portraits.[2]

Millar suffered from a heart condition, which precluded him from war service during the Second World War. This disability led to the later rejection of his application to the National Portrait Gallery by the bigoted director of the time, who would not accept the idea of appointing someone who, unlike him, had not fought in the war. (It was the gallery's loss, since given his interests, he would have made an outstanding curator.[3]) He went as a student to the Courtauld Institute of Art, London University, when the Institute was establishing itself as the leading centre of art history in the country under Professors Anthony Blunt and Johannes Wilde, two distinguished scholars as different in character as it is possible to imagine. Fellow students were such figures as Professor John White and Dr Anita Brookner. He was awarded an Academic Diploma. He was very much a protégé of Anthony Blunt, with whom he went on to have a very harmonious professional relationship. (He was surprised and shocked by the revelations in 1979, but remained a friend and occasional visitor to Blunt who was then living in purdah.) Although not a member of the staff, he remained very much a presence at the Courtauld, giving lectures when required. His enthusiasm for what interested him was infectious, above all for portrait painting in England in the seventeenth century. Van Dyck needed no boosting, but the present writer can remember to his surprise being kept awake and absorbed during a lecture delivered on a hot summer's afternoon on later English seventeenth-century portrait painters. At about the same time there was an annual summer outing for staff and students to Althorp. Millar emerged from a room at one point declaiming excitedly to all those willing to listen, 'There is almost a good Hudson in there', when, it has to be admitted, even a good Thomas Hudson would be unlikely to quicken the pulse of most people.

There was a more personal matter to retain his interest in the Institute, since among the undergraduates he lectured was his future wife, Delia Mary Dawnay (1931–2004). The Courtauld being the small world it was

---

[2] Email to the present writer, 30 May 2016.

[3] Later he had the satisfaction of serving as a trustee of the gallery for many years (1972–95), but even this was not without its moment of drama. When his favoured candidate for the directorship was passed over, he resigned, but rescinded his decision just before his resignation was accepted at the next meeting of the trustees.

in those days, it was something of a public courtship. It was mischievously rumoured that Millar waited before proposing until it was learnt that she got a first, which she duly did. Unintentionally their engagement introduced a note of humanity into that austere temple of higher learning, when shortly afterwards he, on arriving at Home House, the then elegant home of the Institute, leaped up while she ran down Robert Adam's semicircular staircase: they hurtled into in one another's arms on the landing. The whole incident was witnessed by, among others, the somewhat bemused Professor Blunt and Dr Whinney. The marriage took place at the Queen's Chapel, Marlborough Gate, London, on 21 January 1954. Thereafter Delia deserved a first for being the perfect spouse, loving, encouraging and sharing in every aspect of his life. As her contribution to scholarship in the royal cause, she produced a very impressive two-volume catalogue of *The Victorian Watercolours and Drawings in the Collection of Her Majesty The Queen* (London, 1995) in which he took great pride and for which she received a CVO. She sadly died from cancer before him in 2004, having happily seen an advanced copy of the Van Dyck catalogue (see below), in which she had helped so tirelessly; his part is dedicated to her. Among the set of photographs of contemporary British art historians made by their eldest daughter, Lucy Dickens, there is a very telling image of her parents (reproduced here); he, in shirtsleeves, is seated commandingly at a table with his papers spread out in considerable disarray before him, while she stands, mentally on tiptoe, at the end of the table, ever ready to jump in with assistance.[4] No Pamina was ever closer to her Tamino than Delia was to Oliver.

At first they lived in a grace and favour apartment in Friary Court, St James's Palace, but when a pram appeared at the door—they had three daughters followed by a son—they exchanged city life for suburban country life. They bought a house in the attractive village of Penn, in Buckinghamshire, which was to become one of the most expensive places to live in Britain. From there, dressed like a country gentleman in well-tailored tweeds and invariably wearing a Newbury hat and a silk scarf tied loosely around his neck—'doggy' was how Brigid Brophy described him—Millar travelled into London on the Chiltern line to Marylebone, that elegant, bijou station almost exclusively reserved for those who live in the shires. Tall and thin, with a slight stoop, he cut a distinguished figure as he hastened through the streets of St James's.

[4] A set is in the National Portrait Gallery, London, accessible on online: http://www.npg.org.uk/collections/search/portrait-list.php?search=sp&sText=Oliver Millar (accessed 9 December 2016).

He began his career as a member of the Royal Household in 1947, when, as the first full-time employee in the history of the Surveyorship, he was appointed Assistant Surveyor of the King's Pictures by Anthony Blunt. He became Deputy Surveyor in 1949 and, on Blunt's retirement in 1972, he was appointed Surveyor of the Queen's Pictures, and finally in 1987, a year before he retired, he was appointed, justly in view of all he had achieved, the first Director of the Royal Collection. During these years he advanced from being appointed MVO in 1953, to CVO in 1963, to KCVO in 1973, and finally in 1988 on the day of his retirement, just before his farewell party at Buckingham Palace, he was made GCVO. Shortly after his retirement he wrote an essay entitled 'Caring for the Queen's pictures: surveyors past and present', which in view of its autobiographical references and inferences can be regarded as his 'last will and testament'.[5]

Previous Surveyors, working part time and with other demanding jobs to occupy them, did not achieve much presence within the Royal Household. As Assistant Surveyor, a post created for Millar since Benedict Nicolson was still nominally Deputy Surveyor, he faced the challenge to establish what in today's jargon would be called a power base, from which he could operate with accepted authority. Starting from scratch, with his status no higher than that of a midshipman on a battleship, it took time, determination and diplomacy. For most of his career his office was limited to two narrow rooms off the State Apartments in St James's Palace, one of which was filched from the Examiners of Plays and both of which barely contained the numerous inventories of the collection. Content to work on his own, he spent his days there in happy isolation apart from the presence of a devoted part-time assistant, Mrs Gilbert Cousland.

Of all the previous holders of his office going back in time to Abraham van der Doort in 1625, the one he admired most was the artist Richard Redgrave (1804–1888) for his 'devotion to painting, dedication to the welfare of the pictures in his charge, and professionalism in matters of conservation and display, when allied to his modesty, integrity and—perhaps most of all—his capacity for unrelenting hard work'.[6] Millar might well have been describing himself.

---

[5] *The Queen's Pictures: Royal Collectors through the Centuries*, exhibition catalogue by Christopher Lloyd, National Gallery, London, 1991, pp. 14–27, from which numerous quotations below are taken.

[6] O. Millar, 'Redgrave and the Royal Collection', in S. Casteras and R. Parkinson (eds.), *Richard Redgrave 1804–1888* (New Haven, CT, and London, 1988), pp. 86–7.

At that stage he came under the aegis of the Lord Chamberlain's Office. As he wrote, it was 'eccentric that the administration of a great collection should have been to a large extent in the hands of a succession of charming retired Lieutenant-Colonels of the (generally 1st) Foot Guards' who 'were delightful to work with'. One of them was the Comptroller of the Lord Chamberlain's Office, with whom he played golf on Sunday mornings, an engagement which could have done Millar's budget no harm. As a result of his attention to their professional relationship, he could modestly note that 'By the end of our long association he may have come to realise that it is not impossible for an art historian at least to try to be a competent administrator and even to master the rudiments of financial management.' Millar, unlike Blunt who never fitted happily into the social side of the role, was the perfect discreet courtier, at ease in royal company, but never obsequious and, occasionally, capable of quietly noticing some inadequacies in his 'employer', as he liked to call her.

After many years of building up and consolidating his department, 'the formal break with our old colleagues [which] was overdue' came about at last in 1987 as a result of a report commissioned by the Queen on the organisation of the Royal Household from the consultancy firm, Peat Marwick. This, acknowledging the achievements of the Surveyor of Pictures, recommended the creation of a new Royal Collection Department, a sixth Department of the Royal Household, which should be administered independently from the Lord Chamberlain's Office. This brought the vast collection of paintings, drawings, works of art, library, well over 200,000 objects in total, under a single directorship, which, as has been said, was inaugurated by Millar. At the same time more spacious quarters, shared with Works of Art, were provided in Stable Yard House.

Although as Surveyor he was responsible for a group of pictures which any museum director in the world might be proud to have in his charge, he did not have the latter's absolute control over his collection, but was the servant of a monarch and her household, who had to be tactfully consulted and ultimately obeyed over questions of where pictures hung. As he said, 'A surveyor has no prescriptive right to be consulted when rooms are redecorated at Buckingham Palace or Windsor', or on what was lent out to outside exhibitions. The royal family may not be connoisseurs, but they have their favourite pictures and do not like them to be removed, even temporarily, from their private rooms. The Queen, for example, speaks possessively of her favourite picture in the whole collection, Rembrandt's *Shipbuilder and his Wife*, or of Gerard ter Borch's *The Letter*, which hangs in her private dining room and was, as she likes to relate, always admired for its silk dresses by her couturier Norman Hartnell on his professional visits to Buckingham Palace. An understandable reluctance to lend had to be overcome by diplomacy and by persuasion that the purpose of the exhibition was serious. Nearer to home were the loans to the new gallery created, with much input from Millar, at Buckingham Palace in 1962, which allowed, among other things, the temporary display of pictures from that palace not normally seen by the public. (A greatly enlarged gallery was opened in 2002.)

At a lower level tact and firmness—'a flask of healing oil is as important a part of a Surveyor's kit as his torch and measure'—was required when dealing with the superintendents and housekeepers of the royal palaces, who often tended to think that they had the right to deal with the pictures as they saw fit. 'I vividly remember going into the Picture Gallery [at Buckingham Palace] one summer afternoon to discover that *all* the pictures had been taken down on instructions from the Superintendent who, a few years earlier, stuck adhesive labels to the *surfaces* of the pictures so that they would be readily identified in the event of fire.'

Perhaps the greatest testimony to Millar's love of pictures under his control was his concern for their conservation. When he arrived he found no overall awareness of the need for care among the staff. Terrible things had happened: 'Even in modern times a Superintendent did not scruple to slice a large piece off the top of a group by Zoffany or to reduce a fine pair of large Winterhalters so that they would fit better into a room at Balmoral,' or when 'the Superintendent at Windsor, early in Queen Victoria's reign, cut down Gainsborough's lovely full-length group of the three eldest princesses'. Now when pictures were reduced in size, the unseen part of the canvas was folded over to be protected for posterity.

And then there were the daily hazards of palace life to be constantly guarded against. The painting by Wootton hanging above the equerry's tea-time kettle boiling away undetected; the large Rubens, placed over a serving table with, before its recent cleaning, its darkened surface reflecting the traces of menus of past times; or the three paintings by Stubbs which were left hanging exposed on the walls when painters were at work in the room.

As Millar claimed, 'Nothing in the history of the Surveyorship has been more beneficial to the pictures than the establishment of the studio at St James's Palace. Proper standards of conservation and maintenance of the pictures can be established.' And since then most of this work is now carried out at a greatly enlarged conservation studio, with a full-time staff, in Windsor Great Park, where care is up to museum standards.

Millar oversaw the beginning of a general programme of cleaning and restoration, which had never happened in the past. And his care for the collection was extended to considerable research so as to provide frames suitable both for the picture itself and where it hung. 'We were always anxious, for example, to remove as many as possible of the unattractive frames, made by William Thomas, in which Prince Albert reframed all the (predominantly Dutch and Flemish) pictures in the Picture Gallery at Buckingham Palace.'

Millar ends the account of his and his predecessors' career on a lyrical note. 'A Surveyor', as he says elsewhere 'the best job in the world':

> will learn to appreciate the shrewdness of the advice once given by a very wise colleague: it doesn't matter how much you enjoy your job, what *does* matter are the footsteps you leave for a successor to tread in. And to work on the royal pictures and their past does lead you along some delightful tracks: from the footpath beside the Dee, where you try to get the blood going after an April's day's work in Balmoral, through many other enchanted spots to the sunlit rooms and passages of Osborne, where, posing as a convalescent, you can work by the hour in the shadow of Prince Albert. It is wise to avoid distractions and outside commitments, to scorn delights and live laborious days with the pictures themselves; and when, in theory, you retire, to look forward, as Redgrave did in *his* retirement, to visits from friends who told him 'something about his beloved pictures in the royal palaces'.[7]

Alas, as many a retiree has found, such conversations can lead to painful discoveries, such as, for example, when one learns that the carefully designed arrangement of the fourteen views of Venice by Canaletto, the *Prospectus Magni Canalis*, displayed in the Long Corridor at Windsor Castle, is now dispersed, having been 'criticized as hung by one with the instincts of a stamp collector'.

Millar had devoted so much of his life and achieved so much in developing the care and study of the collection that he found it difficult to hand over happily to his successor, to whom he unquestionably gave a hard time. Whereas Millar had pencilled in for the latter many hours to be spent, as he himself had done, at the Public Record Office transcribing documents—various areas to be covered are specifically suggested—Christopher Lloyd saw it of more consequence in these changing times to spend time making the collection more widely known by lecturing throughout the world on what was in his care.

No less impressive than his curatorial successes was the degree of scholarship Millar introduced into the study of the collection. In the past

[7] Lloyd, *The Queen's Pictures*, p. 27.

there had been a number of inadequate catalogues, devoted to the holdings in the different palaces. Blunt, however, started a more substantial programme of cataloguing the pictures, following what was already under way with the drawings at Windsor Castle, but little had actually been achieved until Millar took over the responsibility for carrying out the work.

It was characteristic of Millar, as a scholar of detail, that he began his research on the Royal Collection by the laborious editing of the MS catalogue of pictures drawn up during the reign of Charles I by Abraham van der Doort, the first Surveyor of the Royal Collection.[8] 'I cannot exaggerate the pleasure, or the wealth of insights gained, in simply copying out Van der Doort's manuscripts', but many art historians, especially in view of the illegibility of the latter's handwriting, would be more likely to agree with Millar's *arrière-pensée* that 'it is exhausting work'. (Millar's later handwriting was hardly more legible than Van der Doort's and earned him the polite but firm request from one of the Queen's private secretaries: 'Could you please use a typewriter.'[9]) Van der Doort's manuscripts were vital in establishing much about the early years of the collection, such as authorship, provenance and where the pictures were displayed. Some years later Millar followed this archival work up with the publication of the inventories and valuations of the goods belonging to the royal family which were sold at the time of the Commonwealth, which were of no less importance in the cataloguing of the collection.[10]

There had been a number of summary catalogues of the pictures, divided by residence rather than by school, but none reached the standard expected in the second half of the last century. He began with *The Tudor, Stuart and Early Georgian Pictures in the Collection of H.M. The Queen* (London, 1963), in which the hero was Van Dyck, whose presence in the British School, it has to be said, was somewhat questionable. It covered a period about which he could claim prime authority, with the minor figures being treated as thoroughly as the more important artists. This was followed by *The Later Georgian Pictures in the Collection of H.M. The Queen* (London, 1969), of which the stars were Gainsborough and Lawrence. He gave a richly descriptive account of the artistic as well as court life of the times. He completed his cataloguing of the British School

---

[8] O. Millar, 'Abraham van der Doort's catalogue of the collection of Charles I', *Walpole Society*, 37 (1960), 1–243.

[9] Recorded by C. Lloyd, 'Millar, Sir Oliver Nicholas (1923–2007)', *Oxford Dictionary of National Biography*, http://www.oxforddnb.com/view/article/98814 (accessed 9 December 2016).

[10] O. Millar, 'The inventories and valuations of the King's goods 1649–1651', *Walpole Society*, 43 (1972), 1–443.

with the largest section of all, *The Victorian Pictures in the Collection of H.M. The Queen* (Cambridge, 1992); it was a period in which he felt less assured, but the result maintained the high standard of the previous volumes. The most substantial part of the collection was the Queen's collection of portraits, often of a mediocre quality, but the collection was enlivened by likenesses of her favourite animals, above all of dogs, and the multi-figured pictures of numerous royal ceremonies so enjoyed by the Queen, which have been meticulously catalogued by Millar.

Over almost thirty years he catalogued in all 2,336 paintings. As well as the intellectual task this posed a physical challenge, since Millar firmly believed that every picture must be carefully examined in the original, both back and front. This work, far from being carried out under ideal museum conditions in laboratories, had to be undertaken *in situ*; many pictures were hidden away in attics, distant corridors and storerooms, and had to be lifted off the walls and then replaced, more often than not by him alone. Sometimes the work was carried out in arctic conditions, with pleas to a housekeeper to keep on a little heating heartlessly ignored. His status as guardian of the Queen's pictures did not 'cut much ice' with the hardened and no doubt philistine Resident Factor at Balmoral.

He had a great feeling for the quality and character of a painting. The collection of British pictures, and those deemed to come into the category as by foreign artists working in England, is predominantly made up of portraits, for the art of which Millar had an innate understanding, a quality particularly apparent in his introductions to the catalogues. Given the enormous range between the very good and very bad in the works he had to cover, he always maintained a keen eye for the quality of a painting, at one moment writing that Benjamin West's 'figures appear to be modelled in cardboard', or, scraping the barrel, castigating John Pettie's portrait of Bonnie Prince Charlie, as an image 'more at home on a tin of Edinburgh rock in Princes Street', while, at the other end of the scale, praising the state portrait by Gainsborough of Queen Charlotte for showing 'incomparable sensibility and skill, with tenderness, a latent gaiety and a magic sense of poetry', or lauding Lawrence for having created 'one of the most dazzling sets of portraits in the ancient tradition of the *Hommes Illustres*', which now hang in Waterloo Chamber at Windsor Castle.

Although his catalogue entries are not to be faulted where the provision of basic information about a picture is concerned, paying particular attention, for example, to the existence of copies, they tend to be undernourished in providing the kind of general discussion about a picture now favoured in most catalogues. Although to some extent he made up for this in his long introductory essays, he was sometimes cavalier in giving sources for items of fascinating information, which could, given the extent of his knowledge, be difficult to track down. When remonstrated with, he did not show much sign of repentance.

To catalogue the pictures from the continental schools, outside scholars were commissioned to undertake the work. For these Millar acted as an inspired *cicerone*, and, when they submitted their results, they found him a demanding but appreciative editor. On inspection tours they were led by him, invariably with a torch in one hand and a tape measure in the other, at a smart pace through the royal palaces from basement to attic. Progress was usually accompanied by quick-fire conversation relating to anything from the painting in question to general topics of the day. There was no lingering in the corridors or encouragement to look at other treasures on the way to one's goal. At the end of a morning, say at Buckingham Palace, the cataloguer would, greatly stimulated but somewhat breathless, be deposited at the Privy Purse Door, leaving Millar free to go off and enjoy a pre-luncheon gin and tonic with other senior members of the Royal Household.

As the Royal Collection exhibition programme gradually built up speed, Millar was increasingly called upon to contribute essays to the catalogues, which at the time, by convention, remained unsigned. And to round out his overall study of the collection, he produced a comprehensive, fluently written history of the collection from the Tudor times to the present day in *The Queen's Pictures* (London, 1977), published on the occasion of the Queen's Silver Jubilee. His concise style allowed him to include a vast amount of information and pithy comment. He had a firm grasp of history and was not tempted by virtue of his position to see monarchs of the past through royalty-tinted glasses: Charles I, 'as a ruler, obstinate, devious and self-deluding'; Queen Anne, 'the dullest and meanest of the Stuarts'; Frederick, Prince of Wales, 'an irritating irresponsible scatterbrain'; George IV, 'a self-indulgent and neurotic wastrel'. But when it was deserved, and this of course was the point of the book, he was eloquent in his praise for their achievements as patrons and collectors. The stars of the collection are unquestionably Charles I and George IV, but he showed great sympathy for George III.

What was remarkable was that his work for the Royal Collection amounted to only one part of his scholarly output, which was wide in what it covered of seventeenth- and eighteenth-century British art. His approach to works of art was traditional connoisseurship, concentrating on the object itself, and not studied, as in the so-called new art history, in a wider sociological or theoretical context.

Early in his career he collaborated with Margaret Whinney, under whom he had studied during his Courtauld days, in publishing *English Art, 1625–1714* (Oxford, 1957), in which he wrote with great fluency on the painting of the period, including a very good chapter on the miniature. The only other survey he ever undertook was the memorable exhibition at the Tate Gallery, London, entitled *The Age of Charles I: Painting in England, 1620–1649* (London, 1972), which brought together a rich display of paintings, drawings, sculpture, engraving, miniatures and medals created during that epic period of British patronage and collecting. Arranged by carefully chosen themes, it was an example of a truly successful didactic exhibition, which offered an illuminating conspectus of its subject.

Basically he was by temperament happier writing about an individual artist. In 1951 he arranged and catalogued an exhibition at the Tate Gallery entitled *William Dobson 1611–1646* (London, 1951). It was the first of two other shows devoted to a previously underrated artist who immediately followed Van Dyck but in his own individual way. He wrote about Rubens only once but to good purpose in the Charlton Lecture on Art, published as *Rubens: the Whitehall Ceiling* (Oxford, 1958), elucidating for the first time that marvellous composite oil-sketch, now in the Tate Gallery, London, which adumbrated the designs for no less than seven of the nine scenes which make up the decoration of the ceiling of the Banqueting House in Whitehall. This attracted a compliment from one of the sternest of Rubens scholars, Julius Held, who wrote that 'every student of the complex of questions connected with it will forever more be in debt to his [Millar's] studies'.[11]

In 1978 he arranged a pioneering exhibition of the paintings and drawings of Sir Peter Lely, at the National Portrait Gallery. The catalogue provided an up-to-date account of the artist's life and work that was to be the subject of a complete catalogue, never completed, which was to occupy Millar's last years.[12]

Moving into the eighteenth century, he wrote at the beginning of his scholarly career a short book about Gainsborough, *Thomas Gainsborough* (London, 1949), 'the best and most beguiling of English painters', as he

---

[11] J. Held, 'Rubens' Glynde Sketch and the installation of the Whitehall Ceiling', *The Burlington Magazine*, 112 (1970), 274.

[12] The catalogue is being completed by Diana Dethloff, who was helping Millar before his death.

was later to call him, and who must surely have ranked as number two in his pantheon of painters. This was followed by a well-informed study of *Zoffany and his Tribuna* (London, 1967), a picture in the Royal Collection brimming over with portraits of British on the Grand Tour and the works of art which they were admiring, which called for the precise identification of the kind which was Millar's forte. Because there was so much relevant information about the picture, this was in fact an excursus of his catalogue entry to be published shortly afterwards in *The Later Georgian Pictures in the Collection of H.M. The Queen*.

But unquestionably, where painting was concerned, the love of his life was the work of Sir Anthony van Dyck, and most particularly his portraits of English sitters. Over the course of fifty years he acquired a profound knowledge and, even more importantly, a deep sympathy with and understanding of the artist which, from 1967, was warmed daily by the sight of Van Dyck's fine portrait of *Princess Mary, Princess Royal, and later Princess of Orange* hanging on his own walls.[13] If he never wrote the substantive monograph on the artist, for which his admirers always hoped, he nevertheless made a major contribution to the subject.

He first became publicly involved in the artist in 1953, when he was responsible for choosing the thirty-seven works by Van Dyck that were a major part of the great exhibition of Flemish art held at the Royal Academy. Serious scholarship began with the first volume of the Royal Collection, which contains no less than twenty-six paintings by the artist, many of superb quality. But he gave freer rein to his feelings about the artist in the memorable exhibition of *Van Dyck in England* at the National Portrait Gallery, London (1982), which brought together sixty-five paintings as well as a group of drawings. Millar's love and understanding of the artist is revealed in the catalogue. The introduction is a masterly account of the artist's entire life and the entries contain some of the most eloquent words he wrote about the pictures themselves. As an example of his empathy, one can cite his evocation of the portrait of Lady Ann Carr, Countess of Bedford, in the collection of The Lord Egremont, at Petworth:

> in every way one of Van Dyck's most magical portraits: the subtle sense of movement in the figure as the sitter moves imperceptibly forward is enhanced by the momentarily frozen movement in the hands, by the flutter of the scarf, 'A Lawne about the shoulders thrown', the stirring of the curtain and the trembling

---

[13] After his death the picture was accepted under the Acceptance in Lieu scheme and appropriately allotted to the Historic Royal Palaces, and displayed, beside the sitter's father, Charles I, at Hampton Court Palace, where it is now suggested it originally hung.

of the rose-bush. The handling of the face and hair is exceedingly delicate and fresh, and the slight asymmetry in the sitter's eyes adds to the sense of a living sitter facing the painter. The rose at her breast and the single pearl lying over her womb probably indicate that the Countess is pregnant.[14]

The culmination of his work on Van Dyck came with his contribution to the *catalogue raisonné* of the artist's paintings, which brought him together with three other scholars.[15] It has to be admitted that this major project had a long and painful birth. One scholar, apart from being very dilatory in finishing, worked, to Millar's understandable disgust, only from photographs. For him it was an article of faith that judgements of connoisseurship had to be made on the basis of studying the original painting. But no less pertinent to the difficulties was the fact that, where Van Dyck was concerned, Millar was, as he was the first to admit, 'a cat that walked by himself'. At one point he was fired from the project by his fellow authors and had to be coaxed back. His part in the magnum opus, in which he was responsible for the work executed in England, included the largest number of works in any section of the volume and, moreover, as far as connoisseurship was concerned, it was, given the numerous authentic repetitions, variants and copies by other artists, the most difficult part of the *oeuvre* to study. His entries continued the approach of the exhibition catalogue, with numerous inspired perceptive characterisations of individual works, while the introductory essay gave a consummate overview of the last decade of the artist's life.

A notably hard-working man of great energy, he was a warm and loyal friend, generally courteous to anyone with whom he had dealings; he was always generous with knowledge and help to the young. But he was a more complex character than his usual friendliness and geniality might lead one to suppose, so that it was disconcerting, without warning, to come up suddenly against a severely critical vein in his character. He could be impulsive in his reaction to events and he sometimes regretted what he had said or done, and was fulsome with apologies. His standards were high and he had a clear idea how something should be carried out. If there was any variance, the other party could expect to be told in no uncertain if not brutal terms where they were failing. If you submitted something

---

[14] National Portrait Gallery, *Van Dyck in England*, no. 41. Were it not for its length, I would have quoted his masterly analysis (no. 11) of *Charles I on Horseback with M. St Antoine*, a picture, still in the Royal Collection, which he knew so well and which had hung in St James's Palace.
[15] S. J. Barnes, N. de Poorter, O. Millar and H. Vey, *Van Dyck, a Complete Catalogue of the Paintings* (New Haven, CT, and London, 2004).

you had written to him, the experience was undoubtedly beneficial to the accuracy of your MS but his criticisms were likely to be delivered with a sharp application of the schoolmaster's rod, particularly when it related to a subject dear to his heart. The present writer once had the temerity, or perhaps the foolishness, to ask him to read something he had written about Van Dyck and was seared by his response, although Millar did have the grace to say a few nice words when the booklet was published. Clearly he felt some guilt over his possessiveness about Van Dyck, since following the publication of *Van Dyck, a Complete Catalogue of the Paintings* he wrote a curious, exculpatory letter to *The Burlington Magazine*, expressing indebtedness to some fourteen scholars and conservators, whom he had failed to acknowledge adequately if at all in the book itself.[16] In his very last published work, a review of a book about *echt* Millar territory, Charles I's collection, he relentlessly dissected with a scalpel what, to him, were 'its errors, its repetitions, its prejudice, its tiresome analyses of motives, its overstretched interpretation of events, its flights of imagination and inverted scenarios'.[17] Let it not be said that Sir Oliver departed this world with his critical faculties diminished.

Millar was an interesting mixture of grandeur and attractive simplicity. It is a moot point whether he was a snob. He certainly was partial to people living in historic houses with pictures hanging on their walls, but that could be regarded as an expression of professional curiosity. His children recall being taken out on a weekend afternoon to call unannounced at some substantial house in the vicinity. The surprise of the owners at their unexpected and unknown visitor was soon deflected by Millar's charm and by the fact that he knew very much more about their house than they did. This aspect of his character was amusingly parodied by Sir Michael Levey: 'I must also mention that I lunched with Oliver whose tour of Scotland in the summer had taken in various recherché, difficult of access Scottish castles, etc. "But, of course," he kept saying, "*you* know Fergus McCluskie and his house, I'm sure, Michael." By the end of the meal, otherwise agreeable, I had, truthfully, denied knowing about 20 lairds, 7 castles, 6 houses half-designed by Adam and a quantity of dowagers living on islands in the middle of lochs in or around the

---

[16] O. Millar, 'The Van Dyck Catalogue', *The Burlington Magazine*, 146 (2004), 553.
[17] O. Millar, 'Jerry Brotton, *The Sale of the Late King's Goods: Charles I and his Art Collection*', *The Court Historian*, 12 (2007), 71–80. The *coup de grâce* was Millar's denial of the author's acknowledgement of having received help from the former. I am indebted to Simon Jervis for bringing this review to my attention.

Trossachs. "Just those people who have Balmoral" I feel like murmuring at the umpteenth enquiry.'[18]

His numerous non-professional interests and pastimes were clearly defined and gave substance to any social conversation you had with him. Dickens and Trollope were among his cherished authors, but *Emma* was his favourite book. In music Mozart was the most loved of composers; while he lived in London, he could hardly have missed a single concert given by the London Mozart Players. As he revealed on *Desert Island Discs*, he also liked a sprightly military tune of the kind he must have frequently heard through his office window.[19] He was a competent draughtsman, who greatly enjoyed sketching and designed his own Christmas cards. His early letters were often illustrated with what he had just seen when travelling. He loved gardening, and all the aspects of nature with which he was surrounded; he was a dab hand at identifying a bird on the wing or on canvas. In sport, golf, as has already been mentioned, was much enjoyed. He was a member of the MCC and his passion for the game was illustrated by the annual match at Penn, which he set up and took with great seriousness, when he led his own local eleven onto the pitch against a visiting team, made up largely of art dealers and captained by his old friend, Evelyn Joll, a Director of Agnews. And in later life, his grandchildren gave him much pleasure. His was a very English life. Lunching with him was to engage in an exhilaratingly brisk *tour d'horizon* of many of these topics, not forgetting the world of art history and the foibles of colleagues, which he treated with detached amusement but never malice.

On the morning of 10 May 2007 he went to Christie's to inspect a painting by Sir Peter Lely, often thought, but not by Millar, to be identifiable with 'Madam [Nell] Gwynn's picture naked with a Cupid', painted for Charles II. Afterwards, on his way to lunch at the National Gallery with two former colleagues, he collapsed and died from a heart attack, just near the bench in the garden in St James's Square where he had often enjoyed a sandwich lunch with his wife.

He was elected a Fellow of the British Academy in 1970. He was a Trustee of the National Portrait Gallery (1972–95), the National Art Collection

---

[18] Letter to the present writer, 16 October 1984.
[19] Broadcast on 4 June 1977. His favourite was the Countess and Susanna's duet ('Sull aria') from Act 3 of Mozart's *Marriage of Figaro*. Music also played: excerpts from Haydn's Symphony no. 100 (Military); Mozart's Piano Concerto no. 21; Purcell's *Indian Queen*; Gilbert and Sullivan's *Patience*; Britten's *Little Sweep* and a song by him; and *Lilliburlero* played by the Regimental Band of the Coldstream Guards.

Fund (1986–98) and National Heritage Memorial Fund (1988–92), as well as serving on the boards of a number of other organisations connected with the arts.

CHRISTOPHER WHITE
Fellow of the Academy

Note. Sources drawn upon for this memoir include: K. Rose, *Kings, Queens and Courtiers: Intimate Portraits of the Royal House of Windsor from its Foundation to the Present Day* (London, 1985), p. 210; 'Editorial', *The Burlington Magazine*, 130 (1988), 507–8; Obituaries in *The Times* (12 May 2007), the *Daily Telegraph* (14 May 2007), *The Independent* (16 May 2007, by Christopher White), the *Guardian* (17 May 2007, by Tom Corby), *The Burlington Magazine*, 119 (2007), 554–5 (by Michael Levey) and Christopher Lloyd's in the *Oxford Dictionary of National Biography* (see note 9). I am grateful for help from Lucy Dickens, Professor Brian Allen, Professor Christopher Brown, Sir John Guinness, Simon Jervis and Christopher Lloyd.

MARILYN SPEERS BUTLER

Marilyn Speers Butler
1937–2014

MARILYN BUTLER WAS THE LEADING British romantic scholar of her generation, whose books *Maria Edgeworth: a Literary Biography* (1972), *Jane Austen and the War of Ideas* (1975), *Peacock Displayed* (1979) and *Romantics, Rebels and Reactionaries* (1981), as well as numerous essays and articles, introductions and editorial collections, redefined our understanding of the period and its literature. Displaying an immense knowledge gleaned from wide reading across disciplinary boundaries, her books and articles have stood the test of time, and are still read with pleasure by students and researchers alike, more than a decade after her publishing career was sadly terminated by illness. Their boldness, accessibility and urbanity aptly represent Marilyn's engaging personality, her irreverent wit and love of intellectual argument. The guiding principle of her historical criticism was that 'the writings of the past ask for an educated reading, as far as possible from within their own discourse or codes or cultural system'.[1] This was a creed that challenged the 'New Critical' and subjectivist principles that guided post-war literary study, as well as the structuralist and post-structuralist criticism that sought to displace it in the 1970s and 1980s. Marilyn always read far beyond the received canon, questioning the very concept of 'romanticism' itself as it was understood by twentieth-century critics: Paul Hamilton puts it nicely when he writes about the relationship between the canon and the archive in which 'must reside the alternatives that made the canon a choice, a risk, an election, a

---

[1] M. Butler, 'Against tradition: the case for a particularized historical method', in J. McGann (ed.), *Historical Studies and Literary Criticism* (Madison, WI, 1985), p. 43.

political act ... official literary history is [always] shadowed, in Butler's work, by other possible literary choices and histories'.[2]

Central to her project of challenging the canon of six romantic male poets was her critical reassessment of the role of women writers, whether established figures such as Jane Austen, then lesser-known women such as Mary Wollstonecraft and Maria Edgeworth, and no one else perhaps did more to bring about this fundamental step change in contemporary understandings of romanticism. Although her relationship to 1970s feminism (and indeed to the politics of the British New Left) was more that of a critical fellow-traveller than of a wholehearted partisan, Marilyn never tired of reminding fellow academics that 'students of literature, like readers of novels, are predominately female, a demographic fact which male producers of literary criticism forget at their peril'.[3] But her liberal, 'second-wave' feminist convictions informed her professional trajectory as well as her work: as the first female King Edward VII Professor of English at Cambridge, and as Rector of Exeter College, Oxford (she was the first woman head of a traditionally all-male college), she energetically challenged the 'glass ceiling' limiting the career development of women academics. If her published scholarship has influenced a whole generation of male as well as female critics, she also deserves special credit for having inspired women academics to challenge the barriers that still effectively block female advancement.

Although Marilyn Butler's professional career was centrally located in the 'golden triangle' of Oxford, Cambridge and London, she was in fact something of an interloper, which undoubtedly influenced her 'devolutionary' understanding of romanticism. She was born Marilyn Speers Evans on 11 February 1937 in Kingston upon Thames, to Trevor (later Sir Trevor) Evans and his wife Margaret (née Gribbins). Her father commuted into central London to work as the redoubtable industrial and labour correspondent for the *Daily Express*. (Apparently Kingston was chosen because it was the destination of the only train that left Fleet Street after 4 a.m., the hour of the *Express*'s last edition.) Before entering journalism Trevor Evans, who hailed from a family of Welsh-speaking coalminers, had worked down the Abertridwr pit in Glamorgan. The Welsh connection explains why, at the outbreak of war in 1939, Marilyn was evacuated

---

[2] P. Hamilton, 'Introduction', in H. Glen and P. Hamilton (eds.), *Repossessing the Romantic Past* (Cambridge, 2006), p. 3.
[3] M. Butler, *Jane Austen and the War of Ideas* (Oxford, 1975; reprint with new introduction, 1987), p. xxvi.

with her English mother and brother to board with her father's cousins at New Quay in Ceredigion. In an unpublished auto-obituary written for Dr Jane Mellanby of St Hilda's College, Oxford, Butler gives a wonderful glimpse of how she 'acquired a permanent sense of Welshness from a childhood spent on this coast, with its long sandy beaches and spectacular caves. More Evans cousins, living further inland, ran a pub with smallholding attached. Memories included falling off a haystack, luckily accompanied by a bale of hay, feeding swill to pigs and (illegally) drinking warm milk fresh from the cow. School instruction was in Welsh and English.'[4] As a girl she might unknowingly have crossed paths with Dylan Thomas, who was also living in New Quay in the early 1940s:[5] by the end of the war she spoke fluent Welsh and had acquired what her son Ed calls her 'internal Celt'. She was already a prodigious reader, and her cousin Val Atkinson recalls that after 'lights out' in New Quay 'she would serialize books that she had read for me. I remember "The Three Musketeers": I realize now she could only have been seven.'[6] Through her father, Marilyn made the acquaintance of many Labour Party luminaries, and that Welsh socialist background is glimpsed in a revealing aside in her 1983 review of a book by Raymond Williams. Although she was generally admiring of Williams's work (see below), a characteristically acerbic note is struck when she writes of Williams's 'dignified detachment, which his friends think of as magisterial, and others think of as ponderous'; little sympathy is given to his claim to 'belong with an illiterate and barely literate majority'. 'The boy from Abergavenny Grammar School', Butler retorts, 'never sounds like the type of Welsh autodidact who emerged from the Mechanics Institutes, or—as my own father remembered his fellow workers in the pit, to the disbelief, it must be confessed, of his children—who walked about the mountainsides after chapel, debating philosophy.'[7]

Returning to Surrey after the war, Marilyn attended Wimbledon High School between 1947 and 1954 as a non-fee-paying, eleven-plus student. Here she received some inspiring teaching, and the year after her arrival managed to beat the rest of the school in a general knowledge quiz (her precociousness might be explained by the fact that the journalistic household

---

[4] Unpublished Auto-Obituary for Dr Jane Mellanby, St Hilda's, Oxford. No pagination. Thanks to Heather Glen for procuring me a copy.
[5] As pointed out by Mary-Ann Constantine in her unpublished paper 'Marilyn Butler and romantic Wales', *Marilyn Butler and the War of Ideas: a Commemorative Conference*, Chawton House Library, 11–12 December 2015.
[6] Marilyn Butler *Memorial Service Pamphlet*.
[7] M. Butler, 'Literature and the left', *London Review of Books* (18 August 1983), pp. 2, 4.

in Kingston received six newspapers every day). Despite this minor triumph, Butler later quipped that 'she would not recommend adolescence if there were a viable alternative', a sentiment no doubt shared by many. In 1955, in a more considerable triumph, she won an exhibition to St Hilda's College, Oxford, following her elder brother Richard (born 1935, who had gone up to Durham) to become the first family members to attend university: although initially set to study History, she was 'turned' by an inspiring production of Shakespeare's *Coriolanus*, fascinated by the way in which the play 'made the outcome seem inevitable, while the history [as related in Plutarch] made it seem accidental'. This made her opt to study English Literature instead, as 'the artistic representation of history'.[8] She later recalled that she 'found Oxford dreamlike, medieval and utterly ravishing. I think I was forty before I grew out of my teenage infatuation with the place.'[9]

There is no doubt that she blossomed in mid-1950s Oxford, rising to the challenge of tutorials with the formidable Dame Helen Gardner, as well as Anne Elliott, Dorothy Whitelock and Celia Sisam. The highly traditional Oxford curriculum was supplemented by her involvement with the Critical Society, which provided a forum in which 'young faculty, graduates and undergraduates (Wallace Robson, Christopher Ricks, Emrys Jones, Roger Lonsdale, Gillian Thomas [later Gillian Beer]) read papers and argued'. She embraced the manifold opportunities of university life, writing for *Isis* and *Cherwell*, and working backstage on a number of significant theatrical performances. But politics, and the rise of the New Left, seems to have dominated her extra-curricular activities, even if, as Stuart Hall archly recollected, she was 'not a student radical, but very very intelligent'.[10] The Suez affair and the Soviet invasion of Hungary energised the undergraduate political scene, and she was an active participant in the Socialist Club, where Gabriel Pearson (later a boyfriend), Raphael Samuel and Stuart Hall were active debaters, joined a year later by the Canadian philosophy student Charles Taylor. She marched to Aldermaston with a copy of *Paradise Lost* in her bag—she had two days to read it for a tutorial—and recalled that 'My social life, my love life and my education all coalesced after Suez, and made a kind of sense of the rest of my time at Oxford.' Pearson and his circle were involved in *Universities and Left Review*, soon to be rebranded as

---

[8] J. Wallace, 'The sociable revolutionary', *Times Higher Education* (15 September 1995), p. 1.
[9] M. Butler, 'An undergraduate at St Hilda's', unpublished memoir. My thanks to Heather Glen for providing me with a copy.
[10] Wallace, 'The sociable revolutionary', p. 2.

New Left Review, and centrally concerned with the relationship of politics and aesthetics: the formative influence of this connection on her thought is underlined in Marilyn's recollection that 'theirs was a style of criticism which was more historical and sociological than the "close reading" or "new criticism" I had been taught'. Despite distancing herself from aspects of the *New Left Review* circle in her later work, it was undoubtedly a major influence.

In an illuminating reflection on her own intellectual formation at Oxford (in the 1987 introduction to a new edition of *Jane Austen and the War of Ideas*), Butler recalled her impatience with what she called 'the airless nirvana created of Austen's world' by academics such as Lionel Trilling and F. R. Leavis. 'We British students of the late 1950s were extraordinary battered, it now seems to me, by exhortations to rise to moral challenges' in the light of Suez and the invasion of Hungary: politicised by the writings of 'Osborne, Amis, Wain, and (my circle's favourite) Doris Lessing... [we] hardly needed our academic seniors to tell us to be serious. What did seem surprising was their apparent belief that the moral life should be led privately or domestically behind closed doors.'[11] By her third year she was on an intellectual high, one negative effect of which was the start of the insomnia that dogged her through adulthood. Her husband David remembers often waking up in the middle of the night with the light turned on next to him, as Marilyn scribbled down in a notepad what she referred to as her 'night thoughts', and the BBC World Service often provided nocturnal relief when she was at conferences.

She made many close women friends at St Hilda's, but in a sense this was a 'pre-feminist' decade. In her memoir of college life, she reflected that 'our contemporary Dennis Potter wrote a play a decade later about a miner's son like himself who goes to Oxford. Like Braine, Osborne et al, [first generation Oxonians of this generation] seemed to think cultural alienation was a problem unique to working-class boys, but middle-class girls also encountered it, and for us the issue of virginity became a key.' In general, she felt that her talented female set at St Hilda's in the end underperformed, except for those who pursued graduate study in the USA. 'What seems odd now, even appalling, is that we did not seem to feel knowledge would change us, empower us, make us valuable to ourselves and to others.' Of her five St Hilda's friends who married and had children, she alone was able to return to professional life afterwards: Oxford women still felt abashed to aspire to serious leadership roles. She graduated with a First in 1958.

---

[11] Butler, *Jane Austen and the War of Ideas*, p. xiii.

After Oxford, she worked briefly as a supply teacher for two months in an unruly South London secondary modern school, followed by a year as Assistant English Mistress at the Perse Girls' School, Cambridge. But journalism beckoned and, winning a place in a BBC trainee scheme in News and Current Affairs, from 1960 she worked in newsrooms in London and Manchester, and then as a BBC talks producer. Journalism influenced her clear, jargon-free academic style, and her love of the summary précis, avoiding dense, intellectually allusive formulations: she described her writing as the product of 'the daughter of a man who wrote for 12 million people every day'.[12] This was particularly inexplicable for American admirers, especially 'New Historicists' who were accustomed to more highly conceptualised writing: a leading exponent, Marjorie Levinson, praised her 'cool descriptive style' and tried to argue that 'the absence of theory from Butler's work is, I believe, (I speak of reasons and meanings, not purposes and causes), an act of sabotage'.[13] Such a view seems unconvincing, as she simply preferred to write the way that she spoke, and never regarded herself as an academic saboteur, although she would have happily accepted the role of iconoclast. A more personal outcome of her brief period with the BBC was her engagement and marriage in 1962 to the noted psephologist David Butler (knighted in 2011), a political commentator and Fellow of Nuffield College, Oxford, whom she had 'put on air'. This was the start of a happy fifty-two-year marriage, based on a companionable and affectionate relationship between two people of very different characters, but who always supported and complemented each other. Marriage was one of the reasons why Marilyn abandoned journalism in order to return to Oxford to begin doctoral work, but she always emphasised that this was a conscious career choice rather than wifely self-sacrifice. She had originally planned to write a book on Jane Austen and politics (the topic of one of her undergraduate essays), but David suggested that she turn her attentions instead to the writings of his great-great-aunt, the neglected Irish novelist Maria Edgeworth. The family connection, he concedes, might have been something of a carrot in their courtship: after all his sister Christina Colvin was working at the Bodleian on Edgeworth's correspondence, and proved an invaluable support to Marilyn's research.

The completion of her DPhil in 1966 helped secure her a Research Fellowship at St Hilda's, and after some revision it was published as

---

[12] Wallace, 'The sociable revolutionary', p. 2.
[13] M. Levinson (ed.), *Rethinking Historicism: Critical Readings in Romantic History* (Oxford, 1989), p. 4.

Maria Edgeworth: a Literary Biography in 1972, and was awarded a British Academy prize. In the acknowledgements, Marilyn thanks her supervisors Roger Lonsdale and Rachel Trickett, while also acknowledging an 'incalculable debt' to Christina Colvin. No previous biographer had enjoyed access to Edgeworth's 2,000-plus letters, and the almost equally large body of letters of members of her immediate family; consequently, they had been over-dependent on the filtered correspondence published in the authorised *Memoir* of 1887. Marilyn certainly knew that she wasn't dealing with a minor writer here: she later insisted that, despite a tendency by some Irish critics to underrate Edgeworth as an English, Protestant and 'colonialist' figure, 'she can claim to be Ireland's most innovative, prolific, and influential writer between Swift at the beginning of the eighteenth century and Yeats at the end of the nineteenth century, and its most distinguished writer of any period'.[14] She particularly warmed to the Irish works such as *Castle Rackrent, Ennui, The Absentee* and *Ormond*, in which Edgeworth 'subversively ... brought Irish humour and French wit into conjunction'.[15] Moreover, the fact that Edgeworth (rather than Austen) was her launch pad turned out to be formative for Marilyn's subsequent research, a point to which I will return.

David's support during the first eight years of their marriage enabled her to give birth to and raise three sons, Daniel, Gareth and Edmund, to finish the Edgeworth research, and to begin work on the book that became *Jane Austen and the War of Ideas*, published in 1975. She was freed from the time-consuming demands of teaching that usually make life especially difficult for women academics simultaneously trying to start their careers and their families. In a 1995 interview with Jennifer Wallace, Butler stated that 'the inevitable interruptions from small children did not spoil the reading of Jane Austen, because Austen usefully did not write 'such long books' and she kept herself to 'finite chapters' that could be read in between transporting children to and from school.[16] Her scholarly achievement was recognised by her first tenured academic appointment in 1973 (at the age of thirty-six) as Fellow and Tutor in English of St Hugh's College, Oxford, and the decade that followed proved to be immensely productive. It was also a ground-breaking appointment for women in the heavily male-dominated university: Helen Watanabe remembered that 'her wise counsel

---

[14] M. Butler, 'General introduction', in J. Desmarais, T. McLoughlin and M. Butler (eds.), *Novels and Selected Writings of Maria Edgeworth*, Vol. 1 (London, 1999), p. vii.
[15] M. Butler, 'Introduction', in M. Butler (ed.), *Castle Rackrent and Ennui* (Harmondsworth, 1992), p. 8.
[16] Wallace, 'The sociable revolutionary', pp. 3–4.

was very much appreciated when we were designing and setting up Women's Studies at Oxford. She really changed things—academically, structurally and personally.'[17] In a 1986 article, Ros Ballaster praised Marilyn for her role in establishing the Woman's Writing Paper in 1985 (with Dr Julia Briggs), claiming that she was 'one of the few senior women fellows at Oxford ... and probably the only woman fellow prepared to stick her neck out for feminist work in the English Faculty'.[18]

The importance of *Jane Austen and the War of Ideas* lay in its historically contextualised and political readings of the novels, skilfully demonstrating how Austen gave flesh to the ideological values of British conservatism during the *kulturkampf* triggered by the French Revolution. Butler's historicism, however, looked rather different from that associated with Marxism, which she criticised for economic determinism, and an overreliance on 'monolithic categories of historical explanation'.[19] By contrast she denominated her own empirically grounded work as 'particularized criticism', based as it was on painstaking archival recovery, insisting that because 'a genre is an established code, a medium of communication already learned by writer and reader; to participate with Jane Austen, we have to be ready to re-learn the code her first readers already knew'.[20] The book pays tribute to Austen's artistic achievement, the way she 'uses irony and verbal nuance to give her a dramatist's detachment, so that the consciousness is only one actor in a total drama' (p. 293). *Pride and Prejudice* and *Emma* are judged as the greatest novels, to the extent that they are 'critical of the consciousness, and test their heroes by their actions' (p. 296). At the same time, she writes that Austen's 'happy endings cannot resolve the clash of values which she sets out to describe, because it is hardly the power of art to resolve them. Art merely mimes its resolutions, without real intent or power to deceive' (p. 299).

But much of the book's originality arises from the fact that Austen's art is measured and compared with that of the cosmopolitan Anglo-Irish novelist Maria Edgeworth, providing a radically different cultural perspective upon romantic literature from Austen's 'home-counties' English

---

[17] *Memorial Service Pamphlet*.

[18] R. Ballaster, 'The singular woman', *News from Nowhere*, 2 (October 1986), 28–9.

[19] Although in the 1987 retrospect she acknowledges her failure to cite the work of Raymond Williams, whom we have already seen her criticising for his views on working-class Welsh literacy: here Butler recognized that Williams 'could at least have been cited as evidence that historicism and an extreme degree of abstraction do not have to go together': Butler, *Jane Austen and the War of Ideas*, p. xviii.

[20] Ibid., p. xxxi. Henceforward pagination given in text.

model. Austen could have opted to follow Edgeworth's French, Enlightenment example as a novelist, rather than the English tradition of the 'proper lady' writer (the term coined by Mary Poovey), in trying to pull the novel out of the partisan conflict between Jacobins and anti-Jacobins in the 1790s, but 'she left it largely alone' (p. xxxviii). This was clearly an ideological choice on Austen's part, a function of what Butler described as her deep-grained English conservatism: 'the reforms she perceives to be necessary are within the attitudes of individuals; she calls for no general changes in the world of the established lesser landed gentry' (p. 2). At the same time, Butler's approach reminds us that Maria Edgeworth and Sir Walter Scott, the leading anglophone novelists of Austen's time, were Irish and Scottish respectively, although Austen's rising star would increasingly reclaim the 'Englishness' of English literature in the nineteenth and twentieth centuries, eclipsing both their reputations.

Butler's third book was *Peacock Displayed: a Satirist in Context* (London, 1979) which, although the least widely read of her works today, marked another crucial stage in her intellectual development, shaping much of her subsequent thinking about romanticism. Focusing on the relatively unknown figure of Thomas Love Peacock, learned, classical, liberal, secular and above all a satirist, Marilyn offered a new perspective for understanding the Shelley, Byron and Keats generation. Peacock's erudite mockery of the irrationalism and conservative inwardness of Wordsworth's *Excursion* or Coleridge's *Biographia Literaria* was for Butler a key to the concerns of the post-1810 writers. *Nightmare Abbey* and *Melincourt* are brilliant comic satires on the self-absorption of post-war romanticism and its melancholy cult of poetic genius; novels of ideas no less than those of Edgeworth, they expose the idols of the age by subjecting them to conversational critique and intellectual satire, the liberal writer's arsenal in waging 'a war of ideas'. As Stuart Tave noted in an insightful review, the book was at its best when revealing Peacock's reading in his contemporaries, demonstrating Butler's magisterial knowledge of romantic periodicals (later developed in her 1993 essay 'Culture's medium: the role of the review', still the best short study of Romantic periodicals).[21] According to Butler's reading, Tave writes, '[Peacock] is a writer dependent on contemporary intellectual conflicts to which, with his method of literal textual quotation, he can continually allude'. Where this documentary context was not forthcoming, however, as in *Maid Marian*, the analysis

---

[21] M. Butler, 'Culture's medium: the role of the review', in S. Curran (ed.), *Cambridge Companion to British Romanticism* (Cambridge, 1993), pp. 120–47.

could succumb to blandness, because 'lacking a genuine movement of ideas in England currently expressed in one or more controversial documents'.[22] Tave suggests that one of the risks the book runs in attempting to resurrect Peacock's reputation is to present an author who 'may seem to require a more highly specialized knowledge and become a more academic property': in other words, Peacock's chance of resurrection was over-dependent on a scholarly reconstruction of his intellectual context because (unlike Austen or Edgeworth) his works could not stand alone.[23] Sadly, this caveat has been borne out by the fact that Peacock, unlike many other 'marginalised' figures resurrected by Butler (Edgeworth, Wollstonecraft, Edward Williams, Southey), has never quite made it to the top table of the new romantic canon, despite the obvious attractions of a novel such as *Nightmare Abbey* for initiating a university course on the romantics.

The same reviewer noted presciently that *Peacock Displayed* contained another 'bigger book inside struggling to get out ... an intellectual history of the period from the 1790s to the 1830s [focusing] on the central figure of Shelley'.[24] That book was Marilyn Butler's magisterial survey *Romantics, Rebels and Reactionaries: English Literature and its Background 1760–1830*, published two years later in 1981 in Oxford's Opus series (selling in paperback at a modest £3.95). Along with the Austen book, it is still the most widely read of her works, and has stood the test of time, regularly featuring on university course reading lists. *Romantics, Rebels, and Reactionaries* was dedicated to questioning the unitary definition of romanticism, and its canonical study as practised mainly in North America: its principal targets were Harold Bloom and other members of the Yale School, Northrop Frye, and M. H. Abrams. 'For Bloom and for critics like him,' wrote Butler, 'poets as poets exist primarily in their internalized imaginative worlds, and in relation to one another, which is why the two great writers who most favour imagination [Blake and Wordsworth] are allowed to set the pattern for the rest.'[25] She pleaded instead for literature as a 'collective activity', 'powerfully conditioned by social forces, what needs to be and what may be said in a particular community at a given time—the field of the anthropologist, perhaps, rather than the

---

[22] S. Tave, 'Review of Marilyn Butler, *Peacock Displayed*', *Nineteenth-Century Fiction*, 35 (1981), 548.
[23] Ibid.
[24] Ibid., p. 549.
[25] M. Butler, *Romantics, Rebels and Reactionaries: English Literature and its Background, 1760–1830* (Oxford, 1981), p. 185. Henceforward pagination given in text.

psychologist' (p. 9). The first couple of chapters ('The arts in the age of revolution' and 'Art for the people in the revolutionary decade: Blake, Gillray, Wordsworth') established a broad, interdisciplinary context for the core chapters, addressing the effects of the French revolution and the British reaction to it, arguing that the writing that immediately preceded and followed the revolutionary and Napoleonic wars represented English literature 'at its most glorious'.

The book is polemical in tone, addressing prose writing and the novel, graphic satire and print culture as well as poetry; it is rather light on close reading, in accord with a survey aimed primarily at undergraduates. Butler established an influential distinction between the first romantic generation's immersion in popular culture (ballads and popular prints), compared to the more classically orientated, high cultural pursuits of the second generation of Keats, Shelley, Byron, Peacock and Hazlitt, with their 'cult of the south'. Developing the impetus of the Peacock book, critical sympathy is shifted from Wordsworth and Coleridge (perhaps over-identified here, as elsewhere in Marilyn's criticism, with reactionary solipsism) to the Shelley–Peacock circle, 'the English liberal writers of the post-war period' who are valued for being 'extrovert not introvert, and pagan not Christian' (p. 124), albeit 'in tone much less optimistic than their pre-war precursors' (p. 125). Michael Rossington, Marilyn's PhD student at this time, senses that she had a strong personal identification with Shelley in particular, and his much-misunderstood politics; 'an almost intuitive understanding of what Shelley was up to, tactically, I mean, the strategic impulses that motivated him, his extraordinary range of reading and his relentless making of connections'.[26] Chapter 4, 'Novels for the gentry: Austen and Scott', takes as its focus a reaction on the part of the English novel against radical sensibility, which is dismissed as 'egotistical, solipsistic and potentially anarchic' (p. 104), and in support of re-establishing traditional social hierarchies, the hallmarks of these two great conservative writers of the second decade. In Chapter 6, Butler returns to the familiar trope of 'the war of the intellectuals', once again giving her favourite Peacock central stage with his satire *Melincourt*; and in a brilliant contextualised reading of Keats's *Hyperion* she proposes that 'the poetic mode of the years from 1817 to 1822 probably produced more great works than any comparably short time in our literature', to the extent that it was simultaneously 'formalistic and experiential, traditionalist and progressive' (p. 154).

---

[26] Personal e-mail correspondence, 18 December 2016.

Despite its extraordinary range and boldness in resetting the agenda for romantic studies, however, *Romantics, Rebels and Reactionaries* now looks quite canonical compared to some of Butler's subsequent work: it paid little attention to women or labouring-class writers, said little about empire and orientalism, and used the term 'English Romanticism' boldly throughout to describe writing from the whole archipelago. So, for instance, while the fourth chapter 'Novels for the gentry' rang the changes by situating Jane Austen's novels between Edgeworth and Scott, it saw no need to finesse geopolitical differences between Ireland, England and Scotland, perhaps surprising for a book dedicated to restoring nuanced literary contexts. Butler concluded with a telling critique of the theoretical mindset of her own profession, which she compared rather unfavourably with that of the historian: 'going out to look for "Romanticism",' she animadverted, 'means selecting in advance one kind of answer. No intellectual discipline, certainly not philosophy, condones such a procedure, while the historian has no foolproof protection against it. But he has some safeguards in his empiricism, and in a methodology which gives weight both to the collection of evidence and to analysis as opposed to synthesis' (p. 186). This was provocative stuff for a literary-critical generation that had been raised on Derrida and De Man.

Reviews of *Romantics, Rebels and Reactionaries* were mixed, although most recognised that this was a book with a difference that would have the power to shape subsequent discussion, for better or worse. Tony Boorman complained (in a sardonically titled review 'Collectivizing the romantics') that 'in Mrs Butler's panoramic survey [...] no one is admitted ever to have said anything highly characteristic of himself; the writers of the past are now allowed only to have said things highly characteristic of the age they lived in'.[27] He proceeded to condemn it as a 'determinedly anti-humanist book, which is founded on the contention that, in an almost literal sense, the works of Romantic literature are children of the age; they are group productions, and "had no first author"'.[28] The tools of critical discrimination seemed absent; the creative quiddity of the individual author was ignored by Butler's blanket historicism. Marshall Brown made a similar point in his strictures on Butler in his 1991 study *Preromanticism*: 'Where history makes literature in this fashion, it seems safe to say, literature does

---

[27] T. Boorman, 'Collectivizing the romantics: English literature and its background 1760–1830', *English*, 31 (1982), 151.
[28] Ibid.

not make history.'[29] But Butler was defended from charges of reductionism by Michael Scrivener, a more sympathetic reviewer, who wrote that 'one leaves her history not with a smug sense that each text can now be pigeonholed into a social category, but with a new sense of wonder, since the literature is now mediated primarily not by our own contemporary notions of what constitutes "Romanticism" but by the remarkable culture created by men and women who lived in a different era, with their own urgent concerns.[30] Christopher Ricks concurred, noting in his review for the *London Review of Books* that '[t]he spirit of Marilyn Butler's excellent book on the Romantics is itself that of citizenship: of belonging to a civilised community, cultural and intellectual, which one helps to sustain and is sustained by'.[31] There is little doubt that Ricks's and Scrivener's positive judgements have prevailed.

Remarkably enough, *Romantics, Rebels and Reactionaries* was Marilyn's last published monograph, although the posthumous publication in 2015 of her *Mapping Mythologies: Countercurrents in Eighteenth-Century British Poetry and Cultural History* (edited by her close friend and Cambridge colleague Heather Glen), presents another full-scale study completed when she was at the height of her powers, but never finally revised for publication. The book was written during her tenure of a three-year British Academy Readership that she was awarded in 1982, which she later recalled enabled her to initiate 'a more generalised exploration of Romantic period writing, considered both as intellectual history and commercial age culture'. *Mapping Mythologies* laid the groundwork for two other books that she never managed to complete: a sequel volume on Shelley, Byron and Orientalism, and a study of eighteenth-century women writers. It appears that research on the second, sequel volume prompted her to defer the publication of *Mapping Mythologies*, perhaps so that the two books might be published together. But in the end, all three projects were stalled by her massively increased workload after taking up the Cambridge Chair: they might have been completed in retirement if she hadn't been tragically overtaken by illness, so it is wonderful to have even one of them now before the public. *Mapping Mythologies* (not incidentally

---

[29] M. Brown, *Preromanticism* (Stanford, CA, 1991), p. 15.
[30] M. Scrivener, 'Review of *Romantics, Rebels, and Reactionaries*', *Criticism*, 24 (1982), 286.
[31] C. Ricks, 'Citizens', *London Review of Books*, 3, 21 (19 November 1981), 7. These remarks on the contemporary reviews are indebted to my Glasgow colleague Matthew Sangster's unpublished paper 'Romantics, rebels and reactionaries: past, present and future', presented at *Marilyn Butler and the War of Ideas: a Commemorative Conference*, Chawton House Library, 11–12 December 2015.

Butler's original title) starts with an analysis of the eighteenth-century 'country party' poets James Thomson and Thomas Akenside, before proceeding to study the imagining of 'alternative versions of the nation' in the writings of Thomas Gray, Collins, 'Ossian' Macpherson, Thomas Chatterton, Edward Williams ('Iolo Morganwg'), Blake, Burns and Wordsworth. These poets are commonly distinguished by their interest in 'non-Christian mythologies—stories from ancient times and often from foreign parts, which convey the social and religious practices and beliefs of an alien society'.[32] But popular antiquarianism—the eighteenth-century version of native cultural anthropology or folklore studies—also looms large in the story that the book tells, and Butler unearths an alternative and indigenous version of tradition underpinning British poetry in these decades, quite different from that of the official metropolitan culture of Church and State.

In her introduction, Glen suggests that *Mapping Mythologies* was Marilyn's answer to criticism of the historicism of *Romantics, Rebels and Reactionaries*, to the extent that it addressed 'a series of writers who saw the poet as maker of history, often in a peculiarly literal sense… Her concern is less with the ways in which their writings were shaped by their historical circumstances than with their understandings of those circumstances and the creative strategies that are manifest in the works they produced in response to them.'[33] This said, it is not the book that we might (at least with hindsight) have expected her to write in the early 1980s, to the extent that it is entirely dedicated to male poets, most of them (with the exception of Blake and Wordsworth) largely active in the eighteenth century, rather than in the romantic period proper. In my view, the book's real significance lies in a polemical bid to present a new theory of eighteenth-century poetry based on an 'intricate, diverse and stressful relationship' between the metropolitan centre and its provincial and national peripheries, especially Wales and Scotland, which play important roles in the story that she tells, with creative energy generated by the popular traditions of the peripheries. Its principal historical target is Thomas Warton's massive three-volume *History of English Poetry* (1774–81) which, buttressed by an influential lineage of critics from Johnson through Arnold to Eliot and Leavis, established the English critical mainstream. In this respect, *Mapping Mythologies* anticipated the rise of 'archipelagic' or

---

[32] H. Glen, 'Introduction' to M. Butler, *Mapping Mythologies: Countercurrents in Eighteenth-Century British Poetry and Cultural History* (Cambridge, 2015), p. 6.
[33] Ibid., p. 19.

'Four nations' criticism that transformed our sense of British and Irish cultural history in a devolutionary era, a point to which I will return below.

Along with the publication of an edited anthology, *Burke, Paine, Godwin and the Revolution Controversy* (Cambridge, 1984: still in print and widely used in university courses on romanticism), writing *Mapping Mythologies* brought to a close what Marilyn described as the most prolific period of her academic career. Important and often seminal as were her subsequent publications, they appeared as essays, journal articles, critical introductions, lectures and editions, building on the achievements of her four published monographs but moving into new territory in offering a revised picture of the romantic period. It is much easier to make sense of this brilliant but scattered corpus in the retrospective light of *Mapping Mythologies*; it is like exploring a submerged continent that's been suddenly uplifted from the ocean bed to reveal formerly scattered islands as connected ridges and massifs.

This change of pace in Marilyn's research was, ironically, a result of public and professional recognition of her outstanding achievements. In 1986 she was appointed to the prestigious King Edward VII Chair of English Literature at Cambridge, describing this chair as having 'a special aura, partly because England (unlike Scotland) has no other Regius chair in English, partly because of the high standing of Cambridge English'. She recalled her seven years as holder of the Edward VII Chair, and her Fellowship of King's College, Cambridge, as 'the most stimulating of her professional career—but in scholarly terms also the most frustrating', owing to the weight of professorial responsibilities, which she exercised with great diligence. Her international reputation was consolidated by visiting fellowships at Caltech in 1984 and Chicago in 1992, and she lectured internationally at most of the top dozen American universities, and in Australia, India and Western Europe.[34]

I first got to know her during this period, when I was still a Cambridge doctoral student, and can well remember being struck by her engaging personality, her immense learning and irreverent humour. She was an energetic presence at seminars and lectures, insisting on always asking at least one question, and was in the habit of scribbling down notes on filing cards, upon which she would subsequently draw for her lectures and articles. I recall her input at the King's College Intellectual History Seminar (which she convened with Antony Pagden and Stefan Collini) as one of the intellectual highlights of my early career years as a junior lecturer in the

---

[34] Quotations here are from Butler unpublished 'Auto-Obituary ...'.

English Faculty (the other highlight was my supervisor John Barrell's graduate seminars in King's). But I also remember the informal Marilyn: post-seminar sessions in the pub, a long half-an-hour discussion of Byron and orientalism on King's Parade, when I was beginning research in that area, leaving me wondering if she would be late for some important meeting as a result of her affection for informed chat about her current obsessions. She was always approachable and eager to listen, and willing to share her insights and opinions—even the latest faculty gossip—with graduate students and early career researchers: this was in marked contrast to some others of her rank and academic celebrity, who often left us tongue-tied, preferring to cultivate a remote charisma rather than intellectual sociability. The clouds were already gathering over British academia, however, even in the privileged realms of Oxbridge, and Marilyn later regretted that her professional maturity coincided with 'an unprecedented period for universities of costsaving and externally-imposed change'. She found herself diverted into 'vastly-amplified systems of appraisal and assessment, in her own universities or as an external advisor', sitting on national committees such as the Arts Council Literature Panel and the Council for University English. But she still found time for frequent appearances in the national press or on BBC radio, commenting on literature or educational topics: she understood the meaning of 'impact' long before it entered the official vocabulary of HEFCE and the AHRC.[35]

Despite the pressures of her professorial duties (not to mention 'a lot of driving through Milton Keynes', given that her family home was in Oxford),[36] her intellectual productivity continued unabated, albeit in a rather different mode from the earlier 1980s. Her 1985 essay 'Against tradition: the case for a particularized historical method', written after she had completed work on *Mapping Mythologies,* sought to explain some of the methodological principles of her criticism. The essay was published in the American critic Jerome McGann's collection *Historical Studies and Literary Criticism*, underlining the important connections between McGann's critique of 'Romantic Ideology' and Butler's 'particularized' historical method, but also major differences in terms of their engagement with theory. One of her more acerbic performances, this essay lambasted the ahistoricism of North American romanticists such as Bloom, Abrams and Frye (by now familiar targets), and repeated her strictures on Marxism, although it had more positive things to say about the 'Cambridge

---

[35] Ibid.
[36] 'A singular woman', *The Times*, 28 May 1986.

School' of Quentin Skinner, John Dunn, J. G. A. Pocock et al., despite their tendency to represent 'ideas passing, by the old bad unexplained process, from one Great Thinker to the next'.[37] Although nowhere evoked directly, the influence of the great English socialist historian E. P. Thompson is evident in the essay's bid to appropriate 'customs in common' (the alternative native traditions explored in *Mapping Mythologies*) from the clutches of the Right, as well as defending them against New Left modernisers and Althusserians: a presence she acknowledged when she later wrote 'I have long thought [Thompson] one of the most significant, persuasive models for how to write on the literature of the past.'[38]

Butler also took issue here with Eric Hobsbawm and Terence Ranger's influential collection *The Invention of Tradition* (Cambridge, 1983), for what she took to be a condescending and constructivist tone in its treatment of tradition *tout court*. For example, the editors and some of the book's contributors tended to equate Scottish and Welsh romanticism with inauthenticity, or what Leith Davis, Ian Duncan and Janet Sorensen describe as 'a mystified—purely ideological—commitment to history and folklore' in the service of Celtic nationalism.[39] 'A Welsh woman like myself', responded Marilyn, in a passionate (although doubtless somewhat tongue-in-cheek) appeal to personal experience, 'has been brought up to hear massed male choirs extolling the unique merits of "gwlad beirdd a chantorion": ours is the land of bards and singers, says the third line of our national anthem (composed in 1856). It comes as a shock to find that Welsh "traditional" music appears to be no more than a bastardised version of the pop tunes of the 1700s, which in their actual origins were Italian, German, or much more unfortunate, English.'[40] But 'inventing a tradition maintains your legitimacy, and someone else's lack of it; your mythical past is your defensive strategy in a real present ... a polemic with particularly strong motives for hiding the circumstances which brought it into being'.[41] All traditions are 'invented' earlier or later, but that doesn't make them any less real or potentially empowering, especially for minority nations and sub-cultures.

In her 1989 essay 'Repossessing the past: the case for an open literary history', a revised version of her inaugural lecture as Cambridge's King

---

[37] Butler, 'Against tradition: the case for a particularized historical method', p. 45.
[38] M. Butler, 'E. P. Thompson's second front', *History Workshop Journal*, 39 (1995), 72.
[39] L. Davies, I. Duncan and J. Sorensen, 'Introduction', in L. Davies, I. Duncan and J. Sorensen (eds.), *Scotland and the Borders of Romanticism* (Cambridge, 2005), p. 1.
[40] Butler, 'Against tradition: the case for a particularized historical method', p. 38.
[41] Ibid., p. 39.

Edward VII Professor of English Literature in November 1987, Butler further refined her position in this respect. Because the lecture was (rather cheekily, given the grandiose occasion) focused on Robert Southey's forgotten orientalist poem *Thalaba the Destroyer*, it had plenty to say about post-colonialism and the critique of orientalism, in the wake of Edward Said's influential 1978 study. (At the time I was working on the book that became *British Romantic Writers and the East*, largely inspired by Marilyn's pioneering scholarship, and I well remember the excitement with which I heard her original lecture.) In resurrecting Southey as the forgotten member of the Lake School triumvirate, companion and collaborator of Wordsworth and Coleridge, she shifted English romanticism eastwards, underlining Southey's fascination with exoticism and the literature of imperial conquest, manifest in densely footnoted, experimental epics such as *Madoc*, *Thalaba* and *The Curse of Kehama*. Such epics, in an implicit challenge to the canonical centrality of Wordsworth, 'quer[y] the formalistic belief in the autonomous great poem, as well as the post-Romantic faith in the independence of the great poet'.[42] Above all, she approved of Southey because he was 'contentious rather than reassuring, common rather than genteel, provincial rather than metropolitan, international rather than national'.[43]

'Repossessing the past' continued Marilyn's campaign against current notions of a unitary romanticism, and some of its targets were the same. But she also struck a new note in distancing herself from British metropolitan culture: 'most literature does not speak for the official, London-based "nation". It expressed the view of a sect, a province, a gender, a class, bent more often than not on criticism or outright opposition. For literary purposes, the British Isles have always been what the Australian poet Les Murray recently termed them in the present day, "the Anglo-Celtic archipelago". As a social institution, literature models an intricate, diverse, stressful community, not a bland monolith.'[44] I think that is a wonderful formulation, although one that hasn't received due credit: Butler's name isn't even mentioned in Robert Crawford's *Devolving English Literature* (Oxford, 1992) nor in Davies, Duncan and Sorensen's *Scotland and the Borders of Romanticism* (Cambridge, 2004), both important works which certainly develop the spirit of her critique. Her essay also invoked

---

[42] M. Butler, 'Repossessing the past: the case for an open literary history', in M. Levinson (ed.), *Rethinking Historicism: Critical Readings in Romantic History* (Oxford, 1989), p. 83.
[43] Ibid., p. 72.
[44] Ibid., p. 69.

Peter Burke's magisterial study *Popular Culture in Early Modern Europe* (London, 1978), which positively exemplified what she calls 'Social Baconianism', as well as privileging the Celtic periphery as the site of European romanticism's 'discovery of the people' in the late Enlightenment.

The interest in alternative traditions of 'Repossessing the past' was later followed up by brilliant essays on Robert Burns (in Crawford's *Robert Burns and Cultural Authority*) and 'Popular antiquarianism' in Iain McCalman's *Oxford Companion to the Romantic Age*,[45] which presented a new cast of intellectual heroes in the perhaps unlikely shapes of Francis Grose, Joseph Ritson, Francis Douce and William Hone. Burns (himself a popular antiquarian, and friend of Grose), she proposed, 'is the first of our cultural nationalists, through his brilliantly imagined construction of modern Scotland. In drawing together a nation, he both anticipates Scott and outdoes him.'[46] In a similar vein, her 2000 essay 'Irish culture and Scottish Enlightenment: Maria Edgeworth's histories of the future' memorably described Edgeworth's novelistic art as being 'tuned into the vast, open-ended conversation that was Hume and Smith's metaphor for modern society'.[47] Butler here argued that for the Edgeworths in their defence of popular culture and language, the *Essay on Irish Bulls*, 'there is no British culture as such. Four distinct peoples inhabit the British Isles: English, Scottish, Irish and Welsh, each with a history and cultural traditions, oral and written. Regardless of government and its institutions, it is from their cultural particularity that they define themselves against the others.'[48] Now, in 2016, Marilyn Butler's 'stressful' version of the Union looks more apposite than Linda Colley's influential account of 'forging the nation' in her 1991 book *Britons*, which told how a unitary Protestant Britain transcended internal differences by rallying against a common French enemy, but at the cost of leaving a question mark over the place occupied by Catholic Ireland, not to mention underestimating the importance of English Dissent.

In 1994, after much soul-searching, Marilyn Butler took up the Rectorship of Exeter College, Oxford, partly to be back in Oxford with

---

[45] M. Butler, 'Popular antiquarianism', in I. McCalman (ed.), *Oxford Companion to the Romantic Age: British Culture 1776–1832* (Oxford, 1999), pp. 328–38.

[46] M. Butler, 'Burns and politics', in R. Crawford (ed.), *Robert Burns and Cultural Authority* (Edinburgh, 1997), p. 111.

[47] M. Butler, 'Irish culture and Scottish enlightenment: Maria Edgeworth's histories of the future', in S. Collini, R. Whatmore and B. Young (eds.), *Economy, Polity, and Society: British Intellectual History 1750–1950* (Cambridge, 2000), pp. 160–1.

[48] Ibid., p. 169.

David, but also because she sincerely believed that she could better fight the good fight as the first woman head of a traditionally male Oxbridge college than in the Cambridge English Faculty. When that bastion of male privilege the Oxford and Cambridge Club refused her membership (the first time it had rejected a head of college), David loyally resigned his membership in protest. Her auto-obituary recalled that 'her new College provided distinctive rewards of fellowship and civility, but also new claims on time. She reverted to praising the Isis more highly than the Cam, and managed to remember her grandchildren's birthdays. The row of box files labelled with the names of her unpublished books has cost her literary executors unconscionable time.' After her retirement in 2004, Exeter appointed another woman as Rector, Frances Cairncross, which was a great vote of confidence in Marilyn's pioneering role. Frances wrote that 'she was the ideal predecessor. She left me a College that had been transformed by her warmth, her perspicacity and her scholarship. I am lucky and proud to have inherited her mantle.' Marilyn Butler was elected a Fellow of the British Academy in 2002.

Building on her earlier achievement as General Editor (with her friend and colleague Janet Todd) of the seven-volume edition of *The Works of Mary Wollstonecraft* (London, 1989), Butler's major literary endeavour in these busy years was editing (with Mitzi Myers, before the latter's tragic death in 2000) the twelve-volume *The Novels and Selected Works of Maria Edgeworth* (London, 1999–2003), again for Pickering and Chatto. The Edgeworth edition opens with a seventy-three-page 'General introduction' by Marilyn, and as well as being General Editor she had an editorial role in more than half of the volumes. Editing was doubtless more easily combined with her Rectorial duties, easily picked up and laid down during gaps in her busy schedule, in comparison to sustained scholarly writing. In her introduction, she asserts that 'an edition is not the place to engage in passing critical debates or possibly idiosyncratic interpretations. It is a place for setting out any evidence on why a text came to be written, how it was written, what it alludes to, and if possible what contemporary, now-obscured question it was answering.'[49] Both the Wollstonecraft and Edgeworth editions were major and lasting contributions to recovering the voice of women writers in Anglophone romanticism. Throughout the 1990s she also produced accessible and original introductions to novels by Edgeworth, Godwin, Mary Shelley and Austen—her introduction to

---

[49] M. Butler, 'General introduction', *The Novels and Selected Works of Maria Edgeworth*, Vol. 1, p. vii.

Frankenstein, for example, is a brilliant account of the novel's engagement with vitalism and the romantic life sciences. Another major legacy for contemporary scholarship was the *Cambridge Studies in Romanticism* series, of which she was founding editor, in partnership with her close friend Professor James Chandler of the University of Chicago: initiated in 1990 with studies by Mary Favret and the present author, it now runs to over ninety volumes. As the series manifesto proclaims of British romanticism, 'outside Shakespeare studies, probably no body of writing has produced such a wealth of response or done so much to shape the responses of modern criticism'. Dedicated to publishing work that combined theory with new literary-historical research, *Cambridge Studies in Romanticism* showcased 'the work of both younger and more established scholars, on either side of the Atlantic and elsewhere'. Josie Dixon, series editor for Cambridge University Press, remembers her openness to first monographs based on PhD theses; the author's status was less important to her than the quality of their ideas. She also wrote a lengthy revised *Oxford Dictionary of National Biography* entry on Jane Austen about this time, which took nearly a year to complete, possibly because of the as-yet undiagnosed illness against which she was already struggling.[50]

Shortly after Marilyn resigned her Rectorship in 2004, all her plans for a happy and productive retirement were shattered when she was diagnosed with Alzheimer's, a tragic turn of events that both she and her family endured with great courage and perseverance. This cast a shadow over the otherwise happy event of the 2006 publication of her Festschrift volume, *Repossessing the Romantic Past*, edited by Heather Glen and Paul Hamilton (Cambridge, 2006). Her extensive circle of friends, and the wider scholarly community, were deeply saddened by her premature and forced retirement from public life: it was some comfort to know that she was being lovingly cared for by David and her family, as it became increasingly less possible for friends to visit her. The sudden death of her son Gareth, a successful BBC radio producer, from a heart attack at the age of only forty-two, was another terrible blow. As Josie Dixon put it, it is sadly ironic that a career based on language should have ended in silence, especially given Marilyn's tremendous sociability and gift of communication. But she lives on in her writings, and for those who had the privilege to know her, reading her books and articles is akin to hearing her conversation as it was in her prime: generous, clever, sociable, funny and, above

---

[50] M. Butler, 'Jane Austen (1775–1817)', *Oxford Dictionary of National Biography*, http://www.oxforddnb.com.view/article/904 (accessed 23 January 2017).

all, articulate. Her life was movingly celebrated in a memorial service at Exeter College Chapel on 24 April 2014 (she died on 11 March), with the eulogy given by David, and her sons Dan and Ed, and addresses by Heather Glen and Jeri Johnson. Many of her friends, colleagues, former students and admirers gathered for a commemorative conference entitled 'Marilyn Butler and the war of ideas' at Chawton House Library on 11–12 December 2015. Participants were heard to remark that the crackle of ideas and the social warmth of the occasion were a result of Marilyn's invisible presence as she circulated among her old friends and sparring partners: it is certainly a conference that she would have enjoyed as much as we all did. She is greatly missed.

NIGEL LEASK
Fellow of the Academy

Note. Special thanks are due to the following people for assistance in writing this memoir: Ros Ballaster, Sir David Butler and Edmund Butler, Claire Connolly, James Chandler, Stefan Collini, Mary-Ann Constantine, Josie Dixon, Paul Hamilton, Heather Glen (to whom I owe the greatest debt!), Jon Mee, John Mullan, Michael Rossington and Matthew Sangster. Many others have also contributed indirectly, especially the participants at the Chawton House Conference in December 2015.

BEATRICE EILEEN DE CARDI

Beatrice Eileen de Cardi
1914–2016

BEATRICE DE CARDI, WHO DIED on 5 July 2016 aged 102, achieved the remarkable feat of filling in many of the gaps in our knowledge of the archaeological record over a vast area which stretched from the Persian Gulf to the Khyber Pass. She was able to do this mainly by survey, and then went on to establish the relative chronology of some of the new wares she identified by means of judicious excavation. In addition, she traced some of the connections between her new sites and other better-known ones which provided absolute dates for the new material. She achieved all this without the benefit of permanent institutional backing and never held an academic post, although she was generally acknowledged to be a talented and professional archaeologist. Unusually, she had a second parallel life, until her official retirement, as an outstanding administrator. After retirement she devoted herself solely to archaeology.

Beatrice was born, just before the outbreak of the First World War, on 5 June 1914, to a Corsican father and an American mother. She was the second of two daughters. She claimed that one of her earliest memories is of being in the cellar of their house in Ealing during an air raid with her mother dressed in what sounds like full evening dress. Apart from this the war had little impact on her. From an early age Beatrice wanted to be a ballet dancer and, although ill health prevented this, the training she received may well have been the reason for the upright posture and slightly imperious air which stayed with her all her life.[1]

---

[1] The information on B de C's life until she joined the Council for British Archaeology comes from an interview she gave to Dr P.-J. Smith of the McDonald Institute Cambridge in 2009.

At nine she was sent to St Paul's Girls' School where Kathleen (later Dame Kathleen) Kenyon was head girl. She did so well that after two years she was moved up a whole class, not an unalloyed benefit as she missed a year and, she claimed, no one filled in the gaps in her knowledge of English grammar. In spite of this her published reports in later life were clear and precise, so she plainly overcame the problem. Ill health forced her to leave St Paul's before she reached the top form, and she became an invalid for some years until she outgrew a problem with her heart.

When her health improved she was accepted at University College London (UCL) to read for a general arts degree as she was unsure what she wanted to do in life. While there she attended some lectures by Dr R. E. M. (later Sir Mortimer) Wheeler on Roman Britain. It seems to have been these lectures and several seasons digging at Maiden Castle during her vacations that triggered the love of archaeology which was to shape much of her working life. It also taught her what were then the most advanced and 'scientific' methods of digging and recording the evidence. Wheeler was to remain a crucial figure in her life for many years. Sadly, just before she graduated, Beatrice's father died unexpectedly, leaving the family with no income and a heavily mortgaged house. The staff at UCL suggested that she took a secretarial course in order to improve her employment prospects, and it was while she was completing the course that Wheeler invited her to become his secretary at the Museum of London.

Wheeler was not an easy person to work for, but Beatrice made many friends in the museum world and helped with both the fieldwork and the secretarial work involved in compiling the museum's medieval catalogue of artefacts and buildings. With the outbreak of the Second World War all the male members of staff were called up and Beatrice became temporary Museum Assistant in charge of the storage of important objects and the arrangement of temporary exhibitions of the rest, until the air raids forced the museum to close. Amongst other duties she had to visit the coronation robes in storage in Buckinghamshire to make sure the moths were not getting at them. It was her friend Molly Cotton FBA, with whom she had worked at Maiden Castle, and who later was closely associated with the British School at Rome, who, in 1944, rescued her from this tedium; Molly was by then working in the Ministry of Economic Warfare.

Molly Cotton was looking for someone 'unflappable' to act as assistant to the newly appointed Representative in China of the Allied Supplies Executive of the War Cabinet, a Foreign Office appointment. His name was J. T. Asquith, and he and Beatrice met briefly in London where the appointment was confirmed; an arrangement was made to meet again in Calcutta in a month's time. The Museum of London agreed to loan her for the period of the war, and Beatrice set off in a Sunderland flying boat with five army officers and an elderly rear admiral. The journey took four days, and they were able to see the aftermath of the battle of El Alamein as they flew over North Africa and to catch glimpses of Baghdad and the Makran coast of Iran before landing in Calcutta. A hectic sixteen months followed, travelling all over western China and between China and India, crossing the Himalayas in a DC3, a notoriously dangerous flight.

Asquith's brief was not only to screen all supplies to China from the Sterling Block but also to take care of the 1939–41 loans to China and the 1944 Sino-British Credit. He was confronted by irreconcilable objectives, with the British Government being anxious to keep supplies to a minimum and the Chinese determined to extract as much as possible. Applications for goods and machinery had to be investigated in relation to the projects for which they had been sought, a process involving much travelling in the interior of western China. In addition, cargo arriving in India often went astray and had to be tracked down anywhere between Karachi and Assam.

Living conditions were fairly squalid when they first arrived, and Beatrice persuaded the Embassy to move her from her first lodgings by scraping the lice off her bedroom walls and presenting them to the Chargé d'Affaires in an envelope. He quickly found her a new room at the British Council, then directed by Joseph Needham, the distinguished Sinologist and later Fellow of the British Academy. Beatrice was included in high-level meetings by Asquith and had the opportunity to meet several Chinese government ministers. Dr Wong Wen-hao, the head of the War Production Board and Minister of Economic Affairs, was a geologist by profession. He was keenly interested in archaeology and told her much about Neolithic pottery in Kansu and Shensi.

In 1945 de Cardi was sent to India alone to explain changes in loan procedures to Indian officials. She remembers that she was given a lift to Delhi in the private plane of General Carton de Wiart and was made to wear a parachute which was much too large for her. The crew pinned it together with safety pins, assuring her that they would not hold if there was an emergency. However, all went well, and while in Delhi she managed to see Wheeler who was working there.

Allied victory in Japan saw her back in London with her job in China abruptly terminated. When she went back to the Museum of London, she found, much to her surprise, that her job had been filled and there was no vacancy for her. The museum had agreed to keep her job open for her until the end of the war, but saw VE Day as that end and so felt free to refill the post. On impulse she applied to the Board of Trade and was appointed as an Assistant UK Trade Commissioner to New Delhi, the first woman to hold such a post. After the war the promotion of British exports was of paramount importance and de Cardi enjoyed the challenge. She also managed several meetings with Wheeler, who by this time was Director General of Antiquities in India.

De Cardi spent about nine months in New Delhi, and because of her interest in archaeology was usually deputed to take visiting businessmen around archaeological sites in the vicinity. As the partitioning of India drew near, the staff of the Trade Commission office was given the choice of either staying in India or transferring to the new Pakistan. De Cardi opted for Pakistan, enticed there largely by the Indus civilisation, and found the post in Karachi an exciting one. As the capital of a new country, it was the international diplomatic centre until eventually Islamabad was built.

While there she learnt that Burmah Shell was prospecting in Baluchistan, where there was reported to be a large number of archaeological sites. During the war Stuart Piggott, later professor of archaeology at Edinburgh and a Fellow of the British Academy, had identified some very distinctive painted pottery in the reserve collections of the Central Asian Antiquities Museum. When his next local leave came, with the help of a local taxi driver he had been able to identify the same ware on four sites in the Quetta area. His findings were published in *Ancient India 3* (1947) with the title 'A new prehistoric ceramic from Baluchistan'. Wheeler sent de Cardi a copy of the article, which triggered her interest. She determined to spend her next leave trying to establish the full range of this sophisticated and distinctive pottery.

When she discussed this with Wheeler, he told her that the region was much too dangerous for her to work there, but with characteristic determination she insisted and eventually Wheeler gave way. He also persuaded the new Department of Archaeology to lend her the services of Sadar Din for a month. Sadar Din had worked as foreman on excavations by both Sir Leonard Woolley and Wheeler and he proved invaluable, teaching her the importance of studying the local terrain closely to identify the best locations for sites.

The conditions in 1948 were rough, but it is said that de Cardi emerged from her tent every morning looking pristine with not a hair out of place and wearing her characteristic scarlet lipstick. It is also said that she slept with a pistol under her pillow. When Wheeler quizzed her about the lipstick, she replied tartly that it stopped her lips from getting chapped. She was able to show that the so-called Quetta ware also occurred about 100 miles south from the Quetta region into the northern Jhalawan.[2] A considerable number of new sites, of all periods from the Neolithic to the Islamic period, was also identified for the first time.

The survey was finally abandoned on the advice of local officials who deemed the area too dangerous for her to work in. She was unable to return until 1957, when she continued her survey with a small team which included Pakistani representatives, David Trump as archaeologist, and George Barrington, who was in effect her 'dragoman' taking care of the car and all the practical arrangements, as well as acting as interpreter. He was later to accompany her on many of her expeditions and became an important figure in her life. The most significant excavation was that at Anjira, where a good sequence was established which at a later date was linked to the sequence at Mehrgah where C14 dates were available. These showed that the Anjira sequence probably began in the early fourth millennium.

Her carefully published exploration results and excavation reports have been at the foundation of all later work in that region. All archaeologists working anywhere in western Pakistan or the Iranian borderlands will of necessity consult her most original and detailed fieldwork. No pottery collections were made on the Islamic sites she identified, but the rest of the ceramics were closely studied and published in great detail at a later date. By then much more comparative data was available from new work by the French and the Americans in Afghanistan and Seistan, which enabled her to put the pottery in its proper context.[3] A final report appeared in 1983, by which time important connections with Baluchistan from these areas had been demonstrated. The pottery she had collected was donated to the Institute of Archaeology, now part of UCL, which handed it on to the British Museum.

Having had to leave Baluchistan in 1948 because of security concerns, she soon made a lightning dash to Afghanistan to try to find the northern limits of Quetta ware. On her return to her post she found a telegram from Kathleen Kenyon FBA, the excavator of Jericho, telling her that the newly

---

[2] See B. de Cardi, 'The British Expedition to Kalat 1948 and 1957', *Pakistan Archaeology*, 1 (1964), 20–9; B. de Cardi, 'Excavation and reconnaissance in Kalat West Pakistan – the prehistoric sequence in the Surab region', *Pakistan Archaeology*, 1.i (1965), 86–183; B. de Cardi, 'A new prehistoric ware from Baluchistan', *Iraq*, 13 (1951), 63–75.
[3] B. de Cardi, *Archaeological Surveys in Baluchistan*, Institute of Archaeology Occasional Publications no. 8 (London, 1983).

created Council for British Archaeology (CBA) was advertising a post as Assistant Secretary and suggesting that she applied for the job. As her mother had become seriously ill and de Cardi wished to return to London, she applied and was appointed.

Her twenty-four years at the CBA saw it develop from a small, largely unpaid group of people concerned about the state of British monuments of all sorts after the war, into a fully professional body, with professional staff, which today plays a major role on the national scene. When asked what her proudest achievement was at the CBA, de Cardi replied that it was having helped many students to pursue their interest in archaeology. Key to this was a number of publications, such as the *Calendar of Excavations* which listed all the digs up and down the country that were looking for staff, both amateur and professional. Many students got their first taste of fieldwork in this way. Later, the *Calendar* expanded to include some overseas excavations as well. In addition, there was the *Archaeological Bibliography* and a growing number of Research Reports. De Cardi was also instrumental in the recognition of industrial archaeology as an integral part of British Heritage and co-ordinated a conference on this theme. Her post was upgraded and she became the Secretary with a very large S, often acting as spokesperson for the Council. It goes without saying that the CBA office and the council meetings worked without a hitch and, partly as a result of this achievement, she was universally admired. On her retirement in 1973 she was awarded the OBE in recognition of her work, and on her 100th birthday the CBA's main office building in York was renamed after her as Beatrice de Cardi House.

While in London she became a Fellow of the Society of Antiquaries in 1950 and remained an active member until her death. She became a Director in 1980 and a Vice-President of the Society in 1996. She also saw the importance of the Society's own collections and was instrumental in reorganising and cataloguing them. She was awarded the Society's Gold Medal in 2014 in recognition of her contributions. She was also a member of the Antiquaries' 'Cocked Hat' dining club, and is remembered as 'very convivial' by a fellow member. Some of de Cardi's papers were bequeathed to the Antiquaries.

One of the attractions for de Cardi of the job at the CBA was the fact that they were happy to let her accumulate her leave so that she could return to Baluchistan for a reasonable period in the summer, as she did in 1957 when her second survey was carried out (see above). She was to confess that she preferred survey to excavation and had an insatiable curiosity about what lay beyond the horizon. She was also curious to establish the links westwards into Persian Baluchistan of her Baluchi pottery and to explore some of the east–west valleys of southern Iran, which she felt had been important arteries of communication.

With this in mind she decided to excavate at the site of Bampur in south-east Iran with a small team which once again included George Barrington, two archaeologists and a representative of the Iranian archaeological service. The site lay on the river of the same name in the fertile Bampur valley which ran east–west, and which had first been recognised as an important route by Sir Aurel Stein in 1932. The site was dominated by the ruins of a fine fortress on an impressive tell or mound. It was not possible to explore the main mound, but Stein had sunk a trial trench into its lower flanks where he had identified some interesting painted pottery. De Cardi expanded and completed his trench to ground level and sunk a second one nearby. Six prehistoric levels were identified with badly disturbed later levels above and a few Islamic graves. No complete architectural units were identified, but a number of rooms with mudbrick walls, one of which contained a fine kiln, was found. It was clear that the figurative pottery of the four lowest levels had many similarities both to the pottery from her earlier surveys to the east and further afield to wares from Afghanistan, especially with Mundigak in the south-east of that country. The Italians excavating in Seistan, north of Bampur, were soon to find another link in this chain of contacts at the site of Shahr-i-Sokhta.

Level V at Bampur saw a marked change in the direction of the external contacts of the site from approximately north to east–west. The painted pottery now had some similarities with Kulli/Harappan wares to the east. Grey incised pottery and one or two pieces of grey stone jars appear for the first time and belong to the so-called Intercultural style, at home to the west. This pottery seems to be a copy of similar stone vessels and has designs which could be matched to those on containers found in the Persian Gulf and into southern Iraq. The Danes were finding very similar sherds on Umm-an-Nar island off the north coast of the Emirates and at Hili and Bat inland. The network of contacts which linked southern Iraq, the Persian Gulf, south-eastern Iran and even the Indus valley in the third millennium BC was coming slowly into focus in part at least owing to de Cardi's work. Later, the links were to be extended to central Asia.

Professor Lamberg-Karlovsky, Professor of Archaeology and Ethnology at Harvard University, who was surveying another section of the Bampur valley and was later to dig at nearby Tepe Yahya, knew de Cardi and her work well and admired her as a pioneer in regions that were, at the time, an archaeological no-man's land. He also praised her rapid and complete publication of her results.[4] As always, her main interest was in the pottery which was meticulously recorded with admirable drawings.

It was natural that de Cardi decided to follow her grey ware into the Gulf, and 1968 found her in the United Arab Emirates (UAE). It was fortuitous that as a result of a conference in Bahrain to mark the opening of the new museum there, a decision was taken to set up the Committee for East Arabian and Gulf Studies with Sir Mortimer Wheeler as its president and Richard Barnett FBA of the British Museum as its chairman.[5] The committee was later to become the Society for Arabian Studies and is now called The British Foundation for the Study of Arabia. Its aim was to facilitate British expeditions to the region. De Cardi served as President to the Society and the Foundation for a considerable length of time. The new committee was approached by Michael Rice who had been commissioned to build a museum in Qatar, although little was known about the archaeology and history of the state and there was nothing to put in such a museum except for some stone tools discovered by a Danish expedition. Rice asked for help in setting up a survey, to be paid for by the government of Qatar, to remedy this situation, and Wheeler had no hesitation in suggesting de Cardi to lead the project. Needless to say, this had to be achieved in a very short period of time so that the museum could open on schedule.

De Cardi set to work in 1972 to gather together a team, which comprised her long-time friend, George Barrington, as before in charge of all the practical arrangements, Professor Claudio Vita-Finzi FBA, geomorphologist, and three archaeologists. The government of Qatar provided Land Rovers, buses and even a caravan, advice on local conditions and help with recruiting labourers. In spite of a personal tragedy, when George Barrington was killed after falling from a horse, de Cardi once again proved her professionalism by concluding the survey successfully and providing the necessary artefacts for the museum. Perhaps the most significant find was the presence of distinctive Ubaid pottery at a coastal site called al-Da'asa. This pottery originated in Mesopotamia,

---

[4] B. de Cardi, 'Bampur 1966', *Anthropological Papers of the American Museum of Natural History*, 50 (1970), 233–70.

[5] M. Rice, 'Beatrice de Cardi: an appreciation', in C. S. Phillips, D. T. Potts and S. Searight (eds.), *Arabia and its Neighbours: Essays on Prehistorical Developments Presented in Honour of Beatrice de Cardi* (Turnhout, 1998), pp. 233–6.

southern Iraq, and dates to the fifth millennium BC. It had never been found so far south before, and the find raised questions about the nature of the contacts.

A glance at the final publication,[6] which is dedicated to George Barrington, illustrates the range of the finds made, from Stone Age tools to the remains of an Islamic town. The book also includes articles by major scholars who had not been members of the original expedition on additional aspects of history and archaeology. It is still an important resource after forty years.

After the completion of the Qatar survey de Cardi continued to survey and excavate in different parts of the UAE and Oman, often in difficult terrain, sometimes alone and sometimes with other scholars like Brian Doe. She was to develop a special fondness for Ras al Khaimah, whose ruler was the same age as she was. Even after she ceased to excavate she made annual visits to the museum there until she was well into her nineties, helping to analyse and catalogue the material in its collection. In the early days she also assisted in survey work. She will be much missed by the museum staff—and its cats!

In recognition of her enormous contribution to the study of the heritage of Ras al Khaimah she was awarded the Al Qasimi Medal in 1989. Other awards followed, including that of a golden dhow in full sail which was presented to her in 2009 at a conference to mark fifty years of archaeology in the Emirates. Regrettably, she was to find that she had a new role towards the end of her life, that of reminding the governments and rulers of the Gulf States of the importance of preserving their unique heritage, which faced many threats in the face of rapid and sometimes uncontrolled development.[7]

Towards the end of her life many other honours were awarded in recognition of her work. In 1994 she was made an Honorary Fellow of University College London, where she had been an undergraduate, and an honorary Visiting Professor at UCL's Institute of Archaeology. In 1998 a Festschrift was published in her honour, including contributions from scholars across Europe on a wide range of topics.[8] In 2002 she was elected a Fellow of the British Academy, sealing her acceptance by the academic establishment, something she must have relished.

---

[6] B. de Cardi, *Qatar Archaeological Report. Excavations 1973* (Oxford, 1978).
[7] B. de Cardi, 'Overview', in D. T. Potts, Hasan Al Naboodah and P. Hellyer (eds.), *Archaeology of the United Arab Emirates* (London, 2003), pp. 18–21.
[8] Phillips, Potts and Searight, *Arabia and its Neighbours*. This Festschrift contains a list (possibly incomplete) of de Cardi's publications.

De Cardi was a brave, determined, fiercely independent and somewhat formidable woman. She maintained her interest in her field all her life and was attending lectures until shortly before her death. She also had highly developed managerial and diplomatic skills, but there was another side to her. After the death of her elder sister she lived alone in a flat just off Kensington High Street where she entertained her circle of friends of all ages with cake and conversation. She wrote a pamphlet about Corsica where her father was born, and asked for the Corsican 'anthem' to be played at her funeral. She was one of the rare people of whom others said that when talking to her they completely forgot the age difference. She had a special gift for relating to younger people. She loved cooking and cats, and had an extensive collection of recipe books. She also made many of her own clothes with material usually bought from souks in the Gulf. She was always immaculately turned out with her make-up carefully applied. She apparently liked kippers for breakfast and watching professional wrestling.

It is difficult to summarise the main achievements of such a long and varied life, but there are perhaps three areas for which she will be specially remembered. She played an important part in making the CBA an integral part of the British heritage sector and was responsible in large measure for the rediscovery of the prehistory of the southern Gulf and for its preservation. More broadly, she played her part in beginning to clarify the complex network of connections over an area which stretched from Arabia to the Indus valley. Her work will remain seminal for many years.

HARRIET CRAWFORD
McDonald Institute, University of Cambridge

Note. This memoir would have been impossible without the help of many people. My warmest thanks to Dr P.-J. Smith for the transcript of her interview with B de C and for permission to use it. Many thanks too to Mike Heyworth, Mike Pitts and Cherry Lavell at the CBA, Dr Bob Knox, Professor Rosemary Cramp FBA, Professor Norman Hammond FBA, Professor Lamberg-Karlovsky, Carl Phillips, Sarah Searight, Kamil MacLelland and Christian Velde, all of whom illuminated different aspects of Beatrice de Cardi's extraordinary life. I am also grateful to the librarian of the Ancient India and Iran Trust in Cambridge for her help with books.

PAUL LANGFORD © *Lincoln College, Oxford 2017*

Paul Langford
1945–2015

PAUL LANGFORD HAD A NOTABLE influence on how the political history of eighteenth-century England was written and thought about; and he had no less marked an impact on the academic institutions to which he belonged and whose shape and future he helped to determine. Equally effective as a tutor encouraging pupils to make the most of their abilities, and as a chairman leading fractious committees towards consensus and decision, he was nonetheless a strikingly self-contained and self-motivated man. Formidably well organised, and a person of obvious good sense, he seemed always to know his own mind and what he was about, and to be moving methodically towards his goals without any hesitation, deviation or particular fuss. It was a recipe for sustained academic success in a career which brought him both public recognition and considerable private fulfilment.

I

His roots lay in South Wales, in the Vale of Glamorgan, and in Gloucestershire, in the Forest of Dean. He was born in Mid-Glamorgan Hospital, Bridgend, on 20 November 1945, the elder son of Frederick Wade Langford and his wife, Olive (née Walters), who were then living in Llanharan. By the time he was ten they had moved twice and finally settled in Cinderford in the Forest of Dean, which remained the family home. Paul no doubt owed much of his determination and drive to his father, a Welsh Methodist who was evidently a man of some ambition. He was a successful manager for the Co-operative Society in Gloucestershire, and an effective public speaker who became a major figure in the committees and activities of the Rotary Club, not only there but nationally. The son must have delighted his father in 1957 when he won a scholarship to Monmouth School, then a notable direct grant school, and was soon 'much admired for his calm, measured judgment' in the debating society. At the time Monmouth had a fierce reforming headmaster, Robert Glover, and two renowned history teachers, Robert Parry and Brian Stevens. Stevens taught an A-level Special Subject on the Elder Pitt, which sparked off Paul's interest in the period he was to make his own, while leaving him with a lasting detestation of Pitt himself.[1] Glover once horrified him by turning up with some guests at the Speech House Hotel in Cinderford, where he was working as a waiter and breaking school rules. The headmaster made no comment until Paul's last day at Monmouth. Congratulating him on winning an exhibition to read history at Oxford, he simply remarked that he was 'a very fine historian' but 'a bloody awful wine waiter'.[2] The exhibition was at Hertford College, but before taking it up he took a year off, part of it spent in Lichfield doing some teaching, part in France polishing up his spoken French (he was soon to be equally fluent in German).

When he arrived in Oxford in 1964, Hertford was scarcely a college renowned as a nursery of first-class historians, but he can hardly have required much nursing. He was awarded a scholarship at the end of his second year, and it was a piece of good fortune (or perhaps it was good management) when Felix Markham, Hertford's Modern History tutor, arranged to send him to John B. Owen at Lincoln College for tuition on eighteenth-century England, and particularly on his Special Subject, 'Britain and India in the Age of Warren Hastings'. The two clearly hit it off, and Owen quickly came to admire him as 'the ablest pupil I have had in over twenty years'.[3] While still a student, Paul also had the good fortune and great good sense to meet and get to know his future wife, Margaret Edwards, whose father was a Forester (that is to say born within the registered boundaries of the Forest of Dean) and a gardener famous there for his carnations. While Paul was at Hertford, she was training to be a teacher at Hereford College of Education, and in vacations they both

---

[1] Richard Carwardine, 'Address' at Memorial Service, 30 April 2016. On Pitt's 'personal ruthlessness beyond any politician of his age', see P. Langford, *A Polite and Commercial People: England 1727–1783* (Oxford, 1989), p. 225.
[2] Carwardine, 'Address'.
[3] Lincoln College Oxford Archives [hereafter LCA], 'Paul Langford fellow's file' [hereafter PL file], J. B. Owen to the Rector, 17 April 1969 and 15 March 1970.

worked in that same Speech House Hotel in Cinderford, visited castles all over the country together (a passion of Paul's later replaced by one for the houses of the landed aristocracy) and went to the theatre in Stratford-upon-Avon whenever they could. She also remembers how hard he worked in term-time, particularly in the run-up to Finals, when he had potential examination questions arranged on separate index cards, with an outline of possible answers neatly attached, and then, with her help, memorised them. Thus effectively equipped, he obtained the expected first-class degree in 1967, 'one of the best firsts of his year with consistent first-class marks throughout the range of papers', Markham reported.[4]

He immediately began work for a DPhil, with Owen as his supervisor, on 'The first Rockingham administration, 1765–6', a topic which Owen had suggested. A series of appointments at Lincoln quickly followed, a Grimshaw senior scholarship in 1968, a junior research fellowship in 1969 and finally a tutorial fellowship, in effect a permanent appointment, when Owen moved to a chair in Calgary in 1970 and Paul was elected in his place. He was supported for the tutorial fellowship not only by Owen and Markham but also by the powerful voice of Dame Lucy Sutherland, Principal of Lady Margaret Hall, who had supervised him for a year and found his work 'distinguished and indeed remarkable in so young a scholar'. The fact that she had herself begun research on Rockingham and Burke, and published her first academic article on the subject, gave her recommendation special weight.[5] There were also reports on him from Robert Shackleton and others who had been impressed by his conversation at dinner, or by a paper he had read to a seminar.[6] Favourable opinions were being gathered in.

That there were several of them says something about Paul's reputation at this early stage; and there were two other features of his seemingly inevitable progress which appeared striking to his contemporaries beginning historical research at much the same time. One was the fact that he was working on a topic in high political history at a time when the tide was running against it, and doing so with a 'quiet, modest, unassertive,

---

[4] LCA, PL file, Felix Markham to the Rector, 16 March 1970.
[5] LCA, PL file, Dame Lucy Sutherland to the Rector, 13 March 1970; A. Whiteman, 'Lucy Stuart Sutherland (1903–1980)', *Proceedings of the British Academy*, 69 (1983), p. 616. Paul naturally contributed to her Festschrift, taking as his subject 'The Rockingham Whigs and America, 1767–1773', in A. Whiteman, J. S. Bromley and P. G. M Dickson (eds.), *Statesmen, Scholars and Merchants: Essays in Eighteenth-Century History Presented to Dame Lucy Sutherland* (Oxford, 1973), pp. 135–52.
[6] LCA, PL file, letters to Vivian Green 5 January, 8 May 1970.

but determined conviction that what he was doing was the right kind of thing, however unfashionable'.⁷ The other—itself an unfashionable if not quite unheard of thing at the time—was the speed with which he finished his doctorate, in just over three years, despite shouldering the burdens of a tutorial fellowship for one of them. He was awarded the DPhil in 1971. He had already married Margaret on 22 July 1970, in Lincoln College chapel, filled with her father's specially grown orange carnations for the occasion. The college was to be his academic home for the rest of his career.

II

For almost thirty years, until 1998, he was an assiduous college tutor, and for most of that time Lincoln's senior history tutor, occupying the handsomely panelled 'Wesley Room', as was wholly appropriate for an eighteenth-century historian and one born into a Methodist family.⁸ There he could be observed at work by curious tourists (though usually only at the appointed times), and there he taught his undergraduate pupils, often singly when they were from Lincoln, generally in pairs when they came from other Oxford colleges, and a growing number did so as his reputation increased. All of them started off in some awe of him as he sat in his wing-backed chair, tips of fingers touching, eyes half-closed, while they read their essays. But he was listening attentively, making the odd note and then always encouraging them to improve their own arguments: 'he seemed to have a genius for getting you to realise you had picked up more about a subject than you thought you had'.⁹ For many years, with one or two colleagues, he held a faculty seminar on the eighteenth-century Special Subject which was the lineal descendant of the one he had studied himself as an undergraduate, now reformed and rechristened 'Politics and empire 1763–86' and then 'Politics, reform and imperial crisis, 1774–1784'. In that setting also, and in the pub to which they adjourned afterwards, he treated

---

⁷ Blair Worden to the author, 17 May 2016.
⁸ As V. H. H. Green established, this was not in fact Wesley's room in his early days in Lincoln, where the Holy Club met and Methodism had its origins, but he may have occupied it during his later years as a Fellow: P. Langford, 'Vivian Hubert Howard Green (1915–2005)', *Oxford Dictionary of National Biography*, http://www.oxforddnb.com/view/article/94873 (accessed 12 May 2016).
⁹ Tim Knowles, 'Address' at Memorial Service, 30 April 2016; Guy Rowlands to the author, 10 June 2016.

students very seriously and in much the same style. He 'never talked down to them, wasn't didactic, just learned'.[10]

Unusually for a college tutor at the time, he did very little undergraduate teaching outside his chosen century. Although he gave tutorials on European as well British history between 1700 and 1800, he rarely ventured outside those dates. He was single minded in the use of his time, in teaching as in research, and determined to make himself, as he very soon became, the acknowledged Oxford expert on his own territory. Not surprisingly, he attracted a growing number of graduate students eager for his supervision, often eight at a time, and as many as ten at one point in the early 1990s.[11] He had joined Peter Dickson in running the faculty's eighteenth-century graduate seminar, and arranged for it to meet in what he called the 'appropriately Augustan splendour' of the Beckington Room in Lincoln; and he played a large part, along with Leslie Mitchell and Joanna Innes, in making it a seminar where graduate students felt comfortable and happily contributed—not always a characteristic of such occasions in Oxford. Here too, and at the dinners with students which followed, he showed a disarming willingness to listen, accompanied by what one participant calls 'a delicious wry smile which could speak volumes: sometimes hinting at scepticism, sometimes a quiet recognition of things well done, and sometimes a smile about the sheer pleasures of scholarship'.[12]

These were some of the qualities, understated but quietly effective, which helped to make him so persuasive in the academic politics of his college and faculty, especially when they were backed up by his obvious and life-long conviction that sensible people ought to be able to reach a consensus on what was best for the general good.[13] Early on he won some fame as a negotiator in Lincoln when he was 'parking ombudsman' (a role which fell to the junior fellow), and quickly settled previously insoluble arguments about which fellows should have rights to the college's few spaces off Turl Street. But that was small beer. Once he was sure of his ground, he was eager to promote more permanent reforms, and ready to tread on toes when it was necessary. He was a notably reforming Senior Tutor of Lincoln from 1977 to 1980, building on the work of his predecessor to raise the academic performance and reputation of the

---

[10] Joanna Innes to the author, 20 September 2016.
[11] LCA, PL file, Langford to Robert Fox, 25 September 1992.
[12] Sir David Eastwood to the author, 11 August 2016.
[13] Compare his remarks on 'high politics', below, p. 131.

college by tightening up the system of 'collections' (written examinations) which undergraduates were supposed to take at the beginning of every term. He also added to the college's tutorial resources (and helped the early career development of younger scholars) by persuading it, against some opposition, to introduce three short-term 'junior tutorial fellowships', later to be termed Darby Fellowships.[14]

The story was much the same in the faculty. As chairman of the examiners in the Final Honour School of Modern History in 1979, he was able to get his colleagues to agree on an ingenious scheme 'to increase the amount of double-marking (which everyone agreed was needed) without breaking the examiners' backs (which everyone feared)'.[15] In 1981 he persuaded a faculty meeting to recognise the reality of the decline in language teaching in schools, and require candidates taking the Modern History preliminary examination in their first year to study one text in a foreign language rather than two, as had been the previous rule. At the time this seemed the most radical of revolutions to the old guard, but it had long been campaigned for, and it did not prevent Paul's election as chairman of the Modern History faculty board in 1986. He was plainly a man who had judgement and good sense. He also had staying power. Doing his bit for public education more widely, he was a Senior Examiner in History at 'A' Level for the Oxford and Cambridge Schools Examinations Board every summer from 1970 right through to 1983.

Nothing was allowed to get in the way of his own research and writing, however. After his thesis was finished, he produced three books in very short order. The thesis itself, published as an Oxford Historical Monograph in 1973, was quickly followed in 1975 by a short monograph on the Excise Crisis and in 1976 by a volume on British foreign policy in the eighteenth century.[16] All were well received. One reviewer of *The First Rockingham Administration* thought the author was to be congratulated on tackling an unappealing subject so well. The anonymous reviewer in the *Times Literary Supplement* made clear the historical minefield between 'Namierite' and 'Whig' interpretations through which the author had ventured cautiously to tread, but found the book 'lively throughout' and sometimes 'beautifully provocative'. This reviewer was no less an authority on Whig interpretations than Sir Herbert Butterfield, though Paul may

---

[14] LCA, College Order Book, 1978–9, and associated committee papers.
[15] Blair Worden to the author, 18 May 2016.
[16] P. Langford, *The First Rockingham Administration, 1765–6* (Oxford, 1973); P. Langford, *The Excise Crisis: Society and Politics in the Age of Walpole* (Oxford, 1975); P. Langford, *The Eighteenth Century, 1688–1815* (London, 1976).

well not have known it at the time.[17] Reviews of *The Excise Crisis* were less qualified. It was immediately welcomed as a classic study, resting on substantial original research and throwing wholly new light on Walpole's political limitations and his misjudgement of public opinion.[18] The book on foreign policy, by contrast, was explicitly intended for students, providing them with a running commentary so that they could set foreign policy squarely in the overall domestic context, where it belonged.[19] It did precisely that, as the pencilled underlinings in the several well-thumbed copies still on the open shelves of the Bodleian Library demonstrate.

Meanwhile, in 1974, Lucy Sutherland had persuaded him—instructed might almost be a better word—to take on his next major scholarly preoccupation, as General Editor of the *Writings and Speeches* of Edmund Burke. She was keen to see it follow the great Cambridge/Chicago edition of Burke's *Correspondence*, which had been edited by Thomas W. Copeland, and Oxford University Press had agreed to take it on, despite the fact that it never had the substantial American funding behind it which had supported the *Correspondence*.[20] The task of General Editor was hence a daunting one. Nonetheless, with his characteristic drive, Paul got the whole edition moving:

> Above all, he personally undertook the invaluable preliminary work of surveying the vast holdings of Burke drafts, notes and fragments in the libraries at Sheffield and Northampton. It was his sense of the extent to which authentic versions of speeches could be reconstructed from this manuscript material that constitutes the claim of the edition to have made original contributions on a massive scale to the Burke canon.[21]

He also showed how the job should be done by himself editing one of the first two volumes to appear, volume 2, *Party, Parliament, and the American War, 1766–1774*.[22] This was hailed as a major scholarly achievement, scrupulously edited to standards of which Burke himself would have

---

[17] John Carswell in *English Historical Review*, 90 (1975), 446–7; Sir Herbert Butterfield in *Times Literary Supplement*, 20 July 1973, p. 833.
[18] E.g., John Carswell in *Times Literary Supplement*, 24 October 1975, p. 1253.
[19] Langford, *Eighteenth Century*, p. vii.
[20] T. W. Copeland, A. Cobban and J. P. Boyd (eds.), *The Correspondence of Edmund Burke* (Cambridge and Chicago, IL, 10 vols., 1958–78); Oxford University Press Archives, correspondence between Thomas W. Copeland, Lucy Sutherland and Dan Davin, 19 July, 13 September, 29 September 1972, kindly shown to me by Hollie Thomas.
[21] Peter Marshall to the author, 1 June 2016.
[22] P. Langford and W. B. Todd (eds.), *The Writings and Speeches of Edmund Burke*, vol. 2 (Oxford, 1981). The other volume published in 1981 was volume 5, *India, Madras and Bengal, 1774–1785*, edited by P. Marshall, associate editor of the series, and W. B. Todd.

approved and an auspicious start to an important series.[23] With later volumes Paul kept a close eye on progress, but generally left their editors to get on with it unless they showed signs of never finishing.

Once his own volume was out of the way and the spade-work done for the whole edition, therefore, he was able to turn to less demanding projects. One was his contribution to the eighteenth-century volume of the *History of the University of Oxford*, 'Tories and Jacobites 1714–1751'.[24] Another was his chapter on the eighteenth century in the *Oxford Illustrated History of Britain* (Oxford, 1984), edited by Kenneth O. Morgan, which has a claim to be the most widely read piece of prose he ever wrote, since it was reissued by the Press in various guises down to its appearance in 2000 as *Eighteenth-Century Britain: a Very Short Introduction*.[25] There were other essays of his at the time which seemed to indicate that something more exciting might be in the offing, especially a path-breaking piece on 'Property and "virtual representation" in eighteenth-century England' in 1988.[26] Anyone who saw him in these years hard at work in the Upper Reading Room of the Bodleian in term-time, or in the two dozen and more provincial record offices he visited in the vacations,[27] knew that he must be engaged on some large enterprise. But there was no prior indication of how substantial an advance on his earlier work it would turn out to be, both in the breadth of its historical vision and in the depth of its scholarship, until the appearance in rapid succession of the two books which made his name and by which he will always be remembered. The new breadth of vision was prompted by an invitation from John Roberts, the General Editor, to write a volume in the recently planned 'New Oxford History of England', and it produced *A Polite and Commercial People: England 1727–1783* (Oxford, 1989). The fresh focus for his scholarship became evident when he received a later invitation to give the prestigious Ford Lectures in 1990, and this resulted in *Public Life and the Propertied*

---

[23] E.g., John Brewer in *Times Literary Supplement*, 23 October 1981, p. 1233; Colin Brooks in *English Historical Review*, 99 (1984), 196–7.

[24] L. S. Sutherland and L. G. Mitchell (eds.), *The History of the University of Oxford*, vol 5: *The Eighteenth Century* (Oxford, 1986), pp. 99–127.

[25] P. Langford, *Eighteenth-Century Britain: a Very Short Introduction* (Oxford, 2000).

[26] P. Langford, 'Property and "virtual representation" in eighteenth-century England', *Historical Journal*, 31 (1988), 83–115. For another sign of new interests, see his 'Thomas Day and the politics of sentiment', *Journal of Imperial and Commonwealth History*, 12 (1984), 57–79.

[27] He applied for College funding to visit at least twenty-four Record Offices in these years (and also to do research in libraries in the USA): LCA, PL file, letters 1983-88. Leslie Mitchell commented to me that whenever he visited a fresh archive in the provinces, 'Paul had invariably been there first'.

Englishman 1689–1798 (Oxford, 1991). It was predictable of Paul that his New Oxford History volume was the first of the series to be published, and that *Public Life and the Propertied Englishman* was sent to the press as soon as the last of his lectures had been delivered.

III

The two books, on which he must have been working simultaneously, were very different in style and content, the first a novel interpretation of a whole society, with particular focus on the two themes in its title (taken from William Blackstone), the second a massive work of dense scholarship on a particular and particularly important topic. (He had hoped to publish a shorter synopsis alongside the latter, in the shape of the Ford lectures more or less as delivered, but the Press demurred.) *A Polite and Commercial People* deliberately set out 'to emphasize the changes which occurred in an age not invariably associated with change'; and to underline the role as agents of change, not of a small aristocracy, but of 'a broad middle class whose concerns became ever more central to Georgian society and whose priorities determined so much both of debate and action'. Britain was no longer a traditional society in any sense. It was a 'plutocracy' in which 'power was widely diffused, constantly contested, and ever adjusting to new incursions of wealth, often modest wealth'; and it was held together by the commerce and politeness which were essential elements in what Paul called 'the peculiar modernity of the Hanoverian age'.[28] There was nothing very unusual in pointing to new kinds of commerce and consumption when explaining rapid social change in the eighteenth century; but the stress on the importance of polite modes of behaviour in regulating and conferring status across a broad social range was novel. It made politeness central to historical understanding of the eighteenth century for the first time.

The overall effect of the book was therefore to turn attention away from a landed elite and established church towards the middling and commercial classes who had left as indelible a mark on manners and attitudes as on the economy and politics. Paul confessed that the result was 'a bias perhaps' (p. xi), and there were reviewers who thought that sections of society above or below his very large middle class got short shrift, but all of them welcomed the book as giving new life to a much

---

[28] P. Langford, *A Polite and Commercial People: England 1727–1783* (Oxford, 1989), pp. xi, 25.

neglected period of English history. It contained some nicely quotable phrases in the author's most assured style, to the effect, for example, that 'a history of luxury and attitudes to luxury would come very close to being a history of the eighteenth century' (p. 3). It was also very witty. Until we read Langford's treatment of them, few of us ever supposed that the intricacies of English politics in the 1750s could be so entertaining. One review concluded that he had set a standard 'in terms of scholarship, liveliness and sheer historical craftsmanship' which later New Oxford Histories would find it difficult to match.[29]

Public Life and the Propertied Englishman presented more of a challenge to its audience, a book, one reviewer said, that was 'wonderful to own but dreadful to read', because it was chock full of the results of original research undertaken in every corner of England. John Brewer agreed that it deployed 'a learning that is as formidably deep as it is breathtakingly broad', and while it might not be an easy read, it was 'an astonishing achievement, a new anatomy of eighteenth-century England'.[30] Langford's anatomy was based once again on the broad middle ranks of society, and he concentrated here on the importance of their property, the many forms which it took and its role in giving them political identity and agency, in what was increasingly a propertied rather than a status-based society. In his Preface he was careful to make clear where he differed from the views taken by other historians of the eighteenth century:

> I hope in some measure to have provided a corrective to the view that Georgian politics was overwhelmingly controlled by its aristocracy, as conventionally defined ... and to argue that our perception of eighteenth-century life has been dictated rather too much by the patronage preoccupations of the gentry, by the retrospective appeal of plebeian revolt, and by the long-standing English obsession with party politics.[31]

Here he was not only distinguishing his interpretation from the old Namierite paradigm of an eighteenth century dominated by the power and patronage of its landed aristocracy, which had never had any appeal for him.[32] He was also separating his approach from more recent interpre-

---

[29] Linda Colley, in *Times Literary Supplement*, 20 April 1990, p. 415. For longer, considered, reviews see J. Innes, 'Not so strange? New views of Eighteenth-Century England', *History Workshop*, 29 (Spring 1990), 179–83; and N. Rogers, 'Paul Langford's "Age of Improvement"', *Past and Present*, 130 (February 1991), 201–9.
[30] Daniel A. Baugh, in *Albion*, 25 (1993), 325–7; John Brewer, in *History Today*, August 1992, 53.
[31] P. Langford, *Public Life and the Propertied Englishman 1689–1798* (Oxford, 1991), pp. vi–vii.
[32] J. B. Owen commented that Paul's doctoral thesis on Rockingham 'steered carefully between the eulogies of Macaulay and his Whig successors on the one hand and the strictures of Namier and John Brooke on the other': LCA, PL file, Owen to the Rector, 15 March 1970.

tations in terms of political parties and popular radicalism which were equally far removed from Namier's model.³³ As he explored how property was defined, contested and defended at every level of the political structure, he had come to realise the special character of the politics created by the growth and diversification of a large and propertied governing class. As he said in his Preface, his research in the archives, local as well as central, had led him away from 'high politics' to an appreciation of 'politics in its fullest and authentically "highest" sense, as the means by which communities organise themselves for what they perceive to be the public good'.³⁴

He was also at pains to explain that he was, as he had always been, 'a political historian concerned primarily with relationships of power and influence, with the ways in which individuals and groups obtained and exercised authority'.³⁵ He acknowledged a great debt to social historians (and he might have added economic historians) who had illuminated some of the relationships between property, social class and power which contributed to the peculiar character of Georgian society. But he was never very sympathetically disposed towards their kinds of history, despite his own interest in property and its social distribution.³⁶ He did not need to be. He was a political historian through and through, and *Public Life and the Propertied Englishman* had a major impact across the whole field because it was demonstrably authoritative in its own terms. It spoke to different historical constituencies and offered all of them new arguments and a vast amount of new material to ponder. Critics might find fault with its neglect of one or another kind of property, or of the centre as opposed to the localities on which it lavished so much attention, and question whether property was quite so overwhelming a political preoccupation as its author seemed to suppose.³⁷ It was sometimes underappreciated also because its arguments were too buried in its text. But it was, and remains,

---

³³ He had made clear where he agreed and disagreed with one important contribution to these debates when reviewing John Brewer's *Party Ideology and Popular Politics at the Accession of George III* (Cambridge, 1976) in *English Historical Review*, 92 (1977), 617–22.

³⁴ Langford, *Public Life and the Propertied Englishman 1689–1798*, p. ix. In *Polite and Commercial People* (p. 5) he had made much the same point about 'the politics of politeness' being 'the pursuit of harmony within a propertied society'.

³⁵ Langford, *Public Life and the Propertied Englishman*, p. ix.

³⁶ He once dismissed an important book on urban history by an economic historian, which I had praised in his hearing, because one or two of its statistics seemed to him based on wholly unreliable contemporary sources.

³⁷ On some of these issues, see J. Innes, 'Politics, property and the middle class', *Parliamentary History*, 11 (1992), 286–92.

undeniably a great book. There was no disputing the fact that it made all those working on the eighteenth century 'think differently and think better', and together with the recent Oxford History it marked 'a historiographical breakthrough in our understanding of eighteenth-century England'.[38]

Academic honours naturally followed. Paul was elected a Fellow of the British Academy in 1993, and awarded an ad hominem Readership in Oxford in the following year. In 1996, when the University's policy on professorial titles changed, he was one of the first to be promoted to that status. Never content to rest on his laurels, however, he was already contemplating another 'major book' and embarking on the necessary research. The working title was 'Manners and Character: the British Portrayed, 1700–1850'.[39] Intended to draw on the voluminous printed material recording foreign representations of the inhabitants of the British Isles, its theme may have been suggested to him by some of his work on manners for *A Polite and Commercial People*, and by the further work on manners being generated by a new seminar for Master's students given with Joanna Innes on 'Polite society in eighteenth-century Britain' which ran from 1993 to 1999. An early fruit of the research was an entertaining and enlightening Raleigh Lecture for the British Academy in 1996 on 'Politics and Manners from Sir Robert Walpole to Sir Robert Peel', which pointed, for example, to the decline of formality in English politics between the days when Walpole's birthday was 'a ceremonial event second only to that of royalty' and the early nineteenth century when 'politicians chose to remain gentlemen, exposed to a parliament of gentlemen, and a public of would-be gentlemen'.[40] That was followed by other papers drawing on similar material, on 'British politeness and the progress of western manners: an eighteenth-century enigma', on 'Manners and the eighteenth-century state: the case of the unsociable Englishman' and on 'The English as reformers: foreign visitors' impressions 1750–1850'.[41] The

---

[38] Sir David Eastwood to the author, 1 Aug 2016; Julian Hoppit, review in *Journal of Modern History*, 66 (1994), 139–42.
[39] LCA, PL file, application for the title of professor, 19 December 1995.
[40] P. Langford, 'Politics and manners from Sir Robert Walpole to Sir Robert Peel', *Proceedings of the British Academy*, 94 (1996), pp. 103–25.
[41] In, respectively, P. Langford, 'British politeness and the progress of western manners: an eighteenth-century enigma', *Transactions of the Royal Historical Society*, 6th ser., 7 (1997), 53–72; P. Langford, 'Manners and the eighteenth-century state: the case of the unsociable Englishman', in J. Brewer and E. Hellmuth (eds.), *Rethinking Leviathan. The Eighteenth-Century State in Britain and Germany* (Oxford, 1999), pp. 281–316; P. Langford, 'The English as reformers: foreign visitors' impressions 1750–1850', *Proceedings of the British Academy*, 100 (1999), pp. 101–20. See

last of these opens with a book on 'England and the English' published in German in 1818, translated from a French text which was itself translated from an English text ostensibly written by a Spaniard, but in fact written by Robert Southey.

The source material was, to say the least, difficult to handle, quite apart from its sheer volume and the predictable problems of separating out representations of the Welsh, Irish and Scots from those of the English. The book which finally emerged after much research, *Englishness Identified: Manners and Character 1650–1850* (Oxford, 2000), was striking for its use of little-known material in French and German, and given other pressures on the author's time it is a minor miracle that it appeared as soon as it did. Yet it contained little by way of scholarly apparatus or precise analysis of how far the representations and stereotypes it reported might be taken to reflect English reality. Paul was depressed when it received cooler reviews than his previous books,[42] but the whole project seems to have been one still without clear boundaries or a fixed central focus. It was better suited to be the source of stimulating essays on diverse subjects than the foundation for a third work of major historical significance.

IV

By the time *Englishness Identified* appeared, however, Paul's whole career, rather than just his historical research, was changing direction. In 1995 he had become a member of the British Academy's Humanities Research Board, the body initially set up to administer the Academy's funds which came from government for postgraduate awards and for other research programmes, and which finally—after much uncertainty about the direction of government policy and some controversy within the Academy itself—evolved into the Arts and Humanities Research Council.[43] When John Laver, the first Chairman of the Board, was about to step down in

---

also P. Langford, 'Manners and character in Anglo-American perceptions, 1750–1850', in F. M. Leventhal and R. E. Quinault (eds.), *Anglo-American Attitudes: from Revolution to Partnership* (Aldershot, 2000), pp. 76–90.

[42] For example, David A. Bell in *London Review of Books*, 22, no. 24 (14 December 2000), pp. 26–7; C. Dallett Hemphill, in *Journal of Social History*, 35 (2002), 1000–1002.

[43] J. Herbert, *Creating the AHRC. An Arts and Humanities Research Council for the United Kingdom in the Twenty-First Century* (London: British Academy, Occasional Paper 12, 2008), p. 5 and passim. Herbert's narrative traces the stages by which the Board became a fully fledged Research Council, and is useful as an interim history, but the topic would merit a much fuller account.

1998, Paul was the unanimous choice of the committee appointing his successor. In his application he had been clear about the challenges of the post and about its attractions for him, given his experience. He noted that recent changes in government policy would radically alter the context within which the Board operated. It would require a new strategy to ensure that it was properly responsive to the needs of all the disciplines within its domain, and not, as it often appeared, representative only of academics in the 'golden triangle'. He stressed that he wanted to continue with his own research in order to retain academic credibility, and he commented on the frustrations he had found in Oxford when Senior Tutor of a college and vice-chairman of a faculty board, and which he would be glad to leave behind:

> In my estimation, the more parochial units [in a university] are not necessarily the least taxing. One of the features of Oxford life is the extent to which individuals can find themselves having to exercise a large measure of personal responsibility with a minimum of bureaucratic support and among colleagues of extremely diverse disciplines. Not the least of the attractions of the [Humanities Research] Board is that the support is a great deal better and the diversity markedly less.[44]

The administrative support was indeed a good deal better, especially from Michael Jubb, the Director of Programmes, whom Paul had encountered when Jubb was doing doctoral research into fiscal policy under Walpole, and with whom he now formed a close partnership. In the summer of 1998 they worked together on plans to implement 'heads of agreement' between the English Funding Council (HEFCE) and the Academy on how proposed new funding of some £8m should be handled, before he formally took up his post on 1 October.[45] The post had changed since he applied for it, and it would change further before he left. He was now to be Chairman and Chief Executive of an 'Arts and Humanities Research Board' which still lacked independent legal status and was responsible to the Academy and to HEFCE. He had taken leave from his posts in college and university, but he had to keep both of them regularly informed since the likely length of his absence altered from a total of four years to three and his employer shifted from the Academy to the Funding Council, as political circumstances changed.[46] The goalposts must have

---

[44] LCA, PL file, Langford to the Rector with draft application for HRB post, 23 June 1997.
[45] Herbert, *Creating the AHRC*, pp. 18–19.
[46] LCA, PL file, Langford to A. P. Weale and Rees Davies, 14 October 1997, 7 October 1999; P. W. H. Brown to Nigel Berry, 30 January. 1998.

seemed to be moving throughout what turned out to be his short but remarkably busy two-year tenure.

By the end of his first year, the new Chairman was able to report that the AHRB now had a budget of over £50m, and that agreement had been reached to ensure that future funding would come from all the Funding Councils and not just HEFCE, so that the Board was 'able to serve the whole of the United Kingdom, just as the science and social science research councils do'. It was 'a defining moment for the future of arts and humanities research'.[47] By the end of his second year, he could report that there had been progress in building up an independent administrative base in Bristol, that the Board had enjoyed twice as much funding as in the previous year, and that it had taken on new responsibilities from HEFCE in the shape of funding for Museums and Galleries. The first Research Centres had been launched, extra funding had been devoted to awards for research leave, and a new Resource Enhancement scheme, intended to make important resources more widely available to researchers, had been advertised. The aim was 'to realise potential' by supporting existing researchers and departments of high quality as well as by funding new centres of activity. It was now 'an explicit aim of the Board and its funders to develop towards full Research Council status', and it had adopted a Corporate Plan for the next five years which would support their case.[48]

In order to achieve all this Paul had to win the support of several constituencies. The most important initially was the chief funding council, HEFCE, whose leaders found him much easier to deal with than some members of the Academy who had earlier been suspicious about the implications of movement towards research council status. With Paul at the helm, one of those involved in the negotiations remarks, 'the environment changed completely' because he saw 'the bigger picture and embraced it' and so got the AHRB 'off to such a flying start'.[49] He also had the perhaps more difficult job of managing a committee structure within the Board in which there were traditional tensions between disciplines, as between archaeologists and classicists, and in which newcomers from the Performing and Visual Arts had to be persuaded they were fully at home. Here his natural skills as a chairman came into their own. He recognised

---

[47] AHRB, *Annual Report 1998–9*, p. 2.
[48] Herbert, *Creating the AHRC*, p. 23; AHRB, *Annual Report 1999–2000*, pp. 2–3; AHRB, *Corporate Plan 2000–2005*.
[49] Bahram Bekhradnia to the author, 5 July 2016.

that board members had different interest groups behind them, listened to all of them and reached, if not consensus, then broad agreement, because he had what John Morrill describes as 'that priceless gift of always being in it for others and not for himself', so that his complete lack of self-interest or any disciplinary prejudices always won the day.[50]

Finally, and not least demanding in terms of energy, he had to be an effective advocate for his Board and its activities to universities, colleges and researchers across the United Kingdom. He visited forty institutions in his first year as Chairman, and he and Jubb between them had been to over a hundred by the end of the second.[51] He had to reassure some of the more conservative strands in humanities scholarship that the advent of the AHRB did not mean some enforced transformation of scholarly processes and priorities but offered new opportunities, and at the same time explain to them some of the problems which came with success when extra funding and publicity led to vastly increased numbers of applicants and success rates fell.[52] In this environment it made a big difference for the new institution that its foundations were laid by a scholar of unquestioned authority as well as an administrator of uncommon creativity. He had been determined from the start to make the AHRB a Research Council in waiting, to develop a national strategy, consult widely, establish a full complement of programmes and show their social and cultural benefits to the country as a whole.[53] To have done most of that in only two years was, even by his own standards, quite an achievement.

V

It was inevitable that Paul's abilities would attract the attention of head-hunters and institutions looking for new chief executives, and they might well have thought him ready for a move. In the course of his second year at the AHRB it became clear that acquiring research council status would, sooner rather than later, mean a separation of the roles of Chairman and Chief Executive in accordance with approved principles of corporate governance; and in October 1999 he was asked to stay on, but only for a third year.[54] It would have been understandable if the prospect

[50] John Morrill to the author, 8 July 2016.
[51] AHRB, *Annual Report 1998–1999*, p. 3; Herbert, *Creating the AHRC*, pp. 22–3.
[52] Herbert, *Creating the AHRC*, p. 21.
[53] Michael Jubb, cited in Carwardine, 'Address'.
[54] Herbert, *Creating the AHRC*, p. 23; LCA, PL file, Langford to Rees Davies, 7 October 1999. In

held little appeal for him. He was in any case already being offered other opportunities. He came close to appointment to at least one vice-chancellorship, but was not in the end successful; and he was approached about becoming the head of at least two Oxford colleges, one of them his own. He was elected Rector of Lincoln in November 1999, to take up office in the autumn of 2000.

The statement which he submitted to Lincoln in advance of his election, at the request of the college Governing Body, makes an instructive contrast with his application for appointment to the AHRB two years earlier. It referred again to some of the political frustrations of Oxford's collegiate system, but demonstrated a new sense, learned from his recent experience, of how they might be overcome. He made it clear that he saw the Rectorship of Lincoln as 'an efficient rather than dignified part of the constitution' (though it should be added that he turned out to be pretty good at the dignified parts of the job too). It was the Rector's task to propose policies in response to the fundamental questions faced by all colleges trying to shape their own future in a hostile financial and political environment. There was an evident need for a policy for the size and shape of Lincoln and for its role in research. There should be a 'professional manager' in charge of academic administration across the college. There should be professional financial planning embracing all the college accounts, and a clear strategy for fundraising and development. The Rector, in short, was a leader 'crucial to the effective functioning of a college as a community'—not quite a chief executive, perhaps, but more than simply a chairman.[55] The Governing Body clearly approved, and if there were a few sceptics, they could scarcely say they had not been warned of what was to follow.

From the start, he had the indispensable help of a professional Bursar, Tim Knowles, who had once been his pupil, and who supervised all college accounts and financial planning: recent Bursars had been tutorial fellows with other responsibilities. Within a year there was also a professional Senior Tutor, Anne-Marie Drummond. She was responsible for all academic administration, including student admissions, and hers was only the second such appointment in an Oxford where dons had historically preferred to take turns administering one another. She had been a junior research fellow in Oxford, but more recently an administrator in

---

the summer of 1999 there seems to have been some discussion about a separate Chairman of the Board: AHRB, draft minutes of meeting of 2 July 1999, made available to me by Michael Jubb.
[55] LCA, PL file, statement for the Governing Body, 8 November 1999.

Oxford and two other universities. The Rector and the new officers led discussion of what became a 'Strategic Plan 2001–2006', accepted after some debate by the Governing Body. It included an explicit emphasis on the need to maintain and if possible improve academic performance while eliminating an operating deficit, and so far as was practicable to make the college financially self-sufficient.[56]

By the time Paul retired in 2012, much of this had been achieved. The value of the college endowment had more than doubled and financial security been assured. The academic performance of students, when judged by examination results, had noticeably improved. There were new academic posts, and new buildings, finished, taking shape or planned, small ones inside the college, much larger ones, for graduate students, for example, in college properties elsewhere. Little could have been done without substantial financial support, from alumni and from charitable trusts with which the college was connected, and that was only forthcoming because the Rector had been able to win their confidence and support. What appealed to them were the clear-headed realistic goals which he incorporated into a 'Vision 2007–2027' of how the college should be when it celebrated its six hundredth anniversary: self-governing, self-sufficient, and academically one of the leading colleges in the university.[57] As so often in his career, his personal stature had made all the difference.

When he returned to Oxford, he continued to play a part in the affairs of the British Academy, including chairing the committee representing both social sciences and humanities which set out to demonstrate the contribution they made to the national wealth in *That Full Complement of Riches* (2004). He also began to play a role in the government of the university, sitting on its council for six years and agreeing in 2002 to chair the joint committee with Oxford City Council which mounted a bid for Oxford to become a European City of Culture. The bid failed, but this was another piece of chairmanship which won plaudits from all sides, 'town' as well as 'gown'. In the end, however, he found the university's bureaucracy 'rather wearisome'. The governance of Lincoln, he added, 'was another matter'.[58] His continuing collaboration with his publishers, Oxford University Press, was also another matter. In 2002 he edited for them the eighteenth-century volume in a new *Short History of the British*

---

[56] The Strategic Plan was published together with remarks from the main college officers in *Lincoln College Record 2001–2002*, pp. 7–16.
[57] Knowles, 'Address'. Paul reviewed his own 'Twelve Years of Rectorship' in *Lincoln College Record 2011–2012*, pp. 66–8.
[58] *Lincoln College Record 2011–12*, p. 66.

Isles, and in the same year he completed the demanding work he had begun in 1997 as Consultant Editor for the eighteenth-century section of the *Oxford Dictionary of National Biography*, published in 2004. Working with associate editors for particular subject areas, and with three in-house research editors (all of whom had been his undergraduate or graduate pupils), he was responsible for choosing authors to write some 1500 new biographies and replace or revise 4000 old ones. His particular contribution, as one might expect from his publications, was the greater emphasis now placed on India and America, and on non-metropolitan society in England and Scotland, including such matters as entrepreneurship, crime, intellectual life and the role of women as agents of informal political influence.[59] The decisions he most enjoyed making, however, because he had completely free rein, were which lives he should write himself. His two choices were both notorious challenges for their biographers. The life of Horace Walpole (in 14,000 words) reflects Paul's fascination with a 'complex and somewhat ambivalent personality' he first encountered when he read W. S. Lewis's great edition of the *Correspondence*.[60] The biography of Burke (21,000 words), a more predictable choice, is a superbly rounded portrait of the man whose character had preoccupied Paul for longer than any other eighteenth-century figure.[61]

Burke 'clearly grew on him', Peter Marshall has observed, and reflection on Burke's life at this time seems to have been part of another shift in Paul's historical interests, away from manners and representations, and back towards political power and how it was exercised, particularly at the centre, back to 'high politics' in other words, which had never lost their appeal for him. In some of his publications he continued to draw on the storehouse of evidence collected for *Englishness Identified*,[62] but he had begun to plan a book of essays on prime ministers from Walpole to Blair, which would have had much to say about changes in how government was managed over the centuries, changes of substance as well as style. He became a member of the Editorial Board of the *History of*

---

[59] Information from Philip Carter.
[60] See his review of volumes 37 to 39 in *English Historical Review*, 91 (1976), 433. P. Langford, 'Walpole, Horatio, fourth earl of Oxford (1717–1797)', *Oxford Dictionary of National Biography*, http://www.oxforddnb.com/view/article/28696 (accessed 12 January 2017). He later wrote the life of another somewhat eccentric figure for the online ODNB: Vivian Green, his former colleague at Lincoln: Langford, 'Vivian Hubert Howard Green (1915–2005)'.
[61] P. Langford, 'Burke, Edmund (1729/30–1797)', *Oxford Dictionary of National Biography*, http://www.oxforddnb.com/view/article/4019 (accessed 12 January 2017).
[62] E.g. P. Langford, 'South Britons' reception of North Britons, 1707–1820', *Proceedings of the British Academy*, 127 (2005), pp. 143–69.

Parliament in 2004 (and was its chairman from 2008 to 2012); and his 2005 'History of Parliament Lecture' on 'Prime Ministers and Parliaments: the long view', gives a foretaste of what that book might have offered if he had been able to complete it. It had some good jokes, about there being 'no counting of noses' in the younger Pitt's cabinets because only one nose ('as large as the steeple of Strasbourg') counted, for instance, and about Rockingham spending a year in office without plucking up the courage to speak in parliament at all. But there were also more serious reflections, on fluctuations in the importance of the cabinet and the relative power of the incumbents of 10 and 11 Downing Street, for example, and on the modern evisceration of 'what is still called local government'.[63] It was as polished a performance as any of his earlier public lectures, and as masterly a demonstration of the depth of learning on which he was always able to draw.[64]

Despite all this writing on modern and not so modern political history, it is difficult to discern precisely where Paul's own political sympathies lay. As a young man he would have said they were firmly with the liberal left, and although he may have moved towards the right over time he was a long-standing member of the Oxford branch of the Association of University Teachers. It seems clear from his publications that he never had much sympathy for conventional radicals such as John Wilkes, but he had no sympathy at all for the arrogance and prejudices of the English ruling elite. It is telling that the quality in Burke which he chose to focus on in the *Oxford Dictionary of National Biography* was Burke's 'detestation of those who made abusive uses of the power entrusted to them'.[65] It seems likely that he sympathised most with the middling propertied English men and women, the polite and commercial people of his *Oxford History*, and with their successors who were to be found where he and his wife had grown up, in the farming and small-business communities of the Forest of Dean. In their youth, as in the later eighteenth century, such people were more likely to have been 'chapel' than 'church', but Paul himself was never a particularly religious man. His Methodist ancestors would scarcely have approved of someone who at one time owned a sports car and even bought

---

[63] P. Langford, 'Prime Ministers and parliaments: the long view, Walpole to Blair', *Parliamentary History*, 25 (2006), 382–94.
[64] A similar example, originally given as a seminar paper, is his last historical publication, P. Langford, 'Swift and Walpole', in C. Rawson (ed.), *Politics and Literature in the Age of Swift: English and Irish Perspectives* (Cambridge, 2010), pp. 52–78.
[65] Peter Marshall to the author, 1 June 2016.

a weekly lottery ticket, as he did.⁶⁶ For him religion was a matter of local practice and local loyalties, sanctioned by time. As Rector he naturally attended college chapel regularly, just as he had been an active member of the church and community when he and his family lived in Berkshire, where Margaret was headmistress of a successful Church of England primary school, and he took his turn mowing the grass in the churchyard.⁶⁷ But that too was part of politics in the 'highest sense', as he had defined it in his magnum opus, the politics to be found in the Forest of Dean as much as in an Oxford college, where there were 'communities organising themselves for what they perceive to be the public good'.⁶⁸

VI

The life and loyalties of a small college therefore meant a great deal to Paul and Margaret when they moved into the Rector's Lodgings. They entertained every student to drinks at least once a year, and Paul had formal meetings with each of them every term to discuss their progress with their tutors. Since he played the piano himself (and at one time the viola), he naturally encouraged the musical life of the College, raising funds for choral scholarships and for a fellowship in music shared with another college, and planning a garden building with space for musical and theatrical performances. When Margaret retired as head of Streatley School in 2003, they began to look ahead to the time when Paul might do the same and they would move out of the Lodgings. In the past, they had often had a house in the country: in the 1970s Dorothy Cottage on the edge of the Forest of Dean, and from the later 1980s houses in Berkshire so that their son Hugh could attend Margaret's school, first Lutyens Cottage, Westridge Green, and then Valpys at Ashampstead, where they were able to walk on the Downs and entertain colleagues from London as well as Oxford when Paul was at the AHRB. Now they were able to return to the Forest, buy The Orchard, a handsome spacious house in Hope Mansell near Ross-on-Wye, in 2005, and start planning.

They took particular pleasure in laying out and improving the garden. 'Gardening' was the only recreation Paul acknowledged in *Who's Who*, and for him that included the heavy work of building paths and steps and

---

⁶⁶ Information from Joanna Innes.
⁶⁷ Information from Margaret Langford.
⁶⁸ Langford, *Public Life and the Propertied Englishman*, p. ix.

digging drainage trenches, dressed 'like a scruff', Hugh remarked, which would have surprised those accustomed to his habitual suit and tie when he was in Oxford. In the country, however, and especially on long walks with his cairn terrier, he was able to relax and to release some of the pent-up tensions of a busy working life. (They were normally visible in Oxford only in his habit of clenching and unclenching his fists when some issue or person tried his patience.) He did not, of course, stop thinking and writing about history when in the country. He had taken up swimming himself when Hugh did, and even became a qualified referee for the Amateur Swimming Association in order to have a role; but when not refereeing he was to be seen working on an A4 pad beside the pool, and he did the same at home in front of a TV set. The Orchard naturally had a library, with his books double-banked on purposely designed shelves, so that once he had retired as Rector he could dedicate himself to family life, write the next book, play the piano, dig in his garden and walk his dog. It was an attractive prospect.

It was not to be. By the beginning of 2011 he seemed increasingly unwell, stricken with what was eventually diagnosed as vascular dementia; and after a short period of leave from the college which had already been planned, he retired as Rector in September 2012.[69] The college elected him an Honorary Fellow, as Hertford College had earlier done, and Lincoln named the garden room which he had planned for musical performances the Langford Room in his honour. He had already been awarded honorary degrees by the University of Sheffield and the new University of Lincoln. It may well be that the academic news that gave him most satisfaction towards the end was the report that the final volume of the edition of Burke's writings and speeches had at last, with Peter Marshall's help, been completed. When published it contained a dedication to him as the Editor of the edition 'who planned it at its outset and guided it to its completion'.[70]

Having been cared for devotedly by Margaret as his illness took its toll, he died on 27 July 2015 soon after being admitted to Ross Community Hospital. He was buried like his parents at Yew Tree Brake Cemetery in Cinderford, in the Forest he had always loved. There was a memorial service in the University Church, Oxford, on 30 April 2016, attended by friends, colleagues and students, and by representatives of the many institutions to which he had belonged and whose history he had influenced.

---

[69] LCA, PL file, letter to the Sub-Rector, 13 December 2011.
[70] P. J. Marshall and D. C. Bryant (eds.), *The Writings and Speeches of Edmund Burke*, vol. 4: *Party, Parliament and the Dividing of the Whigs 1780–1794* (Oxford, 2015).

His had been a life of unusually varied personal and public achievement; and although he was in many ways a very private person, he was someone it was always a pleasure to meet and to talk to, and a man it was impossible not to remember and admire.

PAUL SLACK
Fellow of the Academy

Note. I owe thanks to a large number of Paul's friends and colleagues for information and advice, among them Bahram Bekhradnia, Susan Brigden, Philip Carter, Richard Carwardine, Peter Dickson, Anne-Marie Drummond, Sir David Eastwood, Robert Faber, Perry Gauci, Joanna Innes, Michael Jubb, Tim Knowles, Peter Marshall, Leslie Mitchell, John Morrill, Keith Robbins, Guy Rowlands, Sir Keith Thomas, Nigel Wilson and Blair Worden; and I am indebted to the Rector of Lincoln College, Henry Woudhuysen, and the College Archivist, Lindsay McCormack, for facilitating my use of the College archives. Paul's family, Margaret and Hugh Langford, have helped me most of all.

There are appreciations of Paul's life and work in Perry Gauci, 'Paul Langford (1945–2015)', *Lincoln College Record 2014–2015*, pp. 68–9; Leslie Mitchell, 'Oxford Donnery at its best', *The Oxford Historian*, 10 (2012), p. 29; and Paul Seaward and Robin Eagles, 'A tribute to Professor Paul Langford FBA', http://www.historyofparliamentonline.org, 13 August 2015 (accessed 9 January 2016). A portrait of him by June Mendoza hangs in Lincoln College Hall. There will be a full bibliography of his publications in P. Gauci and E. Chalus (eds.), *Revisiting the Polite and Commercial People: Essays in Georgian Politics, Society and Culture in Honour of Professor Paul Langford* (Oxford, forthcoming 2019).

GEOFFREY NEIL LEECH

Geoffrey Neil Leech
1936–2014

GEOFFREY LEECH (ALWAYS CALLED Geoff by colleagues and students) made major contributions to a broad range of topics in language research: the linguistic study of literature, the development of semantics and pragmatics, description of the grammar of English and the development of corpora, large computer-readable databases of language. Linguists reviewing his life tend naturally to focus on the areas closest to their own specialisms, and it can be difficult to get a sense of the full range of his work, especially since he never really dropped one of these topics when he focused on another. He left a detailed, engaging and reflective 'academic autobiography' for a collection compiled for The Philological Society.[1] I will draw on this autobiography to trace his career (all quotations from Leech without footnotes are from this source), but will note later the problems it presents for a biographer, especially because of his inveterate modesty.

Early years and University College London

Leech was born on 16 January 1936, in Gloucester. His parents were Richard and Dorothy Leech, and he had an older brother, Martin. The family moved to nearby Tewkesbury when his father, a bank clerk, got a job as a bank manager. Geoff went to Tewkesbury Grammar School; he

---

[1] K. Brown and V. Law (eds.), *Linguistics in Britain: Personal Histories* (Oxford, 2002), pp. 155–69. I have also drawn on his unpublished brief history of the Department of Linguistics at Lancaster: G. Leech, *Sketch of Departmental History, 1974–1997* (Lancaster, 1997).

notes that Roger Fowler, who would join him at University College London (UCL) and go on to become an influential scholar in stylistics and critical linguistics, was at the same school in a lower form. He was already devoted to the piano; he considered studying music further. He clearly learned a broad keyboard repertoire early on; he remarked in his later years that the music one learns before one is sixteen sticks permanently in one's memory. He says that in his National Service, from 1954 to 1956 in the RAF, 'I . . . spent most of my time shorthand typing in West Germany.'

In retrospect, it was a crucial factor in the direction of his career that he then went to UCL, which in the 1960s attracted many of the key figures in the study of the English Language. He attributes this important decision to chance:

> My father happened to drink in the same pub as Professor A. H. Smith, who was Quain Professor of English at University College London (UCL) and who happened to own a weekend cottage in a village near Tewkesbury. As a favour to my father, Professor Smith gave me an interview at his country cottage, but I must have offended him when I said I really wanted to study French! However, he offered me a place in his department.

There was no Linguistics Department at UCL from 1956 to 1959, when Leech did his BA in English Language and Literature, but there was a long-established Phonetics Department. He was taught by A. C. Gimson and J. D. O'Connor, and heard lectures by Daniel Jones (who had retired ten years earlier) and J. R. Firth, who had retired from the School of Oriental and African Studies just before Leech arrived at UCL. Leech chose a syllabus with a strong historical language component.[2] It included a course on detailed analysis of literary texts with Winifred Nowottny.[3] It also included 'Old English, Middle English, Old Norse, and English Philology'. Leech did not pursue these periods of English in his later work, but it could be argued that they shaped his approach to language, leading to his studies of comparative corpora and language change fifty years later. His studies probably also account for his lifelong interest in the study of place names; he always kept up with scholarship in this area even though he did not publish in it. And he was always ready to assume that anyone who had studied English must have a similar broad knowledge of

---

[2] David Crystal, who was an undergraduate at UCL a few years after Leech, describes the course in more detail in D. Crystal, *Just a Phrase I'm Going Through: My Life in Language* (London, 2009), Chs. 6–8.
[3] W. Nowottny, *The Language Poets Use* (London, 1962).

language history. Once, when I misspelled 'Windermere' on an invitation, he remarked that the mistake was easily made, but I would always get it right if I remembered that it was an Anglo-Saxon genitive.

Leech said his record as an undergraduate was 'undistinguished', but he seems to have impressed many people around him, and in 1959 he was awarded a scholarship to do an MA in English as a research degree, in the newly formed Communication Research Centre. He took up the study of the language of television commercials, as part of a group project (Eugene Winter, later an influential text linguist, was working on press advertisements). He made little progress, lacking methods for dealing with these texts, and for eighteen months he suspended his studies and taught in a London secondary school.

In 1961, he met and married Frances Anne Berman (Fanny). She was a Psychology graduate, also from UCL, with a strong mathematical turn. She would be closely involved with corpus work in the 1970s, and later at Lancaster completed an MPhil in Computing (1988) and a PhD in Linguistics (1999), both on probabilistic methods of parsing. They had two children, Thomas (born 1964), now a barrister in London, and Camilla (born 1967), now an interior designer in Oxford.

He was able to return to full-time study in 1962, with a research studentship funded by ATV, one of the then-new commercial television companies. This was the period of his first reading in linguistics, including books on structuralist (that is, pre-Chomsky) approaches to syntax then coming from the USA. It was a line of study suggested by Randolph Quirk, who had just returned to UCL from Durham. His MA thesis was submitted in 1963, and a version was published in 1966 as *English in Advertising*,[4] in a new Longman series edited by Quirk.

English in Advertising was the first book to take advertising language seriously. In a period when there were many popular attacks on advertising, Leech said, 'This book is written in a spirit of neutral inquiry, with the purely linguistic object of describing what British advertising language is *like*' (p. 3: his emphasis). The data are largely those of his MA thesis, 617 advertisements broadcast from December 1960 to May 1961, with additional press and poster advertisements. Most of the book is devoted to describing the grammatical and lexical characteristics of 'standard advertising English', but perhaps the most interesting chapter, entitled 'Creative Writing', deals with ways in which ads violate orthographic,

---

[4] G. Leech, *English in Advertising: a Linguistic Study of Advertising in Great Britain* (London, 1966).

grammatical and semantic conventions, including the use of figurative language, setting the scene for much later linguistic study of advertising discourse. A section on 'rhyme and rhetoric' links to his next book, on poetic language. In this first work he already shows signs of the accessible style and broad systematic approach that would characterise his many later books.

Even before he finished his MA, Leech was offered an assistant lecturer's post in the English Department at UCL in 1962, which he described as 'another piece of immense good fortune'. He was assigned to teach Rhetoric, a course that was and is unusual in UK universities, though widespread in the USA. It had apparently previously focused on the classical tradition 'and had been reputedly the dullest course offered by the Department'. With his broader background in communications research, he set aside traditional rhetorical lists and taught instead 'literary language (especially the language of poetry) from the modern linguistic point of view'. Later he would return to rhetoric, broadly conceived, when he included 'The Rhetorical Principle' in his *Principles of Pragmatics*.

The course also led to another book, *A Linguistic Guide to English Poetry*.[5] It was presented as a textbook, with exercises for discussion at the end of each chapter. But it is also a broad scholarly attempt at synthesis between traditions of literary criticism (William Empson, I. A. Richards and a note in almost every chapter to Nowottny), linguistic analysis (Fowler, Halliday and the most recent books of Chomsky), rhetorical traditions (via Cleanth Brooks and R. P. Warren), and continental structuralism, including a useful introduction to the Prague School. The literary theory he was using as a context is now dated, with its basis in the New Criticism, but everything about stylistics, including such concepts as foregrounding, is still taught today. He was acutely aware of the likely scepticism of some literary scholars, but he was modest enough to acknowledge the assistance of *The Penguin Book of Quotations* to locate some illustrations. The acknowledgements, to Randolph Quirk, but also to Frank Kermode, Roger Fowler, Sidney Greenbaum and of course Winifred Nowottny, suggest that such a book could not have been written at that time anywhere but UCL. Like *English in Advertising*, the book was proofread by his father-in-law George Berman, indicating a network of family support for the young scholar.

From his early publications, one might have thought that he would base his research firmly in literary stylistics. It was on the advice of

---

[5] G. Leech, *A Linguistic Guide to English Poetry* (London, 1969).

M. A. K. Halliday that he took up studies in semantics. Halliday had recently arrived from Edinburgh, and was then Director of the Communication Research Centre with Leech as Assistant Director. But he did not follow the approach that Halliday was then developing into Systemic Functional Linguistics, a framework that has had huge international influence. Instead Leech pursued a semantic theory that was, in his words, 'based on autonomous semantic and syntactic representations, linked by mapping rules'.

Leech was awarded a Harkness Fellowship for 1964–5 (he recalls Isaiah Berlin grilling him as part of the selection panel) and chose to take it at MIT, then the centre of world linguistics. This experience did not lead him, as one might have expected, to become a missionary for generative linguistics in the UK. Chomsky was away, but he met the core of young linguists who would develop Generative Semantics. Leech did not follow this approach either, and the remark in his autobiography, 'I found the intensely intellectual atmosphere there somewhat uncomfortable', suggests he may not have enjoyed the rather rude, self-assertive and aggressive style of academic argument that seems to have been characteristic of these debates.[6] He noted that the most useful course he took there was Barbara Hall (Partee) lecturing on the mathematical and logical basis of linguistics, a course that may have been useful later in engaging with the work of his colleagues on corpus analysis. After these intensive studies, he, Fanny and the one-year-old Tom went tent-camping for three months, an exciting time exploring a nation then undergoing rapid change.

When he returned to the UK, he worked on a monograph on semantics. It is interesting, in terms of UK academic life in the 1960s, that he thought of it as a monograph first, and only later thought of turning it into a PhD thesis. He received a PhD in 1968, with the thesis entitled 'An Approach to the Semantics of Time, Place, and Modality in Modern English', and revised it as a book, again for Longman.[7] Characteristically, he dismissed it in his autobiography: 'This book was out of print in a very few years, and it is hardly read today.' It is probably true that work in formal semantics dates much more quickly than work in stylistics or pragmatics. But it is also true that from 1970 to 1975 it was cited by just about every major scholar

---

[6] H. R. Harris, *The Linguistics Wars* (Oxford, 1993).
[7] G. N. Leech, *Towards a Semantic Description of English* (London, 1969, and Bloomington, IN, 1970).

in semantics, including, for instance, a long and approving quotation in a key paper by Arnold Zwicky and Jerrold Sadock.[8]

Two other closely interwoven strands of Leech's research began at UCL in the 1960s and continued in his career at Lancaster: the collection of data of language use and the development of an up-to-date academic descriptive grammar. He worked with the Survey of English Usage, a project founded by Quirk and involving David Crystal, Jan Svartvik and Sidney Greenbaum; part of this work was used in the London-Lund Corpus of spoken English, carefully transcribed for prosody using a system devised by Quirk and Crystal.[9]

For Leech, the most important outcome of this project was the work with Quirk, Svartvik and Greenbaum on *A Grammar of Contemporary English*,[10] which he said grew out of a 'need for a reconciliation between theory and practical pedagogy in the study of English grammar'. For the first but not the last time in his career, we see Leech's remarkable talent for collaboration with equals, even after he had moved to Lancaster and Svartvik to Lund. His own estimation of the result was characteristically modest:

> Largely because of Quirk's leadership, and in spite of countless arguments between members of the team, the collaboration was more successful than we had dared to suppose. The book, in spite of its weaknesses, became well known throughout the world as a source of descriptive information on English grammar.

John Sinclair (who did not always see eye to eye with Leech) said later that the *Grammar of Contemporary English* 'pensioned off the great European grammars because it was up to date, reasonably sensitive to modern ideas about language and language-teaching, and tried to say something about most things in grammar'.[11] This work and its successors meant that Leech remained in very regular contact with his UCL colleagues after he went to Lancaster. And even apart from his ongoing collaborations with them, much of his work over the next forty-five years would carry on practices and habits of mind that began at UCL. I will return to some of these practices and habits later.

---

[8] A. M. Zwicky and J. M. Sadock, 'Ambiguity tests and how to fail them', in J. Kimball (ed.), *Syntax and Semantics 4* (New York, 1974), pp. 1–36; quotation p. 10n.

[9] R. Ilson, 'The Survey of English Usage: past, present—and future', *ELT Journal*, 36 (1982), 242–7.

[10] R. Quirk, J. Svartvik, G. Leech and S. Greenbaum, *A Grammar of Contemporary English* (London, 1972).

[11] J. Sinclair, 'Taxonomy of the tongue: review of *A Comprehensive Grammar of the English Language*', *Times Literary Supplement*, 28 June 1985, p. 715.

Lancaster

In 1969, Geoff, Fanny, Tom and Camilla moved when he took up the post of Senior Lecturer at Lancaster University, which had been founded only four years before, and which was still something of a building site in Bailrigg. The English Department at Lancaster had been founded in 1965, by Professor Bill Murray, with the aim of linking language study and literary study, and all literature students took courses on both historical and contemporary studies of the language. There were then only four lecturers teaching linguistics in the department. At thirty-three, Leech was already a major figure in the field, with three books on three widely separated areas of analysis, and he was seen as a great catch (as shown by the fact that he was immediately promoted to Reader).

We have already seen that he did not let up his pace of work when he moved. But he must at some times have wondered what he had got himself into. In 1971, a controversy between Bill Murray and David Craig, one of the lecturers, caused a deep split in the department, leading to demonstrations, national news reports and the departure of some members of the department. It was clearly a very painful time for Leech, who had been thrust into a responsible role as leader of a section of the department, and who had a very strong sense of principle in academic practices. David Crystal, formerly one of his UCL colleagues, was also dragged into it as External Examiner. One of the results of the 'Craig Affair', as it was known, was the hiring of more linguistics lecturers, including Mick Short and Jim Hurford.

It also led eventually to the splitting of the English Department, and in 1974 what had been a Linguistics Section became the Department of Linguistics and Modern English Language, with Leech, now promoted to Professor, as its first Head. He also played an important role in the way the department developed as a community, in all its social activities; for instance, he was a keen player in staff–student and departmental cricket teams (I am told he was a medium-pace bowler and a strong batsman).

Despite many offers over the years, Leech spent the rest of his career at Lancaster. The prospectus from the first year of the department lists him as a specialist in semantics, but he would teach a wide range of undergraduate and postgraduate courses on grammar and stylistics, and was in fact willing to teach on almost any language topic. From 1977 to 1985, he reduced his time at the university to 50 per cent so that he could work on his books and develop computer corpora. Christopher Candlin had set up the Institute for English Language Education in 1977, with Mike Breen as

Deputy Director, an independent unit that would offer in-sessional and pre-sessional courses in English and do teacher-training projects; it led to many international contacts for the department. Leech served as Chairman from 1985 to 1990, an unlikely role but one that shows his concern with the pedagogical applications of grammars. (He says in his departmental history that Charles Alderson, the Director, did all the work and devised the strategy in that period.) From 1997 to 2001 he was appointed Research Professor. Though he notes with relief that he only served as Head for one slightly extended term, he was always a quiet but energetic presence in the department. He never tried to construct the department in his image, and welcomed new colleagues in all areas, but we all looked up to him, whatever our specialisms.

One of the ways Leech contributed to the global standing of his department was in his visiting appointments at other universities. After the political tensions in the department, it was probably with some relief that in 1972 he took up a visiting professorship at Brown University in Providence, Rhode Island, and, as we will see, this turned out to be crucial to his work on corpus construction. In 1977, after his stint as Head of Department, he led one of the first teaching delegations to China, a country that then seemed remote and perhaps irrelevant to an English Department. One direct result was that Yueguo Gu came to the department as an MA and then as a PhD student, studying with Leech; he is now Head of the Contemporary Linguistics Department of the Chinese Academy of Sciences. An indirect result was a long line of contacts with Chinese universities. Leech later held visiting professorships in New Zealand, Australia, France and several times in Japan, a country with which he had a particular affinity.

Leech was elected to Fellowship of the British Academy in 1987, after *A Comprehensive Grammar of the English Language* and the completion of the LOB (Lancaster–Oslo/Bergen) Corpus. Two years later, he was made an Honorary Fellow of UCL, a mark of respect of which he was particularly proud. He had honorary doctorates from the University of Lund (1987), the University of Wolverhampton (2002), Lancaster University (2002) and Charles University in Prague (2012).

The research projects he accomplished in his time at Lancaster were so varied, I will deal with them under separate headings: Reference Grammars, Stylistics, Semantics and Pragmatics, Corpora and the wide range of work he did after his formal retirement. I will then draw out some of the themes that run through these diverse areas of research.

Reference grammars

Though the authors of *A Grammar of Contemporary English* may have thought their ten-year task was more than enough for any team, the project kept developing after publication in 1972. Quirk and Greenbaum fulfilled the pedagogic remit of the project by publishing a student grammar based on the big grammar. In 1975, Leech and Svartvik published *A Communicative Grammar of English*,[12] which was in tune with the move to communicative language teaching at the time, 'relating forms and structures of language to their meaning and use'. (His colleagues Christopher Candlin and Mike Breen were among the main proponents of this approach.) Mick Short said that in writing this grammar, 'The authors took over a seminar room during the summer vacation and worked a series of 18-hour days.'[13] Though the popularity of the communicative approach has passed, we can see from online comments that *A Communicative Grammar*, in its third edition, augmented with corpus results, is still widely and gratefully used.

Much later, in 1985, what was planned as a second edition of the big grammar became a very different book, *A Comprehensive Grammar of the English Language*, which at 1,722 pages was twice as long as its already huge predecessor. In a review, Flor Aarts said:

> What distinguishes it from previous reference grammars of English (apart from breadth of coverage) is that it not only states the facts but attempts to provide explanations whenever it is possible to do so without involving readers in the intricacies and formalisms of modern linguistic theories.[14]

David Crystal has described the considerable efforts it took for four strong-minded and very well-informed grammarians to collaborate successfully; his own task was making sure that all the terminology of the separate sections was consistent. And Crystal also stressed, as Leech himself never would, the key role that Leech took in these working practices.

Even after this twenty-year and apparently definitive project, with its many spin-offs, Leech's work on descriptive grammars was not done. With Douglas Biber, Stig Johansson, Susan Conrad and Edward Finegan, he was part of the team that produced between 1992 and 1999 the *Longman*

---

[12] G. Leech and J. Svartvik, *A Communicative Grammar of English* (London, 1975).
[13] M. Short, 'In memory of Geoffrey Leech (1936–2014)', *Language and Linguistics*, 23 (2014), 306.
[14] F. G. A. M. Aarts, '*A Comprehensive Grammar of the English Language*: the great tradition continued', *English Studies*, 2 (1988), 163–73.

Grammar of Spoken and Written English.[15] As this list of names would suggest, it is a grammar based on corpus data; it acknowledges that it borrows 'the grammatical framework of concepts and terminology' (p. viii) from that of the *Comprehensive Grammar*, but for the first time it could note, for instance, whether a usage was more common in one genre (such as face-to-face conversation) or another (such as news reports). While the other authors drafted chapters (four each by Biber and Johansson), Leech's role, with Biber, was 'primary editorial responsibility for the whole book' (p. vii). Quirk says in his Foreword that 'Biber was lucky in having as his partner in the massive task, both of general design and of implementing detailed insights, a scholar of Geoffrey Leech's stature in the fields of semantics, pragmatics, grammatology, and computational linguistics' (p. v). Because of its empirical base, its impact has gone beyond that of earlier reference grammars. One reviewer said that 'Amongst its many merits perhaps the highest distinction of this grammar lies not so much within the book itself but in the fresh methodological impetus that it gives to the disciplines of English linguistics and grammar writing more globally.'[16] One aspect of this impetus was in the way it showed the centrality of corpus research, not just to lexicography, but to a whole range of linguistic issues.

Stylistics

At Lancaster, as at UCL, Leech taught a course on literary stylistics, but at Lancaster he taught it jointly with Mick Short, who had been one of the first students in English at the new university. They taught it together until 1988, and Short would continue to revise the course, radically, over thirty years, often in collaboration with colleagues new to stylistics, finally developing an online course based on it. They worked on a companion to *A Linguistic Guide to English Poetry*, which would become *Style in Fiction*.[17] Like the earlier volume, it was presented as a textbook, with accessible introductions to linguistic approaches. It was more systematic than its predecessor in presenting a method of analysis, a checklist of features to analyse and suggestions on cautious quantitative approaches

---

[15] D. Biber, S. Johansson, G. Leech, S. Conrad and E. Finegan, *Longman Grammar of Spoken and Written English* (London, 1999).

[16] M. Krug, 'The *Longman Grammar of Spoken and Written English* (review)', *English Language and Linguistics*, 6 (2002), 379–84.

[17] G. N. Leech and M. H. Short, *Style in Fiction: a Linguistic Introduction to English Fictional Prose* (London, 1981, second edition 2007).

(one section is called, 'The Uses of Arithmetic'). But it too went far beyond textbook presentation; for instance, the chapters on fictionality and fictional worlds, on mind style (the way the prose suggests the state of mind and point of view of the narrator) and reported speech and thought were innovative then and have been enormously influential since. The acknowledgements suggest the range of the work, to Quirk again, and Roger Fowler again, to Lancaster literary colleagues Richard Dutton and Joan Lord Hall, and linguistic colleagues James Hurford and Willie van Peer.

Though he had worked on the large group project of the grammar, this was the first monograph on which he had collaborated, and he was working with a colleague who was also strong willed and who had his own ideas and literary tastes. (The eclectic range of examples is one of the delights of the book; no need for a book of quotations here.) The two authors themselves have different styles, but I for one do not see the joins in the text. Leech commented that (his emphases):

> Compared with other books, this book was particularly difficult *to write*, but also most satisfying *to have written*. . . . I was especially fortunate in having, in Mick, a co-author with whom I could work closely and well, though inevitably not without disagreements.

I will return to this talent for collaboration later. While Short continued research on stylistics, Leech was drawn away (rather regretfully) to other issues, returning to stylistics after he retired. In 2005, the book won the Silver Jubilee Prize of the Poetics and Linguistics Association (PALA) as the most influential book in the field since the organisation had been founded in 1980. A revised edition with an additional chapter appeared in 2007.

Semantics and pragmatics

The first book Leech published at Lancaster was *Meaning and the English Verb*, which would have two more revised editions.[18] It was an introduction to the area of semantics he had studied in his thesis and his first semantics monograph. He also wrote the advanced textbook *Semantics* for a Penguin series edited by David Crystal, which would also have a revised edition.[19] Most readers probably know his work on semantics

---

[18] G. N. Leech, *Meaning and the English Verb* (London 1971, second edition 1987, third edition 2004).
[19] G. N. Leech, *Semantics* (London, 1974) and the second edition *Semantics: the Study of Meaning* (London, 1981).

through these works, which are easily accessible to non-specialists and students.

Through the late 1970s, he published working papers, essays and talks working on the boundary between semantics, the study of meaning considered as part of the language system, and pragmatics, the study of meaning in use in specific contexts. As he noted (in the 1981 edition), 'Twenty years ago pragmatics, if it was mentioned at all, was regarded as a convenient dustbin to which to consign annoying facts which did not fit theories. Now it is one of the most vigorous areas of linguistic research.'[20]

The area is even more vigorous now, with more publications (and bigger conferences) than for any other level of linguistic analysis. It was already developing a broad, philosophical version based largely at European universities; Jacob Mey established the *Journal of Pragmatics* in 1977, and Herman Parret, Marina Sbisà and Jef Verschueren had organised in 1979 the first of the conferences that would lead in 1986 to the International Pragmatics Association (Leech spoke at that conference).[21] But part of the reason pragmatics established itself in the curriculum of linguistics was the publication in 1983 of Stephen Levinson's *Pragmatics* and Leech's *Principles of Pragmatics*.[22] Both are presented as textbooks (Levinson's in the Cambridge University Press red series, Leech's again in the Longman Linguistics Library, now co-edited by Leech). Both were accessible, at least in opening chapters, for beginners, but both also went on to substantial new contributions. As one might expect, they covered both Speech Act theory and Paul Grice's logic of conversation (Grice's 1968 lectures were then available only in part). But Levinson extended the field to Conversation Analysis (offering the best short summary) while Leech dealt with some of the same interactional issues by proposing a Politeness Principle to complement Grice's Cooperative Principle. Grice proposed that participants in conversation assumed such maxims as Quantity ('make your contribution as informative as is required for the purposes of the exchange'); Leech added such maxims as Tact ('(A) MINIMISE COST TO OTHER, (B) MAXIMISE BENEFIT TO OTHER.') and explained how they could be used to interpret utterances. Between Levinson's and Leech's textbooks, students and researchers had a wide range of

---

[20] Leech, *Semantics: the Study of Meaning*, p. 319.
[21] J. Verschueren, 'IPrA, the International Pragmatics Association, at 25', *Semiotix*, 10 (2011), http://semioticon.com/semiotix/2011/10/ipra-the-international-pragmatics-association-at-25/ (accessed 10 January 2017).
[22] S. Levinson, *Pragmatics* (Cambridge, 1983) and G. N. Leech, *Principles of Pragmatics* (London, 1983).

approaches to key issues in analysis of language use. Leech's work was especially influential in formulating a line of work on 'linguistic politeness' that had been developing since a paper by Robin Lakoff in 1973, an approach that contrasted in many ways with that of Penelope Brown and Stephen Levinson.[23] More broadly, he put 'Interpersonal Rhetoric' at the centre of linguistic analysis. As with stylistics, he largely set this line of work aside, while the citations and applications piled up, but he returned to politeness in his last book.[24] Lancaster has remained a centre for pragmatics research, with the work of Jenny Thomas and Jonathan Culpeper.

Corpora

In 1970, Leech had proposed to his Lancaster colleagues that the newly emerging group of linguists could 'make its mark in the world' by developing a corpus of British English. The project, founded as the 'Computer Archive of Modern English Texts' (CAMET), was modelled on the one-million word corpus of American English developed by Henry Kučera and W. Nelson Francis from 1961 to 1967 (usually called the Brown Corpus). The six months at Brown had given Leech a chance to learn more about the practicalities of corpus building.

A corpus is a machine-readable collection of written and/or spoken language use. (The Survey of English Usage was still a print-only resource.) Anyone who worked on computer corpora then will say how much easier it is now, with more usable interfaces and media and huge processing power; the process then meant compiling huge stacks of punch-cards or reels of paper tape, both of which were unforgiving of even the slightest errors inputting data or handling the media.

The new corpus of British English would be based on the same categories of written texts as the Brown Corpus (including, for instance, several press genres, several fiction genres, religion, learned and academic writing, skills and hobbies and humour). Each genre would be made up of sets of texts of 2,000 words. Mick Short recalled that in the early years

---

[23] R. Lakoff, 'The logic of politeness; or, mind your p's and q's', *Papers from the Ninth Regional Meeting of the Chicago Linguistics Society* (Chicago, IL, 1973), pp. 292–305; and P. Brown and S. Levinson, 'Universals in language usage: politeness phenomena', in E. Goody (ed.), *Questions and Politeness: Strategies in Social Interaction* (Cambridge, 1978), pp. 56–289.

[24] For a careful and even-handed assessment of Leech's contribution to pragmatics, see J. Culpeper, 'Geoffrey Leech, 1936–2014: the pragmatics legacy', in J.-O. Östman and J. Verschueren (eds.), *Handbook of Pragmatics* (Amsterdam, 2015), pp. 1–17, available at https://benjamins.com/online/hop2/ articles/lee1 (accessed 17 January 2017).

of the project, Geoff and Fanny would be in the department every weekend working on the corpus.[25] But it went very slowly, not only because of the technical challenges but also because of problems getting permission to use texts. Publishers, who had no idea what a 'computer corpus' might involve, insisted on full payment for copyright, even though they would only be used as part of a database, not used as a way around buying a copy of the book. The solution to this seemingly intractable problem came from an unexpected source. Stig Johansson was a Leverhulme Scholar in the department in 1976, working on the project (and apparently his wife, Faith Anne, was also drafted in to the work). When Johansson took up a post at Bergen, he 'offered to take the project to Norway'. In 1977, Randolph Quirk (UCL), Jan Svartvik (Oslo), W. Nelson Francis (Brown), Stig Johansson (Bergen) and Leech met in Oslo to found the International Computer Archive of Modern English (ICAME). Leech found that London publishers were much more likely to grant free rights when asked in a letter from the secretary (Johansson) of this impressive-sounding organisation based in Norway, than when asked by 'an inmate of a provincial northern university'. But of course ICAME was not just a source of letterhead stationery; forty years later it is a large learned society, with an important annual conference and a journal.

What was now the LOB Corpus was completed in 1978, but it was only the beginning of thirty years developing new corpora, annotating these corpora and, crucially, developing tools that would enable users to access these resources. This work was a collaboration with Roger Garside in Computing, in what in 1984 became the Unit for Computer Research on the English Language (UCREL). The next step was a project (1978–83), funded by the Social Science Research Council, in collaboration again with Stig Johansson, to tag the corpus with the part of speech of each word. (The categories are actually much more detailed than just verb or noun, so for instance JJR is a general comparative adjective and VVD is the past tense form of a lexical verb.) This would clearly make it much more useful in studying grammatical patterns, but it was too large a task to be done manually, finding each phrase and determining the role of that string in that phrase. The software developed relies on an algorithm similar to a Hidden Markov Model for assigning likely tags based on probabilities of transitions from one tag to the next. For the model to work, it needed to be trained on one corpus (in this case Brown), to learn

---

[25] M. Short, 'In memory of Geoffrey Leech (1936–2014)', *Language and Linguistics*, 23 (2014), 307.

the frequencies of transitions, and then applied to another corpus (LOB), where the tags were unknown. The CLAWS (Constituent Likelihood Automatic Word-*tagging* System) tagger was developed by a team that included Eric Atwell (now in Computer Science at Leeds) and Ian Marshall (later in Information Science at East Anglia), as well as Roger Garside and Fanny Leech.[26] It has had a huge influence on later corpus projects, as has the idea of a training corpus and a test corpus.

A third stage of the project, funded by the Science and Engineering Research Council (1983–6), was an attempt to apply similar probabilistic methods to the parsing of the corpus—that is, labelling its grammatical structure (such as subject, predicate, noun phrase, subordinate clause). This is a much more difficult problem, and it was a major focus of Natural Language Processing in the 1980s and 1990s. The Lancaster team started with a 'Treebank' built up by Geoffrey Sampson over many hours of laboriously parsing a section of the corpus by hand, to provide a basis for training the probabilistic parser. The project continued from 1987 to 1991 as a collaboration with IBM. Unlike the tagger, it never did produce a practical tool that would process the whole corpus with reasonable accuracy, but it did pioneer methods that would be used by other teams on bigger projects (for instance the Penn Treebank).

The twenty years of work produced an enormously useful corpus and tools for using it, but it produced little in the way of scholarly publication to compare to the stream of outputs in Leech's other lines of work. Perhaps the greatest contribution of the CAMET/UCREL team was in developing new ways of working, and in focusing on key standards for the work. The Lancaster group developed a recognisable approach to corpora. As a comparison, the group led by John Sinclair at Birmingham gathered a very large corpus with any digital resources available, without worrying about the structure of the corpus, and preferred un-annotated texts in developing COBUILD and the Bank of English. Those choices were motivated by their aim of supporting lexicography. The Lancaster group, following Brown, developed carefully designed and balanced corpora, with annotation that would allow much more complex analysis of the data. One benefit of this approach was that the LOB Corpus could be compared to the Brown Corpus to find differences in British and American

---

[26] I. Marshall, 'Choice of grammatical word-class without global syntactic analysis: tagging words in the LOB corpus', *Computers and the Humanities*, 17 (1983), 139–50; see also R. Garside, G. Leech and G. Sampson, (eds.), *The Computational Analysis of English: a Corpus-Based Approach* (London, 1987).

English, because the corpora were designed to be comparable. Much later, comparable corpora of more recent English texts were developed at the University of Freiburg (Freiburg-Brown or FROWN and Freiburg-LOB or FLOB), and comparable corpora of earlier periods were constructed to allow for historical comparisons. None of this would have been possible if it had not been decided at the beginning to focus on careful specification of what the one-million word corpus contained, instead of just trying to get as many words as possible.

Leech worked on many different corpus projects in the 1990s, the most important of which was the British National Corpus (BNC). Produced by a consortium of Oxford and Lancaster Universities, with Longman and Oxford University Press, the BNC was two orders of magnitude larger than LOB, with 100 million words, 10 per cent of which were from hard-to-gather spoken sources. Funding included grants from the Science and Engineering Research Council, the Department of Trade and Industry, the British Academy, Longman, Chambers and Oxford University Press. The team at Lancaster included Tony McEnery in Linguistics, Paul Rayson in Computing and many other researchers. When the immediate work on that project was completed, Leech was involved in initiatives to establish standards for corpora in Europe, making them much more usable. Leech was less involved in corpus work after 2001; a series of projects led by Tony McEnery led finally to the ESRC-funded Centre for Corpus Applications to the Social Sciences (CASS). One of the many projects of this Centre is Spoken BNC2014, allowing comparisons across the twenty-five intervening years.

Computer corpus work involves careful coordination of teams and attention to detail; Leech said it has 'a tendency to monopolise the time of anyone who becomes seriously involved in it'. It also involves a great deal of time in frustrating pursuit of funding and apparently unproductive meetings. He often expressed regret at the work, particularly in pragmatics and stylistics, which he had to set aside while leading corpus projects. But corpus linguistics may be his broadest area of impact. In 2016, the university was given the Queen's Award to Higher Education for its corpus work over forty years.

Retirement

The Department of Linguistics and English Language at Lancaster (as it is now called) is a relatively young institution, and Leech was the first person to retire from it, in 2001. He had already reduced his teaching to complete some of his research projects. He noted in his autobiography, 'I have extricated myself gently from the pressures of running large-scale research projects and large-scale research teams.' As we will see, that does not mean that he stopped doing research. Nor did he stop being part of the department; he retained an office as Emeritus Professor, came in about once a week, met visitors, sometimes supervised research students and helped out the department in a number of tasks. He was a cheerful presence, and many colleagues turned to him for advice. But it was clearly a big transition both for him and for the department he had shaped.

He and Fanny had moved in 1987 from a modern house in Lancaster, where Tom and Camilla had grown up, to a manor house dating from 1700 in the market town of Kirkby Lonsdale. They had a great deal to do in their sympathetic restoration and decoration of the house, and Leech always took great pleasure in its interiors and gardens. They also became very actively involved in their new community. Leech offered his services as organist to the small, beautiful churches in the villages around the town (such as St Peter's, Leck), and over the years built up a church choir. This gave him a chance to play every week the music he loved, and it also brought energy to what would have been dwindling congregations. Fanny also sang in the choir, and it was part of what brought them into their new community.

Though he no longer led new projects, he kept up his energetic output of publications, with eight books and forty-seven articles after his retirement. The core of this work was in historical comparison of grammar between parallel corpora. With Paul Rayson and Nick Smith, he worked on a comparison of LOB and the Freiburg-LOB Corpus (FLOB) that sampled the same genres of texts thirty years apart. He also compared across the two matching corpora of Brown (US English) and LOB (British). And he worked on projects compiling matching corpora from 1931 to take the comparison back further (with Paul Baker compiling a corpus from 1901). This work was funded by the Arts and Humanities Research Board, the British Academy and the Leverhulme Foundation, in smaller projects with less administration. The work led to major books with Smith, and with Christian Mair and Marianne Hundt, who had developed the Freiburg corpora;[27] it also led to many articles and chapters and a series of conference talks. As he said, 'It enabled me to do what I think I do best – which is descriptive study of the English language, not leading-edge language technology.'

He also returned to the two lines of work, in stylistics and pragmatics, that had been sidelined by his all-consuming career in corpus analysis. He collected his earlier studies of literary language and, whenever he got the opportunity, did new ones; his last conference talk, at the Poetics and Linguistics Association in the month before he died, was 'Styles of (im) politeness: a comparison of Ishiguru's *Remains of the Day* and Albee's *Who's Afraid of Virginia Woolf*. He also completed one more major book on politeness, taking up some of the challenges that had been made to his work and that of Brown and Levinson in the thirty years since *Principles of Pragmatics*, developing new accounts of politeness in such speech acts as apologising and requesting and, again, looking at historical change.[28]

The publications from 2001 to 2015 would be impressive for any academic. As one would expect at this stage of a career, there were also many new editions, Festschriften to write for, interviews and plenary addresses. But he seems to have been able to focus, for the most part, on the work he enjoyed doing, and where he thought he had the greatest contribution to make.

Personal traits

I have listed as many of Leech's achievements as I could fit in this space. But the achievements do not explain why he was so much admired and loved by colleagues and by academics around the world. In looking over the many tributes after his death, in print, in person and online, I find repeated mention of some aspects of his personality recognisable to anyone who knew him.

Modesty

Every personal account of Geoff Leech mentions his modesty, and some go on to say how appropriate this trait was in someone who had written

---

[27] G. Leech, M. Hundt, C. Mair and N. Smith, *Change in Contemporary English: a Grammatical Study* (Cambridge, 2009).
[28] G. N. Leech, *The Pragmatics of Politeness* (Oxford, 2014).

at length about the Maxim of Modesty as essential to interpreting interpersonal rhetoric: 'MINIMIZE PRAISE OF SELF: MAXIMIZE DISPRAISE OF SELF.'[29] His history of the department manages to avoid much mention of his own central role in it, and his autobiography plays down any contribution or talent of his own, as Jonathan Culpeper noted:

> His own background and abilities come across [in his own account] as being 'small', even 'undistinguished' or with 'weaknesses', whilst any notable achievements in his career are by 'good fortune' or 'accident', and positive evaluations from others are clouded with modal expressions such as 'apparently' or 'seems'.[30]

Of course, such modesty is only noticeable when one has great achievements to play down.

The other side of this tendency to self-deprecation was a genuine interest in whomever he was talking to (what he called in the *Principles of Pragmatics* the 'Maxim of Tact'). Whether he met a famous scholar, a new junior colleague, a PhD student or a visitor from a foreign university, he would focus on what his interlocutor had done and was doing. This respect for others made an enormous impression, especially on people who might have felt uncertain about their status when they met him. I do not know whether he learned this modesty from his family, his school or from his early collaborators, but it struck everyone who met him, so it must not be very common among famous academics.

Collaboration

Leech had a gift for collaboration, which he must have learned from the apprenticeship he had with Randolph Quirk and others at UCL. There are not many accounts of the practices of the team working on the Survey of English Usage and on *A Grammar of Contemporary English*, but Quirk seems to have combined personal commitment to the project with acknowledgement of the abilities of the other participants, whatever their professional status, and enormous demands for hard work. The grammars, the corpora and the later historical studies were all collaborations, as were many edited collections. Mick Short has commented on their work together on *Style in Fiction*:

---

[29] *Principles of Pragmatics*, p. 136.
[30] Culpeper, 'Geoffrey Leech, 1936–2014: the pragmatics legacy'. Obituaries by Mick Short and Christian Mair also help give a picture of how he was seen by colleagues: Short, 'In memory of Geoffrey Leech (1936–2014)'; and C. Mair, 'Geoffrey N. Leech (16 January 1936–19 August 2014)', *Corpora*, 10/1 (2015), 5–9.

> Perhaps not surprisingly, Geoff Leech managed to get by with less sleep than most. I can remember when he and I were writing *Style in Fiction* that, when we had agreed who would draft each of the next two chapters, at the end of my first night's work I would have, say four or five draft pages but would find a completed first draft of Geoff's next chapter in my pigeonhole the following morning.[31]

In the edited collection that I did with him and Jenny Thomas, I recall being flattered to be asked to participate, and then I recall very clear planning and deadlines, and his leading by example, nudging us to do our part of the work by doing his own part quickly and without any fuss or complaint.

Detail

Mick Short also said, 'He was more painstaking and careful of detail than anyone I have ever met.' Without an overall aim, such a painstaking approach could make someone pedantic, but in the big reference grammars, and the comparisons of corpora, it meant he could marshal a wide range of examples and leave room for the oddity or exception. It may be this attention to detail that made him constitutionally unable to convert to the linguistics he encountered at MIT.

Usefulness

Leech was not an applied linguist; he was primarily motivated by scholarship, not by the desire to improve language teaching or dictionaries. But he was always concerned to make the work useful. The most obvious example of this concern was the string of student versions of the grammars and the simpler handbooks and glossaries he produced, usually in collaboration, throughout his career. The first book, on advertising, would be useful to any practitioner, as his work on stylistics was useful to students of literature. He positively enjoyed teaching, and as soon as he retired he took up a part-time job at the University of Bangor teaching stylistics. Once when I sent around an e-mail asking if anyone in the department could cover a couple of lectures in sociolinguistics, he was the only one to respond, saying that it was not his subject, but he would work it up if I needed help. This is not what one expects of the most senior professor in a department, but it was precisely because he was the most senior professor that he felt he should take on such responsibilities.

---

[31] Short, 'In memory of Geoffrey Leech (1936–2014)', 308.

Steel

Though Leech was always modest, though he avoided conflicts, had a quiet voice and seldom spoke first in a discussion, everyone who knew him recognised something steely in his personality. He had very strong principles about linguistics, education and the right way to treat people, and if these principles seemed to be violated he could be very angry. It was not a shouting, e-mailing, threatening kind of anger, but a very firm and definite response, and though it was rare, one remembered it.

Music

Leech loved music. He did not mention it in his academic autobiography (which was academic after all) and of course he never showed off his knowledge or talent (see Modesty, above). It was just part of his life and, as nearly as I can tell, it was always part of his life.[32] The one reference to music I have come across in his academic work is in an example of everyday linguistic creativity in his book on advertising:

> A friend saw me carrying a copy of Bach's *Klavierübung* ('keyboard exercise') and remarked (referring to the difficulty of the pieces) that they were 'not very übungy'.[33]

The point he is making is about his friend's wit and how it worked in the conversation, not about his music. The same division between his academic and musical lives seems to have applied at church, where he was seen as an organist and worshipper, and some members of the congregation were surprised to hear at his funeral about his academic renown. While he did not make a point of his musical skill in his academic life, he was always happy to play at departmental events, whether accompanying singing or

---

[32] His wife Fanny adds that 'He came from an environment that was the "Three Choirs Festival", the three choirs being Gloucester, Worcester and Hereford. His father Richard had been chief chorister at Gloucester, his uncle had been the organist for Worcester and later for the most important church in Canada, and his nephew again was the chief chorister for Gloucester. From the age of twelve, he and his father shared the position of organist at Bredon parish church. In his late teens he was entered for a scholarship for the Royal Academy in piano. The great Herbert Howells told him his improvisation was not good enough and begrudgingly Geoff settled for the academic life. When I met him a little later he still had feelings of regret! ... Nearly every day of our married life, Geoffrey would play a CD and demand that I guess what it was and who played what – he was so good. Geoff was at his best when he played chamber music when his nervousness would completely disappear, and he would shine as the marvellous pianist that he was!'

[33] Leech, *English in Advertising*, p. 176.

joining in sketches; he played at the department's fortieth anniversary celebrations, and he played at PALA in the month before his death.

*****

Geoffrey Leech died on 19 August 2014. He was in his office, meeting a PhD student, in the middle of a conversation. A funeral was held at St Peter's, Leck; the three eulogies were by Lord Shuttleworth, representing the church community, Tom Leech, representing the family, and David Crystal, representing the field of linguistics. The vicar said it was just the sort of service Geoff would have wanted: no sermon and lots of music. The Department of Linguistics and English Language also had an event celebrating his career, attended by colleagues, friends and admirers from around the world. For me, one of the most moving parts of the memorial held by the department were the songs offered with piano accompaniment by three of his colleagues. I can imagine Geoff fidgeting nervously at all the praise in the talks, but enjoying entirely the duet on Purcell's setting of Dryden's 'Let us wander'.

GREG MYERS
Lancaster University

CLAUS ADOLF MOSER

Claus Adolf Moser
1922–2015

Early life

CLAUS MOSER WAS BROUGHT TO ENGLAND by his parents as a thirteen-year-old German boy. He was born on 24 November 1922 and died at the age of ninety-two as Baron Moser of Regent's Park. His appropriate title changed during that interval, but to friends and acquaintances alike he was always known as 'Claus' and that is how he will be designated here. He was born in Berlin into a prosperous and cultured family. His parents were Ernst and Lotte Moser, who were both Jewish. Ernst was a successful banker; his mother was a talented pianist; he had an older brother, Heinz Peter.

Even though Claus did not become a professional musician, he clearly inherited his skill as performer and his passion for classical music from his mother's side of the family. Music was an integral part of his life and, as we shall see, found an outlet throughout his life.

His parents foresaw that trouble was brewing for the Jews in Germany and in 1936 they removed the family to England, where they set up home in Putney, London. Claus was then thirteen years old and, having had the benefit of an English governess, the new language presented no particular problem as early extant letters show. He was sent to Frensham Heights School, a progressive independent co-educational boarding school, near Farnham, Surrey, which proved to be hospitable to refugees. This provided an ideal place for Claus; it fostered his musical talent and provided a happy environment which he greatly enjoyed. At the appropriate time he sat the Oxford and Cambridge School certificate in which he obtained five credits and two passes. This was a good, though by no means outstanding, result but it was achieved after only two years in what was, after all, Claus's second language and a foreign country. However, the School Certificate was particularly significant, in view of later developments, because it gained him exemption from the London Matriculation examination which was necessary in order to embark on a degree course of London University.

In 1940 Claus was interned as an 'enemy alien' at Huyton, Liverpool. The only evidence we have for his subsequent interest in statistics is the experience he gained of social investigation by assisting a mathematician who wanted to keep records of the characteristics of the internees there. He was soon released, because of his age, in the autumn of 1940. With the support of his headmaster he applied for late entry to the London School of Economics (LSE) to study for the BCom degree. It is believed that his father favoured training for a career in the hotel business so we may surmise that a degree, ostensibly in commerce, might have seemed an acceptable alternative. Whatever the truth of that hypothesis, it is clear that, after some correspondence, he entered the LSE in November 1940. At that time the LSE had been evacuated to Cambridge and Claus was allocated lodgings at 5 Trumpington Street at a weekly charge of 35 shillings. Apart from his studies, on which he received excellent reports from his teachers, Claus was very active in the Students' Union which, according to his tutor, did not significantly impinge on his academic work. This activity evidently included music, because it was the Union which recommended him for the Jessie Mair Prize awarded for his musical activities.

Before long Claus took steps to transfer to the BSc (Econ) degree which ran in parallel with the BCom. For the transfer to be possible it was necessary to satisfy the first year BSc (Econ) requirements, and Claus was clear about how this could be done. The structure of both degrees was similar. There was a Part I examination in both taken at the end of the first year followed by a Part II extending over the following two years on which the class of honours was awarded. In order to satisfy the requirements of the BSc (Econ) Part I, a course on the British Constitution was necessary, and Claus had thoughtfully anticipated this by attending the lectures for this course. By means of this and other measures, a successful transition was negotiated and for the next two years Claus became a candidate for the BSc (Econ) degree with special subject Statistics. The reason for choosing Statistics was presumably his experience of his aforementioned rudimentary social statistics gained during his internment, but it was certainly justified by his Part II results. He was also awarded a 'post Inter' Leverhulme scholarship which covered some of his fees.

In the Part II examination Claus obtained first-class honours and was awarded the Farr Medal and Prize for the best first. (During wartime it was said to be not possible to strike the medal because of restrictions on the use of silver, but Claus was assured that the award would be listed in the records. Later it emerged a medal could be struck after all.) Additionally he was awarded a Gerstenberg Studentship in Economics, but this was not taken up.

This was 1943, and when he graduated there were very limited options available. One possibility was to volunteer for service in the armed forces and the other was to obtain a post as a statistician in work of national importance. He received rather conflicting advice on the latter option; it appeared that there was a shortage of mathematical statisticians but no shortage of economic statisticians—which is how Claus would have been classified. Carr-Saunders, the Director of the LSE, was strongly in favour of volunteering for active service not least because it might be counted in Claus's favour when he applied for naturalisation after the war. In the event Claus 'joined up'. He applied for aircrew duties, but was rejected on the grounds that if he was shot down over enemy territory his German origins might cause complications. Hence, he became a ground crew member in which category he served in a number of capacities such as interpreting and, latterly, helping to evaluate the results of Allied bombing. He reached the rank of sergeant. On the last day of the war he was involved in a serious car accident close to the Belgian–German border which resulted in a prolonged hospital stay, initially nearby and subsequently at the specialist and innovative plastic surgery unit set up by Sir Archibald McIndoe in East Grinstead, Sussex.

The transition from a private school and university to the non-commissioned ranks of the RAF was a major step. It was one thing to flourish in an environment in which one excelled and was 'deservedly popular' among fellow students and quite another to rub shoulders with people whose background was very different. He quickly recognised the reason for this unease and, once he adjusted to the new situation, the initial difficulties were resolved.

At the end of the war the need for his services ceased, but there were complications about the date of his demobilisation. This took place in batches, and Claus calculated that his release was going to be too late for the beginning of the academic year. This mattered because he had been offered a post at the LSE from the beginning of October. However, early release could be obtained if a good case could be made. This was achieved, and he started his academic career on the staff of his old department as an Assistant Lecturer in Statistics, as he had hoped. At one stage prior to this he had contemplated proceeding to take a PhD, but this possibility was quickly superseded by the opportunity to join the staff.

Starting as an assistant lecturer, Claus moved through the grades at a steady pace, attaining a professorship in 1961. Progress was not automatic and the procedure varied somewhat over time as the relationship between London University and the Schools changed. The assistant lecturer grade was normally thought of as probationary and appointment to it was usually for three years, with a possibility of a fourth year in cases of doubt. Claus progressed to the grade of lecturer on 1 October 1949 after three years. For several years around this time he was involved with the International Statistical Institute, which he served as part-time Executive Officer of the International Statistical Education programme, being granted the necessary leave for the purpose by the LSE.

Promotion to the higher grade of reader (or senior lecturer for that matter) was not automatic and could occur only when the lecturer's performance justified it. In Claus's case the University conferred the title of Reader in Social Statistics after only six years on 1 October 1955. The case was made by the School in glowing terms, with the letter of support saying that 'he had done extremely well in his subject'. In 1957 he was invited to fill a temporary appointment (to work on a programme of family living studies) in the Statistics Division of the International Labour Office based in Geneva for a whole session (1957–8), and permission was granted.

The final promotion to Professor of Social Statistics took effect from 1 October 1961. In this case promotion would have depended on the research record as well as on teaching and general ability. In view of what follows, this can be conveniently dealt with as a whole.

The publication record falls in two parts. The first dates from first appointment until his move to the Robbins Committee (while a professor) and the second from that point until he moved to government service.

The early part shows a steady record of publication, including one paper jointly with Alan Stuart, on reviews of empirical studies of sampling methods. This is what one might have expected from someone at the beginning of their academic career. In addition, and more importantly, there was the highly successful book *Survey Methods in Social Investigation*, first published by Heinemann Educational Books. This first appeared in 1958 and was reprinted eight times until the second edition appeared in 1971. By this time Claus was Head of the Government Statistical Service (GSS) and he was helped in preparing the new edition by Graham Kalton, who remained as a joint author for at least seven further reprintings.

Kalton had been an undergraduate in the Statistics department, graduating in the year that the first edition was published. He later moved to the University of Michigan and then to WESTAT in Maryland. This book was originally based on a course given at the LSE and is therefore better regarded as a record of teaching rather than of research. It is comprehensive, authoritative and beautifully clear, and well deserved its wide readership and the 'classic' status it acquired. The principal changes in the second edition were the division of the original chapter on 'Principles of Survey Design' into two new chapters and a new chapter on 'Experiments and Investigations'. The authors later discussed the possibility of a third edition, but this would have required a major revision that they were not in a position to undertake. It was undoubtedly the most successful of Claus's publications in terms of sales, as he himself once remarked. Apparently Heinemann made no special provision for sales in America, otherwise the sales might have been even greater.

The big step in Claus's research career began with his appointment as statistical adviser by Lionel Robbins in connection with the work of the Robbins Committee set up in 1961. This event probably shaped the whole course of Claus's later career. The government decided to conduct an enquiry into the future of higher education in the UK. It asked Lord Robbins, Professor of Economics at the LSE, to chair the committee, and henceforth it became known as the Robbins Committee. Lord Robbins was convinced that his report should be a means to an evidence-based policy and hence that it must depend on data, much of which did not then exist. Accordingly, he asked Moser to join the Committee as its statistical advisor. In the event Claus was much more than advisor and he became intimately involved with its work and took part, for example, in all of its overseas visits. In the report Claus's key role is acknowledged as follows: '...and to our statistical adviser, Professor C. A. Moser, without whose dedicated labours it could not have been conceived, let alone brought to fruition'.

The Committee was concerned with two major questions: (1) 'How was the likely demand for higher education in the future to be met?'; and (2) 'How could enough good quality teaching be provided and how should it be financed?'. In order to provide a base for its deliberations Claus decided to conduct three surveys. One was of students, another was of teaching staff and the third was of twenty-one-year-olds whether already in higher education or not. The results of this research were published in five appendix volumes to the main report and these have been widely considered since as a model of relevant evidence, clearly presented. This work was the responsibility of Claus and proved to be the bedrock of his future as a renowned social statistician.[1]

When the committee finished its work in 1963, those who had worked with Claus on this project formed the nucleus of the Higher Education Research Unit which Claus set up at the LSE in 1964 under his directorship, with Richard Layard as Deputy Director.

Government service

Around 1966 the Director of the Central Statistical Office (CSO), Sir Harry Campion, was due to retire and thought was being given to his replacement. Claus was seconded for three years by the LSE to the Civil Service, where his existing wide experience of public affairs made him an ideal choice. Claus's move from the LSE to the Civil Service seemed natural because his existing experience with the Robbins Committee had demonstrated his capabilities, in particular the fact that he had been the architect of the formidable body of empirical evidence which successfully overcame the entrenched opposition which existed, in many quarters, to the recommendation of the Robbins Committee that the university system be expanded. This achievement would have made him particularly attractive to a government sympathetic to that recommendation. He therefore succeeded Sir Harry Campion.

When Claus moved to the Civil Service he actually had two distinct roles. He was head of the Government Statistical Service (GSS), which was the professional grouping of government statisticians. He was also head of the CSO, which dealt principally with matters relating to the collection and publication of economic statistics. The CSO was under the wing of the Cabinet Office and, in that role, Claus reported to the Prime Minister. During some of his time in the post the Prime Minister was Harold Wilson who, as a fellow statistician, Claus felt to be generally supportive and understanding of the issues he was dealing with. Informally, Claus also saw himself as a general statistical advisor to the government.

The most complete account of Claus's time in, and views on, government service is expressed in his own words in his presidential address to

---

[1] The full report is available online at http://www.educationengland.org.uk/documents/robbins/robbins1963.html (accessed 31 January 2017); this does not include the appendices, some of which were published with the report and others as separate volumes by HMSO in 1963—Cmnd 2154.

the Royal Statistical Society. This address, entitled 'Statistics and public policy', was delivered on 7 November 1979 and published in the society's *Journal, Series A* the following year.[2] After briefly thanking those who elected him and making some reference to his earlier experiences, the bulk of the address is devoted to a wide-ranging account of the GSS. The timing of the address was ideal in that it was given shortly after he had moved to N. M. Rothschild and Sons but while the events of that time were still fresh in his memory. It is comprehensive in its coverage, lucid in its exposition and fully alive to both the successes and failures of his efforts.

The overriding impression which one gains is of the enormous organisational feat of managing what came to be a very large professional organisation (roughly 600 professional staff) and making it fit for the role which it was called upon to fulfil. This called for considerable talents of which only glimpses had been seen in his previous roles, though they must have been latent. Any final assessment of Claus's contribution to government statistics must focus on his ability to see things in a broad context and on his ability to fashion and direct others to achieve long-term objectives.

The titles of the main section headings of the address were 'Integrity', 'Quality', 'Organisation', 'Priorities' and 'Relations with the Public'. Under each heading he gave a penetrating analysis of his successes and failures. There is one area where he faced a problem which continued to exercise him for many years afterwards. This concerned the relative merits of a centralised and decentralised service. The business of government is carried out by separate departments each under the direction of a minister. At one extreme each department effectively could have its own statistical service answerable to its own head. At the other there would be a central statistical service, centrally managed. In practice many compromises are possible. In the United Kingdom there is, and was, a hybrid system but with the balance much in favour of a decentralised version. In a centralised system all statisticians are centrally recruited and managed, and this is certainly more convenient from the point of view of the head of the service. A decentralised service makes for a much closer link between statisticians and the departmental staff who are responsible for delivering government policies.

Within the service he was recognised as a good and considerate manager of staff. Claus was convinced that statisticians in the government should not simply be 'backroom boys' but needed to be outgoing and

---

[2] C. A. Moser, 'Statistics and public policy', *Journal of the Royal Statistical Society, Series A (General)*, 143 (1980), 1–32.

more 'extrovert'. They were to be participants rather than spectators in policy making. Accordingly, when invitations to speak were offered he despatched some of his senior staff to universities in an attempt to get that message across to potential recruits to the GSS. This was sometimes done through talks to those about to graduate (in the guise of seminars), which provided a ready-made vehicle.

Part of his role was to implement the proposals made by the House of Commons Estimates Committee, which involved the creation of the Business Statistics Office and of the Office of Population Censuses and Surveys (OPCS). The latter combined the Government Social Survey with the Registrar General's responsibility for large-scale censuses.

One of Claus's innovations was the introduction of the publication *Social Trends*. This first appeared in 1970, edited by his colleague Muriel Nissel at the CSO, and it has since been emulated elsewhere. This publication provides an annual picture, through tables and diagrams, of the state of society which complements that given by the older and more familiar economic series. Given the musical accomplishments of both the then Prime Minister (Edward Heath) and Claus, it was particularly appropriate that the publication should have been launched with a performance by the Amadeus String Quartet, whose second violin player was Siegmund Nissel, husband of Muriel.

The integrity of government figures is vital for the credibility of the whole enterprise. This requires that there should be no manipulation, however subtle, by those for whom the figures are produced. This has required, for example, that there shall be generally accepted fixed publication dates for all series. There were a number of occasions when the integrity of the service was threatened by the attempt to gain short-term advantage on the part of the government. On one oft-quoted occasion, Claus stood firm when it was suggested that the cost of some jumbo jets should be spread over several months rather than be recorded in the month in which purchase actually occurred. The effect of making the change would have had a beneficial effect on the Balance of Payments figures and might have affected the outcome of the imminent general election. It would be going too far to claim that Claus was alone in taking a stand against this but there is no doubting his resolve. He considered it essential that government statistics be above such things. That it was, and still is, reflects the leadership that Claus provided, and on more than one occasion such things became matters of resignation.

Earlier on, towards the end of his secondment, there was great government satisfaction with the progress that Claus had made in reorganising and driving forward the work of government statistics, but it was clear that a longer period was needed to bring this promising start to fruition. The LSE was therefore approached and asked to consider whether the secondment might be extended for a further two-and-a-half years. There followed extensive discussions between the parties culminating in a meeting between the Prime Minister (Harold Wilson) and the Director of the LSE (Sir Walter Adams) at 10 Downing Street. The upshot of all this was that the LSE felt that it could not extend the period of leave, but it came up with a counter-proposal that Claus should resign from his Chair and that he would be appointed as a Visiting Professor at the School. Claus, himself, was torn in two directions, on the one hand by his loyalty to, and affection for, the School and on the other by his desire to continue with his work at the CSO. The proposal was finally agreed; Claus resigned his chair, became a full-time civil servant and a Visiting Professor at the LSE. The latter appointment was under the usual terms and conditions, but there was no fixed emolument and it ultimately came to an end in 1975. This appointment provided the opportunity for him to remain associated, in particular with the Higher Education Research Unit, but involved no fixed duties.

The School made a further attempt to bring Moser back when in 1971 it indicated that, under new University regulations, it was prepared to create a new Chair of Statistics specifically for Claus, beginning in the session 1972–3, but although this was attractive he declined on the grounds that there was much else that he wished to do in the Civil Service.

Rothschilds

In 1978 Claus left government service and joined Rothschild Bank, where he was Vice-Chairman from 1978 to 1984. When it was known that Claus was moving to the world of banking, one of his senior colleagues in the GSS wryly remarked that a suitable leaving present might be a book with some such title as *Teach Yourself Banking*. Claus, of course, brought his detailed first-hand knowledge of the workings of government as a considerable dowry to his new employer. The wisdom of Rothschild's decision to recruit Claus was evident in the part which he took in the bank's desire to be appointed as investment consultants to the government of Singapore. This was a tricky negotiation as three other financial institutions were believed to be competing for the consultancy. The instability of sterling around this time, among other things, had caused the government of

Singapore to think hard about the management of its reserves, many of which were held in sterling. Claus, together with two other members of Rothschild's staff, travelled to Singapore to be interviewed on the application. They had made several previous visits to obtain information. It so happened that Dr Goh Keng Swee, the Chairman of the Monetary Authority of Singapore, had been Moser's tutee when he had been a student at the LSE many years previously. They were close personal friends who shared an interest in music. However, this fact appeared to have counted for little in the negotiations. The interview consisted of two parts—the first was with Dr Goh and others and the second with the Prime Minister, Dr Lee Kuan Yew, who would make the final decision. For this, the last stage, the party was ushered into the Prime Minister's office and Claus calmed the nerves of his colleagues by remarking, rather breezily, that he had considerable experience of dealing with prime ministers. But all of this was to no avail in the searching questioning which followed. Dr Lee quickly exposed the fact that Claus lacked experience of investments. Nevertheless, in spite of any apprehension, Dr Goh later informed them that Rothschild's would be appointed for a trial period of six months.

Claus chaired the Economist Intelligence Unit from 1979 to 1983. This is a unit within the Economist Group which carries out research and publishes papers under contract, especially on matters of economic concern. Coming shortly after Claus's term as Director of the CSO there could hardly have been a stronger candidate for the job. He also chaired the *Economist* Board for a time.

Wadham College

In 1984 Claus made his final career move, this time to be Warden of Wadham College, Oxford, where he remained until his retirement in 1993. This was a return to the academic world but a very different one from that in which he began at the LSE many years before. He himself said that 'Of the various careers I've had, my nine years at Wadham have been the happiest of all. I love being with students and in the company of academics.' It was the academic environment in which he felt at home with its daily contact with scholars of all ages. As Warden it was his responsibility to chair meetings of the governing body, which he did with the benefit of many years' experience; however, he did not rely on past experience alone but, characteristically, on a sure foundation of knowledge based on prior reading of the papers and consultation with the relevant officers of the College. Although he was also making a major contribution to the running of the Royal Opera House at this time, his effort was equitably apportioned between these two responsibilities. Weekends were, as throughout his life, packed with entertaining and various social activities. His musical talents contributed enormously to the musical life of a College which had not been previously conspicuous in that direction. He made no distinctions between people and this, particularly, appealed to undergraduates. He quickly saw the need for Wadham College to raise its endowment, and he was happy to use his many connections in the financial world as targets when the begging bowl went round. During this period his statistical activities were very much in the background, but while in Oxford he was enlisted to chair a University committee on the future of Statistics in the University. He also served a term as Pro-Vice-Chancellor between 1991 and 1993. He reached the retirement age for Wadham College in 1993 at the age of seventy.

Music

On the public scene Claus exercised his managerial abilities in the service of music. He was appointed to the Board of Directors of the Royal Opera House in 1965 and he succeeded to the Chairmanship in 1974. On the completion of that appointment in 1987, the Royal Opera House put on a performance of Mozart's *The Marriage of Figaro* in honour of Claus to mark his retirement as Chairman. His successor in the Opera House Chair was Sir John Sainsbury. During his working life, and beyond, he supported many musical causes.

Although never a professional musician, there were numerous occasions when Claus gave amateur piano performances at the LSE and elsewhere. It must have been rare for anyone to combine a lifelong interest in music with the personal and managerial expertise which Claus could bring to bear in any field. As well as his close link with the Royal Opera House, his musical interests also included membership of the governing body of Royal Academy of Music and of the BBC Music Advisory Committee, the London Symphony Orchestra where he was also a member of the Education Committee, and the Yehudi Menuhin School, among other similar activities.

It was mischievously claimed (incorrectly) that it was necessary to play a musical instrument to be employed in the Higher Education Research

Unit at the LSE. In later years, it was said, the transition occasioned by the replacement of Harold Wilson's government (with which Claus's sympathies lay) by Edward Heath's was made easier by the latter's musical accomplishments. In later years, when Claus appeared as a guest on the BBC's *Desert Island Discs*, it was clear that his main musical interest was in the great classical composers in the Bach and Mozart tradition.

Throughout his career he showed that blend of arts and sciences of which many have extolled but few have exemplified so completely.

Other activities

Claus Moser acquired many honorific posts during his career. Some were held in parallel with his main occupation, some began during his active career and carried on into retirement, and others were taken up during retirement. Any attempt at an exhaustive listing would almost certainly contain omissions; one estimate suggests that it may have run to upwards of forty. Almost all arose naturally from his professional and other interests linked to his background. Some have been mentioned already.

On retirement he became chairman of the British Museum Development Trust for ten years, where he oversaw the fundraising that culminated on 6 December 2000 in the opening of the award-winning Great Court, designed by Foster and Partners. After completing the term he became chairman emeritus.

He also supported Jewish and related charities, statistical and general academic interests, musical enterprises and organisations concerned with his wider general educational concerns. On the charitable side he was a trustee of the Paul Hamlyn Foundation and The Rayne Foundation.

Claus was president of the British Association for the Advancement of Science (as it was then known) in 1989–90 and he used his presidential address to show his concern for education at a very different level to university education with which he had been mainly involved. In his view young people in the UK were poorly prepared to take their place in the world of work and a radical examination of the situation was urgently needed. He proposed that a Royal Commission be set up to look into the matter, but this request was declined by the government. It is a measure of the seriousness of the situation that he, himself, in July 1991 set up a National Commission on Education under the auspices of the British Association to implement his proposal. The scope of the enquiry and the depth of Claus's own concern is clearly set out in that Commission's terms of reference:

> In the light of the opportunities and challenges that will face the United Kingdom in a changing world over the next 25 years, to identify and consider key issues arising from: the definition of educational goals and assessment of the potential demand for education and training, in order to meet the economic and social requirements of the country and the needs and aspirations of people throughout their lives; and the definition of policies and practical means whereby opportunities to satisfy that demand may be made available for all, bearing in mind the implications for resources and institutions and for all of those involved in the education and training system; and to report its conclusions and recommendations in such manner as it may think fit.

It would be surprising if these words did not express Claus's own thinking on the subject.[3] He became chairman of the Basic Skills Agency in the late 1990s.

Throughout his life Claus continued to use, and to have used, the designation *statistician* in any list identifying his professional roots. Equally, he continued to be regarded as a statistician by the statistical community. It was therefore entirely appropriate, and expected, that he should become President of the Royal Statistical Society for the normal two-year term from 1978 to 1980. The President was not envisaged as a mere figurehead. He was expected to chair the monthly meetings of Council and its Executive and to chair the 'Ordinary' meeting which normally followed. At an Ordinary Meeting a paper was 'read' and discussed, first by a proposer and a seconder of the vote of thanks, followed by contributions from the floor. The other duty was to deliver a Presidential address. In Claus's case this was on 7 November 1979 and it was entitled 'Statistics and public policy'. After the usual formalities it was entirely devoted to a reflection on the author's still-recent experience of eleven years in the GSS (as covered elsewhere in this memoir). The vote of thanks was normally proposed by the President's predecessor in office, who in this case happened to be the Director of Statistics in the Home Office—who had been responsible to Claus. In particular from her we learnt that Claus's attempts to bring statisticians into the limelight had not always been met with universal approval outside GSS circles. There had been cynics who, privately, expressed the view that some statisticians would have been better left in the backroom!

---

[3] The report was National Commission on Education, *Learning to Succeed* (London, 1993).

Claus continued his association with the academic world throughout his life. He received honorary degrees from the Open University among others, but it was to Keele that he made his most lasting contribution and with which his name is particularly associated. He was Chancellor from 1986 until 2002. The Chancellor is the ceremonial head of the University and is normally most visible at the annual degree ceremonies. This was a considerable honour, but Claus took a particular interest in the progress of the social sciences at Keele. This is commemorated in the Claus Moser Research Centre building, which cost £3.5million and houses researchers in the humanities and social sciences; it was opened in the presence of Claus in 2008. A Claus Moser Memorial Lecture was given at the University on 4 May 2016 by John Pullinger, the current head of the GSS. This had the same title—'Statistics and public policy'—as Claus's original presidential address to the Royal Statistical Society in 1978, and described the indebtedness of Pullinger personally and the service generally to Claus's pioneering work, focusing particularly on the continuing need for integrity and quality in the data produced. Pullinger described the radical change over the last thirty to forty years in the ease with which data can now be produced.

As already noted, Claus was Pro-Vice-Chancellor of the University of Oxford from 1991 to 1993; another notable appointment in the academic sphere was as Chancellor of the Open University of Israel from 1994 to 2004. He was elected a Fellow of the British Academy in 1969.

Claus retained an affection for the LSE, in which he had developed his academic career. Apart from having served as a Visiting Professor soon after moving to government service, he became a member of its governing body from 1977 to 2006, and when that term came to an end he was accorded the new emeritus title along with other similarly eminent members retiring at the same time. The government of the LSE is now in the hands of a Court of no more than one hundred Governors each serving for a term of five years. As in most such institutions, much of the business is done through committees, and Claus took his share.

Soon after moving to the CSO in 1965 Claus was made a CBE, and he moved on to a knighthood (KCB) in 1973. He was elevated to the peerage in 2001. Tony Blair, the Prime Minister at the time, aimed to alter the composition of the House of Lords by introducing a new variety of peer who became known as 'People's Peers'. Inclusion in the approved list was to be by application and then selection. The initial list, published in 2001, consisted of fifteen names recommended to the Queen by the Prime Minister. There was some criticism that the list lacked the 'common touch' since all had already achieved some distinction, but Claus was the oldest. The peerage was conferred and Claus became Baron Moser of Regent's Park in the Borough of Camden. Despite his left-leaning politics he sat on the cross-benches, from which he made many contributions drawing on his own experiences.

Assessment

There is no doubt that Claus was a remarkable man who could have succeeded in any of a number of spheres. His original status as a refugee is often used to illustrate how he overcame the initial disadvantages of his family's move to England. It is certainly true that the initial adaptation to the circumstances of life in a new country must have required a greater than average measure of adaptability. But he was admirably prepared for this by his near-perfect command of English, his innate natural ability and the ease with which he entered into personal relations on all fronts. This combination of personality and ability marked all stages of his career and contributed to his success in all of them. In the Civil Service, especially, he was able to develop that easy self-assurance which made for good relations with ministers and senior civil servants. This ability also stood him in good stead later in his career.

The move from the LSE to the Civil Service was the turning point in his career. At the LSE he had made steady progress up the academic ladder and was already a professor by the time he left. Had he remained it is probable that his career would have moved in a managerial direction, and he could easily have acquired any of the various offices which senior academics are often called upon to occupy. There is little doubt that he could have become a vice-chancellor of another university. Whether such a career would have offered the range and variety of challenges which came his way in the Civil Service and beyond is very doubtful. The LSE made strenuous efforts to reclaim his services at the end of his initial term in the GSS, but Claus courteously declined and subsequent history can vouch for the wisdom of this decision. His particular combination of talents needed a wider field for their fruitful exercise.

A gap in his knowledge, to which he often referred, was his lack of mathematics—as distinct from numeracy. As far as the latter was concerned, he was very keen on playing with numbers and he was highly numerate in all other senses of the word. He recognised the general importance of a facility for manipulating and comprehending the meaning of numbers and regretted the lack of numeracy in contemporary society. However, there is no evidence that Claus had had any formal training in mathematics itself beyond school, and the BSc (Econ) degree at LSE certainly contained very little at that time. It was certainly possible to lecture in Statistics, as Claus did, without any systematic knowledge of mathematics. Yet it was clear that things were changing, as Claus discovered when the late Sir Maurice Kendall was appointed to the second chair of Statistics at the LSE. Sir Maurice was, perhaps, the leading UK figure in the world of mathematical statistics and the implications of this soon became clear. At the first annual meeting of the department following his appointment to agree the teaching programme, Sir Maurice said that he thought that all courses should be taken in rotation by all staff. It thus fell to Claus to teach a course on the Analysis of Variance and Covariance which would have had a substantial mathematical content. Claus protested, but was told that all members of the department should be able to teach any course. Accordingly, Claus took the course for three years, 'mugging up', as he put it, the material beforehand and escaping quickly at the end of each lecture lest any student should wish to ask a question! Years later, when they travelled the world together and both had left the LSE, Claus felt that he and Maurice had arrived at a degree of mutual understanding, but Sir Maurice evidently continued to see mathematical thinking as fundamental to life in general. Once, after seeing an opera by Handel together, Sir Maurice remarked that it was all rather trivial, and to prove his point he set the first chapter of his famous *Advanced Theory of Statistics* to music in the style of Handel. Claus dryly remarked that such a score might now be quite valuable, if it was still extant. This anecdote illustrates the fundamental division which was then becoming apparent in statistics between different ways of looking at the world, now almost forgotten. Claus was one of the survivors of that earlier way of looking at the subject and he remained acutely aware of this, as I was reminded when he brought the matter up at a lunch to celebrate his ninetieth birthday given by the Statistical Dinner Club. The conversation turned on whether the ideas of statistics were essentially mathematical. He did not denigrate the mathematical approach, as did some of his contemporaries, but recognised his own limitations in that direction. I was reminded of this in the 1970s when Lord Rothschild, his then boss, said that he wanted to learn some probability theory 'to keep his mind sharp'. Claus declined the invitation to be his tutor and sent him to me instead, when Rothschild ascended, somewhat furtively, by a back stair of the St Clement's Building of the LSE for a weekly session.

To understand why lack of mathematics was sometimes a concern for some statisticians it is necessary to sketch some of the background to the development of the subject. In the beginning the subject of Statistics was primarily concerned with detecting patterns in social and economic data. Very often the data would be presented in tables or as time series and the statistician's job was to discern their meaning. Around the year 1900, in the wake of the Darwinian revolution, Karl Pearson and his colleagues at University College London were studying the patterns of variation displayed by populations of biological objects. These conformed to a variety of simple shapes which could be described by simple mathematical forms. A little later, statisticians turned their attention to inference from random samples. Probability theory, on which both developments depended, is a branch of mathematics. In such ways mathematics gained entry to statistics and modern mathematical statistics was born. This greatly enhanced the power and scope of what had been largely a descriptive science. In various ways, by the 1960s mathematical statistics became the dominant strand of the subject. One could do a great deal without any reference to real data and mathematicians did not hesitate to do this! This led to a cleavage in the subject which was sometimes (and inaccurately) described as between applied and theoretical statistics. To a large extent mathematics has now given way to computer science as the favoured tool for handling variation. In following the traditional terminology Claus declared himself to be, and was, an applied statistician. His knowledge of and facility with mathematics was very limited, as he frequently acknowledged. His strength lay in collecting, tabulating and interpreting the message conveyed by aggregate data without the necessity of much reference to mathematical theory.

Claus was firmly on the non-mathematical side of the great divide to which we have just referred, and this was evident in the section of his presidential address to the RSS entitled 'What kinds of statisticians?'. He referred to the fact that almost all recruits to the GSS had been trained in university departments of Statistics and were firmly based on the mathematical version of the subject. This left them ill prepared for the real world of government service which was firmly located near the more empirical part of the spectrum. Claus himself, in that address, had described Statistics as the 'science of doubt'—or, equivalently, as to do with 'chance and its measurement'. The nub of the problem lay in the fact that the doubt and uncertainty with which the government statistician was concerned was much wider. The sort of uncertainty faced was broader than that on which mathematical statisticians, reared almost exclusively on probability theory, have habitually dealt. Claus's own solution, proposed in that address, was in the direction of grafting what was lacking onto existing courses, but perhaps he failed to see how deep-rooted the difficulty was. The problem has been ameliorated slightly since then because Computer Science has more recently posed a different but equal set of challenges to what the subject of Statistics actually is. In that ambiguity lies the inherent difficulty of locating Claus's true place within Statistics and his contribution to it.

*****

Claus met his future wife, Mary Oxlin, while they were both students at the LSE but they were not married until 1949. They had three children, Kath, Sue and Peter, all born in the 1950s. Claus loved spending time with his family, sharing walks on Sundays, music-making and holidays, and Mary played an invaluable and supportive role in very many aspects of his life. Mary is half Swiss and spent her early childhood in Arosa near Chur, Switzerland. Claus and the family went there on holiday every summer, inviting friends to join them in the chalet in the mountains where Mary grew up. It was while there on holiday that Claus had a stroke and died on 4 September 2015, aged ninety-two.

DAVID BARTHOLOMEW[4]
Fellow of the Academy

Note. When writing about a man with such a wide range of abilities and accomplishments it is impossible to do him justice without drawing on the help of many friends and colleagues. Among those who have materially contributed to this memoir are Lord Richard Layard, Professor Howard Glennerster and, especially, Kath Moser, Claus's elder daughter. To them and all others not named I extend my warmest thanks.

---

[4] David Bartholomew died in October 2017.

JOHN DAVID YEADON PEEL

John David Yeadon Peel
1941–2015

[T]he modest time-depth of an anthropologist's personal acquaintance with another society seems to sharpen his capacity to appreciate the balance of continuity and change in its history over the longer span. (Peel, 2016b, 549)[1]

DOES THE SENTIMENT APPLY as well to another person as to another society? John appears fully formed in the accounts of the personal acquaintances of his early career. His own writings tell a similar story of consistency. The demeanour, mannerisms, opinions, habits of speech, restless energy and relentless memory of the younger man are those of the established professor I met in the early 1980s. It would take a family memoir to get to the bottom of an ageless entirety that was not, in either constancy or character, wholly of his times. I remarked to Tom McCaskie at John's funeral that although John and I were separated by a decade in age, the difference always felt like a generation. Amused, because they were a mere five years apart, Tom confessed the same: John's personality, as he nailed it, was formed before the cultural watershed of the 1960s. A small pointer, but it's uncommon nowadays, when even prime ministers are (not necessarily warmly) referred to as Maggie, Dave and Tony, to be known affectionately by initials. JDY or JDYP seemed at home in a generation of men with initials—W. H. Auden, T. S. Eliot, G. M. Trevelyan—but a monographic acronym trumps even these and has something heraldic about it. The effect hinged around the prescience of that 'Y'.[2]

---

[1] All John Peel's publications referred to in this memoir are listed in date order at the end.
[2] John also claimed to be the real John Peel in contradistinction to a well-known DJ, born John Ravenscroft, who adopted the name in 1967 as cover when working for a pirate radio station.

I have tried to follow John's life story chronologically, but its robust threads have wanted to disregard the timely order of things, so I have had to allow them some licence. John seems, whichever way you order it, fully present in every moment of his life.

*****

Born in Dumfries, West Lowland Scotland, on 13 November 1941, John David Yeadon Peel was mostly raised in the English Midlands as the oldest of the two sons and two daughters born to (Nora) Kathleen Peel (née Yeadon, died 1988) who had married their father in 1939. When John was a youngster, the family moved to suburban Sutton Coldfield once his father, E. A. (Edwin Arthur) Peel (1911–92), a talented artist in oils and later in watercolours, left the University of Durham in 1950 to become Professor of Education at the University of Birmingham, a post he held until 1978, serving as President of the British Psychological Society in 1961–2 (Anon, 1963). Education ran in the family: John's paternal grandfather and -mother were both teachers. A painting by his father of John and his two sisters in their childhood backyard held pride of place over the mantelpiece of John's last home; I never asked him why he was parading a union flag across it. John was to take a University of London DLitt, or higher doctorate, by publication in 1985 on the grounds—so he told friends, though additional more complex motives seem likely—that his father's doctoral robes should not go to waste. The avoidance of waste is telling in the filial gesture: hard work and steadiness were likely to have been qualities formed in John by his father (which John later looked for and valued in others). Edwin Peel was Liverpool—or more exactly Everton—born (whence John's support for that football team) but educated in Yorkshire; his *Dictionary of National Biography* entry (Tomes, n.d.) describes him as a 'craggy-faced Yorkshire man', whose principles of education owed much to observing his four children grow through the lens of Jean Piaget's developmental theories of learning.[3]

I suppose John's attention must have been drawn to this coincidence, since I cannot visualise his ear pressed to a transistor radio listening to alternative rock on Radio London in the 1960s.

[3] John's sister Susan confirms this, as does Peel Snr's work on the growth of thinking during adolescence, described by him as an empirical investigation building on the conception that Piaget expressed of a working through of some of the irreconcilabilities between the actual and the possible in young adults' experience of the world (E. A. Peel, 1971). This seems at odds with Caroline Ifeka's (2015) statement that Peel Snr rejected Piaget's theories (2015). For Peel Snr's papers at the University of Birmingham, see http://calmview.bham.ac.uk/Record.aspx?src=CalmView.Catalog&id=XUS105 (accessed 6 January 2017).

Reaching adolescence and adulthood in the 1950s, at thirteen the young research subject became a Foundation Scholarship boy at King Edward's School, Birmingham, which professes (on its website) to cater for clever and committed students willing to learn to love study and pursue excellence. No question of their success in either selection or outcome. Directly from school, John won entry as a Higgs Scholar to Balliol College, Oxford in 1959, graduating in 1963 with a first in 'Literae Humaniores', fluent reading-Latin that never left him and a commitment to the study of original texts, which included, as I learned only after his death, an enthusiasm for heraldry, sketching and colouring coats of arms collected in albums. The habit of thinking about families, including his own, dynastically preceded John's experience of Africa where it found a comfortable home. While he may have specialised in 'human learning', divine learning was just as close to the heart of a lifelong Anglican. Together, human and divine studies thoroughly prepared him to study Christianity comparatively.

From Oxford, John continued his studies immediately at the London School of Economics (LSE) where, remarkably, a PhD in Sociology was written in three years that included research in Nigeria (predominantly in Lagos and Ibadan in 1964–5). Quite why and how he found himself a sociologist studying religious change among the Yoruba in Nigeria I have not heard explained satisfactorily, and I regret that I never thought to ask him. Even Tom McCaskie's (2005, 30) accounts shed no definitive light on this, though he remarks that John's path may well have been blocked at Oxford, while sociology was considered an exciting and expanding field in the 1960s. John's father probably played some role in refining an initial interest that was likely to have been rooted in religious change and the history of Anglicanism rather than in intensive knowledge of the Yoruba. John's sister Susan recalls their father returning from trips to Africa as an external examiner bearing what seemed to them exotic gifts and recollections. The wide interests of his mentor, LSE Professor of Sociology Donald MacRae, must have been part of the attraction of moving there, and these may have been influential if the doctoral project was not formed fully. But it still seems a leap for a young scholar to make—and to be permitted to make—from 'Greats', or 'Classics', to the sociology of religion in West Africa; not one that would be countenanced by today's 'standards of excellence' for all that they are supposed to emphasise interdisciplinarity. Yet the happy outcome was that John discovered in the Yoruba a people of the scale, historical complexity and contemporary importance to engage the wide range of his curiosities for the remainder of his life, in fact to do so increasingly, and Yorubas gained in him their finest modern social historian or historical ethnographer. And, as they grew in his affections, John identified the qualities that made the Yoruba exceptional in Africa south of the Sahara, and delineated these in ways, to which I shall return in more detail, that were to prove challenging to his comparative sociology. One of the three major ethnic groups of Nigeria, Africa's most populous country, Yoruba also live in the neighbouring countries of Benin and Togo, as well as providing the identity of choice of many North, South and Caribbean Americans. John was cautious about the last, American, category. 'I use "Yoruba" in the conventional sense', he wrote in his final book:

> as used by the vast majority of self-described Yoruba, namely people who have the Yoruba language as their mother tongue or who, even if they have lost it or live outside the Yoruba homeland, still have close links with those who do, like the children of Yoruba parents who have moved abroad. But I do not count as Yoruba people of some other backgrounds who have assumed Yoruba names or who refer to themselves as Yoruba in the context of their practicing *oriṣa* religion. (2015a, 284, fn.1)

Population figures have to be estimates given these circumstances of wide distribution and fuzzy categorisation, but a Yoruba population of around forty million is a common claim and provides some sense of scale.

To return to my sequential narrative, John's first book, based on the LSE doctorate he had submitted during his twenty-fifth year in 1966 as 'A sociological study of two independent churches among the Yoruba of Nigeria', became a modest modern classic, charting the rise of 'Aladura', the churches of 'those who pray', notably the Christ Apostolic Church and the Cherubim and Seraphim, during the forty-odd years before his research, to which an emerging urban, lower middle class turned for help with 'this-worldly' problems of health and well-being and, in doing so, turned away from mission-introduced Anglicanism. The book radically rewrote theories of conversion by pointing first to the enduring importance for African religions of the means to deliver effects now, in the world of the living, rather than promising blessings deferred to the world to come, and second to the 'reasonableness' of these means that made them attractive to converts. Well before the later twentieth-century upsurge in popularity of Pentecostalism and of the gospel of prosperity, John noted that Christian poverty was already an unwelcome message. *Aladura: a Religious Movement among the Yoruba* (1968) provided ethnographic grist to the anthropologist Robin Horton's influential theory of the 'rationality' of African conversion launched in a 1971 article that was largely a recapitulation and generalisation of John's book. The original print run of 2,000 copies sold out in ten years, respectable sales for a specialist monograph that was well reviewed. But John became dissatisfied with the overwhelmingly sociological character of his analysis and, as a thick file at the International African Institute (IAI) attests, was never able to rouse sufficient enthusiasm to write the substantial postscript needed for a planned reprint.

Notwithstanding his reservations about it, *Aladura* had the tone and breadth of reference that remained characteristic of John's later work. These qualities are already in the doctoral thesis which had been revised relatively lightly to become the book. Apart from dropping a couple of short sections concerned with definitional issues around sects and syncretism, and slightly toning down the Weberian references, the main changes occurred in the framing introductory and concluding sections, though even here not in their entirety, where a predominantly historical perspective on similarities gave way to one based in sociological comparison. The book concludes by noting that two transitions (one from primitive to world religions, and the other the religious response to the change from rural to industrial societies) which took place a millennium apart in Europe, occurred together in Africa. The first saw religious and cosmological thought differentiated; the second brought about a separation between religious and social allegiances (1968, 299). After citing examples that include Hellenised Jews at the birth of Pentecostalism, George Eliot's evocations of a dissenting congregation and miners in South Wales, and noting common tendencies in rationalisation between them, John's parting paragraph abruptly dissents from what has gone before: 'Although we aspire to relate systems of ideas to the social situations which gave them birth, the ideas live their own life. Of all elements of a social system, ideas are the most likely to find root in a novel situation.' Perhaps, he writes, it is the 'particularity of beliefs' that counts, which are summed up in the words of the Yoruba politician Chief Obafemi Awolowo: 'They believed in the potency ['efficacy' in the thesis] of prayer' (1968, 300).

Much of John's later work is foreshadowed here, not just his concern for the degree of effective independence of ideas, which remained in a creative tension with his concern for their social contexts, but in more specific ways his intuitions about a modern Yoruba elite being made in his time and the importance to them of Awolowo's example, the role of the forgotten pastors and village evangelists in spreading Christianity (1966, 101), the place of Christianity in the making of Yoruba identity and self-characterisation, and the largely accommodating relations between

Yoruba Christianity and Islam (1966, 232–3). John's later work would also pursue parallels for which a classical education had prepared him: between Yoruba and Greek city states, or between the impact of Christianity on Roman and Yoruba cults. A consequence of this way of formulating questions was that, as he came to know the anthropologists better, absorbing their theories and methods, John never suffered from their later concerns about exoticism. Yoruba were not exotic for John who accommodated them welcomingly within his capacious view of universal human history and sociological comparison, allied to an equal curiosity about parish-pump politics. *Aladura* was the first in the trilogy of works on Yoruba religion that will be the most enduring aspect of John's achievement. But for all it became apparent to him later, and inklings of it are evident with the wisdom of hindsight, nothing indicates this design was consciously present from the outset.

John did not return soon to West Africa. While still researching his PhD, he had accepted a lectureship in Sociology at the University of Nottingham.[4] There, at an Anglican chaplaincy tea party, he met his first wife, Jenny (Jennifer Christine Pare), like him from the Midlands, in her case Leicester, then a doctoral researcher in Psychology (PhD 1972). They married in 1969. Having quickly completed the revision of his thesis for submission as a monograph by November 1966, John was already at work on a biography and a volume of selected writings by Herbert Spencer (1971, 1972),[5] once the most influential of British Victorian social theorists; another man of the Midlands but by then fallen into understandable neglect. Mastering their nineteenth-century context in order to contribute to the wider 'sociology of knowledge', and reading the entirety of Spencer's prolix and repetitive writings, John showed that Spencer's evolutionary views attracted Victorians, and flattered their self-image, for the same reasons that they lost appeal in the twentieth century. Wondering how much of the correspondence of this curious and self-obsessed man was lost, John commented dismissively from his consultation of three small extant collections that 'Spencer does not appear to have been a particularly interesting or revealing correspondent' (1971, xii). Photographic evidence suggests that around the time he was labouring in Spencer's cause John cultivated sideburns of Victorian luxuriance: perhaps

[4] This is apparent from a letter sent to his sister Susan in October 1964 which finds him living in Kuti Hall, a student residence at the University of Ibadan, where he was teaching four hours a week and fully engaged both in research and socialising.
[5] The conclusion to the book version of *Aladura* contains a citation of Spencer's autobiography not in the thesis version (1968, 299, fn.13).

an indication of his veering, if vicariously, towards the participatory methods of ethnography? In all likelihood trying his patience, Spencer nonetheless credentialised John as a sociologist. His theoretical inclinations would have drawn him more enthusiastically to the German tradition, notably Max Weber, the favoured thinker of his doctoral supervisor Donald MacRae, who was to write the Fontana Modern Masters volume on Weber (MacRae, 1974), but John considered his German language not up to an appreciation of that great thinker through his original texts. A near-native grasp of documents was essential. Each year until his retirement, John delivered a course on the history of social thought, predominantly from the mid-eighteenth to mid-twentieth centuries, insisting that students read primary texts (in translation for the continental European theorists) rather than mugging up pre-digested summaries from secondary sources. The texture of the real thing mattered. Introducing first-year students to this canon was a privilege, and not the chore he regretted that it seemed to some colleagues. Even if John tried to be even-handed, Max Weber emerged annually as the hero of his survey. I stood in on the occasions John was unavailable to lecture, and eventually I inherited his course along with its philosophy. Though here again, the connecting threads have moved me ahead of the story.

After four years in Nottingham, and with the publication of the Spencer volumes imminent, John returned to the LSE as a lecturer in Sociology. This tenure was brief (1970–3) because he was invited to Nigeria as a Visiting Reader in the newly formed Department of Sociology and Anthropology at the University of Ife, which itself had been founded only in 1961–2, immediately after Independence (and was to be renamed the Obafemi Awolowo University in 1987, after 'Awo', the Yoruba Nigerian politician cited in concluding *Aladura*, who played a prominent role in its establishment). John's two years spent at Ife (1973–5) with his wife and young family were crucial to his development as a Yoruba scholar, both for the enduring friendships with members of the post-Independence, intellectual elite formed then, and for the researches on which his second ethnographic monograph would be based.

Ijesha, and its capital Ilesha, the subject of the second Yoruba book, lie only 20 miles from Ife, allowing John to travel back and forth from the university for longer and shorter periods of research. The monograph on Ijesha would differ from *Aladura* with respect to both its subject and method. It is a history book, concerned specifically with how one kingdom became Nigerian in the course of becoming Yoruba. So it is also a book about identity and the importance of history both objectively and subjectively to processes of identification. The foundation of the book is a mass of documentation: several surveys were undertaken by a team of interviewers in 1973–5 and again, during repeat fieldwork, in 1979. The testimonies of around a hundred interviewees were transcribed; some of them were interviewed repeatedly and at considerable length. Notwithstanding what John considered shortcomings in method (notably sampling), *Ijeshas and Nigerians: the Incorporation of a Yoruba Kingdom, 1890s–1970s* (1983) was the first of his books to clinch the African anthropology double of the Amaury Talbot Prize of the Royal Anthropological Institute in the UK and the Melville J. Herskovits Prize of the African Studies Association in the USA. One big question was settled for John when the book demonstrated the complementarity of anthropological and historical methods for the study of African societies (a question that had preoccupied anthropologists' disciplinary attention but is now justly forgotten). Two decades later, the book's career was to culminate in another honour, when the *SOAS Alumni Newsletter* (No. 26, Winter 2003) announced, presumably at John's prompting, that the Owa-Obokun, or King, had appointed him a chief of Ijeshaland, with the title *Bapitan* or 'father of historians'. A year earlier, as his friend from the early days of his doctoral research, Bolanle Awe, recalled in her obituary, republication of John's *Ijesha* book had

> occurred during the period of the birth of the Ijesa Cultural Foundation; this was a society founded by a few of us with the aim of sensitizing the Ijesa to the significance of their history and culture. Unfortunately, this book went out of print before many Ijesa could have access to it. We felt that its publication in Nigeria would provide a launching pad for this Foundation. John Peel readily gave us the copyright and agreed to donate the proceeds to the development of Ijesaland. We were able to publish a Nigerian edition in 2002; it was launched, with a great deal of fanfare with the Owa Obokun of Ijesa kingdom and a large host of Ijesa dignitaries from all over Nigeria in attendance. It became a highly prized book in their private libraries.

So John became part of the history he had set out to study.

Again, the momentum of the life has caused my account to run ahead of itself, so I must backtrack. On return from Nigeria in 1975, John had become Charles Booth Professor of Sociology at the University of Liverpool, a post he combined with sundry academic-cum-administrative tasks, including departmental headship (in 1975–81 and again in 1984–5, after a gap to take up a Visiting Professorship in Anthropology and Sociology at the University of Chicago in 1982–3) and Deanship of the Faculty of Social and Environmental Studies (1985–8). John saw these responsibilities as part of an academic 'vocation', a calling in Max Weber's broadening of the religious sense, integral to a rounded career of teaching, research and writing, and to a duty of care for the future of his disciplines and towards his colleagues, particularly younger colleagues. He extended this sense of responsibility outside the university to various editorial positions, most enduringly for the IAI, as editor of its quarterly journal *Africa* between 1979 and 1986, founding general editor from 1985 until his death of its monograph series, the International African Library, of which the fiftieth volume has lately been published, and as its Chair of the Board of Trustees from 2003. John's mentorship of younger scholars was both generous and fastidious. Whether or not they were his own doctoral supervisees, he would rewrite clumsy English, sometimes from second language variants over which he sighed, rearrange paragraphs and refine arguments; all this by annotation in the margins of their drafts, his handwriting as small, precise and spiky as his comments were detailed and unsparing. He was determined, as he often put it, 'to get them through it', whatever 'it' was: a thesis submitted or revised, journal article published or book polished. Mention of 'being edited by John' raises a wry smile in most who underwent the process and emerged with their texts honed and their scholarly instincts sharpened. John's editorial interests extended to type fonts and book covers about which he had strong ideas. Although he did not get his way, he wrote to the novelist Barbara Pym, then also in charge of publications at IAI, when he submitted *Aladura*, suggesting that 'a design incorporating a motif of a bible and handbell would be striking as well as appropriate' (22 May 1968). What he got was a plain cover in a dark sienna yellow, but the International African Library gave him ample later opportunities to see his preferences into print.

It was in the first half of the 1980s, as a contributor to *Africa* and at various conference and workshop meetings while I worked at the University of St Andrews, that I gradually came to know John. My serious publication history got under way when he accepted what was a rarity in *Africa*, a two-part article, and one submitted by a scarcely published author whom he did not know. John always backed his opinions, and he never grudged attention to other scholars who delayed his own projects. He also kept keen and consequential recollection of those who rejected his advice on less than convincing grounds. Rightly so, since his judgement was sound more often than not, and he had nothing to give that he valued more highly, or gave more generously, than his time. Even if occasionally he was not right in his advice, he was fundamentally correct about the etiquette: it was ungracious not to acknowledge a senior scholar giving his attention so selflessly. Without prejudices about race, class, nation, ethnicity and so forth, John was deeply prejudiced in matters of character. Someone he felt to be basically worthy and of good will—a 'trooper' was a term of high, and ungendered, praise—would be supported in the face of what others might construe as exasperating failings; but it was as well not even to mention the name of anyone he considered idle, self-serving or dishonest, albeit none of these precluded his rueful acceptance of their being clever. With few exceptions, characters tended to stay in the categories into which John had decided to fix them.

Tom McCaskie, who became a close friend to John in the mid-1980s, has written about the critical impact during the following decade of his Ife sojourn on John's career (McCaskie, 2005). I never knew the house on the Wirral Peninsula, across the Mersey from Liverpool, where John and Jenny raised their boys, and where he painted over the door a coat of arms hybridised from both their antecedents, but by report it was a comfortable base with a garden study conducive to John's concentration.

The editorship of *Africa* allowed John to refine the attributes of a disciplinary anthropologist and add them to those of comparative sociologist and historian. It was through the IAI that he met his closest Nigerian friend, J. F. (Jacob) Ade Ajayi. That was in 1975 when Ajayi became Chairman of the Council of the IAI, the year after the Directorship had passed from Daryll Forde to David Dalby. By 1979 it was thought that the Institute had over-extended itself and was facing bankruptcy (Peel 2015b). Dalby was deposed, in his own words, by 'an internal coup d'état'.[6] So far as John was concerned, only Jacob Ajayi's clear-sighted resourcefulness had saved the Institute, a service he never forgot, nor allowed others to. John particularly admired 'the stability of interlocking moral attachments' based in family, community, historic wisdom, nation and religion that grounded Jacob (2015b, 746). Like John, Jacob was inclined to recognise continuities and respond to loyalties. Together they assembled the volume of essays to commemorate their mutual friend Michael Crowder (1992). Over forty years, John became a friend and ally not just of Jacob, but of the family: Jacob's wife Christie (née Aduke Martins) and their children: Yetunde, the first of four daughters, Niyi their son, and Funlayo, Titilola and Bisola. When he was invited to deliver an eightieth birthday lecture for Jacob Ajayi at the University of Lagos in 2009, John chose the topic 'Islam and Christianity through the prism of Yoruba history' to pay tribute to the generally peaceful accommodation between

---

[6] https://sites.google.com/site/daviddalbyorg/biography (accessed 6 January 2017).

Yoruba Christians and Muslims. He stayed a last time with the Ajayi family in Ibadan on his final visit to Nigeria in April 2015 to offer his condolences on Jacob's death, and to lecture on the occasion of the ninetieth birthday of Sir Olaniwum Ajayi, a lawyer and close associate of the Yoruba leader Obafemi Awolowo. His subject matter was both broadened and harked back to the previous lecture when he took as his topic 'Religion and the future of Nigeria: lessons from the Yoruba case'. I shall return to the three lectures John delivered in Nigeria after his retirement. On John's death, Christie sent one of the earliest letters of condolence, recalling the last occasion on which she and the family had been welcomed in his home by John in May that year. Her son Niyi, a London-based surgeon, spoke eloquently on behalf of the family at John's memorial meeting the following June. The relationship between the two men and their legacies will continue when John's books are gifted to the Jadeas Educational Trust founded by Christie and Jacob.

Explaining this relationship and its importance, I have again been made to run ahead of the life story. To go back, I met John a few times in the 1980s. One of the earliest of these occasions was at the University of St Andrews workshop on 'Comparative method in social anthropology' convened in December 1983 by Ladislav Holy, to which John contributed 'History, culture and the comparative method: a West African puzzle' (1987), an essay reworked recently as the first chapter of his final book. We spoke there about ethnicity, the subject of my own paper in that volume. A few years later, I listened to John's brilliant paper on 'The cultural work of Yoruba ethnogenesis' at the 1987 annual conference of the Association of Social Anthropologists devoted to 'History and Ethnicity' (1989). We also chatted at one or more of the congenial residential gatherings that Dick Werbner still organises annually in the Lake District as the 'Satterthwaite Colloquium on African Religion and Ritual', certainly at the 1985 meeting since I find among my papers one by John under the title 'Religion and the state in the West African forest' from that year, an outline of a comparative project he never pursued that would have involved Yoruba, Asante and perhaps also Benin and Dahomey. All academic careers, John consoled me later, have their share of uncompleted plans. I think those few occasions, and the editorial communications around my article in *Africa*, were about the sum of our dealings before we became colleagues. I had accepted a lectureship at the University of London's School of Oriental and African Studies (SOAS) in October 1987 but did not move until the following year (the department at St Andrews being too small to leave once the academic year had started). In

1989 (as part of an education funding deal the details of which I cannot now recall) John was transferred to SOAS as Professor of Anthropology and Sociology with reference to Africa. Richard Rathbone has noted how this struck us all as an immense coup for the school, and a particular delight for Richard and me as West Africa specialists. After his first year, John became Dean of Undergraduate Students (1990–4), with Richard as his postgraduate student counterpart, throwing his energies into a complete overhaul of the teaching structure. They were a burly pair, and I privately thought of them as SOAS's version of the City's protective Gog and Magog; Richard recollects them being likened less flatteringly by one colleague to a pair of nightclub bouncers. It was a packed decade: John was elected a Fellow of the British Academy in 1991 and served later as Chair of S3 between 1997 and 2000, and as a British Academy Vice-President, 1999–2000. During the same period, he was also President of the African Studies Association of the UK, 1996–8, which made him its first posthumous recipient of a Distinguished Africanist Award in 2016.

John had moved from the bachelor flat he had initially rented on moving to London in a purpose-built block at The Angel, Islington, with metal stairs around an internal courtyard which struck me as a suitable set for a re-enactment of *West Side Story*, to an appropriately eccentric and homely property alongside the Archway Bridge. Archway—or more accurately the replacement for the original viaduct—crosses, and gives its name to, the concrete canyon through which traffic on the A1 heads in and out of London. It must be one of the capital's busiest roads, but the end-of-terrace property abutting and high above it was always quiet. John occupied the ground floor of this eyrie, reached up a winding and over-grown path, where a spacious living and dining area led onto a secluded and watery back garden where he could indulge his passion for plants. Reversing conventional domestic arrangements, the bedroom was on the basement floor, along with a large office. This setup provided ample room for hospitality, as guests were able to make themselves comfortable on sofas and armchairs while he shuttled between the kitchen and the dining table in the spacious living–eating room. Red wines and hearty stews were the staples. At John's memorial, his friend Sophie Baker read Elizabeth David's classic recipe for cassoulet in recollection of these times.

Alongside responsibilities within SOAS and beyond, throughout the 1990s John was regularly visiting Birmingham to research what would be his greatest book and the centrepiece of the trilogy on Yoruba religion, *Religious Encounter and the Making of the Yoruba* (2000). It was the perfect match: the missionisation of the Yoruba, largely by the Yoruba, during the nineteenth century and under the Anglican auspices of the Church Missionary Society. Everything had prepared him for this. The Church Mission Society Archive was housed in the library of the University of Birmingham, the city of John's upbringing and the university of his father's professorship. It contained, among other treasures, the journal extracts that missionaries were asked to send at regular intervals, which read across the decades with an immediacy John found similar to ethnographers' fieldnotes. He could stay in Birmingham with his close friends from the Centre for West African Studies, the Ghana specialists Lynne Brydon and Tom McCaskie, and Paulo Moraes de Farias and Karin Barber, she the doyenne of Yoruba literary studies in the UK. Fieldwork in Nigeria was called for and undertaken in 1994, during which John became vividly aware of the scale of the Pentecostal movement amongst Yoruba. The Birmingham–London axis was mobilised to gain an Arts and Humanities Research Board project award to study 'The role of the media in the constitution of new religious publics in Yorubaland' between 1996 and 1999, as an undertaking jointly between SOAS, where it was led by John and Louis Brenner, and the University of Birmingham, in the persons of Paulo and Karin. This project supplied some of the wider context to John's last two books.

Religious Encounter continued to document, among other matters, the vital role that Yoruba intellectuals, initially predominantly Christians, had played in the creation of a collective Yoruba ethnic identity from the myriad sometimes violently competing states and statelets of the nineteenth century. More broadly, Nigerians, John argued, played a crucial part in making and transforming the collective identities that were critical to post-colonial politics. In this respect, John's history of the nineteenth century connected with his experience of living alongside the Yoruba elite during the twentieth century. Because he did not give it explicit book-length treatment, the significance of John's ethnographically anchored history of the making of a Yoruba elite is easy to overlook, but it is a recurrent concern, particularly evident in the wonderfully engaged reading of Wole Soyinka's memoir of his father, *Isara*, that John composed for the Festschrift for Adrian Hastings (2002). Like *Ijeshas and Nigerians* before it, *Religious Encounter* did the 'double' with the award of the Talbot and the Herskovits Prizes on the two sides of the Atlantic: a double double achievement so far unique to John.

As he entered the new century, John was already at work on the third book of the Yoruba religion trilogy. It was to appear posthumously in 2016 as *Christianity, Islam and* Orișa *Religion: Three Traditions in*

Comparison and Interaction; all but the proofs and index were completed before his death. By now the shape of the trilogy was before him clearly. The final book would make good his relative neglect of Yoruba Islam which, outside Lagos, predominated in the northern areas of Yorubaland that were less familiar to him. In common with other observers, notably themselves, he was struck by the relatively scant importance in comparison to bonds of family and place that Yoruba had historically attributed to differing confessional identities. But relations between Christians and Muslims were polarising both inside and outside Nigeria. The book begins with the evidence of Michael Adebolajo, London born of Yoruba Christian antecedents, hacking to death a soldier on the streets of the capital in the name of Islam. This could not, John writes, or perhaps not yet, have happened in Nigeria. Adebolajo was radicalised in London. Within Nigeria, conflict between Yoruba Christians and Muslims remained rare and is actively downplayed. Yoruba do not kill one another over religion, as John had put it in his Olaniwun Ajayi lecture.

Perspectives on '*orişa* religion', as John decided to call it, are also distinct and different inside and outside Nigeria: for self-identified Yoruba in the Americas, Yorubaland is the source of African gods, essential attributes of Yoruba culture and identity; but these gods are for the most part disregarded or disparaged by ordinary Yoruba in Nigeria who consider themselves Christians and Muslims, members of world religions and, for all that some aesthetic and imaginative space may be found for their historical or 'traditional' beliefs, definitely not pagans. John's last book has ambitions wider than Yorubaland, since it draws upon his increasing certainty about the differing historical trajectories of the world religions that were set in motion in their early years and which the comparative sociology of religion would demonstrate. Seen in these terms, Christianity and Islam differed by virtue of their contrary relations to political power at the time of their inception.

The shape of a trilogy also becomes apparent retrospectively in the identities of the dedicatees of John's Yoruba religion books: the first volume, *Aladura*, for his parents; *Religious Encounter* for his three sons; and *Three Traditions*, the final volume, dedicated to his second wife Anne and to the six grandchildren born in his lifetime and any more who would not meet him. A seventh grandchild, a grandson, was born in February 2017. It may only seem significant with hindsight that the books on Spencer and on the kingdom of Ijesha did not have dedicatees. An over-interpretation? Perhaps, but John's life was patterned consistently by the enduring character of his dispositions. The trilogy, as I suggested earlier, seems already present in the doctoral thesis.

For all that it is engrossing, John's last book is not an achievement of the same magnitude as *Religious Encounter*, which in turn he considered a much better book than *Aladura*. John knew that he did not have the time to complete his final book as he would ideally have liked to, hence the number of chapters recycled from previously published papers, some of them old. The meat of the book is in the substantively new chapters of Part II, which deal with Yoruba Islam but, as he freely admitted, in scholarly terms John did not have the command of sources he enjoyed for Christian history, and by inclination he was less attracted to Yoruba Islam than to Christianity. Frankly its study was a struggle. For all his intense interest, it always felt an obligation, a dutiful, even noble, putting the balance to rights.

*****

John's personal life had been in flux. After a prolonged period of growing apart, or perhaps discovering how unsuited they had been all along, to his regret his first marriage to Jenny was finally dissolved after more than thirty years in 2000. He literally and metaphorically dug himself in at the Archway and created the hospitable place his temperament needed for entertaining and work. He was intensely proud of his three sons—David, who became a consultant oncologist, Tim working in finance in Australia and Francis (Franko) in a development initiative at Imperial College London. He was effusively delighted by his three daughters-in-law and his six grandchildren, most recently a fourth granddaughter born in 2015. Outwardly, and although he knew it was incurable, John treated his diagnosis with a melanoma in 2010 as a nuisance more than a crisis. In the preceding couple of years, he had found happiness after again meeting Anne Ogbigbo, who had been a mature student of ours at SOAS in the late 1990s. As an aid and development professional, Anne was posted to be a Human Rights Officer with UNMIL, the United Nations Mission to Liberia. After five years together, she and John married in 2014, honeymooning in Rome (from where John sent postcards expressing his greater enthusiasm for baroque churches, and Anne's reactions to them, than for classical ruins). His need for treatment prevented John from spending as much time as he wished with Anne in Liberia. On a second visit in December 2010 he had begun the habit of sending monthly 'Letters from Liberia' as email attachments to his personal communications to his friends. Seven more letters were to follow, the last in June 2014. After his death, we assembled them into a short illustrated volume as a souvenir of the day held at SOAS to celebrate his life (2016a). The letters were written with warmth for the people he encountered, enthusiasm for the country, happiness at his life with Anne, but without mention of his illness.

Treatment continued in the forms of surgery and chemotherapy for more than five years; a drug trial in 2012 proved promising and kept recurrence at bay for some time. The operations to excise the cancer were painful but more particularly resented for interfering with the long walks John had always taken. Weekend treks were planned to allow him to set out from a starting point with time to walk all morning to a sustaining pub lunch, then continue for the afternoon, preferably with a stop for tea, before reaching the station from which he would take the train back home. Anywhere between 15 to 20 miles a day was routine. Longer trails were tackled in successive weekends, each resuming the next leg of an itinerary. During annual vacations, extended walks could be undertaken; some of the most satisfying were in France. Continental trips began from the married home of his sister Susan in Paris. John had embarked with passion on a project of visiting the great churches and cathedrals of France with a view to describing them, and the circumstances of his encounters with them, for English-speaking visitors. There was nothing nicer, he beamed, than pottering along secondary roads to imposing feats of architecture from which to retire to a modest nearby café for an invariably excellent lunch. The incomplete project survives as a box of notes, photographs and other church memorabilia.

The end, when it came, was sudden, shockingly so given how long we had all become habituated to it. Its rapidity caught out everyone, even John. But he was prepared spiritually, and died as his classical and enlightenment icons would have wanted to: calmly, thankful for his family, loves, friends and career, and with individual attention to each of many visitors coming to say their farewells and wish him a comfortable passage to ancestorhood. Others will have their own recollections. I had dined in late September with John and Anne at a fish restaurant he liked on Archway. Conversation flowed to all intents normally, though John explained a new difficulty in calling nouns to mind that prevented his completing crossword puzzles. On the positive side, he added, his mathematical faculty seemed unimpaired so he had substituted numbers for words and did Sudoku puzzles instead. The symptom, he knew, resulted from a secondary brain tumour. Our meal was timed by my leaving for Australia where my mother had died. We parted and walked our separate ways home from the restaurant. Anne felt able to return to Liberia. When, back in London, I saw John a month later, Anne had rushed from Liberia that day and he was bedridden. We held hands, he smiled and spoke a few sentences, unaware that I could make no sense of his parting words.

I have been rooting back through old emails to remember John's laughter, sometimes oddly close to a giggle for a man of outward gravitas and solid stature. It meant something had been, was or soon would be afoot. For instance, the sheer glee of writing a letter strongly protesting at the reorganisation of our university which began (I have changed the name of its addressee), 'Dear Director (or Gordon if we must be chummy) …'. John did not feel 'chummy' towards what he construed as foolishness, and he had to struggle to understand disagreement when his own viewpoint was self-evidently correct. This is not to suggest that John always thought he was right: on some occasions (I initially wrote 'many' but given the deceased's respect for facts I ought to stick to them) he sought others' opinions and listened to them intently. He was the most constant supporter of his friends for whom he always wanted and savoured the very best their own best efforts deserved (the idle kept company with the smug and self-satisfied in his estimation). Of one email I sent as his administrative successor at SOAS, and conveying views we shared, he responded instantly and briefly, *'Fortis est veritas et praevalebit!'*—'Truth is strong and shall prevail!' In being first part university town motto from the arms of Oxford, second part Vulgate bible quotation, completely forthright and uncompromisingly supportive, this was quintessential JDYP. You knew he had sent it after rubbing his hands and grinning as he always did when righteous mischief was abroad. In this event, he was wrong and truth did not prevail, but if John agreed then other opinions seemed to matter less. I am not sure whether it is appropriate to recollect it in a British Academy Memoir, but notes on the inadequacies of the Faculty Office support sent to our then Dean were entitled 'Fac. Off.' followed by their number in the series of complaints. John appreciated serviceability in things, people and ideas.

*****

To return to the intellectual achievements of the life, given the monumental books, it is easy to overlook the carefully crafted lectures and articles. John was a brilliant essayist, poised, assured, measured and always lucid. Rereading his work, I wonder whether the essay form was not his ideal medium. Many of the finest started out as occasional lectures. John took unashamed delight in scholarly recognition; the numerous invitations to deliver named lectures meant a lot to him, and most of the domestic honours he might have anticipated duly came his way (along with a few I had never heard of). An honorary DLitt from the University of Birmingham was most valued for what that place and institution had meant to him since childhood. The reader of just a few of the essays will come away with the governing ideas of the career. In 1976, with Robin Horton, a strong defence against a critic of what was called the 'intellectualist' approach to the rationality of conversion in Africa. Two years later (in 1978), an argument for the need to devote attention to translation in development studies, delivered through a close examination of the Yoruba notion of development and enlightenment, *ọlaju*, that referred alike to these qualities and to their emissaries, and in Nigeria particularly apt, as Yoruba saw it, to describe themselves. Tellingly, this was placed in a journal of development studies. In the 1980s, the decade in which he thought most about historical method, there were essays demonstrating the necessity to understand history as an element of reflexivity in the making of the present, and particularly in the making of identities, including ethnic identities, and of course Yoruba identity (1984, 1989). From the 1990s, a concentration on the parts played by Yoruba intellectuals, typically Christians or from Christian families, in creating contemporary Yoruba culture and identity, including, as noted already, a compelling essay of exposition of Wole Soyinka's *Isara* and a related genealogy of the Yoruba intelligentsia dedicated to his friend Jacob Ajayi (1993, 2002). In John's closeness to the contemporary Yoruba intellectual elite, as much as their nineteenth-century forebears, we encounter a quality of relationship rare among Africanist anthropologists with which I want to conclude the intellectual portrait.

By a happy mixture of accident, attraction and accommodation, over time John was able to envisage the Yoruba, at their best, in something like his own best image. For their part, the Yoruba elite returned his regard and welcomed him into their circles, as was apparent both in numerous tributes and obituaries, and in three invitations to deliver named lectures in Nigeria after his retirement in 2007 that mattered greatly to him. Read to predominantly Yoruba audiences in honour of Yoruba famous men, it is unsurprising that these lectures shared and developed a theme of Yoruba exceptionalism. An anthropologist lecturing his research subjects about their own history is worth our attention.

The first of these lectures was delivered in April 2008 in the Chapel of the Resurrection at the University of Ibadan (Unibadan) as the third Memorial Lecture for Bishop Ebenezer Adeolu Adegbola (1918–2004). A year later, in April 2009 at the University of Lagos, the occasion of the second was an eightieth birthday lecture for John's friend Professor Jacob Ade Ajayi (1929–2014). Finally, in April 2015 at Muson (the Musical Society of Nigeria), Onikan Centre, Lagos, a third lecture was delivered on the occasion of the ninetieth birthday of Sir Olaniwun Ajayi (1925–). Respectively, these three Yoruba had played crucial roles in the twentieth-century making of Nigeria as a scholar of religion and Methodist minister (founding Principal of the Methodist Lay Training Institute, Sagamu in Ogun State, and the Director of the Institute of Church and Society, Ibadan); a scholar-administrator (sometime Vice-Chancellor of the University of Lagos and historian of Yoruba); and a prominent lawyer (head of a major law firm and political ally of 'Awo'). They were born more or less within a single decade (1918–29) between the two world wars, and together are evidence in themselves of Yoruba exceptionalism.

These commemorative occasions allowed John to put before audiences in the great cities of Ibadan and Lagos, which had been crucial to his research, what he saw as the contemporary relevance to Nigeria of his books, notably of *The Missionary Encounter*, in 2008–9, and of *Three Traditions*, in 2015. His particular challenge was to do this from the perspective of the Yoruba, and with reference to the exceptional co-existence among them of the triple religious heritage of historic African religion (for Yoruba he chose the more specific term '*oriṣa* religion'), Christianity and Islam. The attractions and repulsions between these three compelled his attention.

The first lecture addresses Bishop Adegbola as a figure on the cusp of the transition between the Nigerian nationalist era, with its high valuation of the African past that ended in 1977 with FESTAC (the second Festival of African Arts and Cultures held in Nigeria), and the debate from 1978 to the present surrounding the role of *sharia* or Islamic law in the Nigerian constitution. As John remarks, he is lecturing in sight of the Great Cross of the Chapel of Resurrection at Unibadan, which became the focus of conflict in 1985 when, during a flashpoint in religious tensions, Muslims demanded it be taken down. Adegbola was a scholar of the Africanisation of the church, that is to say of the attraction of Christianity towards the pole of historic African religion and its concerns. Events had since moved on, but Adegbola contributed to seeing Yoruba religious practice as a 'whole' in its three main varieties, which were like three legs of a stool. But would that balanced agreement to co-existence remain after one of the legs, the most distinctively Yoruba of them, that of *oriṣa* religion, was removed?

The second lecture of the following year presents Jacob Ajayi as the direct descendant, and major historian, of the nineteenth-century Christian intellectual elite of the Yoruba. Picking up the Nigerian national story after the new (but short-lived) constitutional arrangements of 1978–9, John highlighted the ways that 'new and more strenuous forms of devotion on both sides', aided by globalisation, put strain on the historic 'settlement' that was Yoruba co-existence between Christianity and Islam. The strains were exacerbated by some Yoruba politicians who gave salience to religious difference as they tried to mobilise confessional identities electorally. John credits Olusegan Obasanjo, the Yoruba who was Nigerian leader both as a general and as an elected civilian president, with defusing this potential; but he detects a periodisation of Yoruba co-existence, with the implication that this settlement might not have an indefinite term. The new strains of Christianity and Islam shared compelling resemblances, notably in their rejection of historic religion, but also significant differences between the individual aspirations of Christians to health, wealth and children, which closely matched long-standing Yoruba priorities, by contrast with the collective desires of Muslims to purify the *sunna*.

The third lecture, half a dozen years later, has a less optimistic tone, although it opened with the bold claim, cited earlier, that 'No one has ever been killed for their faith in Yorubaland.' The peacefulness of the Yoruba had been assured by the ties cross-cutting religious affiliations within families and localities and by the absence in Yorubaland of the jihadic tradition of the North. The mutual influence between the strands of Yoruba religion was long-standing. The defining figure of Yoruba aspirations during the twentieth century had been the federalist 'Awo', Chief Obafemi Awolowo, whose imprisonment had created the icon of the martyred Yoruba leader. Ironically, this stereotype was now reproduced in the undeserving person of Mashood Abiola, a Yoruba whose martyrdom occurred as a result of imprisonment by the military when he was denied the presidency. John's point is that Abiola, who as a Muslim had endorsed the demolition of the Great Cross in Ibadan, ended his life as a Yoruba rather than either Muslim or Nigerian figure. In terms endorsed by John's doctoral student Wale Adebanwi, Abiola became a 'structural Christian' in the way he was appropriated by the Yoruba elite (Adebanwi, 2014, 136). John remarks that his visit to Nigeria in 1994 was like stepping back thirty years to the imprisonment of Awolowo, then the most prominent Yoruba politician. Perhaps the case of Abiola suggested that Yoruba culture still retained its genius for neutralising the religious tensions engulfing Nigeria?

In this context, John noted also the exceptional success of modernising Yoruba Muslim politicians who had made Lagos the best governed of Nigerian states, embracing the Yoruba concept of enlightenment and development, or *olaju*. But here John's examples encountered a problem. His topic was supposed to be the general lessons of Yoruba experience for Nigeria, but his conclusion tended to draw attention to capacities that, on his analysis, Nigerians other than Yoruba lacked. Islamic reformism, as his final contribution to the journal *Africa* argued (2016d), removed the pursuit of well-being from the public sphere and replaced it with a political theology of purification. On this analysis, the country really was held together by little more than its shared dependence on the distribution of oil revenues without which South and North would have little in common.

John's optimism about Yoruba was based in a cultural exceptionalism that made it difficult for him not to be pessimistic about Nigeria, specifically about the capacity for co-existence between its largely Christian South and that part of the North that identified closely with the historic Sokoto Caliphate and had introduced *sharia*. The culminating volume of John's Yoruba religion trilogy explicitly addresses the triple heritage of the Yoruba, which he saw as a privileged case for the comparative sociological study of the historical trajectories of Islam and Christianity. He called his expertise in human and divine studies, history and anthropology, the past and the present into a final synthesis, but the very success of his demonstration of Yoruba uniqueness, which echoed their own sense of collective selfhood, made this a difficult exemplar for the comparative sociology of African religions.

I mentioned earlier how John had consoled me—when I once lamented the various projects I had been unable to pursue for one reason or another—with the observation that all reasonably productive academic careers must have their share of projects not completed. His own abandoned or uncompleted projects seem to have been the comparative ones both within Nigeria and more widely in Africa which some of his essays begin. Rereading so much of his work—and sadly writing an account like this forces one to find the time to reread only when a friend is no longer alive—is, among other emotions, immensely frustrating. I have questions to ask him. Was it John's keen sense of Yoruba exceptionalism that made his comparative projects impossibly challenging? By coincidence, much of my own research has also concerned a predominantly Nigerian people, far less numerous than the Yoruba, who share with them the self-image of being split almost equally between Christians and Muslims, and who have also managed to sink these religious differences by appeal to shared ethnicity. We never finished a conversation about whether the conditions of this identity outcome remaining viable were similar in these two cases. How could he leave in mid-discussion? As our colleague Kit Davies remarked, knowing John none of us imagined death would have the nerve.

*****

John's funeral (he died on 2 November 2015) took place at St Michael's in Highgate Village, North London, on 20 November, London's highest church where he had been a parishioner and usually attended Evensong, in his view the most quintessentially Anglican of church services. Quiet and without bombast: the hymn 'How great thou art' opened the service, 'Thine be the glory, risen, conquering Son' closed it. The speakers and readers included two of his sons (Francis and Tim), his oldest granddaughter (Josie), his closest confidant (Tom McCaskie) and the vicar (Dr Jonathan Trigg). A eulogy and prayer was delivered by Mabel Kemjika who recounted how she had come to Britain from Nigeria after she had looked after the Peel family, forty years earlier, during their two years in Nigeria. She had married and brought up her family here. She did not mention that she had also provided care for John during his last weeks.

John's ashes were interred the following June, while Anne was home from Liberia, close to what locals call 'Marx and Spencer's corner' in Highgate Cemetery, the resting place of the two great Victorian social theorists. The following Saturday (25 June 2016) we held a commemoration at SOAS – 'J. D. Y. Peel: a celebration of life to the full'—designed to share memories of him as theorist, cook, lover of Corelli's Concerti Grossi, walker, Africanist, honorary Yoruba elder and friend. The speakers included former students and colleagues, opening with Robin Horton, the presiding elder, who set the tone by recounting John's apology for being unable to write his obituary as promised. Anne Peel Ogbigbo brought video of the memorial held in Liberia both inside St John's, where John had worshipped, and outside where the masks came to dance for him. Karin Barber read the *Oríkì*, verses of praise, she had composed for him in Yoruba and in translation.

ORÍKÌ FÚN JỌ́Ọ́NÙ
Erin ti wó, kò le dìde.
Àjànàkú sùn bí òkè;
Gbogbo àgbáyé ń sọ̀fọ̀ olùkọ́ òdodo tó ti lọ;
Baba àwọn onímọ̀ ijìnlẹ̀ gbogbo
Olórí àwọn òpìtàn làntì-lanti
Olọ́gbọ́n tí í mú ẹ̀kọ́ wuni.
Ó mọ ilẹ̀ Yorùbá bí ẹni í mowó
Ìwádìí tó ṣe, ijìnlẹ̀ ni
Ó bèèrè lọ́wọ́ ọba, bẹ́ẹ̀ ló bèèrè lọ́wọ́ọ mẹ̀kúnnù
Gbogbo ènìyàn ló ṣe dọ̀gba-dọ́gba
Kò sẹ́ni tí kò mọ̀ ọ́
Bẹ́ẹ̀ ni kò sẹ́ni tí í ṣaláì-yìn ọ̀ láyé
Ìwé tí o kọ kò lópin
Oore tí o ti ṣe kò lónkà.
Bàbá wa, sùn re.

PRAISE POETRY FOR JOHN
The elephant has fallen, and cannot stand up.
The mighty animal sleeps like a mountain;
All the world laments the passing of the true teacher who has gone;
Father of (=Foremost among) all the deeply versed scholars
Leader of all the great historians
Brilliant one who makes others want to study.
He knew Yorubaland as one knows money
The research he did was profound
He enquired of obas, but he also enquired of ordinary people
He treated everyone alike.
There is no-one who does not know you
Likewise no-one who could fail to praise you in this world.
The books you have written are endless
The good turns you have done are uncountable.
Our elder, rest in peace.

Karin (Àjíkẹ́) Barber

To see us out, Paul Richards introduced the andante from Samuel Sebastian Wesley's great anthem 'Ascribe unto the Lord', as a musician himself explaining why andante was the most difficult of tempos to master; neither too fast nor too slow, it needed to move along at a measured walking pace, unhurriedly but purposefully, just as John did through life. The anthem reaches the conclusion that John expressed of himself, 'Ye are the blessed of the Lord, you and your children.'

RICHARD FARDON
Fellow of the Academy

Note. So many tributes to John have been published that it is difficult to add much factually. As well as drawing upon published obituaries (cited below) and some letters of condolence, and guided by Richard Bartholomew's (2016) excellent bibliography (IAI, 2017), I have also used recollections from John's funeral and from the memorial event held at SOAS on 25 June 2016 as 'J. D. Y. Peel: a celebration of life to the full', which include with her kind permission Karin Barber's praise poem. I am grateful to Stephanie Kitchen for the loan of the IAI publication file on John's *Aladura*, as I am to Toyin Falola for a pre-publication copy of John's 2016 Sir Olaniwum Ajayi lecture, and to Olufunke Adeboye and Yetunde Aina for final copy of John's other two Nigerian lectures. I discussed these lectures at the roundtable devoted to John's work at the 2016 Biennial Conference of the African Studies Association UK where I also benefited from hearing other contributors. The Archivists at LSE were as helpful as they always are. Susan Peel Robert, John's sister, has shared family recollections with me and a letter from the time of John's doctoral research. Members of John's immediate family helped me write an earlier, short obituary in ways that are more fully reflected here. I thank Catherine Davies for her careful reading of my final text.

Given the inconsistency in sources, I have retained Yoruba subscripts but omitted tonal superscripts except in Karin's praise poem and where they occur in the original titles in the bibliography.

References to cited works by J. D. Y. Peel

1966. *A Sociological Study of Two Independent Churches among the Yoruba of Nigeria*, University of London PhD thesis, 574pp.

1968 *Aladura: a Religious Movement among the Yoruba* (London), pp. xii + 338.

1971 *Herbert Spencer: the Evolution of a Sociologist* (London and New York; reprinted Aldershot, 1992,) p. 338.

1972 'Introduction' (vii–li), and selection of *Herbert Spencer on Social Evolution* (Chicago; reprinted Chicago, 1982), pp. li + 270.

1976 (with R. Horton) 'Conversion and confusion: a rejoinder on Christianity in Eastern Nigeria', *Canadian Journal of African Studies*, 10, 481–98.

1978 'Olaju: a Yoruba concept of development', *Journal of Development Studies*, 14, 139–65.

1983 *Ijeshas and Nigerians: the Incorporation of a Yoruba Kingdom, 1890s–1970s.* (Cambridge), pp. xiv + 346.

1984 'Making history: the past in the Ijesha present', *Man* (NS), 19, 111–32.

1987 'History, culture and the comparative method: a West African puzzle', in L. Holy (ed.) *Comparative Anthropology* (Oxford), pp. 88–118. Revised version in J. D. Y. Peel, *Christianity, Islam, and Orișa Religion* (2016), pp. 17–37, 236–40.

1989 'The cultural work of Yoruba ethnogenesis', in E. Tonkin, M. McDonald and M. K. Chapman (eds.), *History and Ethnicity* (London), pp. 198–215.

1992 (co-edited with J. F. Ade Ajayi) *People and Empires in African History: Essays in Memory of Michael Crowder* (London, pp. xxv + 254). Also co-author of 'Introduction', pp. xv–xxv.

1993 'Between Crowther and Ajayi: the religious origins of the modern Yoruba intelligentsia', in T. Falola (ed.), *African Historiography: Essays in Honour of Jacob Ade Ajayi* (Harlow and Lagos), pp. 64–79.
2000 *Religious Encounter and the Making of the Yoruba* (Bloomington, IN), pp. xi + 420.
2002 'Christianity and the logic of nationalist assertion in Wole Soyinka's Ìsarà' in D. Maxwell with I. Lawrie (eds.), *Christianity and the African Imagination: Essays in Honour of Adrian Hastings* (Leiden), pp. 127–55.
2008 'Yoruba religion: seeing it in history, seeing it whole', *Orita: Ibadan Journal of Religious Studies* 40: 1–24. Under the same title, Third Ebenezer Adeola Adegbola Memorial Lecture (Ibadan: Institute of Church and Society), 3pp.
2009 'Islam and Christianity through the prism of Yoruba history.' Distinguished Lectures Series. Lagos: Faculty of Arts, University of Lagos, pp. iv + 23.
2015a *Christianity, Islam, and* Oriṣa *Religion: Three Traditions in Comparison and Interaction* (Oakland, CA), pp. 312.
2015b 'J. F. Ade Ajayi: a memorial', *Africa*, 85, 745–9.
2016a *Letters from Liberia* (London).
2016b 'Time and difference in the anthropology of religion', The Frazer Lecture, Oxford, 9 May 2000, *HAU: Journal of Ethnographic Theory*, 6, 531–51.
2016c 'Religion and the future of Nigeria: lessons from the Yorùbá case', lecture on the occasion of the ninetieth birthday of Sir Oláníwúm Ajàyí delivered on 10 April 2015. *Yoruba Studies Review*, 1, 1–18.
2016d 'Similarity and difference, context and tradition, in contemporary religious movements in West Africa', *Africa*, 86, 620–7.

Obituaries of J. D.Y. Peel

Awe, B. (2016) 'J. D. Y. Peel: a tribute', *Africa*, 86, 382–3.
Falola, T. (2016) 'John David Yeadon Peel, 1941–2015', *Africa*, 86, 379–81.
Gifford, P. (2015) Obituaries by SOAS colleagues,
 https://www.soas.ac.uk/news/ newsitem107075.html (accessed 6 January 2017).
Ifeka, C. (2015) 'John Peel', *ROAPE* online,
 http://roape.net/2016/01/09/obituary-john-peel/ (accessed 6 January 2017).
McCaskie, T. (2015) 'John Peel obituary' *The Guardian*, Friday 20 November 2015, https://www.theguardian.com/science/2015/nov/20/john-peel (accessed 6 January 2017).
McCaskie, T. (2016) 'John Peel: a valedictory remembrance', *Africa*, 86, 374–8.
Marchand, T. H. J. (2016) 'J. D. Y. Peel, 1941–2015', Obituaries online, *Royal Anthropological Institute*, 7 January 2016,
 http://www.therai.org.uk/archives-and-manuscripts/obituaries/jdy-peel (accessed 6 January 2017).
Olukotun, A. (2015) Included in his 'Friday musings …' *Punch*, 6 November.
Rathbone, R. (2015) Obituaries by SOAS colleagues,
 https://www.soas.ac.uk/news /newsitem107075.html (accessed 6 January 2017).
The Times (2015) 'John Peel', 30 November.

Bibliography of J. D. Y. Peel

Bartholomew, R. (2016) 'A bibliography of the works of J. D. Y. Peel 1941–2015', *Africa*, 86, 384–400.

IAI (International African Institute) (2017) 'Addendum to "A bibliography of the works of J. D. Y. Peel (1941–2015)"', *Africa*, 87(2), 445.

Other references cited

Adebanwi, W. (2014) *Yorùbá Elites and Ethnic Politics in Nigeria. Ọbáfẹmi Awólọwọ and Corporate Agency* (Cambridge).

Anon (1993) Note on E.A. Peel's will (*The Independent*, 11 June), http://www.independent.co.uk/news/people/wills-1491163.html (accessed 6 January 2017).

Horton, R. (1971) 'African Conversion', *Africa*, 41, 85–108.

McCaskie, T. C. (2005) 'John Peel', in Falola, T. (ed.) *Christianity and Social Change in Africa. Essays in Honor of J. D. Y. Peel* (Durham, NC).

Macrae, D. G. (1974) *Weber* (London).

Peel, E. A. (1971) *The Nature of Adolescent Judgement* (London).

Tomes, J. (2004) 'Peel, Edwin Arthur (1911–1992)', *Oxford Dictionary of National Biography*, http://www.oxforddnb.com/view/article/51279 (accessed 6 January 2017).

JOHN TILEY

John Tiley
1941–2013

JOHN TILEY WAS BORN IN Leamington Spa in Warwickshire on 25 February 1941, the son of William and Audrey Tiley. His exposure to tax came early: his distinguished father was HM Inspector of Taxes for Coventry 1 District.[1]

John attended Winchester College, where he excelled as a scholar but also lived school life to the full—football, cricket, music, astronomy and the Cadet Force reveal the energy and breadth of interest that he would bring to his later life and career. A passion for sport and music would enrich his life.[2]

When he left Winchester in 1959 he went to Lincoln College, Oxford, where in his second year he won the Winter Williams Law Scholarship by prize examination. Rather than choosing to exercise his considerable abilities in practice, either as a solicitor or a barrister, he chose instead to pursue an academic life. After graduation he stayed on at Lincoln College to lecture in law, before leaving to take up a lectureship at the University of Birmingham. In 1964 he married Jillinda Draper, a newly qualified barrister, later academic and Law Fellow of Lucy Cavendish College, Cambridge. Later that year he was called to the Bar by the Inner Temple, to which he was always devoted and subsequently became a bencher. He intermitted his academic career to do a pupillage with Donald Nicholls.

---

[1] When John was honoured with a CBE in 2003, he carried his father's OBE in his pocket, since his father had been unable to collect it personally: J. Tiley, *Revenue Law*, 6th edn. (Oxford, 2008), p. vi.

[2] See D. Hartnett, 'Foreword', in J. Avery Jones, P. Harris and D. Oliver (eds.), *Comparative Perspectives on Revenue Law: Essays in Honour of John Tiley* (Cambridge, 2008), p. xiv.

Biographical Memoirs of Fellows of the British Academy, XVI, 219–235.
Posted 4 May 2017. © The British Academy 2017.

He moved in 1967 to a fellowship at Queens' College, Cambridge, and an assistant lectureship in the University.[3] Cambridge, and Queens', would remain his home for forty-six years until his death. He held most of the college's senior offices including Senior Bursar and Vice-President. His affection for, and pride in, his college was communicated to visiting scholars who were invited to college dinners in all their splendour, and given personally conducted tours of the college.

In 1984 he was appointed Assistant Recorder on the South-Eastern Circuit and in 1989 Recorder, specialising in family law, a post he held for the next decade.

John was a central presence in the life of the Cambridge Law Faculty. In 1990 he was appointed Professor of the Law of Taxation, the first such in the Faculty. In 1992 he was appointed Chairman of the Faculty, and during his three-year term of office he ensured that his contribution to the Law Faculty was even more than an intellectual one. As Chairman, he oversaw the construction of a new Faculty building to foster the Cambridge community of legal scholars, bringing together the Squire Law Library and teaching and staff accommodation fit to see the expanding Law Faculty well into the future. Owing to his vision, energy, commitment and the closest interest in matters of design and functionality, the new building on the Sidgwick site in West Road, designed by Norman Foster and Partners and formally opened by the Queen with the Duke of Edinburgh in 1996, provides a striking and fitting home for the Faculty. Lying at the heart of law teaching and scholarship in Cambridge, it is described as the hub of intellectual life in the Faculty, for its teaching staff, its students and the many visitors from the United Kingdom and abroad.

Having served as the president of the Society of Public Teachers of Law, now the Society of Legal Scholars, in 1995–6, John's next Cambridge project was to found the Centre for Tax Law as a centre for the teaching of, and research into, tax law. This he did in 2000 with the support of the Chartered Institute of Taxation, the International Fiscal Association Congress Trustees and the accountancy firm KPMG. The Centre, which is located within the Law Faculty building, seeks to promote the study of the law of taxation as an intellectual as well as a practical discipline.

John's distinguished contribution to the discipline of tax law was marked by the academic law community and beyond. He was awarded an LLD by Cambridge in 1995. His work in tax law and policy was formally recognised when he was awarded a CBE in 2003 for services to tax law. His

---

[3] Ibid., p. xii.

outstanding contribution to the academic discipline of tax law received its highest accolade when he was admitted as a Fellow of the British Academy in 2008, the same year as his retirement. In 2008 he was awarded a Leverhulme Trust Emeritus Fellowship for a project entitled 'Developing Tax Law'.

Neither work nor honours ceased on his retirement. It was marked by a Festschrift, and the volume of essays in his honour was published in the following year.[4] The distinction of the contributors reflects John's own. The volume was received, in the words of Professor Roger Kerridge, 'with a mixture of awe and sadness. Awe at a life so well spent, and sadness that this phase is over.'[5]

Having been made a life fellow of Queens', to which he was so committed, and Emeritus Professor in the University, in 2009 he was appointed honorary Queen's Counsel, and in 2011 Winchester College received him *Ad Portas*, a practice of recognising exceptional Old Wykehamists and the highest honour the college bestows. He continued to teach, to write and to organise those workshops and conferences so appreciated by the tax community. With his two sons Nicholas and Christopher and his daughter Mary established with careers and children of their own, John continued, with Jillinda, to travel extensively. This was partly facilitated by constant invitations to visit, personally and professionally, colleagues and past students all over the world.

Tax as an academic subject

John Tiley's paramount professional achievement was to establish tax law as an academic discipline, taking its rightful place not only in the curricula of British universities but also as the subject of rigorous analytical research worthy of a place in the scholarship of law. This feat can only be fully appreciated in the context of the orthodox perception of tax law which pervaded the legal system until well into the twentieth century.

Tax is found universally in the modern world. There is no construct that is more influential on the personal and working lives of both individuals and communities, and no one is immune to its effects. As the Bill of

---

[4] J. Avery Jones, P. Harris and D. Oliver (eds.), *Comparative Perspectives on Revenue Law – Essays in Honour of John Tiley* (Cambridge, 2008).
[5] R. Kerridge, 'Publication review – *Comparative Perspectives on Revenue Law – Essays in Honour of John Tiley*, Edited by J. Avery Jones, P. Harris and D. Oliver', *British Tax Review* (2009), 155–8.

Rights in 1689 laid down that there could be no taxation without the consent of the taxpayer, taxes must be expressed in Acts of Parliament in order to ensure parliamentary consent. Tax statutes state the substance and scope of the charge to tax, any exemptions and allowances, and determine how the tax is to be implemented. As it is constitutionally required to be levied only under the authority of statute, tax is unambiguously law, and it could be thought that its age, nature and importance would make it the exemplar of conventional law and process, standing squarely within the legal system and subject to its values, standards and safeguards. This was, however, not so. Tax law differed from the orthodox model, and in various ways it stood outside the norms of the legal system in the key elements of that structure.

Its prominent constitutional underpinning in parliamentary consent and the liberty of the subject was the first way in which tax law stood apart from other branches of law. It gave it a special nature savouring of public affairs and fundamental rights, with an immensely strong political context and constitutional basis not shared by other branches of law, and was even characterised by a special parliamentary procedure applicable only to such legislation. This public character was generally unfamiliar to the majority of those involved in the practice of law who were in their daily lives more concerned with the private law of property, contract, wills and trusts, and domestic relations between individuals. Secondly, the principle of consent required the charge to tax to be stated as clearly and unambiguously as possible, to ensure that taxpayers were charged only by express and clear words in the legislation. Because of this requirement, and the increasingly technical nature of the subject matter, tax statutes were exceptionally lengthy and highly complex, and necessitated the strictest interpretative approaches by the judiciary. Unlike other branches of law, however, tax law had remarkably little judge-made law, and this constituted a third distinction from other branches of law. For policy reasons, appeals to the regular courts were denied in relation to the direct taxes until the late nineteenth century. Instead appeals were only permitted outside the cadre of professional judges and the resolution of disputes was dominated by untrained lay adjudicators. Not only did this mean that judges only exceptionally had the opportunity to interpret tax statutes, it gave a prominent and enduring role to the executive in the interpretation of tax statutes in the first instance. The level of bureaucratic involvement constitutes the fourth and unique feature of tax law. The complexity of tax law led to its administration by a highly specialised bureaucracy that, in its exclusive understanding of it, and its appreciation of pressing political and economic demands, came to dominate tax law. Furthermore, the implementation of tax law by tribunals possessing an admixture of administrative and judicial functions, and the powerful influence of the officers of the revenue department of the executive, led to its perception as administrative regulation rather than law, and of the issues coming before tax tribunals not as legal issues, but as factual issues of finance and accounting. The intimate relationship between tax law, its implementation and the imperatives of the executive obscured boundaries which were clear in other branches of law.

These four characteristics set tax law apart from other branches of English law to the extent that it was not seen as law in the generally accepted sense of the term. Its perception as part administration, part accountancy and only part law was firmly embedded in British legal culture from the nineteenth century. This equivocal position within the orthodox legal system resulted in the isolation of tax law. This isolation was exacerbated by a certain passivity in regular judicial and legal circles, an unwillingness to get involved with tax. This was partly for all the reasons above, but also because tax law required some specialist accounting knowledge with which, traditionally, lawyers were not comfortable. This not only alienated lawyers from the subject, it also left open an opportunity for accountants to dominate the field, and this they grasped. This further marginalised tax law within the legal establishment and contributed to the inaccessibility of tax law to taxpayers, legal professionals and students of law.

Sitting in this way outside the norms of the legal system in its key elements, at best perceived as distinct from other branches of English law, and at worst as not law at all, tax was not embraced within the academic study of law in Britain. It is this deep-seated perception which John Tiley recognised when he began his career in the mid-1960s. His professional challenge, to which he devoted his academic career, was to bring tax into the mainstream of academic law. John was well aware of the insularity of tax law. He wrote:

> Avoiding a feeling of isolation is important for the good of the academic. Dialogue can be particularly useful with those who find tax materials interesting for their own research, e.g. in jurisprudence and legal reasoning. Tax should be at the forefront of the minds of our political philosophers as the area where their theories can be tested yet, perhaps, because of the reputation our subject has for technicalities, few of them appreciate this.[6]

---

[6] J. Tiley, '50 years: tax, law and academia', *British Tax Review* (2006), 238.

Developing the vision of Professor Ash Wheatcroft, he created and ensured the place of tax law as a field of academic study.[7] He did so in three ways: through his scholarship; through his teaching; and through his leadership.

Scholarship

First, John led by example and grew academic scholarship in tax. He wrote what has become a classic of tax law texts, *Revenue Law*, distinctive on any law library shelf not only by its size but also by the striking colours of the cover, famously chosen by his children and then his grandchildren. The first edition of this majestic work appeared in 1976,[8] when John was a young lecturer at Cambridge, and at the time of his death was in its seventh edition. It was published, from 2000, by Richard Hart. For the fifth and sixth editions John worked with one of his past students, Glen Loutzenhiser, who went on to co-author the seventh edition with him. Thanks to him, John's work lives on, with Dr Loutzenhiser having in 2016 produced the eighth edition.[9] Entitled *Tiley's Revenue Law*, it takes its place in the mould of the classics of English law texts known by their author's name.

Tax texts before *Revenue Law* had almost invariably followed the traditional pattern of stating the legal rules applicable to the taxes in question, often in the form of merely a brief comment on the statutory provision just stated, in exhaustive detail, with a consideration of any relevant judicial decisions and possibly with some calculations where appropriate. The content was rarely contextualised, with the purpose of taxation, the history of its legal framework, wider influences of economics or politics, and the nature of United Kingdom tax law as compared with that of other jurisdictions rarely if ever discussed. This style reflected the status of tax law as the province almost exclusively of tax practitioners; in other words, it accurately reflected the perceived place of tax law on the margins of academic law.

When *Revenue Law* appeared, therefore, it was a revelation. John's approach maintained a rigorous doctrinal core, covering the principal taxes, namely income tax, capital gains tax, corporation tax and inheritance

---

[7] On Wheatcroft, see J. F. Avery Jones, 'Ashcroft, George Shorrock Ashcombe (1905–1987)', *Oxford Dictionary of National Biography*, http://www.oxforddnb.com/view/article/20102 (accessed 11 January 2017).
[8] J. Tiley, *Revenue Law* (London, 1976).
[9] G. Loutzenhiser, *Tiley's Revenue Law*, 8th edn. (Oxford, 2016).

tax. From its first edition it addressed international matters and, increasingly, the impact of European law. For the first time, however, it contextualised tax law within the wider principles of law, and drew on history, economics and political theory, as well as revenue practice, all the time grounding the doctrinal study in an appreciation of underlying policy considerations. Furthermore, he never neglected a comparative perspective when he thought it would be illuminating. His belief in the value of this was confirmed in the titles of both his inaugural lecture,[10] and that of the volume published in his honour on his retirement.[11] He was also more open to the writings of academics in journals and cited such legal literature extensively. *Revenue Law* was continually updated, no small task in view of the technicality and dynamic nature of tax law, but it retained the basic structure which had served him—and its readers—so well, and he ensured that the underlying and largely unchanging principles of tax law formed the core of the book.

It was, nevertheless, a battle to remain true to this intellectual ideal of an academic tax law text for students of the discipline. In the early 1980s, at the time a fourth edition was due, John's vision for the exposition of tax law would take what in his view would be a retrograde step—to turn *Revenue Law* into a book for practitioners. As a result, the more practical and technical topics in the third edition of the text were extracted and developed into *Butterworth's UK Tax Guide*, from 1998 entitled *Tiley and Collison's UK Tax Guide*, and marking the beginning of an eleven-year collaboration with David Collison.[12] It soon found its place as an annual publication, primarily for practitioners, addressing new legal developments, and is now in its thirty-fourth edition.[13] Again, the contextual material which constituted the hallmark of the original text was for a while cast into a separate *Policy Supplement* to be used with the practitioners' guide, but it was soon understood that this marginalised the key element of the text which made it such an effective and valuable work for students of tax law.[14]

In terms of structure and content, *Revenue Law* reached its apotheosis in its fourth edition, published in 2000 by Richard Hart some nineteen

---

[10] J. Tiley, 'The law of taxation in a European environment', *Cambridge Law Journal*, 51 (1992), 451–73.
[11] Jones, Harris and Oliver, *Comparative Perspectives on Revenue Law – Essays in Honour of John Tiley*.
[12] See D. Collison, 'Professor John Tiley; lives remembered', *The Times* (10 July 2013), p. 47.
[13] X. M. Manzano and K. Gordon (eds.), *Tiley & Collison's UK Tax Guide 2016–17*, 34th edition (London, 2016).
[14] R. Kerridge, 'Publication review, *Revenue Law* by John Tiley', *British Tax Review* (2001), 283–7.

years after the previous edition and reuniting in a work of substantial size the doctrinal, contextual and—where appropriate—the practical. John acknowledged the great generosity of the first publishers, Butterworths, who allowed him freely to use the material from the earlier text. Its reviewer, Professor Roger Kerridge, described it as 'a truly outstanding book, a monumental work, one which should be welcomed back with loud rejoicings by all those who are interested in tax law as an academic discipline'.[15]

Writing a tax law text book is a daunting task. In no other area of law are there annual statutes to be incorporated and explained, the consequences foreseen and elucidated, the ever-present danger of a sudden and often unforeseen abolition of sometimes extensive parts of the subject matter, major politically driven initiatives such as the Tax Law Rewrite Project initiated in 1997,[16] the unrelenting growth of the subject in terms of volume and complexity and the need to master it all to the high degree needed to explain it as simply, clearly and accurately as possible.

As always in tax law, periods of transition from one code to another pose particular problems for all students and practitioners of tax, and succinct explanation, analysis and guidance are essential. As the work of the Tax Law Rewrite Project led to a recasting of the income tax legislation, so the successive editions addressed the changes in their full legislative context, beginning with the comprehensive guidance in relation to the new Capital Allowances Act 2001, the Income Tax (Earnings and Pensions) Act 2003 and the Income Tax (Trading and Other Income) Act 2005 in the fifth and sixth editions. The seventh edition, which appeared after an interval of four years, saw the first major restructuring of the work. The bulk and nature of the material had grown to such an extent that the decision was taken to make the principal taxes of the United Kingdom the focus, and to address a number of other matters in a new and discrete text. Corporation tax, the examination of international and European matters and the taxation of savings were accordingly moved to form the basis of *Advanced Topics in Revenue Law*.[17]

While *Revenue Law* and its cognate publications formed the core of John's work and the basis of his reputation across every sector of the tax community of students, academics and practitioners, he refined many of his ideas in a body of scholarship published in the form of discrete articles.

---

[15] For the history of the text, see ibid.
[16] John was a member of the Steering Committee.
[17] The eighth edition, published in 2016, reunited the material in one text.

These, he said, were a 'sideline'.[18] They were published principally in the *British Tax Review*, the *Cambridge Law Journal* and editions of collected essays, and tended to reflect his own particular interests. He published extensively on the subject of tax avoidance,[19] and contributed materially, and with insight,[20] to the adoption by the United Kingdom government of a general anti-abuse rule through his academic writing and his membership of an advisory body established to consider that issue. Tax avoidance figured most strongly in John's publication portfolio partly because it was an ideal candidate for comparative analysis since, unlike many Common Law jurisdictions, the United Kingdom had no statutory anti-abuse provision, preferring a judicial doctrine. He also explored the taxation of the family,[21] estate duty and then inheritance tax, capital gains tax and tax issues in employment law, and wrote on European and international tax perspectives. His substantive articles were supported by masterly case comments and analyses on all the major developments in tax law as they occurred, published over some thirty years in the *British Tax Review* and the *Cambridge Law Journal*. John also contributed regularly to the *All England Law Reports Annual Review*, indeed he did so every year from 1985 to 2012. This work played to his skills and he was a master of the genre—acute, insightful, detailed, knowledgeable and accessible analyses of the court decisions in tax of the year, and expressly intended to bring together the academic and the practical. And all were leavened by the sparkle of irreverence, wit and anecdote.

This body of published work covered the whole spectrum of tax law—its doctrine, history, policy and practice. Neither did John neglect law outside tax. Demonstrating the breadth of his legal expertise, he published in the field of the law of torts, family law and property law, and as early as 1968 wrote *A Casebook on Equity and Succession*.[22]

---

[18] Tiley, '50 years: tax, law and academia', 246.

[19] For example, J. Tiley, 'An academic perspective on the Ramsay/Dawson doctrine', in J. Dyson (ed.), *Recent Tax Problems* (London, 1985), p. 19; J. Tiley, 'Judicial anti-avoidance doctrines: the U.S. alternatives', *British Tax Review* (1987), 180–97, 220–44; J. Tiley, 'Judicial anti-avoidance doctrines: some problem areas', *British Tax Review* (1988), 63–103; J. Tiley, 'Judicial anti-avoidance doctrines: Part 3 – corporations and conclusions', *British Tax Review* (1988), 108–45; J. Tiley, 'Tax avoidance jurisprudence as normal law', *British Tax Review* (2004), 304–31.

[20] J. Freedman, 'Editorial: Professor John Tiley CBE QC (Hon) FBA 1941–2013: an appreciation', *British Tax Review* (2015), 2.

[21] For example, J. Tiley, 'Tax, marriage and the family', *Cambridge Law Journal*, 65 (2006), 289–300.

[22] J. Tiley, *A Casebook on Equity and Succession* (London, 1968).

Teaching

The second way in which John ensured the place of tax law as a field of academic study was through his teaching. He had a clear notion as to the form it should take, a notion which encapsulated his entire approach to tax law. It should, he said, 'be broad and demanding'.[23]

> First and foremost there must be technical competence with a good grasp of the primary sources. That competence can be tested in many ways ranging from elementary computation to planning transactions. However the tax student must go more broadly than technical competence in the current materials. Our subject moves so fast that a failure to understand why things change or have changed or may change in the future will produce someone who has been trained rather than educated, a monkey rather than a Socrates...[24]

Believing that tax law should be taught to undergraduate and not just postgraduate law students, he taught the subject to both cohorts for some thirty years.[25] At Cambridge the Faculty attracted the best young minds to take his courses. He valued the teaching of his subject, believing utterly, as Lord Falconer observed, in the educational value of law,[26] and he was a dedicated, popular, caring and sensitive lecturer and supervisor. Teaching and, above all, inspiring generations of students, his influence was immense. As one distinguished past student observed, 'I am not certain how the tax profession in this country (and sometimes elsewhere) would have fared were it not for the introduction we received in John's rooms in Queens'. We all owe him an immense debt of gratitude.'[27]

Though believing that the teaching of tax law had already achieved 'full academic recognition',[28] he was never complacent.[29] He echoed widespread concerns as to the place of tax law as a university subject. When the fourth edition of *Revenue Law* appeared, he wrote that 'tax is seen to be trying to make a more substantial presence in law curricula', but the qualification was significant. In an article to mark fifty years of the *British Tax Review*, he wrote that '[t]here is much that is good and successful but

---

[23] J. Tiley, 'Preface', *Revenue Law,* 4th edn., reproduced in part in J. Tiley, *Revenue Law,* 6th edn. (Oxford, 2008), pp. vi–vii.
[24] Ibid.
[25] Originally he taught family law in Cambridge.
[26] Lord Falconer of Thoroton, 'Address: Professor John Tiley, Fellow 1967–2013', *Queens' College Record* (2014), https://issuu.com/jw463/docs/queens__college_record_2014 (accessed 5 November 2016).
[27] P. Baker, 'An additional appreciation', *British Tax Review* (2015), 4–5.
[28] Tiley, '50 years: tax, law and academia', 230.
[29] Ibid.

also much that could be better; we must avoid complacency without succumbing to despair'.[30] Some commentators felt that the last decade of the twentieth century had seen a decline in tax teaching, with the impetus and progress resulting from the efforts of Ash Wheatcroft at the London School of Economics in the 1950s petering out by the 1980s. And so powerful was the influence of John's *Revenue Law* text that the absence of an updated edition for nearly twenty years between the third and the fourth was regarded as a material check to the development of tax law as an academic discipline in Britain.[31] It was, indeed, 'both a symptom and a cause' of the decline.[32] The interval between editions was thought to be due to the undermining influence of the persistent perception of tax law as the province of practice rather than academe.

So important was the teaching of tax law to John's vision of its place as an academic subject that he was not content merely to do it, nor to accept that it had achieved the recognition that Wheatcroft had sought, but strove to secure it. With his usual energy and commitment he aimed to increase the number of tax academics in British universities. He fought, successfully, for new funding to support a lectureship in tax law at Cambridge from KPMG, a new tax chair at Oxford and bursaries for postgraduate research. This at least ensured robust teaching of tax law at those institutions, and raised the profile of tax law to promote it as part of the curricula of other British universities.

Leadership

Many, indeed most, academic lawyers would have regarded a career of sustained scholarship and teaching of such breadth, depth and quality as singularly successful. John, however, achieved yet more. It was—thirdly—as an outstanding leader of the tax community that he ensured the place of tax law as an academic discipline.

Through his teaching and his writing, John forged relationships with tax practitioners and academic tax lawyers all over the world, many of them of considerable distinction. In his capacity as visiting professor in Australia, Canada, the United States of America, New Zealand and France he created a network of tax lawyers which stretched across the

---

[30] Ibid.
[31] Kerridge, 'Publication review, *Revenue Law* by John Tiley', 283.
[32] Ibid., 284.

Common Law world and beyond. His voice, and accordingly that of United Kingdom tax law, was heard on the European stage through the European Association of Tax Law Professors, of which he was a founding member. He sustained these relationships and thereby energised the tax community. Nowhere was this better reflected than in the tax workshops he held on a monthly basis at the Centre for Tax Law at Cambridge which he founded in 2000 to encourage tax law scholarship through the organisation of conferences, discussion groups and workshops, and the Cambridge Tax Law Series published by Cambridge University Press. The monthly workshops at Queens' College—perhaps inspired by Wheatcroft's monthly seminars in the 1960s at the London School of Economics— brought together academic tax lawyers from the United Kingdom and other jurisdictions, Treasury officials and colleagues from HM Revenue and Customs. Bringing together legal theory and the practice of tax on topical issues in tax law and policy across a range of jurisdictions, the discussion was often provocative, invariably lively, erudite and practical, and—as with all John's conferences—liberally endowed with laughter and friendly collegiality. Only through his own standing in the international community of tax could he attract participants and speakers of such calibre. And never a session went by without a participant reminding us that he or she had been taught, at some point, by John.

John's belief in progression through discussion and debate, through bringing together all parts of the profession of tax in a congenial setting not only to address the sense of isolation that many tax academics felt but also better to integrate the discipline within academe, would form the guiding ethos of the Centre for Tax Law. The Centre now expressly promotes the study of tax by early career researchers, postgraduates and undergraduates, and supports this by an annual conference on tax law and policy. Another aim is to encourage discussion with other lawyers and university scholars on taxation topics, which is supported by a Tax Discussion Group and occasional seminars.

Not only did John organise group events, he was equally interested in and immensely supportive of colleagues as individuals, at every stage of their careers, in his own university and in other institutions. He facilitated research visits of days, weeks or even years to Cambridge, and supported more permanent positions. His generous willingness to act as referee for academic funding applications and for book proposals, and his acute anonymous—and always constructive—reviewing of articles submitted for publication or presentation, were invaluable to the individuals concerned who will always remain indebted to him.

The history of tax law

John's entire approach to tax law, and that which made him a pioneer in his field, is that he appreciated that for it to take its full and deserved place as an academic discipline it had to break with the orthodoxy of tax writing in the first half of the twentieth century and develop a young field of law by placing it in its full context. He was not an interdisciplinary scholar—he was a doctrinal lawyer and master of his subject. But what he profoundly understood was that intellectual isolation denied tax law the opportunity to flourish as an academic discipline. He knew that a complete understanding of that subject could only be achieved if it was set in its broad legislative, practical and international context. In his work he drew on different disciplines and their sources to explain the nature and place of tax law, an approach that Professor Judith Freedman has described as 'the epitome of the "hybrid methodology"'.[33] A major context, the historical, forms another chapter in John's writing where he challenged the insularity of tax law and made yet another material contribution to its status as an academic discipline. His contribution to the legal history of tax is the least written about, and arguably the most pioneering, aspect of his work. This was a field which, until very recently, was the province of a handful of scholars, sitting uncomfortably in pure (and to some extent, legal) history owing to its highly technical nature, and eschewed by pure law for the same reasons that excluded it from orthodox law curricula. Were it not for individual enlightened editors of the *British Tax Review* in the last quarter of the twentieth century—notably John Avery Jones, David Oliver, Erica Stary and, later, Judith Freedman—scholarly work in the legal history of tax would have reached a very small audience indeed.

Adopting the view which pervaded his approach to tax law, and just as he encouraged his students to range widely across disciplines in their attendance at lectures according to interest, so he understood the value of legal history in establishing tax law as an academic discipline. John had been taught and mentored by A. W. Brian Simpson, one of the greatest legal historians of his generation,[34] as a student at Oxford, and indeed he had himself taught the subject at Birmingham at the beginning of his

---

[33] J. Freedman, 'Establishing the foundations of tax law in UK Universities' in Jones, Harris and Oliver, *Comparative Perspectives on Revenue Law – Essays in Honour of John Tiley*, p. 290.
[34] On Simpson, see C. McCrudden, 'Alfred William Brian Simpson 1931–2011', *Biographical Memoirs of Fellows of the British Academy*, 11 (Oxford, 2012), pp. 547–81.

academic career. John saw that the history of tax law transcended even the fundamental role of tax in the constitution, being 'so much more ... than the execution of kings or other seventeenth century struggles'.[35] Governments needed to learn: 'one lesson from history', he wrote, 'is that it can save us from reinventing the wheel. Another lesson, no less important, is to know when not to change the wheel.'[36] The story of tax law needed to be studied and recorded, in its full richness, depth and rigour, and the Tax Rewrite Project made that need all the more urgent. Only through its history could the purposes, nature and substantive doctrine of tax law be properly understood. Fundamental concepts and institutions in tax—from the definition of income (or absence of it) to the jurisdiction of tax tribunals—could only be explained historically, and only historically could patterns of change and development be discerned. Such studies involved the bread and butter of tax lawyers, namely such matters as legislative drafting, statutory interpretation, bureaucratic administration and the practicalities of the implementation of a tax. And it would inevitably require the exploration of the social, political and wider legal context of such issues. John saw, too, that the converse was true. Not only would such research enable tax lawyers to grasp the essentials of their subject, it would open tax law to wider academic scholarship. It would lead to a recognition that tax law could inform and illuminate other discourses in history, social policy, politics and government.

Seizing the challenge and the opportunity, John sought to encourage work on the history of tax by establishing the Cambridge Tax Law History Conference in 2002. It was begun under the auspices of the Centre for Tax Law which John had founded two years before. This conference has become a biennial fixture for all academic and practising tax lawyers with an interest in the legal history of tax. The conference attracts academic tax lawyers from many different jurisdictions, as well as historians, accountants and economists, whether postgraduate students, early career researchers, established scholars or retired colleagues, and invariably includes colleagues from HM Revenue and Customs. It is widely accepted by participants that it is one of the most inclusive, friendly, enjoyable, eclectic and stimulating conferences in the calendar of academic conferences in both tax and legal history. Through the good offices of Jillinda Tiley, the conference is held at Lucy Cavendish College. John was particularly keen to ensure that the numbers did not grow beyond the accom-

---

[35] J. Tiley, 'Preface', *Studies in the History of Tax Law*, 1 (Oxford, 2004), p. vii.
[36] J. Tiley, 'Editorial, tax law history forum', *British Tax Review* (2007), 210.

modation offered by the main meeting room in the college—namely forty—to maintain its informal and supportive ethos, and this is being continued by Professor Peter Harris, John's friend and colleague for over a decade, and Dr Dominic de Cogan who, in the testing circumstances of John's death, and with the gratitude of the tax history community, took upon themselves the task of continuing with the conference.

John eloquently and perfectly evoked the spirit of the conference:

> Over two perfect English September days in 2002, a group of some 40 interested people gathered together for the first Tax Law History Conference ... Our days were passed in the beautiful surroundings of Lucy Cavendish College and the air was heavy with the scents of a Cambridge Edwardian garden in late summer. No less perfect and no less intoxicating were the technical discussions as we sat and listened to the speakers and talked among ourselves.[37]

It was a founding principle of the conference that papers would not be restricted to a theme,[38] and this has been continued to this day. As a result, the presentations are diverse, reflecting a range of historical periods, topics, sources and, indeed, disciplines. They address both the substantive doctrine of tax law (the primary purpose of the conference programme) and the more general history of taxation (a study with a longer academic pedigree). The first volume set the tone: from the sixteenth century to the twentieth; from Tudor estate planning to Victorian tax tribunals; from Britain to Australia via Israel and Hong Kong. John himself contributed to the first conference, with a presentation on the taxation of imputed income from land. Over the next ten years, a wide range of taxes was considered from a variety of perspectives—stamp duty, income tax, capital gains tax, estate duty, excess profits tax, excise duties, poll taxes, the danegeld and the land tax, and, occupying a borderline region, tithes. The perspectives adopted were equally diverse—often doctrinal, as in examinations of the concept of total income, or the remittance basis for foreign income and the taxation of charities, but also philosophical, as with the model of taxation in the age of enlightenment and the influence of Montesquieu; social, as with the development of the tax professions or the impact of the window tax on public health; biographical, as with a study of Edwin Seligman, indicating what is set to be a growing field. The ethos was not merely interdisciplinary but international. Tax treaties, for example, provided a fruitful subject of discourse, but the domestic taxes of individual jurisdictions were increasingly the subject of presentations.

---

[37] Tiley, *Studies in the History of Tax Law*, p. vii.
[38] Although within each published volume the papers are grouped by theme.

The United States, Canada, the Netherlands, France, Germany, Algeria, Malta, New Zealand and China were in due course added to the jurisdictions explored. The sources upon which these papers were based were rich and varied. John's preoccupation, however, was how much there was to be done, in the history of tax as in the establishing of tax as an academic subject. For example, and though this is an aspect yet to be presented to the conference, he even saw the importance of oral history in the record of the history of tax.[39] As he said, 'if the technique is sound for social history it must also be valid for the institutional and technical history of our subject'.[40]

From the beginning, the conference proceedings were published as fully formed academic pieces, in a volume after each conference and edited by John. The *Studies in the History of Tax Law* have found a unique place within the discipline, supported from their inception by Richard Hart. John died as the sixth volume was going to press. The publisher wrote on that occasion that John 'was immensely proud of this series, which will remain a monument to his energy, vision and passion for tax law and scholarly enquiry more generally'.[41] On behalf of all the contributors, John Avery Jones wrote that 'we shall remember him for his inspiration and encouragement of the study of the history of tax law in organising these conferences and the volumes that record them'.[42]

Epilogue

The circumstances of John Tiley's tragic and untimely death on 30 June 2013 at the age of seventy-two remain utterly baffling to all who knew him. The shock and pain of his passing was felt beyond his close and devastated family, and affected the entire tax community in this country and across the world. For those fortunate enough to have known John, he was a warm, welcoming, wise, loyal and valued colleague. He had the rare gift of making us all feel we were his friend, and he inspired not just respect, but loyalty and affection. But his influence will be felt beyond this generation. He was, as Lord Falconer described him in his memorial address, 'a giant in academic law, a pioneer and transformer in the study

---

[39] J. Tiley, 'Preface', *Studies in the History of Tax Law*, 1, p. vii.
[40] Ibid.; Tiley, 'Editorial, tax law history forum', 210.
[41] J. Tiley (ed.), *Studies in the History of Tax Law*, 6 (Oxford, 2013), p. vi.
[42] J. Avery Jones in ibid., p. vii.

of Revenue Law'.[43] His immense scholarship reflecting his powerful intellect, his energy, enthusiasm and geniality, made him not only one of the leading tax lawyers of his generation, but a driving and uniting force in the world of tax law. As a committed and inspirational teacher, a superb communicator, an outstanding scholar and a visionary leader in his discipline, his influence on the national and international community was immense—on the career paths of individuals, both in practice and in academia, on individuals' approach to tax law and, above all, on creating and maintaining tax law as a true academic discipline. Just as Joseph Schumpeter had demonstrated that tax was the prism through which the essential values of any society are distinguished and revealed, so John demonstrated that the true nature of tax could only be discerned through a material engagement with the imperatives leading to its final legal expression, and its interaction with other disciplines thereafter. Isolation and independence, however, are distinct. Much as John valued the contextual approach, he did not allow economics, accountancy, history, sociology or political theory to dominate or threaten the independence and integrity of tax law. It was this unique holistic approach to tax which made John the author of tax law as an academic discipline.

CHANTAL STEBBINGS
University of Exeter

Note. I am indebted to Mrs Jillinda Tiley and Dr John Avery Jones CBE for their comments on the memoir while in draft form, and to the written tributes of many individuals at the time of John's death, notably Lord Falconer of Thoroton and Professor Ellis Ferran at the memorial service for John in Queens' College Chapel,[44] and Professor Judith Freedman.[45]

---

[43] Lord Falconer of Thoroton, 'Address: Professor John Tiley, Fellow 1967–2013', *Queens' College Record* (2014), https://issuu.com/jw463/docs/queens__college_record_2014 (accessed 5 November 2016).
[44] Ibid.
[45] J. Freedman, 'Editorial: Professor John Tiley CBE QC (Hon) FBA 1941–2013: an appreciation', *British Tax Review* (2015), 1–4 at 2.

CHRISTOPHER NUGENT LAWRENCE BROOKE

Christopher Nugent Lawrence Brooke
1927–2015[1]

I: Introduction

PROFESSOR CHRISTOPHER BROOKE, who died on 27 December 2015 aged eighty-eight, was one of the most prolific and influential medieval historians of the past seventy years. He held the title of professor for nearly sixty years, which may well be a record: he obtained his first Chair at the age of twenty-nine, at Liverpool, and later taught at Westfield College, London, and at Cambridge. The time-span of his publications was even longer, for he published his first article (jointly with his father) in 1944, and he remained active in scholarship to the end. At a time when the writing of medieval history has increasingly become dominated by ever more specialised monographs, Christopher Brooke demonstrated the importance of reaching out to a wider audience by way of well-illustrated surveys and much-used textbooks, although he was also a master of exact scholarship, with an especial penchant for the editing of Latin texts. His very successful *From Alfred to Henry III*, published when he was thirty-two years old, had the great virtue of looking at England both before and after 1066.[2] *Europe in the Central Middle Ages* displaced a standard account of the same period written by his own father; but it amply reflected a broadening in the study of the period beyond the popes and emperors who had dominated earlier

---

[1] Parts I, II and V of this memoir were written by David Abulafia, Part III by Henry Mayr-Harting and Part IV by David Luscombe.
[2] References to all the works written or edited by Christopher Brooke that are mentioned in the text can be found at the end of this memoir; the footnotes mainly concern items by other authors, although some specific references to pages in works by CNLB are included.

writing to take in the social and economic history of Europe. In *The Twelfth-Century Renaissance* he made sensitive use of literary texts, dwelling with obvious approval on the tolerant world view of the great German poet Wolfram von Eschenbach, author of *Parzival*.

He wrote elegantly and clearly, resisting the invasion of jargon; and he was not much interested in what is grandly called 'theory', recognising much of it as the recycling of old ideas in highly ornamented new clothes. Sometimes, indeed, he wanted to tell a story, for example about Héloise and Abelard; but the analysis that accompanied the story was beautifully expressed and rich in insights. Yet he was perfectly open to new developments in the writing about the Middle Ages pioneered by such historians as Georges Duby in France, as can be seen in his book *The Medieval Idea of Marriage*; and he was greatly respected in Italy. His profound sense of place was expressed not just in his writings about Cambridge but in the history of medieval London he co-authored with Gillian Keir during his Westfield days.

He also demonstrated that medieval historians need not be confined, as has so often been the case, either to British or to European history, and that they have to take into account visual evidence as well as the texts of which he himself was so fond: illuminated manuscripts, architecture, archaeological remains. This might sound obvious today, but was much less so when the stern tradition of German medieval scholarship guided students towards the technicalities of charters and chronicles, sometimes barely moving beyond the intricacies of the documents themselves. Yet he was also an outstanding editor of texts, serving as one of the editors of *Nelson's* (later, *Oxford*) *Medieval Texts*; his own editions of the letters of Gilbert Foliot (a famous figure in the Becket controversy) and of the great scholar John of Salisbury established standards that were rightly hard to follow.

To cap all this, he was a prolific historian of other periods as well, with a book about Jane Austen and her era to his credit, as well as a series of studies of the medieval and modern history of Cambridge University, which was his first and his last home. When he was elected Dixie Professor of Ecclesiastical History at Cambridge in 1977 he was aware that his was one of the few Cambridge chairs tied to a college Fellowship, in this case at Emmanuel; but he was also entitled to return to his beloved Caius as an ex-Fellow, which he did. He greatly softened the blow to Emmanuel by graciously offering to write a new history of that college, which followed on from a perceptive history of Gonville and Caius that navigated diplomatically through some of the crises and conflicts of the twentieth-century college. He was also an active Fellow of the British Academy, having been elected in 1970, and he served as President of the Society of Antiquaries in 1981–4; he was awarded the CBE in 1995. He was particularly proud of the innovation he introduced as President of the Ecclesiastical History Society: that each annual conference should have a particular theme, so that out of them came not random miscellanies but volumes of proceedings that possessed overall unity.

He was a handsome man, with a rather slight figure and an intense stare that, far from being intimidating, was inquisitive and welcoming. His care for his students and younger colleagues at the three universities where he taught was legendary; he was generous with books and advice, but he also knew when to stand back and let younger historians do things their own way. He kept an eye on them during their careers, and, if their children should happen to come up to Cambridge, he welcomed the next generation too to his sixteenth-century room in Gonville and Caius College, plying them with generous glasses of amontillado. Although he was deeply immersed in the three universities where he taught, he enjoyed escaping to his house at Ulpha in the Lake District. There he and his wife Rosalind could find the time, space and peace to write and to take delight in one another's company.

This memoir is built around his early life in Cambridge, his period at Liverpool, his output as a scholar and his return to Cambridge via London. The account of Cambridge necessarily lays emphasis on his sense of belonging to his college and to the university, which was such an important part of his identity—one might almost say his birthright. Moreover, this memoir can only attempt to capture some aspects of the life and career of a historian who had an extraordinary range of interests and, correspondingly, exercised enormous influence on the world of scholarship.

II: The Cambridge years, 1927–56

Fortunately Christopher Brooke's early life can be traced in some detail, since when he was about eighty years old he wrote an account of it for the college annual record, *The Caian*, entitled 'Memories of Caius'. There he admitted that his memory might sometimes be at fault ('I must emphasise at the outset, as a historian the fallibility of human memory'); but it is the best source that we have, and will be used extensively here.[3] Christopher

---

[3] C. N. L. Brooke, 'Memories of Caius', *The Caian: the Annual Record of Gonville and Caius College Cambridge*, 1 October 2007–30 September 2008, 123–39.

Nugent Lawrence Brooke was born on 23 June 1927; his father, Zachary Nugent Brooke (1883–1946), was himself a Lecturer in, and later Professor of, Medieval History at Cambridge and a Fellow of Caius.[4] Zachary Brooke had been educated at St John's College, Cambridge, and in 1908, at the start of his own career, he had had doubts about the offer of a Fellowship at a college that did not, at that time, have the special reputation in History that was to develop very much later. In fact, the Brooke family had longstanding family links with St John's: an earlier Zachary Brooke, Z. N.'s great-great-grandfather, had been born in 1715 or 1716, became Lady Margaret Professor of Divinity at Cambridge, and served as a chaplain to King George II. The entry in the *Oxford Dictionary of National Biography* notes that this Zachary 'delivered sermons of remarkable complacency' before his royal patron; then, when he became Lady Margaret Professor he gave no lectures, although this was considered the normal way to profess (or not to profess)—the painfully frank author of the entry being none other than C. N. L. Brooke.[5]

Z. N. Brooke became a pillar of his new college. The impression he leaves is of a serious-minded, somewhat stern individual, and his sense of dedication to his work was certainly inherited by all three sons, Michael (born in 1921), Nicholas (1924) and finally Christopher.[6] Z. N. Brooke had married the daughter of A. H. Stanton, rector of Hambleden, Henley-on-Thames, in 1919; she had nursed him through a bout of trench fever during the Great War, in which he served for four years, rising to the rank of captain. On her mother's side she was a Cripps; and her cousin rose to fame as Sir Stafford Cripps, the Labour politician. Christopher was baptised in Caius chapel on 2 August 1927; since there was no font in what had been for centuries a celibate community, the priest who officiated, his grandfather Herbert Stanton, made use of the Master's rosebowl. With such a background, Christopher possessed a sense of his connection to the college, of belonging, that none of its other alumni could match.

---

[4] M. D. Knowles and H. C. G. Matthew, 'Brooke, Zachary Nugent (1886–1946)', *Oxford Dictionary of National Biography*, http://www.oxforddnb.com/view/article/32095 (accessed 20 January 2017); H. Cam, 'Zachary Nugent Brooke, 1883–1946', *Proceedings of the British Academy*, 32 (1946), 381–93.

[5] C. N. L. Brooke, 'Brooke, Zachary (1715/16-1788)', *Oxford Dictionary of National Biography*, http://www.oxforddnb.com/view/article/3557 (accessed 20 January 2017).

[6] C. W. Previté-Orton, 'Zachary Nugent Brooke 1883–1946', *Proceedings of the British Academy*, 32 (1946), 381–93.

When he was very young, he naturally did not quite understand what the college and university were all about. Sir Noel Malcolm remembers being told this story by Christopher:

> When he saw his father going off to some college feast wearing an all-scarlet gown, he asked why he was dressed like that, and his father said 'It's because I'm a Doctor of Letters.' Since the colour was (more or less) pillar-box red, little Christopher became convinced that his father had a part-time job in the evenings, going off to the Post Office and kindly sealing up all the letters that had got opened or damaged in the post.[7]

In his college memoir he described the parties the Master's wife organised for the children of Fellows, and had fond memories of the asparagus sandwiches. There was also the Christmas party that was mainly attended by college bedmakers, during which the Fellows' children would put on a pantomime, which was a challenge for a shy child. Christopher also enjoyed several months that his family spent in a Queen Anne house at Heacham, on the Wash, when he was seven years old. The house had been presented to his successors as Masters of Caius by Dr Davy, who died in 1839. Later, it became a country house for the use of Fellows, and the Brooke family was able to stay there while their new house in Wilberforce Road, Cambridge, was being built. The house at Heacham is no longer a college property, but in those days it was staffed by servants; there was a private bathing machine on the beach nearby.[8]

Brooke was educated at Winchester College, where he was a scholar and was inspired by excellent 'dons', as the masters were called; like another distinguished medieval historian, Nicholas Brooks FBA, he benefited particularly from the teaching of Harold Walker, a talented amateur archaeologist.[9] Walker could be severe even with his favourite pupils. Once, when he had apparently confused possession and proprietary law cases in an essay on the reign of Henry II, Walker wrote in the margin: 'I see, Brooke, that you are still capable of gamma'. He remained loyal to his old school, sending his own sons there and taking an interest in its fortunes. By the age of fifteen his schoolteachers and his father had helped to propel him down the path of historical research. While still at school, he collaborated with his father, who already allowed him free use of his fine library, in writing an article on Hereford Cathedral dignitaries; and in

---

[7] Personal communication from Sir Noel Malcolm FBA.
[8] Brooke, 'Memories of Caius', 125–6.
[9] B. Crawford, S. Keynes and J. Nelson, 'Nicholas Peter Brooks, 1941–2014', *Biographical Memoirs of Fellows of the British Academy*, 15 (2016), pp. 23, 28–9.

1945, aware that some of the printed texts they had used were seriously defective, ZN took CNL along on a research visit to Aberystwyth, where the archives of Hereford Cathedral had been deposited during the war, leading to a second joint article. The ultimate aim of their research was to produce a new edition of the letters of Gilbert Foliot, which Christopher eventually achieved (with Dom Adrian Morey), and which is discussed later in this memoir.

From Winchester Christopher won another scholarship which took him back to Caius in October of the same year. Caius was part of his identity, but the college also posed challenges. Christopher pondered his religious beliefs, and found himself increasingly attracted by Roman Catholicism. He became fascinated by the work of Jacques Maritain and ideas of natural law, seen from a Catholic perspective; one of the impulses was his overwhelming sense of horror at the end of the Second World War when he discovered the fate of Europe's Jews; and this led him to deeper philosophical and theological reflection.[10] He had barely arrived at the college when he found himself closeted with Eric Heaton, the college chaplain (Heaton would later become Dean of Christ Church, Oxford). Christopher admitted that he did not intend to attend the college chapel, since he was interested in becoming a Catholic. Not disconcerted, Heaton reproved Christopher with the words 'I think God is a sufficiently large person to be worshipped in Caius chapel.' Thereafter he and Heaton spent much time studying the New Testament (and attending Caius chapel) together. The words he used to describe his religious path are revealing:

> Guided through many evening talks by his incisive mind and insight into the nature and fruit of New Testament criticism I became a convert to the Anglican Church in which I had been reared, and found in the quiet daily routine of Caius chapel a new spiritual home.[11]

He also found a different sort of peacefulness in the gramophone evenings arranged by his father's younger colleague, Philip Grierson, another future FBA, who had no time for chapel. Grierson held open house on many evenings after Hall (in later years he would switch from records to tapes of rather dreadful science fiction films); but Christopher took no part in college sport and was definitely a 'reading man'.

---

[10] I owe this point to Professor Miri Rubin, who kindly sent me a copy of her eloquent and moving address at the Memorial Service for Christopher in Great St Mary's Church, Cambridge, on 5 November 2016.
[11] Brooke, 'Memories of Caius', 127.

His attachment to Caius became all the greater because his father died suddenly while he was an undergraduate and the college, worried that his mother had been left with limited means, carried most of the responsibility of paying for his education. Otherwise he felt that he quite simply might not have been able to stay at Caius.[12] In any case, Christopher now depended upon his college entrance scholarship and his leaving scholarship from Winchester. Beyond Caius, he benefited from the protection of his father's friends, notably Dom David Knowles, who had forgiven him for leaving a precious pile of his research notes on a bus at the age of fifteen. He was recruited by Knowles and his father to join their project of drawing up an inventory of the heads of religious houses in medieval England and Wales. This, like the edition of Foliot's letters, was a research project that he saw to completion a number of years later. Although what has been said so far might make the trajectory of his academic career seem obvious, the lecturers who impressed him most in his first and second years were two future FBAs of great distinction: Michael Oakeshott, then a History Fellow of Caius, who taught papers in political thought, and M. M. Postan, the imaginative, enthusiastic and colourful Professor of Economic History, who was a colleague of Knowles at Peterhouse.[13] Indeed, he was to collaborate later with Postan in the production of an edition of two important documents in medieval English economic history.

Despite his strong interest in what both Postan and Oakeshott had been teaching him, the decisive move towards the topics that dominated his career took place in his third undergraduate year, when he took David Knowles's Special Subject on St Francis and the friars. He was introduced to Knowles's research student, Rosalind Clark, and tea in Caius and Girton was eventually followed by their engagement, their marriage and their lifelong devotion to one another: 'I have been Rosalind's research assistant from those days till now.'[14] Still, straitened resources meant that they could not marry until he had finished his military service, where he

---

[12] Brooke, 'Memories of Caius', 129. On the other hand, the new *Oxford Dictionary of National Biography* notes with commendable exactitude that his father had left £10,012 9s 1d after probate (Knowles and Matthew, 'Brooke, Zachary Nugent (1886–1946)'), which was quite a sizeable sum in those days, the equivalent of nearly £400,000 when Christopher died in 2015. This would include the value of the architect-designed house in Wilberforce Road, Cambridge; but even so it is possible Christopher had a romantic view of how he had been kept going by the college, when he already held the necessary scholarships and his mother had some money in the bank.
[13] N. Johnson, 'Michael Joseph Oakeshott, 1901–1990', *Proceedings of the British Academy*, 80 (1991), 403–23; E. Miller, 'Michael Moissey Postan, 1899–1981', *Proceedings of the British Academy*, 69 (1984), 543–57.
[14] Brooke, 'Memories of Caius', 131.

eventually became a captain in the Royal Army Educational Corps. Even before he received his commission, in 1949, he was elected to a Research Fellowship at Caius. He returned to his mess from a rather tricky encounter with his commanding officer to find a letter from Sir James Chadwick, the Master of Caius, offering him a Fellowship out of the blue. This was before the elaborate system of formal applications, submission of a dissertation and probing interviews for Research Fellowships had come into being; and it was before the days when a PhD degree was the sole passport to an academic career—he did not have one, and when he was lecturing in the History Faculty at Cambridge only one of his medieval colleagues, the crusade historian R. C. Smail, had actually completed a PhD in History.

Just about able to afford getting married (on a stipend of £300 per annum), Christopher was enchanted by the opportunity to dine with the other Fellows, even if he and most Research Fellows found the cost of port at dessert beyond their means. He was excited to have free access to the Senior Combination Rooms where his father had preceded him, and to be able to mix on equal terms with Sir Ronald Fisher, Joseph Needham and other luminaries who were then Fellows. But he also witnessed the irritation of the younger, and some more senior, Fellows at the existence of a closed inner circle that ran the college through the Council of thirteen members whose origin could be traced all the way back to Dr Caius's sixteenth-century statutes. Although the agenda of what became known as the Peasants' Revolt (named after Peter Bauer, the eminent economist) is often said to have been the provision of a proper bathroom for Bauer, who lived in college, Christopher recognised that the real division lay between those who saw the college as primarily a place of teaching and those who gave priority to their research, while being well aware that good research fuels good teaching.[15] Beyond that, the rebels sought to make the government of the college more democratic, by denying Council members what were in effect permanent places on the Council, and by rotating membership among the Fellows instead; and the four-year Research Fellowships were opened up to candidates from outside the college. The peasants won, and all Fellows of Caius are peasants now—something of which Christopher approved. On the other hand, he was clearly uneasy about the lack of access for, or interest in, the Fellows' families. Even when he returned to Caius in 1977 wives were only permitted to attend one dinner at the start of the calendar year, gorgeously entitled Bishop Shaxton's Solace, and even then a College Order decreed that it should be

[15] Brooke, 'Memories of Caius', 134.

no better than an ordinary High Table dinner—an order that was, however, consistently ignored.

Christopher's career seemed to be heading in a predictable direction. Before long he had swapped his Research Fellowship for the post of College Lecturer (that is, Teaching Fellow), and had been appointed to an Assistant Lectureship in the History Faculty. At a time when there was no very strong pressure to publish anything (one of his colleagues produced four articles in a forty-year career), he set a different example, producing volume one of *The Letters of John of Salisbury* in 1955. Like many of his other works, this was a product of collaboration, even though again and again Christopher took on the major burden right through to proof-reading without, however, complaining or claiming special credit. As the rising medieval historian of his generation, he was, not surprisingly, seen as good professorial material, even though he was still in his twenties. And the fact was that professors were paid better; with a growing family Christopher had to think of such considerations. He was also aware that openings for his wife in Cambridge were virtually non-existent in those days, even though she had written an excellent PhD thesis on early Franciscan government which was accepted for publication by Cambridge University Press.[16] So the call from Liverpool proved powerful enough to tear him away from the college that he loved. He had to break the news to the Master, the eminent physicist Sir James Chadwick, a man of few words. He found Chadwick in the Master's study puzzling over a scrap of paper, and announced that he was leaving. Chadwick's response was 'Well, that's a relief!' for, rather than paying attention to Christopher, he had been deciphering a note about something quite different.

III: The Liverpool years, 1956–67

Christopher Brooke arrived in Liverpool as Professor of Medieval History at the extraordinarily young age of just twenty-nine, but with a remarkable scholarly achievement already behind him. The previous Professors of Medieval and Modern History had been at daggers drawn; they had to use separate staircases in the School of History. They both departed at the same time, so that Christopher, to whom feuding was totally alien, was joined by the charming and genial Northern Irishman, David Quinn, as Professor of Modern History, and peace at once descended on the School.

---

[16] R. B. Brooke, *Early Franciscan Government: Elias to Bonaventure* (Cambridge, 1959).

As one might have imagined, there was a small 'old guard' at Liverpool who resented a brilliant young man from Cambridge being brought in over the heads of established locals (not that the scholarly and saintly Alec Myers, the senior member of the department and an established local, was like this at all); and one of them once said to me disparagingly that there would always be something of the innocent choirboy about Christopher. Colour was given to this idea by a true story with a wide currency in the university. Early in his time at Liverpool, there was an overhauling of the History syllabus, and new letters were attached to the courses. Christopher had suddenly exclaimed in the midst of his colleagues of both departments, 'we haven't got a French Letter!' David Quinn slapped his thighs and snorted with laughter, though he was not backed up by his modernist colleagues who all kept straight faces.

When it came to academic politics, however, Christopher was far from innocent. The 1960s were a period of university expansion, and whenever David Quinn came forward with figures to show that Modern History needed another one or two lecturers, Christopher was ready with figures to show that Medieval History needed the same. With his perfect Wykehamist manners, Christopher could run rings round practically all the other Arts professors when it came to any matters of university politics. For eleven years, the Department of Medieval History benefited from his inspired leadership. His methods were in no way dirigiste. He did it all by scrupulous fair-mindedness, by taking an interest in his colleagues and listening to them, and by his own general sense of direction. He never treated departmental meetings as occasions to dictate to his colleagues; one could say what one liked provided one spoke responsibly; he was remarkably open to criticism himself, if it were stated dispassionately. In the Senior Common Room of the School, a sizeable room and a wonderful institution for bringing medievalists and modernists together, he would be regularly at tea, which he liked very weak, and would participate in any conversation going, whether about history or about life; but he never gossiped, and still less did he engage in character detraction. His own ears were always close to the ground, but if he ever gave way to an apparent indiscretion, it was something everyone else had known for at least six months. His humanity and skill in dealing with personal matters was shown in high degree when he saw that he would have to obtain a Senior Lectureship for Robert Markus, and also saw how hurt Dorothea Oschinsky, who had until then published very little, would be if she were left behind. So he coaxed out of her—there is no other word for it than coaxed—her fine and important edition of Walter of Henley's *Husbandry*.[17]

---

[17] D. Oschinsky, *Walter of Henley and other Treatises on Estate Management* (Oxford, 1971).

For myself, an early example of how Christopher treated his colleagues came on the day I was interviewed and appointed. My appointment sent me into transports of delight, not least because I had already read much of what he had written, and had even acquired his then recently published *Letters of John of Salisbury*, volume one, as part of a college book prize. He drove me down to Lime Street Station, and—what was this!—my professor-to-be had seized my case, and having sent me to buy a ticket (for which the university would pay), rushed off to find me a good place in the train. The following June I returned to Liverpool to make arrangements about lectures and so on, and I stayed with him and his family at their beautiful seventeenth-century manor house at Willaston on the Wirral. I took to Rosalind at once. She was amusing; she was hugely intelligent and perceptive in a slightly wacky sort of way; and while I was to meet some professors' wives who spoke as if they were the oracles of their awesome husbands, what one got from her was pure unadulterated Rosalind. Their three boys were lively but delightful. The oldest, Francis (who was tragically to be carried off by a rare blood disease when he was only about forty) was then four. Christopher cycled to Willaston Station every day, and came to Liverpool by train via the Mersey Tunnel. Distinguished professors, particularly youthful ones, did not grow on every tree in Willaston, and it was said that if Christopher arrived slightly late on his bicycle, the Willaston stationmaster would hold up the train.

The Brookes, including Francis, Phil and Patrick, were a very hospitable family. I had a chance sometimes to repay their hospitality in an unusual way. Rosalind's parents lived in south Cornwall, and when the family went on holiday there, they would pack the sleeping children into their estate car, together with two large dogs, at three in the morning, and stop for breakfast at the house of my mother in Bristol, where I would make huge quantities of scrambled egg and toast (I was still a bachelor while at Liverpool). After breakfast, Christopher would take the dogs for a walk, accompanied by whichever of the boys wanted to go; while Rosalind, who was not as discreet as her husband, and I would stay in and chat. My mother always enjoyed these occasions.

His eleven years at Liverpool (1956–67) were among the happiest and most creative periods of Christopher's life. They were also one of the most fruitful for his scholarship; they included his magnum opus, *The Letters and Charters of Gilbert Foliot*, together with its companion book, *Gilbert Foliot and his Letters*, which had appeared four years earlier. Both were co-authored with Dom Adrian Morey, a former pupil of and collaborator with Christopher's father. But it was clear (anyhow to myself) that the lion's share of both works was Christopher's. He was an empiricist rather than a philosopher as an historian, at least in his time at Liverpool. The first chapter of the earlier book is entitled 'The Problem'. This is not an attempt to establish a conceptual framework, nor to justify a methodology; it raises a human problem: how to reconcile the golden opinions of Foliot, expressed by contemporaries, with the personal nastiness of his opposition to Thomas Becket. The second chapter is about the genre of letters, and about how much personal responsibility Foliot had for his own letters. There follow chapters which give a wealth of original insight into the development of the twelfth-century English Church. A later chapter concerns the forgeries of Gloucester Abbey while Foliot was abbot there (1139–48). Sir Richard Southern said of Vivian Galbraith (one of the assessors for the Liverpool chair in 1956), that he 'ignited at the sight of a charter'. Christopher ignited at the smell of a forgery. Yet together with this sniffing-out went an interest in, and a large degree of sympathy for, those responsible for forgeries. It is that understanding which makes this chapter a classic discussion of forgery. The next chapter is about Foliot's opposition to Becket, a masterpiece of empathy. It shows incidentally that Christopher was by no means inclined to avoid political theory when it was relevant.

The edition of *The Letters and Charters of Gilbert Foliot* appeared in Christopher's last year in Liverpool; it had dominated his work during his whole time there. Christopher would later be involved, from its start (1973), in the British Academy project for the publication of the English Episcopal *Acta*, diocese by diocese; he became chairman of the project after Christopher Cheney's death in 1987. His and Morey's large volume had appeared six years before 1973, and was a major force in kick-starting the Academy project. Twelfth- and early thirteenth-century episcopal charters have to be laboriously collected from the various sources of the beneficiaries—their archives, monastic and other cartularies, later copies made by antiquaries and so on. Before bishops had copies of their own documents kept in episcopal registers, mostly from around the late thirteenth century onwards, collecting their *acta* is the principal way of shedding light on important areas of the English and Welsh Churches after the Norman Conquest, such as who controlled appointments to benefices, who were their patrons lay and ecclesiastical, who constituted the personnel of its higher clergy, who formed the dynamic groups in the fast-growing diocesan administration and what were the economic foundations of its churches. Fundamental to handling episcopal *acta* was dating them as closely as possible, for they rarely carried a date. Here Christopher excelled. As the edition of both the *acta* (or formal documents) and the letters (the latter giving the volume an almost unique importance) of a peculiarly interesting and long-lived bishop (abbot of Gloucester, 1139–48; bishop of Hereford, 1148–63; bishop of London, 1163–87), this edition of a bishop's documents is easily the most important for the twelfth century.

In the introduction, one sees immediately the relish for palaeographical, codicological and diplomatic technicalities. But these are no mere technicalities; there is not a scrap of pedantry in this introduction, nor in any of Christopher's scholarship. They concern the manuscripts of the letters and some of the charters made for Foliot himself, which enables us to peer into the most intimate world of Foliot and his circle. As to the texts themselves, with their English running-titles and notes, all one can say of this superb edition is that one could almost write a history of the English Church for fifty years, vividly and in fascinating detail, from this volume alone. The notes, often about matters of dating, are never forced in where not strictly necessary.

Gilbert Foliot was the main, but not the only, focus of Christopher's scholarly attention while he was at Liverpool. In 1960 the Northamptonshire Record Society brought out M. M. Postan's and his edition of the *Carte Nativorum* of Peterborough Abbey, a volume very interestingly discussed by Edmund King in his fine obituary of Christopher.[18] These documents give an exceptional insight into fourteenth-century peasant land transactions through the abbey's attempt to record and control them. Postan originally transcribed the (Latin) texts and wrote a magisterial account of their evidence in the Introduction. Christopher analysed the manuscript, checked the texts, provided the English running-titles (or abstracts) and the notes, mainly about dating and identifications of places and individuals mentioned in the texts. He did all this within a matter of weeks at the end of 'a hectic first year in Liverpool' in 1957. As he explained in a letter to Joan Wake, General Editor of the Society, he did not wish to overwhelm the text with notes, but nonetheless to make the meaning of the documents as plain as was compatible 'with reasonable economy of editing'. This may be taken as the leitmotif of everything that Christopher edited.

From about 1960 until the late 1980s he was one of the General Editors, at first with Vivian Galbraith and Roger Mynors, of the *Nelson's* (later *Oxford*) *Medieval Texts*, perhaps the most distinguished and important British series of scholarly texts (with English translation) from

---

[18] E. King, 'Professor Christopher Nugent Lawrence Brooke, CBE FBA', *Northamptonshire Past and Present*, 69 (2016), 89–91.

the Middle Ages. Christopher was a hands-on General Editor, sometimes necessarily so; and his diplomatic skills were occasionally very much required, as I remember, and as can be seen, for instance, in the acknowledgements at the beginning of the *Magna Vita Sancti Hugonis*.[19]

During his years at Liverpool, Christopher wrote a number of more popular books: *From Alfred to Henry III*; *The Saxon and Norman Kings*; and *Europe in the Central Middle Ages*; followed not long after his departure by *The Twelfth Century Renaissance*. There were those who thought that he was publishing too many of this sort of book for his own good; but he probably saw it as his duty as a professor to spread the understanding and enjoyment of medieval history as widely as possible. In the 1960s the University of Liverpool was much more closely related to the local community than was the case with Oxford or Cambridge, and Christopher would go here, there and everywhere giving talks, which were very popular. None of these books was what one could call a pot-boiler. For instance, the first chapter of *The Saxon and Norman Kings*, on king-making, made a lasting impression on me, as did much of *Europe in the Central Middle Ages*, such as the wonderful pages on Gerbert of Aurillac's letters. All these books are attractively written and with a fresh slant, even on well-known topics. Christopher once said to me in conversation that it was important to learn to write quickly when one was in one's twenties, adding that his father had not so learnt and thus had never written as much as a scholar of his calibre should have done. To my horror I heard myself say that if I had written just one book as original and marvellous as his father's *The English Church and the Papacy*, I would be well content.[20] He was embarrassed by what may have seemed an implicit criticism of himself, though totally unintended; but he did not take umbrage and answered me (unconvincingly) that what one should understand was that that book was the fortunate breakthrough of one year rather than the result of many years of cumulative scholarship.

During his time in Liverpool, Christopher was working on other projects which would only come to fruition in later publications—on London, on the heads of religious houses (an outstandingly useful compendium covering the period of Knowles's *Monastic Order*), and on the revision of Wilkins's *Concilia*.[21] It is impossible to discuss in detail all his important

---

[19] D. L. Douie and H. Farmer (eds.), *The Life of St Hugh of Lincoln*, vol. 1 (Edinburgh, 1961), p. vi.
[20] Z. N. Brooke, *The English Church and the Papacy from the Conquest to the Reign of John* (Cambridge, 1931).
[21] D. Knowles, *The Monastic Order in England: a History of its Development from the Times of St Dunstan to the Fourth Lateran Council, 943–1216* (Cambridge, 1940; D. Wilkins, *Concilia Magnae*

articles. He was drawn into some of the fictions, chronicle and documentary, concerning Welsh churches, through his work on Gilbert Foliot and the involvement of Gloucester Abbey in the story. Two witty articles on all this appeared in *Studies in the Early British Church* and in *Celt and Saxon: Studies in the Early British Border*. They represent his unwillingness to rest, where there was skulduggery in the case, until he had got to the bottom of it. His contribution to one of these books, in which he argued that the *Book of Llandaf* was a forgery, drew the fire of an irate Welsh reviewer. Christopher used to enjoy quoting one sentence of this review: 'Wrong again, Mr Brooke!'[22] He rarely took umbrage at criticism; he once said to me that one of the advantages of publishing a book was that you thereby often elicited useful criticism. He asked me to read an early draft of his article on the Wix Charters, distinguishing the forgeries from the probably genuine. My response was that it was fascinating, but rather inchoate as an article; only three weeks later, in his busy schedule, he showed me the final version. It was the utterly coherent article, with everything lucidly explained, which went into the Doris Stenton Festschrift, published by the Pipe Roll Society.

Perhaps of all his articles, the one that most moved me had nothing to do with forgeries, 'St Dominic and his first biographer', reprinted in his *Medieval Church and Society*. During his time in Liverpool, Christopher held a seminar on Saints Francis and Dominic. This owed its inspiration in good part to the work of Rosalind on the friars. Of the three principal forms of university teaching in the arts, lectures, tutorials and seminars, Christopher was an excellent lecturer; the reports of the few tutorials he was able to give were glowing; but as the taker of a seminar, he was one of the two or three best that I have ever encountered. Of the three forms, it is the hardest to bring off successfully. He did it not by being magisterial, but by creating an atmosphere in which it was possible for anyone to say what they thought; a rather smoke-filled atmosphere, it may be added, in which he stubbed out his cigarettes into an ashtray which had the shape of a rotund friar. His article is about the contrast between Francis and Dominic, and how Francis's personality was the reference point for the early development of his order, whereas Dominic and his biographer, Jordan of Saxony, sank his personality in the order and its General

---

Britanniae et Hiberniae (London, 1737); see also his co-edited *Councils and Synods* listed at the end of this memoir.

[22] J. W. James, 'The *Book of Llandav*: the Church and See of Llandav and their critics', *Journal of the Historical Society of the Church in Wales*, 9 (1959), 5–22.

Chapter. The climax of the article is especially poignant, on how, by a sudden inspiration and act of courage, Dominic turned his back on preaching to the Cathars (against whom he had not had much success) and dispersed his order from Toulouse to the whole of Europe, particularly to such university cities as Paris and Bologna, with the implication that the profoundest possible study of theology was the surest way to counteract heresy.

One of the qualities which Rosalind and Christopher shared was this capacity for deep human insight—in life as well as history. Rosalind's interpretation of how Brother Elias should have been so trusted by Francis, and yet later, in his own way of life, should have so abandoned Francis's ideal of poverty, is an example. She explained this by Elias needing someone like Francis to hold up his personality and spirituality, and, lacking Francis's sustaining power after the saint's death, collapsed morally. Rosalind and Christopher were ideally suited to each other, both by complementarity and by like-mindedness.[23] The only time anyone witnessed anything approaching acrimony in their dealings with each other was over a route to be taken by car on one of our annual study weeks for the second-year undergraduates at Attingham Park in Shropshire. The students in the car wittily noted that during the argument there was an especially large number of 'darlings' flying around.

In his inaugural lecture delivered at the University of Liverpool in 1957, the unfortunately entitled 'Dullness of the Past', Christopher made a plea for combining the specialism of amassing and analysing evidence, 'which gains for the historian an uneasy respectability from the kindlier logical positivists', with the enlargement of human understanding.[24] One may stand in awe of his spectacular gifts as a diplomaticist, or documentary critic; but what made him a great historian, as it made his mentor and teacher David Knowles, was above all the breadth of his human understanding.

IV: Christopher Brooke as scholar and author

Christopher Brooke's prodigious output of scholarly publications, firmly and accurately rooted in documentary evidence and supported by a rare level of skills in palaeography and diplomatic and the study of art, archaeology and literature, began early. His work was always enlightened by

---

[23] R. B. Brooke, *Early Franciscan Government*; also her *The Coming of the Friars* (London, 1975).
[24] C. N. L. Brooke, *The Dullness of the Past; an Inaugural Lecture* (Liverpool, 1957).

human and religious understanding and sometimes beautifully illustrated with photographs, some of them taken by Christopher himself. It came to embrace best-selling outline histories and new editions with new English translations of medieval Latin texts of the highest interest, and he rarely made a mistake.

He was a precocious child. Even at the age of ten he helped his father, Z. N. Brooke, with the proofs and index of his *History of Europe, 911–1198*, published in Methuen's 'History of Medieval and Modern Europe' series in 1938. He was, he said, his father's apprentice who at the age of fourteen or so gave up collecting engine numbers and began collecting archdeacons instead. He was early interested in problems of chronology but had a scare in 1942 at the age fifteen or so when he left on the top of a bus irreplaceable notebooks containing years of enquiries made by the distinguished monastic historian and family friend Dom David Knowles into the careers of the heads of medieval religious houses, and which the young Brooke was meant to transcribe. Fortunately a swift pursuit on foot led to their recovery and eventual publication. Years later in 1972 these lists, much extended and largely by Christopher himself and also by Vera London, appeared in *Heads of Religious Houses, England and Wales, 940–1216* and a second edition followed in 2001 with further new material. With his father he had published two papers before he reached his twentieth birthday, one in the *Cambridge Historical Journal* (1944; supplement in 1946) on Hereford Cathedral dignitaries in the twelfth century, the other in the *English Historical Review* (1946) on Henry II, Duke of Normandy and Aquitaine.[25] His first solo publication, on the Canterbury forgeries, appeared in the *Downside Review* (1950–1).[26]

His interest in the history of medieval religious life was developed in his final year as an undergraduate student of history at Cambridge when he took the Special Subject on St Francis of Assisi taught by Professor David Knowles. While still in his twenties he joined M. M. (later Sir Michael) Postan in the publication of an edition, made by W. T. Mellows and P. I. King for the Northamptonshire Record Society, of *The Book of William Morton, Almoner of Peterborough Monastery, 1448–1467* (1954).[27] William Morton's Book, which is found in the British Library MS Cotton,

---

[25] Z. N. Brooke and C. N. L. Brooke, 'Henry II, Duke of Normandy and Aquitaine', *English Historical Review*, 61 (1946), 81–9.
[26] C. N. L. Brooke, 'The Canterbury forgeries and their author', *Downside Review*, 68 (1950), 462–71 and 69 (1951), 210–51.
[27] M. M. Postan, C. N. L. Brooke, W. T. Mellows and P. I. King, *The Book of William Morton, Almoner of Peterborough Monastery, 1448–1467* (Northampton, 1954).

Vespasian A XXIV, is a rare private account book of the almoner (or land-agent) of Peterborough Abbey in the mid-fifteenth century who managed the abbey's properties and its two homes (or hospitals) for old people. Christopher provided the notes and a fine Latin and Middle English glossary, had a share in the making of the indexes and also wrote a substantial introduction on which Postan gave advice as well as making a contribution (pp. xxxi–xxxvii). The introduction includes a detailed description of the Cotton MS and brings the reader close to William Morton 'in the intimacy of office and counting house, wrestling with addition and subtraction and petty cash in the regular humdrum of affairs' (p. xi). It gives many a glimpse also into the relations of the monks of Peterborough with their neighbours, tenants and servants. A 'meticulous man in a meticulous age' (p. xliv), William Morton comes out well from a penetrating assessment. Continuing work on the history of Peterborough Abbey in collaboration with Postan resulted in the publication in 1960 by the Northamptonshire Record Society of an edition of the *Carte Nativorum: a Peterborough Abbey Cartulary of the Fourteenth Century.* The *nativi* were the villein tenants of the abbey and there was much work to be done in dating the charters, carefully identifying persons and properties and, for Christopher in particular, the writing of a detailed description of the MS (Peterborough, Dean and Chapter 39), the compilation of the abstracts and notes, and the preparation of a glossary.[28]

An edition of the letters and charters of Gilbert Foliot had been planned by his father, Z. N. Brooke, and independently by Dom Adrian Morey, OSB. Zachary Brooke died, however, in 1946 and the edition was made by Dom Adrian, monk of Downside Abbey and Headmaster of the Oratory School, in collaboration with Christopher. It was published in 1967 as *The Letters and Charters of Gilbert Foliot, Abbot of Gloucester (1139–48), Bishop of Hereford (1148–63) and London (1163–87)*, but the work was preceded by a book, jointly written by Christopher and Dom Adrian, on *Gilbert Foliot and his Letters* (1965). The two had collaborated earlier on an article which appeared in the *English Historical Review* in 1948 when Christopher was only twenty-one or so and which was on letters which Gilbert Foliot wrote as abbot of Gloucester and concerning the troubles in Cerne Abbey in the 1140s and the exasperating complications which they stirred.[29] Morey was the older man: in 1937 he had

---

[28] Christopher, who was a member of the Society's Publications Committee until 1974, gave considerable help in the production of other volumes in the series.

[29] C. N. L. Brooke and A. Morey, 'The Cerne letters of Gilbert Foliot and the Legation of Imar of Tusculum', *English Historical Review*, 63 (1948), 433–52.

produced a landmark book on one of Foliot's contemporaries, Bartholomew, bishop of Exeter. In Foliot Morey and Brooke both found a man who 'combined in himself to an exceptional degree the ideals, the prejudices and the paradoxes of his age': an ascetic monk, an abbot, a capable bishop, a scholar, an inspiring preacher, but a highly controversial figure who attracted a stream of golden opinions but was held by others to be a scheming Pharisee and a harsh controversialist who 'was involved in forgery and practised unashamed nepotism' (p. 1). Foliot's letters are a valuable source for the anarchy of Stephen's reign and the bitter conflicts which saw Foliot forcefully opposing Becket and loyally supporting Henry II. The book is absorbing to read and no reader can fail to see the wealth of original enquiries which went into its making, especially into an exceptional number of episcopal charters, often unprinted and often spurious, out of which historical detail is squeezed and the framework of administrative activity made visible. The various branches of Foliot families in twelfth-century England are established, and the personnel who ran Foliot's chapters and household in Hereford and London—the deans, precentors, archdeacons, canons, schoolmasters, clerks, chaplains and others—are listed and thoroughly documented.

This book, invaluable as it is on its own for Gilbert and his letters, serves as a companion to the edition of 283 letters and 193 charters which aimed to print the letters and charters, 'as nearly as possible, as they left the hands of Gilbert Foliot or his clerks and passed into those of their recipients' (p. 29). A single manuscript, Bodleian E Musaeo 249 (27835), contains most of the letters but many letters and charters had to be uncovered in scattered libraries and archives. The texts are supported with a wealth of analysis of their scribes, their dating and diplomatic, their authenticity and circulation, as well as of the people who figure in them and of the papal letters that were addressed to Foliot. Gilbert's writing-office is miraculously brought to light: 'it was a school for church government as well as an administrative headquarters' (p. 28).

For twenty-eight years from 1959 to 1987 Christopher was one of the General Editors of the flagship series *Nelson's Medieval Texts* (NMT) which in 1966 became *Oxford Medieval Texts* (OMT). The other General Editors of NMT were V. H. Galbraith and Sir Roger Mynors. After this became OMT Galbraith and Mynors retired and the future of the series was precarious. But Christopher was joined as General Editors by Diana Greenway and Michael Winterbottom; they did well to ensure that it kept going, maintained standards and, by the time of Christopher's own retirement in 1987, had reached smooth waters. Christopher left a very considerable mark on both series through editions and translations he made himself, through the reworking of editions published earlier and through his selfless dedication to the review of other editions accepted for publication. He saw through to publication forty-seven volumes, by which stage the series had established itself as one of the essential landmarks of medieval studies, a new Rolls Series but with translations facing pages of Latin text. His own crowning personal achievement in the OMT series is his completion, in two volumes with over 1,100 pages, of an edition and translation of *The Letters of John of Salisbury*, John being the very well-connected, highly cultured and witty diplomat who served two archbishops of Canterbury, Theobald and Becket, and who tirelessly shuttled between Canterbury and the papal curia. The letters introduce us to the great personalities of the day and to the great crisis that resulted in Becket's death. *The Early Letters (1153–1161)*, edited by W. J. Millor, SJ, and H. E. Butler and revised by Brooke, were published in NMT in 1955. The work had begun as a thesis by Fr Millor under the supervision of Butler. The General Editors of the series, Galbraith and Mynors, explained that the foundation of this volume was 'a text of John of Salisbury's letters with very full collations of the manuscripts and short notes, the work of Dr W. J. Millor, S. J. ... the credit of producing this entirely new and reliable text is his ... The translation was undertaken by the late Harold Edgeworth Butler, professor of Latin in University College, London, until his lamented death suspended the enterprise' (p. vii). Christopher, they continued, expertly and unselfishly checked and completed the translation, worked out afresh the dates and order of the letters (the letters themselves being undated) and provided introduction, notes and appendices. Mynors described the manuscripts and the previous editions. For Christopher this was a wonderful opportunity which led to his becoming a third General Editor of NMT in 1959. In 1986 the volume was reprinted by the Clarendon Press in the OMT series with *corrigenda* supplied by himself. These include a courteous acceptance of the sweeping away by R. W. Southern of Christopher's 'attractive theory' that the first collection of John's letters (the letters from 1153–61; letters 1–135) formed a packet which John sent sometime in 1161 or 1162 to his close friend Peter of Celle, abbot of Montier-la-Celle near Troyes.[30] *The Later Letters (1163–1180)*,

---

[30] See Southern's review in the *English Historical Review*, 72 (1957), 495: 'My own impression is that both the manuscripts which form the basis of this edition go back to rough drafts of the letters, preserved on separate sheets of parchment with one or more ... letters on each.' For Brooke's response see *The Letters of John of Salisbury*, I (1955), pp. ix–xii, and the *corrigenda* in the reissue of vol. I in 1986 on pp. 297–8. This was not the only occasion on which 'nemesis

bearing the names of Millor and Brooke (letters 132–325), were published in OMT in 1979. A story which circulated, that Brooke translated a letter a day before breakfast, has about it the ring of truth.

Of Christopher's work for OMT three further volumes are particularly memorable. He contributed a new introduction and revised notes to a new edition and translation by Sir Roger Mynors of M. R. James's edition of Walter Map, *De nugis curialium – Courtiers' Trifles* (originally published in 1914). This book is an extraordinary conglomeration of stories of different kinds that was written in the late twelfth century by an archdeacon of Oxford whose brilliant and amusing reworking of earlier materials found in writers as far apart from each other as Cicero and Geoffrey of Monmouth was read at the time by almost no one. In 1990, in collaboration with Martin Brett and Michael Winterbottom, Christopher also produced for OMT a revision of Charles Johnson's edition (NMT, 1961) of Hugh the Chanter's *History of the Church of York, 1066–1127*. In an introduction Christopher outlined the passions aroused by the primacy dispute between Canterbury and York and the fascination and importance of the largely hidden world of the cathedral chapters of England and France in the early twelfth century, a time when family life faded away from there, clerical celibacy became the norm, and most canons became absentees. Third, some fifty years after first being published by David Knowles (Nelson Medieval Classics, 1951) Christopher published a revision of Knowles's edition of *The Monastic Constitutions of Lanfranc* (2002). For this he collated a MS not used by Knowles (Hereford Cathedral Library, P.V.1) and also wrote a new chapter on the audience for the work, its date and the sources used.

Christopher's exceptionally energetic dedication to the discovery, study and publication of the records of the medieval English Church focused especially on the period to which his father had devoted most attention in his celebrated book on *The English Church and the Papacy from the Conquest to the Reign of John*, of 1931. In an edition of this book issued in 1989 Christopher provided a new Foreword in which he wrote about the transformation of studies of the English Church in the twelfth

struck' in the pages of the *English Historical Review*: in the following year Southern showed that the Canterbury forgeries of a series of papal privileges which were intended to boost the primatial authority of the see of Canterbury over the see of York, and which Christopher had believed to date from Lanfranc's time, belonged to the 1120s. See R. W. Southern, 'The Canterbury forgeries', *English Historical Review*, 73 (1958), 193–226, Brooke, 'Canterbury Forgeries', and also Brooke, Foreword to the 1989 edition of Z. N. Brooke, *The English Church and the Papacy from the Conquest to the Reign of John*, p. xv.

century brought about largely by the study of papal decretals. But Christopher himself gave most attention to the documents of the English Church itself. With Martin Brett and Dorothy Whitelock he cooperated in the preparation of *Councils and Synods with other Documents relating to the English Church, I, 871–1204* (1981). He was primarily responsible for documents, especially canons of councils, from the period 1135 to 1204, a period when Henry I, Stephen and Henry II all issued charters of liberties, when the Constitutions of Clarendon were issued, when many councils were presided over by papal legates and when the primatial claims of Canterbury and York were in dispute. Most of this material, which fills over 300 pages, was edited from manuscripts.

More substantial still was Brooke's vigorous work on the English Episcopal *Acta* project of the British Academy (EEA) which collects and publishes the records of English bishops from the late eleventh to the thirteenth century, thereby projecting light into hidden corners of medieval history and revealing the Church at work on its ordinary routines and preoccupations. Forty-four volumes have been published so far, and nearly twenty editors have been at work bringing the original materials and later copies of these together from many scattered libraries and archives. The initial impulse sprang from Sir Frank Stenton in the late 1920s. Christopher Cheney gave indispensable leadership until 1986, but when Christopher Brooke became chairman of the British Academy's EEA Committee a very great burst of activity was to follow. The General Editorship of the project, now in the hands of Philippa Hoskin of the University of Lincoln, was from 1973 to 2005 in those of David Smith of York, and Christopher's deep attachment to the project is particularly shown in the warm appreciation of David Smith's work which he expressed in a volume of studies presented to him by friends in 2005.[31] Here Christopher outlined the development of the EEA project: fashionable monographs, he wrote (pp. 3–4), eventually bite the dust but documents reclaimed provide the bone structure of the past and its chronology and are the crucial foundation for the work of a historian. In return in 2012 the editors of EEA volumes paid their tribute to Christopher for the tireless energy and extraordinary care he had spent on drafts of almost every volume by presenting him with a token of their collective gratitude and affection. This took the form of a sumptuous volume of *Facsimiles of English Episcopal Acta*, a collection of plates intended to illustrate the most

---

[31] C. N. L. Brooke, P. Hoskin and B. Dobson (eds.), *The Foundations of Medieval Ecclesiastical History: Studies Presented to David Smith* (Woodbridge, 2005).

characteristic features of the surviving original acts of the bishops of the English sees edited in EEA.[32]

Running almost in parallel with EEA was the *Le Neve, Fasti Ecclesiae Anglicanae* project for the period 1066–1300. Nine volumes listing officials of the English dioceses were published by the Institute of Historical Research, London, between 1968 and 2003. Christopher took a constant and active interest in the project from its first days, contributing to its editors copious draft lists and notes of documentary references of his own. As Diana Greenway FBA, the editor of several volumes, wrote, Christopher was one of the 'early Fathers' of the project, always responding speedily, helpfully, patiently and encouragingly to her pleas for information and advice and also devoting much time to reading and commenting on volumes to their great benefit.[33] For volume 1 (1968) at least, which lists the early dignitaries and prebendaries of St Paul's Cathedral, London, Christopher's contribution was a continuation of the work of his father, Z. N. Brooke.

Christopher was far more than an antiquarian producing lists and indexes. He wrote a number of very successful outline histories and monographs to serve the purposes of students and a wider public. These include *From Alfred to Henry III, 871–1272* in 1961 and *The Saxon and Norman Kings* in 1963. The central place among these histories is surely the volume *Europe in the Central Middle Ages 962–1154* in Longman's *General History of Europe*, which came out a year later and was translated into French and Spanish. Here, as in his other books, he was unabashed in seeing political history and written documentary evidence as only a tiny part of the rich historical deposit of these creative centuries. For a full and coherent narrative of these centuries he referred readers to his father's *History of Europe from 911 to 1198* for which some decades earlier he had helped with the proofs and index. But Christopher set out 'to sketch the life of the age under every aspect which can now be viewed' and in his preface to the second edition he faced down critics of the first: 'to make the politics of the central Middle Ages the core of this book would run counter to all my convictions of what is most worth studying' (pp. xiv–xv). To this end he brought alive the cultural movements of the time—city life, the schools, learning and theology, Latin and vernacular literature, courtly romances, law, architecture and art.

---

[32] M. Brett, P. Hoskin and D. Smith (eds.), *Facsimiles of English Episcopal Acta, 1085–1305* (London, 2012).
[33] *Le Neve, Fasti Ecclesiae Anglicanae 1066–1300*, vol. 4 (London, 1991), Acknowledgements.

Almost all these elements are to be found in a book written in his London years with Gillian Keir, *London, 800–1216: the Shaping of a City*. This points clearly to an approach to history that attaches less importance to political events, which are briefly summarised, and more to other features such as markets, crafts, streets and churches with many comparisons made with other European towns and much use of evidence from archaeology, topography and numismatics. In *The Twelfth-Century Renaissance* (Thames and Hudson's *Library of European Civilization*, 1969), he combined copious pictures, quotations from written sources and the evidence of archaeology to raise questions, open windows and propose interpretations of cultural changes in the twelfth century and to reveal the achievements of a selection of creative thinkers, writers and artists. At the time of publication the copious display of colour photographs in a historical work was still unusual but Thames and Hudson were changing that and *The Twelfth-Century Renaissance* has a high ratio of illustrations (132) to pages of text (192). The questions raised were general ones but fundamental: was the civilisation of the twelfth century derivative or creative?; what did the different parts of Christendom contribute to it?; and so on. The book relies on key figures around whom discussion is constructed. These were favourites with Christopher: the parodist Geoffrey of Monmouth, the satirist Walter Map, the philosopher Peter Abelard, the lawyer Master Gratian, the sculptor Gislebertus, the poet Wolfram von Eschenbach and others. And the discussions centred on the schools and theology, literature and humanism, canon law and the church, architecture and art, and literature both vernacular and Latin. The book is rich in humorous dismissals. Of Geoffrey's *History of the Kings of Britain* Brooke writes that 'what appeared to be serious history, and was intended (perhaps not very seriously intended) to be read as serious history, was in fact a substantial work of fiction' (p. 10).[34] And of Thomas Becket's biographer William FitzStephen he writes that he combined 'genuine appreciation of the past, pagan and Christian' with 'an astonishing wealth of ignorance' (p. 10). Not every reader of the book takes to its sometimes flowery style. The movement we call the twelfth-century renaissance, he wrote (no doubt with one of his hikes in the Lakeland fells in mind), 'is as if we stood on the slopes above a valley between lofty hills: across the valley is a road

---

[34] The dismissal was in part also directed against R. W. Southern. See C. N. L. Brooke, 'Geoffrey of Monmouth as a historian', in C. N. L. Brooke, D. E. Luscombe, G. H. Martin and D. Owen (eds.), *Church and Government in the Middle Ages. Essays Presented to C. R. Cheney on his 70th Birthday* (Cambridge, 1976), pp. 77–91, and R. W. Southern, 'Aspects of the European tradition of historical writing, 1', *Transactions of the Royal Historical Society*, 5th Series, 20 (1970), 173–96.

running up the further slope and over the hills opposite to us. We cannot see clearly where it comes from, nor the route it takes when it has crossed the hill and gone out of our sight'—and so on for several more lines on p. 192. But the book is most successful when it opens the windows which C. H. Haskins had left untouched in his classic book on *The Renaissance of the Twelfth Century* (1927): vernacular literature, art and architecture.

In the foreword to *The Structure of Medieval Society* (1971)—in its format similar to the earlier *The Twelfth-Century Renaissance* and produced by the same publisher[35]—Christopher reflected on the changing preoccupations of historians as they came to dwell less on wars, political alliances, constitutional developments and written documents, and more on the presentation of visual background, 'a change'—there is a touch of exaggeration in what follows—'that can only be paralleled in the second half of the nineteenth century when trains and steamers made it easy to travel and everyone began to know their Europe' (p. 8), but now 'a new wave of travel by air and plane has been accompanied by incredible [sic] developments in photography and reproduction' (p. 9). Historians have 'tried to make the Christian civilisation of Europe in the Middle Ages more significant and more comprehensible to the readers of today. The keyword to our conception of history is civilisation' (p. 10). As Christopher wrote this his thoughts may have turned to Kenneth Clark's outstandingly successful and lavishly illustrated BBC television series *Civilisation* (1969)—and also to summer holidays and sightseeing on the Continent with family, car and camera.

In his and his wife's *Popular Religion in the Middle Ages. Western Europe 1000–1300* (1984) they explored together the wide spectrum of popular religion by which they meant the religious aspirations of lay people and of the groupings they formed, their attachment to relics, pilgrimages, saints, the sacraments, churches and their ornament, preachers, the Bible and belief in the life to come. The Brookes stopped short of folklore, superstition and witchcraft; they also in this book kept the religious orders and the papacy at arm's length. Rosalind Brooke's own book on *The Coming of the Friars* (1975) had in any case said much about the religious orders, especially in the twelfth century. On the other hand, the religious outlooks and practices of largely illiterate lay people,

---

[35] The content of *The Structure of Medieval Society* was taken from Christopher's contribution to J. Evans, *The Flowering of the Middle Ages* (London, 1966), another book with attractive photographs published by Thames and Hudson. Joan Evans' interests in medieval art closely matched Christopher's own.

although they could rarely be studied through their own writings, could be reconstructed from other sources, often physical, and also often of great beauty, provided that these are approached critically and are seen with medieval eyes, and provided that the 'unlearned' and the 'learned' elements in society are seen to overlap each other and to be themselves divided into many different layers. The Brookes's outlook on medieval religion was a sympathetic one: medieval religion seemed like a dark force sometimes, but at others like a great shaft of light. Much of it was unpopular in the sense that it provoked dissent, repression and persecution, but this did not provide the Brookes with their main narrative. As in so many other books of theirs, the repertory of examples on which they drew to illustrate an argument is extraordinarily wide in type, time and place. They had favourites, nonetheless, to which they turned with especial enthusiasm and wove into a rich and lively tapestry, among them the anchoress Christina of Markyate, the poet Wolfram von Eschenbach and the churches which they themselves visited (and photographed) in Rome and Assisi, Winchester and Conques.

The Medieval Idea of Marriage (1989) is one of the best of the many contributions Christopher made to social and cultural history and to the reconciliation which he desired between the two. Social history fuelled by imaginative literature—by the stories of Lancelot and Guinevere or Tristan and Isolde or the Wife of Bath or Romeo and Juliet—would not do. To be used as historical evidence literature must first be treated as literature, but although literature's factual basis is often elusive, unlike Peter Laslett, the leader of the Cambridge Group for the History of Population and Social Structure, he did not see 'drama and the novel [as] red herrings set across the track which leads to the actual history of human societies' (p. 173). Nor art, for all works of art are themselves historical documents no less than the parish registers which provided the foundations for the work of the Cambridge Group. He had had the idea of writing a history of medieval marriage for more than a quarter of a century, during which time an enormous 'industry' had grown up, attracting experts who, Brooke thought, did not always understand each other. Hence *The Medieval Idea of Marriage* emerged as a smaller book than was originally envisaged, but one that brought together a series of vignettes and case studies as a means to harmonise different approaches with a focus on the period from 1100. Inheritance and family structure were not his main concern, nor is there much in the way of statistical evidence to which a historian of the central Middle Ages may usefully turn. The note of warning struck firmly here against a trend in social science history arose from a passionate belief that a deeper knowledge of the inwardness of human nature was needed to understand the variety of motives that lead a man and a woman to choose to enter or to leave marriage, and that for this a historian must use his or her imagination and gain fluency in other disciplines such as literature, art, theology and law. He wrote: 'when we are served statistics deliciously cooked we are wise to scatter over them the herbs and spices of imaginative literature very finely ground and sieved' (p. 22). For literature Brooke turned to the correspondence of Héloise and Abelard, Chrétien de Troyes, Wolfram von Eschenbach, Chaucer and Shakespeare; for art to paintings and church porches; for theology to the Bible, Augustine, Jerome and Peter Damian; and for law to Gratian and Pope Alexander III. For case studies he went in many directions, to Christina of Markyate, Richard of Anstey, the canons of St Paul's Cathedral in London, the Capetian kings, Henry VIII and elsewhere, including the early-fourteenth century Register of the Inquisition for Montaillou, which gave Christopher the opportunity to reply to a distinguished contemporary French historian, Emmanuel Le Roy Ladurie, whose book on *Montaillou* he admired but found too credulous of records of marriages which, although authentic, were not lacking in gossip or exaggeration.[36] In the course of the book Brooke also took on Georges Duby whose two books on medieval marriage—*Medieval Marriage* (1978) and *The Knight, the Lady and the Priest* (1984)—were proving popular and influential, largely on account of the two 'models' of marriage which Duby had constructed and which Brooke sought to corrode.[37] The first of the two sets of attitudes to marriage outlined by Duby was that of the kings of France in the eleventh and twelfth centuries who sought marriage to provide themselves with male heirs and for personal satisfaction, and who changed their wives if they were unsatisfactory. The second was that of the clergy of the early medieval church. Duby saw the two models as opposites; Brooke did not. For Brooke a central fact of this period was the willingness of the lay aristocracy to allow the Church and the papacy to take over jurisdiction of the law of marriage and to act as umpires when difficulties arose.

Collaboration with the photographer Wim Swaan resulted in a number of books which presented numerous new photographs of high quality accompanied by texts written by Christopher. The earliest of these is

---

[36] E. Le Roy Ladurie, *Montaillou* (Paris, 1975; English transl. by B. Bray, London, 1978).
[37] G. Duby, *Medieval Marriage* (London, 1978) and *The Knight, the Lady and the Priest* (London, 1984).

The Gothic Cathedral, published in 1969, a weighty book to which he contributed a short historical introduction on the cathedral in medieval society. The golden age of coffee-table books was opening; but for students of history such books often offered visual perspectives on the past that had hitherto been far less accessible to them. Swaan's sumptuous photographs, nearly 400 of them, also fill *The Monastic World 1000–1300*, published by Elek in 1974 with a fairly conventional but quite substantial outline history written by Christopher and tracing the remote origins of monasticism in early Christian Egypt, the establishment of Benedictine monasticism in Western Europe and the orders of friars that followed, with a relatively brief assessment of monasticism since the Reformation bringing the book to a conclusion. Here plates and text dance together. As Christopher rightly observed, 'the dialogue between the literature and the buildings of medieval monastic communities was a theme too little developed by historians' (p. 7). It is not obvious why the reissue of this book in 1982 by Omega Books was given a new title, *Monasteries of the World: the Rise and Development of the Monastic Tradition*, as the book is not concerned with world history.

Further collaboration with Swaan resulted in *A History of Gonville and Caius College* (1985) with a detailed historical outline from the fourteenth century to 1984 written by Christopher. It also resulted in *Oxford and Cambridge* (1988, with Roger Highfield). This book sets buildings at the forefront of the history of Oxford and Cambridge as prime expressions of changing aspirations and tastes. Christopher's contributions to the history of these two cities and universities and to the history of his own college went far beyond the making of glossy books or fascination with historic medieval buildings. Most of *Oxford and Cambridge* is concerned with post-Reformation history down to the mid-twentieth century, and eleven out of the twenty-one chapters of the *History of Emmanuel College, Cambridge* (1999, with Sarah Bendall and Patrick Collinson) are by Christopher and cover a wide span from the medieval proto-history of the College as a Dominican friary to the College in the 1990s. Christopher was also the prime mover and the General Editor of *A History of the University of Cambridge* (1988–2004). He called that *History* a modest, serviceable frigate beside a great battleship, *The History of the University of Oxford*, which had been launched by Oxford University Press and enjoyed the support of paid staff. The Cambridge *History* has only four volumes, four contributors and received no support from the Cambridge History Faculty—Christopher found this 'painful'. He supplied each volume with a new preface and remarkably himself wrote volume 4 (1993) which was devoted to the university between 1870 and 1990 and ran to more than 600 pages. The preface to this volume seems to anticipate criticism which duly came: 'I have dwelt at length on some seminal figures ... and on some crucial buildings and institutions ... Perhaps their share is disproportionate; but if we are to understand anything of a very complex subject we need from time to time to go deeply into this or that person or institution.' The preface to volume 2, the last volume to appear, includes a particular riposte to John Prest who, in a review, gave his opinion that the volume had concentrated on the heights and ignored the rank and file.[38] Here Brooke settled scores with other reviewers too who thought that in his own volume there was more narrative and exposition than analysis: 'the truth is', he wrote, 'that my closely woven analyses of student backgrounds ... were less readable than my vignettes of the men and women who have made Cambridge internationally famous.' Brooke firmly restated his belief in the importance of reflection in the work of a historian, writing that his own studies of major figures reveal 'the element of reflection which I thought and think the chief mark of my volume'. And he went further to defend his 'frequent references to my own memories and experiences' which 'generously gave the reviewers ... some amusement ... though with less generosity none gave me credit for my purpose—which was precisely to underpin a broad survey of an enormous subject with as much authentic evidence as possible.' He took a swipe too against Lord Annan who 'failing to use the index ... was astounded to find no mention of Lord Adrian'.

Christopher had an inexhaustible ability to collaborate with others whose work he reviewed and also inspired. He always generously acknowledged his debts, above all to his father, his wife and David Knowles.[39] But these were his contemporaries. He also had an intimate understanding of the figures of the past on whom he reflected most, and he had a detailed knowledge of the places in which they once lived and worked and of the sights they saw. If transported in time he would have found his way round the buildings of medieval Cambridge, Gloucester or London with ease, and he would have swiftly recognised and struck up conversation with

---

[38] J. Prest, review of Brooke (1993) in *Journal of Ecclesiastical History*, 46 (1995), 344–6.

[39] Examples of this *pietas* include C. N. L. Brooke, B. H. I. H. Stewart, J. G. Pollard and T. R. Volk (eds.), *Studies in Numismatic Method Presented to Philip Grierson* (Cambridge, 1983), the revised edition (with D. E. Luscombe) of D. Knowles, *Evolution of Medieval Thought* (London, 1988), and (with R. Lovatt, D. E. Luscombe and A. Silem) *David Knowles Remembered* (Cambridge, 1991).

some of the people he met.[40] Had he been cornered awkwardly with Foliot or Becket or Geoffrey of Monmouth he would have parted from them on the best of terms. Had he the chance to talk with John of Salisbury about the times they lived in and the books they had read or with Pope Alexander III about changing attitudes to marriage, they would have gained as much from their conversations with him as would he with them.

V: In London and back in Cambridge, 1967–2015

Liverpool did not offer the opportunities for Rosalind that the Brookes might have hoped; the idea that husband and wife might be employed in the same department was, in those days, unthinkable. The chance to take up a chair at London University was bound to be attractive; it would bring the Brookes much closer to the great libraries and enable them to become involved in the lively seminars of the Institute of Historical Research. Rosalind might even be able to pick up some teaching at other colleges, though in the event this only happened here and there.

Christopher deployed all the skills he had displayed at Liverpool once he was at Westfield. Determination combined with diplomacy won the day at staff meetings, which were fuelled by his sherry bottles. Brenda Bolton overlapped with Christopher during her first two years as a Lecturer at Westfield, and she has testified to the energy and enthusiasm that he brought to the college. Westfield was undergoing significant changes: the college began to admit men three years before he arrived, and Christopher thoroughly approved of mixed institutions. He was less sure that the introduction of science courses at the college was a good thing, but he pressed hard for the teaching of art history, in support of his close colleague Nicolai Rubinstein FBA, the eminent scholar of Renaissance Florence. There was a general policy that students should study something in their first year different from what they knew already, and this drew many to medieval history; exciting lectures by Christopher and his colleagues convinced a good many that it was worth taking medieval papers in later years as well. But perhaps the most memorable episodes were the frequent trips—to Wells, to Chichester or indeed his famous walk around medieval London, conducted at so fast a pace that some student

---

[40] See, for the abbey of Gloucester, Brooke, *Gilbert Foliot and his Letters*, p. 82, and for medieval churches inside and outside the City Walls of London, Brooke and Keir, *London, 800–1216. The Shaping of a City* (London, 1975), pp. 143–8.

stragglers were almost left behind. Their loyalty to him, and his affection for them, did not fade even when he had left London for Cambridge, and he was always glad to see them and to hear from them.[41]

My first, indirect, contact with Christopher occurred at the age of thirteen when I received a school prize on leaving my prep school, and found in a small Richmond bookshop his *From Alfred to Henry III*. My great passion in those days was archaeology, but that embraced Anglo-Saxons and Vikings, and I liked the idea of a book that examined what happened both before and after the Norman Conquest. Then, at my next school, St Paul's, I discovered that this, along with his *Europe in the Central Middle Ages*, was to be one of our A-level textbooks; my own introduction to medieval history, and my turn away from ancient to medieval history, thus owed much to his books, as well as to inspired teachers who invited him to come and speak at the school. I remember that I button-holed Christopher after his lecture and accused him of misunderstanding some points made by R. W. Southern (which I had probably misunderstood, in fact); he remained very civil. Indeed, he invited a group of us, all Oxbridge candidates, to visit Westfield College so we could see what a university was like, even if we had no intention of applying for a place there. Typically, he took enormous care to make sure that we were well looked after, and invited some of us to sit in on his tutorials.

Much later, when I was a graduate student, he discovered that we had a common interest in the Norman Kingdom of Sicily—he was studying a remarkable ivory reliquary put together in Sicily and preserved in Cornwall—and invited me to lunch in London at one of his favourite restaurants, Bertorelli's, in Charlotte Street. In an extensive article, 'The Reliquary of St Petroc and the ivories of Norman Sicily', Christopher traced the story of the relics, which involved a not uncommon tale of theft and restitution, and his collaborator Ralph Pinder-Wilson, a specialist in Islamic art from the British Museum, concentrated on the ivory casket in which the bones of St Petroc lay. His genial generosity towards a doctoral student who was not from his own university was entirely typical; so was his awareness that the sort of research that needed to be done on the ivory casket crossed the traditional boundaries between disciplines—and a good opportunity to make use of evidence from what would now be called 'material culture' was worth seizing.

Christopher remained a frequent visitor to Caius all the time he was at Westfield. Indeed, he was a candidate for the Mastership in 1976, when

---

[41] I am grateful to Dr Brenda Bolton for information about Christopher's time at Westfield.

Professor H. W. R. (later Sir William) Wade FBA was elected by the Fellows. His lack of success did not induce rancour. That he hoped to return to Cambridge eventually was clear. He might well have succeeded Christopher Cheney as Professor of Medieval History in 1972; but one of the electors, Walter Ullmann, suddenly threw his hat into the ring—one did not easily gainsay Walter. By the time the chair fell vacant again, Christopher was safely installed as Dixie Professor of Ecclesiastical History and Professorial Fellow of his old college. That was when I came to know him best, as first a Fellow of Caius and then as a colleague in the History Faculty. Christopher had arrived back in Cambridge a year before Jim Holt FBA was elected to the Chair of Medieval History. Christopher and Jim were very different personalities. Holt was energetic and determined, but he could be brusque, and had spent his career in universities where the word of the Professor (with a capital P) was law. His predecessors, Walter Ullmann FBA and Christopher Cheney FBA, had rather opted out of Faculty affairs, and Holt was determined to raise the profile of medieval history; but it is doubtful whether he ever understood the egalitarian principles that made it difficult for the senior figures in the Faculty (even G. R. Elton) to pull rank. Christopher had more subtle ways of achieving his aims. There was steel beneath the velvet exterior, as Eamon Duffy has noted: he could be obstinate in defence of his subject area and principles, but he was also a diplomat who deplored aggressive talk at the Faculty Board (which for a time he chaired) or other meetings. After Sir James Holt was succeeded by Barrie Dobson FBA in 1988, he found himself in a different role—not just as wise counsellor to Holt's successor, but as a force for peace among the rather fractious group of medieval historians, for Dobson was unhappy in Cambridge and was disappointed to find that the first loyalty of his colleagues tended to be their college rather than an amorphous Faculty housed in one of Cambridge's ugliest and least usable modern buildings. There was a visible contrast between Dobson the outsider and Brooke the insider, accentuated by the fact that by then most or all of the other medieval historians could also be described as insiders. Christopher was rather more effective than Barrie in dealing with the tensions and rivalries that existed among the medieval historians.[42] In particular, Christopher took an interest in the College Teaching Officers, a group peculiar to Cambridge: Teaching Fellows of

---

[42] W. M. Ormrod, 'Richard Barrie Dobson, 1931–2013', *Biographical Memoirs of Fellows of the British Academy*, 13 (2014), pp. 121–42, which on pp. 134–5 rather underestimates Dobson's discontent with Cambridge.

colleges (often with tenure) who did not hold a university post, despite the great distinction of several of them. Unlike some senior historians, he did not treat them as second-class citizens.

As a Professorial Fellow of Caius, Christopher was not involved in college teaching; but he more than made up for that in taking on a horde of graduate students from every college. Miri Rubin has described the experience:

> To a doctoral student just arrived from Jerusalem in the summer of 1981, Christopher Brooke offered the perfect welcome. Even before we got down to the supervision of my research in medieval history, Christopher imparted a great deal of local knowledge to make me comfortable in my new world: how to pronounce Norwich or Gonville and Caius; how best to address those who held sway over college archives and libraries and on whom my research would depend; how to drink sherry and nibble a Bath Oliver biscuit with decorum. In short, Christopher made a stranger into a neighbour, and ultimately into a friend.[43]

On the other hand, his administrative duties were heavier than most other professors in the Humanities, since he was expected to be active in the Divinity Faculty as well as the History Faculty—indeed, his predecessor as Dixie, Gordon Rupp, had spent most of his time in Divinity rather than History. He was co-convenor, with P. N. Brooks, of the Church History seminar that took place in the old Divinity School opposite St John's. Eamon Duffy has described what very often used to happen there:

> Good humour and courtesy were the hallmarks of his chairmanship of the Church History seminar, the humour greatly enhanced by the fact that invariably, as soon as Christopher had introduced the speaker, a benign and temporary narcolepsy descended upon him. His eyelids would droop, his head would descend slowly towards the table before him, and he would fall deeply asleep. Equally invariably, he would wake shortly before the end of the paper, and would be ready with an apposite, pointed and well-informed question to start the discussion.[44]

Whether or not he was really asleep, he had good reason to feel tired: anyone trying to make an appointment with him would see him take out a *Cambridge Pocket Diary* so thick with densely scrawled engagements that it was a miracle he could work out what he was doing on any particular day, however excellent his manuscript reading skills—but this was the

---

[43] Quoted with kind permission from Miri Rubin's address at the Memorial Service for Christopher.
[44] From Eamon Duffy's address at the Memorial Service for Christopher, with Professor Duffy's kind permission.

workaholic Christopher who took his typewriter or sets of proofs on holiday, while still finding plenty of time for the family; and this was the Christopher who rose every morning at five o'clock, which helps to explain his prodigious achievement in publication.[45]

Christopher's hospitality was constantly on view in his college. After his return to Caius he occasionally dined on High Table, though he tended to be rather silent, almost shy, and did not take a prominent part in the sometimes colourful and provocative banter among the Fellows. He did not really form part of any of the social circles within the college. On the other hand, I doubt whether any other Fellow has ever invited so many guests to lunch, which was, of course, a tribute to the fact that so many people wanted to consult him, and that he was involved in so many research projects. (I was a particular beneficiary, since this enabled me to know scores of medieval historians from all over the world whom I would not otherwise have met.) Rosalind often came along as well, not so much as a college wife as in her capacity as a distinguished scholar in her own right—even so, there was never an official position for her in any of the colleges, although she did a certain amount of college teaching. Christopher took great pride in her writings and was especially delighted when she received the degree of Doctor of Letters. His short memoir in the college annual carries a colour illustration of Christopher and Rosalind in their scarlet festive gowns (one of which may well be the gown Z. N. Brooke had worn and that young Christopher thought proved he was a part-time postman, while the other is almost certainly David Knowles's gown); they can be seen disporting themselves in Caius Court, against the backdrop of the sixteenth-century Gate of Honour, close to where Christopher had his college room.

Christopher worked hard behind the scenes on behalf of those in whom he believed, and his patronage was extremely valuable to those in search of academic positions, since his opinions were trusted. He also extended his kindness to scholars who were competent rather than exciting, because he valued their presence and willingness to work hard; and he was constantly busy raising funds for worthwhile research projects —to give an example from the realms of excellence, he argued powerfully and persuasively to obtain funding from the British Academy and Caius for the late Mark Blackburn's position as assistant to Philip Grierson, which led to the publication of the first volumes of the massive study of

---

[45] Information from Philip and Patrick Brooke.

Medieval European Coinage based on the Grierson collection in the Fitzwilliam Museum, Cambridge.

Christopher loved Caius with passion; and yet there was an undeniable ambiguity in his thoughts about the college. In his memoir he wrote:

> Caius has Life Fellows, and they have (in principle) as much say in the running of the college as their younger colleagues. They have long experience – so they tend to think they know better. Some of them, however, also remember what it was like to be young, and try to keep quiet and leave it to those who are closer to the students, closer to the coal-face of learning and research, more in tune with the needs of the present, to take the initiatives.[46]

In this spirit, he could be quite acerbic about some Fellows who held political views, or views about the college and university, of which he did not approve. The admission of women to the college soon after his arrival brought him (and it must be said, just about all the Fellows) great pleasure. He did not share Elton's bizarre doubts about the intellectual capacity of all female historians apart from Helen Cam, which the Regius Professor of History enjoyed expressing. His egalitarian attitude to women also comes across in his book on Jane Austen, published in 1999, which provides a historian's perspective on the social mores of the eighteenth century: attitudes to love, marriage and social status then and further back in time. (His aim was not to compete with the large body of literary criticism that already existed, but he had firm views about how a historian might and indeed should make use of works of literature.) This work was further stimulated by the fact that three of his colleagues in Caius, the social and economic historians Neil McKendrick, Brian Outhwaite and Vic Gatrell, were also interested in using this type of source material in their studies of seventeenth-, eighteenth- and nineteenth-century Britain. Even more, his interest in Jane Austen was aroused by the knowledge that hers was the world with which his ancestors the Johnian divines would have been perfectly familiar.

Christopher's love for his college was very distinctive: Caius was part of his identity in a way that it could never be part of the identity of those who were not hereditary Caius historians brought up around its courts and keeping-rooms—by the 1970s relatively few Fellows had been Caius undergraduates, most having arrived from other colleges or universities. Christopher's attachment to Caius was reflected in his rather romantic vision of the early history of the college that was built on the interpretations offered by two previous historians of Gonville and Caius, John Venn

---

[46] Brooke, 'Memories of Caius', p. 134.

and Dr Caius himself: a small community of poor scholars who inhabited Gonville Hall, the original institution, in the late fourteenth and fifteenth centuries, dependent for all the many improvements to the early college on generous benefactors, and lucky to survive the turmoil of the late Middle Ages.[47] This was probably to underestimate the esteem in which Gonville Hall was held as far away as Avignon and Rome, and it does not explain why the early Fellows were able to accumulate maybe 700 manuscripts (of which up to half still survive), a larger library than the university itself; but his reverence for a community of poor scholars reflected his interest in medieval monks and friars who had sacrificed material wealth for a life of learning—his view of the early college was a way of connecting with medieval religious values he deeply admired. He was, as Eamon Duffy has pointed out, in many ways a traditionalist. His traditionalism extended beyond the college. Duffy recalls how Christopher considered that 2.15pm was the sacred time at which Faculty Board meetings would begin, and even when a radically minded Chairman of the Divinity Faculty moved meetings to 2.00pm Christopher would still arrive not a moment before 2.15. He was not the sort of Oxbridge don who fashionably proposes to throw all ceremony to the winds; but he understood that ceremony works when it has meaning. Indeed, he injected additional meaning into the party held in the University Combination Room in Cambridge to celebrate the publication of the first Festschrift in his honour, in 1993: he had somehow managed to filch a set of proofs, goodness knows from where, and was able to comment graciously on all the contributions, as a return tribute to all the authors (every one of whom was present at the event, even at the cost of crossing the Atlantic to attend).[48] Not surprisingly he was presented with yet another Festschrift to celebrate his eightieth birthday, as well as being honoured with the fine collection of facsimiles mentioned already.[49]

The premature death of their son Francis on 15 March 1996 was a great shock to the Brookes, but they were sustained by their devotion to one another and to a growing brood of grandchildren, as well as by their religious faith. For both Christopher and Rosalind, their last years were troublesome in other ways, with stays in hospital caused by Christopher's

---

[47] J. Venn, *Caius College* (Cambridge, 1901), one of a series of histories of all the colleges in Oxford and Cambridge.
[48] D. Abulafia, M. Franklin and M. Rubin (eds.), *Church and City: 1000–1500: Essays in Honour of Christopher Brooke* (Cambridge, 1992).
[49] M. Rubin (ed.), *European Religious Cultures: Essays Offered to Christopher Brooke on his Eightieth Birthday* (London, 2008).

circulation problems and Rosalind's blood disorders. But they remained remarkably cheerful, and when Rosalind died late in 2014 Christopher insisted on saying a few words at her funeral in Caius chapel, even though he was by now wheelchair-bound. Nonetheless, he continued to work on the charters of Archbishop Theobald into the very last months of his life. He saw his own death as the path to reunion with his beloved wife, and passed away on 27 December 2015 surrounded by his family. Although it could barely contain those who had come to show their respects, his own funeral took place, as he had always wished, in the chapel of the college that he had always seen as his second home.

DAVID ABULAFIA
Fellow of the Academy

DAVID LUSCOMBE
Fellow of the Academy

HENRY MAYR-HARTING
Fellow of the Academy

Note. We should like to thank Philip and Patrick Brooke, Professor Anna Sapir Abulafia, Dr Brenda Bolton, Dr Martin Brett, Professor Eamon Duffy FBA, Dr Diana Greenway FBA, Sir Noel Malcolm FBA, Dr Nigel Ramsay, Professor Miri Rubin, Professor Peter Spufford FBA and Professor E. M. C. van Houts for the information they have very kindly supplied.

List of publications by C. N. L. Brooke mentioned in this memoir

This does not pretend to be a full bibliography of Christopher Brooke's writings. For a bibliography up to 1991 see D. Abulafia, M. Franklin and M. Rubin (eds.), *Church and City, 1000–1500: Essays in Honour of Christopher Brooke* (Cambridge, 1992), pp. 333–9; more recent publications have not yet found a bibliographer. Rather, the list is confined to books, text editions and articles mentioned in this memoir, listed alphabetically. Where CNLB was a co-author his name has been placed first.

Books

A History of Emmanuel College Cambridge (Woodbridge, 2000).
A History of Gonville and Caius College (Woodbridge, 1985).
A History of the University of Cambridge, vol. 4: *1870–1990* (Cambridge, 1993).

Europe in the Central Middle Ages (London, 1964, and subsequent new editions).
From Alfred to Henry III (Nelson History of England, vol. 2, London, 1961).
Gilbert Foliot and his Letters [with A. Morey] (Cambridge, 1965).
Jane Austen: Illusion and Reality (Woodbridge, 1999).
London 800–1216: the Shaping of a City [with G. Keir] (London, 1975).
Medieval Church and Society: Collected Essays (London, 1971).
Oxford and Cambridge [with R. Highfield and W. Swaan] (Cambridge, 1988).
Popular Religion in the Middle Ages: Western Europe 1000–1300 [with R. B. Brooke] (London, 1984).
Studies in Numismatic Method Presented to Philip Grierson [ed. with B. H. I. H. Stewart, J. G. Pollard and T. R. Volk] (Cambridge, 1983).
The Dullness of the Past: an Inaugural Lecture (Liverpool, 1957).
The Foundations of Medieval Ecclesiastical History: Studies Presented to David Smith [ed. with P. Hoskin and B. Dobson] (Woodbridge, 2005).
The Gothic Cathedral (London, 1969).
The Heads of Religious Houses: England and Wales, 940–1216 [with D. Knowles and V. London] (Cambridge, 1972; revised edition, 2001).
The Letters and Charters of Gilbert Foliot [with A. Morey] (Oxford, 1967).
The Letters of John of Salisbury, vol. 1: *Early Letters (1153–61)* [with W. J. Millor and H. E. Butler], (London, 1955; new edn with corrigenda, Oxford, 1986).
The Medieval Idea of Marriage (Oxford, 1989).
The Monastic World 1000–1300 (London, 1974).
The Saxon and Norman Kings (London, 1963).
The Structure of Medieval Society (London, 1971).
The Twelfth-Century Renaissance (London, 1969).

Editions

The Book of William Morton, Almoner of Peterborough Monastery, 1448–1467 [ed. with M. M. Postan, W. T. Mellows and P. I. King] (Northamptonshire Record Society, vol. 16, Northampton, 1954).
Carte Nativorum: a Peterborough Abbey Cartulary of the Fourteenth Century [ed. with M. M. Postan] (Northamptonshire Record Society, Northampton and Oxford, 1960).
Councils and Synods, with other Documents Relating to the English Church, vol. 1: *AD 871–1204* [with D. Whitelock and M. Brett] (Oxford, 1981).
Hugh the Chanter, *History of the Church of York, 1066–1127* [revised edn, with M. Brett and M. Winterbottom of volume originally edited by C. Johnson, London, 1961] (Oxford, 1990).
The Letters and Charters of Gilbert Foliot, Abbot of Gloucester (1139–1148), Bishop of Hereford (1148–63) and London (1163–87) [with A. Morey] (Oxford, 1967).
The Letters of John of Salisbury, vol. 1: *Early Letters (1153–61)* [with W. J. Millor and H. E. Butler], (London, 1955; new edn with corrigenda, Oxford, 1986); vol. 2, *The Later Letters (1163–1180)* [with W. J. Millor] (Oxford, 1979).
The Monastic Constitutions of Lanfranc [revised edn of volume originally edited by D. Knowles, London, 1952] (Oxford, 2002).
Walter Map, *De Nugis Curialium – Courtiers' Trifles* [with R. Mynors] (Oxford, 1983).

Articles

'Brooke, Zachary (1715/16–1788)', *Oxford Dictionary of National Biography*, http://www.oxforddnb. com/view/article/3557 (accessed 20 January 2017).

'English Episcopal *Acta* of the Twelfth and Thirteenth Centuries', in M. J. Franklin and C. Harper-Bill (eds.), *Medieval Ecclesiastical Studies in Honour of Dorothy M. Owen* (Woodbridge, 1995), pp. 41–56.

'Episcopal Charters for Wix Priory', in P. M. Barnes and C. F. Slade (eds.), *A Medieval Miscellany for Doris Mary Stenton* (Publications of the Pipe Roll Society, vol. 36 for the year 1960, London, 1963), pp. 25–43.

'Geoffrey of Monmouth as a historian', in C. N. L. Brooke, D. E. Luscombe, G. H. Martin and D. Owen (eds.), *Church and Government in the Middle Ages. Essays Presented to C. R. Cheney* (Cambridge, 1976), pp. 77–91.

'Henry II, duke of Normandy and Aquitaine' [with Z. N. Brooke], *English Historical Review*, 61 (1946), 81–9.

'Hereford Cathedral dignitaries in the Twelfth Century' [with Z. N. Brooke], *Cambridge Historical Journal*, 8 (1944), 1–21; and 'Hereford Cathedral Dignitaries in the Twelfth Century—Supplement', *Cambridge Historical Journal*, 8, (1944–6), 179–85.

'Memories of Caius', *The Caian: the Annual Record of Gonville and Caius College Cambridge*, 1 October 2007–30 September 2008, 123–39.

'Philip Grierson 1910–2006' [with Lord Stewartby], *Proceedings of the British Academy*, 150 (2007), 79–104.

'St Dominic and his first biographer', *Transactions of the Royal Historical Society*, 17 (1967), 23–40.

'St Peter of Gloucester and St Cadoc of Llancarfan', in N. Chadwick (ed.), *Studies in the Early British Border* (Cambridge, 1963), pp. 258–322.

'The Archbishops of St David's, Llandaff and Caerleon-on-Usk', in N. Chadwick, K. Hughes, C. N. L. Brooke and K. Jackson (eds.), *Studies in the Early British Church* (Cambridge, 1958).

'The Canterbury forgeries and their author', *Downside Review*, 68 (1950), 462–71, and 69 (1951), 210–51.

'The Cerne letters of Gilbert Foliot and the Legation of Imar of Tusculum' [with A. Morey], *English Historical Review*, 63 (1948), 433–52.

'The Reliquary of St Petroc and the ivories of Norman Sicily' [with R. Pinder-Wilson], *Archaeologia*, 104 (1973), 261–305.

Books published in his honour

D. Abulafia, M. Franklin and M. Rubin (eds.), *Church and City: 1000–1500: Essays in Honour of Christopher Brooke* (Cambridge, 1992).

M. Brett, P. Hoskin and D. Smith (eds.), *Facsimiles of English Episcopal Acta, 1085–1305* (London, 2012).

M. Rubin (ed.), *European Religious Cultures: Essays Offered to Christopher Brooke on his Eightieth Birthday* (London, 2008).

MICHAEL JOHN MUSTILL

Michael John Mustill
1931–2015

MICHAEL MUSTILL WAS ONE OF THE finest lawyers of his generation, as Queen's Counsel at the Commercial Bar, as a judge of the Queen's Bench Division, as a Lord Justice of Appeal and finally as a Law Lord, a member of the Judicial Committee of the House of Lords. He was ennobled as Lord Mustill of Pateley Bridge. Unlike some other life peers he did not take his title from the place where he had simply acquired a second home. He took it from the name of the town in Yorkshire where his mother had grown up, and where he died, having spent all the time he could there towards the end of his life.

Michael Mustill was a Yorkshireman, and was proud of it, although only those who knew him well were particularly aware of it. He was born on 10 May 1931 in Leeds in the West Riding of Yorkshire, and died in Pateley Bridge on 24 April 2015. Pateley Bridge had been the home of his mother Marion Summersgill Mustill (née Harrison) and of her parents and grandparents since at least as far back as the 1850s, and Mustill inherited Sandholme Cottage from his parents. Many of his mother's relations still live in and around Pateley Bridge. Mustill's great-great-grandfather, Alfred Mustill, was a smallholder in Cambridgeshire who moved to Yorkshire before 1875. By 1881 he was a police constable in Goldsborough. He had three sons. The two younger sons, Joseph (b. 1872) and Alfred (b. 1875), made a living in Boroughbridge as manufacturers of mineral water. The oldest, Clement Michael (1871–1944), went to Geneva as a young man, where he learnt the hotel trade. He was a head waiter for much of his life. He suffered an accident in his later years which left him unemployed, although he lived until the age of 73.

Biographical Memoirs of Fellows of the British Academy, XVI, 281–299. © The British Academy 2017.
Posted 14 November 2017. © The British Academy 2017.

Mustill's father, also called Clement Mustill (1903–93), was the son of the head waiter. He trained as an engineer and worked his way up from adversity to become the managing director of Jackson Boilers in Leeds. He was the chairman of the Leeds Northeast Conservative Association which chose Keith Joseph as its candidate for the constituency, overcoming some resistance to the choice of a Jewish politician. Sir Keith was heard once to say that Clement Mustill would have been the MP if he had come from a less humble background: the truth was that Clement could not afford to sit in Parliament.

Michael's mother Marion was quite as impressive as his father. Her father ran a grocery: he was highly esteemed and loved locally, a pillar of the community and musical. Like Clement, Marion Mustill was a lifelong Conservative, and she served for many years as a councillor in Leeds. She was an accomplished pianist (as in a lesser way was Mustill himself) and an associate of Trinity College, London.

Between them, with the help of scholarships, Mustill's parents managed to educate him at private boarding schools, first at the Wells School, Ilkley, from the age of eight (1939), at Stancliffe Hall, Derby, from the age of eleven (1942) then at Oundle School from thirteen to eighteen (1944–9). Oundle was not an upper-class school: it was mainly the place for the gifted sons of well-to-do merchants, although its reputation was such that H. G. Wells, Siegfried Sassoon and Robert Graves also sent sons there. The standard of teaching was very high: in chemistry, for example, he once wrote home that his class had manufactured polonium, well known nowadays as a lethally radioactive substance. At Oundle he took part in every activity which was on offer. He discovered a talent for shooting and tennis, and he conducted the house orchestra, having learnt to play both the cello and the piano. Several essays have survived from his time at Oundle, one on the subject of death, and another on a text from the Book of Daniel which led him to reflect on the appalling consequences of the atomic bombing of Hiroshima and Nagasaki. The essays are remarkably mature for a teenager, and the ideas that he had formed at that time matured in later life into his more profound thoughts on such subjects as mentally disordered offenders and the termination of the lives of patients in a vegetative state.

After leaving Oundle School, he spent two years of National Service with the Royal Artillery between 1949 and 1951. He had a reputation for being clumsy and ill-dressed as a soldier, but in spite of this, to his surprise, he was commissioned second lieutenant and became ADC to a general, who greatly enjoyed Michael's company and had a high regard for him. William 'Rusty' Park, Professor of Law at Boston University, has an anecdote from this time:

> During one of Michael's visits to Boston we took in a baseball game together. The Red Sox, our local team, were playing their sworn rivals, the New York Yankees. Michael revealed that during his army service he sometimes narrated baseball games for American troops stationed in England. Then with frightening precision he imitated noises for a host of plays: the whoosh of an infield fly ball before being caught by the second baseman; the thud of a slow runner tagged while trying to slide into third; and the smack of a home run hit by a right-handed batter on its way to clearing the left-field wall at Fenway Park. Enough to cause envy in the best radio sound effects.

After his National Service he went on to St John's College, Cambridge (1951–4) to read mathematics, supported by an open scholarship and a state scholarship. But he realised that although he had been taught to a very high standard in mathematics, he was not so exceptionally gifted as to warrant spending three years studying it, and on the advice of his tutors he decided to read law. He was awarded the George Long Prize for Jurisprudence and, by St John's College, a McMahon Law Studentship to help with his studies for the Bar. However, his degree was not as good as had been expected, no doubt because, as he said in later life, he found the study of the law as an undergraduate subject pretty dull. But he read and attended lectures prodigiously outside the law, and made many friends, including actors and writers, who stayed with him for life. After the great earthquake in the Ionian Isles in 1953 he went alone and at his own expense to Kefalonia, supported later by charitable funds raised by his mother. For this he was thanked for his services by the Greek government. From this experience he derived great affection for Greece and for Greeks. Later as counsel he had many Greek shipowners as clients, most of whom had neither the wealth nor the sophistication of an Onassis or a Niarchos—but he got on well with all of them.

After his graduation he spent time working for Slaughter & May, a leading firm of solicitors in the City. This gave him an insight into the life of a working solicitor which stood him in good stead in his time as a barrister and as a judge. At the Bar he worked well in a team with solicitors, and as a judge he was more understanding than many others in his position of the pressures under which solicitors conduct litigation.

He was called to the Bar by Gray's Inn in 1955 and in the autumn of that year he became the pupil of Michael Kerr at 3 Essex Court Chambers (later Sir Michael Kerr, a Lord Justice of Appeal), who became a lifelong friend. Michael Kerr was at that time an overworked but highly paid junior barrister. He was the son of the renowned German writer and critic Alfred Kerr, and the sister of Judith Kerr, the author of *The Tiger Who Came to Tea* and *Hitler Stole My Pink Rabbit*. The Kerr family fled from Berlin in 1933, first to Switzerland, then to Paris and finally to England, where Michael Kerr attended a public school and then, for a year, Clare College, Cambridge. He was interned for a time in the Isle of Man in 1940, but ended the war in the RAF, still classified as an enemy alien, but speaking fluent German, French and English. The head of the chambers was Alan Mocatta QC (later Mocatta J.) and among the other members were Eustace Roskill (later Lord Roskill), John Megaw (later Lord Justice Megaw), John Donaldson (later Lord Donaldson, Master of the Rolls) and Robert (Bob) McCrindle, who ranked high among the most talented advocates of his time. Anthony Lloyd (later Lord Lloyd) joined soon afterwards and was for years afterwards Mustill's constant opponent in the law courts, and eventually a colleague in the House of Lords.

Mustill was taken on as a tenant at the end of his pupillage and despite the shortage of work at the Commercial Bar at that time was soon busy attending cases in the Commercial Court and in the Court of Appeal. Michael Mustill was pupil master to a whole generation of barristers, among whom was Nicholas Phillips who later became Master of the Rolls and President of the Supreme Court and whose sister Caroline became Mustill's second wife.

From the outset Mustill's method as a lawyer was, if not unique, at the very best level of his contemporaries. The conventional view of the common law at the time was that it was the best system of law that could be imagined, because it was based on decisions on individual cases as they came before the courts and was therefore not based—as were other systems of law and particularly the systems of civil law which prevail in Europe and elsewhere—on speculative reasoning about hypothetical cases. The classic statement of this point of view was that of Oliver Wendell Holmes that 'The life of the law has not been logic; it has been experience.' For Mustill this was a strength but also a shortcoming. The strength lay in the focus on the practical issues in the case before the court, and the experience that the court could, with the help of counsel, bring to bear on them. But Mustill had a profound view that the legal decision of practical questions could not be divorced from a systematic and logical analysis of the underlying legal principles. In his view, the weakness in the common law lay in the fact that systematic development of principles of law depended on the chance that cases arose which enabled the court to deal with them. In contrast, systems of law based on civil or Roman law were able to absorb more readily ideas based on principle, independently of the facts of actual cases, because it depended principally on the work of legal scholars, not on the decision of judges. Mustill felt this to be a serious limitation on the development of the common law. It was never enough for him to decide a case. He needed to know where the decision would lead in other cases, and why.

He never started by assuming that the answer to any particular problem was to argue from the propositions decided by the reported cases. His instinct was always to treat the question he was attempting to answer as part of a wider set of questions, to which an answer could only be found by resorting to norms other than those derived from the legal precedents. Sometimes these were legal norms of more general application which underlay or sometimes contradicted those which were derived from the decided cases. There was also to him a basic principle that rules should be consistent unless the doctrine of precedent dictated otherwise—and, as one can see from the reasoning in some of his judgments, consistency meant not only consistency between decided cases on the point in question but also consistency between the logic of decisions in different but related fields of law. He was, for example, much troubled by the fact, which so far as is known he never had the opportunity to articulate in any reported case, that administrative law had different principles from arbitration law, and gave rise to different results in similar cases.

As an advocate he was not a great orator. Quite the reverse. His style of argument as counsel was low key. The days of Marshall Hall and Norman Birkett were long past. He sought to persuade not by rhetoric but by the strength of his argument and the skill with which he handled the evidence. His voice was in the tenor range or perhaps upper baritone, but it was tinged, scarcely perceptibly, by a Yorkshire intonation, and a constant sense that he was on the point of saying something amusing. In private his wit and good humour burst forth the whole time, but in court, both as an advocate and as a judge, he maintained a purity of language and thought which was exemplary. He had the characteristic, which too few advocates have, of pausing before he answered a difficult question from the bench: this gave the impression, in his case quite correctly, that he wished to be sure of his answer before he gave it. He had a most disarming smile when he was challenged from the bench—the same smile that he gave to his friends in private. His prose style was not only beyond reproach, but maintained a freshness and fluidity which few lawyers in modern times have equalled. He often spoke of himself as a simple craftsman of language, but he was in truth supreme in his field and dedicated this craft to the exposition of the law. In this he was pre-eminently successful, not only in the felicity of individual phrases, but in his ability to pace the development of an argument through its exposition in several themes, its development and recapitulation. The pace was sometimes slow, but it built up seamlessly from basic propositions to what was often a complex and far from basic result: his argument was clearly articulated, and in the end it led to conclusions which, so far as legal conclusions ever can be, were intellectually convincing. All of this he achieved without the slightest hint of rhetoric or bombast.

He taught his pupils that the first minute of an argument was the one that really counted: it was the moment at which you aroused the interest of the court in your case and told them why the merits were on your side. In his last years as a junior he often demonstrated to his pupils how to put this into effect before the Queen's Bench Masters, an overworked but admirable body of junior judges dealing with matters which did not need to be decided by the judge himself. In those days they had an appointment list after lunch for short applications in an area of the Law Courts known as the 'Bear Garden'. Many barristers made the mistake of sauntering in and assuming that the Masters would listen patiently and respectfully to their arguments, not realising that they had a huge workload and dreaded the *longueurs* of appearances by counsel. Not so Mustill. When his case was called on he would enter at the trot with his papers open in front of him, explaining why he was there and what he wanted before he had even passed through the door. By the time he had crossed the carpet and reached the Master's desk he had virtually completed his submissions. Many opponents were quite blown off course by his whirlwind attack.

He had a great ability to break down a legal problem by analysis of every possible permutation of circumstances, in contrast to the usual forensic method of the advocate, who typically concentrates on arguments to defeat those of the opposite side. This skill was not deployed in argument, but it served to anticipate contrary arguments and difficult questions from the bench. It was, however, very much a feature of his academic writing, which he regarded as a quest for the correct—or at least the best—answer to every foreseeable variation of the question at issue. For questions requiring multiple answers, he would often construct elaborate algorithms and spreadsheets. These rarely saw the light of day in any of his published work,[1] but they enabled him to be confident that he had

---

[1] The 1996 Goff Lecture, City University, Hong Kong, entitled 'Hong Kong 1996—too many laws?', *Asia Pacific Law Review* 6 (1998), 1–21, is a notable exception. It is illustrated by no fewer

covered the subject from every angle, and to seek out the general principles underlying a seemingly disorganised set of legal rules. Although the scaffolding was usually dismantled once the general principles had been established, the fact that it was the underpinning of the general principles gave consistency and coherence to what he wrote.

His most accomplished work of this kind was published as 'Multi-party arbitrations: an agenda for law-makers'.[2] The problems of multi-party arbitrations were very much to the fore at that time and had been discussed at length by the Departmental Advisory Committee on Arbitration Law, of which he was the chairman. One of the weaknesses of arbitration, particularly at the international level, was its inability to harness together related disputes between different parties, operating under different national laws and under different contracts. The discussion of the problems to which this gave rise was not always well organised and the proposed solutions were correspondingly ineffective. Mustill's paper set new ground rules for the discussion in a comprehensive and ordered framework, and asked the fundamental questions which needed to be answered. It was, frankly, a masterpiece. The shape of the whole subject had been set. But the answers have still to be found.

*****

The formal milestones of Mustill's career after he was called to the Bar can be set out quite briefly before we turn to consider his contribution to the development and exposition of the law, which will be the subject of most of the remainder of this memoir. Other significant appointments and honours will be mentioned in their proper context.

He became a QC in 1968. In 1972, he was appointed Recorder of the Crown Court, a precursor to being made a High Court Judge of the Queen's Bench Division in 1978. From 1981-4 he was Presiding Judge on the North Eastern Circuit and, from 1984-5, Judge in Charge of the Commercial Court. In 1985 he was appointed Lord Justice of Appeal and admitted to the Privy Council, and in 1992 was made Judge of the Appellate Committee of the House of Lords, and appointed Lord of Appeal in Ordinary.

From the start of his judicial career, as a part-time Recorder, Mustill came into contact with the criminal law, a field in which he had played virtually no part as counsel. He sat in criminal cases, both as a High Court Judge in trials before juries and as a member of the Court of Criminal

---

than eight diagrams showing the relationship between the various topics under discussion, and is characteristic of Michael's habitual methodical approach when tackling a complex subject.
[2] *Arbitration International*, 7 (1991), 393–402.

Appeal and, as we shall see, when he reached the House of Lords he turned his mind to some of the more perplexing issues in that field. He was particularly pleased to be appointed Presiding Judge on the North Eastern Circuit, which included his home town, Pateley Bridge. It was during his time on the North Eastern Circuit that he tried at Newcastle five conjoined cases concerning the liability of shipyards for industrial deafness suffered by men who worked in the yards.[3] The trial lasted four weeks and resulted in a judgment of nearly fifty pages. It demonstrated what those who had seen his work as counsel already knew, that he was completely at home with complex technical evidence, and particularly skilful at summarising and evaluating it. The judgment was not appealed, and formed the basis for settlement of a large number of other cases which turned on similar facts.

The number of reported judgments given by Mustill during his judicial career runs to over 800, and there must be hundreds more unreported judgments. The most widely used online database for law reports has 209 cases in the House of Lords, 74 in the Privy Council, 582 in the Court of Appeal and 78 in the High Court (where fewer cases are reported). They cover a wide range of subjects, grouped by the database into twenty-four separate (but to some extent overlapping) categories. There are over fifty reported cases in the categories Crime (227), Commercial (102), Contract (93), Finance (68), Land (94), Public Law (89) and Transport (54). This breadth of decision is not in itself unique but it does show the great variety of cases in which a long-serving judge can be called upon to demonstrate his ability as a lawyer. It is notable in Mustill's case how very few of his decisions in the lower courts were overruled or disapproved.

*****

If asked to identify Mustill's greatest contribution to the law outside the Bench most lawyers, certainly those who work in the field of commercial disputes, would point to his comprehensive account of the law of arbitration, published originally in 1982 by Butterworths under the title *The Law and Practice of Commercial Arbitration in England and Wales*, with the short title *Commercial Arbitration*.

This was published before the explosive growth in international commercial arbitration which has taken place in the last thirty years or so. It was based on Mustill's great experience in appearing as counsel in arbitra-

---

[3] *Thompson v Smiths Shiprepairers (North Shields) Ltd.* [1984] Q.B. 405.

tions, most of which were domestic, in the sense that they took place in London, although they covered among other things shipping, insurance and commodity disputes, and therefore frequently involved parties from abroad. There was already a substantial amount of international arbitration, particularly arbitrations under the Rules of the International Court of Arbitration of the International Chamber of Commerce based in Paris, where Mustill also appeared as a silk in some of the heavier cases.

The only textbook which had been kept up to date when Mustill started work on the book was a reasonably workmanlike analysis of the reported cases, but it was by no means complete or accurate and contained little discussion of matters of principle, particularly if there were few or no reported cases to form the foundation of such a discussion. Mustill therefore resolved to write a book which was founded on his own comprehensive re-reading of the reported cases, which went beyond the reported decisions in discussing important and fundamental matters of principle, and at the same time gave guidance to the participants in arbitrations on matters of practice, which were rarely mentioned in the decided cases but in which he had a wealth of valuable experience. It is not possible to pinpoint exactly when he started work on the project but it was probably around the time that he took silk in 1967. Almost from the start until publication of the first edition in 1982, he had a commitment from Butterworths to publish it, which they loyally and patiently stood by through the many years of gestation. Eventually it became common knowledge that the book had been in preparation for some fifteen years, during which time Mustill was known to be writing it in the relaxing surroundings of the Ardèche, but that it had still not been forthcoming. This led to Mustill's then wife suggesting that the following quotation from Anthony Trollope's novel *Ralph the Heir* should appear in the introductory pages, as it did:

> Nevertheless, let us hope that the change of air may tend to future diligence and that the magnum opus may yet be achieved. We have heard of editions of Aristophanes, of Polybius, of the Iliad, of Ovid, which have ever been forthcoming under the hands of notable scholars, who have grown grey amidst the renewed promises which have been given. And some of these works have come forth, belying the prophecies of incredulous friends.

Mustill's main resource when writing the book was a complete collection of the Lloyd's List Reports, which has since 1919 published law reports of interest to the maritime and insurance communities, but which had not been systematically noted up in the current textbooks. In his spare time he read through these and noted them up from start to finish, and during the long vacation would often load up his car with as many of the volumes as he could manage and take them away with him, usually to France, latterly to the Ardèche where he spent much of his free time.

He was a subscriber all his professional life to the *Revue de l'Arbitrage*, the leading French periodical in the field, which was a valuable source of French doctrine and jurisprudence. His practice was to summarise articles and law reports which he felt were of interest, and sometimes to photocopy them in their entirety. The results went into a series of what he called 'shoeboxes', which is what many of them were. They also contained scribbled notes written by Mustill to himself on topics which occurred to him from time to time: some of these were indecipherable even to Mustill himself. As time went on he relied on pupils and other young colleagues to conduct preliminary research and to go through the shoeboxes, categorising them by subject matter, and sometimes writing draft material for him to work into completed text. The last of these was the author of this memoir. But the fact is that the substance although not the shape of the first edition was substantially the work of Mustill himself. Although his co-author wrote more of the second edition and quite a large part of its later companion volume,[4] Mustill always proved able to contribute a large amount of material of the very highest quality—usually it must be said at the last minute—and in a state of some editorial disarray as had been the case with his manuscript of the first edition. *Commercial Arbitration* had many innovative features, and the discussion that follows covers only those topics which can truly be said to be innovative, rather than improvements in presentation and accuracy over other contemporary texts on the subject of arbitration.

Probably the most conspicuous innovation was that the book did not confine itself to propositions of law derived from the decided cases. That was not Mustill's way. He never hesitated to offer an opinion on questions to which the reported cases gave no answer, with such degree of hesitation or certainty as he though fit. In this he was not unique. Other law books, particularly those written by academics, had taken the same line. What was unique about Mustill was that he not only dealt with speculative issues of law, but also with troublesome issues of practice. There is scarcely a page in the book which could not be used to illustrate this. A good example is his discussion of the practice of 'stopping counsel', well known to judges and advocates, but unnoticed in any other textbook. This is the

[4] M. J. Mustill and S. C. Boyd, *The Law and Practice of Commercial Arbitration in England*, 2nd edn (London, 1989); M. J. Mustill and S. C. Boyd, *Commercial Arbitration. 2001 Companion Volume to the Second Edition* (London, 2001).

practice, common in the law courts, of telling counsel that he need make no further submissions when the court is in his favour and his opponent has already had the opportunity to put his case in full. The discussion in the text is a good example of what Mustill was able to contribute from his own experience as counsel and as a judge:

> The practice of stopping counsel is a useful one, but it should only be used when the arbitrator's decision is in a party's favour. It should not be used as a way of cutting short a long winded argument when the arbitrator has decided against the party making the submission: to stop counsel in this situation and then to decide against him might well amount to misconduct. The best course in this situation is for the arbitrator to summarise in his own words the submission which is being made so as to understand that he has understood it, even if he does not necessarily agree with it: few advocates will go on repeating themselves once they are sure the point has been understood.[5]

The book abounds with practical observations of this kind, which is no doubt why for many years it was the standard textbook for those seeking admission to the Chartered Institute of Arbitrators.

The book contained many innovations in terms of the analysis and exposition of the law. The very first chapter, described as a 'Descriptive introduction', was a new idea of giving a bird's-eye view of the entire subject. It was a summary of the English law of arbitration, as described in more detail in the rest of the book. This was aimed not only at non-lawyers (of whom many were in those days, and still are, appointed as arbitrators in England) but also at foreign lawyers who increasingly were to become involved in arbitrations in London and in arbitrations abroad conducted under English arbitration law. The second chapter, headed 'What is an arbitration?', was an equally innovative idea, which dealt systematically with a subject that until then had received little attention. It was a topic which had been the subject of two quite recent decisions of the House of Lords, but the discussion went far beyond the relatively narrow issues involved in those decisions.

Chapter 3 contained a discussion of the laws governing an arbitration in which Mustill, probably for the first time, identified four separate laws which may potentially be involved in a case raising questions of the conflict of laws: (1) the proper law of the contract, which governs the substantive rights of the parties to the contract; (2) the proper law of the arbitration agreement, which governs the obligations of the parties to submit their disputes to arbitration and to abide by its outcome; (3) the

[5] Ibid., pp. 307–8.

curial law, which governs the procedure to be applied; and (4) the proper law of the reference, which is the contract law governing a particular reference under the arbitration agreement. This has now become the standard classification.

Chapter 12 discussed 'The residual jurisdiction of the court'. This was a subject of some complexity, and its boundaries had not been properly explored. Its importance to the work as a whole was in situations where the arbitration had broken down. Could or should the court take over the dispute in such a case? This was of relevance to later chapters, discussed below, which explored the possibility that the arbitration agreement might come to an end because of the doctrines of abandonment or frustration. Its significance in this context, it may safely be said, had not before been noticed.

The final section of the book, entitled 'Problems and remedies', and forming more than a third of the whole work, discussed the powers of the courts to enforce arbitration agreements and in various other ways to support the arbitration, so to ensure that it is properly conducted, and to supplement the powers of the arbitrators where they are absent or defective. Previous works had not attempted to deal separately or comprehensively with these powers, preferring instead to treat them as incidental to the discussion of individual subjects, such as the duty of the arbitrator to act impartially and fairly, which *Commercial Arbitration* dealt with as separate topics already discussed in earlier parts of the book. Two developments of importance had taken place before the book was published. First, the Arbitration Act 1979 had done away with the much-criticised special case procedure, which was until then the main method of inviting the courts to decide questions of law arising out of an award. This was clumsy and expensive, and had latterly led to an avalanche of applications to the court. 'Problems and remedies' began with a history of the judicial control of arbitrations, itself a novelty, and a full discussion of the 1979 Act and how it had been applied in practice, together with a quite new discussion of the use of reasons for an award, and what they should contain. Second, there had been two recent decisions of the House of Lords relating to the problem of putting an end to arbitrations which had dragged on for years with little or no effort on the part of the claimant to bring them to a conclusion. The argument in the first case was that the arbitration agreement might come to an end by abandonment, or through the doctrine of repudiation, and in the second that it might be discharged by the doctrine of frustration. The use of contractual doctrines as a solution to a well-known practical difficulty undoubtedly was in large part the result of ideas which he had formed and discussed with colleagues while he was still at the Bar. In the end the use of these doctrines turned out to lead to a dead end, but the two cases enabled the House of Lords to consider for the first time the extent to which an arbitration agreement could be analysed as if it were an ordinary contract.

As a coda to the work, there were two appendices on new subjects. The first was a compilation of cases on the issue of what was a question of fact or a question of law, or belonged to the category of 'mixed fact and law', which could only have been written by an author who, as Mustill had done, had read and noted up virtually every case on the law of arbitration decided in the previous seventy-five years. It remains a valuable resource for those who have to persuade a court to grant leave to appeal on a question of law, or to resist an application for leave. Second, he contributed a short account of the doctrine of 'Manifest Disregard' under United States law, derived wholly from cases decided in the USA. This has proved to be of less value, but it was incidental to the discussion in the body of the book of ways in which an award might conceivably be challenged by procedures other than by way of appeal. It strikingly illustrates Mustill's readiness and ability to think outside the confines of English law.

By the time of the second edition in 1989, to Mustill's great pleasure, the sales of the book overseas were as great as those in England. Largely because of this, his name was as familiar to overseas lawyers as it was to English ones. It has been said that he delivered addresses and took part in arbitration colloquia in some twenty countries. His influential monograph on multi-party arbitrations has already been mentioned, but it was his monograph 'The new *Lex Mercatoria*: the first twenty-five years' which perhaps had the greatest influence of all his published addresses on the theory of international arbitration law.[6]

In the twenty-five years leading up to the publication of this monograph in 1987 there had grown up among academic lawyers—mainly but not exclusively from civil law countries—the concept of a transnational and non-national body of law supposed to represent the law of commerce and of merchants (hence *lex mercatoria*). The main advantage of this body of law was said to be its independence from the particular rules of any one national system of law and its supposed origins in the usages of trade and commerce. Mustill dealt with the subject by posing a series of questions: What is the *lex mercatoria*?; What kind of law is it?; When does

---

[6] M. J. Mustill, 'The new *Lex Mercatoria*: the first twenty-five years', *Arbitration International*, 4 (1988), 86–119.

it apply?; Does it empower the arbitrator to decide in equity?; What is the relation between *lex mercatoria* and national law?; What are the sources of *lex mercatoria*?; What are its rules?; and How is it to be ascertained? Each question was answered methodically with compendious references to the published material, mainly in French. Finally he asked:

> Does [the *lex mercatoria*] provide the businessman with a set of rules which is sufficiently accessible and certain to permit the efficient conduct of his transactions? Is the *lex* manifestly superior, in its content and methodology, to establish national systems of commercial law? If so, is its superiority so obvious that it can now be said to have imposed itself, whether by the very fact of its existence or by a notion of implied consent, on the international business community as a whole, and on all transactions in which it is not expressly excluded? In short, has the lex mercatoria stolen the international commercial scene, pushing national laws into the wings? In each case, the detached observer must, I believe, be driven to answer 'no'. More sympathetically, he might add '... or at least not yet'.[7]

Since this monograph was published, the *lex mercatoria*, although not without its adherents even now, has not prospered as a practical tool for resolving commercial disputes. The first edition of *Commercial Arbitration* was followed by a second in 1989 and a Companion Volume in 2001. They contained valuable new material on the theory of arbitration and on the underlying concepts of the Arbitration Act 1996.

As a result of his work on arbitration law Mustill was awarded the degree of LLD (Doctor of Laws) by the University of Oxford. This was not an honorary degree. It was awarded for his important and original academic work in *Commercial Arbitration*, which he had been invited to submit for examination for the LLD. It is scarcely surprising that he was awarded this degree, given the quality of his work in *Commercial Arbitration*, and the fact that the material it contained was the equivalent of several theses or dissertations, perhaps four or five in all. He was also appointed an Honorary Fellow of St John's College, Cambridge, the Yorke Distinguished Visiting Fellow and Arthur Goodhart Visiting Professor of Legal Science, Cambridge, from 2003–4 and Honorary Professor of English Law at Birmingham University. He was Honorary President of the Chartered Institute of Arbitrators from 1994–7, a vice-president of the Court of Arbitration of the International Chamber of Commerce, and a President of the International Law Association. Mustill was elected a Fellow of the British Academy in 1996.

---

[7] Ibid., p. 117.

In 1985 Mustill was appointed by the UK government as chairman of the Interdepartmental Advisory Committee on Arbitration. Under Mustill and two later chairmen (Lord Steyn and Lord Saville) the work of the Committee eventually led to the drafting and enactment of the Arbitration Act 1996. The preparatory steps, which took place under Mustill's chairmanship, were to participate in the drafting of the UNCITRAL[8] Model Law on Arbitration, and to make recommendations as to whether the final draft should be adopted by the UK. The 'Response to the UNCITRAL Model Law', published in 1989,[9] recommended that that there should be a new and improved Arbitration Act which should comprise a statement in statutory form of the more important principles of the English law of arbitration expressed in language which was sufficiently clear and free from technicalities to be readily comprehensible to the layman and which should so far as possible have the same structure and language as the Model Law. After a number of false starts this recommendation led to the Arbitration Act 1996.

Following his retirement from the Bench, Mustill was much in demand as an arbitrator in international commercial and investment disputes, but the principle that arbitration is confidential makes it impossible to discuss these cases.

*****

Apart from his work on arbitration, Mustill made contributions as a judge to many varied fields of law. This is however true of most judges who have served long periods on the Bench. But it has already been said that Mustill's special contribution was not in deciding cases as they happened to arise for decision, but as a systematic analyst of the law, in which his skill rarely had an opportunity to be invoked in his reported decisions, which had perforce to focus on the case in hand, but in his published books and lectures. Out of the very many exceptions to this, two cases stand out, each of which illustrates Mustill's profound analysis of the relationship between law and ethics, or to put it in a structural framework, the relationship between the Courts and Parliament in matters of social policy.

---

[8] United Nations Commission on International Trade Law.
[9] Advisory Committee on Arbitration Law, *A New Arbitration Act? The Response of the Departmental Advisory Committee to the UNCITRAL Model Law on International Commercial Arbitration* (London, 1989).

The first is the *Spanner* case,[10] which involved a prosecution under the criminal law of offences against the person of male sado-masochists who had consensually engaged in private in a series of the most revolting acts of perverted harm against one another. Mustill's dissenting judgment quashing the convictions was portrayed by the media, as it still is, as a defence of such practices. Nothing could be further from the truth. Mustill was careful not to express any personal view about the moral dimension of the case, although the tone of his judgment makes it clear that he was disgusted by the evidence. His opinion is encapsulated in the following extract from his judgment:

> ... since this prosecution has been widely noticed it must be emphasised that the issue before the House is not whether the appellants' conduct is morally right, but whether it is properly charged under the Act of 1861. When proposing that the conduct is not rightly so charged I do not invite your Lordships' House to endorse it as morally acceptable. Nor do I pronounce in favour of a libertarian doctrine specifically related to sexual matters. Nor in the least do I suggest that ethical pronouncements are meaningless, that there is no difference between right and wrong, that sadism is praiseworthy, or that new opinions on sexual morality are necessarily superior to the old, or anything else of the same kind. What I do say is that these are questions of private morality; that the standards by which they fall to be judged are not those of the criminal law; and that if these standards are to be upheld the individual must enforce them upon himself according to his own moral standards, or have them enforced against him by moral pressures exerted by whatever religious or other community to whose ethical ideals he responds.[11]

The second case is the decision of the House of Lords in the *Bland* case.[12] This concerned a young man who had been seriously injured in the Hillsborough disaster, where scores of people attending a football match had died or been injured in a catastrophic crush caused by a failure of crowd control. Bland had survived, but in a 'persistent vegetative state', incapable of any normal human function. The issue was whether the doctors could let him die, or as it was put 'kill him', by withdrawing life support in the form of food and water. Killing him might amount to murder or at least to manslaughter. The House of Lords decided that the principle of the sanctity of life would not be violated by withdrawing invasive life support to which he had not consented and which was of no

---

[10] *R v Brown* [1994] 1 AC 212, named the Spanner case after Operation Spanner, the investigation which led to it.
[11] Ibid., p. 273.
[12] *Airedale NHS Trust v Bland* [1993] A.C. 789.

benefit to him. Mustill delivered a judgment which is masterly in describing the role and limits of the courts in deciding questions which have not only a legal but also an ethical and moral dimension. Following this decision he was appointed a member of the House of Lords Select Committee on Medical Ethics.

His interest in the moral and ethical side of the law was reflected in his maiden speech in the House of Lords, which was on the subject of mentally disturbed offenders. He had written an article in 1992 which was founded on the trouble he had felt in sentencing such offenders. When trying criminal cases, he had been notoriously cautious about imposing sentences of imprisonment, to the point of being regarded as a soft judge. He was particularly troubled by the sentencing of mentally disturbed offenders, and by the seriously inadequate treatment available to them in the penal system. He gave much time to organising, through the Mental Health Foundation, conferences of a kind never held before at which prison governors, senior members of the judiciary, social workers, probation officers, academics and psychiatrists could pool their experience towards finding ways to improve the system.

After his retirement Mustill had the ambition to write a book analysing the principles of the criminal law, but ill health and overwork prevented him from achieving this. This was a great loss to the criminal law. Mustill considered parts of the criminal law, particularly in the field of offences against the person, to be illogical and sometimes even incoherent. He was not alone in this, and the subject would have benefited greatly from Mustill's systematic and panoptic approach to fundamental questions of principle. His experience of the criminal law, by then very wide by any standard, was not greater than a good many other judges, but his intellectual capacity to make sense of it all was unrivalled.

Mustill was an editor for many years of *Scrutton on Charterparties and Bills of Lading*,[13] then one of the two standard works on shipping law, and of Arnould on *Marine Insurance*,[14] the leading work in its field. During his time at the Bar he was one of the leading practitioners in these fields, in which his experience and knowledge were second to none. A substantial number of his reported judicial decisions are in these two fields, particularly

---

[13] A. A. Mocatta, M. J. Mustill and S. C. Boyd, *Scrutton on Charterparties and Bills of Lading*, 17th edn (London, 1964), 18th edn (London, 1974), 19th edn (London, 1984).
[14] M. J. Mustill and J. C. B. Gilman, *Arnould's Law of Marine Insurance and Average* 17th edn (London, 2008).

from his time as judge of the Commercial Court, and as an appellate judge.[15]

For at least the last forty years of his life Mustill had an ambition to write an account of what he always called the case of 'the second Kumar', but is usually known as 'the Bhawal case'. This was a case which ran for years in India and eventually came before the Judicial Committee of the Privy Council in London. A short account of this astonishing history is that Ramendra Narayan Roy, the second Kumar of Bhawal, the ruler of a huge estate in Bengal, had in his youth spent most of his time hunting, in festivities and with women, having several mistresses. By 1905 he had contracted syphilis. In 1909 he went to Darjeeling to seek treatment but was reported to have died there at the age of twenty-five and to have been cremated. Around 1920–1 a religious ascetic appeared in Dhaka covered in ashes, and gradually relatives and the local people became convinced that this was the second Kumar. He said he had lost his memory and had recovered in the jungle, where a guru had taken him into his care. In legal proceedings in India two judgments found that he was indeed the second Kumar, and the Privy Council upheld their decisions.[16] The case was a *cause célèbre* in Bangladesh, comparable to the case of the Tichborne Claimant in what is now England many years earlier, but with much more colourful detail and with far wider repercussions for the estate.[17]

In the end the book never appeared in print. The saddest thing about this was the discovery after his death of a box with all his research for the book he wanted to write. In the bottom of the box were all the photographs and documents he had had copied from the House of Lords library collection. He was convinced that he had lost his copies, and he had searched far and wide to locate the originals, which by then had been destroyed: but the copies were there all the time.

*****

---

[15] See for example *Pan Atlantic Insurance Co Ltd v Pine Top Insurance Co Ltd* [1995] 1 AC 501, a leading case on the principles of material non-disclosure in insurance law.

[16] *Devi v Roy* [1946] AC 508. The report summarises the facts of the case and the decisions of the Indian courts.

[17] The claim to the Tichborne baronetcy captivated the public for several years in the 1860s and 1870s, and resulted in the claimant being sentenced to fourteen years' hard labour for perjury. There is the briefest account of the trial of the claim itself in *Tichborne, Bart v Sir Pyers Mostyn, Bart* (1872–3) L.R. 8 C.P. 29 but no official report of the trial itself.

Michael Mustill was married in 1960 to Beryl Davies: they separated in 1979 and divorced without children in 1983. After the separation he was introduced by her brother to Caroline Phillips, whom he married in 1984. Her brother is Lord Phillips of Worth Matravers, a former pupil of Mustill and the first President of the Supreme Court. Mustill is survived by his second wife and by his two sons of that marriage, Thomas and Oliver.

STEWART BOYD
Essex Court Chambers

ROBERT BRIAN TATE

Robert Brian Tate
1921–2011

Life

BRIAN TATE WAS A MAJOR FIGURE IN Hispanic studies, as much at home in Catalan and Latin as in Spanish. He was born in Belfast on 27 December 1921 and died on 21 February 2011. He was educated at the Royal Belfast Academical Institution: the school was unusual in offering Spanish at this period, and produced a number of eminent Hispanists (among them F. W. Pierce). In 1939 he began studies at Queen's University, and in his second year left for war service in India, Nepal and Burma; while out east he began learning Arabic. In the company of General Slim he was one of the first to enter Rangoon in 1945. On graduation in 1948 with a first in French and Spanish, his teacher Ignasi González i Llubera (1893–1962) encouraged him to go to Barcelona and Girona (in Catalonia) to do research. (This was early in the Franco regime, when Catalan politics and Catalan studies in general were suppressed.) His MA thesis at Queen's University was 'The Life, Works and Ideas of Cardinal Margarit' (1949), and his PhD (also Queen's University, 1955) was 'The Influence of Italian Humanism on the Historiography of Castile and Aragon during the Fifteenth Century'. After teaching at Manchester (assistant lecturer, 1949–52) and Queen's (lecturer, 1952–6) he was appointed reader at Nottingham in 1956 and was professor (indeed, the first professor of Spanish at Nottingham) from 1958 to 1983; dean of the faculty of arts 1976–9; professor emeritus in 1991. In the late 1970s Tate was also a great supporter of the development of Portuguese studies at Nottingham, a discipline which is still going strong at the University. He married Beth

(Elizabeth Ida Lewis) in 1952. Tate was a founder member of the Association of Hispanists of Great Britain and Ireland and with Geoffrey Stagg hosted the first conference of the Association at Nottingham; he was president 1983–5: for his presidential address at Leeds in 1985 his only visual aid was 'Narrationem expellas furca, tamen usque recurret' written on a blackboard, this appropriation of Horace's 'Naturam . . .' (Ep. I, 10, 24) pointing to the literary qualities of historiography. He was a founder member and later president of the Anglo-Catalan Society, a committee member of the Asociación Internacional de Hispanistas, corresponding fellow of the Secció Històrico-Arqueològica of the Institut d'Estudis Catalans (1964), Real Academia de la Historia (1974) and Reial Acadèmia de Bones Lletres (1980) and honorary fellow of the Asociación Hispánica de Literatura Medieval. He was elected Fellow of the British Academy in 1980. He also founded and edited the Pergamon Hispanic Series and was founding committee member and honorary president of the Association of Teachers of Spanish and Portuguese (East Midlands Branch).

He was the recipient of two Festschriften: one from his Nottingham colleagues and pupils, edited by Richard A. Cardwell (*Essays in Honour of Robert Brian Tate from his Colleagues and Pupils*, Nottingham, 1984) and a more wide-ranging volume, edited by Ian Michael and Richard A. Cardwell (*Medieval and Renaissance Studies in Honour of Robert Brian Tate*, Oxford, 1986). The publisher of the latter was Joan Gili (1907–98), Catalan exile and man of letters.[1] The Tate Lectures at Nottingham were founded in his honour: the fourteenth, 'White Faces/Black Masks: Gender and the Zombie Gothic in Pedro Costa's Down to Earth', was given in 2017 by Professor Hilary Owen (University of Manchester), a Tate alumna.

Historiography

Although Brian Tate was a highly accomplished expert in Hispanic studies in their broadest sense, he was especially interested in Spanish history as well as in medieval and early modern Spanish historiography. One of his major contributions to the field is to have shown how the history of the late Middle Ages and the early Renaissance in Spain entailed complex processes

---

[1] Correspondence relating to the volume is in Senate House Library University of London, Joan Gili / The Dolphin Book Company papers, MS. 1197/27/5.

of transition and dissemination. Indeed, Tate's doctoral dissertation (submitted in 1955) already assessed the extent to which late medieval historical writing in Spain reflected the penetration of the new humanistic ideas emerging from Italy. A movement based on the recovery, interpretation and imitation of ancient Greek and Roman texts originating in Italy towards the middle of the fourteenth century, humanism has long been recognised to have spread to the farthest recesses of Europe within the period of a century and a half. Enquiries into the impact of Italian humanism in Western Europe have not, however, been immune to critical preconceptions. If this is true of the dissemination of the humanist movement in Northern Europe, the nature of the penetration of humanist interests into Catalonia has also very often been subjected not only to the preconceptions of the critics who studied it but also to previous scholarly practice. Particularly controversial has been the question of the date and true extent of such penetration.

Traditionally, research into the spread of Italian humanism in Catalonia has been marked by a tendency to overemphasise the humanist credentials of early followers of the intellectual trends pioneered by Italian humanists. This is best exemplified by the figure of Bernat Metge (*c*.1350–1413), the creator of a rich and cultivated prose in Catalan. In the first four decades of the twentieth century—when a series of distinguished scholars coined the term 'Humanisme català' ('Catalan humanism') to denote an alleged early vernacular humanism at the heart of late medieval Catalan literature—Metge was heralded as a fully fledged humanist. Later, more nuanced accounts of the advent of humanism in Catalonia have pointed out the highly problematic nature of the 'Humanisme català' cultural construct. As Brian Tate's mentor Jordi Rubió i Balaguer emphasised, the term 'humanism', when applied to the Catalan-speaking lands, should be reserved for the activity of a group of Latin authors writing in the last quarter of the fifteenth century. Among these belongs the historian Joan Margarit i Pau (*c*.1421–84), on whom Tate published his seminal *El Cardenal Joan Margarit i Pau: vida i obra* (Barcelona, 1976). Tate continued to work on Margarit until the last years of his life: in 2006 he contributed a paper on the subject to a conference on 'El Cardenal Margarit i l'Europa quatrecentista' organised at the University of Girona.

Tate's 1976 monograph attends both to Margarit's intellectual background and to his key Latin historiographical tract, the ten books of the *Paralipomenon Hispaniae*, lengthy passages from which were made available here for the first time. Educated at the Spanish College in Bologna, Margarit travelled to the Congress of Mantua (1459–61) as a representative of John II of Aragon. The Congress, which had been summoned by Pope Pius II in response to the fall of Constantinople, allowed Margarit to make the acquaintance of several Italian scholars who inspired him to undertake the study of the antiquities of the Iberian Peninsula. To that end, Margarit wrote the *Paralipomenon Hispaniae* ('Lost Chronicles of Hispania', begun in the 1460s), devoted to the history of Hispania up to the time of Augustus. An outspoken critic of the merely 'bearable' ('tolerabilis') Rodrigo Jiménez de Rada, who, in his *De rebus Hispaniae*, had appropriated the Gothic theory, Margarit focused his research on the distant past of the country, a period which he labelled as the 'forgotten' age. As Tate showed, underlying Margarit's interest in the Ibero-Roman period is the concept of a Hispanic ethnicity antedating the Visigothic kingdom. Margarit approached his subject in a scholarly way: for instance, in his researches into the ancient geography and anthropology of the Iberian Peninsula, he drew on reliable sources and visited the ancient sites and ruins himself. Taking pride in having immersed himself 'in the histories and geographies of the ancient world', Margarit consulted the latest (Latin) translations of Greek authors such as Strabo, Appian and Plutarch, as well as Roman geographers like Pomponius Mela.

As well as the sources, contents and ideology of the *Paralipomenon*, Tate was also interested in the circulation of the text after Margarit's death. In his essay 'The rewriting of the historical past: *Hispania et Europa*' (1996), Tate examined Sancho de Nebrija's collective edition of four fifteenth-century partial historical narratives in Latin crucial for a knowledge of Spanish history, which also included the *Paralipomenon*. As Tate brilliantly demonstrated, the compilation—dedicated to the future Philip II in 1545—was a clear attempt to put into the public domain a cluster of basic texts of the history of Spain written in the previous century. Aimed, through the choice of Latin, both at a local and international readership, it also served a very political function. Tate concluded that the primary theme of the authors included was Spain's cultural and political precedence over other European nations. This was an old aspiration of the Spanish monarchy since the reign of Ferdinand and Isabella. The issue of who should be appointed to write the history of Spain and how the deeds of the Spaniards should be made known abroad had long preoccupied the Spanish royal house. It became crucial on the threshold of the Spanish domination of European politics. Tate's examination—first in his *Ensayos sobre la historiografía peninsular del siglo XV* of 1970, and subsequently in several papers published in the 1980s and 1990s—of the controversies surrounding the choice of the official chronicler by the Catholic Monarchs is informed by his deep understanding of the ideologies and narrative strategies of late medieval Spanish historiographers. As he showed, the role of royal historian became increasingly coveted, and several candidates—Antonio de Nebrija, Alfonso de Palencia and Lucius Marineus Siculus (all of whom merited in-depth studies by Tate)—presented their credentials for the job. The position was finally awarded to the Andalusian Nebrija, who was regarded by Ferdinand as more to be trusted than his Italian counterparts to put across the political message of the monarchy resulting from the unification of Aragon and Castile in 1492.

Don Juan Manuel and other Spanish editions

Tate produced three editions of Old Spanish texts alone, and the *Libro de los estados* in collaboration. Although all these works have been studied as examples of literary prose written in accord with contemporary rhetorical ideas, their interest for Tate was clearly historiographical. As he wrote in the Introduction to *Claros varones* (p. x), 'The principal aim of the historiographical study is not far distant from that of the literary critic: to approach the text in question as a product of the historical and cultural situation of the times, to set forth the conditions in which it was written, to extract the political, social, and moral lessons, and to study the means by which the author intended to persuade his audience.' He began in 1965 with the *Generaciones y semblanzas* of Fernán Pérez de Guzmán (*c*.1377–*c*.1460). This was an early contribution to the Tamesis series, founded by John E. Varey, which had published its first volume only a year before. In the early years contributors were largely based in British universities.

The *Generaciones y semblanzas* is a collection of brief sketches (Tate himself thought it debatable whether they were character sketches) of Castilian magnates of the reigns of John II and Henry IV (1406–74). Tate based his text on Escorial MS Z-III-2, collated against other manuscripts and the *editio princeps* of 1512. So influential was Tate's edition that a review of a subsequent edition by José Antonio Barrio Sánchez (Madrid, 1998) proclaimed: 'This must be considered an ancillary edition to Tate's. It does not know any manuscript or early print which he did not know, and does not cite any bibliography since 1965.'[2]

---

[2] *Boletín bibliográfico de la Asociación Hispánica de Literatura Medieval* (www.ahlmboletin.es), 13.2 ficha 793.

His second edition was of the *Claros varones de Castilla* of Fernando del Pulgar (*c*.1436–*c*.1492). It appeared in 1971, with a revised Spanish edition in 1985. This too is a series of sketches of great men. Tate took as his base text the incunable (Toledo: Juan Vázquez, 24 December 1486), collated against other early editions; the existing manuscripts seem to derive from the incunable. Tate was insistent that times had changed between the two works and that the authors differed in politics if not in technique. Pulgar took the form of his work from Pérez de Guzmán and the title is derived from the earlier author's verse *Loores de claros varones*. Pérez de Guzmán was a nobleman, Pulgar a commoner; the period of conflict of the reign of Henry IV had by Pulgar's time given way to greater stability under Ferdinand and Isabella; 'The *Generaciones*, written in a period of unresolved tensions, ends on an anguished note. The *Claros varones*, a work completed after a civil war and in the middle of the Granada campaign, aims to fortify the spirit and reconcile all factions' (translated and summarised from Pulgar 1985, p. 62).

The common element to these two works is that they were biographical sketches of ultimately Suetonian inspiration. In contrast to the Catalan historians whom Tate studied, critics have not been quick to discern humanistic elements in these works.

A third edition was of the text known in the single manuscript—New York, Hispanic Society of America, MS HC: 371/164—as *Directorio de príncipes* (1977). This, a mirror of princes, addressed to the Catholic Monarchs, is now known to be a section of the *Espejo de corregidores y jueces* of Alonso Ramírez de Villaescusa. The Exeter Hispanic Texts series in which it appeared was founded by Keith Whinnom as an outlet for critical editions of early texts that were not attractive to commercial publishers.

Tate also wrote extensively on the works of the aristocrat and author Don Juan Manuel (1282–1348), who was a major political figure of the time. The nephew of Alfonso X and much influenced by him, he wrote chiefly on statecraft. The old critical judgement of Marcelino Menéndez y Pelayo (1856–1912) was that he was 'el primer escritor de nuestra Edad Media que tuvo *estilo* en prosa' ['the first writer of our Middle Ages to have *style* in prose'; his emphasis]. He was a classic from the earliest days of Spanish literary history, although Ian Macpherson commented in about 1987 on 'the boom in Juan Manuel studies which has taken place since the early 1970s'. His most famous work, read in schools in Spain and a staple of the university curriculum in Spain and Britain, was *El conde Lucanor*, fifty exemplary tales framed by the dialogue of Count Lucanor and his counsellor Patronio. In a later article of 1986/7, Tate identified the name Lucanor in a French romance. However, his especial interest was in the political-historical element in the author's work. An article of 1972 showed how three apparently traditional stories in *El conde Lucanor* on the tensions between the *vita activa* of the statesman and the *vita contemplativa* of the religious were informed by recent historical cases of noblemen who retreated into the monastic life. His review article of Daniel Devoto's bibliography of Don Juan Manuel occupied five tightly printed pages of the *Modern Language Review*. Another article which was typical of Tate's interests was a study of the relationship between Don Juan Manuel and his brother-in-law, Don Juan de Aragón, archbishop of Toledo: Don Juan Manuel dedicates the *Libro del cavallero e del escudero* to him, as he knows he is a bad sleeper and will appreciate a trifling book to beguile the hours of insomnia; and he asks him to translate a work of his into Latin, as Don Juan Manuel as a knight pretends to have no Latin (an obvious pose): here we may note the close relationship between literature and history, and the relations between Castile and Aragon.

His monument however is the edition of the *Libro de los estados*, edited with introduction and notes by R. B. Tate and I. R. Macpherson (1974; revised edition in Spanish in 1991). This is a survey of the three estates (those who pray, those who fight and those who labour) and their obligations. The frame derives from *Barlaam and Joasaph*, but as so often with Don Juan Manuel it is not known which version or versions he knew. Macpherson (1934–2011) was professor of Spanish at Durham: this was their only collaboration.

The edition, beautifully printed and bound in a sober dark blue, was uniform with various other editions of Spanish texts which were published by the Clarendon Press around this time, although they appear not to have been considered a series: Calderón, *El médico de su honra* edited by C. A. Jones (Oxford, 1961), the *Poema de Mio Cid* edited by Colin Smith (Oxford, 1972) and of course Tate's own edition of Pulgar. These editions had their critical matter in English; in the case of *Estados* even the interior headings supplied by the editors were in English. The introduction gave an account of the author's life and works, and of the nature of the text and its transmission (there is in fact only one manuscript (Madrid, Biblioteca Nacional, MS 6376, mid-fifteenth century); it is quite common for Old Spanish texts to be preserved in few witnesses, and these considerably later than the date of composition). The volume closes with a vocabulary of hard words. Tate and Macpherson's edition stood head and shoulders above those of previous editors from Gayangos and Benavides (both 1860) to Castro y Calvo (1968), of whom they comment:

'The text displays such an unusual quantity of transcriptional and printers' errors as to make it useless to the philologist and at times incomprehensible to the general reader' (p. lxiii).

The philological study was almost certainly by Macpherson (although as we have seen Tate was an expert editor of medieval texts in his own right) and the extensive annotations a collaboration: the frequent citation of Old Catalan texts for the purpose of comparison (Arnau de Vilanova, Ramon Llull et al.) was certainly attributable to Tate. The editors acknowledge that they have benefited from the draft edition which Ignasi González i Llubera had left unfinished at his death: another indubitably Tatian contribution. (The typescript of González i Llubera's edition is in the Special Collections of Queen's University Library.) (Incidentally, like Tate himself, Don Juan Manuel was culturally as Aragonese as Castilian: he was for instance the first Castilian imitator of Ramon Llull's *Llibre de l'orde de cavalleria*, which he cites as 'algunas cosas que fallé en un libro' ['some things which I found in a book'].)

Estados was reissued in revised form in the Clásicos Castalia series, to be found in all Spanish bookshops and schools. This time Macpherson's name appeared first; the critical matter was naturally in Spanish; the biographical section was expanded, the treatments of the language of the manuscript and the debt of *Estados* to the Barlaam legend were abbreviated.

Alfonso de Palencia

Another of Tate's long-term interests was the figure of Alfonso de Palencia, Italian-educated humanist and Hellenist (1423–92), and—most importantly for Tate—chronicler. Tate's first publication on him in 1975 was focused on his historiography. In 1984 he edited his Latin epistles with Rafael Alemany Ferrer. He also studied the *Batalla campal de los perros contra los lobos*—a political allegory on the battle of the dogs and the wolves—written by Palencia in Latin (now lost) and translated by him into Spanish. Palencia was outspoken as an historian, and his attitude to the faction of Isabella the Catholic in the civil wars of 1475–9 was hostile. Accordingly, the publication of his Decads (more properly *Gesta Hispaniensia ex annalibus suorum dierum collecta*) was troubled. A great step forward was the publication by Tate, again with a collaborator, this time Jeremy Lawrance. Two volumes came out to great acclaim, but the project seems once more to have stalled. Although Tate continued to write on Palencia until the end of his life (his last study was published posthumously in 2013), this edition was the culmination of decades of interest.

Palencia was indubitably a humanist: probably educated by Alonso de Cartagena, by 1450 he was in the service of Cardinal Bessarion; in Rome he studied under George Trapezuntius. His humanist training is apparent in the fine *littera antiqua* he wrote: ten of his holograph manuscripts are extant, probably the earliest autographs of any Spanish author. As royal chronicler and Latin secretary he was an eye-witness to the turbulent political events of his day. His work is one of the most important sources for our image of his age. Secretary and chronicler to Henry IV of Castile in 1465, in the nobles' revolt Palencia defected to the camp of 'Alfonso XII', and after Alfonso's death in 1468 backed Isabella, becoming official chronicler to the Catholic Monarchs. Palencia grew suspicious of Isabella's ambitions for full royal power and the Queen sacked him in 1480 in favour of Fernando del Pulgar; he ended his life as a cleric.

Palencia's schema for his history of Spain developed over time, but the final plan was for eight decads (groups of ten books, not years). Decad I covered the Pre-Roman period: this is extant. Decad II, on the Roman to Moorish periods, is lost. Decad III was to cover the Christian Reconquest but seems never to have been written. Decads IV–VI are extant and cover the years 1440–74. Decad VII, extant, concerns the beginning of the reign of the Catholic Monarchs and the Portuguese war. Decad VIII, on the War of Granada, was left unfinished. Tate and Lawrance's project was to edit the three decads devoted to 1440–74, which they term 'Decads I–III'. The two volumes which have appeared, cited by the editors as 'Dec. I', occupy the place in Palencia's final scheme of Decad IV (years 1440–68). This is the first and only published edition of the text. Only the *Cuarta década* had been published in Latin and Spanish, by José López de Toro, in two volumes (Madrid, 1970–4). The edition of the Real Academia de la Historia, prepared in 1835–7, proved abortive, as Tate studied in 1989. Historians have commonly relied on Antonio Paz y Melia's translation of 1904–9.

The text is preserved in eighteen manuscripts and one fragment (Madrid, Biblioteca Nacional 19439 (M) is an autograph first draft of Dec. 1 Prologue to Dec. 1.ix.8, with interlinear and marginal corrections and additions). Sixteenth-century scholars record the existence of an authorial revision (*minuta*) from which, the editors convincingly argue, all other witnesses descend. They conclude that the extant witness closest to this *minuta* is A-P, divided between Leon, Centro Don Bosco (formerly Astudillo, Residencia Salesiana), unnumbered MS, and Paris, Bibliothèque nationale, MS nouv. acq. lat. 2058. The editors chose M as their base text. The editors respect Palencia's *usus scribendi*. Palencia's orthography is very correct by humanistic standards, using the *e caudata* for *ae*. The text is presented with a facing modern Spanish translation, exhaustive philological and historical notes and a comprehensive index. It is to be regretted that the edition of the remaining text has run into the sands: Tate himself was anxious to find younger colleagues to bring the project to completion.

Catalonia

In his speech to acknowledge the award of the doctorate *honoris causa* from the University of Girona in October 2004, Brian Tate recalled how the teaching of Spanish and Hispanic culture had been introduced in Belfast in 1918. The university's governing body had set their mind originally on a Chair of Russian, but the Revolution had thrown them into a mild panic and they decided that Ignasi González i Llubera, the first holder of the Chair of Spanish in the university, would run a less dangerous department. An eminent linguist and a scholar of medieval Arabic and Hebrew texts who also venerated the classics, González i Llubera was convinced that the history and the culture of the Iberian Peninsula were multilingual and that the products of the interweaving of traditions between Castilian, Portuguese and Catalan could not be properly understood without reference to them. These perceptions shape, for example, Tate's extraordinary study on the medieval kingdoms in the Iberian Peninsula published in Peter Russell's *A Companion to Spanish Studies* (London, 1973).

González i Llubera was to leave a deep mark on Tate, who completed his degree in French and Spanish at Queen's in 1948. It was González i Llubera—together with another Catalan exile, Josep M. Batista i Roca—who persuaded Tate to pursue postgraduate study in Catalonia and to concentrate on the work and ideas of the diplomat, historian and cardinal-bishop of Girona Joan Margarit (*c*.1421–84). Tate's researches in the archives of Barcelona and Girona, where, on his own admission, he was the only foreign scholar and where he was to learn Catalan ('my first second language', as he once described it), formed the centre of his Master's thesis submitted in 1949. Tate's dissertation, entitled 'The Life, Works and Ideas of Cardinal Margarit', was the first major work on this Catalan figure and was later published by the Institut d'Estudis Catalans,

Barcelona, as *El manuscrit i les fonts del 'Paralipomenon Hispaniae'*; it won him the Francesc Cambó Prize from that institution in 1954. Girona was to remain Tate's Hispanic university. He was regularly invited to lecture there and in 2002, on the occasion of a colloquium on Joan Margarit, he bequeathed his collection of 1,000 books and working papers, chiefly on Catalan humanism, to the Institut de Llengua i Cultura Catalanes of the University of Girona. Fittingly, arrangements for the relocation of Tate's research and archival material—which was undertaken by Tate's Catalan friends, who drove between Catalonia and Nottingham— were made by one of Tate's closest collaborators at Girona, Professor Mariàngela Vilallonga, a leading scholar of Latin humanism in Catalonia, who also pronounced Tate's *laudatio* at the close of the conference. Currently held at the university library, Tate's volumes and research documents (not to mention his abundant correspondence with prominent scholars since the 1950s) have already inspired a wave of essays by postgraduate students which will shed light on the history of British Hispanism in the second half of the twentieth century. This constitutes a fair tribute to Tate's close connection with the University of Girona and the city itself. As Tate stated in his doctoral acceptance speech, 'here in Girona I began my work, and here I end it'. He regarded the doctorate *honoris causa* conferred upon him by the university as his most favoured of all his awards.

During his time in Catalonia in the late 1940s Tate came under the spell of the eminent bibliographer and cultural historian Jordi Rubió i Balaguer (1887–1982), whose commitment to Catalanism had led to his ban from a university position by the Francoist authorities after the end of the Spanish Civil War. Alongside other prominent Catalan scholars such as Ferran Soldevila (1894–1971), Rubió i Balaguer filled the gap left by the official Spanish university system by providing clandestine tuition in his own apartment to groups of interested students on the literature and historical institutions of medieval and Renaissance Catalonia. In private conversations Tate often referred to the spirit of camaraderie shared by all the students who attended Soldevila and Rubió i Balaguer's classes. 'Jordi Rubió i Balaguer,' he once orally recalled, 'was a kind and soft-spoken man, whose ironic remarks however could sometimes be rather sharp. He once reprimanded me for arriving a few minutes late by pointing out that "here tuition begins on time". We were all aware that Rubió i Balaguer's mischievous use of the adverb "here" was meant as a strong rebuke of the stagnated and centralized Spanish university system, from which he had been separated and which we were all eager to forget even if it was only from time to time.'

Equipped with a modest grant provided by Rubió i Balaguer, Tate started to build a broad network of contacts with Catalan historians of the time such as Ramon Aramon i Serra and Santiago Sobrequés, senior, some of whom were to remain good friends until his death. Throughout the years Tate's relations with Catalan intellectuals and Catalan institutions grew. He was elected Corresponding Fellow of the Institut d'Estudis Catalans (1965) and of the Reial Acadèmia de Bones Lletres de Barcelona (1988). In 1995 he was awarded the Premi Internacional Catalònia de l'Institut d'Estudis Catalans 'for his studies on Catalan humanism, and for his contribution to cultural relations between Catalonia and Britain'. The committee's decision was no doubt informed by Tate's efforts to promote knowledge of Catalan culture abroad. He was invited to lecture on Catalan topics at a number of American universities. He published articles on the Valencian Vicent Climent and Joanot Martorell, and he contributed reviews of modern editions of several of the Catalan classics to British journals. Having helped to found it, he served as president of the Anglo-Catalan Society for a number of years. Alongside Alan Yates, he organised the Third International Colloquium on Catalan Language and Literature held at Fitzwilliam College, Cambridge, in 1973. The last gathering of this kind taking place before Franco's death in November 1975, the event brought together Tate's old friends and collaborators such as the above-mentioned Batista i Roca as well as Joan Gili, one of the co-founders of the Anglo-Catalan Society, under whose auspices the proceedings of the conference were published in a handsome volume by The Dolphin Book Co. in 1976.

Until his retirement in August 1983 and beyond, when he was still connected as Professor Emeritus to the Department of Hispanic Studies at Nottingham, Tate always strove to share his love of Catalan language and culture among colleagues and students. He was known to speak with authority on the *modernista* architects Lluís Domènec i Muntaner and Antoni Gaudí, and he delighted departmental and school gatherings with subjects as diverse as the fifteenth-century Valencian poet Ausiàs March, the Catalan revolt of 1640 and George Orwell's *Homage to Catalonia*.

The International Brigades

Orwell and the fate of those British soldiers who participated in the Spanish Civil War were a long-standing preoccupation of Tate. In the summer of 1996 he single-handedly organised a colloquium in Nottingham to mark the sixtieth anniversary of the outbreak of the conflict. The event proved a stimulating gathering, plentiful in ideas, discussions and enthusiasm. It was meticulously planned by Tate, who invited local undergraduate and postgraduate students, British academics and Catalan scholars alike. The concluding plenary lecture was given by his old friend Joaquim Nadal, historian and former mayor of Girona, and it examined the aftermath of the Civil War in Catalonia. A group of former British members of the International Brigades, the paramilitary units set up by the Communist International to assist the Second Spanish Republic in 1936, was also invited. Though not directly involved in the conflict, Tate always took an interest in the role played by the International Brigades during the Spanish Civil War. In the autumn of 1996 he joined in the various tributes organised to mark the crucial and bloody Battle of the Ebro in Gandesa, southern Catalonia, and he accompanied some of the former members of the International Brigades to Barcelona and Madrid, where they were granted Spanish citizenship at a public ceremony. At home in Beeston, near Nottingham, Tate owned a large selection of visual material of Spanish Civil War-related subjects, including interviews with several British Brigaders and films of the meetings in Madrid and Gandesa which had taken place in 1996. All this rich documentation has been preserved by the International Brigade Memorial Trust[3] and is now available to scholars and members of the public for research. It constitutes yet further proof of Tate's enduring love of Catalonia and of its history.

Pilgrimage

Another area of interest to Tate, on which he began to publish quite late in his career, was the pilgrimage to Santiago de Compostela. He was a member of the Confraternity of Saint James from its early days, served on the Confraternity's Research Working Party—which met twice a year at Birmingham University—and represented it on the Xunta de Galicia's Committee of Experts. His publications on pilgrimage were solidly historical rather than personal. His first book on the subject recorded the journey which he undertook with his son Marcus, *The Pilgrim Route to Santiago* (1987), sumptuously illustrated with photographs by Pablo Keller. He loved to describe how they would leave their rooms before dawn to drive by jeep to some scenic spot to capture the atmospheric morning light, and

---

[3] See www.international-brigades.org.uk/ (accessed 27 January 2017).

then drove hard to the next location to wait for the evening light; the Tates themselves do not figure in any of the pictures. There followed an edition of Constance Mary Storrs, *Jacobean Pilgrims from England to St. James of Compostella: from the Early Twelfth to the Late Fifteenth Century* (1994). Constance Storrs died in 1990, and her MA thesis of 1964 formed the basis for the book, which Tate persuaded the Xunta de Galicia to publish. Tate also edited, with Thorlac Turville-Petre, *Two Pilgrim Itineraries of the Later Middle Ages* (1995), one in verse originally published in *Purchas His Pilgrimes* in 1625 and that of 'Master Robert Langton Clerke (1470–1524)'. Shorter contributions were an article of 1993 and a lecture, 'Pilgrimages to St James of Compostella from the British Isles during the Middle Ages'. This last was published by the Confraternity of Saint James, to whose *Bulletin* Tate also contributed reviews of Spanish books. The pilgrimage of life grew more meaningful and gave him strength as he grew older and his health declined. At his funeral the pilgrim hat rested on his coffin and scallop shells were cremated with him. His ashes were buried beneath a stone inscribed 'Soldier, Scholar, Pilgrim'.

*****

Tate's personality did not extend into his academic writing. He is remembered as an active conference-goer, open to the work of younger scholars and eager to participate in debate. He liked the theatre and wine and was a skilful sportsman. Dr Fiona Maguire recalls an incident that demonstrated Tate's indomitable spirit. The 2005 conference of the Association of Hispanists was held in Valencia and included a day trip to Peñíscola. Despite being in his eighties, Brian scaled the ramparts of the medieval castle. As Fiona climbed the stone steps of the castle and emerged onto the open flat roof area, nobody else was around and she suddenly spotted Brian lying on the floor, surrounded by the ramparts. She did not see him fall but found him on the ground. He was conscious and keen to get up and she helped him; other people from the group started arriving on the roof then and also helped. He made a complete recovery.

He was elected Fellow of the British Academy in 1980. One of his last publications was a paper on the academies of Great Britain and Ireland, delivered at a conference on 'The world of the academies, yesterday and today'. An informative survey of the role played by learned societies in Great Britain and Ireland since 1645, Tate's essay should partly also be read as a personal account of his life as a scholar. In the preliminary remarks to his paper—before referring to his long connection with the city of Seville, the conference location and the birthplace of Alfonso de Palencia—Tate exhibited his characteristic humour. By virtue of his name, he stated, he was bound to devote himself to the study of Hispanic history and letters. This was revealed to him by the illustrious Argentine literary historian María Rosa Lida de Malkiel in the first letter she sent him in the 1950s. To Tate's astonishment, Lida de Malkiel explained that he was the only Hispanist whose name ever occurred in *Don Quixote*. Indeed, towards the end of the novel, the following words are written by Cide Hamete, the fictional author created by Cervantes as the chronicler of the adventures of his hero:

> Tate, tate, folloncicos
> De ninguno sea tocada;
> porque esta impresa, buen rey,
> para mí estaba guardada.
>
> [Beware, beware, you scoundrels,
> I may be touched by none:
> This is a deed, my worthy king,
> Reserved for me alone].[4]

A fitting tribute to Tate's outstanding contribution to Hispanic studies.

BARRY TAYLOR
The British Library

ALEJANDRO COROLEU
ICREA–Universitat Autònoma de Barcelona

Bibliography

Although his publications to date were listed in *Medieval and Renaissance Studies in Honour of Robert Brian Tate*, ed. Ian Michael and Richard A. Cardwell (Oxford, 1986), pp. xi–xiii, the following bibliography is intended to be exhaustive.

Books and critical editions

Joan Margarit i Pau: a Biographical Study (Manchester, 1954).
Fernán Pérez de Guzmán, *Generaciones y semblanzas*, ed. R. B. Tate (London, 1965).
Pierre Vilar, *Spain: a Brief History*, tr. R. B. Tate (Oxford, 1967; 2nd edn., 1977).

---

[4] Miguel de Cervantes, *The Adventures of Don Quixote*, translated by J. M. Cohen (Harmondsworth, 1950), II, lxxiv, p. 939.

Ensayos sobre la historiografía peninsular del siglo XV (Madrid, 1970).
Fernando del Pulgar, *Claros varones de Castilla*, ed. R. B. Tate (Oxford, 1971; revised Spanish edn, Madrid, 1985).
R. B. Tate and I. R. Macpherson (eds.), Don Juan Manuel, *Libro de los estados* (Oxford, 1974; revised Spanish edn, Madrid, 1986).
El cardenal Joan Margarit, vida i obra (Barcelona, 1976).
Directorio de príncipes: (HSA MS HC: 371/164), ed. R. B. Tate, Exeter Hispanic Texts, 16 (Exeter, 1977).
Alfonso de Palencia, *Epístolas latinas*, ed. R. B. Tate and R. Alemany Ferrer (Bellaterra, 1982 [1984]).
[with M. Tate], *The Pilgrim Route to Santiago*, photographed by P. Keller (Oxford, 1987).
Pilgrimages to St James of Compostella from the British Isles during the Middle Ages, E. Allison Peers Publications; Lectures, 4 (Liverpool, 1990).
Constance Mary Storrs, *Jacobean Pilgrims from England to St. James of Compostella: from the Early Twelfth to the Late Fifteenth Century*, ed. R. B. Tate (Santiago de Compostela, 1994).
Two Pilgrim Itineraries of the Later Middle Ages, ed. R. B. Tate and T. Turville-Petre; photographs by M. Tate ([Santiago de Compostela?], [1995]).
Alfonso de Palencia, *Gesta hispaniensia: ex annalibus suorum dierum collecta*, ed. R. B. Tate and J. Lawrance, 2 vols (Madrid, 1998–9).
Pilgrimages to St James of Compostella from the British Isles during the Middle Ages (London, 2003).

Articles

'Joan Margarit, Bishop of Gerona', *Speculum*, 27 (1952), 28–52.
[with A. Fernández Torregrosa], 'Vicent Climent, un valenciano en Inglaterra', *Estudios de Historia Moderna*, 6 (1956–9), 3–56.
'Italian humanism and Spanish historiography of the Fifteenth Century', *Bulletin of the John Rylands Library*, 34 (1951/2), 137–65.
'Spanish medieval literature', *The Year's Work in Modern Language Studies*, 14 (1953), 124–9.
'El manuscrit i les fonts del *Paralipomenon Hispaniae*', *Estudis Romànics*, 4 (1953/4), 107–36.
'Nebrija the historian', *Bulletin of Hispanic Studies*, 34 (1957), 125–47.
'The literary persona from Díez de Games to Santa Teresa', *Romance Philology*, 13 (1959–60), 283–304.
'Rodrigo Sánchez de Arévalo (1404–1470) and his *Compendiosa Historia Hispanica*', *Nottingham Medieval Studies*, 4 (1960), 58–80.
'An apology for monarchy: a study of an unpublished fifteenth-century Castilian historical pamphlet', *Romance Philology*, 15 (1961/2), 111–23.
'A humanistic biography of John II of Aragón', *Bulletin of Hispanic Studies*, 39 (1962), 1–15.
'Four notes on Gonzalo García de Santa María', *Romance Philology*, 17 (1963/4), 362–72.

'A humanistic biography of John II of Aragon', in *Homenaje a Jaime Vicens Vives* (Barcelona, 1965), I, pp. 665–74.
'Introduction' to T. S. Eliot, *Quatre Quartets*, versió catalana de Lluís M. Aragó (Palma de Mallorca, 1965).
'Joanot Martorell in England', *Estudis Romànics*, 10 (1967), 277–81.
'Adventures in the Sierra', in G. B. Gybbon-Monypenny (ed.) *'Libro de buen amor' Studies* (London, 1970), pp. 219–29.
'Don Juan Manuel and his sources: Ejemplos 48, 28, 1', in *Studia Hispanica in honorem R. Lapesa*, 3 vols (Madrid, 1972), I, pp. 549–61.
'The Medieval Kingdoms of the Iberian Peninsula', in P. E. Russell (ed.) *Spain: a Companion to Spanish Studies* (London, 1973), pp. 65–105; revised Spanish edn, *Introducción a la cultura hispánica, I. Historia, arte, música* (Barcelona, 1982), pp. 83–130.
[with A. M. Mundó], 'The *Compendiolum* of Alfonso de Palencia: a humanist treatise on the geography of the Iberian Peninsula', *Journal of Medieval and Renaissance Studies*, 5 (1975), 5–12.
'Daniel Devoto, *Introducción al estudio de don Juan Manuel y en particular de "El conde Lucanor"* (Valencia, 1972)', review article, *Modern Language Review*, 71 (1976), 671–5.
'La obra literaria de don Juan Manuel y el infante don Juan de Aragón', in *Actas del quinto Congreso Internacional de hispanistas* (Bordeaux, 1977), II, pp. 819–28.
'Who wrote *Don Quixote*?', *Vida Hispánica*, 25 (1977), 5–12.
'The Infante Don Juan of Aragon and Don Juan Manuel', in I. Macpherson (ed.), *Juan Manuel Studies* (London, 1977), pp. 169–79.
'Political allegory in fifteenth-century Spain: a study of the *Batalla campal de los perros contra los lobos* by Alfonso de Palencia', *Journal of Hispanic Philology*, 1 (1977), 169–86.
'Ottavio di Camillo, *El humanismo castellano del siglo XV* (Valencia, 1976)', review article, *Modern Language Review*, 73 (1978), 444–7.
'La geografía humanística y los historiadores españoles del siglo XV', in P. S. N. Russell-Gebbett (ed.), *Belfast Papers in Spanish and Portuguese* (Belfast, 1979), pp. 237–42.
'The civic humanism of Alfonso de Palencia', *Renaissance and Modern Studies*, 23 (1979), 25–44.
'Roger Boase, *The Troubadour Revival: a Study of Social Change and Traditionalism in Late Medieval Spain* (London, 1978)', review article, *Modern Language Review*, 75 (1980), 211–14.
'Margarit i el tema dels gots', in *Actes del Cinquè Colloqui Internacional de Llengua i Literatura Catalanes* (Barcelona, 1980), pp. 151–68.
'Descripción de un Ms. perdido de las Crónicas del canciller Ayala', *Incipit*, 1 (1981), 81–4.
'El *Tratado de la perfección del triunfo militar* de Alfonso de Palencia (1459): La villa de discreción y la arquitectura humanista', in R. B. Tate (ed.), *Essays on Narrative Fiction in the Iberian Peninsula in Honour of Frank Pierce* (Oxford, 1982), pp. 163–76.
'Alfonso de Palencia y los preceptos de la historiografía', in *Nebrija y la introducción del Renacimiento en España: Actas de la III Academia Literaria Renacentista* (Salamanca, 1983), pp. 37–52.

'Las *Décadas* de Alfonso de Palencia: un análisis historiográfico', in J. M. Ruiz Veintemilla (ed.), *Estudios dedicados a James Leslie Brooks* (Barcelona, 1984), pp. 223–41.

'La sociedad castellana en la obra de Alfonso de Palencia', in *Actas del III Coloquio de Historia Medieval Andaluza* (Jaén, 1984), pp. 5–23.

'El cronista real castellano durante el siglo quince', in *Homenaje a Pedro Sáinz Rodríguez* (Madrid, 1986), III, pp. 659–68.

'The *Lusiads* of Camoens and the legacy of Virgil', in R. A. Cardwell and J. Hamilton (eds.), *Virgil in a Cultural Tradition: Essays to Celebrate the Bimillenium* (Nottingham, 1986), pp. 77–85.

'*El conde Lucanor*: the name', *La Corónica*, 15 (1986–7), 247–51.

'The relic and the icon', *Confraternity of Saint James Bulletin*, 25 (January 1988), 20–3; 26 (March 1988), 8–10.

'Spanish literature: biography', in J. R. Strayer (ed.), *Dictionary of the Middle Ages*, XI (New York, 1988), 432–5.

'Spanish literature: lost works', in J. R. Strayer (ed.), *Dictionary of the Middle Ages*, XI (New York, 1988), 442–5.

'Alfonso de Palencia and his *Antigüedades de España*', in A. Deyermond and I. Macpherson (eds.), *The Age of the Catholic Monarchs, 1474–1516: Literary Studies in Memory of Keith Whinnom* (Liverpool, 1989), pp. 193–6.

'Las *Décadas* de Alfonso de Palencia: del manuscrito a la página impresa', in M. C. Carbonell (ed.), *Homenaje al profesor Antonio Vilanova* (Barcelona, 1989), I, pp. 689–98.

Joanne Land, *English Pilgrim Routes to Santiago de Compostela, I: Droitwich to Bristol*, with a general introduction by Brian Tate (London, 1989).

'Guidelines for a critical edition of the *Decades* of Alfonso de Palencia', *La Corónica*, 18, 1 (1989), 5–18.

'El Humanismo en Andalucía en el siglo XV', in A. Collantes de Terán Sánchez and A. García-Baquero González (eds.), *Andalucía 1492. Razones de un protagonismo* (Seville, 1992), pp. 213–41.

'Alfonso de Palencia: an interim biography', in A. Deyermond and J. Lawrance (eds.), *Letters and Society in Fifteenth-Century Spain. Studies Presented to P. E. Russell on his Eightieth Birthday* (Llangrannog, 1993), pp. 175–91.

'Las peregrinaciones marítimas medievales desde las Islas Británicas a Compostela', in Fernando López Alsina and Serafín Moralejo Alvarez (eds.), *Santiago, camino de Europa. Culto y cultura en la peregrinación a Compostela* (Santiago, 1993), pp. 161–79.

'Robert Langton, pilgrim', *Confraternity of Saint James Bulletin*, 45 (January 1993), 19–32.

'La historiografía del reinado de los Reyes Católicos', in C. Codoñer and J. A. González Iglesias (eds.), *Antonio de Nebrija: Edad Media y Renacimiento* (Salamanca, 1995), pp. 17–28.

'The rewriting of the historical past: *Hispania et Europa*', in A. D. Deyermond (ed.), *Historical Literature in Medieval Iberia*, Papers of the Medieval Hispanic Research Seminar, 2 (London, 1996), pp. 85–103.

'The rewriting of the historical past. *Hispania et Europa*', in J.-P. Genet (ed.), *L'Histoire et les Nouveaux Publics dans l'Europe Médiévale (XIIIe-XVe siècles). Actes du *colloque international organisé par la Fondation Européene de la Science à la Casa de Vélasquez, Madrid, 23–24 avril 1993*, Collection Histoire ancienne et médiévale, 41 (Paris, 1997), pp. 241–57.

'The official chronicler in the fifteenth century: a brief survey of Western Europe', *Nottingham Medieval Studies*, 41 (1997), 157–85.

'Poles apart – two official historians of the Catholic Monarchs – Alfonso de Palencia and Fernando del Pulgar', in J. Mª. Soto Rábanos (ed.), *Pensamiento medieval hispano. Homenaje a Horacio Santiago-Otero* (Madrid, 1998), I, pp. 439–63.

'Camões, Luíz Vaz de', in P. F. Grendler (ed.), *Encyclopedia of the Renaissance* (New York, 1999), I, pp. 336–7.

'"Laus urbium": praise of two Andalusian cities in the mid-Fifteenth Century', in R. Collins and A. Goodman (eds.), *Medieval Spain: Culture, Conflict, and Coexistence: Studies in Honour of Angus MacKay* (Basingstoke, 2002), pp. 148–59.

'Las Academias en el Reino Unido e Irlanda', in E. Vila Vilar and R. Reyes Cano (eds.), *El mundo de las Academias, del ayer al hoy* (Seville, 2003), pp. 69–78.

'Biography', pp. 173–5; 'Carbonell, Miquel', p. 200; ,Galíndez de Carvajal, Lorenzo', pp. 351–2; 'García de Santa María, Alvar', pp. 354–5; 'Gersonides', pp. 360–1; '*Gesta Comitum Barcinonensium*', p. 361; 'Historiography: annals and chronicles, Fifteenth Century', pp. 395–8; 'Margarit i Pau, Joan', pp. 542–3; 'Marineo Sículo, Lucio', pp. 543–4; 'Palencia, Alfonso de', pp. 630–1; 'Pedro Mártir', pp. 638–9; 'Pulgar, Fernando del', pp. 684–5, in E. M. Gerli (ed.), *Medieval Iberia. An Encyclopedia* (New York, 2003).

'Una "década" de Alfonso de Palencia recobrada: la segunda parte de las *Antigüedades de España*', *Boletín de la Real Academia de la Historia*, 93: 307 (2013), 5–25.

TONY JAMES WILKINSON

Tony James Wilkinson
1948–2014

TONY WILKINSON SADLY PASSED AWAY, after a long battle with cancer, on 25 December 2014, at a very youthful sixty-six years of age. He was born in Essex on 14 August 1948. He trained first as a geographer, studying for a BA at Birkbeck College, London University, from 1966 to 1969, then for his MSc in Canada, at McMaster University, from 1970 to 1972, where he studied the hydrology of overland water flow in the Canadian Arctic. Moving into a career in Archaeology, he always remained grounded in his geographical knowledge, specialising in Landscape Archaeology. His first employment as an archaeologist followed, excavating in the south of England, notably at the highly innovative excavations at Fengate with Francis Pryor, then with Geoffrey Wainwright and the English Heritage Central Excavation Unit. The reputation of both of those projects for hard work and hard drinking would not faze Tony, who was always wiry, athletic, sociable and possessed of a great sense of humour.

Early research into the development of the physical landscape and changing human settlement in his native Essex (see Wilkinson and Murphy, 1986) continued into the late 1980s, although the major final publications were to appear much later, after he had discontinued fieldwork in Britain (Wilkinson and Murphy, 1995; Wilkinson et al., 2012). In 1973 Tony began his first fieldwork season in the environment that he would make his very own—the Middle East—supporting David Whitehouse's project in Siraf, southern Iran (the final publication being Whitehouse, Whitcomb and Wilkinson, 2009). Here from the start, and then in subsequent seasons working with similar field projects in Oman, in the Gulf and in Syria, he pioneered the detailed analysis of landforms, landscape change, the patterning of human artefactual and architectural debris across the countryside and built-up settlements, and the changing modes of land-use, in ways never before conceived, but which would eventually become the accepted ideal for state-of-the-art landscape archaeology in the Middle East and the wider Mediterranean. Tony's home base was Lincoln, where he lived with his first wife, Judith O'Neil, an archaeologist and photographer.

In 1989 he was appointed Assistant Director of the British School of Archaeology in Iraq, a post he held until 1992, but worsening political conditions had already closed that country for field research after 1991. Fortunately Tony gained a position as Research Associate, eventually achieving the rank of Associate Professor, at the prestigious Oriental Institute in Chicago (1992–2003), where he founded the Center for Ancient Middle Eastern Landscapes (CAMEL). In 1995 he married Eleanor Barbanes, an archaeologist who subsequently collaborated with Tony on many of his field projects as well as several publications (Wilkinson et al., 2005, 2007; Wilkinson and Barbanes, 2000; Wilkinson, Peltenburg and Barbanes Wilkinson, 2016; Wilkinson and Wilkinson, 2016) From this Chicago base he relaunched his tireless walking and studying the landscapes for numerous archaeological expeditions in Turkey, Syria and Yemen.

In 2003 Tony moved to the University of Edinburgh as Lecturer, where his achievements were rapidly noted, leading to a Chair in 2005. He transferred to a Professorship at Durham University in 2006, where he remained until his very untimely death. Apart from his major contribution at Durham to teaching and research in Archaeology, Tony was a significant figure in the University's Institute of Advanced Study, where he served as one of its directors. Landmarks during this period included the Society of American Archaeology Book Award in 2004 and the James R. Wiseman Book Award of the Archaeological Institute of America, both for his 2003 masterpiece—*Archaeological Landscapes of the Near East*—as well as election as a Fellow of the British Academy in 2008 and the award in 2009 of the John Coles Medal for Landscape Archaeology.

If we turn to evaluate Tony's research trajectory, the early experience of the Canadian Arctic and then the semi-submerged landscapes of Essex already provide the hallmark of his career as an archaeological explorer of complex and often harsh environments. Despite concentrating on fieldwork for many high-profile projects in the Middle East, Tony did not forget his obligation to write up his early Essex landscape studies. The two much later volumes, written in collaboration with Peter Murphy, have lost none of their significance through much-delayed publication (Wilkinson and Murphy, 1995; Wilkinson, 2012). Indeed their late appearance gave Tony time to incorporate insights gained in the Levant, discovering 'sunken ways' in Essex. Walking was both a hobby and a professional key to his approach to Archaeology. Whilst traditional excavation, especially in the Middle East, involved burying yourself ever deeper into vast tell mounds, Tony wanted to map and take apart the human-impacted landscapes around cities, villages and farms, where the traces of diverse land-uses still survived to as penetrating a scientific eye as his. In his first Middle Eastern field campaign at Siraf, Tony's alertness to signs of human presence in the landscape perceived a potential pattern of meaning in vast carpets of broken ceramics and other domestic debris radiating out from ancient settlements, seemingly not representing buildings or cemeteries. He was later to test his proposition that they were fossil marks of extensive manuring practices through mapping their shape and density and test-pitting below the soil surface. From this visual clue he could develop, as was customary with him, more elaborate structures of meaning: collecting numerous similar cases around the Eastern Mediterranean and beyond and dating their deposition convinced him that they were rare phenomena in time, and were especially to be associated with peaks of population and hence the need to increase food production (Wilkinson, 1989). Since then, large-scale landscape manuring carpets have been mapped and analysed in almost every country in Europe and the Mediterranean, with Tony's pioneering work always the original inspiration.

Equally innovative, and also due to his unique eye for detail in the landscape, was his discovery of radial depressions surrounding prehistoric and historic towns, especially in the semi-arid steppes of Syria. In analogy to the traditional pre-tarmac country paths and roads in England, he termed these 'hollow ways' and, sometimes in conjunction with manuring carpets, he was able to interpret these as fossil remnants of the major paths taken by ancient farmers out to their fields, and shepherds to outfield grazing, and hence indicative of the areas of most intense land-use around tell communities. Meanwhile, since so many of the fossil land-use features were clearest from the air, Tony pioneered the use of satellite photographs when he was working on the North Jazira Project, initially using the assistance of the British Petroleum company.

The move to Chicago initiated a phase in Tony's career where much greater funds for research became available, allowing him to gather and analyse more and richer data. CAMEL, which he created at the Chicago Institute, became one of the first major institutions to gather and interpret satellite images, which by then were becoming far more easily available, especially the CORONA 'spy photos', which were declassified in 1995. As usual, however, Tony would not be content with merely adding remote-sensing to existing ideas of landscape history—he was already looking for new approaches to add to his analytical toolkit. In 2002, in collaboration with the Argonne National Laboratories, he was awarded National Science Foundation funding to develop a computer-based modelling of the dynamics of ancient Mesopotamian society, tying in his own knowledge of landscape and land-use history with the rich textual sources. Although published long after he had left the United States, this led to a major edited volume which appeared in 2013—*Models of Mesopotamian Landscapes: How Small-Scale Processes Contributed to the Growth of Early Civilizations* (Wilkinson, Gibson and Widell, 2013). Taking his earlier insights into land-use and overpopulation even further, here Tony developed mathematical models of the rise and fall of societies in ancient north Mesopotamia. The full incorporation of the 'social', and the innovative use of 'agent-based modelling' to reintroduce individual decisions into reconstructions of past societies, shows how far Tony was from being simply a geomorphologist or land-use historian. In fact in an even now much-cited major paper of 1994, he proposed a model for the rise of small city-states in North Mesopotamia, while at the same time setting up a series of models for food production and population levels which could assist in identifying the degree of sustainability of large central-places and their smaller satellite communities (Wilkinson, 1994).

The year Tony left Chicago for Edinburgh University was a culminating moment: it saw the publication of his magnum opus, certainly his masterpiece, *Archaeological Landscapes of the Near East* (Wilkinson, 2003). Here he brought together his encyclopaedic knowledge of the many historic landscape types in the macro-region, to compare and contrast the long-term dialectic between the dynamic physical landscape and changing forms of human society over this vast expanse of varied landforms. No one else could have written such a work; no one had anything like his experience throughout the macro-region, or the layer upon layer of knowledge and ideas about how to make sense of such a magnificent story. It will come as no surprise that this volume was awarded two prizes in the succeeding two years.

Some of the major projects on which Tony was a key staff member as the Landscape Archaeologist included the early research at Siraf and several field seasons in Oman, which gave rise to articles with a wide impact. However, his key involvement with excavation and survey at

Kurban Höyük in Turkey and then at Tell Sweyhat in Syria led to two significant volumes under his own name—*Town and Country in Southeastern Anatolia* (Wilkinson, 1990) and *On the Margin of the Euphrates: Settlement and Land Use at Tell Sweyhat, and in the Upper Lake Tabqa, Syria* (Wilkinson, 2004) respectively. A third volume, entitled *Settlement Development in the North Jazira, Iraq* (Wilkinson and Tucker, 1995), resulted from his collaboration with David Tucker on a survey in northern Iraq. The Jazira Project was the first Middle Eastern survey where standard site-focused survey was accompanied by 'offsite survey' where artefacts were plotted and sampled across the entire landscape outside settlement foci, and this was to influence survey practice in the whole region permanently. After the move to Chicago, Tony was busy running field surveys—usually in association with excavations—in Turkey at Titris Höyük and the Amuq Plain, then in Syria in the Balikh Valley, at Tell Brak and Tell Hamoukar, as well as carrying out several field seasons in Yemen. His brief time at Edinburgh University nonetheless led to his participation in two major projects, the Land of Carchemish Project in collaboration with Edgar Peltenburg, published in the monograph, *Carchemish in Context* (Wilkinson et al., 2016), and a collaboration with Eberhard Sauer on the Gorgon Wall survey in northern Iran—*Persia's Imperial Power in Late Antiquity: the Great Wall of Gorgon and the Frontier Landscapes of Sasanian Iran* (Sauer et al., 2013). His most recent projects, marking his arrival in Durham University, included a survey project collaboration with Graham Philip—the 2008–12 Fragile Crescent Project —an ambitious effort to identify and analyse long-term patterns of settlement, land-use and societal changes over 2,500 years beginning in the fourth millennium BC. Utilising geophysical data in conjunction with the archaeological record from numerous regional surveys across a broad swathe of the Middle East, most of which were conducted by Tony himself over the course of his forty-five-year career, this project was the one he viewed essentially as his magnum opus. Along with a publicly accessible online database, this project has published papers in journals including *Levant, Journal of World Prehistory, Quaternary International, PLos ONE* and *Quaternary Science Reviews.* A second project with his former Edinburgh colleague Eberhard Sauer—*Persia and its Neighbours*—has examined the landscape of the Sasanian Empire (third–seventh centuries AD) in Iran, Georgia, Azerbaijan and Oman, and the research strategies and data collection techniques devised by him for this project have continued to be implemented in the field, but regrettably without the benefit of his presence as this project continues.

Finally to the man. We have seen how bright and forward-looking Tony Wilkinson was in his research. One always looked forward eagerly to a new paper or book from his pen; it would be full of surprises, ideas and approaches one had not thought of, while immediately making you want to go out and use or test them in one's own landscapes. He was not only a great collaborator, easily measured by the global response to his passing from sympathy letters and numerous obituaries, but he liked to involve students in his work, allowing them enough scope so that so many went on to run their own surveys and landscape reconstructions under his inspiration. His sadness at the eruption of wars throughout the Middle East would result in action: he stayed in close touch with former colleagues in the various countries he had worked in; he was one of the first archaeologists to visit Iraq after the fall of Saddam Hussein in order to inspect the damage to heritage in 2003; and soon after arriving in Durham he and his wife Eleanor hosted a meeting of Iraqi archaeologists whose work and monuments were threatened by conflict—a conference funded by a grant gained by Eleanor.

Apart from his official hobby 'walking', until the late 1980s somehow Tony found time to play blues harmonica in the Bamboo Beat band in various gigs across England, and even into the 1990s, while at the University of Chicago, Tony would occasionally join in open-mic nights at the local blues club around the corner from his apartment on Woodlawn Avenue. Later in life he took enormous pleasure in playing the vintage guitar he had bought in England in 1973, and although his academic responsibilities occupied more of his time as his administrative responsibilities increased, music remained an obsession through to the end of his days. But most important of all, Tony was a modest and kind man. He was not to be drawn into the 'odium archaeologicum' of personalised arguments about methods and theories, but calmly presented his position alongside views he often did not agree with. Despite his immense knowledge and profound experience, he wore his learning lightly and was a delightful companion whether in academic meetings, in searing temperatures in the hottest parts of the Middle East or in the pub. There really was no one like him: he is simply irreplaceable as a beacon of ever-advancing research skill in Landscape Archaeology, wherever it is practised.

JOHN BINTLIFF
University of Leiden and Edinburgh University

References

Sauer, E. W., Rekavandi Omrani, H., Wilkinson, T. J., and Nokandeh, J., *Persia's Imperial Power in Late Antiquity: the Great Wall of Gorgan and the Frontier Landscapes of Sasanian Iran* (Oxford, 2013).

Whitehouse, D., Whitcomb, D. S. and Wilkinson, T. J., *Siraf: History, Topography and Environment* (Oxford, 2009).

Wilkinson, T. J., 'Extensive sherd scatters and land-use intensity: some recent results', *Journal of Field Archaeology*, 16 (1989), 31–46.

Wilkinson, T. J., *Town & Country in Southeastern Anatolia: Settlement and Land Use at Kurban Höyük and Other Sites in the Lower Karababa Basin* (Chicago, IL, 1990).

Wilkinson, T. J., 'The structure and dynamics of dry-farming states in Upper Mesopotamia', *Current Anthropology*, 35 (1994), 483–520.

Wilkinson, T. J., *Archaeological Landscapes of the Near East* (Tucson, AZ, 2003).

Wilkinson, T. J., *On the Margin of the Euphrates: Settlement and Land Use at Tell es-Sweyhat and in the Upper Lake Assad Area, Syria* (Chicago, IL, 2004).

Wilkinson, T. J., Gibson, M. and Widell, M. (eds.), *Models of Mesopotamian Landscapes: How Small-Scale Processes Contributed to the Growth of Early Civilizations* (Oxford, 2013).

Wilkinson, T. J. and Murphy, P. L., 'Archaeological survey of an intertidal zone: the submerged landscape of the Essex coast, England', *Journal of Field Archaeology* 13 (1986), 177–94.

Wilkinson, T. J. and Murphy, P. L., *Essex: Hullbridge Survey Project Volume 1:c. The Archaeology of the Essex Coast* (Essex County Council, 1995).

Wilkinson, T. J., Murphy, P. L., Brown, N. and Heppell, E. M., *The Archaeology of the Essex Coast, Volume II: Excavations at the Prehistoric Site of the Stumble* (Essex County Council, 2012).

Wilkinson, T. J. and Tucker, D. J., *Settlement Development in the North Jazira, Iraq: a Study of the Archaeological Landscape* (Baghdad, 1995).

Joint publications of Eleanor and Tony Wilkinson referred to in the text

Wilkinson, T. J. and Barbanes, E., 'Settlement and settlement patterns in the Iron Age: the Syrian Jazira', in G. Bunnens (ed.), *Essays on Syria in the Iron Age, Ancient Near Eastern Studies Supplement 7* (Louvain, 2007), pp. 397–422.

Wilkinson, T. J., Peltenburg, E., McCarthy, A., Wilkinson, E. B. and Brown, M., 'Archaeology in the Land of Carchemish: landscape surveys in the area of Jerablus Tahtani 2006', *Levant*, 39 (2007), 213–47.

Wilkinson, T. J., Peltenburg, E. and Barbanes Wilkinson, E. (eds.), *Carchemish in Context: the Land of Carchemish Project 2006–2010*. Themes from the Ancient Near East, BANEA Publications Series Vol. 4 (Oxford, 2016).

Wilkinson, T. J. and Wilkinson, E. B., 'The Iron Age of the Middle Euphrates in Syria and Turkey', in J. MacGinnis, D. Wicke and T. Greenfield (eds.), *The Provincial Archaeology of the Assyrian Empire* (Oxford, 2016), pp. 213–28.

Wilkinson, T. J., Wilkinson, E. B., Ur, J. and Altaweel, M., 'Landscape and settlement in the Assyrian Empire', *Bulletin of the American Society for Oriental Research*, 340 (2005), 23–56.

Publications from the Fragile Crescent Project

Lawrence, D., Philip, G., Wilkinson, K., Buylaert, J. P., Murray, A. S., Thompson, W. and Wilkinson, T. J., 'Regional power and local ecologies: accumulated population trends and human impacts in the northern Fertile Crescent', *Quaternary International Online* (2015), http://dx.doi.org/10.1016/j.quaint.2015.06.026 (accessed 5 March 2017).

Lawrence, D., Philip, G., Hunt, H., Snape-Kennedy, L. and Wilkinson, T. J., 'Long term population, city size and climate trends in the Fertile Crescent: a first approximation', *PLoS ONE*, 11 (2016), e0152563.

Lawrence, D. and Wilkinson, T. J., 'Hubs and upstarts: pathways to urbanism in the northern Fertile Crescent', *Antiquity*, 89 (2015), 328–44.

Smith, S., Wilkinson, T. J. and Lawrence, D., 'Agro-pastoral landscapes in the zone of uncertainty: the Middle Euphrates and the North Syrian Steppe during the 4th and 3rd millennia BC', in M. Bonacossi and D. Harrassowitz (eds.), *Settlement Dynamics and Human-Landscape Interaction in the Dry Steppes of Syria. Studia Charubensia*, 4 (2014), 151–72.

Wilkinson, T. J., Galiatsatos, N., Lawrence, D., Ricci, A., Dunford, R. and Philip, G., 'Late Chalcolithic and Early Bronze Age landscapes of settlement and mobility in the middle Euphrates: a reassessment', *Levant*, 44 (2012), 139–85.

Wilkinson, T. J., Philip, G., Bradbury, J., Dunford, R., Donoghue, D., Galiatsatos, N., Lawrence, D., Ricci, A. and Smith, S., 'Contextualizing early urbanization: settlement cores, early states and agro-pastoral strategies in the Fertile Crescent during the fourth and third millennia BC', *Journal of World Prehistory*, 27 (2014), 43–109.

STROUD FRANCIS CHARLES MILSOM

Stroud Francis Charles Milsom
1923–2016

STROUD FRANCIS CHARLES MILSOM, known since childhood as 'Toby',[1] was the pre-eminent historian of English law in the twentieth century. The penultimate male descendant of the Georgian Milsoms who gave their name to Milsom Street in Bath, and of the Victorian Milsoms who founded the music company there, he was born on 2 May 1923, the second son of Harry Lincoln Milsom (1889–1970), Secretary of the London Hospital in Whitechapel, and Isobel Vida ('Babs'), daughter of the Hon. W. E. Collins MC of New Zealand.[2] Harry had met Isobel in Cambridge at a Trinity College May Ball, while she was still a pupil at Wycombe Abbey, and they married in 1915. Toby always spoke fondly of them. They were clearly a happy family, imbued with good humour, and comfortably situated, with a house in Wimbledon and a larger house ('Carn Du') in Rock, Cornwall.

Harry had the foresight to enter both his sons as candidates for admission to Trinity College in 1929, when Toby was six. But the path to Cambridge was not smooth. Toby's schooldays at Charterhouse were, by his own account, unhappy. He was not a sportsman, and he was not exceptionally distinguished academically. But he enjoyed the sciences, and seemed set on a scientific career of some kind. Then calamity befell him. While staying at Rock in April 1938, the inquisitive schoolboy risked an

---

[1] His first name was registered on birth as George, but changed at baptism. Stroud was the forename of an uncle, Francis that of his paternal grandfather, and Charles that of his paternal great-grandfather.
[2] A. C. Fox-Davies, *Armorial Families: a Directory of Gentlemen of Coat-Armour* (Edinburgh, 1929), pp. ii, 1361.

unwise investigation of something on the beach which exploded and fractured his skull, puncturing the frontal lobe of his brain and bringing him close to death. A risky operation by the eminent neurosurgeon Professor H. W. B. Cairns of Oxford, followed by many others during a seriously unpleasant year in hospital, left him with a permanently cleft forehead but with his formidable mental faculties unimpaired. Indeed, there was a theory—which he sometimes hinted at himself—that his imaginative gifts may have been somehow released by the trauma. It was an encouraging sign when, during his recuperation, he cultivated his hobby of inventing gadgets seemingly inspired by Heath Robinson.[3]

Disaster struck the family again in 1940, when Toby's elder brother Darrell was killed in an aircraft collision, only months after receiving his commission as a Pilot Officer.[4] The hopes of the family were now pinned on Toby. He had been at the bottom of his advanced class on returning to school, a year behind his contemporaries; but he passed the school examinations required for university entrance, and in 1941 duly followed his father to Trinity. Whether or not it was the result of wartime conditions, there was no interview—a reassuring letter from the housemaster was sufficient—and no prior discussion of what he might study. He went up with a trunk full of science books, intending to read Natural Sciences, but his tutor disabused him of that on arrival. His Mathematics were not good enough. The next suggestion, that he might read English, was brushed aside with the observation that he would surely not want to become a schoolmaster. So he was pushed into Law, the last refuge in such cases.

To everyone's surprise, Milsom began to shine in this new line of study, with starred firsts and prizes in both parts of the Tripos,[5] and a brief first

---

[3] E.g. machines to let him pick things off the floor. This was not a new-found inclination. In 1937 he had invented a fretwork frame for holding crossword puzzles cut from newspapers—this was illustrated in *The Times*, with a letter from his father which shows more than a hint of the humour which Toby inherited.

[4] He was killed on 29 March in a collision between two Gloster Gladiators. Born in 1919, he had gone to the RAF College at Cranwell, rather than Cambridge (as intended), on leaving school. There was a third calamity when Harry Milsom, the father, lost an eye and narrowly escaped death following a Territorial Army explosives demonstration at Padstow.

[5] He was placed in the first class in the Law Qualifying Examination in 1942 and awarded a college prize. The following year, in Part IB of the Law Tripos, his was the only distinction (colloquially known as a starred first) and he was awarded the George Long Prize in Roman Law. In Part II of the Tripos in 1944 he was one of two candidates awarded distinctions, and shared the George Long Prize for Jurisprudence with the other.

publication in the *Cambridge Law Journal* in his second year.⁶ A few years later Harry Hollond, a venerable Law fellow of Trinity, reflected on this strange turn of events in a letter to T. F. T. Plucknett:

> Milsom is a very odd case. For one thing he had a hole blown in his forehead by an explosion, and [for] another he was just an ordinary average boy at Charterhouse in school subjects, and his housemaster was amazed when at the end of his first year here he achieved an unprecedented performance in the Law Qualifying Examination. He adds to his ability a quite outstanding charm, and his modesty is almost absurd.⁷

After graduating in 1944, Milsom worked until the end of the war as a temporary civil servant in the Naval Intelligence Division of the Admiralty, scrutinising aerial photographs in Oxford. He then returned to Cambridge and read for the Bar, being tutored at the weekends by R. E. Megarry (later Sir Robert Megarry FBA). He was awarded a Cassel Scholarship by Lincoln's Inn,⁸ was called to the Bar in 1947, and envisaged a career at the Chancery Bar, perhaps pursuing his scientific inclinations by specialising in patent work. But scholarship was pulling in another direction, and in 1947 he obtained a Commonwealth Fund Fellowship to study for a year in the United States. Since the most eminent legal historian across the Atlantic (S. E. Thorne) was then in England, it was arranged that he should go to the Pennsylvania Law School in Philadelphia to study under George L. Haskins. The original plan was to work on bailment, but Haskins suggested the early history of judicial review instead.⁹ Milsom set to work and wrote a dissertation on the subject in under a year.¹⁰

The dissertation was a remarkable piece of work, revealing Milsom's ability to peel away misconceptions and rethink the past from the original sources. He began work with the writ of error, which had never been a satisfactory procedure, since it was tied rigidly to the formulaic wording of the plea roll. But 'those who laid the foundations of the common law

---

⁶ *Cambridge Law Journal*, 8 (1943), 206, a case-note on *Murray v Parkes* [1942] 2 KB 123. A second followed, *Cambridge Law Journal*, 8 (1944), 331–2, on the more important case of *Glasgow Corporation v Muir* [1943] AC 448.
⁷ Letter of 28 September 1948. This letter, found in Milsom's papers, must have come from Plucknett's papers.
⁸ This was worth £600. It more than paid for his admission and call fees, and for his pupillage.
⁹ Letter from Haskins to Milsom, 12 July 1947.
¹⁰ While there he wrote a review of F. Schulz's *History of Roman Legal Science* (Oxford, 1946), published in *University of Pennsylvania Law Review*, 96 (1947), 299–301, which already displayed something of his characteristic way of thinking. His main criticism was that Schulz assumed everything the Roman jurists wrote must have been the lucid expression of accurate thought.

were intelligent men', and Milsom concluded that 'something at some time must have gone wrong, that there must have been an unperceived degeneration'. He decided that the key to the story lay in the more obscure procedure called 'false judgment', which no one had correctly grasped:

> Accounts of the process of false judgment are to be found in many text books; all are in substantial agreement, and all, as it has transpired, are unsatisfactory. For the most part they are based upon a passage in Glanvill, and if the present writer is correct almost every word of that passage has been misunderstood ...

He concluded that false judgment had been the prototype of proceedings in error, and largely responsible for the procedure's defects. Its dominant characteristic, a legacy from the Anglo-Saxons, was the idea that the judge who judged unjustly had committed a fault for which he ought to be punished. False judgment focused not upon the rights of the parties, but upon the wrongs of the court, and therefore upon its record. Various consequential developments altered the role of the record, causing serious long-term difficulties. The dissertation concluded with some modest disclaimers, the last of which was quietly subversive: 'The writer does not believe that the story which he has tried to tell has any significance in modern affairs at all except perhaps this, that it furnishes new illustrations of the great part, both good and ill, played in legal development by the forces of misunderstanding and confusion.'

On Milsom's return, the essay was submitted for a prize fellowship at Trinity College, the examiners being Plucknett and Thorne, the foremost historians of English law at the time. They were bowled over by it, and Milsom was given the fellowship without difficulty.[11] Plucknett reported that it was many years since he had read anything on legal history with such pleasure and admiration: 'It would be most unfair to describe this dissertation as showing "high promise", for in fact it is a work of notable achievement.' He had recognised the distinct qualities which were later to characterise Milsom's published work:

> at numerous points I have noted suggestions and speculations which could only have proceeded from the application of a mature and penetrating mind to a rich store of historical knowledge. This fertility in suggestion is balanced by a keen sense of the difference between proof and probability and complete intellectual honesty (as on p. 118). There are several valuable discussions in which the meaning of words is analysed (e.g. *recordum, curia*), and a passage on p. 134 which

---

[11] He was also awarded the Yorke Prize the following year, the examiners being Plucknett and Sir Cecil Carr. There is a copy of the essay in Trinity College library, and Milsom's own copy will be placed in the Centre for English Legal History, Cambridge.

briefly touches upon the psychology of legal decision shows how thoroughly the author has entered into the thought of the thirteenth century lawyer. In short, this is a mature study ... the author keeps steadily on his course, and constructs his argument in English which is careful, correct and unpretentious. It is a pleasure in these days to read an essay so free from clichés and jargon.

Haskins recommended publication, subject to some work on the manuscript records, which of course were not available in Philadelphia. Plucknett, too, was in no doubt that it should be published as a book,[12] and Milsom's Yorke Prize was awarded on condition that the manuscript be prepared for the press. Milsom duly began to delve into medieval plea rolls in the Public Record Office, amassing piles of expensive photographs, but he was diverted by other work and left the revision too long. A proposal for publication was still with Cambridge University Press in the 1960s, and as late as 1971 he wrote to the Press that he would like to 'preserve the intention and possibility of producing it'.[13] But there is no evidence that he ever began the revisions.

Mindful of the impermanence of his prize fellowship, Milsom did not in 1948 dare to abandon all thoughts of the Bar, and in his first year he served a pupillage in Chancery chambers with J. W. Brunyate, himself a former prize fellow of Trinity.[14] The precaution proved unnecessary,[15] because in 1949 he was appointed a University Assistant Lecturer at Cambridge, and in 1952 he was promoted to the tenured position of Lecturer. He immediately started buying books on legal history,[16] and in

---

[12] Letter to Derek Hall, 19 September 1949: 'A new fellow of Trinity Cambridge has a book in preparation, which I have seen ... he is S. F. C. Milsom, and it is a good book.' Cf. S. E. Thorne to Harry Hollond, 16 June 1963, referring to 'his unfortunately still unpublished but often-quoted paper on judicial review'. There are only a few remarks on the subject in S. F. C. Milsom, *Historical Foundations of the Common Law*, 1st edn. (London, 1969), pp. 47–8; this book is hereafter referred to as *HFCL*.

[13] Letter of 15 March 1971 ('although the fundamental work is there, it needs a good deal done to it. I was actually without a copy of it for many years until recently, because my copy was being used by the late Helen Cam'). He asked for more time, on the grounds that writing the Maitland Lectures (1972) was more important to him.

[14] Brunyate's clarity of legal thought and exposition made a deep impression on Milsom: see S. F. C. Milsom, 'F. W. Maitland', *Proceedings of the British Academy*, 66 (1980), p. 274. He wrote several works, including a posthumous edition of Maitland's *Equity* (based on lecture-notes). The chambers were at No. 4, Stone Buildings, Lincoln's Inn.

[15] He did earn a fee of 50 guineas for a joint opinion written in 1949, with Professor E. C. S. Wade, supporting the Government's claim to sovereignty over the Ecréhos and Minquiers islets, on the strength of records stretching back to the time of King John. The International Court of Justice decided in favour of the United Kingdom: *France v United Kingdom* [1953] ICJ 3.

[16] Among the earliest were *Bracton's Note Book*, bought in January 1949, and the first eight volumes of the *Curia Regis Rolls*, bound in March 1949.

1951 laid out £100 for a set of 'quarto' year books. Odd as it seems in retrospect, the subject of Legal History, which had until 1949 been a paper in Part II of the Law Tripos, was dropped from the syllabus at the very moment of his appointment. This was ostensibly the outcome of a Tripos reform, but the true reason was that the subject had previously been taught in an old-fashioned manner which failed to attract students.[17] The result was that Milsom lectured on Legal History only for the postgraduate LLB course,[18] though from 1950 he also gave lectures on Personal Property for the Tripos. He reminisced that his lectures were scheduled at 9am, and he usually began preparation at midnight, so that they were 'fresh off the cooker, as it were'. Most of his teaching, however, would have taken the form of college supervisions, doubtless in a wider range of subjects.

Trespass and the forms of action (1949–54)

The original reason for putting aside the prize essay was that Milsom had become concerned, while preparing his first LLB lectures in 1949,[19] about the traditional background account of English legal history as enshrined in Maitland's *The Forms of Action at Common Law*. The 'forms of action' were the procedural formulae, or writs, into which plaintiffs' facts had to be fitted in order to originate lawsuits in the royal courts, and they had seemed to provide an eternal conceptual framework for the common law. Maitland's little manual had come to be treated as gospel, and had been the basis of Cambridge teaching, though it was put together posthumously from lecture notes and never intended for publication. It was a concise introduction to the classical system, which had survived almost until Maitland's own time: still essential learning for a Victorian law student, but not a convincing explanation of how or why the myriad structure of peculiarities had first evolved. 'To one whose boyhood had been excitedly concentrated upon the natural sciences', Milsom later recalled, the 'lack

---

[17] The Tripos course had been taught in Milsom's undergraduate days by H. E. Hollond of Trinity, the Rouse Ball Professor of English Law, whose lectures were said to have been far from popular, and seems last to have been taught in 1948–9 by K. Scott.

[18] From 1950 to 1955 jointly with M. J. Prichard, a fellow of Gonville and Caius College, who obtained a starred first in the LLB in 1949 after attending Milsom's first class. Mr Prichard's recollection is that Milsom gave most of the lectures.

[19] See 'Not doing is no trespass' (n. 26, below), 105 n. 5 (a discussion with Hollond), and 113 n. 33 (a discussion with Prichard).

of any credible connections between phenomena' was unsatisfying.[20] Milsom revealed his uncertainty about the traditional story in 1949, when reviewing a book about thirteenth-century procedure without writ.[21] Procedure by plaint or bill had long been regarded—reading history backwards—as an odd exception to normal common-law procedure, a form of extraordinary justice comparable to equity. But in fact it was the norm before the writ system began, and Milsom saw that an understanding of how such lawsuits worked, and how causes of action were framed independently of writs, ought to be the principal key to understanding how and why the writs came into being.

The same book review alluded briefly to the origins of the writ of trespass, and it was with trespass that the doubts mainly began. Generations of law students had been taught, and indeed it had become the law, that there were two principal torts: trespass, a forcible wrong (committed 'with force and arms against the king's peace'), and 'case',[22] a miscellaneous and ever-expanding category of non-forcible wrongs. It was widely believed that trespass had been recognised first, and that—as the 'fertile mother of actions' (Maitland's immortal phrase)—it had somehow begotten case, though quite how this happened was controversial. Milsom's difficulties with trespass were further explored in 1953 when, in a review of A. K. R. Kiralfy's *Action on the Case*,[23] he criticised the author's confusion over the action's origins. Kiralfy had assumed that there was in the thirteenth and fourteenth centuries 'a definite wrong called trespass', whereas the word probably just meant 'wrong' in a general sense, as in the Lord's Prayer.[24] On Milsom's view, the origin of case ceased to pose any problem if non-forcible wrongs and trespasses *vi et armis* were both seen as species of trespass remediable through two different forms of writ, the special form (actions on the case) and the general. The 'force and arms' found in the general writs had a jurisdictional rather than a juridical

---

[20] S. F. C. Milsom, *Studies in the History of the Common Law* (London, 1985), p. ix: this book is hereafter referred to as *Studies*. Cf. the opening remarks in his unpublished Harris Lectures at Indiana University (1974): '... My first attempt in life was to be a natural scientist; and I have never lost the scientist's craving for an almost visible simplicity of mechanism.'
[21] *Law Quarterly Review*, 65 (1949), 259–63, belatedly reviewing H. G. Richardson and G. O. Sayles (eds.), *Select Cases of Procedure without Writ under Henry III* (London, 1941). The editors had not understood the significance of their material in the way Milsom did.
[22] This was an abbreviation of 'action on the special case', or 'trespass on the case'.
[23] *Cambridge Law Journal*, 11 (1951), 464. There was a similar criticism in the review of C. H. S. Fifoot's *History and Sources of the Common Law: Tort and Contract* (1949), in *Cambridge Law Journal*, 10 (1950), 482.
[24] A further development of this thinking was that criminal misdemeanours were also trespasses, in the same sense, but divided from 'tort' by jurisdiction and procedure: *HFCL*, p. 43.

explanation; lesser wrongs were at first beneath the notice of the king's judges, though they were trespasses none the less. Trespass had been split in two for purely practical reasons but with big unforeseen consequences.[25] This was the core of Milsom's discovery about the personal actions, an insight which he acknowledged had been prompted by one of Professor Hamson's lectures in 1947.[26]

Milsom expounded the theme more fully in his first major paper, 'Not doing is no trespass' (1954).[27] The theory that trespass simply meant wrong, and that 'trespass on the case' was a constituent species rather than something generically different, not only did away with the problem of its origin but also removed a major difficulty relating to its later expansion into the field of contract. The use of 'case' to remedy passive breaches of promise—'the most spectacular exploit of case'—had been resisted in the fifteenth and sixteenth centuries, supposedly (according to the received theory) because 'nonfeasance', not doing anything, did not remotely resemble forcible trespass and could not easily be accommodated by analogy. In reality, as Milsom pointed out, it had never been wholly true that 'not doing is no trespass'.[28] The innkeeper who did not protect his guest's goods from theft, or the tenant whose failure to repair his stretch of sea-wall led to a flood, had both been made liable by the use of special writs of trespass devised in the time of Edward III. Not doing could be a trespass, if there was a duty to act; but the medieval view was that, if the duty to act was essentially contractual, the plaintiff should use one of the pre-existing contractual remedies (the writs of covenant, debt and detinue). Many plaintiffs, however, could not use covenant, because they did not have the necessary document under seal, and they did not like to use debt or detinue because (unless there was a sealed bond) the debtor could avoid liability simply by swearing an oath. It was arguably wrong to evade these procedural requirements by treating a breach of contract as a tort, but the exploit was brought off by emphasising the economic damage

---

[25] Cf. *HFCL*, p. 271 ('the common law of torts was permanently disfigured by coming to the king's courts in two instalments'), and p. 345 ('The modern tort of negligence resulted from the confluence of two streams which had been separated in the first instance only by the jurisdictional division that produced "trespass" and "case" ...').

[26] Hamson had drawn attention to a telling case of 1309, in which a special action with no allegation of force and arms was described in the report simply as 'trespass': S. F. C. Milsom, 'Not doing is no trespass: a view of the boundaries of case', *Cambridge Law Journal*, 12 (1954), 106 n. 7 (*Studies*, p. 92); *Baker and Milsom: Sources of English Legal History*, 2nd edn by J. Baker (Oxford, 2010), pp. 669–71.

[27] Milsom, 'Not doing is no trespass', 105–17; *Studies*, 91–103.

[28] The aphorism was well known to lawyers from a case reported by Sir Edward Coke in 1610.

suffered by reliance on the good faith of the promise, which could be presented as a kind of deceit; and this led in turn to the mysterious doctrine of consideration.[29]

Milsom's new way of looking at trespass put paid to Maitland's *Forms of Action*, at any rate for the formative period of the common law. As Milsom wrote half a century later:

> Maitland saw England as a legal Galapagos insulating native evolution from Roman contamination. We now know that he pressed the Darwinian analogy too far, seeing the whole development of English law in terms of monstrous species, the 'forms of action ... living things ... The struggle for life is keen among them and only the fittest survive'.[30] It is one way of picturing what was going on from the sixteenth century to the nineteenth ... But Maitland extended the vision to earlier times, and so hid what had really been rational argument about legal categories.[31]

Legal history had thus suddenly begun to change. Fifoot's *History and Sources of the Common Law* (London, 1949) would (as Milsom acknowledged) revive students' interest, by allowing them to read the arguments in the old cases at first hand.[32] Then Kiralfy's *Action on the Case* (London, 1951) had pointed to the importance for scholarship of the later plea rolls, which had been completely unexplored, and of the records of local courts in showing how law was thought of away from Westminster. Milsom hailed it as 'a vast and heroic labour', albeit presented as 'aggregations of important facts rather than as narratives'.[33] But both writers had failed to connect the facts convincingly. By misunderstanding 'trespass', they had misunderstood the role of the early forms of action: 'It is not the nature of plaster that determines the shape of the cast.'[34] It was Milsom who had begun to supply a convincing narrative which joined up the facts.

---

[29] Milsom would later characterise consideration as 'a coherent theory of contract mutilated by its passage through tort': *HFCL*, p. 315.

[30] A quotation from P. & M. (n. 53, below), p. 561.

[31] S. F. C. Milsom, 'Maitland', *Cambridge Law Journal*, 60 (2001), 268–9. Cf. *HFCL*, p. 25: 'since the mechanisms of change within the common law had been to allow one writ to do the work formally [*altered in 1981 to* formerly] done by another, the whole process came to be seen as an irrational interplay between "the forms of action". It was not. It was the product of men thinking.'

[32] Review in *Cambridge Law Journal*, 10 (1950), 481. Milsom here offered some scathing comments about the old way of teaching legal history 'as a mass of assertion and conjecture taken entirely at second hand, learnt by heart, and rarely understood ... To learn the subject like that is almost a waste of time.'

[33] Review in *Cambridge Law Journal*, 11 (1951), 466.

[34] Ibid.

Marriage, and Oxford (1955–64)

Milsom's work was briefly interrupted by a change of personal circumstances and a geographical relocation. During a severe illness which confined him to his rooms in Trinity College, the other Law fellows had asked Irène Radzinowicz to keep an eye on him, and they had become close. Irène (formerly Ira) was the daughter of Witold Szereszewski (1879–1943), a Polish architect, and in 1933 (aged sixteen) she had married a criminologist, Leon Rabinowicz (1906–99—later Sir Leon Radzinowicz FBA), who taught at the Free University of Warsaw. They came to England in 1938 to study the English penal system, thereby escaping the fate which befell both her parents.[35] Irène had helped her then husband with the research for the first volume of his *History of English Criminal Law* (London, 1948), which earned him a fellowship of Trinity, but the marriage had proved painful for Irène and it ended in divorce. With Toby she found a remarkable rapport. They married in 1955, and supported each other unfailingly for forty-three years. Irène was to manage his life, type up his hieroglyphic drafts,[36] read his proofs, compile his indexes and travel the world with him. She was also reputed to chivvy him into finishing things which he was disinclined to release.[37] But in 1955 it was not possible to remain in Cambridge after marrying the wife of another fellow, and so Milsom resigned his fellowship, accepted a temporary lectureship at the London School of Economics, and moved with Irène to a 'miserable flat' in Chiswick. The *Cambridge Law Journal* was now out of bounds, the editor (a fellow of Trinity) having declined to publish any more of his work on the ground that he did not want to offend Radzinowicz.[38]

---

[35] Milsom wrote to the present writer on 30 April 2005: 'They came for her Jewish father in the small hours, shot him in a street in Warsaw, and would not let his body be taken away for burial. Her good Catholic mother just disappeared, presumably to be killed in a camp.' Her father had been reduced to working as a warehouseman, and was killed in the Umschlagplatz from which Jews were transported to Treblinka.

[36] By his own account, 'She contrived to type almost everything I ever wrote, but used to say my manuscript was just an aid to telepathy ...': letter to Fiona Baker, excusing his handwriting, 15 July 2003.

[37] Hollond wrote to Irène on 5 August 1969, concerning *HFCL*: 'P.S. After finishing this letter, I read it to Marjorie, who commented: "you haven't said anything about Irène's contribution towards the successful appearance of Toby's book" ... So I add this p.s. to assure you how fully aware we are of what the book owes both to your stimulus and to your co-operation.' Milsom once told M. J. Prichard that she would sometimes order him back to work from more relaxing pursuits such as fretwork.

[38] Letter to the present writer, 15 December 1985, adding: 'Irène and I could, as it were, have sunk'. The editor was Professor C. J. Hamson, who nevertheless remained on friendly terms with Milsom.

The difficulties were soon overcome. Through the intervention of a London colleague (Professor L. C. B. Gower), the editor of the *Law Quarterly Review* (A. L. Goodhart) agreed to take anything he wrote. Then, the following year, he was offered a fellowship of New College, Oxford,[39] where he became settled with Irène in a beautiful college house in New College Lane. As was then usual at Oxford, he was teaching around sixteen hours a week, and from 1959 he also served as dean, responsible for discipline. His pupils from that time remember with fondness both his directness in encouraging high standards, where appropriate,[40] and the generous help he gave to those with less appetite for legal scholarship than himself. One of the latter recalled being asked each week whether or not he had done any work, in between rowing, and on giving the usual evasive answer would be told, 'Never mind, sit down, have a sherry, and I will tell you all about it.'[41] Many acknowledge the lifelong personal influence which he (and Irène) exerted on them.

Meanwhile, in the vacations, Milsom continued with his work on the personal actions. He had searched through the plea rolls for examples of trespass cases, and the result was a trilogy of articles, 'Trespass from Henry III to Edward III', which appeared in the *Law Quarterly Review* in 1958.[42] The use of plea rolls had been pioneered by Kiralfy and G. O. Sayles,[43] but Milsom's approach went beyond the collection of specimens. The articles drew some private criticism for their dense technicality,[44] but they further strengthened the case Milsom had made in 1954 about trespass, and added some general conclusions. Legal historians had been

---

[39] He succeeded to the Law tutorship which J. B. Butterworth (later Lord Butterworth) vacated on becoming bursar.

[40] C. J. Perrin CBE recalls that Milsom wrote on one of his first essays, 'Assertion is no substitute for reasoning, and especially when the assertion is wrong.'

[41] C. Russell, 'My legal life', *Lawyer Monthly* (June 2014), 30–1.

[42] S. F. C. Milsom, 'Trespass from Henry III to Edward III', *Law Quarterly Review*, 74 (1956), 195–224, 407–36, 561–90; *Studies*, pp. 1–90.

[43] Sayles drew attention to the high proportion of trespass cases in the King's Bench rolls under Edward I: *Select Cases in the Court of King's Bench under Edward I*, vol. ii (57 London, 1938), pp. xlii–xliii. But he regarded trespass as 'this "mitigated" felony on the borderland of tort'.

[44] E.g. Hollond to Milsom, 3 November 1958: 'I venture to suggest that when you publish further articles in the LQR you should look at them for a moment through the eyes of a probable reader and when necessary enlighten by a note ... (e.g. *op. se*)'. Cf. Hamson to Milsom, 23 October 1963: 'I remember reading your prize dissertation on the Origins of the Writs of Error—a truly astonishing affair which made the story uncannily clear and plausible and exciting, and I missed a comparable effect in the LQR articles. But the cause most probably is that Error was the work of a very young man who did not bear the burden of knowledge which you now have and who was therefore willing and able to tell the story in a manner much more debonnair, and much less appropriately no doubt. It is I am sure as foolish to regret that as to regret *les neiges d'antan*.'

looking for conceptual developments, a growing body of remediable wrongs starting with forcible trespass, 'but we come nearer the truth if we suppose a fixed body: what increased was the proportion remediable in royal courts'. The real story was about jurisdictional boundaries, and the strategies for getting round them.

It was in 1958 also that Milsom first became actively involved with the Selden Society.[45] Plucknett asked him if he would take over the editing of *Novae Narrationes*, which had been begun in 1933 by Dr Elsie Shanks in parallel with her proposed glossary of Law French. It was a guide to the French forms of oral pleading in the various forms of action, probably intended for use at moots in the nascent inns of court or of chancery.[46] The French text was Shanks's, but Milsom revised the translation heavily in order to make legal sense of it, and wrote a long introduction surveying all the actions represented in the text, commenting on the formulae in the light of reported discussions and early treatises on procedure. The massive volume appeared in 1963. It was full of recondite learning, and few have read it from cover to cover; but Milsom later considered it as a kind of starting-point,[47] and was grateful that the unsought task had compelled him to confront many aspects of the actions which he might not otherwise have thought significant. The exercise convinced him that editing texts could be more fruitful than writing monographs:

> In a monograph the writer sets the agenda and will dot i's and cross t's in the existing learning. In an edition the document sets the agenda, and (if he lets it) it may lead the editor into original thought. In my own case I'm sure it was brooding over the forms in *Novae Narrationes* that was mainly responsible for any idea I ever had.[48]

That was obviously an exaggeration, but Milsom's appreciation of the importance of editing coincided with the aims of the Selden Society, of which he became Literary Director, in succession to Plucknett, in 1964.[49]

---

[45] He had discussed with Plucknett as early as 1952 an edition of Holkham Hall MS. 245, discovered by Thorne, a collection of entries from the plea rolls from 1296 to 1317. He obtained photographs of it, probably because it contained numerous error cases. But Thorne advised against an edition, and the idea was dropped.

[46] Shanks disagreed with Milsom on this, but subsequent research on moots in the inns suggests that Milsom was right.

[47] Letter to Biancalana, 22 August 1997: 'Research [while at Oxford], mostly in vacations, was on the history of the personal actions (on which I also gave lectures), and then (which I have always thought of as my main starting-point) trying to make sense of the forms in Novae Narrationes.'

[48] Letter to the present writer, 12 December 2001.

[49] He held the office until 1980, and served as President in the Society's centenary year (1987).

London (1964–76)

Milsom also succeeded Plucknett in 1964 as Professor of Legal History at the London School of Economics.[50] Plucknett had been the first holder of the chair, created in 1931,[51] and Milsom was the obvious successor. Freed from college teaching and decanal responsibilities, Milsom was highly productive in the London years, and in 1967 he was elected a Fellow of the British Academy. During the same period he was a regular summer visitor to New York University and Yale, where he taught legal history courses.[52]

The year after he arrived in London he accepted an invitation by Cambridge University Press to produce a new edition of 'Pollock & Maitland', then in its seventieth year.[53] Tinkering with Maitland's hallowed words was unthinkable, and so he decided instead to write a long critical introduction.[54] Published in 1968, it turned out to be one of his major works, and much of his later writing would be concentrated on Maitland— whom he greatly admired as the founder of his subject,[55] but whose writings some historians seemed to treat as unchallengeable. He began the introduction by remarking on the longevity of Maitland's book; it was being reprinted 'not as a dead masterpiece but as a still living authority'.

---

[50] His candidacy was supported by Thorne, who wrote to Hollond on 16 June 1963, 'In my opinion Toby is the most promising legal historian in England today, and it was in these precise words that I urged his name upon Kahn-Freund when he visited me here ....'.

[51] Plucknett died in 1965, and Milsom's insightful memoir was published in S. F. C. Milsom, 'Theodore Frank Thomas Plunknett 1897–1965', *Proceedings of the British Academy*, 51 (1965), 505–19; *Studies*, 279–93. He was (according to Milsom, in an interview in 2009) 'a very nice man, totally removed from the world'; but he lost his mind a few years before his death, and it was rumoured that the LSE authorities had to forge his signature to a letter of resignation.

[52] He made nineteen visits to teach legal history in the United States: five to New York University (a relationship initiated by A. L. Goodhart), nine to Yale, three to Indiana, one to Harvard and one to Colorado. He visited China in 1979 as part of a British Academy delegation, and lectured in Japan in 1981 under an exchange scheme between the Academy and the Japan Academy.

[53] F. Pollock and F. W. Maitland, *History of English Law before the Time of Edward I* (Cambridge, 1895; revised edition, 1898), referred to hereafter as *P. & M*. This was mostly written by Maitland, whose name was placed second only in deference to Pollock's seniority at the Bar.

[54] In 1970, at the invitation of the publishers, he was minded to do the same for Plucknett's *Concise History of the Common Law*, 5th edn (London, 1958); but this came to nothing.

[55] He wrote five subsequent pieces specifically about Maitland: Milsom, 'F. W. Maitland'; review of G. R. Elton's *Maitland*, in *Times Literary Supplement*, 28 Feb. 1986, 225–6; S. F. C. Milsom, '"Pollock and Maitland": a lawyer's retrospect', in J. Hudson (ed.), *Centenary Essays on 'Pollock and Maitland'* (Oxford, 1996), pp. 243–59; 'Maitland' (address at the unveiling of Maitland's tablet in Westminster Abbey), *Cambridge Law Journal*, 60 (2001), 265–70; and S. F. C. Milsom, 'Maitland, Frederic William (1850–1906)', *Oxford Dictionary of National Biography*, http://www.oxforddnb.com/view/article/34837 (accessed 28 February 2017).

Yet the splendour of Maitland's achievement had beguiled historians into unthinking dependence, and it was time to attempt 'an essay in heresy, pious heresy, intended to suggest the kind of doubt which it is possible to have about Maitland's picture'. His own account of its genesis is worth quoting:[56]

> CUP agreed to a distant date, then reneged on that and the job had to be done in great haste. The bit on the personal actions came relatively easily; they had been my stamping-ground. Except for Formedon[57] (a casual find when searching plea rolls for trespass etc.) and except for relevant bits in *Novae Narrationes*, I had neither written nor lectured on the real actions. It would hardly do for a relatively young man to express unidentifiable dissatisfaction with the central Maitland gospel (which was as far as I'd got), so what on earth was I to say? Most of it (more or less all at once, but I started with seisin and disseisin) came out of the grey while waiting at Charing Cross for a train home ... Funny how one remembers places ... I could have shown you the bit of wall in the old PRO I walked painfully into when the trespass/case thing came to me.

Milsom's work on the personal actions had indeed already dealt a death-blow to Maitland's view of the forms of action. Maitland had concentrated too much on the procedures developed in the royal courts, and had treated those courts as if they were making law rather than reflecting assumptions already in existence and enforced in other courts. But the same difficulty beset his account of the land law and the real actions, which paid insufficient attention to the feudal jurisdictions which had been the first, if not the only, recourse earlier in the twelfth century. The result was that many features of the land law seemed to have no rational explanation, and had to be accepted as inexplicable archaisms. Even Maitland had admitted puzzlement over 'the mystery of seisin', the concept which lay at its root.

Recovering unexpressed assumptions was the paramount difficulty. There was an almost impenetrable darkness beyond *Glanvill* (*c.*1187/89), the first coherent account of English law, written just before routine judicial records began to be kept. *Glanvill* was mainly about procedure. So much was known about the procedural mechanics of the writ of right

---

[56] Letter to Biancalana, 22 August 1997 (copied to the present writer for information); cf. S. F. C. Milsom, *A Natural History of the Common Law* (New York, 2003), p. xxiii—hereafter referred to as *Natural History*. While working on Thorne's obituary, he had become troubled by an unfounded hint that his introduction had in effect taken over Thorne's ideas and deterred him from turning his Maitland lectures of 1959 (mentioned below) into a book. Thorne had in fact been diverted from the idea of such a book by his concentration on *Bracton*.

[57] S. F. C. Milsom, 'Formedon before *De Donis*', *Law Quarterly Review*, 72 (1956), 391–7; *Studies*, 223–9.

'that with some rehearsal we could manage the law-suit ourselves. But we do not know what it was about, what "the right" was.' Maitland had been misled not only by the later concept of the forms of action but by the seeming continuity of all legal institutions and terminology. He had relied too often on the 'the majestic work of Bracton',[58] a massive academic work of the thirteenth century, the author of which had not witnessed the beginnings of royal justice and had in any case perceived the legal system 'with eyes not representative of his own time'.[59] Maitland had, moreover, unconsciously carried back into the twelfth century the legal assumptions of the thirteenth—which indeed were still largely those of the Victorian lawyer—and thought of owning land in the same way as one might own a horse. But possessive pronouns are a trap: 'my land' could indicate contractual entitlement rather than property, in the same way as 'my job', 'my bank account', or 'my seat on the train'.[60] Milsom had suddenly seen, while awaiting *his* train at Charing Cross, that seisin and right did not begin as 'flat' or 'horizontal' relationships between equal neighbours, or between people and things, like the Roman *possessio* and *dominium*, but as 'vertical' relationships between lords and tenants. Seen in this way, they were at first more about managerial control than abstract ownership. Seisin could only be derived from a lord; and 'right' could only be a right to hold of a particular lord.

This new vision tied in neatly with the account of inheritance which Thorne had given in a Maitland Lecture in 1959.[61] By the thirteenth century, as in Maitland's time, inheritance occurred automatically on an ancestor's death, by operation of law; even if the rightful heir was for some improper reason excluded, he inherited the legal estate and could

---

[58] *HFCL*, p. 29, adding that 'it is one of the important facts in the history of western thought that [*Brevia Placitata*, a treatise on pleading in French] was to prove fruitful, the latter [*Bracton*] sterile'.
[59] Milsom thought it too sophisticated and too remote from the way lawyers actually thought: *P. & M.*, pp. lxxii–lxxiii. He reviewed Thorne's edition of it sympathetically in *Harvard Law Review*, 74 (1971), 1756–62; but after Thorne's death he wrote that 'history was surely the loser by the diversion of Thorne's extraordinary power of perception. From a fruitful understanding of the nature of the world in which the common law began, he turned to difficult but relatively insignificant puzzles in a heavily corrupted text of questionable value for the study of thirteenth-century English law': footnote to his undelivered Maitland lecture (2007).
[60] This was not spelt out in the 1968 essay but is briefly mentioned in *HFCL*, p. 88 ('Today we think of the ownership of a suburban garden, or even of a great agricultural estate, as being something like the ownership of a motor-car'), and more fully in later discussions.
[61] S. E. Thorne, 'English feudalism and estates in land', *Cambridge Law Journal*, 17 (1959), 193–209. His (much earlier) essay on seisin was in the Maitland tradition: S. E. Thorne, 'Livery of seisin', *Law Quarterly Review*, 52 (1936), 345–64.

sue to recover it in the king's court. But this had not been the starting point. Grants to men and their heirs were frequent enough in the twelfth century, but a putative heir, however strong his claim, had not actually become heir until he had been identified and put in seisin by the lord's court; the heir was the person who actually succeeded, in the realm of fact. The decision by the lord's court was by no means arbitrary, since the default criteria governing the choice were usually clear, but in form it was a managerial decision free from external control.[62] The change in the nature of inheritance would not be visible in the charters and estate histories,[63] but it would profoundly affect the legal historian's understanding of the role of the common-law remedies. Milsom's revision of Maitland carried Thorne's insight further. Seeking to understand the forms of action dealing with real property, he postulated that, when people were expelled from land, the usual culprit was not a third-party villain but the lord: 'mere anarchy might envelop the great, but at the level of the local community are we always to think of neighbour ousting neighbour?'. The primary original sense of disseisin may, in fact, have been the withdrawal of the seisin which only the lord could give, an unseating of his own man. The vertical dimension is what gave seisin the quality which had so puzzled Maitland, a kind of possession but somehow imbued with rightful authority. And this new perspective led Milsom to a different understanding of the real actions, beginning with the writ of right.[64] 'Right' in this context was a greater right to be a lord's tenant than the present incumbent, and the claim was made out by inheritance from someone whom the lord (or the lord's ancestor) had previously put in seisin.[65] It was the lord who had to do right, to make good an earlier grant at the expense of someone he had more recently seised. The assizes of novel disseisin ('the greatest enigma in the history of the common law') and mort d'ancestor could both be explained as remedies devised to challenge more recent actions by

---

[62] This thesis was not universally understood. Milsom wrote to Professor Charles Donahue on 22 June 1997: 'my own belief ... is that the historians misunderstood what Sam was saying: they thought he was claiming there was a change in who actually succeeded to land, not just a change in the perception of an unchanging pattern of succession'. (Cf. similar remarks in Milsom, *P. & M.*, p. 255; *Natural History*, p. xxiv.)

[63] Thorne's lecture perturbed some of the hearers, but he told Milsom in 1968 that 'they won't find charter evidence or the like to disprove it': Milsom to the present writer, 30 June 1997.

[64] A further account was given in *HFCL*, pp. 88–126. This was substantially rewritten in the second edition (1981), pp. 99–151; it was the most heavily reworked part of the book.

[65] Milsom later admitted to not carrying his heresy far enough in 1968. He had originally thought the claimant had to trace title from the earliest of his ancestors known to have been seised, but subsequently realised that it was rather the *latest* of his ancestors to be seised: see *Natural History*, p. 101.

lords or their agents,⁶⁶ before determination of the right, whereas the writs of entry were 'downward' writs for use by lords against people wrongly claiming to be their tenants.⁶⁷ The language of right, seisin and entry, which became embedded in the English law of real property, had thus all begun with 'vertical' feudal connotations which later evaporated. The words remained the same but they changed their meaning, perhaps without everyone noticing. An even more profound, if invisible, effect of the jurisdiction given to the king's courts by means of these writs was the end of the feudal world as a social reality. The end was not foreseen, or imposed, let alone resisted, but was the unintended result of measures originally meant to reinforce the working of feudal custom. The king's courts, looking downwards, had to make decisions of a different kind. They were not second-guessing managerial decisions but developing inexorable rules of law which created abstract ownership, and, since it was their decisions which counted, the lord's role became increasingly irrelevant. The earlier practical arrangements of a feudal society then became 'embalmed in logic',⁶⁸ and all the peculiarities of the common law of real property were left—in Milsom's chemical metaphor—as the residue after the lord was dissolved out. This new understanding has been much discussed and criticised,⁶⁹ but it is generally agreed that medieval English land law can no longer be understood without first coming to terms with Milsom. The test of a changed viewpoint, as he said himself, is 'whether you can see more from it'.

Around the same time Milsom revealed another insight, that 'legal development consists in the increasingly detailed consideration of facts'.⁷⁰ Obvious when put into words, it never had been before. That, perhaps, is the true mark of genius. (He once told the writer of this memoir that he had spent his life saying things that are either obvious or wrong, 'but you

---

⁶⁶ The suggestion as to novel disseisin was at first made tentatively: cf. *HFCL*, p. 118 (two instances of 'perhaps'); in the 1981 edition (pp. 139–43) the case is made more fully but still guardedly. In *The Legal Framework of English Feudalism* (1976), pp. 11–14, it is asserted more firmly, albeit with an acknowledgment that the assize was used for other purposes by the time of *Glanvill*.
⁶⁷ Cf. *HFCL*, p. 120 ('An entry seems to be a coming into land as seen from above, as seen by the lord'). This was pursued further in Milsom's last article, 'What was a right of entry?', *Cambridge Law Journal*, 61 (2002), 561–74.
⁶⁸ S. F. C. Milsom, 'The past and future of judge-made law', *Monash University Law Review*, 8 (1981), 3; *Studies*, p. 211.
⁶⁹ See below, n. 89.
⁷⁰ S. F. C. Milsom, 'Law and fact in legal development', *University of Toronto Law Journal*, 17 (1969), 1–17; *Studies*, 171–89. Cf. *P. & M.*, p. lvii ('Substantive law is the product of thinking about facts. What takes a legal system beyond the mere classification of claims is the adoption of a mode of trial which allows the facts to come out ...'); *HFCL*, pp. 31, 65.

cannot tell which'.[71]) This particular insight led to new explanations of later legal developments, in terms of procedural changes which brought out more of the facts of awkward cases than were contained in formulaic writs and equally formulaic denials. The implications were fully worked out in the revolutionary textbook *Historical Foundations of the Common Law*, commissioned in 1965—as an alternative to revising Plucknett's *Concise History of the Common Law*—and published in 1969.[72] It may have begun life as a projected monograph on the personal actions,[73] but its more ambitious nature resulted from the publisher's request for a textbook. Milsom had new ideas about what such a textbook ought to be. He told the publishers that 'the subject must be sold as the efforts of reason to deal with affairs'.[74] As work progressed, Milsom began to see it as more than a mere introduction to basic information: 'I do believe that the book is coming out, not as a compendium of largely unrelated facts, but as a continuous and intelligible story; and also (do please bury this letter deep in your files) that it is rather important.'[75] It was no longer aimed exclusively at students, and as a provisional title Milsom suggested 'The Growth of the Common Law'.

Historical Foundations was not the sort of textbook from which to learn basic facts and dates, but rather a wholly new vision of the subject. A remarkable tour de force, crafted with immense care and subtlety, and full of memorable epigrams, it is too profound to be taken in one reading[76]—some readers have been known to give up—but it acquired a biblical status among the initiated. It recast the new learning in different words, and carried the stories forward into the early-modern period, making use of Tudor plea rolls as well as law reports. A recurrent theme in the book was the danger to historical understanding of hindsight:

---

[71] Cf. his letter to D. E. C. Yale, 17 February 1974: 'As you know I worry endlessly, and particularly over a topic in which everything fits (or not) with everything else (I had an aunt who managed to do a *Times* crossword entirely wrong)'.
[72] There was a second, much revised, edition in 1981. Many passages were rewritten, and a concerted effort was made throughout to delete unnecessary words.
[73] That project is referred to in S. F. C. Milsom, 'Sale of goods in the fifteenth century', *Law Quarterly Review*, 77 (1961), 257; *Studies*, 105. An autographic note, written later, says it was abandoned around 1970. Some drafts remain for the chapter on the action of debt.
[74] Letter to Nicolas Harrison of Messrs Butterworth & Co., 24 September 1965 ('the twin claims of "piety" and "culture", which have largely kept legal history going among lawyers, have lost their grip, and rightly so').
[75] Letter to Simon Partridge of the same firm, 7 October 1967, explaining the delay in completion.
[76] Thorne wrote to Irène Milsom on 11 August 1969: 'I have read Toby's book with great delight; it is a first-class contribution disguised as a book for beginners: unless the beginners have been doing a lot of reading and thinking, they are not going to get very much [on] first reading ...'.

> Lawyers have always been preoccupied with today's details, and have worked with their eyes down. The historian, if he is lucky, can see why a rule came into existence, what social or economic change left it working injustice, how it came to be evaded, how the evasion produced a new rule, and sometimes how that new rule in its turn came to be overtaken by change. But he misunderstands it all if he endows the lawyers who took part with vision on any comparable scale, or attributes to them any intention beyond the winning of today's case.[77]

The book also provided an opportunity to apply the new learning to other topics, such as equity and trusts. Here too, the lesson was that much of the history had previously been approached backwards. The extra-ordinary jurisdiction of the Chancery had not begun as 'equity' in its later sense: 'Not only was there no equity, as a nascent body of rules different from those of the common law. There was no common law, no body of substantive rules from which equity could be different.'[78] In exercising its jurisdiction without the formalities of the common law, the Chancery was at first concerned with the mechanisms of justice rather than with jurisprudence. The likely cause of equity in the substantive sense was the trust of land, and the need to be consistent in exercising the burgeoning jurisdiction over trusts in the fifteenth century. No one could have foreseen its later doctrinal elaboration. The complexities of springing and shifting uses and executory devises was to make the law of future interests 'the most elaborate folly ever built by logic'; but it was a logic which Milsom set out to unravel.[79]

The book did not aim at completeness, and the omissions reflected the teaching of legal history in law faculties. For instance, there was no attempt to revise Maitland's *Constitutional History*, which remained in print even longer than his other works. In so far as it was about law at all, it was not the kind of law found in the medieval plea rolls and year books.[80] Criminal law was only grudgingly added in at the end, with a robust warning:

---

[77] *HFCL*, p. xii. Cf. ibid., p. 16 ('An immediate problem arises: an immediate solution is found. Nobody can know that the solution will later be seen as the origin of something, or the problem as the effective end of something else'), p. 278 ('lawyers at the time ... could not know, as we do, that a new law of contract was in making for new worlds'), and p. 283 ('Historians looking backwards ... have taken this as a conscious step forward on the path leading to a general remedy ... But lawyers at the time could not see the path they were treading ...').

[78] *HFCL*, pp. 76, 80. This involved some rhetorical overstatement. There were, of course, some substantive rules of common law, such as those which governed inheritance; but equity was not concerned with those.

[79] Ibid., p. 197.

[80] The Press did float the idea of a new edition, but no one dared to take it on. The subject was kept up in some History departments, still relying on Maitland as the textbook, but little original research was done by legal historians after Plucknett.

> The miserable history of crime may be shortly told. Nothing worth-while was created. There is no achievement to trace ... A book concerned with foundations can have little to say about Stonehenge, and the aim of this chapter will be negative: to suggest what went wrong, what was lost, why the subject was not developed.[81]

There were telling contrasts to be made here with the sophistication of private law, and these proved Milsom's general point about the mechanisms of change: in a sphere where those mechanisms were absent there was no change, no means of incremental refinement. Major crimes like murder and theft ('legal monoliths') remained much the same over the centuries, while the rest of the criminal law was beset by piecemeal legislative tinkering. The result was that criminal law 'had by the eighteenth century reached an incoherence which seemed to defy even the modest order of the alphabet; and at its less serious levels was perhaps dependent for its workability on the ignorance of all concerned'.[82] The chapter—and the book—end with a bang: 'Crime has never been the business of lawyers.'[83] The strong language flowing through the chapter was considerably watered down in the 1981 edition. It is a tempting speculation that it was a reaction to the pretensions of Radzinowicz's five-volume *History of English Criminal Law*, which evidently still rankled with Irène.[84]

Historical Foundations earned Milsom the Ames Prize and Medal from Harvard Law School (1972) and the Swiney Prize for Jurisprudence from the Royal Society of Arts (1974). Soon after it was published, he was invited to deliver a series of Maitland Lectures at Cambridge,[85] and decided to pursue further his revisions of Maitland's account of medieval land law, a subject broached in the previous series by Thorne in 1958. Neither lecturer was hostile to Maitland's methodology; they were continuing in the same tradition, and many believe that Maitland would have been readily persuaded by most of what they said. But the revisions went deep, and were unsettling. The lectures were delivered in 1972, during power cuts, and the lecturer (as he recalled) 'peered from a wavering patch of candle-light much as his lectures tried to make out what sort of world

---

[81] *HFCL*, p. 353. The paragraph was considerably modified in the 1981 edition. Cf. *HFCL*, p. 361: 'In criminal matters [the common law] had done no more than systematise barbarity'; this became, in 1981, 'In criminal matters there had been almost no substantive development'.
[82] *HFCL*, p. 365.
[83] Ibid., p. 374. This disappeared in the 1981 edition.
[84] Her assistance with volume I of this was acknowledged in the preface. But she later felt the need to compile a hefty file setting out the extent of her own contributions.
[85] The formal invitation was issued by the Managers of the Maitland Memorial Fund late in 1970.

lies in the darkness behind our earliest legal records'.[86] The darkness of the subject matter did indeed give difficulty to the hearers, and the version printed in 1976 as *The Legal Framework of English Feudalism* was not for the faint of heart.[87] Milsom regarded it as the principal achievement of his career,[88] but it was undoubtedly his most challenging piece of writing, and it has in return attracted challenge from historians, chiefly for its factual assumptions about feudal England before the reign of Henry II.[89] No one, however, has seriously doubted its importance. Sir James Holt, whom Milsom came to regard as his fiercest critic, immediately wrote to him: 'I spent some time on it on Sunday evening and then found that I couldn't put it down. It is a *marvellous* piece of work which will set all sorts of new ideas going.'[90]

Although his years at the London School of Economics were Milsom's most productive, his experience of the School was not entirely agreeable. Service on the General Purposes Committee from 1968 to 1970 put him in the thick of the student troubles,[91] and he also felt that some of his

---

[86] S. F. C. Milsom, *The Legal Framework of English Feudalism* (Cambridge, 1976), p. vii. The copy given to the present writer in 1976 is inscribed to 'John Baker, who supplied the candles'. Milsom's own copy, heavily annotated with further references to the *Curia Regis Rolls*, was specifically bequeathed to the present writer.

[87] Professor J. P. Reid, in *New York University Law Review*, 51 (1976), 911–13, wrote with friendly exasperation: 'While Milsom can turn a phrase with the grace of a Frederic William Maitland, he can obscure a concept with the brilliance of a James Willard Hurst ... If any American lawyer understands this book, it will be marvelous; any general historian, astonishing.'

[88] His file on the lectures contains a note dated 1999: 'It was from these lectures that my most important publication grew ...'. But in the interview which he gave on 11 December 2009 he said there were two to choose between, and *Historical Foundations* was 'the one that made me think the most' and probably the more important.

[89] The principal extended commentaries (by no means all hostile) are R. C. Palmer, 'The feudal framework of English law', *Michigan Law Review*, 79 (1981), 1130–64; R. C. Palmer, 'The origins of property in land', *Law & History Review*, 3 (1985), 1–50; P. R. Hyams, 'Warranty and good lordship in twelfth century England', *Law and History Review*, 5 (1987), 437–503; J. Biancalana, 'For want of justice: legal reforms of Henry II', *Columbia Law Review*, 88 (1988), 433–536; J. Hudson, 'Milsom's legal structure: interpreting twelfth century law', *Tijdschrift voor Rechtsgeschiedenis*, 59 (1991), 47–66; J. Hudson, *Land, Law and Lordship in Anglo-Norman England* (Oxford, 1994), ch. 9; J. Hudson, *The Formation of the English Common Law* (London, 1996), ch. 7; P. Brand, 'The origins of English land law: Milsom and after', in P. Brand, *The Making of the Common Law* (London, 1992), pp. 203–25; P. Dalton, 'The first century of English feudalism', in P. Dalton, *Conquest, Anarchy and Lordship: Yorkshire 1066–1154* (Cambridge, 2002), pp. 257–97.

[90] Holt to Milsom, 21 September 1976. He added: 'I want to re-read it and then I will write to you ...'; but the subsequent letter, if there was one, has not survived.

[91] Milsom to George Reid, 21 June 1978 ('It got me into the firing line in the troubles'). Professor George Garnett recalls that he remained 'very, very angry about the student radicals he had encountered at the LSE in 1968. I recall one account of their provoking a heart attack in one of the caretakers, who had died'. The trouble was not confined to the students. Milsom remembered

colleagues in the Law Department were too busy elsewhere to pull their weight. When he was pressed to take on the convenorship in 1973, the discontent boiled over:[92]

> In my mind, my life will justify itself or not on what I can do for my subject. Few people think worth while the slice of a lifetime needed to attain a useful familiarity with the medieval materials; and one's effective work starts late. It may also stop early. I have had exceptional luck in catching glimpses of a framework different from that upon which earlier work was based. It is important if true, and either I get it out or not. This luck has depended on two qualities: a literal mind (in all other ways a great nuisance) which I shall keep; and a fluke imagination which, like mathematicians and such, I know I shall lose. My fear is that if I turn aside now, I shall not succeed in getting back to it. If that were to happen, I should blame myself; I believe I should be blamed by others; and on my scale of values, even the narrow interests of the School would not have been served.

He did take on the unrewarding task a year later, but by then he was looking for an escape. Not averse to administrative duties in a more congenial setting, he thought a headship of house at Oxford would be a preferable situation, and he pursued active discussions first with Pembroke College (1974)[93] and then with New College (1975).[94] At the same time, Professor Glanville Williams, one of the electors to the Downing Professorship of the Laws of England (Maitland's chair at Cambridge), wrote to enquire whether Milsom would accept it if offered. Not appreciating that there would be a contest, Milsom replied that he would, though he confided to New College that, if forced to elect, he would prefer to become its warden. As it turned out, he was not chosen for either position; but the following year another vacancy at Cambridge enabled him to be elected to the 'Professorship of Law (1973)'.[95] The chair of Legal History at the London School of Economics, despite an impassioned written plea from Milsom to the Director of the School, was thereupon discontinued.

---

a paper handed to him by a young revolutionary, 'a really nasty, beautifully written piece of work' which he felt sure had been penned by a colleague.

[92] Milsom to John Griffith, 20 August 1973.

[93] He withdrew because the college could not make up its collective mind. He wrote to Derek Hall on 9 November 1974: 'they have seen me four times and Irène three ... it does not seem right to hang about any more'.

[94] He wrote to Herbert Nicholas, fellow of New College, 28 May 1975: 'Of course it is something I would like to be. It is also, so far as one can tell without having tried, something I would like to do. I am woolly headed enough to be capable of attachment to institutions, and since I was orphaned at my first college, Irène and I have a special affection for New College.'

[95] The innominate chair had been created in 1973, and was occupied by Kurt Lipstein (previously an *ad hominem* professor) until his retirement in 1976.

Return to Cambridge (1976–90)

In 1976 Milsom returned with Irène to Cambridge. His lawyer friends at Trinity College would have welcomed him back there, but it was reported that other fellows would be reluctant to offend Radzinowicz, and that it would be 'socially awkward for anyone to have two husbands in the same College'.[96] Milsom therefore accepted a fellowship of St John's College instead. The possibility of confronting the social awkwardness continued to plague him while in Cambridge, but he found solace in the friendly welcome at St John's and nearly became its master in 1978.[97] He contributed not only to the governance of the college but resumed the supervision of undergraduates, a voluntary service for which generations of undergraduates had reason to be grateful. One recalled that, in the late 1990s, 'he was old but ageless ... you were carried on a journey through years of legal history in the company of a guide so knowledgeable that no matter how confusing the topic had seemed before entering his rooms, you left feeling enlightened and privileged to have been taught by such a master'.[98]

In his later years he turned his mind to the implications of his discoveries for historical jurisprudence. The theme was developed in the Addison Harris Lectures at the Indiana Law School, Bloomington, in March 1974, which he intended to become a small book.[99] Fashion, he observed, had replaced historical jurisprudence with semantic and philosophical studies: 'a confident age does not want any lessons from history, and does not like the lessons that history seems to teach'. But perhaps his new perspectives could do for jurisprudence what they had done for the history of the common law. It was wrong to assume that law just grows, while remaining all the time the same sort of thing as today. That may have been true for centuries, but not for ever. Maitland's 'survival of the fittest' view of the forms of action had proved unsatisfactory; but there

---

[96] Patrick Duff to Irène Milsom, 9 October 1975 and 5 January 1976.
[97] He was willing to give up his chair for this, though not his research: letter to George Reid, 3 November 1978. He wrote to John Hall, one of the Law fellows, in June 1978: 'I am vain enough to imagine I have some of the appropriate qualities of heart if not of head, and therefore that the idea is not inherently absurd', but he thought the circumstances of his marriage might offend religious sensibilities. In fact the main obstacle was that he had only been a fellow for two years.
[98] Recollection of Isobel Hoyle (BA 1998).
[99] This is indicated by a draft preface. The title of the lectures was 'Legal Development Analyzed', and there were two sections, 'Law and Morals' and 'Elementary Concepts'. Milsom abandoned the book after Indiana University declined to arrange for its publication.

were other models of legal evolution, the prime example being the shift from seigniorial management to a scheme of abstract rules worked out by lawyers and imposed by superior courts. Between the thirteenth century and the 'golden age' of the nineteenth, the common law had indeed developed in a linear fashion, under the influence of a learned profession, through the increasingly detailed consideration of factual situations. Law became a discipline akin to Mathematics, in which answers could be worked out by reasoning, as in later Roman law. The Roman and the common law, said Milsom, were both about rights between equals, 'because the two societies could afford those terms'. But that development was largely over. The disappearance of the jury in civil cases had weakened the distinction between law and fact, so that clear legal principle was disappearing in a myriad single instances, and 'longer judgments cite more cases to settle smaller cases less clearly'.[100] And, whereas the jury had been 'index-linked' to the standards of the times, trial by judge alone worked differently. The judgments of individual judges made minute accretions to a body of book-learning which could only be changed by legislation. Moreover, increasing legislative control over citizens meant that English law was reverting to the early medieval model in which upward claims against authority were more significant to most people than the enforcement of abstract rights of property and contract. Milsom pursued these themes further in unpublished lectures in 1978 and 1980,[101] and then in the Wilfred Fullagar Lecture delivered at Monash University, Melbourne, in 1981.[102] They achieved a wider readership in *A Natural History of the Common Law* (New York, 2003), based on lectures given in New York in 1995.[103] This elegant little book is by far the most accessible introduction to Milsom's theories about legal history. But his jurisprudential work, though of the first importance, was largely ignored by the professors of

---

[100] Milsom, 'The past and future of judge-made law', 9; *Studies*, p. 217.

[101] The Cambridge inaugural lecture, 'A Historian's View of English Law Today', 7 February 1978 (the typescript is marked characteristically: 'Not published—and should not be'); 'Changing Role of the Law—A Historian's View' (St John's College Lecture, University of East Anglia, 1980). A brief foretaste had appeared as 'The vitality of the law', *New Law Journal*, 199 (1969), 607–9.

[102] Milsom, 'The past and future of judge-made law', 1–14; *Studies*, pp. 209–22. This is chiefly concerned with the relationship between courts and juries.

[103] The Carpentier Lectures, delivered at Columbia University, were originally entitled 'A New Essay in Historical Jurisprudence'.

jurisprudence.[104] It seemed either that no one was listening or that the historical detail was too esoteric for pure philosophers.

Milsom was less upset by that than by the criticisms of his revision of Maitland, which suggested an unbridgeable gulf between legal historians with a legal education and those without. The sense that no one outside the law school seemed to connect with what he was saying played increasingly on his mind from the 1970s onwards. He was particularly troubled by the remark of one leading historian that he ought to 'do it all properly, with names',[105] evidently misunderstanding what Milsom took to be a virtue, shared with Maitland.[106] It was a point which never ceased to irritate him, and it came increasingly to symbolise for him the narrowness of much historical scholarship:

> [T]he orthodoxy of the last half-century by which most kinds of historian project essentially still and close-up pictures, assembling all the evidence for narrow subjects in short periods, is inimical to comprehending the largest legal developments ... As in the natural sciences, fundamental propositions stand or fall not with single facts but with their power to explain all the facts.[107]

Historians of both kinds observed the same facts, which were rarely in dispute; the difficulty was to get inside people's heads and see that the legal records and documents often concealed changes in the meaning of the words, and in contemporary perceptions of what was really happening.[108] Milsom addressed this explicitly in a lecture given to the Anglo-American Conference of Historians in 1978,[109] in which he set out to 'consider, in the context of medieval rights in land, the relationship

---

[104] Not, of course, by legal historians. A. W. B. Simpson wrote that Milsom's papers on the mechanisms of legal change were 'important contributions not only to history but to legal philosophy' and deserved a wider readership than they had enjoyed: review of *Studies* in *Times Literary Supplement*, 5 September 1986, 985.

[105] He wrote to Biancalana on 22 August 1997: 'even I, blessed with Dr Johnson's "stark insensibility", have been shocked by some of the things that have been said to me e.g. that I ought to make public recantation'.

[106] Cf. Milsom's review of Elton's *Maitland* (n. 55 above), 225–6: 'neither the legal historian nor the lecturer on modern law can ever find the case which illustrates the truly elementary point ... It was too simple to happen, or to be identifiable among records in common form. The point to be communicated is central, beyond doubt, reflected in all the real cases; but there is no way to communicate it clearly except to turn dramatist.' He returned to the point more insistently in Milsom, '"Pollock and Maitland": a lawyer's retrospect', pp. 252–6.

[107] Milsom, *Natural History*, pp. 75–6; and cf. ibid., pp. 121–2 n. 1 (on names). Milsom was also critical of historians' indexes, which too often concentrated on names rather than ideas.

[108] This was also the theme of Milsom, '"Pollock and Maitland": a lawyer's retrospect'. It was pursued further in the projected Maitland Lecture which he prepared in 2007 but never delivered. He admitted to the present writer that 'the thought of a guaranteed (if infuriated) audience for my current effort is a real temptation'; but he had second thoughts about giving it as written.

[109] 'Politics and Jurisprudence in Medieval Land-Holding' (unpublished typescript).

between what people were up to, and what lawyers were thinking about, and what actually happened'. Milsom wrote on his copy of the lecture, 'The audience were all historians, and they listened with the incomprehension to which a lawyer grows accustomed.' He had always portrayed himself as a heretic,[110] the 'lonely figure in some Bateman drawing, the man who thinks that Maitland was wrong'.[111] No doubt this began as the absurd modesty of his youth, a polite way of proclaiming the importance of his discoveries.[112] Later he saw himself as really enduring condemnation, like lawyers Thorne and Hall before him,[113] and the imagined failure of his teaching to penetrate history faculties caused serious disappointment in later life. He seemed unable to believe that he was held in such high esteem, even by those who did not accept everything he had written.

It was with the same troublesome 'divide' in mind that Milsom accepted from the Oxford historians the daunting challenge of delivering the Ford Lectures in 1985–86 on 'Law and Society in the Twelfth and Thirteenth Centuries'. These explored further the transition from the world of feudal management to that of abstract law, dealing in turn with 'The falling value of knight service', 'Perceptions of property', 'Property and pay', 'Capital and income', the 'Inconvenience of change' and the arrival of 'A rule of law'. They made a deep impression on the hearers, and Milsom intended to prepare them for the press; but he never finished the task, and in 2004 wrote despairingly that they 'still cannot be reduced

---

[110] He did so in 1958, when sending out offprints of his trespass papers, and he described his introduction to *P. & M.* (1968) as an essay in 'pious heresy'. In speaking about Maitland at the British Academy in 1980, on 5 November, he expressed unease about the ready availability of bonfires on that evening.

[111] Milsom, 'F. W. Maitland', 267; *Studies*, p. 263.

[112] This was made explicit in a letter of 18 May 2002 to the present writer (accompanying a draft paper on writs of entry): 'Vanity of course, but I should not have persevered with this whole 3-D saga if I was not vain enough to think it important. Heresy is serious when it questions assumptions rather than facts.'

[113] In the undelivered Maitland lecture (2007) he reflected that 'damaging to the history of personal actions was historian Plucknett's failure to see the point of lawyer Derek Hall's manuscript readings of two words in the year book report of the *Humber Ferry Case* ... For lawyers they turned what had seemed a woodenly formalistic quibble into an elementary proposition about the legal analysis of the facts; and this played a part in the (overdue) replacement of Maitland's vision of English law as evolving in a Darwinian struggle between "the forms of action".' For the 'failure' see T. F. T. Plucknett, *Concise History of the Common Law*, 5th edn (London, 1956), p. 470.

to a publishable state, and should not be published', a view from which others may choose in the fullness of time to dissent.[114]

One area where his advocacy was unquestionably effective was the plight of the Faculty of Law at Cambridge. His chairmanship of the Faculty Board (1986–8) brought out the latent flair for leadership which had once attracted him to the idea of a college headship. He soon saw beyond the daily detail to the deep-seated problems facing the Faculty, and in 1987 he prepared a long and forceful paper for the University authorities setting out the grievances as he saw them. The Faculty had less than four per cent of the University's academic staff to teach about eight per cent of its students, the worst ratio of any Law Faculty in the country; lectures had to be given on three widely separated sites; the Squire Law Library was congested and due to run out of space in three years; the office facilities ('a cubby-hole') and the level of staffing were quite inadequate. These problems were, no doubt, a result of the ever-growing imbalance of resources between Humanities and Sciences, but Law was demonstrably suffering more than other subjects.[115] Milsom's persuasive presentation of the Faculty's case began a long dialogue, continued by his successors, which led to a new building, finally opened by the Queen ten years later, and a substantial increase in the Faculty's resources.

Milsom's retirement in 1990 more or less coincided with his wife's increasingly serious loss of memory. By the time of her death in 1998 she hardly knew who he was. There were no children. Her death left him desolate, and a spinal stroke in 1991 reduced his confidence in going out. He had always been a lone scholar, who did not care to discuss his nascent ideas or share his drafts with anyone but Irène, and—perhaps as a result of shyness—he conducted himself with a slightly distant courtesy which seemed to come from another age. Yet he was committed to collegiality, and always uplifted those around him with his wit and infectious sense of humour. It was therefore distressing for his many friends and colleagues, who held him in affection as well as esteem, that for the last ten years before his death on 24 February 2016 he became increasingly reclusive. But the great work had already been done. Among his many honours were

---

[114] He discussed publication with Oxford University Press in 1986, and gave them some hope of a manuscript later in the year. But only three of the lectures were ever written out in full. Notes survive in 'delivery format' for all six, and also the text of a preliminary lecture about 'the divide'.

[115] The draft case was circulated to the Faculty Board on 2 December 1987.

an honorary benchership of Lincoln's Inn (1970), a silk gown (1985) and honorary degrees from Glasgow (1981), Chicago (1985) and Cambridge (2003). His contribution to the way legal historians think—even those who do not agree with him—has been incalculable. While most historians of the law and legal institutions have contented themselves with establishing details, Milsom altered the entire framework of thought. Legal history was not for him simply the jumble of technical facts which he had been taught, or a form of social history obscured by lawyers' jargon, but nothing less than 'the intellectual history of society'.[116]

JOHN BAKER
Fellow of the Academy

Note. Unless otherwise stated, the correspondence and unpublished lectures referred to in this memoir were found in Milsom's papers, which were deposited with the writer by his executors. Of great help also were the interviews with Milsom which were conducted between October and December 2009 by Lesley Dingle of the Squire Law Library, Cambridge, and posted on the Library's website (https://www.squire.law.cam.ac.uk/eminent-scholars-archive/professor-stroud-francis-charles-toby-milsom—accessed 28 February 2017).

---

[116] Milsom, 'Maitland', p. 270 ('it is not just part of social and economic history. To use uncomfortably large words it is the intellectual history of society').

DAVID RUSSELL HARRIS

David Russell Harris
1930–2013

HOLDING ACADEMIC POSTS IN GEOGRAPHY and later in archaeology, David Harris believed that knowledge was universal and conducted research that was multidisciplinary and interdisciplinary. He was greatly influenced by Carl Sauer at the University of California, Berkeley, whose teaching introduced him to cultural geography, human ecology and anthropology. David taught geography in the University of London and made close contact with colleagues in anthropology. His enquiries asked big questions associated with the domestication of plants and the origins of farming, setting detailed case studies into their global context. His publications in the 1970s opened the way for new ecological approaches in archaeology. His research, writing and teaching at the Institute of Archaeology in London embraced environmental archaeology and palaeoecology. Many students were inspired by the breadth of his vision and his clear and challenging delivery. A highly efficient organiser of international conferences, David Harris displayed great skill as an exacting editor of their proceedings. Exercising more influence among archaeologists than among geographers, he pioneered new approaches to the understanding of early subsistence systems and strove to promote innovative scientific methods to elucidate fundamental questions about the human past.

Biographical Memoirs of Fellows of the British Academy, XVI, 363–385. © The British Academy 2017.
Posted 14 November 2017. © The British Academy 2017.

Geographical career

From London to Oxford and then to California

David Russell Harris was born in north-west London on 14 December 1930, the third child of Herbert and Norah Harris. Herbert Harris had been a Nonconformist minister in Oxford but lost his faith and retrained as a medical doctor. In keeping with his principles, he had been a conscientious objector during the First World War, undertaking civilian service by working on a farm, where his interest in the countryside, plants and wildlife had been reinforced. This keen interest he communicated to his four children by telling them about Charles Darwin and taking them on country walks.

David received his secondary education as a boarder at Saint Christopher School in Letchworth, a progressive establishment, coeducational and vegetarian, with a pupil-centred approach. Oscar Backhouse, his geography teacher, organised caving, hill walking and mountaineering expeditions. At Saint Christopher, David met Helen Wilson who would become his wife. As a teenager he was very impressed by *What Happened in History* (1942), by V. Gordon Childe. Many years later he recalled: 'I was already a geographer in the making, and Childe's revelatory little book added a new dimension of deep time to my fascination with distant places.'[1] David studied biology, English, geography and history for his Higher School Certificate examinations, but was frustrated by the European focus of the history syllabus since he craved the global view. Straight after school, he did his national service, spending eighteen months in the Royal Air Force.

With an open exhibition, David entered University College, Oxford, to read geography. His real love was anthropology and archaeology, but these disciplines were only offered at graduate diploma level. The geomorphologist Robert Beckinsale was his personal tutor, and Robert Steel mentored him on the political geography of British colonial Africa. Although David was disillusioned by the intellectually restricted concept of geography at Oxford, he greatly enjoyed the geology course given by Colonel K. S. Sandford of Libyan desert fame, and the world ethnology sessions with anthropologists John Bradford and Beatrice Blackwood. David recalled how 'she used to take us to the Pitt-Rivers Museum where

---

[1] D. R. Harris, 'Life at and before the Institute of Archaeology: a personal retrospect', *Archaeology International*, 9 (2005), 10.

she would unlock dusty cabinets and show us their wondrous contents'.[2] In the long vacation of 1952, David, his older brother Esmond and a geographer friend bought an old jeep and drove to the Atlas Mountains in Morocco. Their choice of destination may have reflected David's interest in deserts or it may have been due to Sandford's teaching. David achieved a distinction in his preliminary examinations, and was awarded the Herbertson Memorial Prize. In 1953 he graduated with a BA Honours (second class, second in the list), missing a first because he could not recall a detail of African geography. He received a postgraduate studentship to research 'Water resources and land use in Tunisia' for a BLitt (1955). Seeing Roman ruins and traditional irrigation systems stimulated a growing interest in the ecology and early history of agriculture.

In 1955, David received a King George VI Memorial Fellowship to study in the United States of America, choosing to be based at the University of California in Berkeley. There he was influenced by the cultural geographer Carl Sauer, whose controversial lectures to the American Geographical Society on worldwide agricultural origins and dispersals had been published in 1952.[3] One year later, David enrolled as a doctoral student and took courses in botany, ecology, archaeology and anthropology as well as geography. During vacations, he travelled widely in western North America to gain experience of desert and semi-desert vegetation, and boreal forest and tundra. He wrote many course papers, including two for Sauer. One was on agriculture in prehistoric Europe, which introduced him to the work of Grahame Clark; the other was on the ancestry of the domestic goat. Sauer suggested that the second paper merited publication but David sought advice from Frederick Zeuner who recommended publishing the first part only.[4] The remainder, on the symbolism of scimitar-like horns of wild goats, remained in David's files. Sauer's publications on the use and effects of fire and on early human migrations also impressed David, as did the proceedings of the symposium 'Man's role in changing the face of the Earth', at which Sauer was a prime mover.[5] This wide-ranging work, published in two volumes, anticipated twenty-first-century concerns over exploitation and conservation of global resources.

In 1957, David married Helen Wilson and soon afterwards they left England, crossed the Atlantic on the *Queen Elizabeth*, bought an elderly

---

[2] Ibid.
[3] C. O. Sauer, *Agricultural Origins and Dispersals* (New York, 1952).
[4] D. R. Harris, 'The distribution and ancestry of the domestic goat', *Proceedings of the Linnaean Society of London*, 173 (1962), 79–91.
[5] W. L. Thomas (ed.), *Man's Role in Changing the Face of the Earth* (Chicago, IL, 1956).

Chevrolet in Manhattan and drove it from the East Coast to California, where David was taking up the post of Instructor in the Berkeley Geography department, camping rough all the way. With preliminary examinations over, David prepared to investigate the changing land use of three of the Outer Leeward Islands, conducting his first fieldwork with Helen in 1958: it was not all work, however; they 'usually ended up each day at a beach'.[6] David's study fitted into a larger project of Caribbean enquiry funded by the Office of Naval Research, coordinated by James Parsons at Berkeley. Research in the field, the archive and the aerial photography laboratory led David to declare:

> It is quite clear that the vegetation of Antigua has been drastically altered since the arrival of English settlers in the seventeenth century. How far the vegetation of Barbuda has been changed in this time is less certain. The outstanding problems raised by a study of vegetation in these islands concern the relation of climate and soils to the present cover of vegetation in aboriginal times and the consequences of man's interference with it since then.[7]

Opportunities and experiences in London and beyond

In the autumn of 1958 David returned to teach at Queen Mary College (QMC) in the University of London. As well as biogeography and the geography of deserts, he gave classes on Africa, North America and human and economic geography. He also contributed to the intercollegiate course on plant geography. Lawrie Wright, one of his tutees, remembered that he was 'always cheerful, an enthusiast for the subject, a stickler for correct spelling and punctuation but, above all, a person who was interested in the essays we wrote and recommended new titles to broaden our reading'.[8] June Sheppard found David to be 'a pleasant and amenable colleague, but I was always conscious that he was rather different. The rest of us were all London University products and out of the same mould ... David came from a different world, and I suspect he found us odd.'[9] With his training at Oxford and Berkeley, and much field experience overseas, David was certainly different, holding a global view and striving to elucidate big questions.

---

[6] Email from Helen Harris to Ken Thomas, 23 July 2016.
[7] D. R. Harris, *The Vegetation of Antigua and Barbuda, Leeward Islands, West Indies* (Washington DC: Technical Report, Geography Branch, Office of Naval Research, 1960), p. 70.
[8] Information from Lawrie Wright, 26 April 2014.
[9] Information from June Sheppard, 2 May 2014.

David went back to the Caribbean and spent a further two months there in 1960. While still working on his thesis, he wrote a critical paper on the invasion of oceanic islands by alien plants.[10] Then he obtained a Fulbright Travel Grant to spend the academic year 1962–3 at the University of New Mexico, Albuquerque, with Helen and their two daughters (Sarah, born in 1959, and Joanna, in 1962). When not teaching or writing up, he undertook fieldwork, sometimes with his Oxford contemporary Yi-Fu Tuan, who was working on desert geomorphology. David drew on this experience to write a paper on recent plant invasions in the arid and semi-arid Southwest.[11] In 1963, he submitted his thesis for examination at Berkeley. The three Caribbean islands he had studied were well suited for work in historical ecology since they had not long been settled, and documentary sources for the period of English colonisation were plentiful. With additional information and professional illustrations, his thesis was published by the University of California.[12] Later research, involving scientific dating techniques, shows that human occupation was earlier than David had envisaged.

After New Mexico and summer school at Berkeley, David returned to London in the late summer of 1963. At this time, Henry Clifford Darby, Professor of Geography at University College London (UCL), was seeking a biogeographer to join his rapidly expanding academic staff. He had already met Sauer and considered David as a possible candidate. After presenting his paper on plant invasions to the International Geographical Congress in London, David joined UCL on 1 October 1964. With seventeen staff, his new department was very different from the half dozen geographers at QMC, enabling him to focus his teaching and research. UCL also had a dynamic department of anthropology and the still independent Institute of Archaeology was close by. In due course, David stimulated inter-departmental collaboration by running a culture and ecology seminar with anthropologists, initiating a joint degree in geography and anthropology, and contributing to an interdisciplinary course in human sciences.[13] He worked with the UCL geomorphologist Claudio Vita-Finzi and Cambridge archaeologists on the climate, envi-

---

[10] D. R. Harris, 'The invasion of oceanic islands by alien plants', *Transactions and Papers, Institute of British Geographers*, 31 (1962), 67–82.
[11] D. R. Harris, 'Recent plant invasions in the arid and semi-arid Southwest of the United States', *Annals of the Association of American Geographers*, 56 (1966), 408–22.
[12] D. R. Harris, *Plants, Animals and Man in the Outer Leeward Islands, West Indies: an Ecological Study of Antigua, Barbuda and Anguilla* (Berkeley and Los Angeles, CA, 1965).
[13] This programme was conceived by zoologist J. Z. Young in 1975.

ronment and industries of Stone Age Epirus,[14] and on the erosion of a fragile 'badland' in Greece.[15] His colleagues Ron Cooke and Andrew Warren also studied arid lands and provided David with intellectual support. Under Darby, and then from 1966 under William Richard Mead,[16] the departmental ethos allowed David's research to develop, and the arrival of geographer Paul Wheatley in 1966 was an important source of inspiration. Sharing the Berkeley experience, where Wheatley had taught geography and history, the two men provided complementary teaching in cultural geography, with Wheatley concentrating on urban origins and Harris exploring plant and animal domestication and agricultural origins.[17] Tutees recall that David encouraged them to criticise the innovative works of Peter Haggett, Richard Chorley and David Harvey, since he firmly believed that the 'new geography' should be conceptual as well as quantitative. Postgraduates appreciated his editorial skills as he honed their work. David also collaborated with Wheatley in revising doctoral training along the lines of a North American graduate school. He demonstrated his administrative capabilities as departmental examinations tutor (1966–70) when examinations set by the federal University of London were replaced by assessments arranged by each college. During his years in geography departments, David co-edited *Africa in Transition* for undergraduates, contributing an essay on geographical diversity in unity in North Africa, but all his later books would be aimed at graduate students and researchers.[18]

In 1968, David joined an expedition to take a hovercraft through rivers and rapids from Manaus in Brazil along the Rio Negro, the Casiquiare channel and the River Orinoco in Venezuela to reach the Caribbean. Frequent stops by the hovercraft enabled him to observe vegetation and collect samples of soil and plants. Hating the noise and vibration, he travelled in a dug-out canoe through the Casiquiare and witnessed traditional shifting cultivation. At a Yanomamö settlement on the Rio Ocamo he

---

[14] E. S. Higgs, C. Vita-Finzi, D. R. Harris, A. E. Fagg and S. Bottema, 'The climate, environment and industries of Stone Age Greece: Part III', *Proceedings of the Prehistoric Society*, 33 (1968), 1–29.

[15] D. R. Harris and C. Vita-Finzi, 'Kokkinopilos: a Greek badland', *Geographical Journal*, 134 (1968), 537–46.

[16] H. Clout. 'William Richard Mead 1915–2014', *Biographical Memoirs of Fellows of the British Academy*, 14 (2015), 383–408.

[17] D. R. Harris, 'New light on plant domestication and the origins of agriculture', *Geographical Review*, 57 (1967), 90–107.

[18] D. R. Harris, 'North Africa (excluding Egypt)', in B. W. Hodder and D. R. Harris (eds.), *Africa in Transition; Geographical Essays* (London, 1967), pp. 35–94.

encountered people who cultivated root crops and fruit trees as well as undertaking fishing and hunting. David came to realise that 'the sharp division conventionally made between hunter-gatherers and agricultural subsistence was a gross oversimplification, and that, at least in the tropics, systems that integrated small-scale cultivation with continuing exploitation of wild plants and animals were widespread'.[19]

David took unpaid leave of absence in autumn 1970 to teach at the University of Toronto, where he, Helen and their four daughters (Lucy was born in 1964 and Zoe in 1969) spent six months. David visited various scholars including those at Berkeley, where he was urged to consider a permanent appointment. At the same time, the chair of geography at the Australian National University (ANU), Canberra, became vacant and he was invited to apply. He was flattered by the invitation but decided not to go ahead. Despite constrained finances at UCL, Bill Mead indicated that it would be reasonable to put David's name forward for promotion to Reader in 1971. Mead wrote to the College authorities to support David's case: 'On academic grounds he is well above average—a mature and recognised scholar, with plenty of work in the pipeline and of continuing potential; on departmental grounds, he is an exceptionally capable and effective colleague ... I would prefer him to remain at UCL as a Reader.'[20] In 1972, David received the Back Award from the Royal Geographical Society for biogeographical research. Further invitations to apply for chairs in the USA arrived, but not until 1973 was his Readership in the University of London attained.

Having crossed this hurdle, David applied for a year's unpaid leave of absence as Visiting Fellow at the Research School of Pacific Studies of the ANU to investigate Aboriginal subsistence systems in the Torres Strait region and Papua New Guinea, and in particular the interactions between foragers and farmers. He duly received a Fellowship, but Helen and the children remained in England, travelling out for a couple of weeks at Christmas. In mid-September 1974, he reached Rocky Point in Queensland and wrote to Mead, 'sitting literally under a coconut palm at the back of the beach, with the swash of the Coral Sea sounding gently on the sand'.[21] After a month in the field, he drove 600 miles to the Lockhart River

---

[19] Harris, 'Life at and before', 11; D. R. Harris, 'The ecology of swidden cultivation in the upper Orinoco rain forest, Venezuela', *Geographical Review*, 61 (1971), 475–95.
[20] Geography Department Archive UCL, letter from W. R. Mead to A. Tattersall, dated 15 October 1971.
[21] Geography Department Archive UCL, letter from Harris to W. R. Mead, dated 18 September 1974.

Reserve before flying to the Torres Strait Islands. This enquiry into subsistence horticulture was the start of a decade-long project that continued to expand after David joined the Institute of Archaeology.[22] He concluded that the celebrated subsistence divide or agricultural boundary at Torres Strait was essentially a construct of modern ethnography, which exaggerated contrasts in subsistence practices between Australian 'hunter-gatherers' and Papuan 'agriculturalists', as well as the extent and intensity of agriculture in New Guinea. He suggested that 'since Torres Strait came into existence some 6000 years ago, it has functioned neither as a barrier to nor a bridge for the "transmission" of agriculture into Australia'.[23]

During the late 1960s and 1970s, David participated in interdisciplinary symposia, organised by Peter Ucko, Geoffrey Dimbleby, Colin Renfrew and others, where he presented critical review papers. The published proceedings of these meetings had a major impact on various aspects of research, such as plant and animal domestication, and the origins and diffusion of farming. David explained that, in the first volume, he explored 'an ecosystemic approach to the beginnings of plant cultivation and domestication, in the second the nature of swidden (shifting) cultivation and its relation to settlement, and in the third I proposed an ethnoecological model for the prehistory of tropical agriculture'.[24] While still based in Geography, David participated in other international symposia on the origins of plant domestication in Africa, pre-Hispanic Maya agriculture, and early civilisations in Asia and Meso-America. In the mid-1970s, he was charged with organising the Wenner-Gren Foundation Symposium on Human Ecology in Savanna Environments that met in 1978 at Burg Wartenstein in Austria. As well as making his own contributions, he edited the conference volume.[25]

David's reputation continued to grow and further invitations to apply for chairs arrived, including a tempting request to attend for interview at

---

[22] D. R. Harris and A. J. Barham, *Archaeological and Palaeoenvironmental Investigations in Western Torres Strait, Northern Australia: Final Report to the Research and Exploration Committee of the National Geographic Society* (London: Institute of Archaeology and Department of Geography, UCL, 1987).

[23] D. R. Harris, 'Early agriculture in New Guinea and the Torres Strait divide', in J. Allen and J. F. O'Connell (eds.), *Transitions: Pleistocene to Holocene in Australia and Papua New Guinea, Antiquity (special number)*, 69 (1995), 853–4.

[24] Harris, 'Life at and before', 11; H. Clout, 'David Russell Harris, 1930–2013', *Geographers: Biobibliographical Studies* 35 (London, 2016) provides a full bibliography of David's work.

[25] D. R. Harris, 'Tropical savanna environments: definition, distribution, diversity and development', in D. R. Harris (ed.), *Human Ecology in Savanna Environments* (London, 1980), pp. 3–27.

Berkeley; but a younger and less expensive applicant was selected. James Parsons declared: 'It would have been grand to have had you here. The very thought of it made my imagination soar. And yet I know that it would have been a wrench to move and a very difficult personal decision for you and Helen.'[26] David had to weigh his ambitions carefully against the advantages of an English education for his daughters and the benefits of the National Health Service for the whole family. An attractive opportunity came in 1979, when the Chair of Human Environment at the Institute of Archaeology (still an independent part of the University of London) was about to become vacant. In his letter of recommendation Bill Mead stated:

> For the past decade, David Harris has established a considerable reputation for himself outside the traditional limits of geography as well as within them. In my own view, his research 'took off' with a paper entitled 'Alternative pathways towards agriculture', in this there is displayed a blend of theory and fieldwork, a deep concern with the past and a keen appreciation of contemporary techniques, a wide-ranging spirit of enquiry, and love of detail ... David Harris has proved to be a man of initiative and imagination in administration as well as in research ... He has a positive outlook on life and a pleasant sense of humour. He can be firm when required and does not suffer fools gladly. A happy family background undoubtedly strengthens his capacity for work.[27]

David was duly appointed, but his arrival at the Institute was delayed since he spent October and November visiting Australian universities. His new position opened important challenges in a long career that exemplified his belief that knowledge was universal and that research should be multidisciplinary and interdisciplinary. In 2002, he wrote the following words:

> I cherish the memory of the fifteen years I spent in the UCL geography department ... The departmental ethos permitted—even encouraged—one to pursue a personal research agenda, unrestricted by disciplinary boundaries that were emphasized in some geography departments. I was free to develop my interests in cultural ecology, anthropology and archaeology, without fearing that I was straying unacceptably beyond the bounds of geography—a process that was intensified after the arrival of Paul Wheatley, who became a close friend and a source of inspiration. It was largely due to the UCL Geography department (and my earlier experience at Berkeley) that I have felt academically comfortable working in the fertile fields where geography, anthropology and archaeology

---

[26] Geography Department Archive, UCL, letter from J. Parsons to D. R. Harris, dated 1 March 1977.
[27] Geography Department Archive, UCL, letter from W. R. Mead to P. F. Vowles, Academic Registrar, University of London, dated 8 May 1979.

intersect, and I count myself very fortunate to have spent most of my professional career at UCL.[28]

The Institute of Archaeology

In January 1980 David joined the Institute of Archaeology, at that time one of a number of Senate Institutes of the University of London, with its own internal academic departments.[29] He succeeded Geoffrey W. Dimbleby as Professor of Human Environment and Head of the Department of Human Environment, after a difficult meeting of the appointment board, where his broad range and experience eventually prevailed over the merits of another strong candidate. His appointment provided an immense support for the then Director of the Institute, Professor John D. Evans, whose time was increasingly taken up with outside commitments. David contributed a great deal during those years, though his more managerial style was not to everyone's taste.

His first academic priority for the Department of Human Environment was to develop research and teaching in the archaeobotany of plant macroremains. He already knew that Gordon Hillman had carried out innovative archaeobotanical research in Turkey and had also retrieved a large assemblage of cereal and other charred plant remains from Epipalaeolithic and Neolithic levels at the important site Tell Abu Hureyra in Syria during Andrew Moore's excavation of the site in the early 1970s. Abu Hureyra was a key site for investigating the beginnings of agriculture in south-west Asia, and Gordon's job in the Plant Sciences department in Cardiff left him insufficient time to analyse the plant assemblage fully. So, with the agreement of Gordon's head of department, Alan Smith, David successfully applied in 1981 to the Science and Engineering Research Council's Science-Based Archaeology Committee for a three-year research grant to enable Gordon to work full time on the project at the Institute.

As part of this research, in 1983 David, Gordon and Sue Colledge travelled extensively in Syria and Turkey (accompanied by Tony Legge and Peter Rowley-Conwy in Syria), making ecological surveys and collecting herbarium specimens to develop the Institute's now-renowned comparative botanical and archaeobotanical reference collections. Sue Colledge has

---

[28] Geography Department Archive, UCL, Letter from D. R. Harris to H. Clout, received August 2002.

[29] For a concise history of the earlier years of the Institute of Archaeology see D. R. Harris, 'Sixty years on: the Institute of Archaeology, 1937–97', *Archaeology International 1997/98*, 3–5.

recorded how much she learned from David and Gordon, following in their footsteps as they 'strode across the Syrian steppe', and has emphasised the importance of David's contribution to the trip's success, 'not just his tireless, late into the night, pressing of endless plant specimens, but his knowledge and understanding of the environment and how early use of the natural resources had transformed the landscape'.[30]

David later recalled an incident during fieldwork searching for emmer wheat in a remote area in north-eastern Turkey, when they were stopped at gunpoint by Turkish soldiers who thought they were spying. Sue's diary for 30 April records, 'getting distinctly colder up in the mountains; stopped to look back at the view of the city that had the largest army base I've ever seen in the foreground; David took lots of photos of some interesting land formations in the far distance—our Turkish colleagues looked worried'. They were driven to the military headquarters in a nearby town and incarcerated overnight but were released the following morning after the commandant recognised the surname of one of the group's Turkish colleagues as being the same as that of a major general in the army (she was his daughter). It had been believed that they were Armenian spies.[31]

An important, if less adventurous, development later in 1983 was the appointment of Gordon Hillman to a lectureship in archaeobotany which David had secured through a University of London New Academic Initiatives competition.

The following year he resumed his fieldwork in Australia with his new Institute colleague Tony Barham and others. Two more field seasons of survey and small-scale excavation of coastal middens and relict field systems were carried out on islands in Western Torres Strait and in coastal Papua New Guinea, with the aim of testing his previously developed ideas about past patterns of settlement and subsistence.[32] Their reconnaissance work on the island of Mabuyag led to the mapping and excavation of an area of great past ceremonial significance on the island's south coast. The study of the excavated material with reference to the nineteenth-century

---

[30] Unpublished account of the journey prepared by Sue Colledge for the writing of this memoir.
[31] This was not the last time the search for emmer wheat in Turkey led to trouble. It happened again in 1992 when a group including Helen, Zoe and the Israeli archaeobotanist Daniel Zohary were stopped by suspicious Kurdish soldiers (Helen Harris, telephone conversation, 30 March 2017).
[32] See A. J. Barham and D. R. Harris, 'Prehistory and palaeoecology of Torres Strait', in P. M. Masters and N. C. Flemming (eds.), *Quaternary Coastlines and Marine Archaeology: Towards the Prehistory of Land Bridges and Continental Shelves* (London, 1983), pp. 549–57; and see A. J. Barham and D. R. Harris, 'Relict field systems in the Torres Strait region', in I. S. Farrington (ed.), *Prehistoric Intensive Agriculture in the Tropics* (Oxford, 1985), pp. 247–83.

ethnographic records of past island life formed the basis of a PhD thesis by Barbara Ghaleb Kirby.[33] The significance of the work was further demonstrated and enhanced twenty years later by a team of Australian archaeologists based at Monash University.[34]

Back in Britain, the 1980s were stormy times for archaeology. In 1981 it had been agreed that Britain would organise the next major congress of the International Union of Pre- and Protohistoric Sciences, a long-established organisation that was largely dominated by European archaeologists and their specialist topics. It was to take place in 1986 and be organised by the archaeologist and anthropologist Peter Ucko, an old friend of David's who had recently returned to Britain from Australia, where he had revolutionised the Institute of Aboriginal Studies. This was at the height of the anti-apartheid campaign for an academic boycott of South Africa and in the run-up to the meeting, under pressure from the anti-apartheid movement and the unions, it was agreed to exclude people who worked in South Africa from participation, in defiance of the International Union, whose meeting it was supposed to be. The Union withdrew its support, a move that led to the resignation of the existing organising committee of senior British archaeologists. David, however, 'was supportive of such actions—including within the academic world— and so was fully behind ... [it] in the circumstances'.[35] He joined Peter Ucko's new organising committee to create the first World Archaeological Congress, which took place in Southampton in 1986 and not only had a much broader focus but also included representatives of indigenous peoples whose lives were affected by archaeologists' actions.

One of the participants in the World Archaeological Congress was Professor V. M. Masson, the Director of the Institute for the History of Material Culture in Leningrad and a Corresponding Member of the Academy of Sciences of Turkmenistan, where he had partially excavated a number of Neolithic sites, including the site of Jeitun on the southern edge of the Karakum desert, believed to be the earliest farming site in Central Asia. In the late 1980s the Soviet Union, under Mikhail Gorbachev, was going through the period of 'glasnost', opening up to the outside

---

[33] For a summary see D. R. Harris and B. Ghaleb Kirby, 'Mabuyag (Torres Strait) in the mid-1980s: archaeological reconnaissance of the island and midden excavations at Goemu', in I. J. McNiven and G. Hitchcock (eds.), *Goemulgaw Lagal: Cultural and Natural Histories of the Island of Mabuyag, Torres Strait* (Brisbane, 2015), pp. 283–375.
[34] I. J. McNiven, D. Wright, S. Sutton, M. Weisler, S. Hocknull and J. Stanisic, 'Midden formation and marine specialization at Goemu village, Mabuyag, Torres Strait, before and after European contact', in McNiven and Hitchcock, *Goemulgaw Lagal*, pp. 377–475.
[35] Letter from Helen Harris to Ken Thomas, 30 September 2015.

world, and Masson invited David to come and carry out new excavations that would apply modern methods to the retrieval and analysis of botanical and faunal remains. Despite his many administrative duties, including as Director of the Institute of Archaeology from 1989 (see below), David was determined not to give up fieldwork altogether and this became his last field project. He and Gordon Hillman visited the site in April 1989 and carried out preliminary excavations alongside the Russian and Turkmen team to evaluate the site's potential for environmental analysis. Excavation and related fieldwork continued until 1997, with major field seasons in 1993 and 1994, though Russian involvement gradually declined as the Soviet Union collapsed and Turkmenistan became independent. Unsurprisingly in this climate, enormous administrative, logistical and financial difficulties had to be faced and overcome. It is always difficult bringing together the results of excavations involving contributions from many specialists working in different places and with their own timetables and priorities, but David achieved this in characteristic well-organised fashion with the publication in 2010 of the fieldwork monograph, which included the first modern synthesis of the evidence for the spread of farming into western Central Asia at the end of the seventh millennium BCE.[36]

The Institute of Archaeology joins UCL

As financial pressure on universities grew ever stronger during the Thatcher years of the early 1980s it became clear that the Institute was running up significant deficits and that the University of London Senate was not prepared to keep supporting it. In fact, this was the culmination of increasing problems in the Institute's relations with the central University authorities arising from the decision to admit undergraduates in the late 1960s. In Senate House's view, institutes were essentially static bodies designed to provide facilities for research and certainly did not need more teaching staff. The Institute was told it would have to look after its own future. A number of options was explored but it was pretty clear that joining UCL was the only viable one and David was very keen on it, in contrast to some of his colleagues. In 1986, after a series of negotiations in which he played a major part alongside John Evans, the Director, the Institute merged with UCL; after a period of transition, the Institute's internal departments were dissolved. In 1989 David became Director of the Institute,

---

[36] D. R. Harris, *Origins of Agriculture in Western Central Asia: an Environmental-Archaeological Study* (Philadelphia, PA, 2010). This is the source for the description of the project given above.

which benefitted greatly from his previous experience as a member of the UCL Geography department.

David's legacy as Director of the Institute

His period as Director, 1989 to 1996, left a number of important legacies. Perhaps the greatest, and certainly the most tangible, were the Wolfson Archaeological Science Laboratories and secure artefact store that were built in the basement of the Institute, following a major fund-raising effort, including the auction of Indiana Jones's whip, and opened in 1991. These laboratories have been the foundation of the Institute's subsequent world-leading eminence in archaeological materials science under Professors Thilo Rehren and Ian Freestone. The artefact store has provided the basis for ongoing efforts to put the Institute's massive artefact collections in order. It was also during David's tenure that the Institute took its present shape, with the Classical Archaeologists, the Medieval Archaeologists and the Egyptologists, who had always been in separate departments in UCL, joining the Institute.

A less tangible major achievement but perhaps the most important of all was a 'culture shift' in the Institute towards a clearer focus on excellence in research and in teaching. Or, as one colleague put it, 'he helped change the Institute of Archaeology from a nice but sluggish institution to a strong research centre'. Indeed, he led the way personally, gaining one of the first large research grants in the then new science-based archaeology.

Another aspect of his 'culture-shift' was an expansion of teaching at graduate level, with new MA and MSc degree courses. He also broadened out the academic profile of the Institute in a variety of ways. For example, he appointed the first lecturer in Museum Studies and started the MA in Museum Studies, still one of the Institute's key degrees. Apart from the important appointment in his own field of Gordon Hillman, he also appointed the first lectureship in African archaeology, Kevin MacDonald, and the first post in theoretical archaeology, Cyprian Broodbank, now Disney Professor of Archaeology at Cambridge, who set the pattern for many subsequent Master's degrees with his course 'Themes, Thought and Theory in World Archaeology', which in modified form is still running.

When the time came for David to retire from the Directorship he was determined that his legacy should be built on and extended, and to this end made sure that Peter Ucko, then at the University of Southampton, was appointed as his successor. He knew Peter would be even more radical than he had been himself and he thought that this was what the Institute needed. His success in achieving the appointment was a result of his political abilities and the support of Derek Roberts, then Provost of UCL. The result provoked a storm within the Institute and in the British archaeological world more widely at the time, but it was achieved and David told people approvingly, 'You won't recognise the Institute in ten years' time.' His vision, and the resulting structural changes, created a firm foundation upon which subsequent Directors have continued to build. In short, while he always came across as very urbane and measured, and the very epitome of politeness, those qualities hid a radicalism, vision and determination that, allied to his sheer competence, laid the foundations for the modern Institute.

Nor should his broader administrative contributions be forgotten. In addition to his major role at the Institute, David was also actively involved in the academic and administrative affairs of UCL and the University of London, as well as the wider academic community. Among the latter, the chairmanship (1989–92) of the Science-Based Archaeology Committee (then part of the Science and Engineering Research Council, now under the aegis of the Natural Environment Research Council) and the presidency of the Prehistoric Society (1990–4) stand out as especially important contributions.

As Emeritus Professor of Human Environment at the Institute of Archaeology following his retirement in 1998, David continued to be involved with the Institute, attending seminars and public lectures, and stimulating and encouraging younger colleagues. He was particularly excited by the work of Dorian Fuller, whom he regarded as his intellectual heir in many ways, continuing his commitment to a global view of the subsistence practices of early societies and their implications. Important research and writing continued too, not least preparing the publication of the Jeitun monograph described above. David also founded *Archaeology International*, the 'house' journal of the Institute of Archaeology, editing it from its first issue of 1997/8 to the eighth in 2004/5. In typical fashion, he was still editing his friend and former colleague Jack Golson's book on Papua New Guinea when illness took over.[37] But retirement also enabled him to spend more time on cultivating the large garden at home, practising (in Helen's words) a little of what he preached, growing subsistence crops such as potatoes and beans. He and Helen, who had fitted her career as a French teacher around the demands of David's academic life, stayed in the same house in

[37] Neil Faulkner, eulogy for David Harris at his funeral, 15 January 2014.

Rickmansworth for most of their married life, enjoying the views and sunsets over the valley of the River Chess.

David's teaching at the Institute of Archaeology

By the early 1980s, when David was Head of the Department of Human Environment, the Institute was offering a wide range of courses on different specialist aspects of environmental archaeology, but the central course for any programme in this field was his own 'Resources and Subsistence', a module that cut across the boundaries of these 'specialisms' to address the broad issues of understanding global subsistence systems, how humans had managed their land-use and used plants and animals as subsistence resources. It was an entirely unique course stemming directly from David's academic background and research interests, combining the approaches of ecological geography, anthropology and archaeology. The course took as its focus the main categories of organic resources exploited by humans as food, and examined the systems by which food is procured. The scope was remarkable, both in geographical range and David's sheer breadth of knowledge about plant and animal use in a diverse range of ecosystems. For many fledgling archaeology students these were the most fascinating and memorable hours in the lecture theatre. They learnt, for example, how bitter manioc was detoxified in South America using a *tipiti* expandable basket, pulled down to draw out the toxin, so the grated manioc could be made into cakes and baked—and, incidentally, how the extracted poison could be used for tipping hunting arrows, or adding to low waters to stupefy fish. And there can have been no other archaeology students in the UK at the time learning about how Torres Strait Islanders undertook short-term food storage by tethering green turtles to boats and shorelines, or how prehistoric fishers in the Hawaiian Island chain constructed boulder fish traps for use at low tide. His main message for environmental archaeology students, however, was the importance of considering whole systems in the explanation of past subsistence: he demonstrated how the predictabilities of resource distribution, productivity, reproduction, seasonality and yields, combined with ethnographic perspectives on social practices, resource selection and preparation, were powerful tools for the environmental archaeologist. He encouraged students not to be shy of a lack of firm archaeological data and demonstrated how building models of subsistence systems led to the construction of testable hypotheses that put detailed fieldwork and laboratory studies in context. In short, David's teaching was an enthusiastic distillation and sharing of his immense knowledge and deep thought gained from his lifelong research and interests.[38]

David's teaching inspired generations of Institute of Archaeology students. Many undergraduates and particularly Master's students during the 1980s and 1990s got hooked by the questions posed in his teaching and the logic of the interdisciplinary approaches he advocated. Since his death, a number of past MSc students now in academic posts in various parts of the world have posted online tributes to his teaching. One, now a senior researcher at the Royal Botanic Gardens at Kew, states: 'I first came in contact with David through his "Resources and Subsistence" MSc module at the Institute, a fascinating world tour of food production practices, all based on first-hand observations, and a compelling demonstration of the virtues of the worldwide, comparative, rigorous approach that David took.'[39]

Broader influence: David Harris and the origins of agriculture[40]

Through his writings, edited volumes[41] and conference organisation, David influenced generations of environmental archaeologists, ethnobotanists and archaeobotanists, by promoting a comparative and world approach to the diversity of pathways from foraging to farming. This began with his 1967 paper 'New light on plant domestication and the origins of agriculture',[42] an ambitious review of all the key regions globally, from Eurasia to Africa and the Americas. In this paper he sought to update the global view of his supervisor Carl Sauer by drawing on a greatly expanded evidence base, both from botanists working on crops and the genetics of domestication and from archaeology. Unlike Sauer, Harris was a polycentrist and he

---

[38] The description of David's teaching is taken from an unpublished account of it prepared by Louise Martin for the purpose of this memoir.

[39] Mark Nesbitt, Comment on http://archaeobotanist.blogspot.co.uk/2014/01/in-memoriam-professor-david-r-harris.html, made on 6 January 2014 (accessed 18 April 2017).

[40] The detailed review in this section of David's contribution to understanding the origins of agriculture has been edited from an unpublished text provided by Dorian Fuller.

[41] D. R. Harris (ed.), *The Origins and Spread of Agriculture and Pastoralism in Eurasia* (Washington, DC, 1996); D. R. Harris (ed.), *The Archaeology of V. Gordon Childe: Contemporary Perspectives* (London, 1994); and D. R. Harris and G. C. Hillman (eds.), *Foraging and Farming: the Evolution of Plant Exploitation* (London, 1989)—all originating from international symposia that David had organised. Those who contributed to his edited collections soon became aware of how very exacting an editor he was; some felt that he had virtually rewritten their contributions and, in so doing, improved them immeasurably.

[42] D. R. Harris, 'New light on plant domestication and the origins of agriculture: a review', *Geographical Review*, 80 (1967), 90–107.

concluded that the origin of agriculture was not a revolution nor driven by a single environmental change, but that 'the beginnings of cultivation were slow and complex processes involving varied and gradual adjustments between man and the land over long periods of time in many different habitats'.[43] He highlighted that hard evidence was still meagre for most of the world and for most plants, calling for more genetic and ethnobotanical studies of minor cultigens and more archaeology beyond the then established centres of southwest Asia and Mesoamerica. His brief reviews of the evidence from China, Southeast Asia and Africa now appear remarkably prescient.

It was the innovative ideas that David had developed on the origins of agriculture in tropical forest regions, drawing on deductions from ecology, biogeography and ethnography, that first brought him to the attention of archaeologists, with his 'Agricultural systems, ecosystems and the origins of agriculture',[44] delivered at a multidisciplinary seminar on domestication at the Institute of Archaeology in May 1968. This chapter was a conceptual one and can be regarded as his first landmark contribution to this field; it continues to gather regular citations. In it David explores variations in cultivation in terms of their biodiversity and how it transformed pre-existing natural ecosystems. Most often agriculture represents a reduction in diversity, or ecological specialisation, but in some cases, especially tropical slash-and-burn systems, the opposite could be true and agricultural systems maintained or enhanced plant diversity. This insight suggests quite different potential pathways from foraging to managed agricultural systems in different parts of the world. David also observed that most known transitions to farming occurred initially in quite diversified natural ecosystems, such as tropical forest-savanna or the Mediterranean zone of south-west Asia, rather than more monotonous vegetation zones, like the Eurasian steppe. He went on to draw attention to the fundamental difference between seed culture and vegecultural food production. In addition, he began to formulate some biogeographically informed rules that could predict where in the world agricultural origins were likely to have occurred. This offered an opportunity to escape an ascertainment bias in early agriculture research, by which archaeologists focus on regions of known origins (the Near East, Mexico), find evidence

---

[43] Ibid., 107
[44] D. R. Harris, 'Agricultural systems, ecosystems and the origins of agriculture', in P. J. Ucko and G. W. Dimbleby (eds.), *The Domestication and Exploitation of Plants and Animals* (London, 1969), pp. 3–15.

for origins there, and then conclude that those are the only primary centres for agricultural origins, without comparable evidence from elsewhere. In this chapter, as in his subsequent works, David took a balanced and global view of what evidence there was and where gaps in research, in various regions or on various species, continued to limit knowledge.

In this landmark chapter he also deduced that as underground tubers represented a survival strategy for some plants growing in seasonally dry tropics, it was in these regions, the forest savanna margins, that the early use and cultivation of many tuber crops should be sought, including Asian and African yams, as well as Neotropical tuber crops. He predicted that in these zones small-scale fixed plot horticulture or 'proto-cultivation' could be expected. This idea was developed further in a journal article,[45] and in the specific context of Africa,[46] but his general framework and predictions have had their greatest impact through inspiring and informing multidisciplinary archaeology in the lowland tropics of the New World,[47] and the highland tropics of New Guinea.[48] Piperno and Pearsall attribute to Harris an explanation for the delay between an early start of tropical cultivation and fully sedentary village life, in contrast to the more closely tied transition in seed cropping systems, as tropical cultivation was higher in diversity and closer to natural systems, and began under lower population densities.[49]

David's next landmark paper, 'Alternative pathways to agriculture',[50] was a global synthesis of archaeobotanical and archaeozoological data on origins, but also a framework for comparing different subsistence systems and trajectories of change. It was organised around resource types—grass and forb seeds, nuts, roots and tubers, fish and aquatic mammals, herd ungulates—and for each category explored documented variation in processing, storing, producing and reproducing such resources, drawing on a mixture of ethnographic and archaeological cases. For example, wild

---

[45] D. R. Harris, 'The origins of agriculture in the tropics: ecological analysis affords new insights into agricultural origins and suggests a fresh evaluation of the limited archaeological evidence', *American Scientist*, 60 (1972), 180–93.

[46] D. R. Harris, 'Traditional systems of plant food production and the origins of agriculture in West Africa', in J. R. Harlan, J. M. J. De Wet and A. B. Stemler (eds.), *Origins of African Plant Domestication* (The Hague, 1976), pp. 311–56.

[47] D. R. Piperno and D. M. Pearsall, *The Origins of Agriculture in the Lowland Neotropics* (New York, 1998).

[48] E.g. T. Denham, 'Envisaging early agriculture in the Highlands of New Guinea: landscapes, plants and practices', *World Archaeology*, 37 (2005), 290–306.

[49] Piperno and Pearsall, *The Origins of Agriculture in the Lowland Neotropics*, p. 22.

[50] D. R. Harris, 'Alternative pathways toward agriculture', in C. Reed (ed.), *Origins of Agriculture* (The Hague, 1977), pp. 179–243.

seed gathering by Native Americans of the recent past in the Great Basin was compared with broadcast sowing of millets in north China and early Neolithic cereal growing of the Near East, highlighting the importance of different harvesting techniques in allowing intensification and selecting for domestication. This paper provides a framework for systematically comparing subsistence practices and considering the feedbacks between particular practices, resource productivity and potential pressures that might select for changes leading to domestication. In this paper he also proposed four alternative models for how different stresses—environmental changes, human impacts on the environment, resource competition, and population density increase—might push wild food procurement systems towards food production. Issues relating to growing population density and the emergence of sedentism were explored in a subsequent paper on 'settling down',[51] which acts as a supplement to 'alternative pathways'.

David's third landmark paper explored both Darwinian and ecological interactions between plants and people.[52] In it he outlined an 'evolutionary continuum' between foragers and farmers, framing key stages that can be expected in any chronological pathway between hunting and gathering and agricultural economies and in particular the necessary intermediate stage of 'pre-domestication cultivation'. While a few scholars had noted or implied the likelihood of finding evidence for plant cultivation without the botanical changes recognised as domestication,[53] it was arguably Harris that really made 'pre-domestication cultivation' part of the accepted archaeological lexicon. It is now quite routinely explored as an analytical framework by archaeobotanists working in various world regions.[54]

---

[51] D. R. Harris, 'Settling down: an evolutionary model for the transformation of mobile bands into sedentary communities', in J. Friedman and M. J. Rowlands (eds.), *The Evolution of Social Systems* (London, 1978), pp. 401–17.

[52] D. R. Harris, (1989) 'An evolutionary continuum of people-plant interaction', in Harris and Hillman, *Foraging and Farming*, pp. 11–26.

[53] E.g. H. Helbaek, 'The palaeoethnobotany of the Near East and Europe', in R. J. Braidwood and B. Howe (eds.), *Prehistoric Investigations in Iraqi Kurdistan* (Chicago, IL, 1960), pp. 99–118; R. I. Ford, 'The processes of plant food production in prehistoric North America', in R. I. Ford (ed.), *Prehistoric Food Production in North America* (Ann Arbor, MI, 1985), pp. 1–18.

[54] E.g. Piperno and Pearsall, *The Origins of Agriculture in the Lowland Neotropics*; Denham, 'Envisaging early agriculture in the Highlands of New Guinea'; S. Kahlheber and K. Neumann, 'The development of plant cultivation in semi-arid West Africa', in T. Denham, J. Iriarte and L. Vrydaghs (eds.), *Rethinking Agriculture: Archaeological and Ethnoarchaeological Perspectives* (Walnut Creek, CA, 2007), pp. 320–46; D. Q. Fuller and L. Qin, 'Water management and labour in the origins and dispersal of Asian rice', *World Archaeology*, 41 (2009), 88–111.

However, he was concerned to make clear that he was not supposing 'pre-ordained steps on a ladder' nor irreversibility, but rather that a gradient existed in terms of 'increasing input of human energy per unit area of exploited land'.[55] In other words, there was an intensification trajectory inherent in the transition to agriculture. His main aim with his model of an evolutionary continuum was to 'clarify the general terminology' and it did so by disentangling changes in plants (domestication) from changes in human activities (cultivation, agriculture). While he sketched a history of how domestication had been conceptualised in archaeology and botany and built on earlier insights of a wide range of scholars, his model, presented as a table, laid a new foundation for a clearer and more structured approach to using archaeological evidence to document domestication. A comparison of the archaeological literature prior to this paper and that which came after suggests that the conflation of finding domestication and finding agriculture was typical through the 1980s and broke down from the 1990s onwards.

The influence of David's 'evolutionary continuum' is evident in three ways. First, as already noted, one finds it referred to as a framework for the transition to farming across many disparate world regions, from New Guinea to the Neotropics, from Africa to Eastern Asia. Second, the history of citation of this paper charts an impressive trajectory, such that within twenty years it had easily outstripped his earlier landmark papers. Through his later career he often returned to this model and made minor modifications;[56] indeed, he worked on a final revision as an encyclopaedia entry in his last year, published posthumously.[57] Finally, by early in the twenty-first century, the phase of pre-domestication cultivation that was theoretically central to the evolutionary continuum started to be recognised through empirical archaeological evidence.[58]

[55] Harris, 'An evolutionary continuum of people–plant interaction', p. 12.
[56] E.g. D. R. Harris, 'Themes and concepts in the study of early agriculture', in D. R. Harris (ed.), *The Origins and Spread of Agriculture and Pastoralism in Eurasia* (London, 1996), pp. 1–9; D. R. Harris, 'Domesticatory relationships of people, plants and animals', in R. Ellen and K. Fukui (eds.), *Redefining Nature: Ecology, Culture and Domestication* (Oxford, 1996), pp. 437–63; D. R. Harris, 'Evolution of agroecosystems: biodiversity, origins, and differential development', in P. Gepts, T. R. Famula, R. L. Bettinger, S. B. Brush, A. B. Damania, P. E. McGuire and C. O. Qualset (eds.), *Biodiversity in Agriculture: Domestication, Evolution, and Sustainability* (Cambridge, 2012), pp. 21–56.
[57] D. R. Harris and D. Q. Fuller, 'Agriculture: definition and overview', in C. Smith (ed.), *Encyclopaedia of Global Archaeology* (New York, 2014), pp. 104–13.
[58] E.g. G. Hillman, R. Hedges, A. Moore, S. Colledge and P. Pettitt, 'New evidence of Lateglacial cereal cultivation at Abu Hureyra on the Euphrates', *The Holocene*, 11 (2001), 383–93; G. Willcox, 'Charred plant remains from a 10th millennium B.P. kitchen at Jerf el Ahmar (Syria)', *Vegetation History and Archaeobotany*, 11 (2002), 55–60; E. Weiss, M. E. Kislev and A. Hartmann,

In exploring and illustrating the evolutionary continuum, David produced a number of empirically based syntheses on the transition to farming and settled life in the Near East. The first of these is represented by the Kroon Memorial Lecture delivered in May 1990 and subsequently published.[59] In this he probed the history of research on domestication leading up to his evolutionary continuum model and drew on his 'alternative pathways' paper to suggest how wild cereals and pulses were more readily intensified and domesticated than the tree nuts, like acorns, that were inferred to be co-staples during the Epipaleolithic.[60] In subsequent years he updated his syntheses of both Near Eastern plant domestication and subsequent agricultural expansion involving the integration of livestock,[61] and the expansion of growing agricultural populations.[62] His final revised synthesis of agricultural origins and early dispersals in the Near East constituted a key chapter in his monograph of the Djeitun field project.[63] While these syntheses drew on the slowly expanding empirical record, they also recorded a major shift in thinking on causation by attributing the beginning of pre-domestication cultivation to the push factor of climatic aridification brought on by the Younger Dryas at the end of the Pleistocene. Indeed, exploring the evidence for a global climatic event at the Younger Dryas, and its potential as a factor driving parallel evolution of agriculture, for example in south-west Asia and China, was an important addition to his later syntheses.[64] While the role of the Younger Dryas continues to be debated, David's strong conceptual framework, represented by the three landmark papers identified above, has left a lasting legacy on

---

'Autonomous cultivation before domestication', *Science*, 312 (2006), 1608–10; D. Q. Fuller, (2007) 'Contrasting patterns in crop domestication and domestication rates: recent archaeobotanical insights from the old world', *Annals of Botany*, 100 (2007), 903–24.

[59] D. R. Harris, *Settling Down and Breaking Ground: Rethinking the Neolithic Revolution* (Harlem, 1990).

[60] Harris 'Alternative pathways toward agriculture'.

[61] D. R. Harris, 'The origins of agriculture in southwest Asia', *Review of Archaeology*, 19 (1998), 5–11; D. R. Harris, 'The spread of neolithic agriculture from the Levant to western Central Asia', in A. D. Damania, J. Valkoun, G. Willcox and C. O. Qualset (eds.), *The Origins of Agriculture and Crop Domestication* (Aleppo, 1998), pp. 65–82.

[62] D. R. Harris, 'The expansion capacity of early agricultural systems: a comparative perspective on the spread of agriculture', in P. Bellwood and C. Renfrew (eds.), *Examining the Farming/Language Dispersal Hypothesis* (Cambridge, 2002), pp. 31–40.

[63] D. R. Harris, *Origins of Agriculture in Western Central Asia: an Environmental–Archaeological Study* (Philadelphia, PA, 2010).

[64] E.g. D. R. Harris, 'Climatic change and the beginnings of agriculture: the case of the Younger Dryas', in L. Rothschild and A. Lister (eds.), *Evolution on Planet Earth: the Impact of the Physical Environment* (London, 2003), pp. 379–94.

the interpretation of the growing empirical evidence for domestication processes and transitions to agricultural economies.

The excellence of David's academic contributions was recognised in various ways throughout his career. His awards in his earlier career in Geography have already been mentioned. In 1982 he was elected a Fellow of the Society of Antiquaries; he was made an Honorary Fellow of University College London in 2000 in recognition of his services to UCL; and his distinguished contributions to scholarship were recognised in 2004 when he was elected a Fellow of the British Academy. It was entirely appropriate that he was a member of two of the Academy's sections: Archaeology, and Anthropology and Geography. In that position he was at home.

STEPHEN SHENNAN
HUGH CLOUT
Fellows of the Academy

Note: Helen Harris and her daughter, Lucy, generously discussed David's life and work with Hugh Clout on 22 April 2014; further information is taken from the tribute delivered by Neil Faulkner at David's funeral on 15 January 2014. In addition to the contributions made by Helen Harris, Sue Colledge, Dorian Fuller and Louise Martin noted in the text this memoir is also based on the work of Ken Thomas, including the obituary he wrote for *Archaeology International*.[65]

---

[65] K. Thomas, 'Professor David Russell Harris (1930–2013)', *Archaeology International*, 17 (2014), 7–11, DOI: http://dx.doi.org/10.5334/ai.1701.

MICHAEL JOHN ARTIS

Michael John Artis
1938–2016

MICHAEL ARTIS WAS BORN in Croydon on 29 June 1938 to Violet and Cyril, the name Artis reflecting Huguenot origins. He was never one for sitting on formality, and was known universally as 'Mike'. The family later moved from London to Blackpool, where Mike was to acquire the northern accent which was to puzzle his colleagues at the European University Institute when he moved there later in his academic career.

It was in Blackpool in the early 1960s that Mike met Lilian Gregson, then a research assistant at the Blackpool Infirmary, and they married in 1961. Their first daughter, Rosamond, was born when Mike was at Adelaide University and she was one of more than six children born to faculty members there around that time. It was a very happy and lively period in their life with many social functions involving large numbers of children. Their second daughter, Hilary, was born after their return to the UK. In their early years at Swansea many Australian friends visited Mike and Lil, and enjoyed their hospitality. However, the marriage ended and they divorced in the mid-1970s.

While at Swansea, Mike fell in love with the Economics Departmental Secretary, Shirley Knight, and they married after Mike moved to Manchester. Shirley's children, Mark and Jacqui, accompanied them to Manchester and Mike welcomed them and was a great help to them both. Mike had made many lifelong friends in Australia and they maintained their close relationships with Lilian, Ros and Hilary, while remaining in touch with Mike and his new family. Mike and Shirley later moved to Florence where they seemed especially happy. Four years after returning to Manchester Mike became very ill, and Shirley was a strong support, as were his daughters.

Mike was what would be described as a 'bright spark'. He shone at school in Blackpool, winning a place at the top local grammar school (Baines Grammar School). From there, Mike gained a scholarship to Magdalen College, Oxford, to read PPE from 1959 to 1961. His tutor at Magdalen was David Worswick, whom Mike held in great affection and respect.

The Oxford Institute of Statistics

On graduation, he was encouraged to join the Oxford Institute of Statistics, and his ability was recognised by Tommy Balogh (later Lord Balogh). It was under Balogh's supervision that he began work on his first book and published his first journal article in 1961.

First journal article

In this first journal article, 'Liquidity and the attack on quantity theory', in *The Bulletin of the Oxford University Institute of Statistics* (Artis, 1961), he tackled an issue in monetary economics relating to the 1959 Report of the Committee on the Working of the Monetary System (the 'Radcliffe Report'). Although that committee included two academic economists, Professors Cairncross and Sayers, its conceptual basis was largely hidden from sight, with no equations or formal analysis. Mike's article, in our view the best commentary on Radcliffe, provided an interpretation of its underlying framework, effectively delineating the issues for an academic audience; it was appropriately reprinted in the volume on *Readings in British Monetary Economics* (Johnson, 1972).

The Radcliffe Committee's major conclusion was that money did not matter in economic policy. If the government sought to control its quantity, substitutes would emerge so rapidly that any attempt at control would prove pointless. This seemed to run directly counter to Milton Friedman's contemporaneous claim that 'inflation is always and everywhere a monetary phenomenon'.

In the UK the Radcliffe Committee's assessment met with a mixed response. Economists, such as Victor Morgan, insisted that a fundamental difference exists between money and other financial assets and were highly critical of the Report's emphasis on liquidity as the appropriate focus of policy. To them, the money supply seemed more readily quantifiable and less amorphous than what the Report called the 'state of liquidity', a term which seemingly embraced confidence, incentives and attitudes incapable of precise measurement.

It is on this point that Mike entered the scene. He drew attention to three main features. First, when considering the quantity theory of money one should distinguish between what he called the 'naïve' and 'sophisticated' quantity theory. Second, he then took the analysis further by drawing on American analysis of money substitution. Third, he built on that analysis to provide a different interpretation of liquidity and money in terms of the quantity theory.

As he noted, 'the Committee was in no doubt that variations in money supply could be offset, in their effect on price levels, by variations in the velocity of circulation, adding moreover, that "we ... cannot find any reason for supposing ... that there is any limit to the velocity of circulation" (para. 391)' (Artis, 1961, 345). To make sense of this (arguably extreme) position, it is necessary to consider the 'sophisticated quantity theory', as Mike called it, and his interpretation of the Radcliffe Committee's attack on it.

In his article, he argues that the Committee's emphasis on the 'whole liquidity position' paralleled US research on the impact of non-bank financial intermediaries in monetary policy by Gurley and Shaw (1956, 1960). In terms of the standard Keynesian model, the growth of non-bank financial intermediaries is analytically equivalent to an improvement in bond liquidity (Patinkin, 1961), which makes bonds a better substitute for money, causing the demand curve for money both to shift leftwards and become more interest elastic.

The scenario proposed by Mike Artis, as a rationale for the Radcliffe position, was that the shifts in the demand for money due to the emergence of non-bank intermediaries were not autonomous, accidental events, but were in fact institutional developments induced by monetary tightening, a potentially greater challenge to the quantity theory of money.

This illustrates a hallmark of Mike's career, a (then young) scholar combining in a measured way a variety of explanatory approaches and interpretations within an encompassing conceptual framework. In this case, it is perhaps ironic that, despite the Radcliffe Committee's emphasis on 'liquidity', the analytical framework employed was that of the quantity theory and the demand and supply of 'money'.

His first book

A second article appeared two years later, on 'Hire purchase financial houses' (Artis, 1963a). Following the Radcliffe Report there was interest in sources of 'liquidity' outside the banking system, and this led directly to a discussion of such non-bank intermediaries in Mike's first book, *Foundations of British Monetary Policy* (Artis, 1965).

Foundations was concerned not with monetary policy but with the development of those fundamental and institutional relationships underlying the authority and ability of the Bank of England to initiate and implement monetary policy. While these institutional factors take many forms and are continually changing, the analysis was centred on three 'basic' arrangements, these being the Bank's relationship with the apparatus of government, its own internal organisation and its relationship to the financial system. In the last case, Mike observed that the Bank's control of the financial system rested heavily on informal persuasion, rather than upon statutory provisions.

While the book covered the years 1939 to 1963, now distant history, he was sufficiently prescient to pick several major changes afoot in the 1960s, for example the beginnings of the Euro-dollar and Eurobond markets. These markets were to transform the City from the vestiges of the sterling area into a major, indeed the leading, international financial centre for foreign exchange, international bank loans and bond issues, and trading activities and derivatives. The Bank's use of 'its weight to encourage a revival of the international status of the London capital market on an "entrepôt" basis' (Artis, 1965, 77), often in the face of US opposition, testifies both to the central role of the Bank, and Mike's early recognition of it.

Foundations was, effectively, Mike Artis' PhD. At this juncture Oxford distanced itself from the American PhD system, so that one instead wrote a book. However, by the date of publication, Mike had left Oxford and had become a Lecturer in Economics at the University of Adelaide.

The move to Adelaide

In 1960 Harold Lydall, Deputy Director of the Oxford Institute, had become dissatisfied with the Institute and went to Australia, first to the University of Western Australia, and then to a Chair at the University of Adelaide, heading a department in his words 'full of young talent'. Harold then head-hunted Mike, who joined in 1964.

There Mike formed his friendship with Robert (Bob) Wallace, whose time at Oxford overlapped with Mike's. That led to a shift in the direction of Mike's research as he and Bob began to study Australian fiscal policy, a topic which, in comparison with Australian monetary policy, had attracted little academic attention. Meanwhile Bob and Mike became two of the four foundation members of what was initially the University of Adelaide at Bedford Park, which was later to become Flinders University.

They presented the first fruits of this research at an Australian and New Zealand Association for the Advancement of Science (ANZAAS) conference in January 1967, but the bulk of the work came out later, as two chapters (the only ones) on fiscal policy (one conceptual, the other empirical), in a compendium (edited by Neil Runcie) on *Australian Monetary and Fiscal Policy* (Artis and Wallace, 1971). The section 'Assessing the fiscal impact', the analytical contribution, deserves to be remembered as a seminal paper. They argued that the main macroeconomic function of the Budget should be to influence overall demand and GDP (functional finance). By this criterion the summary indicators of the 'thrust' of the annual Budgets used by Australian Treasurers since 1945 were all judged to be woefully inadequate, and much the same was true of academic work. It was then proposed, along Keynesian analytical lines, how the effect of Budgetary measures on the economy might, and should, be measured. Based on these analytical tools, the authors then turned in the second chapter to an historical assessment of all Australian budgets between 1945 and 1966. Endorsing their work, their ANZAAS discussant, John Nevile, noted that their fiscal multipliers were very similar to his, obtained from a large-scale econometric model.

Mike continued to use his expertise in fiscal policy in his later career. In 1972 he wrote a chapter (Artis, 1972) on 'Fiscal policy for stabilisation' as used by the Labour Government in 1964–70 (finding that it was distorted in practice by the failure to counteract balance of payments weakness and by the need to support the subsequent 1967 devaluation), and it became one of the themes he extended while in his first years at Manchester University.

Return to the UK

The Prices and Incomes Board

The UK Government referred the question of the system and level of bank charges to the National Board for Prices and Incomes (NBPI) on 22 June 1966. Aubrey Jones, its Chairman, invited Mike to join the Inquiry as Consultant, and immediately following the ANZAAS conference Mike left Flinders University to return to the UK. There is no internal evidence, nor indeed any acknowledgement (to him or any other assistant), of his work for the NBPI. But his own subsequent accounts suggest that he played an active role, and that his time in Australia had left its mark. He recalled that 'his close and direct questioning of one of the witnesses provoked the response "Are you an Australian or something?".'

When the NBPI Report on Bank Charges (Report No. 34) was completed (1967), it was critical of the cartelised rate structure in the banking system, lack of competition and the practice of maintaining hidden reserves. When much the same field of enquiry opened up in the following year by the referral to the Monopolies Commission of the then proposed merger between Barclays and Martins Banks, it was natural for Mike, given this prior experience, to write a review of this second Report for the *Bankers' Magazine* (Artis, 1968), again critical of the same subjects. These reports helped to set the climate of ideas that led up to the Competition and Credit Control reform in 1971. Mike's assessment was that technology would change banking dramatically and that the structure of fees and charges needed to be reformed. This was correct, but his views were often ignored. When asked how he felt about that by an Australian colleague, Mike replied that 'some people like one's work and others don't. I would be really concerned if people I liked didn't like my work. Otherwise, I stick to my own standards.' Although never again working in Australia, the Adelaide connection continued; for example, once at Swansea his first visitor was Dr Barry Hughes of Flinders University, and his second was Mervyn Lewis (co-author of this memoir).

The National Institute

Later, in October 1967, Mike joined the National Institute for Economic and Social Research (NIESR), initially as Assistant Editor of the *National Institute Review*, but with a clear expectation of taking over from Blackaby, who had been its Editor since it began in January 1959. Worswick, Director of NIESR, had taught Mike at Magdalen, and was aware of his abilities. Mike arrived just in time to participate in publishing the November 1967 issue. He then took over as Editor in August 1968, bolstered by a newly formed Editorial Board. A year later, in November 1969, he edited the fiftieth issue of the *Review*, marked for the occasion by a newly designed cover and a somewhat revised layout, as well as an Introduction by Lord Roberthall.

In those years, neither the detailed forecasts of the Treasury, nor (even more closed to the public) of the Bank of England, were published. A major role for the NIESR, and for its *Review*, was to provide publicly accessible forecasts for the remainder of the current year, and for the next year, of likely economic developments in the UK ('The Home Economy') and in the World Economy. Besides the forecasts, special articles expanded on functional relationships and forecasting methods, or were the research subjects of academics seconded to the NIESR or of particular interest to the staff.

Mike Artis, assisted by Bob Nobay, wrote one such special article on 'Two aspects of the monetary debate' (Artis and Nobay, 1969) in which (following various studies in the USA) they used reduced-form regressions comparing the relative efficacy of fiscal and monetary changes. They found that fiscal measures, rather than monetary ones, appeared to be 'more powerful and certainly the quicker acting'. That result probably gave some comfort to the NIESR staff. Their forecasts gave little, or no, emphasis to monetary data, and the NIESR stance was firmly Keynesian, anti-monetarist, and pro-incomes policies.

Mike Artis was by preference and training a macro-monetary economist, rather than a professional econometrician or model-builder, and most of the technical work in developing and extending the model(s) then used by the NIESR was taken on by others, more specialised economists such as Ray Byron (another link to Adelaide), George Fane and Mike Surrey. Nevertheless, Mike was a highly competent and efficient applied economist and, with his prodigious work rate, played a full role in the, inevitably largely judgmental, process of moving from a model printout to a fully articulated forecast. At the Southampton Conference (1969) on Short-Run Econometric Models, it was Mike who gave the paper on 'Short-term economic forecasting at NIESR' (Artis, 1970).

By May 1972, however, Mike had been at the Institute five-and-a-half years, and had participated in nineteen issues of the *Review*. Being Editor does not leave much time for original, personal research and during these years he had authored only three academic papers. It was time to move on.

University of Wales, Swansea: 1972–6

Harry Johnson had returned to the UK to take a Chair at the London School of Economics (LSE) in 1966. On arrival at LSE, he gathered a group of younger monetary economists, several of whom, notably David Laidler and Michael Parkin, were willing to challenge the mainstream Keynesian approach to inflation (i.e. via incomes policies). In 1969 Harry founded the Money Study Group (MSG).

Although Mike Artis and the NIESR were, institutionally, supporters of Keynesian analysis and incomes policies, he was nonetheless essentially a monetary economist, and prepared to assess all arguments on their merits. Consequently, he gravitated towards Harry Johnson's coterie of monetary economists. David Laidler writes (personal correspondence):

> From its very beginning in 1969 he [Mike] was a regular participant in Money Study Group activities. He was at all the big conferences that produced volumes (Hove, Sheffield, LSE, Bournemouth) and he was also a major player in the editing of *Readings in British Monetary Economics* that went out as edited by Harry Johnson and an MSG Committee. In my memory, the point about Mike was that, though a bit of a Keynesian cost-pusher among the monetarists, he was open minded and willing to listen as well as talk. Also, and very important, he knew a lot more about the institutions and details of data than any of the rest of us (his stint at NIESR presumably gave him this) and in this respect he was a particularly good influence!

One of these monetary economists, and close to Harry, was Bob Nobay, who had been a research economist at NIESR when Mike arrived in October 1967. They jointly wrote the 1969 *Review* paper, and edited together three conference volumes.

Almost all of the available main writings on monetary analysis then emanated from the USA. To provide a somewhat equivalent UK set, Harry encouraged the MSG to provide *Readings in British Monetary Economics*. The selection of papers to be included was made by Artis, David Croome, Norman Gibson, David Laidler, Marcus H. Miller, Bob Nobay and Michael Parkin, the leading young UK monetary economists of the day, and included no fewer than five excerpts from Mike's own work.

So it was no surprise that, aged thirty-four, Mike was appointed to a Chair at Swansea, starting in September 1972. In doing so, he completed a triumvirate of monetary economists similarly appointed: E. Victor Morgan (1945–66), Edward (Ted) Nevin (1968–85) and Mike (1972–6). Interestingly, Victor Morgan left Swansea for a Chair at Manchester, and so did Mike in due course.

Those who met Mike know that he possessed a keen, if understated, sense of humour. His dry wit was in evidence (as reported by Hughes) in the opening remarks of his 1973 inaugural lecture. Noting that he was the Professor of Applied Economics while Nevin was simply Professor of Economics, Mike inquired whether that was because Ted's economics was supposed to have no application.

One of Mike's students from Adelaide University was Mervyn Lewis (then an Economics Senior Lecturer there), who was part of an Honours Money class of two in 1964; he spent six months in Swansea and six months in Manchester. Upon arriving in Swansea, Artis suggested that it was worth looking into the determinants of the UK demand for money. This was a happy turn of events, as their collaboration then resulted in four articles, two books and three chapters in books. Although these publications also covered a time when they had Chairs in Manchester and Nottingham respectively, it makes sense to discuss them here.

After Milton Friedman in 1956 defined the quantity theory (of money) as essentially a theory of the demand for money, estimating demand for money functions became all the rage for at least the next two decades. There were three issues: (i) Friedman's empirical hypothesis that the demand for money is highly stable; (ii) his contention that 'money matters' for the economy; and (iii) that important factors govern the supply of money that do not affect the demand function.

Artis and Lewis' first paper, in *The Banker* (1974), examined the stability of the demand for money. It was given at an MSG meeting at LSE in November 1973, memorable to the authors because they had to catch a return train to Swansea. However, an IRA bomb scare meant that they were trapped in King's Cross, the deepest tube station, with all escalators switched to coming down. Somehow they managed to run up a bank of down escalators (not recommended) in order to catch a taxi to Paddington.

In this article, they considered recent concerns about the stability of the demand for money. If such a relationship is relatively stable, then this supports monetary control policies. Indeed, from the late 1960s onwards the monetary authorities increasingly emphasised monetary aggregates. In common with other similar research, the Bank's equations in Goodhart and Crockett's (1970) *Bulletin* paper appeared to rest on three basic ideas. First, the amount of money which people and business firms wish to hold varies directly with the flow of money income, and inversely with the interest rate. Second, it was assumed that transactors in aggregate can always obtain the money balances that they require, so that the money supply is determined by demand. Finally, the concept of 'partial adjustment' was incorporated—the idea that people will not move to their desired long-run money holding immediately but will take time to do so.

It was widely believed in the City that these research findings (published under the title 'The importance of money') may have heralded a new approach by the Bank:

> Recent UK monetary policy has placed increased emphasis on control of monetary aggregates, a policy based, it seems, on an official assumption that there is a stable demand for money. (Artis and Lewis, 1974, i)

On this basis, and given that during the two years to mid-1973 the quarter-to-quarter rate of growth of the money supply on the M3 definition averaged 22.0 per cent per annum, and for M1 averaged 14.7 per cent, the task that Artis and Lewis set themselves was to check how far that pattern of monetary growth could be accounted for by demand for money functions as fitted in the 1960s.

So, the authors began by re-estimating twelve variants of the standard demand function, 1963 QII–1970 QIV. By normal statistical criteria, the equations obtained seemed realistic and well-determined, with satisfactory overall fits. But their forecasting ability, whether for M1 or M3, having been quite good for 1971, was disastrously bad for 1972 and the first two quarters of 1973, with the money supply massively exceeding the forecast demand for money.

Several explanations were offered. Even after allowance was made in the demand equations for three factors that could have shifted the demand for money (Certificates of Deposit, bond price variability, the 'own' rate on money), the massive overshoot remained. This left a further possibility, namely that the money supplied may have been in excess of that demanded, producing subsequent pressures on asset prices, incomes and the balance of payments until the desired ratio of money to nominal income became restored. This latter was basis of the authors' other two articles on this topic.

To explore the excess money supply idea, they had first to refute the view that the extant stock of money must be demanded. It is, obviously, held but not necessarily demanded, except temporarily in the process of moving from one equilibrium to another. If new supplies augment the money stock fast enough, transactors could find their money holdings in excess of expectations. The dissipation of excess monetary holdings through portfolio adjustment and spending—over time—could be temporarily overwhelmed by further unexpected monetary increments.

The contrary view that the supply of money was necessarily demand-determined was, most likely, because of the Bank of England's policy of stabilising the rate of interest (at varying levels). Given this policy, the Bank would then have to supply the money to validate it, rendering the money supply demand-determined.

However true of the 1960s, Artis and Lewis (1974) contended that the conditions of 1972–3 offered an inhospitable context for this latter view. Highly expansionary budgets, the floating of the pound, the abolition of advances' controls and changes of tactics in the gilt-edged markets all suggested reasons why the stock of money might not be determined by demand but rather in excess of it. If so, the standard demand function would be incorrectly specified, and its failure unsurprising.

In their *Manchester School* article (Artis and Lewis, 1976), they advanced two alternative models, both recognising that money demand may have been adjusting to money supply rather than the opposite. In the first model, money income is assumed to bear the adjustment. An increase, say, in the money stock raises the actual ratio of money to income relative to the desired level. Discrepancies between actual and desired money holdings set in train a rearrangement of expenditures, output, and prices until the ratio of money to income is brought to the desired level. The model specified that this scenario would likely occur over time, and allowance was made for factors that may interrupt the adjustment and constrain money-holders' ability to reach equilibrium. In fact, on the estimates obtained, the adjustment appeared 90 per cent complete after twenty months, and the parameters of the model seemed to be affected less by the inclusion of data for 1971 and 1972 than the standard model.

In their second approach, they assessed whether the rate of interest (rather than income) could provide the market-clearing mechanism, at least in the short run. With interest rates being the dependent variable, they effectively turned the equations 'the other way round'. Overall, they contended that their model results indicated that changes in the money supply could generate partial adjustments of income and interest rates, thereby challenging the conventional notion that the money market always clears in the short run. The results were consistent with the view that changes in the money supply had been interacting with a relatively stable demand function.

Their third paper, in *Economica* (Artis and Lewis, 1984), sought an alternative approach to the issue of stability. Paish (1959) and Dow (1959) presented evidence in their Radcliffe submissions of an inverse graphical relationship between the consol rate and the ratio of money to income (the inverse of the velocity of money). Artis and Lewis replicated this and then added the out-of-sample observations for 1958–81. With the exception of 1973–6, their regression line fitted the extra-sample data extremely well, suggestive of long-run stability of the demand for money, provided that the observations for the mid-1970s could be accounted for. Artis and Lewis attributed this to supply shocks that forced the private sector off its demand curve until the disturbance became eliminated via the induced adjustment of prices, incomes, interest rates and the money supply itself, restoring the ratio of money to income to its original path.

Their work had an enduring impact in a number of respects. First, they appear to have been the first to have challenged the view—described by them as fallacious—that the stock of money must be demanded, and that the supply of money was necessarily demand-determined. Second, following on from this argument, they helped usher in a strand of monetary analysis based on 'buffer stock money' and 'disequilibrium money'. Third, turning the equations 'around the other way' appeared to provide more realistic lag structures.

Such research then led them to write two books on monetary policy. The first, *Monetary Control in the United Kingdom* (Artis and Lewis, 1981), was focused, in addition to reviewing research on the demand for money, on the nature of bank intermediation and its implications for monetary control. The second, *Money in Britain* (Artis and Lewis, 1991), was widely used by students, influencing a generation of monetary economists. The book also devoted more attention to the European Monetary System (EMS), the Exchange Rate Mechanism (ERM) and European Monetary Union (EMU). The latter emphasis led, when the ERM broke down in August 1993, to them being invited by the *Oxford Review of Economic Policy* to evaluate the experience and its implications (Artis and Lewis, 1993: 'Après le déluge: monetary and exchange-rate policy in Britain and Europe'). They argued, accurately, that a 'quick' move to EMU could be a solution attractive to Europe (sans Britain), Thereafter, for much of the rest of his career, such European issues were to occupy a lot of Mike's attention.

The University of Manchester: 1975–95

In May 1975, while still at Swansea but in the process of moving to Manchester, Mike was summoned to Paris (along with one of the authors of this memoir, Charles Goodhart) to meet Dr Jim Cairns, then Treasurer in the Australian Labor Government. Cairns had become unhappy with the liberal, market ideology of both the Treasury and the Reserve Bank of Australia, and was now looking for an outsider to become Governor of the Reserve Bank who would help him to shift the allocation process from a pure market system to a planned system based on social priorities. The name of Artis (and that of Goodhart) had been suggested to him by Geoff Harcourt (again an Adelaide connection, a leading Australian academic who advised the Labor Government). In the note for the record at the time for the Bank of England Goodhart wrote (2 June 1975):

> Professor M. (Mike) Artis is much more in sympathy with Cairns, knows Australia, and was a minor adviser of Whitlam and an ALP member when there. He is a good, well-balanced monetary, macroeconomist: he edited the National Institute Review before going to Swansea. Cairns, in a longer interview with him, made more effort to attract him, discussing terms of pay, etc. He would seem a sensible choice in the circumstances, whereas I would guess that Cairns has now put me among the unacceptable 'market' men. However Artis is doubtful whether he should go any further on personal grounds (family worries, doubts about the responsibility, etc.).

In the event, however, both Cairns and the Labor Government soon ran into political troubles, and the chance for Mike (or Charles Goodhart) to become Governor of the Reserve Bank of Australia—though always a long shot—evaporated.

In 1974 David Laidler and Michael Parkin were becoming frustrated with their positions at the University of Manchester. They faced continuing uphill battles to get their (more monetarist) papers published in top English journals. In particular, their battle to have their paper on 'Inflation' in the *Economic Journal* (Laidler and Parkin, 1975) was epic. Pay scales at Manchester were restricted. The UK academic scene was limited in comparison with that in North America.

Enter Harry Johnson. He used his influence, and connections with Grant Reuber there, to help resettle David and Michael in the University of Western Ontario, in 1975. But that left a huge gap at Manchester. Harry knew just who could fill that gap. Within the pecking order of UK universities, Manchester lay above Swansea. Thus, Mike was happy to move, even though Manchester was then known for fractious infighting between the Marxist and mainstream wings of its Economics faculty. Moreover, Mike must have seemed especially well suited for his new position, since he disliked conflict and could comfortably interact with almost everyone.

Once Mike arrived in Manchester he began to diversify his research fields further away from his earlier concentration on monetary economics. His first foray outside that field in Australia had been into the study of fiscal policies there described above. He continued this work on fiscal issues with two self-authored papers, and others with Marcus Miller, Chris Green and Robin Bladen-Hovell, Elias Karakitsos and Barry Dwolatzky, examining the effects of fiscal policies and undertaking simulations with the Treasury and NIESR models.

The second additional field which Mike entered in these early years at Manchester was the form and existence of a UK wage equation, involving two overlapping papers; the first, with Marcus Miller, was on 'Inflation, real wages and the terms of trade' (Artis and Miller, 1979); the second, his own, was 'Is there a wage equation?' (Artis, 1981). The starting point was that the Phillips curve, relating wage inflation to unemployment, had broken down in the context of worsening inflation through the 1960s and 1970s. This had been replaced by two alternative hypotheses—the augmented expectations version of the Phillips curve, and the target real wage model. Neither of these, however, proved 'robust' in the face of empirical testing, leaving open whether any reliable wage equation could be found.

This was a period when monetary targetry, even if only of the pragmatic variety, was in vogue. Most of the prior analytic work had been for the United States, which approximated to a closed economy. How would targets operate in an open economy context, such as the UK? This was the subject which Artis and David Currie (1981a) analysed in an *Oxford Economics Papers* paper, reprinted in a volume edited by Eltis and Sinclair (Artis and Currie, 1981b). Their overall conclusion was (Artis and Currie, 1981a, 196):

> for a small open economy in which cost-mark-up pricing dominates, stabilisation of the nominal exchange rate (by means of suitable changes in domestic monetary policy) offers rather better prospects for price stabilisation than do monetary targets. Only if disturbances to the economy arise primarily from changes in the general level of foreign prices are monetary targets likely to be clearly superior, and we would not regard this as the relevant case for the UK.

Having then covered monetary and fiscal policies in his research, together with wage determination, Mike felt ready to pull all of these strands together in a textbook, *Macroeconomics* (Artis, 1984). The blurb on the back cover concluded:

> The volume seeks to convey a useful macroeconomics—one that is suited to policy applications. Diagrams play a large role in the exposition although the use of formal mathematics is kept to the minimum needed for a rigorous exposition.

In fact, the role of diagrams was understated, for they probably played a larger role than in any equivalent book. A lot of the book was relatively standard: IS/LM with the addition of a BB curve for the Balance of Payments, credit counterparts for the money supply, and, for much of the volume, prices and wages were treated as fixed in Keynesian style. Perhaps the most original contribution was the emphasis on asset accumulation and wealth as determinants of long-run equilibria. While the volume may not have added greatly to his academic reputation, it put his name before many future macroeconomists and, being reprinted at least twice in 1986 and 1989, the royalties may have helped. It was only later after Mike moved to Italy that money became more plentiful.

Meanwhile, Mike continued to be sought out as editor, par excellence, taking over Prest and Coppock's *The UK Economy: a Manual of Applied Economics* when those authors wanted to hand over the baton, and his first edition of many came out in 1986 (Artis, 1986). The fourteenth edition (1996), for example, had some eleven chapters by nine authors on a variety of aspects of the British economy, one of which was written by Mike, jointly with Harvey Armstrong, on 'The UK and the European Union'. Indeed, from the mid-1980s onwards Mike's academic interests turned sharply towards European institutions and policies, and their relationship to the UK. Mike was never an abstract theorist and, as an applied economist, wanted to direct his economic knowledge and skills to the leading issues of the day.

From Mike's vantage point these concerned whether the volatility of exchange rates and interest rates had changed after EMS, whether exchange rates had become more predictable, whether there was less sign of misalignment in real exchange rates, whether there was more policy convergence, and more convergence in wage rate adjustment, and finally whether capital controls still played a major role in stabilising the fixed, but adjustable, pegged system. In order to employ the most advanced non-parametric econometric techniques he teamed up with Mark Taylor to produce no less than ten subsequent joint papers in the years 1988 to 1995, five of which found that short-run exchange volatility had declined, that EMS misalignments had not fallen and currency substitution had not risen. Three papers on the role of exchange controls were inconclusive, while two papers explored the consequences of exchange rate misalignment.

There were two other strands of Mike's 'European' and 'international' research at this time. One examined what appeared to be very different responses of German wages to unemployment (i.e. an old-style Phillips curve) than in France, Italy or the UK. The other strand considered the advantages of international coordination to stabilise exchange rates, most notably the Chatham House paper with Sylvia Ostry and his own paper (Artis, 1989). Artis and Ostry (1986) proposed nominal income targets. Mike always saw exchange rate pegs, in EMS and/or EMU, as a means for gaining commitment to greater disinflationary policies. EMS/EMU was seen as a way of inducing the more lax members to follow German counter-inflationary leadership, a hypothesis advanced in his article with Dilip Nachane in *Weltwirtschaftliches Archiv* (Artis and Nachane, 1990).

Although Mike had not been a forecasting technician, he remained a close participant in the forecasting process. In the mid-1980s and early 1990s this led to two areas of research. The first was the accuracy of macro forecasts. This began with an invitation, likely from Andrew Crockett who was then running the IMF *World Economic Outlook*, to assess the accuracy of the WEO, done in 1988 (Artis, 1988). Besides comparing WEO forecasts with actual outcomes, another yardstick was to compare them with auto-regressive models. Following that, Mike teamed up for the first time with Wenda Zhang, a Chinese economist from Fudan University who had come to Manchester University (and was to become Mike's most important co-author in these decades) to study how WEO forecasts compared with Bayesian vector autoregressive (BVAR) models, resulting in an article and a paper, as well as a 1996 reprise of his earlier IMF study on WEO forecasting accuracy. This latter study assessed how well cyclical turning points could be predicted, a subject that he had written on in 1993 and 1994. Papers with Sean Holly and with Scott Moss and Paul Ormerod continued these themes. At much the same time, with modelling the economy by adaptive (backward-looking) expectations giving way to rational (forward-looking or model consistent) expectations, Mike, along with Robin Bladen-Hovell and Yue Ma, applied such approaches, in an *Oxford Economics Papers* article, to assess the Labour Government's policies on expenditures, tax rates and interest rates, 1974–9 (Artis et al., 1991).

By the mid-1980s Mike Artis' standing as a leading macroeconomist in the UK was being widely recognised. He became a member of the Panel of Academic Consultants at both the Treasury and the Bank of England, and gave a paper to the latter on 'Why do forecasts differ' (1982). He was Joint Managing Editor of *The Manchester School* for eighteen years,

Associate Editor of the *Economic Journal* for ten years and President of the Manchester Statistical Society (1987–9). More importantly, he was elected a Fellow of the British Academy in 1988, as one of the leading applied macroeconomists in the UK. He was then awarded a Houblon-Norman Fellowship at the Bank of England in 1989–90, followed by a Nuffield Foundation Fellowship at Manchester.

As the 1990s progressed, Mike's focus turned increasingly, almost exclusively, towards European issues. This was a decade of great progress on that front. The collapse of the ERM in 1992–3 had not led to a reversion to generalised floating and/or exchange controls, but to a determination of the central political elite to press forward to a single currency, as predicted in the Artis and Lewis (1993) article, culminating in the establishment of a single currency Eurozone on 1 January 1999, and the introduction of euro notes and coins on 1 January 2002.

It was an exercise in political economy, and Mike eagerly participated. Perhaps his most widely read publication was the 1995 OUP book that he edited on *The Economics of the European Union: Policy and Analysis*, initially with Norman Lee (Artis and Lee, 1995), and from 2001 onwards with Frederick Nixson (Artis and Nixson, 2001). In this he wrote the chapter on 'European Monetary Union', first solo and later with Robin Bladen-Hovell (Artis and Bladen-Hovell, 2001). Cohorts of economics students will have read this work. But he wrote many more such political economy studies on the transition to EMU.

On balance, Artis was a keen supporter of greater monetary unification, especially for the main continental countries, though more hesitantly for the UK, since the latter was seen to be more asymmetric in its characteristics. In addition to the obvious advantages of lower transactions costs and less (exchange rate) uncertainty, Mike prized the counter-inflationary and fiscal discipline that such a system would bring, as well as supporting the general idea of greater European unity. The downsides were the loss of an adjustment mechanism, and the Walters critique (that a single zone-wide interest rate would have the perverse effect of stimulating (depressing) more (less) inflationary regions in the zone). In an unhappily prophetic article (Artis, 1992), 'Counter-inflationary policy in the framework of the EMS', Mike argued that the Walters critique could be offset by more stabilising fiscal policy and/or exchange controls, without fully appreciating that politics would usually prevent surplus countries from fiscal expansion or deficit countries from austerity during booms, although a more kindly interpretation is that he was forewarning the European authorities as to what policy levers were needed to be put in place.

With his focus now fixed on European monetary issues, there was a clear attraction to move from Manchester University, in a somewhat Eurosceptic country, where European issues always ranked behind domestic ones, to a newly established centre, the Robert Schuman Centre at the European University Institute (EUI), which specialised in the subject that Mike now took for his own. Moreover, the EUI site (San Domenico near Fiesole outside Florence) is breathtakingly beautiful, and both the academic community and the wider Italian population naturally welcoming.

The European University Institute at Florence

Mike applied in 1994 for the advertised joint position of a Chair in the Economics Faculty, and the (first) economist to join the newly established Robert Schuman Centre for Advanced Studies. The EUI was a good place to go to develop his research agenda. It had a prestigious reputation. Being a graduate Institute it had a favourable salary/teaching requirement trade-off.

He went through the normal interview process, chaired by the first Director of the Schuman Centre, Yves Mény, who was to become a close friend. Yves recalls that Mike was clearly the best candidate, but the proposal to appoint him was not easy as it was the very first case of a joint appointment between a department and the newly established Schuman Centre. At the time, Mike only spoke English and French, the former with a northern accent that apparently some there found hard to understand. He subsequently learned Italian; a good knowledge but initially reticent about speaking. These communication difficulties were, however, fully offset by his kindness and constant availability to students and colleagues.

Mike was appointed to this joint position from 1 January 1995. The term of the Chair was for four years, renewable once for another four years. The main teaching function was the training and supervising of PhD students, of whom Mike had twenty-three during his years there, from cohorts ranging from 1993 to 2002, and from nine countries. Four of these, Fiorella de Fiore, Martin Ellison, Marcel Fratzscher and Mathias Hoffmann, along with Ramon Marimon of the EUI, organised a conference in his honour in June 2016 at EUI. Several of his students collaborated with him in research and publication.

The second main function was to undertake and encourage research, especially on European issues. Mike took part enthusiastically both in his own research, described later in this memoir, and in supporting the research of others. He played an important role in the seminar programme and in the establishment of the Pierre Werner Chair of Monetary Integration, first held by Giancarlo Corsetti. Mike was never pushy, and although a little hesitant at times in the new environment, he got on extremely well with the other economists (and other academics) who followed him there, such as Roberto Perotti, Rick van der Ploeg and Giuseppe Bertola.

His research there mainly followed two separate, but connected, strands, both related to EMU. The first, more technical, set of papers analysed the statistical inter-relationships between the EU economies (and with the United States and Japan), focused primarily on the relationship between the UK and the core countries of EMU—for example, Germany, France, Benelux. The second set consisted of a series of macroeconomic commentaries on the concurrent political economy developments in EMU—for example: Gordon Brown's five tests for UK membership of the single currency; the Stability and Growth Pact; EU unemployment; and an inflation target for the ECB—which were closely followed in policy circles in the UK.

The first set includes a sizeable series of joint papers with Wenda Zhang, who moved to be with Mike at the EUI later in 1995, before subsequently returning (in 1996) to Manchester Metropolitan University. Mike was the senior economist, driving many of the ideas, but Wenda, a mathematical economist, will have done the greater part of the technical exercises. These include works on common European Business Cycles, on Clustering in EMU, on European Interest Rate Linkages and on European Exchange Rate Linkages.

Of these statistical studies, those seeking to assess the extent of 'clustering' between countries are, in our view, the most original and insightful, resulting in countries ranked in their closeness of relationships. While this did not lead to any major surprises (there was a central core European Group, a separate Northern Group—UK, plus Ireland and Scandinavia—and a Club Med Group), it allowed such common understandings to be nicely quantified and graphically displayed in a useful way. In particular, Mike and Wenda were able to show the clusters of countries pictorially as faces, or emoji, where each aspect of the face represented the closeness of each linkage, with Germany, as the anchor country, and North America and Japan disapproving or unimpressed.

Before the ERM was formed in 1979 there was a single world business cycle, largely led by the United States. After 1979, however, there was a core of continental European countries whose economies moved in concert with Germany, the anchor country, but separately from the United States. However, the UK was not in this group. Instead, along with the main Scandinavian countries, its currency continued to fluctuate in conjunction with the United States.

These findings were a challenge for him, since he would clearly have preferred the UK to adopt a much closer European involvement. He had to face the issue squarely and his conclusion in 2000 was that:

> The evidence reviewed in this paper suggests no 'strong' economic case for participation in the EMU. If anything, the organizing framework of the OCA approach suggests that the UK might be right to stay outside; in particular its stochastic experience is different from that of the 'core group' within the Eurozone and on these grounds the UK will need a stabilizing policy instrument. Membership of EMU would remove the possibility of using monetary policy and a floating (or adjustable) exchange rate in that role. Reliance on labour-market flexibility alone is unlikely to be enough and, in the event of joining, there will be a premium on fiscal policy flexibility. (Artis, 2000, 28)

Throughout, the analysis was conducted in terms of optimal currency area theory, following Mundell (1961) and later Krugman (1990). Mike's general concern was whether, in the light of optimal currency theory (OCA), the economic benefits would outweigh the economic costs of joining. Relatively little attention was paid to more political economy issues, though he did not disguise that he himself was highly sympathetic to greater European federalism. For example, in October 1990 he was one of the lead signatories of a letter to the *Independent* outlining the 'Advantages of a Single Currency' and advocating UK participation.

Despite Wenda Zhang's subsequent return to Manchester, the main technical side of Mike's research continued to be on the dating of business cycles, in the UK, the Eurozone and other developed countries, and the linkages (transmission mechanisms) between cycles in different countries, especially in relation to the key anchor countries of Germany and the United States.

As time passed, the econometric and analytical techniques that he used became increasingly sophisticated. A research exercise that had begun using simple cross-correlations between countries moved on to Markov switching auto-regressions and observed transition vector auto-regression models. Subsequently the same techniques were used to explore whether the transitional states of Eastern Europe were well suited (on optimal currency grounds) to join EMU, with a generally positive conclusion.

His research flourished at the EUI and he loved the relaxed, cheerful Italian lifestyle, as well as the food and wine (although he was not a big drinker), yet retained his love of English tea. His stay at the EUI was one of the happiest periods of his life. Even after his renewal finished at the end of 2003, he returned every summer to EUI as a Visiting (Emeritus) Professor from June 2004 until June 2009, unpaid but with full facilities.

One of the more unusual episodes of his research career occurred there in 1997–8. One of his junior colleagues, Marco Buti (now—in 2017—the Director-General for Economic Affairs at the European Commission) and the mayors of two local townships, Fiesole and Pontassieve, had the idea of running a behavioural economics experiment, to issue euro-coins and a euro 'voucher-banknote' in advance of the actual true euro issue in 1999, to see, for example, how the euro and the lira might jointly circulate. Mike was enlisted to act as a senior proponent, to provide greater academic gravitas, and he participated wholeheartedly. The experiment operated as follows:

> The euro symbols were: a one-euro coin, a half-euro coin and a 3 euro 'voucher-banknote'. Following the approval of the Banca d'Italia, they were produced by the Zecca dello Stato and Poligrafico dello Stato (State Mint) and the exchange rate was fixed at 2000 lire for 1 euro. From October 1, 1997 until March 31, 1998 these 'euro symbols' circulated alongside the lira in the municipalities of Fiesole and Pontassieve, which at the time counted 15,000 and 20,000 inhabitants respectively. Once the experiment was over, the two populations had a 3-month time for withdrawal....
>
> Every shop involved in the project received a kit including stickers and displays which had to help identify the business' adherence to the experiment. Other marketing devices were also conceived and included in the kit, which was also sent to the banks: posters, brochures, displays, price lists and price labels.
>
> The project 'Ecco l'Euro!' consisted in fact in a wide range of initiatives including all the economic and social actors of the time on the territory of Fiesole and Pontassieve, in order to address a multiple-objective goal. (Buti, 1998, 1–3)

After his formal position at EUI ended, he stayed on in 2004 as an External Professorial Fellow. In 2005 he was awarded a George Fellowship at the Bank of England, January to July, though he and Shirley continued to live primarily at Fiesole. But then, in 2005, he was approached to take up an Economics Chair and become Director of the Institute for Political and Economic Governance (IPEG) at the Manchester Regional Economic Centre at Manchester University, though he kept close ties to EUI. Consequently, it is not really possible to mark any break between research done at EUI and in his second stint at Manchester. While the main thrust continued to be on economic cycles in different regions and countries, he did open a new research subject with Mathias Hoffmann, explaining why a reduction in home bias, which undoubtedly had occurred as a result of greater globalisation and financial integration, failed to show up in econometric tests.

In the final years of his academic career, Mike found another regular co-author, Toshihiro Okubo from Kobe University. Together they published seven papers, all related to spatial interactions amongst business cycles. There were two new twists in that they studied much longer historical time periods, and they began to explore regional cyclical relationships within countries (for example, the UK and Japan). In both these new sub-fields, Mike worked with others, such as George Chouliarakis and Pahatch Harischandra on cycle synchronisation and with Christian Dreger and Konstantin Kholodilin, on regional business cycles. Having been appointed the Welsh Assembly Visiting Professor at Swansea in 2008, he also researched the timing of cycles in unemployment for each unitary authority in Wales.

The crowning achievement in these later years was the international symposium that he initiated and largely organised on 'Business cycle behaviour in historical perspective', held at the University of Manchester in 2009. Most of the papers presented there were published in a special issue of the *Manchester School* (Volume 79, Number 2, March 2011). Not only did this issue include two of his joint papers but he was also a Guest Editor, and the Introduction came out under his name.

Regrettably, by this time he was no longer capable of continuing his academic career. On the way driving home to his house in Knutsford on 30 October 2009 he suffered a severe stroke. Initially it was hoped that he might recover almost fully, but he was then struck down by a series of hospital infections (for example, MRSA) and became incapacitated, needing 24-hour care. His body was letting him down, yet his colleagues, especially Richard Harrington, and overseas friends who visited him can attest that his brain remained active, but unfortunately his condition deteriorated over time. He died on 8 January 2016.

Assessment

Although Mike Artis was a rounded macroeconomist, it was as a monetary economist, working largely with Mervyn Lewis, that his earlier work will be best remembered. Thereafter, he did more general work on fiscal and wage equations, culminating in his 1984 textbook. But from the mid-1980s onwards his attention shifted towards the assessment of EMU, which he analysed mainly in terms of optimal currency area theory. His chief analytical contribution to the latter lay in the applied empirical study of the regional and country inter-linkages between business cycles. In this area he became a, indeed possibly the, leading international expert.

Those who worked with him will remember Mike as a mentor and teacher who invariably brought out the best from those with whom he interacted. He was always supportive and treated others' views, even those with which he disagreed, with respect. This is perhaps best summarised by a former colleague who said simply 'he was a first class human being'.

CHARLES GOODHART
Fellow of the Academy
MERVYN LEWIS
University of South Australia

Note: An extended version of this memoir, also including a comprehensive Bibliography of Artis' publications, and Acknowledgements of his many friends who helped us prepare this publication, is now available on the website of the London School of Economics, Financial Markets Group, Special Paper Series (http://www.lse.ac.uk/fmg/dp/specialPapers/home.aspx), under the heading M. J. Artis.

References

Artis, M. J. (1961) 'Liquidity and the attack on quantity theory', *Oxford Bulletin of Statistics*, 23, 343–66.

Artis, M. J. (1963a) 'Monetary policy and financial intermediaries: the hire purchase finance houses', *Bulletin of the Oxford University Institute of Economics and Statistics*, 25, 11–46.

Artis, M. J. (1963b) *Foundations of British Monetary Policy* (Oxford).

Artis, M. J. (1968) 'The Monopolies Commission report', *Bankers' Magazine*, 206 (1494, September), 128–35.

Artis, M. J. (1970) 'Short-term economic forecasting at the N.I.E.S.R.', in K. Hilton and D. F. Heathfield (eds.), *The Economic Study of the United Kingdom* (London), pp. 443–62.

Artis, M. J. (1972) 'Fiscal policy for stabilisation', in W. Beckerman (ed.), *The Economic Record of the Labour Government* (London), pp. 262–99.

Artis, M. J. (1981) Is there a wage equation?', in A. S. Courakis (ed.), *Inflation, Depression and Economic Policy in the West* (London), pp. 65–80.

Artis, M. J. (1984) *Macroeconomics* (Oxford).

Artis, M. J. (1988) 'How accurate is the World Economic Outlook? A post mortem on the short-term forecasting at the IMF', in *Staff Studies for the World Economic Outlook* (Washington, DC: International Monetary Fund), pp. 1–49.

Artis, M. J. (1989) 'International economic policy coordination; theory and practice', *Oxford Review of Economic Policy*, 5, 83–93.

Artis, M. J. (1992) *Counter-inflationary Policy in the Framework of the EMS*, Centre for Economic Policy Research, Discussion Paper 649, http://cepr.org/active/publications/discussion_papers/dp.php?dpno=649 (accessed 15 June 2017)

Artis, M. J. (2000) 'One size fits all? EMU and Procrustes', in M. J. Artis, A. Weber and E. Hennessy (eds.), *The Euro—a Challenge and Opportunity for Financial Markets* (London), pp. 19–28.

Artis, M. J. and Bladen-Hovell, R. (2001) 'European Monetary Union', in M. J. Artis and F. Nixson (eds.), *The Economics of the European Union* (Oxford), pp. 290–313.

Artis, M. J., Cobham, D. and Bladen-Hovell, R. (1991) 'The background', 'A model-based analysis' and 'Summary and appraisal', in M. J. Artis and D. Cobham (eds.), *Labour's Economic Policies, 1974–1979* (Manchester), pp. 1–18, 88–103 and 266–77.

Artis, M. J. and Currie, D. A. (1981a) 'Monetary targets and the exchange rate: a case for conditional targets', *Oxford Economic Papers*, 33, 176–200.

Artis, M. J. and Currie, D. A. (1981b) 'Monetary targets and the exchange rate', in W. A. Eltis and P. J. N. Sinclair (eds.), *The Money Supply and the Exchange Rate* (Oxford), pp. 176–200.

Artis, M. J. and Lee, N. (eds.) (1995) *The Economics of the European Union: Policy and Analysis* (Oxford).

Artis, M. J. and Lewis, M. K. (1974) 'The demand for money: stable or unstable?', *The Banker*, 124, 239–47.

Artis, M. J. and Lewis, M. K. (1976) 'The demand for money in the UK: 1963–1973', *Manchester School*, 44, 147–81.

Artis, M. J. and Lewis, M. K. (1981) *Monetary Control in the United Kingdom* (London).

Artis, M. J. and Lewis, M. K. (1984) 'How unstable is the demand for money in the UK?', *Economica*, 51, 473–6.

Artis, M. J. and Lewis, M. K. (1991) *Money in Britain* (London).

Artis, M. J. and Lewis, M. K. (1993) 'Après le déluge: monetary and exchange-rate policy in Britain and Europe', *Oxford Review of Economic Policy*, 9, 36–61.

Artis, M. J. and Miller, M. H. (1979) 'Inflation, real wages and the terms of trade', in J. K. Bowers (ed.), *Inflation, Development and Integration: Essays in Honour of A. J. Brown* (Leeds). pp. 55–86.

Artis, M. J. and Nachane, D. M. (1990) 'Wages and prices in Europe: a test of the German leadership hypothesis', *Weltwirtschaftliches Archiv*, 126, 59–77.

Artis, M. J. and Nixson, F. (2001) 'Introduction' in M. J. Artis and F. Nixson (eds.), *The Economics of the European Union* (Oxford), pp. 1–2.

Artis, M. J. and Nobay, A. R. (1969) 'Two aspects of the monetary debate', *National Institute Economic Review*, 49, 33–51.

Artis, M. J. and Ostry, S. (1986) *International Economic Policy Coordination* (London: Chatham House Papers, 30).

Artis, M. J. and Wallace, R. H. (1971) 'Fiscal policy in post-war Australia', in N. Runcie (ed.), *Readings in Australian Monetary and Fiscal Policy* (London), pp. 351–481.

Buti, M. (1998) *Report of the Scientific Committee on the Euro Experiment*. Unpublished European University Institute document, originally in Italian, translated by M. Buti.

Committee on the Working of the Monetary System (1959) *Report of the Committee on the Working of the Monetary System* (London, Cmnd. 827).

Dow, J. C. R. (1959) 'Memorandum of Evidence submitted by Mr. J. C. R. Dow, on the Economic Effect of Monetary Policy, 1945–57', in *Radcliffe Report: Committee on the Working of the Monetary System, Principal Memoranda of Evidence*, Vol. 3, pp. 76–105, especially Figure 1C, p. 102.

Goodhart, C. A. E. and Crockett, A. (1970) 'The importance of money', *Bank of England Quarterly Bulletin*, 10 (2), 159–98.

Gurley, J. G. and Shaw, E. S. (1956) 'Financial intermediaries and the saving-investment process', *The Journal of Finance*, 11, 257–76.

Gurley, J. G. and Shaw, E. S (1960) *Money in a Theory of Finance* (Washington, DC).

Johnson, H. G. (ed.) (1972) *Readings in British Monetary Economics* (Oxford).

Krugman, P. (1990) 'Policy problems of a monetary union', in P. De Grauwe and L. Papademos (eds.), *The European Monetary System in the 1990s* (London and New York), pp. 48–64.

Laidler, D. and Parkin, M. (1975) 'Inflation: a survey', *Economic Journal*, 85, 741–809.

Mundell, R. A. (1961) 'A theory of optimum currency areas', *American Economic Review*, 51, 657–65.

National Board for Prices and Incomes (1967), *Bank Charges*, Report no. 34, Cmnd. 3292 (London).

Paish, F. W. (1959) 'Memorandum of Evidence submitted by Prof. F. W. Paish, MC, on the "The Future of the British Monetary Policy"', in *Radcliffe Report: Committee on the Working of the Monetary System*, Principal Memoranda of Evidence, Vol. 3, pp. 182–8, especially Chart 1, p. 185.

Patinkin, D. (1961) 'Financial intermediaries and the logical structure of monetary theory', *American Economic Review*, 51, 95–116.

Runcie, N. (ed.) (1971) *Readings in Australian Monetary and Fiscal Policy* (London).

JOHN ADNEY EMERTON

John Adney Emerton
1928–2015

DURING HIS TIME AS REGIUS PROFESSOR of Hebrew at the University of Cambridge John Emerton stood at the forefront of international research on the Hebrew Bible and related disciplines. In addition he assumed significant administrative positions and was tireless in several editorial roles, while at the same time he gave leadership in teaching during a period when the faculties in Cambridge in this field were exceptionally strong.

I

The path to this position was clear enough once he had embarked on his academic studies at Oxford in 1947, but there was nothing in his family background to explain his particular choice of subject for his first degree. He was born on 5 June 1928 in Winchmore Hill in North London as a first son to Adney Spencer Emerton and Helena Mary (née Quin). His father was an accountant with the family firm which became United Dairies. In 1938 the family moved the short distance to an area of Southgate known as Lakenheath, which meant that John attended Minchenden School there. He was clearly successful, gaining entrance to Corpus Christi College, Oxford, to read Theology. This was from the start a response to his strong sense of vocation to the Anglican ministry, fulfilled by ordination some five years later. This vocation was nurtured primarily at school and at the local Anglican church. Some of his Minchenden friends were committed Christians; of them, some were later ordained and Emerton kept in touch with them throughout his life. In addition, the friendly vicar, the church services and the youth group in the strongly evangelical Anglican church local to his home became important to him. They taught him to read the Bible and at first to adopt a rather puritan lifestyle. His tutor at Corpus, Christopher Evans,[1] was certainly an influential figure in educating him initially into wider intellectual pastures.

While studying for his first BA he quickly learned to appreciate in particular the teaching of Hebrew Old Testament texts by the Reader in Semitic Philology in the Faculty of Oriental Studies, G. R. Driver.[2] He was also inspired by the lectures of the Jewish scholar Chaim Rabin. Thus it came about that while completing his formal training for ordination at Wycliffe Hall in Oxford he also studied for a second BA in Oriental Studies. This comprised principally further study in Hebrew (including post-Biblical Hebrew) and Aramaic (including especially Syriac), but other Semitic languages were not ignored as important cognate material; it is remembered especially that while he was attending lectures relevant to an ecclesiastical vocation a grammar of Ugaritic or whatever might well be simultaneously studied under the desk.

Those two years were important in other ways than merely gaining another first class BA to add to his previous one in Theology. He was a member of a student Bible discussion group and was painfully shy in social terms. Another member, a young woman called Norma Bennington, who was studying natural sciences (including the study of crystallography with Dorothy Hodgkin), had accepted an invitation by a member of the group to learn Arabic with him for an hour a week. John inquired whether she might like to add Hebrew to her repertoire. Hebrew being a language in which the greater part of the Bible was written, she agreed, and it was some time before she realised that he had ulterior motives. Eventually matters became clearer and in the long run Hebrew trumped Arabic. John and Norma were married two years after he had left Oxford and by then was in Durham, and, as we shall see, it is difficult now to imagine how his career might otherwise have developed.

Following ordination in 1952 John went for one year to Birmingham as a curate in the Cathedral and also as an assistant lecturer in the University. This was about as close as he ever came to what we might call a conventional church appointment, and a career in that direction was

---

[1] See M. D. Hooker, 'Christopher Francis Evans, 1909–2012', *Biographical Memoirs of Fellows of the British Academy*, XIII (Oxford, 2014), pp. 195–214.
[2] See Emerton's own appreciative biographical memoir, 'Godfrey Rolles Driver, 1892–1975', *Proceedings of the British Academy*, 63 (1977), pp. 345–62, reprinted in C. E. Bosworth (ed.), *A Century of British Orientalists (1902–2001)* (Oxford, 2001), pp. 103–19.

never seriously considered. This should not be misinterpreted to indicate that his ordination was somehow insignificant. As already mentioned, he had a very strong sense of vocation, and although this was never a matter for display in any academic setting it was an underlying motivation behind much of what he did. He always played a supportive role in college chapel or local parish church (he favoured especially conducting the early morning communion service and he was devoted to the 1662 Book of Common Prayer). Moreover as a teacher of many who were making the transition from an uninformed faith to trying to come to terms with the results of responsible biblical scholarship he could be sympathetic, if never compromising, having himself trodden that same path years before.

The procedures for academic appointments in those days were not always quite as they are today. During Emerton's year in Birmingham Professor T. W. Thacker, an Egyptologist with an interest in Semitic studies and Director of the School of Oriental Studies in the University of Durham, wrote to Driver to ask if he knew of anyone who would be capable of teaching Hebrew. In consequence Emerton was appointed as lecturer in Hebrew and Aramaic at Durham. Driver's influence was equally influential two years later when Emerton was appointed as a lecturer in the Divinity Faculty at Cambridge, a post he held for seven years from 1955. All this was without a doctorate or any publications whatsoever, but rested simply on a star-studded undergraduate career which included winning several prizes such as the Canon Hall Junior Greek Testament Prize and the Hall-Houghton Junior Septuagint Prize—the Senior Prize followed a couple of years later—and also being the Kennicott Hebrew Fellow in his last undergraduate year (which no doubt also helped an Anglican ordinand financially).

II

Although Emerton's reputation came over time to be firmly centred on his expertise in many aspects of Old Testament study (and this was the subject he was first appointed to teach in Cambridge), the range of subjects on which he published in those early years is already marked by astonishing breadth. Perhaps surprisingly, several of his first published articles concerned New Testament subjects.[3] He used to enjoy attending the senior

---

[3] Forty-eight of Emerton's articles were published shortly before his death in G. Davies and R. Gordon (eds.), *Studies on the Language and Literature of the Bible: Selected Works of J. A.*

New Testament seminar in those days (led at that time by C. F. D. Moule[4]) and always regretted that pressure of other duties prevented him from continuing with this when he later returned to Cambridge in a more senior position. No doubt several of his earliest articles had a first airing in that setting, not least his proposed explanation for the number of fish—153— recorded in John's gospel as having been caught during one of Jesus's post-resurrection appearances (*SLLB* 41). He reports that he was aware of eighteen previous suggested explanations. His own, a nineteenth, evidently occurred to him in bed one night, as Norma ruefully recalls.[5] The language that Jesus spoke[6] and the Aramaic background of the words of institution in the Eucharist (*SLLB* 40 and 42) are among several other such articles.

Second, two articles relate to the Aramaic portions of the book of Daniel, one of which has become a classic (*SLLB* 31). In the vision described in Daniel 7 the seer sees one 'like the son of man' approaching 'the Ancient of Days', and the importance of this for New Testament scholarship relating to Jesus as well as the history of Old Testament religion is obvious. In his article Emerton developed a whole new way of tackling the question of the origins of this imagery by appeal to the descriptions of the god El and one of his sons, Baal, as known from the second millennium BCE Ugaritic texts. Though Ugarit/Ras Shamra is sited on the coast of modern Syria it is clear that the religion of its inhabitants had much in common with that of the Southern Levant as a whole, often dubbed 'Canaanite'. There are many points of comparison and contrast, in terms of language, literature and religion, with the world of the subsequent Old Testament, and the conclusion of Emerton's study was that 'the enthronement of the Son of man by an aged deity goes back to Canaanite myth and ritual, and that behind the figure of the Son of man lies Yahwe, and ultimately Baal'. How could this be explained, given that we are

---

Emerton (Supplements to *Vetus Testamentum*, 165; Leiden, 2015). Where an article to which I refer in the following is included in this volume I cite it as *SLLB*, followed by the number of the article in the volume. He published a total of more than 130 articles in journals and invited contributions to books.

[4] See W. Horbury, 'Charles Francis Digby Moule, 1908–2007', *Biographical Memoirs of Fellows*, VIII (Proceedings of the British Academy 161; Oxford, 2009), pp. 281–310; among several pages descriptive of the seminar in this memoir, Emerton's participation is noted on p. 291.

[5] The solution involves a somewhat complicated form of *gematria* based on the place names in Ezekiel 47:10 and the mathematical relation between 17 and 153, the latter being the sum total of every number from 1 to 17. It is perhaps not necessary to rehearse all the details here.

[6] See J. A. Emerton, 'Did Jesus speak Hebrew?', *Journal of Theological Studies*, new series 12 (1961), 189–202, and see too his later and broader *SLLB* 44 (1973).

dealing with texts written some thousand or more years apart? Emerton's proposal was that memories of the older mythological narratives were preserved in the Jerusalem cult tradition, the city having been Canaanite/ Jebusite before it fell into Israelite hands. It is now commonplace to detect comparable links between Canaanite and Israelite religious traditions in the Psalms, most obviously, and also elsewhere, not least in apocalyptic literature. While such comparisons were not wholly new with Emerton's article, there can be no doubt with the advantage of hindsight that his work here helped bring such research into the mainstream. It is also of note that in this article he already showed mastery of the Ugaritic sources alongside the Aramaic, and later he was to publish several articles that dealt with particular problems in those texts (e.g. *SLLB* 25, 26 and 28), as well as a useful survey of the field as a whole.[7]

The third area of his early research is one for which he is not, perhaps, always given the credit he deserves, not least because it is centred in a part of the field much less frequently entered. The Hebrew Bible was translated into several languages during the centuries which precede by some way the manuscripts of the Hebrew text which we have available to us now. Printed Hebrew Bibles are usually based on a manuscript from the start of the second Christian millennium, well over a thousand years, therefore, after the time when the texts were first written. Of course, the Dead Sea Scrolls take us back long before that, more or less to the turn of the eras, and although the whole of the Hebrew Bible has not survived among them enough of it has to have transformed our understanding of the preservation and transmission of the text in those early centuries. Despite this, the value of the early translations for textual criticism as well as for the light that they shed on their host communities remains important. Pride of place goes to the Greek translation, usually referred to as the Septuagint. It is of pre-Christian origin and has a complicated transmission history of its own. Emerton contributed to one aspect of that in his early years,[8] but far more innovative was his work on the Syriac Peshitta. The main focus of his attention at first, however, was not a book that was translated from the Hebrew Bible but rather from the Apocrypha, being originally composed in Greek, and thus it is not as widely known outside specialist circles as it might otherwise have been.

[7] J. A. Emerton, 'What light has Ugaritic shed on Hebrew?', in G. J. Brooke, A. H. W. Curtis and J. F. Healey (eds.), *Ugarit and the Bible: Proceedings of the International Symposium on Ugarit and the Bible, Manchester, September 1992* (Münster, 1994), pp. 53–69.
[8] J. A. Emerton, 'The purpose of the second column of the Hexapla', *Journal of Theological Studies*, new series 7 (1956), 79–87; see too his later *SLLB* 43 (1971).

While still the Kennicott Hebrew Fellow in Oxford (and thus while still reading for his second BA), he took up a suggestion from W. D. McHardy[9] that he might undertake a critical edition of the Syriac Peshitta of the Wisdom of Solomon (quite why that particular book is not recorded). This work, which in some respects could be thought of as the equivalent of a doctoral project,[10] occupied him, along with his other teaching and smaller research projects, over the next six or seven years. In his 100-page introduction he documents how he tried to get access to all available manuscript sources in European and American collections, arguing that 'there should be an edition of at least one book for which an attempt has been made to collate every available ms'. These are then described each in turn and grouped into their appropriate textual families. Not all by any means contribute directly to the establishment of the original text (so far as this can be done), but of course they all have their part to play in the history of the Syriac-speaking Church. The edition itself which follows is based on a manuscript from the Ambrosian Library in Milan and is accompanied by a full critical apparatus.

Apart from the importance of this work in its own right, it needs to be set in its context in the history of Peshitta studies. Indeed, this history may partially explain McHardy's original suggestion. In 1959, the year in which Emerton's volume was published, the Peshitta Project was formally established in Leiden in the Netherlands. It had a prehistory, however, for in 1953 at the first Congress of the International Organization for the Study of the Old Testament (which rather remarkably, by the way, Emerton already attended) the Danish scholar E. Hammershaimb proposed that the Organization should consider the question of the preparation of a critical edition of the Old Testament Peshitta. In taking this up, the Organization set up an Advisory Committee under the chairmanship of D. Winton Thomas, Regius Professor of Hebrew in Cambridge, and one to whom Emerton in his Preface pays a handsome tribute for all his support and careful reading of his draft. McHardy was another scholar who was closely consulted at the time, and at the 1956 Congress (the Organization has a Congress every three years) he was invited to serve as editor-in-chief of an accompanying *editio minor*, though he withdrew in

---

[9] McHardy was at that time Samuel Davidson Professor of Old Testament Studies in King's College London, but he lived in Oxford where he had previously been lecturer in Aramaic and Syriac and where he was later to become the Regius Professor of Hebrew. He will thus have been a close colleague when Emerton returned to Oxford in 1962.

[10] In fact in 1960 he was awarded a Cambridge BD for it, a senior degree usually based on published work.

1959 without much having been accomplished. At the Congress held that same year in Oxford under the presidency of Driver, the project was formally established with Professor Piet de Boer of Leiden as editor.

Emerton was already in touch with de Boer as he prepared his edition, and it was a relationship that became even more important later in his career. De Boer was enormously active during the 1950s and 1960s, networking with the widest possible spectrum of scholars in the field of Old Testament and related studies, and he was a real entrepreneur in the matter of establishing publication outlets. More immediately relevant, he was at this time also busy collecting microfilmed copies of manuscripts of the Peshitta from the Middle East as well as from occidental libraries. Among his correspondence,[11] only a part of which is extant, a letter from Driver (22 March 1959) thanks him for 'being so good to Emerton; he is one of my most promising pupils in recent years'. Two relevant letters from Emerton himself survive in that particular collection. In one (18 August 1958), which is principally about some quite unrelated matter, he reports that 'my work on the Peshitta of Wisdom is slowly but steadily nearing completion. I hope to finish it in the next few weeks', and on 11 October he sent the typescript itself with a covering letter saying 'I am very grateful to you for the interest which you have shown in this work of mine. I hope that you will find it satisfactory.' He asked de Boer to consider it for a new monograph series which he had just established, Studia Post-Biblica (which had both Thomas and McHardy on its board at that time). It seems clear from this that de Boer was indeed aware of the work (the Preface thanks him for accepting the work for publication and says that he 'has helped me in several other ways') but that he had not, so to speak, supervised it, as one might otherwise have supposed.

Be that as it may, Emerton's edition clearly served very much as a template for the new project, and he was in close and frequent correspondence with de Boer about his own pioneering contribution to it during its early years.[12] This was an edition of the Song of Songs. About sixty letters from Emerton survive, and the spread of dates (for instance, nothing from 1962 or 1964) suggests that these are not complete. Many of the letters take

---

[11] His archives are housed now in the Leiden University Library. I am most grateful to Professor Arie van der Kooij for facilitating my access.

[12] The files of the Peshitta Project, originally kept in its rooms in Leiden, have now been moved, together with the Project itself, to Amsterdam. I am grateful to several of its former and present research workers (in particular Dr K. D. Jenner) for comments and for permission to access this material and especially to Mr G. J. Veltman for providing me with copies of Emerton's letters there.

more space explaining why he has been delayed by teaching, examining, and other commitments from progressing as fast as he could have wished than on the particular matter in hand, but nevertheless he also reports on weeks or fortnights spent on the work in vacations, collating manuscripts (with de Boer sometimes sending along microfilms or photographs of ones not previously considered), discussing how exactly the apparatus should be formatted, and so on. He is aware that he is in some senses setting a benchmark for those who will follow him and he is anxious constantly to revise his first drafts in the light of lessons learned later. He was also assiduous in fund raising, mainly from Oxford and Cambridge trust funds, to support the publication.

Several times in these letters he states that after the edition of the Song of Songs he wishes next to prepare the edition of Leviticus, and a 1962 article I mention later (*SLLB* 32) suggests that he was already working on this. On 26 December 1961, for instance, he wrote that he hoped (but could not promise) to complete it by the end of 1963. No letter in the collection that I have seen, however, explains why this failed to materialise, nor is it mentioned in the Preface to the edition of Leviticus when it eventually appeared.[13] It can only be surmised that the pressures of time when he moved to Oxford delayed progress and perhaps that when he was elected to the chair in Cambridge he felt that he should devote his main energies to more mainstream Hebrew and Old Testament projects.

When the Peshitta Project published a sample edition in 1966, Emerton's new edition of the Song of Songs stood as the first item.[14] Dr Piet Dirksen, who wrote his doctoral thesis on the Peshitta of Judges[15]

---

[13] D. J. Lane et al., *The Old Testament in Syriac According to the Peshitta Version*, I/ii and II/i b: *Leviticus—Numbers—Deuteronomy—Joshua* (Leiden, 1991).

[14] J. A. Emerton (ed.), *The Old Testament in Syriac According to the Peshitta Version, Sample Edition: Song of Songs—Tobit—4 Ezra* (Leiden, 1966). Interest in this particular book may have been stimulated by his work as part of the team that was responsible for the Song of Songs in the *New English Bible*.

[15] See P. B. Dirksen, *The Transmission of the Text in the Peshitta Manuscripts of the Book of Judges* (Monographs of the Peshitta Institute 1; Leiden, 1972). In his account of the history of the Project Dirksen writes that 'The harbinger was J. A. Emerton's *The Peshitta of the Wisdom of Solomon*, which appeared in the year the Peshitta Project made its start, and may to a great extent be regarded as a model for a number of other studies' (P. B. Dirksen, 'In retrospect', in W. Th. van Peursen and R. B. ter Haar Romeny [eds.], *Text, Translation, and Tradition: Studies on the Peshitta and its Use in the Syriac Tradition Presented to Konrad D. Jenner on the Occasion of his Sixty-Fifth Birthday* [Monographs of the Peshitta Institute 14; Leiden, 2006], pp. 25–37 [29]). For comparable remarks, see P. A. H. de Boer, in the preface to *The Old Testament in Syriac According to the Peshitta Version*, I/i: *Genesis – Exodus* (Leiden, 1977), p. vi.

and later became a director of the Project (1982–93), wrote to tell me that the Introduction to Emerton's edition of *Wisdom*

> provided a framework for ordering and analyzing the textual material for Judges. It might be maintained that Emerton's approach was the only possible way to do this type of analysis anyway, but someone had to find out, clear the path, and set the example for others. That person was Emerton ... Emerton's monograph marks a new start in Peshitta research, called for by the Peshitta Project and, linked with it, the availability of a great many Peshitta mss.

Later, in the light of continuing experience, it was decided that the project should restrict its edition to manuscripts only up until the twelfth century (something with which Emerton himself wholeheartedly agreed;[16] indeed, it is likely that he had been an active participant in the discussions which led to this decision). Both of his editions later appeared in revised format in 1979 (with the revision undertaken by David Lane[17]). The importance of his scholarly contribution to the project in its early years thus deserves wider recognition than it has generally received.

It will be convenient to note here that these editions did not exhaust his contributions to Syriac studies. In addition to a study of printed editions of the Song of Songs (1967), he wrote an influential article with the unpromising title of 'Unclean birds and the origin of the Peshitta' (*SLLB* 32) as a contribution to the unresolved question whether the Peshitta is of Jewish or of Christian origin. Later on he also prepared the best translation available of the Odes of Solomon[18] and accompanied that by two substantial articles (and a shorter one co-authored with R. P. Gordon) in which he discussed specific textual and linguistic points in that text.

In addition to these research projects during this period Emerton also worked on the Biblical text in ways that would be of benefit to the wider church. First, under Driver's chairmanship in the 1950s and 1960s he contributed to the *New English Bible* Old Testament translation, including the Song of Songs and Isaiah. Second, working with Winton Thomas from 1959 to 1962 he helped with the revision of the liturgical Psalter for the Church of England. Third, in the late 1960s and 1970s he was invited by the British and Foreign Bible Society (now the Bible Society) to chair a

---

[16] In a letter dated 13 December 1974 he wrote that he 'agree[s] entirely and enthusiastically with the general changes proposed for printing the text and the apparatus'.
[17] *The Old Testament in Syriac According to the Peshitta Version*, II/v: *Proverbs – Wisdom of Solomon – Ecclesiastes – Song of Songs* (Leiden, 1979). The main differences relate to conformity to the revised terms of reference for the edition.
[18] J. A. Emerton, 'The Odes of Solomon', in H. F. D. Sparks (ed.), *The Apocryphal Old Testament* (Oxford, 1984), pp. 683–731.

Cambridge group of Hebraists producing a translators' translation. This was a version in simplified English to serve as an accurate and reliable basic text for overseas translators in local languages who knew some English but no Hebrew or Greek.

III

When Driver retired in 1962 it was, perhaps, inevitable that Emerton should apply and be appointed as his successor as Reader in Semitic Philology and he became a Fellow of St Peter's College, Oxford. There can be no doubt that it was Driver who was Emerton's closest and most valued mentor and it was appropriate that Emerton dedicated his edition of the Wisdom of Solomon to him 'in gratitude for teaching, encouragement and help'—this despite the fact that Syriac was not a field of Semitic studies to which Driver himself made any very great contribution.[19] They maintained a regular and frequent correspondence on Biblical Hebrew, both of them in almost illegible handwriting, for the rest of Driver's life, each of them consulting and advising the other as equal collaborators and close friends.

Emerton now assumed the mantle of one who taught long hours by reading through large portions of the Hebrew Bible with particular attention to textual criticism and philology. Thus besides many other texts he worked right through Proverbs, for instance, on a three-year cycle, and Psalms on a five-year cycle. There were also classes on such related subjects as epigraphy, Ugaritic and Semitic philology generally. The same continued when, in 1968, he was elected Regius Professor of Hebrew in Cambridge, where he remained for the rest of his career, retiring in 1995. As Regius Professor he was a foundation member of Trinity College until he retired, and he held a Fellowship at St John's College from 1970, renewed until his death. Two or three hours of teaching most mornings was not unusual, and this was sometimes quietly extended to, for instance, taking an individual (as it might be, a New Testament PhD student) through basic Syriac grammar or the like if there was nobody else available to do so.

---

[19] The only exception is his share in the joint edition by G. R. Driver and L. Hodgson of *The Bazaar of Heracleides, Newly Translated from the Syriac and Edited with an Introduction, Notes & Appendices* (Oxford, 1925).

It was out of this teaching schedule that many of his subsequent articles arose. His preparation was so thorough in its attention to the full range of primary sources that he would come up with fresh ideas for the solution of old problems, as well, sometimes, as spotting new difficulties and proposing answers. These 'textual notes', as they have been somewhat modestly labelled (e.g. *SLLB* 10–24), typically took the form of a full explanation of how the received text has been understood in antiquity and in more recent scholarship and of why nevertheless there still remains a difficulty, a survey of relevant evidence from the ancient versions and the possible light shed by related Semitic languages on difficult vocabulary, a rigorous examination of proposed modern solutions by emendation or in other ways, and then a new proposal for a solution from one direction or another. Such studies are naturally of immense value in their treatment of any given passage, and it is helpful to have the ground cleared of so much accumulated discussion so as to sharpen the focus on the nub of the issue. Precision, clarity, sensible caution and exactitude were his hallmarks. Whether his solutions were always convincing is a matter for each to decide. My own impression has been that he was never simply wrong but equally that he was unlikely always to have been right: while some of his solutions are fully persuasive others do not always carry conviction in terms of probability.

That does nothing to lessen the importance of the body of work as a whole, however, because he exemplifies a method that was in need of emphasis during the closing decades of the twentieth century. Until the early decades of the century, scholars confronted with a textual difficulty had little choice but to consult the ancient versions and then either defend the indefensible or propose an emendation which could rarely rise above the level of the conjectural. During the twentieth century knowledge of closely related languages was either added from scratch on the basis of new discoveries (e.g. Akkadian, Ugaritic) or advanced very considerably (e.g. several forms of Aramaic). Evidence from inscriptions in Hebrew also accumulated steadily. (Evidence from Arabic had already been exploited in the medieval period, so that though it was much invoked during the period under discussion it was never likely to prove so fruitful.) In some circles proposals for new meanings of words based on these cognate languages piled up in a completely undisciplined manner, and Emerton was by no means the only scholar to sense the danger.[20] The difference was

---

[20] Mention has naturally to be made of J. Barr, *Comparative Philology and the Text of the Old Testament* (Oxford, 1968); see too E. Nicholson and J. Barton, 'James Barr, 1924–2006',

that his initial enthusiasm for Old Testament scholarship as a whole had been fired precisely by the inspirational teaching of a leader in this field and one to whom he remained loyal and grateful even as he came gradually to question some of his more excessive results. His articles thus evince something of an attempt to do more sympathetic justice to the work of Driver and his colleagues than some other critics allowed, while at the same time being unafraid to combine that with a return to the best procedures of the older school. His method was therefore thoroughly eclectic in the best sense of the word. There is no 'one approach fits all' method but a careful weighing of all possible evidence, leading sometimes down one road and sometimes another towards the favoured solution. Only one with an incomparable command of the wide breadth of sources would be able to achieve this.

Two points deserve mention here. First, Emerton was honest enough to admit that he gradually changed his approach in the direction of moderation during the course of his career. In 1995, the year of his retirement, he served as President of the International Organization for the Study of the Old Testament, with its Congress taking place in Cambridge. In his presidential paper (*SLLB* 1) he reflected on 'Comparative Semitic philology and Hebrew lexicography'. Among other points, he recalls his undergraduate days when he was 'delighted to sit at Driver's feet, excited by every lecture of his that I heard'. At the same time, the Regius Professor then was Herbert Danby, a scholar steeped in Jewish learning and whose reading of the text derived exclusively from an interpretation based on the traditional virtue of careful grammatical study as understood within inherited tradition, represented especially by the great medieval Jewish commentators. 'At the time, I tended to regard Danby's teaching as unimaginative.' Over time, however, Emerton came to a far greater appreciation of Danby's strengths, recognising them as a vital ingredient for sound textual analysis while at the same time developing stricter controls that should govern the comparative philological method, which he sets out at length in his paper. He concludes, 'I believe we need to combine the approaches of Driver and Danby—and also any more recent approaches that have proved their value. In a sense, both Driver and Danby were right.'

Second, Emerton was entirely open to changing his mind if evidence to the contrary was presented. Unlike some who defend their previous

---

Biographical Memoirs of Fellows, VII (Proceedings of the British Academy 153; Oxford, 2008), pp. 25–51.

positions even after they clearly become untenable, his quest was not for his personal reputation but for an honest evaluation of evidence as best it was known. This was dramatically illustrated in the case relating to his assessment of part of the work of his predecessor in the Cambridge chair, D. Winton Thomas, whose help early on in Emerton's career we have already noted. Throughout his time in Cambridge, and even before, Thomas had argued that the Hebrew verb *yada‘* ('to know', as usually understood) actually combined two different words, the second of which (based on Arabic evidence) meant 'be still, quiet, at rest', and in the causative theme 'to make submissive, to humiliate'. This second meaning, which was then also read back into the simple form of the verb, was proposed by Thomas for an increasing number of passages in the Old Testament in a long series of short notes and studies. His theory was widely, though by no means universally, accepted at the time.

Soon after he arrived in Cambridge, Emerton chose to gather all these proposals together and to evaluate them in the light of criticisms which had been made. Since he came to the conclusion that Thomas was usually right, it was a nice appreciative gesture by the newcomer.[21] Years later, however, Professor William Johnstone of Aberdeen read a paper at a conference in Leuven which effectively demolished the most significant parts of Thomas's use of Arabic in this connection and which therefore also rendered most of Emerton's work on the subject redundant.[22] I was present on that occasion and well remember how quickly Emerton insisted that Johnstone should publish the paper in the journal which he edited, *Vetus Testamentum*,[23] and how he himself wrote another article (*SLLB* 6) soon after, revisiting the whole question in the light of this improved understanding. It always seemed to me a rather courageous thing to have done rather than just keeping quiet.

Alongside this textual and linguistic research Emerton also wrote a wide variety of articles on literary and historical problems in the Old Testament. It had been an ambition since his earliest days to write a commentary on the book of Genesis and quite a number of articles

---

[21] J. A. Emerton, 'A consideration of some alleged meanings of *yd‘* in Hebrew', *Journal of Semitic Studies*, 15 (1970), 145–80. We may note too his much later appreciative though not uncritical article 'The work of David Winton Thomas as a Hebrew scholar', *Vetus Testamentum*, 41 (1991), 287–303.

[22] Emerton did not claim expertise in Arabic. He had consulted a colleague in Arabic studies about the matter when he wrote his first article and received reassurance on the subject. Without any malice he later accepted that he had been unintentionally misled in this regard.

[23] W. Johnstone, '*YD‘* II, "Be humbled, humiliated"?', *Vetus Testamentum*, 41 (1991), 49–62.

focused on specific problems arising from that book. He took a relatively conventional position with regard to the history of composition based on four discrete sources, and sometimes he defended this position against alternatives, whether from the more conservative angle that defended its authorial unity or from those who, for instance, dated it all far later than he preferred. Again, however, his choice of subjects for study was far from narrow, and articles could be mentioned that treated subjects relevant to Deuteronomy (a significant piece which has stood the test of time), Judges, Isaiah, the Psalms, Proverbs and Ezra-Nehemiah.

In addition he kept abreast of epigraphic discoveries and their significance not only for linguistic matters but also for wider historical and religious issues as well. One that stands out and has been cited repeatedly concerns the discovery of some inscriptions from Kuntillet 'Ajrud, about 50km south of Kadesh-Barnea (*SLLB* 27; see also 30). As he once said, seeing these on display in the Israel Museum long before their official publication, he came out of the exhibition with the idea for an article in his head. That idea concerned only a question of grammar, however, and fortunately before publishing it he developed it into a major discussion of the question prompted by these inscriptions as to whether the Israelite God Yahweh had a consort Asherah (he argued more than once that the word in these texts is better understood as a reference to asherah as a cult symbol rather than to the goddess herself, while not denying that Asherah was worshipped as a goddess in some forms of Israelite religion).

The spread of Emerton's other academic commitments during his years as Regius Professor, yet to be described, meant that his style of work was best suited to the writing of articles on which he would work with furious concentration for relatively short periods of time. He always hoped that he would be able also to complete three major books—a commentary on Genesis for the New Century Bible Commentary series and commentaries on Song of Songs and Isaiah chapters 28–39 for the International Critical Commentary. To those who knew him best during those years it always seemed questionable whether these would ever be completed, and by the time retirement came his pattern of working was perhaps too firmly established to allow him to break free. I always thought that he would be a superb lexicographer, each entry being, so to speak, a short article, with many lexemes in ancient Hebrew still requiring clarification on the basis of textual and philological research. But any self-respecting academic has more projects in mind than are ever likely to be completed, and like anyone else Emerton deserves to be credited for all his many positive achievements and not for having 'left undone those things which we ought to have done'.

IV

Enough has been said to indicate the astonishing breadth of Emerton's scholarly contributions to the field of Old Testament and related studies. Mostly using the article form rather than more extended studies he touched on a much wider variety of subjects than most of his contemporaries and yet his publications were always marked by a detailed acquaintance not only with the primary sources but also with secondary discussions throughout the nineteenth and twentieth centuries (and including occasional forays earlier as well).

This is far from exhausting an appreciation of his contribution to scholarship during his tenure of the chair in Cambridge, however. Unlike Oxford, Cambridge has been peculiar in not having an established Professor of Old Testament studies in its Faculty of Divinity, so that by convention the Regius Professor of Hebrew in the Faculty of Oriental Studies has assumed responsibility for the different aspects of the subject in both Faculties. Emerton took this responsibility most seriously in both academic and administrative matters. On the latter, though never seeking a position higher up the University ladder, so to speak, he was extremely conscientious in all Faculty matters, never missing a Board meeting in either Faculty if he could help it and at one time chairing them both simultaneously. He was the opposite of the politically astute kind of academic who is able to manipulate the system to the advantage of his or her own pet interests. Rather, his almost innocent openness and sense of fairness towards colleagues in other subjects occasionally meant that others were able to take advantage of his integrity to their own advantage and to his loss. Nevertheless, he ensured the smooth running of the subject for which he was responsible, much to his close colleagues' relief.

In addition to his own research he did all he could to encourage that of others. The team of colleagues in his own areas of expertise, though inevitably changing slowly over the years as some went off to more senior positions in other universities, was of exceptional strength throughout his long tenure, so that many doctoral students from around the world were attracted to study at Cambridge. While the work of supervision was shared out, of course, Emerton had by far the largest number of research students and the roll of his former pupils in senior positions both in this country and overseas is impressive. He was always supportive, working quickly on submitted work and encouraging the particular interests of each rather than pushing them to become effectively his research assistants. He never wanted to establish a 'school' or anything of that sort, and if, as some have claimed, his pupils tend to bear a family resemblance, that will only have been because they were often anxious to follow what they regarded as a path of excellence.

To bring all this activity together, he took over from its founders—Andrew Macintosh, Ronald Clements and Barnabas Lindars—the work of co-ordinating the fortnightly Old Testament Seminar once it moved from its original college setting to the Faculty of Oriental Studies.[24] The seminar not only gave colleagues and doctoral students near the end of their studies a chance to give a preliminary airing to their current work but also attracted other scholars from elsewhere, including not least many from overseas who were on sabbatical in Cambridge or who were invited to present a paper if they were visiting this country for a shorter period. This regular procession of leaders in the field from elsewhere was often the excuse for generous hospitality by John and Norma in their home.[25] It all contributed to the sense of 'buzz' about the subject in the University.

Emerton's international influence was exerted not least by his editorial activity,[26] especially in regard to the quarterly journal *Vetus Testamentum*. This journal was effectively the baby of Piet de Boer during the post-war years. It is clear from the rapid rise in circulation after its first issues in 1951 that there was a market for another international journal to set alongside the German *Zeitschrift für die alttestamentliche Wissenschaft*, though at the same time de Boer made no secret of the fact that, owing to his own wartime experiences aiding the Dutch resistance, he was keen to establish an international forum independent of a journal whose editor during the war was seriously compromised politically. To draw scholars together during the difficult years after the war de Boer had organised an

---

[24] See R. P. Gordon (ed.), *The God of Israel* (University of Cambridge Oriental Publications 64; Cambridge, 2007), p. xi. Gordon comments on the book's dedication to John Emerton that he 'set a standard of contribution from the chair that is rightly remembered as one of its most notable features during the many years that he organized the Seminar'.

[25] Norma has counted 379 such visits in her own diaries (many of them repeats, of course) and she has listed for me the names of 84 scholars from all the inhabited continents except South America.

[26] It deserves mention here that in 1988 Emerton served on a panel of otherwise Flemish-speaking scholars to investigate Dutch theological faculties at universities and theological colleges and to report to the government. This involved nine visits to the Netherlands that year.

international Old Testament congress in Leiden in 1950, and from this successful gathering both the International Organization was established and, at the formal level, *Vetus Testamentum* as its journal, with its editorial board having ultimate oversight of the triennial Congresses. De Boer edited the journal for its first 25 years, and his archives show how assiduous he was in this role. In his report to the editorial board in 1971, however, he comments that, after taking advice from one or two close associates on the board, he had approached Emerton to see if he would be willing to be nominated at the Congress in Uppsala that year to join the board in the expectation that he would assume the task of principal editor when de Boer retired. This all went through smoothly. Emerton joined the board and became Secretary of the International Organization in 1971, and he succeeded de Boer as editor in 1976. He held the post until 1997, his twenty-one years thus falling short by only a few years of de Boer's own exceptionally long period of service.

Although Emerton had help with some of the work of assessing submitted articles, especially from America, he took full personal responsibility for all aspects of the journal's presentation with an insistence on editorial excellence that few could match. Once an article was accepted in principle he would correspond with the author in hand-written letters (he never had a secretary and later he never used email) to ensure that she or he was content with even minor copy-editing details. One American colleague once expressed to me his astonishment at receiving a letter with no fewer than 86 numbered points, inviting improvements on some matters of substance but also recommending that this comma might be replaced by a semi-colon and so on.[27] Emerton insisted (quite rightly) that all secondary works should be cited in the form in which they were first published and only then, if desired, in a translated form. Many (mainly) English-speaking scholars would often document only a translated version. Part of Emerton's routine for many years thus involved teaching in the Oriental Studies Faculty for most of the morning, walking to St John's College (or less frequently Trinity College) for lunch, and then calling in at the University Library on his way back to the Faculty for meetings and the like, in order to track down and document the relevant book and page number in its original language version. All this would

---

[27] When I held the position of Secretary of the Faculty Board in Oriental Studies, which in those days included the drafting of agendas and minutes, a colleague in another subject joked with me that if I was sure to make an odd mistake in punctuation Emerton would be so concerned to have that put right that he would not take any notice of what I was actually reporting so that I could effectively cook the books. It didn't work.

then be typed into the margin of the article before it was submitted to the publisher. He also personally typed out the many short book reviews that he developed as a feature of the journal (and in fact wrote many of them himself; it is difficult to count them, because at first the authors of the notes were not named). The labour involved in preparing a fascicule of 128 pages every quarter (and it was never late), together with the additional work of editing the Supplement series, therefore, scarcely bears thinking about. Some would be dismissive of the value of such chores (and I suspect that there was an element of displacement activity here), but for Emerton it mattered that the leading international journal in his field should maintain the highest standards in every respect of which he was capable. Certainly, the senior editors at the Press (E. J. Brill of Leiden) were grateful that there was nothing for them to have to do editorially and also that the circulation of *Vetus Testamentum* was noticeably higher than its peers.

In addition, for a number of years he was the editor of the (British) Society for Old Testament Study (SOTS) monograph series, from 1964 he was the Old Testament editor (with C. E. B. Cranfield as New Testament editor[28]) for the revival of the venerable International Critical Commentary series, and he was on the less onerous editorial board of the *Zeitschrift für die alttestamentliche Wissenschaft*. These tasks were of a more spasmodic nature but nonetheless important each in its own way.

Sometimes there were signs that the burden was unsustainable. The length of time that submitted articles took to be evaluated could vary. For the most part they were treated in a timely manner, but if for some reason he found them challenging they could lie ignored. There were some submissions to the Supplement series which might also lie unread on his desk for up to a year, and the Congress volumes, which were published in that series, took longer and longer after the Congress itself to appear. Eventually this particular problem was solved by the Supplements being edited by another member of the board. Equally, editorship of the particular series of SOTS monographs for which Emerton was responsible came to be shared with R. E. Clements, who then succeeded him as sole editor. For all that, and however great the loss of time for his own research projects, Emerton's editorial work deserves to be celebrated. Many younger scholars benefited from the attention that he gave to their submissions and

---

[28] See J. D. G. Dunn, 'Charles Ernest Burland Cranfield, 1915–2015', *Biographical Memoirs of Fellows of the British Academy*, XV (Oxford, 2016), pp. 187–204.

the advice he gave them, while the quality of the journal was (and remains) outstanding.

When the Liturgical Commission of the Church of England needed a new translation of the liturgical Psalter in 1970 they asked a member, the English language scholar David Frost, to start a pilot scheme. He enlisted Andrew Macintosh, a Cambridge Hebraist, and they translated twenty-five psalms, which were published in 1973. They were joined by Emerton, who now undertook a major project for the Anglican Church which brought together his detailed knowledge of the Hebrew text of the book of Psalms with the wide variety of problems associated with it and his vocation as a scholar in holy orders. In 1972 he was asked by the Archbishops of Canterbury and York to chair a panel of eight Hebraists: himself, Macintosh and three other Anglicans, a Roman Catholic, a Methodist and a United Reformed Church member, with Frost as an English specialist, to translate a new liturgical Psalter. They worked with remarkable unanimity, and their new version incorporated Macintosh and Frost's earlier psalms. The work lasted six years. It was published as a separate volume, *The Psalms: a New Translation for Worship* (London, 1977), as well as in the *Alternative Service Book* (Cambridge, 1980), and again later as *The Cambridge Liturgical Psalter* (Cambridge, 2013); furthermore, some of its translations were used in the Penguin Classic *The Psalms in English* (London, 1996).

It was therefore a severe disappointment (to put it mildly) that the Liturgical Commission of the Church of England chose to use a different version in the subsequent *Common Worship*. The version they preferred had been developed in the United States on the basis of prior English versions by people with no knowledge of Hebrew. As initially recommended, it contained a number of serious errors and inaccuracies; indeed, this was one of the reasons why an earlier embodiment of the Liturgical Commission had decided against adopting it in 1971. A special meeting on the Psalter was held in July 1998 between members of the Liturgical Commission and a small group of biblical scholars. There was bitter antagonism between Emerton and his colleague Andrew Macintosh on the one side and the Commission members on the other. The Revd Dr Anthony Gelston of Durham University did his best to mediate between them, and probably as a result of this was asked (along with Professor John Rogerson of Sheffield, who chaired the meeting) to vet the text and propose necessary emendations. He has told me privately that 'I think all the absolute errors were removed (they were called the Gelston Noes!), but many of my other suggestions were not adopted … I believe it is a reasonably satisfactory version in its published form.' Despite this, Emerton understandably felt aggrieved that the powers that be in the church which he had sought faithfully to serve had sacrificed what he regarded as their prime responsibility to uphold careful and thorough scholarship in favour of other considerations.

By a deliciously ironical misprint, a review of the new translation in *News of Liturgy*, March 1999, appeared under the title 'The Psalter 1998: A Daft Text for Common Worship'. Emerton, with his colleagues Macintosh and Frost, seized on this to prepare a booklet for the relevant meeting of the Anglican General Synod: *'A Daft Text': The Psalter 1998. A Critique of the New Psalter* (Cambridge and Sydney, 1999). Its aim was to demonstrate that the version proposed by the Liturgical Commission should be dismissed 'as a poor translation of scripture and as a mediocre English version'. It gives a much fuller account than I have offered here concerning the whole history of the production of the text eventually adopted[29] and points out many mistakes and other defects in the version as then available. (It should be noted that this was prior to the version as corrected by Gelston and Rogerson.) The booklet was endorsed by two other members of the original panel, one of whom already was and the other of whom later became a Fellow of the British Academy: the Revd Dr E. W. Nicholson[30] and the Revd Dr W. Horbury. Despite all this effort, General Synod followed the recommendation of the Liturgical Commission, which to an outside observer looks like a triumph of politics over scholarship. Nevertheless the version whose preparation Emerton had overseen went into six national prayer books elsewhere in the world, while in this country it remains as a version approved for use by the church.

V

Emerton's years in Cambridge saw the growth from school to adult independence of his three children, Caroline, Mark and Lucy. It is fair to

---

[29] This includes the astonishing revelation that when the version was originally presented to Synod in 1997 members were assured that it had been checked 'by a group of Biblical scholars from Cambridge'. It turned out that these scholars were candidates for ordination at one of the theological colleges, two of whom had just completed one-year courses in elementary Hebrew. It is scarcely surprising, therefore, that it was later necessary to engage two real scholars, Gelston and Rogerson, for the necessary task, though they had to do their patch-up job under considerable pressure of time.

[30] See J. Barton, 'Ernest Wilson Nicholson, 1938–2013', *Biographical Memoirs of Fellows of the British Academy*, XV (Oxford, 2016), pp. 121–38.

say that the bulk of care for home and family fell on Norma's shoulders, which makes all the more remarkable her own achievement of completing a doctorate in the history of chemistry. When published as *The Scientific Reinterpretation of Form* (Ithaca, NY, 1984), it won the highly prestigious Phi Beta Kappa Society award in Science (1985). I once asked her how she managed to find the time to do this, and she replied quite simply that 'I only darn John's socks in the vacation'.

Norma went on to collect a great deal of material for a book on scientific explanations in the pre-scientific era of the Genesis creation narratives, but time taken in caring for John sadly meant she had to abandon her plans for publication. Given that, as already noted, he had harboured an ambition since student days to write a commentary on Genesis, this means that our loss on this score is double.

Outside home (and away from his beloved cats), the principal focus of Emerton's social life lay in St John's College. Elected as a Professorial Fellow in 1970, he did not hold any major college office, but he was an active supporter of the work in the chapel, assisting there regularly until 2003. He enjoyed dining and participating in the Wine Circle after dinner (it has been said of him that 'vintage port was the object of his profound devotion'[31]), using this, as well as his home, as a base for entertaining colleagues and guests. This was only one of the scenes where his boyish sense of humour could shine; he had an unending supply of humorous stories and jokes and was also an occasional author of limericks. But equally, such relaxed surroundings were the ideal setting for the kinds of gossip which are often the best way in which to advance university and wider academic life.

During the first part of his tenure in Cambridge Emerton did not take sabbaticals, partly because one of his colleagues suffered a serious road accident which left the small department, already reduced by university cuts, very short-staffed, and Emerton was, as already noted, completely committed to ensuring that the full undergraduate syllabus should be taught. In due course, however, he discovered St George's Anglican Cathedral in East Jerusalem, with its associated hospice, and the unrivalled library collections of the Dominican École biblique just down the road. This provided a more than congenial home from home, and from there he was able not only to continue his research but also to maintain the several friendships he had with colleagues in the Hebrew University. Also associated with the cathedral is St George's College, which was no

---

[31] From an obituary in the college's *The Eagle* (2016), 71.

longer able to serve its founding purpose of training for Anglican ordination throughout the Arab-speaking countries of the Middle East. It therefore reinvented itself as a base for thoughtful pilgrims who wanted to have some serious historical and archaeological input into their visits to the Holy Land, and Emerton soon became a very popular adornment to a number of such courses. The recognition of his standing and contribution by his appointment as an Honorary Canon of the Cathedral in 1984 was thus a source of particular pride, and it drew him back to Jerusalem on many subsequent visits for shorter or longer periods.[32]

Honours and distinctions that came his way included a Cambridge DD (1973), an honorary doctorate from the University of Edinburgh (1977), a fellowship of the British Academy (1979) and the award of its Burkitt Medal for Biblical Studies (1991) and a Corresponding Membership of the Akademie der Wissenschaften, Göttingen. A loyal member of the British Society for Old Testament Study, he was elected its President for 1979. Similarly, he was the President of the International Organization for the Study of the Old Testament (whose Secretary he had long been previously) from 1992 to 1995. This concluded with his presiding over the Congress which met in Cambridge in August 1995, thus coinciding, more or less, with his retirement from the Regius Chair. Following his Presidential paper he was presented with a Festschrift to mark the occasion, and another followed fifteen years later after a day at St John's College that was held to mark his eightieth birthday.[33]

Only rarely did he take up invitations to visiting positions abroad. Early on he was Visiting Professor of Old Testament and Near Eastern Studies at Trinity College, Toronto University (1960), and in 1982–3 he was a Fellow at the Institute for Advanced Studies at the Hebrew University of Jerusalem.

In 1986 he acceded to the strong invitation from a former student to spend a term as Visiting Professor at the United Theological College in Bangalore, India. While sitting on an upstairs veranda of his residence there, the door back into the room behind him blew shut and locked.

---

[32] He visited Israel some 39 times in all, including more or less annual visits between 1979 and 2009.

[33] J. Day, R. P. Gordon and H. G. M. Williamson (eds.), *Wisdom in Ancient Israel: Studies in Honour of J. A. Emerton* (Cambridge, 1995); K. Dell, G. Davies and Y. V. Koh (eds.), *Genesis, Isaiah and Psalms: a Festschrift to Honour Professor John Emerton for his Eightieth Birthday* (Supplements to *Vetus Testamentum* 135; Leiden, 2010). The latter, incidentally, includes a fine portrait by John Edwards. These volumes include more or less complete bibliographical records of Emerton's publications with a final update in *SLLB*, pp. 1 and 5.

Unwisely, he decided the best way to extricate himself from this predicament was to drop from an upstairs balcony. Given that he was extremely short-sighted and not especially athletic (though otherwise perfectly fit), almost inevitably he fell, injuring his pelvis. The long-term effect of this accident led from one hip replacement to another. He eventually began to lose free mobility because of arthritis and was reluctant to use a wheelchair in public. Thus in his last two years he was confined to his home, where he enjoyed frequent visits from colleagues and friends. After years of macular degeneration of the eyes he lost his sight, depended on Norma to read to him and effectively gave up on his academic pursuits. He was cared for with loyal devotion by Norma and he died peacefully at home on 12 September 2015, aged eighty-seven.

His legacy was a significant body of work together with a band of pupils, colleagues and friends who were strongly influenced by his example. The number who gathered for his memorial service on 27 February 2016 in St John's College chapel, including not a few from overseas, was testimony to the high regard and, indeed, affection in which he was held.

H. G. M. WILLIAMSON
Fellow of the Academy

Note: I am especially indebted to Norma Emerton for help in compiling this memoir. Among others who have offered information and advice I note with gratitude Graham Davies, Anthony Gelston, Robert Gordon, Arie van der Kooij and Andrew Macintosh. Dutch scholars formerly or currently engaged in work on the Peshitta Project who have provided helpful guidance include Piet Dirksen, Konrad Jenner and Geert Jan Veldman.

MARGARET JOY GELLING

Margaret Joy Gelling
1924–2009

MARGARET GELLING WAS A SCHOLAR OF ENGLISH PLACE-NAMES who published the material for two-and-a-half counties, played a leading role in two major reassessments of the discipline and was widely appreciated for her enthusiastic popularising of the subject in books, lectures and evening classes.

She was born Margaret Joy Midgley on 29 November 1924 in Gorton, Manchester, the youngest child (she had two older brothers) of William Albert Midgley, merchant buyer, and his wife Lucy (née Wallace). The family moved south to Sidcup when she was young, and she attended Chislehurst Grammar School; from 1942 to 1945 she read English at St Hilda's College, Oxford, the first member of her family to attend university. She was taught there by Helen Gardner, with whom she said once that she did not get on particularly well, presumably because of a difference in approach; and by Dorothy Whitelock, who taught her Old English. At that stage Gelling did not specialise in philological aspects of Old English, having no thoughts of a career in that area. After graduating she worked briefly for the civil service, but Dorothy Whitelock presciently recommended her as an assistant to Bruce Dickins, Director of the Survey of English Place-Names, in 1946–51; she worked in that position from 1946 to 1954, and later credited Whitelock with being 'entirely responsible for my involvement in place-name studies'.[1] In this post Gelling was expected to undertake general work for the Survey and for the English Place-Name Society (EPNS), including secretarial duties, but she also started work

---

[1] M. Gelling, *The Place-Names of Berkshire*, 3 vols (Cambridge, 1973–6), I, p. viii.

herself on collections of material, begun by Lady (Doris) Stenton, for the two counties of Oxfordshire and Berkshire. She went on to publish both counties for the Survey, Oxfordshire in 1953–4 (two volumes) and Berkshire in 1973–6 (three volumes); characteristically both publications incorporated innovations within the Survey series.

In 1952 Margaret married the archaeologist Peter Stanley Gelling (1925–83), a Manxman from Marown parish; his father was headmaster of the nearby school of Braddan.[2] Peter's broad interests were centred particularly on the early development of agriculture; to that end he conducted excavations in places as dispersed as Cyprus, Orkney and Peru, as well as England and his native island. Margaret accompanied him to these places, including regularly on training excavations on Orkney, where her motherly care for the team is said to have contributed greatly to overall morale. In later life she considered it a weakness that she preferred en-suite accommodation at a conference, having formerly lived for weeks in a cave high in the Andes. In 1953 Peter was appointed to a lectureship in the Department of Archaeology, University of Birmingham, and they moved to Harborne, where Margaret was to live for the rest of her life; in 1954 she resigned from her post as assistant for the EPNS, and she never held another full-time post. She used to say that her achievements illustrated the benefits of not needing to go out to work. Margaret was glad to learn from Peter's interests when considering agricultural aspects of place-names (including the interpretation of field-names, but not only those), and also in working across the interface between place-names and archaeology, for instance in considering place-name evidence for the Anglo-Saxon settlements in England, and in ensuring that the results of toponymic research were accessible to archaeologists.[3]

Peter Gelling's move to Birmingham was responsible for Margaret's lifelong association with that university, owing partly to the warm reception which she found in three departments there (History, Archaeology and English), and also to her devoted work for its Extramural Department. Margaret was a lifelong socialist, as a result of seeing the effects of deprivation when growing up in London in the 1930s; in the 1950s she switched from the Communist Party to the Labour Party, of which she remained a member. One consequence of her political views was a desire to make the results of scholarship available to people at all levels of education; her

---

[2] D. Kelly (ed.), *New Manx Worthies* (Douglas, 2006), pp. 188–90.
[3] M. Gelling, *Signposts to the Past* (London, 1978; and subsequent editions), Chapter 6, 'Place-Names and the Archaeologist', and *passim*.

commitment took concrete form both in her enduring extramural classes and lectures to local societies all around the country, and also in her books written for a general readership, in addition to her EPNS volumes and scholarly articles. Her experience in adult education not only prompted the writing of such works for wider audiences, but also informed it, by making her aware of the problems and potential misunderstandings that needed to be tackled, and of how to present complex and technical material to a lay readership. Her general introduction to the study of English place-names, *Signposts to the Past*, although it has been rather eclipsed by her later work on landscape and place-names, remains the best such work (among several good ones), both for the general reader and for the scholarly one in related disciplines.[4]

The main work of the Survey of English Place-Names, which has enjoyed the support of the British Academy since its inception in 1924, is to publish historical forms and analysis for the place-names of every English county, showing the development of those names, along with their derivations and the overall significance of the toponymy of the individual counties. In the 1920s and 1930s a county was published almost every year (a few taking two years), in cursory surveys covering the major names and some minor settlement-names, but with little treatment of lesser names. After the Second World War the approach changed significantly, with much more detailed coverage of minor names and field-names; counties therefore required multiple volumes for publication of their detailed material. Gelling's *Oxfordshire* was the second county to be published in this new form, the first having been Cumberland.[5] In addition she characteristically made two innovations in publishing that county, incorporating in the introduction a section on the geology and its influence on the settlement (an innovation which has been generally followed in subsequent counties), and also printing the full texts of the Anglo-Saxon charter-boundaries of the county, though without comment or analysis.[6]

In the other counties which she edited for the Survey, Gelling was similarly innovative. She had worked on Berkshire, for which Lady Stenton had also collected material, in parallel with Oxfordshire, and was able to concentrate fully on it after completing the first county; in 1957 she was

---

[4] Gelling, *Signposts*.
[5] A. M. Armstrong et al., *The Place-Names of Cumberland*, 3 vols (Cambridge, 1950–2); M. Gelling, *The Place-Names of Oxfordshire*, 2 vols (Cambridge, 1953–4).
[6] Gelling, *Place-Names of Oxfordshire*, I, pp. xi–xv (geology); II, pp. 483–90 (charter-boundaries).

awarded a PhD at the University of London for a thesis on the north-western part of that county. The whole county was effectively ready for publication by then, but it had to wait in a queue for volumes covering Derbyshire, the West Riding of Yorkshire, Gloucestershire, Westmorland and Cheshire to appear before it, year by year (twenty-one volumes in total). With characteristic acceptance of the facts, however unpalatable, Gelling set the completed county aside and began work on an entirely fresh one, Shropshire. When Berkshire eventually appeared twenty years later she included in the final volume, as well as the usual analysis of the county toponymy as a whole, a detailed edition and discussion of its Anglo-Saxon charter-boundaries, printing the texts in full and using her later place-name material as an essential aid to analysis and tracing their courses.[7] Anglo-Saxon boundary-clauses have subsequently become a major field of study in their own right, with valuable results for a variety of related disciplines including landscape history and dialectology; Gelling's lead has been followed by others, notably Peter Kitson, Della Hooke and the volumes of the British Academy's series of Anglo-Saxon Charters.

Gelling's third county, Shropshire, had hitherto received very little attention from toponymists, partly because of the particular skills needed for working on it owing to the large numbers of Welsh names (down to the level of field-names) in some of its western parts. Although Gelling never learnt more than basic Welsh vocabulary, she was not afraid of facing difficulties squarely, nor of recognising when she needed advice and seeking help accordingly, so this aspect did not deter her from tackling the county. One of her innovations in collecting material for it was the use of a long-running extramural class, held latterly at Shrewsbury Public Library, for excerpting name-forms from medieval documents there. (She once began a lecture, 'This talk arises out of an adult class which has been running for twenty-five years.') When it came to begin publishing the material she took another new step, making the first volume of the Survey one which covered the whole county, but only its major names (parishes and Domesday manors), and listing them in alphabetical, not geographical, order.

In her introduction Gelling stated her reasons for this new approach. First, the result was a single book which covered the whole county, appealing to general readers in a way which the detailed post-war volumes cannot; and, second, Shropshire in particular has a large number of

---

[7] M. Gelling, *The Place-Names of Berkshire*, 3 vols (Cambridge, 1973–6), III, pp. 615–794.

repeated names (such as Aston, Bourton, Preston, sometimes with distinguishing affixes), and studying those names together as groups both makes it easier to assign the individual early spellings to the right places, and also provides a better opportunity to consider the overall significance of such repetition within the name-stock.[8] A further advantage is that the presentation of the material of difficult names can open up discussion of them, which can then make possible further analysis or revision when they later arise in their geographical place in the subsequent volumes. However, there are also drawbacks to this format. The later volumes for the county necessarily have to refer back to Volume I for the full material and detailed treatment of many major names (since the alternative would be simply to repeat it), so those subsequent volumes are not self-contained for their particular geographical areas; and in terms of the total number of names *Shropshire* Volume I in fact provides considerably less depth of coverage for the county than the less-detailed pre-war volumes had done. It also contains much more detail concerning individual names (for example, in the number of early forms cited) than would be wanted by general readers, so such a volume does not altogether suit the broader readership at which it is partly aimed. An alternative approach which has been adopted by some editors has been to retain the older format for publishing the detailed material and discussion in the Survey volumes, but also to publish a separate book giving brief accounts of the names of the whole county, written specifically for a general readership.[9] Such volumes can cover larger numbers of names, and of greater variety since some of those will be of different kinds from the (historically) major names treated in *Shropshire* Volume I.[10] Both systems have advantages, and preference will depend partly upon the approach of the individual editor; the important aim of both, prompted partly by Gelling's innovation, is to make the results of the Survey accessible to a wider readership than that reached by the traditional volumes, which are necessarily detailed and technical.

Gelling did not live to complete the publication of the material for Shropshire—she died while the sixth volume was at press—but her

---

[8] M. Gelling, *The Place-Names of Shropshire* (Cambridge, 1990), I, p. ix.

[9] Some of these volumes have from 1998 been published in a Popular Series by the English Place-Name Society (see footnote 10), while others had earlier been published elsewhere by the Society's county editors (Dorset, Cornwall, Hampshire, Isle of Wight).

[10] K. Cameron, *A Dictionary of Lincolnshire Place-Names* (Nottingham, 1998); V. Watts, *A Dictionary of County Durham Place-Names* (Nottingham, 2002); B. Cox, *A Dictionary of Leicestershire and Rutland Place-Names* (Nottingham, 2005). Gelling, *Shropshire*, vol. I treats about 470 separate names in 335 pages, whereas Watts's *Durham* treats about 1,200 names in 172 pages.

collections for the remainder of the county are being edited for publication by a team based at the Institute for Name-Studies, University of Nottingham, and at the Centre for Advanced Welsh and Celtic Studies, Aberystwyth.

In parallel with her work for the Survey of English Place-Names, Gelling spent much effort in thinking more broadly about the subject, both within it and also in relation to other disciplines and its presentation to the wider public. In the late 1950s and early 1960s several younger scholars independently started to rethink the question of how place-name evidence can help our understanding of the Anglo-Saxon settlement of England, one of the most difficult but important topics in English history, and one to which it has always been hoped that place-names should be able to contribute significantly, since the toponymy of England changed so thoroughly as a result of that settlement. From the early days of the Survey it had been considered that place-names composed of an Old English personal name plus *-ingas, -inga-* 'people (of)' (as in Reading, Hastings) had a special significance, since they seemed to evoke leaders and their bands of followers, so these place-names were thought to refer to individual pioneer settlers and their retinues. Other habitative names (ones containing a word referring explicitly to the settlement itself, such as *tūn* 'farmstead' or *hām* 'homestead', as contrasted with topographical ones which refer primarily to its natural setting) had also been the focus of work which tried to relate place-names to the early settlements. The work of John Dodgson, Kenneth Cameron, Barrie Cox and Gelling herself in the 1960s questioned some of these long-standing assumptions, partly on the grounds of the distributions of the names, which in the case of names in *-ingas* did not seem to be in the same areas as the growing body of evidence for pagan Anglo-Saxon burials. Gelling's chief contributions to this fresh assessment of the toponymic evidence for the Anglo-Saxon settlement were on the subject of names in *wīchām*, which she suggested did belong to a very early period and referred to sites close to settlements which the Anglo-Saxons recognised as Roman (Old English *wīc* being a Germanic loan-word from Latin *vicus*); and on the place-name evidence for Anglo-Saxon paganism (where the names by definition were created early within the Anglo-Saxon period), for which she regretfully made the corpus of such names rather smaller than had been thought, and also suggested that such names as did refer to pagan sites belonged to a slightly later period, after conversion had begun, rather than to the pre-Christian period itself.

One general result of this reconsideration of the evidence was that some types of name which had been thought to date from the earliest Anglo-Saxon period were no longer thought to do so, or not necessarily; leaving open the question of which names might actually be ascribed to that earliest period. Gelling's second reassessment, which was largely her own work to begin with, served partly to fill that newly recognised void. Rather than habitative names Gelling looked instead at topographical place-names, in which the generic term might refer to a hill, stream, valley or some other aspect of the landscape. These names had generally been considered of little chronological significance, since the landscape terms at their core were mostly in use over a long period; and they had been comparatively neglected as a group. Alongside the suggestion that some of these names might belong among the earliest names of the Anglo-Saxon settlement, she also began a detailed and far-reaching examination of the finer shades of meaning to be discerned in different topographical terms.

Neither of these developments was entirely new. Both John Dodgson, in demoting the significance of population-names for the settlement period, and Barrie Cox had suggested that topographical ones might be significant among the earliest English names.[11] And the possibility of subtle shades of meaning among the various Old English words broadly meaning 'hill', 'valley', and the like had been recognised from the earliest days of the Survey of English Place-Names: the existence of several words apparently having broadly the same meaning invites the speculation that they may have been differentiated, and Gelling herself pointed out that Sir Frank Stenton had suggested in 1924 that the Anglo-Saxons were 'remarkably sensitive to diversities of ground'.[12] This part of Gelling's rethink happened to chime with a broader and growing scholarly interest in landscape, especially its historical aspects, and this side of her work has probably been the one which has become best known, and has also

---

[11] J. McNeal Dodgson, 'The significance of the distribution of the English place-name in *-ingas, -inga-* in south-east England', *Medieval Archaeology*, 10 (1966), 1–29 (p. 5), reprinted in K. Cameron (ed.), *Place-Name Evidence for the Anglo-Saxon Invasion and Scandinavian Settlements* (Nottingham, 1975), pp. 27–54 (p. 29); B. Cox, 'The place-names of the earliest English records', *Journal of the English Place-Name Society*, 8 (1975–6), 12–66.

[12] F. M. Stenton, 'The English element', in A. Mawer and F. M. Stenton (eds.), *Introduction to the Survey of English Place-Names*, 1 (Cambridge, 1924), pp. 36–54 (p. 37); M. Gelling, *Place-Names in the Landscape* (London, 1984), p. 5.

inspired the greatest number of further studies.[13] Subsequently she developed her work further with Ann Cole, a geographer who had attended a weekend class which she gave, and Cole's geographical eye produced much refinement of Gelling's original observations; Gelling's book was republished under a fresh title and dual authorship, with illustrative drawings by Cole which greatly enhanced its message.[14]

In this study Gelling wisely limited her corpus of names, rather than attempting to use the whole body of material to be found in the growing Survey of English Place-Names. She therefore considered only those names (about 19,000 in total) appearing in the *Concise Oxford Dictionary of English Place-Names* by Eilert Ekwall (1877–1964), a classic work which itself used Bartholomew's *Gazetteer* as its main corpus, and thus included the names of most parishes in England, plus those of some other major features; in most counties this corpus also included a high proportion of the manors named in Domesday Book. Gelling assumed, justifiably, that this corpus could be hoped to include a large number of 'ancient settlement-names'.[15] She demonstrated convincingly, first, that names for settlements, probably from a very early period, were often based upon topographical generic words such as *dūn* 'hill' (as in Bredon, Faringdon, Clevedon), rather than incorporating any habitative element, and she suggested the term 'quasi-habitative' for such words, referring to natural features but used for settlements; and second, that many Old English words for 'valley', 'hill' and water features did indeed have precise meanings which could be identified by examining, even today, the landscape to which those names refer. One remarkable example of this topographical precision is Old English *snōr*, which is known in just eight place-names altogether, six in the south-east (London, Surrey and Kent) but also one in each of Cheshire and Lincolnshire. Gelling's analysis showed convincingly that this rare word (from a Germanic stem meaning 'twist') was used of 'a place where a road curves in order to negotiate a rise'.[16] The further implication of Gelling's work on this and other topographical terms, as she realised herself, is that from a very early period the Anglo-Saxons

---

[13] Gelling, *Place-Names in the Landscape*; the Society for Landscape Studies, with its journal *Landscape History*, was founded in 1979; Oliver Rackham's *History of the Countryside* was published in 1986 (London).
[14] M. Gelling and A. Cole, *The Landscape of Place-Names* (Stamford, 2000).
[15] E. Ekwall, *The Concise Oxford Dictionary of English Place-Names* (Oxford, 1936; 4th edn, Oxford, 1960); Gelling, *Place-Names in the Landscape*, p. 4.
[16] M. Gelling, 'The hunting of the Snōr', in A. R. Rumble and A. D. Mills (eds.), *Names, Places and People: an Onomastic Miscellany in Memory of John McNeal Dodgson* (Stamford, 1997), pp. 93–5.

showed a surprising consistency in their linguistic usage across the whole of what was to become England, having arrived with a ready-made topographical vocabulary of great precision, or adapting their existing topographical vocabulary in a consistent way to suit the variety of landscapes which they encountered in this island.

Being based on a limited corpus of material, this work does not always tell a complete story. Gelling suggested that *dūn* 'hill' was not used in names for major settlements after about AD 800; however, the word itself continued to be used both within the language and for creating place-names, until modern times in its later form *down* or *downs* 'rough grazing'. Gelling herself was well aware that such qualifications were inherent in her chosen corpus,[17] but they may risk being overlooked by workers less familiar with the later onomastic material.

These developments within English place-name study have been received with enthusiasm, and they have inspired other workers to look more closely at other topographical aspects of place-names, both within England and in other regions and languages. One lifelong characteristic of her work was her open-minded ability to acknowledge when a received opinion, perhaps held by herself as well as others, was poorly founded, and to see within fresh suggestions or developments the possibilities for future work by herself or others; another was her encouragement and support of younger workers in the field. Her collaboration with Ann Cole in the subsequent development of her own work on the landscape of place-names was only the most striking example of these long-standing habits. Conversely, she was swift to spot when an inquirer did really not want to learn, and she would not waste her time on such people.

Gelling's interest for wider aspects of her subject led her into several related areas of scholarship, not only to study Anglo-Saxon charter-boundaries but also to contribute *The West Midlands in the Early Middle Ages* (Leicester, 1992) to a series on the Early History of Britain, edited by Nicholas Brooks, her close colleague and friend at Birmingham; and through her marriage to Peter to examine the place-names of the Isle of Man, suggesting with characteristic iconoclasm that the evidence for Gaelic there before the Scandinavian settlements is much weaker than has generally been assumed.[18] On this matter her arguments have been found

---

[17] The element *dūn* 'remained in use as a term for field-name and minor name formation, and for features of the landscape, however, till modern times', Gelling, *Place-Names in the Landscape*, p. 142.
[18] M. Gelling, 'The place-names of the Isle of Man', *Journal of the Manx Museum*, 7 (1970–1), 130–9 and 168–75; M. Gelling, 'Norse and Gaelic in medieval Man: the place-name evidence', in P. Davey (ed.), *Man and Environment in the Isle of Man*, 2 vols, British Archaeological Reports,

more persuasive outside Man than within it, where Gaelic is seen as having been the dominant language there since time immemorial.

Gelling's formal career after the move to Birmingham was uneventful, since she did not hold any paid position other than her part-time adult classes. However, her scholarly standing was recognised both nationally and internationally in the unpaid positions which she held: president of the English Place-Name Society, 1985–98; chairman of the Council for Name Studies (subsequently the Society for Name Studies in Britain and Ireland), 1976–9; and vice-president of the International Council for Onomastic Sciences, 1993–9. In 1993 she was made an Honorary Fellow of St Hilda's, her undergraduate college in Oxford; she was awarded the OBE in 1995 and became a Fellow of the British Academy in 1998; and she received honorary doctorates from the Universities of Nottingham (2002) and Leicester (2003). She died on 24 April 2009 and obituary notices for her appeared in the *Guardian*, the *Daily Telegraph* and the *Economist* (4 May, 9 May and 14 May 2009), as well as in scholarly journals.[19] She and Peter did not have children, but they played an important role in the upbringing of her nephew Adrian Midgley, who remained close to her and cared for her in her final illness. Apart from her political activities, her main interest outside her scholarship was gardening, one that she shared with her close onomastic colleague Cecily Clark (1926–92); she regretted that her soil was unsuited to primroses but delighted in the flourishing alpine strawberries. In some ways Gelling was notably modest: while remaining well aware of her own scholarly eminence, she seemed to consider that her success was no more than could be achieved by anyone reasonably intelligent who devoted time and rigour to thinking about the material. Her reaction to the news of a Festschrift in her honour and also a plan for a collection of her own essays, many of which had typically been published in extremely obscure local journals, was a characteristic mixture of this modesty with recognition of her own eminence: she thought the collection of her own essays a 'much better idea'.[20] Her strong and enthusiastic sense of humour does not often appear on the page in

---

British Series, 54 (1978), II, 251–64 (alongside her husband Peter in the same book, and with his evident input into her own article); and M. Gelling, 'The place-names of the Isle of Man', in S. Ureland and G. Broderick (eds.), *Language Contact in the British Isles* (Tübingen, 1991), pp. 141–55.

[19] *Journal of the English Place-Name Society*, 41 (2009), 134–9 (O.J.P.); *Nomina*, 32 (2009), 159–62 (Ann Cole).

[20] O. J. Padel and D. N. Parsons (eds.), *A Commodity of Good Names: Essays in Honour of Margaret Gelling* (Donington, 2008); the collected essays have not yet appeared at the time of writing.

her writings, but was frequently apparent in her dealings with colleagues. While waiting for her to collect her OBE at Buckingham Palace her party was reproved by an official for the mirth emanating from it; those who knew her will suspect that Gelling herself was probably the chief culprit.

O. J. PADEL
University of Cambridge

JOHN RANKINE GOODY
By permission of the Master and Fellows of St John's College, Cambridge

John Rankine Goody
1919–2015

ONE OF THE MOST PRODUCTIVE THEMES addressed repeatedly by Jack Goody during his long and prolific career concerned the 'mode of communication', in particular the impact of literacy. The invention of writing, especially in alphabetic form, enabled a new kind of 'knowledge society' in which people could 'look back' and continuously rediscover the stored wisdom of their ancestors. Goody's mature work reminds us that, in the early twenty-first century, this process is still regrettably segmented across the globe. Educated Europeans are familiar with the rediscovery of classical antiquity in the European renaissance, but few appreciate that Song dynasty intellectuals in China were able to look back in much the same way to Confucian as well as Buddhist classics.[1] The structural similarity of East and West in Eurasia eventually became Jack Goody's dominant theme. But his starting point was the flexibility of oral communication in Africa, where the transmission of knowledge, of political offices and of property, all differed significantly from Eurasian patterns. A transition from Africa to Eurasia structures the central sections of this memoir. But Goody is not to be pigeon-holed geographically and to speak of a transition in his work is not to deny continuity and unity. There was no sudden intellectual shift, but rather a gradual reorientation that coincided roughly with his tenure of the William Wyse Chair in Social Anthropology at Cambridge between 1973 and 1984. The two sections in which I focus more on the professional accomplishments (in as much depth as a short memoir allows) are bracketed by sections in which I elaborate on the life

[1] J. Goody, *Renaissances. The One or the Many?* (Cambridge, 2010).

and character of a man who was acknowledged, even by those unsympathetic to his intellectual positions and personality, as a 'big man' of the academic tribe of social anthropologists.

The apprentice

Jack Goody was conscious of the fact that his rather conventional Home Counties background made him an unusual recruit to a discipline in which middle-class Englishmen were outnumbered by South African Jews, Central European refugees, cosmopolitan aristocrats and 'colonials'. He joked about this by emphasising his mother's Scottish heritage.[2] He was born on 27 July 1919 in London and grew up in Welwyn Garden City and St Albans, where the Roman excavations of Mortimer Wheeler apparently made an impression on him as a schoolboy. St Albans School was almost as ancient and no doubt just as impressive in its own way.[3] Jack's father was a technical journalist and later an advertising manager in an electrical company. His mother worked as a civil servant for the Post Office before her marriage. Both parents valued education highly, and Jack dedicated his first monograph to them.[4] More than half a century later, in the Acknowledgements to his final book, he looked back as follows:

> above all I remember the earlier help of my mother, Lilian Rankine Goody of Turriff (she always retained her maiden name) and of my father, Harold Ernest Goody of Fulham, both of whom left school at sixteen but developed their own interests in work and education and were so pleased when their two sons obtained sizarships and later PhDs (without loans) at St John's College, Cambridge, later becoming Fellows of the College, as they would also have been when they both subsequently became members of the National Academy of the USA.[5]

When Jack went up to Cambridge in 1938 to read English he encountered communists and radicals of diverse social backgrounds. Raymond

---

[2] Jack's second Christian name was her family name. He and his younger brother Richard spent summers in the maternal home in Turriff, Aberdeenshire. Richard Goody is a distinguished atmospheric and planetary physicist and an Emeritus at Harvard University.
[3] Colin Renfrew, the archaeologist who later became Jack's jousting partner in Faculty Board meetings in Cambridge, was a pupil at St Albans School many years later. Ernest Gellner (who succeeded Goody as William Wyse Professor in 1984) completed his secondary education during the war at a different (less prestigious) grammar school in the same town.
[4] J. Goody, *The Social Organisation of the LoWiili* (London, 1956).
[5] J. Goody, *Metals, Culture and Capitalism: an Essay on the Origins of the Modern World* (Cambridge, 2012), p. xvii.

Williams was a contemporary at Trinity College, but Jack established a closer relationship with Eric Hobsbawm at King's.[6] His undergraduate career was interrupted for six years by the Second World War. In several reminiscences, Jack attributed his decision to take up social anthropology to his experiences among Italian villagers in the Abruzzi, where he displayed great valour on the run from the Nazis, who had captured him at Tobruk in 1942.[7] After twice escaping and being recaptured, the second time in Rome, he spent over a year in Eichstätt, a Bavarian prisoner-of-war camp, where he was able to read James Frazer's *The Golden Bough* and Gordon Childe's *What Happened in History*.

The war brought traumas, but it also extended social horizons. When looking back on his adventures in Italy, Jack stressed his encounters with the 'olive skinned peasants'. But the ensuing literary efforts of the young officer to render the vernacular of his fellow soldiers, including British army privates, suggest a revelatory discovery of the diversity of his own society and its class structure. This memoir of the war, the first half of which was written in the camp at Eichstätt, reveals a connoisseur of Joyce: the hero—aka Jack—is called Stephen. When finally demobbed, Stephen is troubled by 'the fuss of relatives' and requests a rail warrant to John O'Groats 'to do his own adjusting, sort out his own cards of identity and social relations'.[8] I think it is possible that Jack Goody might have chosen to take up sociology or perhaps even social psychology, had such options existed in Cambridge at the time.

After completing Part I of the English Tripos in 1946, Jack took a one-year Diploma course in social anthropology, passing with a Distinction. His practical curiosity toward his own British society then deepened during a two-year stint as an Assistant Education Officer in Hertfordshire, with responsibilities for adult education. But research scholarships were not available for sociology. He returned to university in 1949 with the help of a Colonial Social Science Scholarship to study social anthropology, not at Cambridge but at the institute headed by Edward Evans-Pritchard (E-P) in Oxford. This was the year in which E-P delivered a famous lecture calling for a rapprochement between anthropology and

---

[6] Hobsbawm interviewed Goody in 1991 for Alan Macfarlane's digital archive: at http://upload.sms.cam.ac.uk/media/1117872 (accessed 11 July 2017).
[7] In 1997 he revisited the cave where he had taken refuge, following publication of his memoir of these events in Italian translation (*Oltre I Muri*, Rome, Il Mondo). A French translation was published in 2004 (*Au-delà des murs*, Marseille, La Découverte). The English typescript *Beyond the Walls* was published privately by the Goody family in 2012.
[8] Goody, *Beyond the Walls*, p. 77.

history.[9] However, this manifesto had little impact on the courses taught at Oxford. Goody accepted an offer to work on West Africa with Meyer Fortes, who was appointed at precisely this time to be William Wyse Professor in Cambridge. Formally Jack Goody spent the next few years as a Sociological Research Officer for the Gold Coast Government. The winds of change were already beginning to blow: though he still held a commission as an army officer, at his field site Jack promptly joined the local branch of Nkrumah's Convention People's Party. He spent a little over twelve months in 1950–1 among the acephalous, non-literate LoDagaa. This was his collective name for the inhabitants of the two settlements he studied, who he called the LoWiili and LoDagaba. He quickly realised that the old notion of a 'Lobi tribe' was a mirage, since no named groups existed on the ground in this region of north-western Ghana near the Black Volta River. Jack obtained a BLitt from Oxford in 1952 before returning to the district for a further nine months' field research. He was guided throughout this research by Fortes. Looking back, Jack sometimes spoke of the 'five years' he spent in Ghana at this time; but this was a form of amnesia that subsumed the writing-up process in Cambridge. For his wife Joan (née Wright), whom he had married in 1947, and their three young children Jeremy, Joanna and Jane, it perhaps did feel like a continuous five-year absence. The marriage collapsed.

Jack Goody's PhD dissertation was examined in 1954 by G. I. Jones (a veteran of the Colonial Service) and Max Gluckman from the University of Manchester. It secured its author immediate appointment as an Assistant Lecturer in the department that Fortes was consolidating. Jack was promoted to Lecturer in 1959 and elected to a Fellowship at St John's College in 1961. Meanwhile in 1956 he married Esther Newcomb, one of his first graduate students and the daughter of the distinguished American social psychologist Theodore Newcomb. Jack and Esther were a remarkable academic team, both in the field and in Cambridge. They wrote papers together and visited Ghana regularly throughout the first decade of independence, living there continuously from 1964 to 1966 with their daughters Mary and Rachel. Sabbaticals and many university vacations were spent mainly among the Gonja, a more stratified and centralised society than the LoDagaa. Esther also worked with West African migrants in London. While her focus remained firmly on kinship and interpersonal

---

[9] This Marett Lecture modified (and in places contradicted) the thrust of E-P's inaugural lecture just two years before. See the memoir of E-P by John Barnes: J. A. Barnes, 'Edward Evan Evans-Pritchard, 1902–1973', *Proceedings of the British Academy*, 73 (1987), 447–89.

relations, Jack's interests began to diversify, to include precolonial history as well as the challenges of economic development and postcolonial statehood. Together they provided a stream of fresh empirical as well as theoretical insights to complement the Olympian overview of kinship theory provided by Fortes in his Morgan Lectures.[10]

Jack succeeded Audrey Richards as Director of Cambridge's African Studies Centre in 1966. He applied for and was awarded the ScD degree in 1969, and he was appointed Smuts Reader in Commonwealth Studies in 1972. But not everything was plain sailing. Before the Smuts elevation he had failed in an effort to obtain promotion to a personal Readership, and his appointment to succeed Fortes as William Wyse Professor in 1973 was not quite a foregone conclusion. Factional opposition inside Cambridge was one thing (more about this below), but Jack had managed to make a few enemies in Oxford and other places with a say in the matter. Eventually, the depth and breadth of his publications list was decisive. At this stage, Jack Goody was still very much an anthropologist's anthropologist; but his increasing engagement with other academic fields presumably counted in his favour at this moment of disciplinary transition in the wake of empire.[11] It had been a long apprenticeship. Jack paid appropriate homage to his mentor by editing the Festschrift for Fortes that appeared shortly afterwards.[12] His own contribution to this volume, 'Polygyny, economy and the role of women', gave a fair indication of his interests at the time; at this point few had any inkling of the scale of the changes to come.

The Africanist

The hallmark of the Cambridge department built up by Meyer Fortes was 'descent theory', grounded above all in West African ethnography. Critics of the descent theorists, influenced by the path-breaking work of Claude Lévi-Strauss, emphasised prescriptive marriage rules and inter-group

---

[10] M. Fortes. *Kinship and the Social Order: the Legacy of Lewis Henry Morgan* (London, 1969).
[11] One criterion that did not weigh heavily in those days was pedagogical skill. Formal teaching (as distinct from informal supervision and guidance, in which he invested a great deal) was never a priority for Jack Goody. His lectures were often unprepared and his delivery was poor. Even when Prince Charles, the heir to the throne, was sitting in the lecture rooms at the Haddon Library in the late 1960s, it is said that Jack mumbled and rambled much as he always did. The contrast with his lucid and well-crafted books and articles was so strong that audiences sometimes wondered if the awkward lecturing style was a deliberate ploy to reinforce his arguments about the deficiencies of the oral mode of communication.
[12] J. Goody (ed.), *The Character of Kinship* (Cambridge, 1974).

alliances, rather than the character of the kin group (clan or lineage) as a corporation. The alliance theorists were instrumental in popularising structuralist anthropology more generally. They were championed in Cambridge by Edmund Leach, who was recruited by Fortes in 1953 from the London School of Economics (LSE). Leach had studied engineering at Cambridge and worked in China before participating in Bronislaw Malinowski's seminar at the LSE in the late 1930s. His horizons, too, had been greatly changed by the war, much of which he spent in remote regions of Burma. Leach was a born provocateur, ready to tangle with Lévi-Strauss himself on some points, and dismissive of virtually all his contemporaries in Britain. Some of those criticised felt that Leach's preference for rationalist logic was a case of *faute de mieux*. Having lost his Burma fieldnotes and written a well-received book that was not burdened with ethnographic facts, Leach went on to publish a second monograph that was full of them.[13] But *Pul Eliya* was based on just seven months' field research in Ceylon (as it was still called), and Leach did not match the standards of his Africanist colleagues as an ethnographer. He concluded the Ceylon study with a sharp attack on the primacy attached to kinship by the Africanists around him. Leach declared that the institutions of the domestic domain and kinship itself had no autonomy but were constantly refashioned by economic realities, in particular through the system of land tenure.

This sounded like a manifesto for a materialist economic anthropology based on ethnographic data, but Edmund Leach was incapable of pursuing such an agenda and soon moved on to other matters (notably the analysis of biblical myth). In his more general theoretical statements, he disparaged ethnographic 'butterfly collecting' in favour of an eclectic adaptation of the structuralist analysis practiced by Lévi-Strauss, with its origins in Saussurian linguistics. In his much-quoted 1959 Malinowski Lecture titled 'Rethinking anthropology', Leach singled out Goody's early work in northern Ghana as an example of the kind of anthropology that had to be overcome:

> My colleague Dr Goody has gone to great pains to distinguish as types two adjacent societies in the Northern Gold Coast which he calls LoWiili and LoDagaba. A careful reader of Dr Goody's works will discover, however, that these two 'societies' are simply the way that Dr Goody has chosen to describe the fact that his field notes from two neighbouring communities show some

[13] E. Leach, *Political Systems of Highland Burma: a Study of Kachin Social Structure* (London, 1954); *Pul Eliya: a Village in Ceylon; a Study of Land Tenure and Kinship* (Cambridge, 1961).

curious discrepancies. If Dr Goody's methods of analysis were pushed to the limit we should be able to show that every village community throughout the world constitutes a distinct society which is distinguishable as a type from any other.[14]

The Goody work in question here was his BLitt thesis, a revised version of which was published in 1956.[15] One might doubt whether Leach was ever a 'careful reader' of the works of his Africanist colleagues. Be that as it may, by the time Goody published a much-revised version of his PhD in 1962 even the most superficial reader could see that his purpose was hardly sterile classification.[16] Goody agreed with Leach that anthropologists should not limit themselves to writing 'impeccably detailed historical ethnographies of particular peoples'.[17] But rather than generalisation via 'inspired guesswork', as advocated by Leach, Goody wanted the discipline to get back to addressing the big questions of human history, and to do so on the basis of careful analysis of empirical evidence, rather than intuition and logical patterns.

Some in Leach's audience in 1959 and later readers of his lecture jumped to erroneous conclusions about the main protagonists in these Cambridge debates. Leach, the structuralist, was also marked by the Malinowski imprint, joking with his students that for half of the week he remained an old-fashioned functionalist. He upheld the same high standards of field research using local languages as those of the 'journeyman' (Fortes' ironic self-description) ethnographers in the other camp. Certainly there were vigorous debates and occasional misunderstandings between the leading personalities; affairs, and even religious heritage, might have been mischievously invoked on occasion. But looking back, one sees that the tensions between Fortes, Leach and Goody were intellectually productive. They did not impede significant collaborations across the departmental divide, such as a *Cambridge Papers* volume on bridewealth and dowry in which Jack and Stanley Tambiah (ostensibly a card-carrying member of the Leach faction and a rival of Jack's for the Chair in 1973) published complementary studies.[18]

---

[14] E. Leach, 'Rethinking anthropology', in E. Leach (ed.) *Rethinking Anthropology* (London, 1961), p. 3.
[15] Goody, *The Social Organisation of the LoWiili*.
[16] J. Goody, *Death, Property and the Ancestors: a Study of Mortuary Customs of the LoDagaa of West Africa* (Stanford, CA, 1962).
[17] Leach, *Rethinking Anthropology*, p. 1.
[18] J. Goody and S. J. Tambiah, *Bridewealth and Dowry* (London, 1973). For further insight see the memoir of 'Tambi' by C. J. Fuller, 'Stanley Jeyaraja Tambiah 1929–2014', *Biographical Memoirs of Fellows of the British Academy, XIV* (London, 2015), 599–619.

Just as Edmund Leach never questioned the accomplishments of the Malinowskian tradition, so Jack Goody respected the impulses coming from Paris, where expertise on West Africa was as strong as that in Britain for some topics. His French was better than that of his colleagues and he was a frequent visitor as Directeur d'Études Associé at the École des Hautes Études en Sciences Sociales throughout the 1970s.[19] Yet Jack Goody was never seduced by the central precepts of French structuralist anthropology. Of course, for some hard-nosed Anglo-Saxon empiricists the entire Lévi-Straussian school was an unfortunate consequence of the continental preference for armchair philosophising and reluctance to suffer the discomforts of the field. In Jack's case there were more serious intellectual reasons behind the critique. In his formative years he had come under the influence of 'three visiting Professors of Social Theory at Cambridge in 1953–56, Talcott Parsons, Lloyd Warner and George Homans'.[20] All three were primarily sociologists (though Warner also made important contributions to anthropology). Jack was not overwhelmed by Parsonian theory. He was more impressed by Homans' bold ambition to develop a comprehensive science of human groups. If an American sociologist could publish a perceptive overview of medieval English villagers,[21] surely a social anthropologist could make equally valuable contributions from a somewhat different angle? This had some affinity to the 'natural science of society' programme of A. R. Radcliffe-Brown, a Cambridge anthropologist of an earlier generation who had interacted with Warner in Chicago. Jack Goody, though not uncritical of Radcliffe-Brown, always preferred an explicitly comparative, sociological vision of the discipline to that offered by the later Evans-Pritchard. He may also have preferred the politics of a man known in his Cambridge years as 'Anarchy Brown' to the Catholic conservatism of E-P.

These key elements, assembled in Cambridge and cemented during a sabbatical year at the Institute for Advanced Studies in the Behavioral Sciences in Palo Alto (1959–60), were firmly in place by the time Goody published *Death, Property and the Ancestors* in 1962. This work meets the highest Malinowskian-Fortesian standards in terms of presenting fieldwork data. The comparative anthropologist recalls his earlier academic identity by punctuating his work with epigraphs and quotations from English literature. It is also instructive to note early signs of an engage-

---

[19] He also spent many summers in the vicinity of Figeac, in the department of the Lot, returning each year to the same gîte in a tiny hamlet, and later to the house he and Esther bought nearby.
[20] Goody, *Death, Property and the Ancestors*, p. vii.
[21] G. C. Homans, *English Villagers of the Thirteenth Century* (Cambridge, MA, 1941).

ment with English and European history as he draws on Henry Maine and other classical European sources to understand the transmission of property in northern Ghana. His analysis of the dual inheritance system of the LoDagaba showed that it allowed for greater *choice* than that of the LoWiili, the people with whom he spent most of his first stint in the field. The differences had implications both for the corporateness of descent groups and interpersonal relations. All this was new grist to the Fortesian mill, but at the same time it opened up original paths for comparison, of a kind not envisaged by the master. The significant differences between LoDagaba and LoWiili turned on inheritance, but how did the difference in property transmission come about? It could not be explained with reference to the regional ecology, and Goody was not disposed to give credit to speculative evolutionary theories about 'uterine inheritance' as an earlier stage in human evolution; the trend in the savannah of the Niger bend in recent centuries seemed to be in the opposite direction.

To the best of my knowledge, Goody never resolved this question pertaining to the entanglements of regional migration histories. Instead, perhaps piqued by the teasing remarks of Leach, he turned his attention ever more ambitiously to the bigger picture, always with the archaeology of Gordon Childe in the back of his mind and influenced also by the Danish economic historian Ester Boserup. He argued that most of Africa south of the Sahara was characterised by rudimentary technology (the digging stick rather than the plough) and by the relative abundance of land. This was the deeper explanation for an intercontinental contrast with Europe and Asia, where fertile land tended to be scarce, surpluses were larger and property was transmitted to individual heirs, female as well as male, rather than collectively through kin groups. A series of publications elaborated this contrast, culminating in *Production and Reproduction*.[22] By now, both the emphasis on materialist causation and the historical orientation distinguished Goody clearly from Fortes.

This emerging interest in modes of production did not lead Jack Goody to embrace the neo-Marxist paradigms that became fashionable in these years (also largely derivative of developments in Paris in particular the work of Louis Althusser). He did not take kindly to accusations of economic or technological determinism. The idealism of the neo-Marxist stress on the relations of production was little better than Leach's *trompe l'œil* at the end of his Ceylon monograph. Contributing to a symposium

---

[22] J. Goody, *Production and Reproduction: a Comparative Study of the Domestic Domain* (Cambridge, 1976).

on slavery organised by his friend Woody Watson, Jack elaborated a more general suspicion of 'theory':

> ... in rural economy slavery has different implications in the simpler agricultural systems of Africa than in the more advanced ones of the Eurasian continent, under industrial than under craft production. To make such an assertion is viewed by some Althusserians as 'technological determinism' or 'vulgar Marxism'. However the obverse is an equally 'vulgar' form of 'idealism', which can be maintained only by those who have little concern with the interplay of 'theory' and 'research', and who view 'theory' as a body of ready-made constructs insulated from the realm of empirical systems. Such a binary approach to social theory and research has a long tradition in the decontextualized discussion of philosophers. It has little relevance to the dialectical process involved in the study of human society.[23]

One counter move (also a favourite ploy of Ernest Gellner) was to insist on paying as much attention to the means of destruction as to the means of production. You could not understand political formations in West Africa without appreciating the different implications of horses and guns as military weapons (not all regional experts were convinced by Jack's generalisations about this contrast). But the move which had greater significance for Goody's oeuvre concerned the mode of communication and the importance of literacy as a 'technology of the intellect'. This too emerged from his original field research, during which he wrote down a very long myth of the LoDagaba. The Bagre was a secret association and the way in which Jack first gained access and published his materials might not pass muster for the more restrictive ethics committees of our age. This was nevertheless work that gave him the satisfaction of being able to give back something of value pertaining to the past of the societies he had studied so intensively, while the LoDagaba themselves were now firmly focused on constructing new futures. *The Myth of the Bagre* was particularly well received in France, where it appeared in translation.[24] Later recordings of the myth revealed that substantial changes could take place in little more than a decade. Gradually, Goody recognised the deeper implications of oral transmission when compared with writing systems, such as the alphabet invented by the Greeks, which permitted systematisation and scientific procedures. The strong version of this contrast was first outlined in a paper written with his close friend at St John's, the literature scholar Ian Watt. This paper dominated the

---

[23] J. Goody, 'Slavery in time and space', in J. L. Watson (ed.), *Asian and African Systems of Slavery* (Oxford, 1980), p. 17.
[24] J. Goody, *The Myth of the Bagre* (Oxford, 1972); J. Goody (with S. W. D. K. Gandah), *Une Récitation du Bagré* (Paris, 1980).

subject for years and was republished in a volume edited by Jack in 1968.[25] He returned to the theme repeatedly, retracting some of his stronger propositions and the excessive concentration on the case of Greece, which (from his later standpoint) reflected a Euro-centric bias and underestimated the potential of logographic representation.

But the core of the argument was retained and it was central to his answer to the structuralist challenge. Lévi-Strauss seduced his readers into a world of binary oppositions, all predicated on an opposition between 'hot' societies endowed with history (notably those of Europe) and the 'cold' societies which lacked such a past and formed the traditional terrain of anthropology (ethnology). To Jack Goody this always seemed feeble as a philosophy of history. The binary it implied was contradicted by the speed with which a new generation in Africa was adapting to modern systems of education and science. Jack called instead for a renewal of collaboration with historians and archaeologists to understand the multiple paths of human history. In *The Domestication of the Savage Mind* (his most comprehensive riposte to the structuralists—the very title evokes a key concept of Lévi-Strauss), it sometimes seems as if Goody is positing the invention of writing as the key moment in a 'great divide' theory of his own.[26] Translated into at least six major languages by the end of the century, this was probably the book that had most impact during his lifetime.

While these long-term historical interests were beginning to bear fruit, throughout the 1950s and 1960s Goody was also paying his dues to the Malinowskian-Fortesian tribe with publications in quite different genres. His standing as a kinship specialist was first established with a rigorously argued paper on conceptions of incest and adultery (1956).[27] This was published (strange though it seems today) in the *British Journal of Sociology*, as was a later paper on religion and ritual (1961).[28] Further papers in leading anthropological journals dealt with 'the mother's brother and the sister's son' (1959),[29] 'double descent systems' (1961)[30] and 'the

---

[25] J. Goody and I. Watt, 'The consequences of literacy', *Comparative Studies in Society and History*, 5 (1963), 304–45; J. Goody (ed.), *Literacy in Traditional Societies* (Cambridge, 1968), pp. 27–68.
[26] J. Goody, *The Domestication of the Savage Mind* (Cambridge, 1977).
[27] J. Goody, 'A comparative approach to incest and adultery', *British Journal of Sociology*, 7 (1956), 286–305.
[28] J. Goody, 'Religion and ritual: the definitional problem', *British Journal of Sociology*, 12 (1961), 142–63.
[29] J. Goody, 'The mother's brother and the sister's son in West Africa' (Curl Prize essay), *Journal of the Royal Anthropological Institute*, 89 (1959), 61–88.
[30] J. Goody, 'The classification of double descent systems', *Current Anthropology*, 2 (1961), 3–12, 21–4.

circulation of women and children in Northern Ghana' (1967, with Esther Newcomb Goody).[31] During these years, Jack also published papers in a variety of historical journals as well as the social sciences and regional studies outlets. The journal best suited to his growing ambitions was *Comparative Studies in Society and History*, which in addition to the above-mentioned seminal paper on literacy (1963, with Ian Watt) also published wide-ranging surveys of adoption (1969)[32] and 'strategies of heirship' (1973).[33] Seemingly 'arid' exercises to demonstrate that specialist terms could serve a useful purpose if rigorously defined and applied cross-culturally were complemented by the trenchant dismissal of terms that might have taken firm root, but which upon closer scrutiny were too imprecise to be saved for science. His objections to 'ritual' were no doubt prompted by the loose usage of Leach; they were repeated in the 1962 monograph and reformulated in his contribution to an influential volume devoted to 'secular ritual'.[34] Jack's reservations concerning the applicability of 'feudalism' on the African continent prefigured later elaborations of his critique of Eurocentric bias in the historical social sciences.[35] This essay was republished in a wide-ranging collection which showed how far he had come by the end of his apprenticeship. Africa was still at the centre of his work, but the agendas were expanding rapidly.[36]

The world historian

I have stressed that there were no abrupt transitions in Jack Goody's work: the seeds of just about everything he wrote after 1973 can be found in the years preceding his appointment to the William Wyse chair. But along with a shift in the spatial focus from Africa to Eurasia, he strikes out ever more adventurously beyond anthropology and the social sciences in order to address the agendas of historians and archaeologists. Publications in exclusively anthropological journals become increasingly rare. There is an acceleration following his retirement in 1984 when, freed of managerial

---

[31] J. Goody and E. N. Goody, 'The circulation of women and children in northern Ghana', *Man*, 2 (1967), 226–48.
[32] J. Goody, 'Adoption in cross-cultural perspective', *Comparative Studies in Society and History*, 11 (1969), 55–78.
[33] J. Goody, 'Strategies of heirship', *Comparative Studies in Society and History*, 1 (1973), 3–20.
[34] J. Goody, 'Against "ritual": loosely structured thoughts on a loosely defined topic', in S. Falk-Moore and B. Myerhoff (eds.), *Secular Ritual* (Assen, 1977), pp. 25–35.
[35] J. Goody, 'Feudalism in Africa?', *Journal of African History* 4 (1963), 1–18.
[36] J. Goody, *Technology Tradition and the State in Africa* (Cambridge, 1971).

responsibilities, the emeritus is able to concentrate fully on his writing. Jack Goody produced some eighteen new works between 1984 and 2012. Almost all were published in Cambridge. There was a falling-out with Cambridge University Press when it opted to change the name and governance of the monographs series for which he had long served as sole General Editor.[37] Yet he continued to publish his most substantial books with CUP. Several shorter works for wider audiences were commissioned by Cambridge sociologist John Thompson for Polity Press. Rich essay collections appeared in 1997 with Blackwell and 1998 with Verso.[38] The titles of these latter volumes are indicative of another slow shift over the years: from a comparative social scientist who engages with the very latest results of historical demographers, and who supports his generalisations with reference to Murdock's *Ethnographic Atlas* and statistical path analysis, to a historian of culture who is more concerned to provide narrative descriptions of patterns and associations than to measure causal flows. Throughout these decades Jack read incessantly in broad fields of world history; but whenever there was a danger of losing his way in details, he would pull up sharply and reconnect with his Childean master narrative of similarity and difference on the continental scale.

The 1980s brought fresh syntheses of his research into orality and the importance of writing as a technique with far-reaching implications for the organisation of society.[39] But the main area in which Jack continued to break new ground in this decade was property transmission. Not all of his historian colleagues were ready to accept scholarly trespassing of the kind which peaked in his book about the impact of the Roman Catholic Church on family and kin relations in medieval Europe.[40] Yet this was quickly

---

[37] The series *Cambridge Studies in Social Anthropology* published sixty-nine volumes between 1967 (when it was founded by Goody together with Fortes and Leach) and 1990 (when for marketing reasons the title was changed to include 'and Cultural'). In addition, CUP published eleven volumes of *Cambridge Papers* between 1958 and 1982—volumes which served almost exclusively to disseminate the research of department members. These two series did much to project the department's worldwide reputation in its golden age. At CUP, Jack worked especially closely with Patricia Williams (wife of the philosopher). His editorial inputs declined in the 1990s and ceased altogether when he condemned the Press's failure to stand up to political pressure in dropping a monograph on Macedonia (A. N. Karakasidou, *Fields of Wheat, Hills of Blood*, Chicago, 1997). The main series was terminated in 2003.
[38] J. Goody, *Representations and Contradictions: Ambivalence towards Images, Theatre, Fiction, Relics and Sexuality* (Oxford, 1997); J. Goody, *Food and Love: a Cultural History of East and West* (London, 1998).
[39] J. Goody. *The Logic of Writing and the Organization of Society* (Cambridge, 1986); J. Goody, *The Interface Between the Written and the Oral* (Cambridge, 1987).
[40] J. Goody, *The Development of the Family and Marriage in Europe* (Cambridge, 1983).

translated into French and contributed significantly to his reputation there. It was followed in 1990 by a work that pushed back in the direction of Eurasian commonalities.[41] Having shown that Western Christianity did indeed have distinctive features that impacted on kinship and marriage, Jack Goody did not wish to be classified as yet another theorist of the 'European miracle'. All of his African experience, in combination with what he knew of Europe and Asia through reading and travelling, led him to emphasise similarities and comparability across Eurasia. He was critical of the teleological tendency of so many Europeans to search for deep, long-term clues to the global domination exercised by Western Eurasia in recent centuries.

This argument was pursued both inside and outside the sphere of domestic institutions and driven home in several major works with meticulous critiques of the most influential Eurocentric thinkers.[42] These were significant contributions to a larger wave that was taking the discipline of history beyond traditional nation-state and imperial paradigms. Jack's message was clear: the Western passage from antiquity to feudalism had to be placed in a wider Eurasian context. Ideas such as that of renaissance are not relevant only to Europe, and the industrial and scientific revolutions can only be appreciated in the light of earlier contributions in the Near East, and South and East Asia. Jack Goody's world history emphasised oscillation between East and West, 'alternating domination' as he called it.[43]

Most Western scholars continue to think of capitalism and modernity as a product of the last 500 years or so, following European voyages of discovery and the concomitant expansion of global markets. This was followed by two further ruptures: scientific revolution and then (intimately related to the new scientific technologies) the transformation wrought by industrial capitalism, which created a proletariat obliged to sell its labour as a commodity. This basic narrative is common to Weberians and

---

[41] J. Goody, *The Oriental, the Ancient and the Primitive: Systems of Marriage and the Family in the Pre-industrial Societies of Eurasia* (Cambridge, 1990).

[42] The most important are J. Goody, *The East in the West* (Cambridge, 1996), in which he takes aim at Karl Marx and (especially) Max Weber; and J. Goody, *The Theft of History* (Cambridge, 2006), in which Joseph Needham, Norbert Elias and Fernand Braudel are singled out for penetrating critique.

[43] A short synthesis can be found in J. Goody, *The Eurasian Miracle* (Cambridge, 2010); see also the article published in the month of his passing, J. Goody, 'Asia and Europe', *History and Anthropology*, 26 (2015), 263–307. Keith Hart has written an incisive review article encompassing all the major works of the new century: 'Jack Goody: the anthropology of unequal society', *Reviews in Anthropology*, 43 (2014), 199–220.

Marxists alike. Even the Marxist anthropologist Eric Wolf, whose notion of a tributary mode of production is welcomed by Goody as an improvement on the Eurocentric category 'feudalism', privileges the last 500 years and neglects the three millennia which preceded this phase of European domination. But Jack Goody disagreed with neo-Marxist anthropologists (and also historians such as the young Chris Wickham) who thought they could escape the Eurocentric straitjacket by adapting the concept of 'mode of production', and who then compounded their error by privileging the 'relations of production' ahead of the 'forces' (technologies). Instead Jack drew attention to much earlier forms of dispossession. Capital was deployed 'rationally' in earlier millennia by merchants who traded overland as well as by sea, when the economy of western Eurasia (i.e. Europe) was backward in comparison with the east. Rather than focus on antagonistic relations at the point of production, Jack Goody drew attention to increasingly stratified societies and the emergence of 'connoisseurship' in various realms of culture, to complement his earlier analysis of how inequalities were reproduced through property transmission and domestic institutions.

Jack's alternative to the Eurocentric narratives did not change significantly over the years. The argument of his last, most archaeological monograph, which demonstrated the centrality of metal to the 'origins of the modern world', still followed the contours that he had imbibed from Childe in the library of his prisoner-of-war camp.[44] Most of the historical works of the last decades are high-level syntheses packed with empirical data. It is futile to search for innovative causal hypotheses, or specific theoretical foundations. Jack was impatient with crude classifications such as 'structural-functionalist' or 'descent school', and consistently eschewed jargon. Confronted with the abstract texts of non-anthropologists such as Parsons in the 1950s or Althusser in the 1960s, or Foucault in the 1970s and 1980s, he seems to have made a conscious decision to ignore them, no matter how popular they became with other anthropologists. How else would he have found the time to work through several different versions of the Bagre myth? Jack Goody certainly invested a lot of energy in studying the ethnography and languages of Ghana, and in enabling

---

[44] Goody, *Metals*. Although he rejected Childe's unilineal evolutionism (for which he also criticised Marx and Freud), Jack repeatedly adapted the prehistorian's perspective to his own topics; for a notable late instance, see J. Goody, 'Gordon Childe, the urban revolution, and the Haute Cuisine: an anthropo-archaeological view of modern history', *Comparative Studies in Society and History*, 48 (2006), 503–19.

Ghanaians themselves to continue such work.[45] This empiricist disposition persisted in later decades: when postmodern, postcolonial theories became *de rigueur* in anthropological writings, Jack preferred to read ever more widely in world history. Colleagues and students struggled to put a label on his historical books, and on him; the absence of a theoretical framework was perceived to be a drawback. For example, in an otherwise positive review of his last major work, archaeologist Stephen Shennan suggests that the narrative might have been strengthened by an explicit adoption of neo-institutionalist economic history.[46] The suggestion is not at all unreasonable, but in this respect Jack tended to disappoint; theory was either left implicit or it was altogether invisible. Not that he was an intellectual philistine: Durkheim, Marx and Freud were permanent benchmarks (though he was critical of them all). He paid surprisingly little attention to Marcel Mauss. One French contemporary for whom he had great respect was Pierre Bourdieu: Jack arranged for a translation of *Esquisse d'une théorie de la pratique* soon after its publication and it became a bestseller in the Cambridge Studies series.[47]

As I have noted, because Jack Goody placed much emphasis on surplus production and technology in some of his best known works, he was sometimes accused of economic determinism. But in his later books there is nothing deterministic about the way in which technologies of communication and of violence interact with the realm of production. In the end, he was content to leave 'economic anthropology' in the hands of Raymond Firth and the neo-Marxists. What mattered most in the first phase of his career was not the mode of production per se, but the property system and transmission mechanisms in the domestic domain. Having exhausted this theme by 1990, Jack then preferred to explore how the Africa–Eurasia contrast played out in various cultural realms, rather than dig further into the political economy that made the 'Eurasian miracle' possible. Numerous works on food,[48] a massive study of flowers[49] as well as the last book on metals, are all rooted in the basic economic contrasts between Africa and Eurasia. All play down the significance of East–West

---

[45] Jack once calculated that he had spent over a year of his life in painstaking transcription and (re)translation of different versions of the Bagre myth. See S. Grelet, E. Guichard and A. Lalande, 'La matière des idées; entretien avec Jack Goody', *Vacarne*, 49 (Autumn 2009), 12.
[46] S. Shennan, 'Refuting Western uniqueness', *European Journal of Sociology*, 54 (2013), 508–12.
[47] P. Bourdieu, *Outline of a Theory of Practice* (Cambridge, 1977). (Goody arranged for numerous other translations for this CUP series, from Augé and Godelier to Segalen and Zonabend.)
[48] The manifesto was laid out in J. Goody, *Cooking, Cuisine and Class: a Study in Comparative Sociology* (Cambridge, 1982).
[49] J. Goody, *The Culture of Flowers* (Cambridge, 1993).

differences within Eurasia. In some contexts, however, none of the axes for opposition suffice. A reluctance to represent the High God figuratively is a recurring feature of the 'world religions' of Eurasia, but it is also to be found in sub-Saharan Africa.[50] At this point Jack Goody acknowledges that historical accounts of divergent pathways must yield to recognition of cognitive universals: for example, concerning ambivalences (a favourite word) in domains of aesthetics and religion. At some level we are all the same, and binary models of otherness are simply false. However, Jack Goody's attitude to the emergence of a new 'cognitive anthropology' was itself ambivalent. He appreciated the work of scholars such as Dan Sperber and Pascal Boyer, as well as Stephen Levinson in linguistic anthropology; but he was unsympathetic to the emergence of named sub-fields in which conversations with biologists and psychologists would supersede those with other social scientists and historians.

Within Jack Goody's vast compass it is inevitable that some aspects receive more careful attention than others. Labour and exploitation are neglected in his insistence on pushing the origins of capitalism back to the 'merchant cultures' of the Bronze Age. Missing too, especially in the Eurasian context, is the messy business of politics. Perhaps neither production nor politics were particularly interesting phenomena among the LoDagaba, but the development of new forms of market exchange in the Eurasian civilisations was embedded in new forms of polity. Embeddedness was the key term of Karl Polanyi's substantivist economic anthropology, but Jack considered this approach to be flawed by a romantic anti-market ideology. He was influenced by Cambridge historian Moses Finley's account of the 'ancient economy' but in the end he judged Finley's position to be still too close to that of Polanyi (despite Finley's criticisms of the models of his mentor in 1950s New York).[51]

Religion was even more complicated terrain.[52] Jack was initially directed by Fortes to focus on the religion of the LoDagaba and he spent most of his time in the field documenting mortuary rituals. In his definitive 1962 monograph he concluded (against Fustel de Coulanges and Durkheim) that, although religion was certainly embedded in this case, it had no causal priority. This conclusion was echoed decades later when he

---

[50] Goody, *Representations and Contradictions*, Chapter 2.

[51] M. I. Finley, *The Ancient Economy* (Berkeley, CA, 1973).

[52] As far as I am aware, Jack Goody's writings about religion (unlike those of several other influential British social anthropologists of Africa) were not coloured by any personal religious faith. It took him some time and effort to accept that three of his children took up Buddhism in a serious way.

discounted the significance of religious beliefs for the emergence of stratified Eurasian society and divergent histories within the landmass.[53] His criticism of the Weberian thesis of a unique 'Protestant ethic' underpinning the capitalist spirit is undoubtedly justified. But to discount the significance of belief and the institutions of religion altogether is another matter; after all, Jack himself had drawn attention to distinctive features of Latin Christianity and their impact on marriage and the family, as well as outside the domestic domain.[54] He did not engage with the debates about 'multiple modernities' which flourished in the early twenty-first century, nor with their possible roots in the philosophies of the 'Axial Age'. Jack cast the onset of the 'transcendental' rather simplistically as a *hindrance* to the scientific quest. But upholding a basic distinction between Eurasia and Africa, based in economy and technology, need not impede recognition of more complex civilisational histories, both in Africa and in Eurasia, in which a decisive role is played by the 'religio-political nexus'; this nexus receives scant attention in Jack Goody's historical analyses.[55]

The big man

When Jack Goody succeeded Meyer Fortes in 1973, the discipline of social anthropology, in Cambridge as everywhere else, faced an uncertain future. With the end of the colonial empires and the retirements of E-P in Oxford, Firth at the LSE and Gluckman at Manchester, it seemed obvious that an epoch had come to an end. That Cambridge proceeded to reinvent itself as the pre-eminent department in the country owed much to Jack's own prodigious activities in these years (as well as to the above-mentioned creative rivalry with Edmund Leach, who was Provost of King's College between 1966 and 1979 and attracted excellent students with his own unique magnetism). It was clear to us in the 1970s that social anthropology had entered a new era of expansion. The graduate students who turned up in Pembroke Street were admitted to an intimate scholarly community, but their field projects diverged more and more from the kind of face-to-face community of a few thousand inhabitants that Goody

[53] Goody, *The Eurasian Miracle*; Goody, *Metals*.
[54] Goody, *The Development of the Family and Marriage*.
[55] I borrow this phrase from Johann Arnason. See J. P. Arnason and C. Hann, *Anthropology and Civilizational Analysis. Eurasian Explorations.* (New York, forthcoming).

himself had studied in his own apprenticeship.[56] The physical move to new premises around the corner in Free School Lane brought the social anthropologists into the immediate proximity of a similarly expansive sociology. Cambridge's first professor of sociology was John Barnes, an old friend of Jack's, for whom the notion of an intellectual boundary between anthropology and sociology made even less sense than it did for him. Jack was also close to Geoffrey Hawthorn, appreciative of his efforts to push the new department of Social and Political Sciences beyond the narrow paradigms of textbook sociology.

Links to historians had long been important and Jack greatly enjoyed working for many years as a member of the editorial board of *Past & Present*.[57] He was on good terms with Munir Postan as well as Moses Finley, and he was an early supporter of the historical demography developed in Cambridge by Peter Laslett and others. Ties to history took a significant new twist with the arrival of Peter Burke in 1979 to pioneer new styles of cultural history in Cambridge. Jack admired Alan Macfarlane's efforts to bring anthropology and history together, and was instrumental in recruiting him to the Cambridge department. Macfarlane's work, however, later took him in quite different directions.[58] The two men remained close, despite their obvious intellectual differences. For Jack, it was misleading to highlight distinctive features of the English case; even the evidence for East–West differences in marriage patterns within continental Europe (the much debated 'Hajnal line') paled into insignificance when one considered commonalities in the 'woman's property complex' stretching all the way to East Asia.

The upshot was that, far from fading away as some had feared in the aftermath of empire, social anthropology in Cambridge boomed (even if

---

[56] Keith Hart, whose doctoral project in the late 1960s on urban migrants in Accra was supervised by Goody and examined by Fortes, summed up the transformation as follows: 'Jack was in many ways Meyer Fortes' opposite, bringing to his headship the spirit of his own research and writing. He had no respect for disciplinary boundaries, telling us "You must find a question and follow it wherever it takes you". As a result, Cambridge social anthropology became an assemblage of solipsists, with PhD students often pursuing topics unknown to their supervisors.' (K. Hart, 'Professor Sir John Rankine Goody FBA (aka Jack), 1919–2015', *Anthropology Today*, 31, 6 (2015), 27–8.)

[57] He collaborated with Edward Thompson and Joan Thirsk in a comparative volume which emerged from a conference of the Past & Present Society: J. Goody, E. P. Thompson and J. Thirsk (eds.), *Family and Inheritance: Rural Society in Western Europe, 1200–1800* (Cambridge, 1976). This collaboration was doubtless facilitated by the editors' common left-wing political proclivities.

[58] A. Macfarlane, *The Origins of English Individualism* (Oxford, 1978). In a generous memoir available at his website, Macfarlane concludes by describing Jack as 'the man who has shaped my life most ... a constant inspiration'. See http://www.alanmacfarlane.com/ (accessed 11 July 2017).

a price was paid in terms of coherence). The well-established ethnographic focus on Africa was extended with the appointment of specialists on regions such as Amazonia and Melanesia, but work on Europe was also encouraged, including 'anthropology at home' (as it was called by the 1980s). My own case was not so unusual. I wanted initially to go to New Guinea, like many others in the 1970s. But Cambridge had already invested significantly in Melanesia, and Jack Goody urged me to go back to my undergraduate specialisation in the economics and politics of socialist Eastern Europe. Since no one among the core staff, or even in the penumbra of the colleges and other affiliated institutions, had the necessary regional or thematic expertise, Jack took me on himself.

In those days it was taken for granted that the William Wyse Professor was the Head of Department, who would promote its interests at meetings of the Faculty Board (vis-à-vis colleagues in archaeology and physical/biological anthropology) and beyond in the labyrinthine structures of the university. Jack invested much energy at multiple levels, beginning inside the department, where from the very beginning he had to fight his corner if appointments were not to be dominated by Leach.[59] Positions were always scarce: not every Certificate (later MPhil) student could secure PhD funding, not every PhD would become a Junior Research Fellow, not every JRF could be taken on as an Assistant Lecturer, and not every Assistant Lecturer could be awarded tenure. Some of those who missed out saw a typical academic patriarch, scheming and sometimes bullying to get his way. Nor did the unfairness end with tenure: some Cambridge colleges were rich enough to look after their Fellows very well, but the support available to Esther Goody at New Hall was very limited in comparison to that available to Jack at St John's. It was the college system which allowed him to make time for reading and writing. Mornings were generally taken up with teaching and administration in the vicinity of Downing Street and Free School Lane, but after lunch in John's (if no meetings were scheduled) he was usually able to retreat to his famously untidy college room in the New Court block popularly known as the 'wedding cake', where he would work without disturbance through to dinner.

---

[59] The department only took shape as such after his appointment to the chair. Prior to 1973 bureaucracy was minimal and the anthropologists were an informal cluster in a Faculty where archaeologists formed a majority. See J. Goody, 'Anthropology and bureaucracy', *The Cambridge Journal of Anthropology*, 28 (2008–9), 20–2.

Appointments and political battles outside Cambridge did not have the same significance. Jack declined to join the Association of Social Anthropologists and considered its annual conferences too introverted (because they lacked interdisciplinary stimulus). He was a Fellow of the Royal Anthropological Institute (and was awarded its highest honour, the Huxley Memorial Medal, in 1995), but he avoided office-holding. It was the same story in St John's College and also in the British Academy, where he remained loyal to the sociology section that elected him in 1976, after the majority of social anthropologists fissioned to form a new section with geographers. Jack also shunned the American Anthropological Association. The importance of his year in California in 1959–60 was noted above, and he visited the country often enough. But he never became close to the likes of Clifford Geertz, David Schneider or other influential figures in a similarly expansive US cultural anthropology. Like Geertz, Jack Goody started out as a student of English literature. But he was convinced that a British school focused on social relations and emphasising links to a more general comparative sociology and to history had more to offer than the North American predilection for cultural particulars. Geertz visited Cambridge in 1983 to deliver an early version of the argument later published as 'Anti-anti-relativism';[60] but this was at the invitation of Anthony Giddens (who succeeded John Barnes as Professor of Sociology at this time). The lecture was not even advertised in the Department of Social Anthropology, situated next door in Free School Lane.

I think this disdain and lack of hospitality towards Geertz were altogether exceptional. When Marshall Sahlins visited from Chicago at about the same time (invited by Peter Gathercole, the Curator of the Haddon Museum, to present a version of his celebrated Frazer Lecture on the death of Captain James Cook), he was welcomed according to the local cultural script, which included being entertained by Jack and Esther at 8 Adams Road. By the time Jack retired, Esther was securely established as a senior member of the department (given the conventions of that era, she had been obliged to resign her post after his appointment to the Chair; but having provided abundant evidence of her independent scholarly creativity, especially at the interface between anthropology and psychology, she was reappointed to a Lectureship in 1978). The Goodys lived in a large house in Adams Road which they acquired from St John's College (initially leasehold and later freehold). It was ideally suited to the

---

[60] C. Geertz, 'Distinguished lecture: anti-anti-relativism', *American Anthropologist*, 86 (1984), 263–78.

sort of informal suppers and Sunday lunches that Jack and Esther liked to host.⁶¹ Numerous more or less penurious young scholars lodged here over the years. When Jack retired in 1984 he insisted on hosting his own rite of passage (not without morbid jokes about having to endure yet another funeral: hadn't he sat through enough of them during his first field research in Ghana?). House and garden were full to overflowing. Maurice Godelier came over from France, Alan Macfarlane brought his guitar from the Fens, Keith Hart adapted a well-known folk song from Yorkshire to provide a satirical salute, Cesare Poppi and Paul Sant Cassia added Mediterranean accents to the conversations and the cuisine, Stephen Hugh-Jones demonstrated yet again that reports of a continuing feud with the Leach camp at King's were, to say the least, exaggerated, and Gilbert Lewis embodied the continued vitality of anthropology within John's. All of these men were close to Jack, and there were many more. However, to the very end of his life the patriarch liked to stress that women had exerted a greater influence.⁶²

Jack continued to value his room at St John's and his summer holidays in France throughout the peripatetic decades of his retirement. He accepted invitations from all over the world, seemingly indifferent to whether the occasion was a Distinguished Lecture or a run-of-the-mill doctoral examination or consultancy. Though he never warmed to Germany as he did to France (hardly surprising in view of the war), he was a regular guest of the Max Planck Society. On a memorable December evening in 1997 in Berlin, after drinking some decent red wine at the Wissenschaftskolleg, Jack, Eric Hobsbawm and Perry Anderson (three quite different hues of the British academic left) regaled their companions with revolutionary songs. Alas Jack tripped on the way back to his room and was hospitalised for several weeks with a broken hip. He was thus unable to attend a meeting the next day charged with taking the decision

---

[61] Food was also a central theme of his writing for decades. In addition to the 1982 monograph noted above, several chapters and articles are staples in the interdisciplinary field of Food Studies.
[62] A small example: I think he cited the work of Q. D. Leavis on the emergence of the English novel more often than he mentioned the impact of her equally distinguished husband on generations of literature scholars in Cambridge. It is worth bearing in mind that from his school years onwards, Jack Goody spent the greater part of his life as a member of exclusively male or male-dominated institutions. (The two years he spent working for Hertfordshire County Council between 1947 and 1949 were the main exception.) Even after his retirement, High Table at St John's was often an all-male gathering. This is the social context in which to place not only his enduring intellectual fascination with the 'woman's property complex' but also his energetic campaigning for the admission of women to his beloved college (accomplished in 1981). Privately, he was unstinting in the support he gave his daughters to realise their potential.

whether or not to establish a Max Planck Institute for Social Anthropology.[63]

Jack Goody received numerous honorary degrees, medals, prizes and a belated Festschrift.[64] He also responded to a symposium in *Theory, Culture and Society* in which his work was addressed mainly by historians and cultural sociologists.[65] More formal international recognition came as early as 1980 in the USA, when he was elected an Honorary Foreign Member of the American Academy of Arts and Sciences; in 2004 he was elected to the National Academy of Sciences. In France, he was appointed Chevalier (later Officier, and in 2006 Commandeur) of the Ordre des Arts et Lettres. In 2005 he was elevated to a Knighthood by the Queen 'for services to anthropology'.

Lectures and extended stays in prestigious academic bolt-holes equipped with good libraries all functioned to hone Jack's ability to generate texts for staff at St John's to process back in Cambridge. But so did long train journeys, or even airport stopovers where he had only the back of an envelope at his disposal. Mrs Susan Mansfield, Fellows' Secretary at John's, had an almost unique ability to decipher his handwriting. (Fittingly, she was the only non-family invitee when he went to Buckingham Palace to be knighted.) Jack made some use of research assistants for his later books. These writings were shaped not only by promiscuous encounters in seminars and conferences around the world but also by the contingencies of High Table interaction in Cambridge, especially within his own College—and by whatever he happened to have been reading lately.

Jack met the psychoanalyst and feminist Juliet Mitchell in the early 1990s at Yale University. In 2000 Juliet became his wife and her daughter Polly his step-daughter. Summers in France continued, but now at her base at Bouzigues (Herault). When Jack's health deteriorated in the new century, in addition to providing practical help with his writing and editing his texts, Juliet cared for him. Her professional background enabled her to trace the origin of his most intemperate moods to his wartime experiences and she accompanied him on visits to key sites in the Mediterranean. Jack's third family opened new horizons on feminism and changes in British society, while at the same time rekindling his interest in Freud and

---

[63] Fortunately, a second distinguished foreign consultant had been invited: Marilyn Strathern remained sober throughout her stay in Berlin.

[64] D. R. Olson and M. Cole (eds.), *Technology, Literacy, and the Evolution of Society: Implications of the Work of Jack Goody* (Mahwah, NJ, 2006).

[65] M. Featherstone, P. Burke and S. Mennell (eds.), 'Occidentalism: Jack Goody and comparative history', Special Issue of *Theory, Culture & Society*, 26 (2009), 7–8.

his love of English literature. In addition to looking over each other's latest texts, Juliet and Jack read poetry to each other. His unique gravelly voice fell silent on 16 July 2015 in a Cambridge care home.

Conclusion

I have tried to provide a sketch of Jack Goody the human being as well as an indication of the significance of his work. In both respects, my effort is necessarily preliminary. He undoubtedly warrants a full biographical study. In one way or another, Jack Goody's gruff charisma touched just about everyone who came into contact with social anthropology in Cambridge in the second half of the twentieth century. Although I have identified a gradual shift of focus during the 1970s, his work has a high degree of unity. It was rigorously materialist, and at the same time holistic in its embracing of art, literature and science. While reaching out to the humanities, especially in his later books, Jack never abandoned the view that anthropology should contribute to a cumulative social science. Long before the advent of postmodernism made things much worse, he deplored the fact that many sociocultural anthropologists were forgetting their discipline's history and losing their way in 'soggy' jargon.

Jack was one of the last of the colonial ethnographers. His fieldwork was excellent and the touchstone for everything that followed. Ghana never ceased to matter (he visited for the last time with Juliet Mitchell in the new century). But Ghana and Africa were never enough. In terms of intellectual ambition, Jack Goody had more in common with predecessors such as James Frazer and 'Anarchy' Brown than with most of his contemporaries and successors in anthropology. His scholarship was also shaped by sociologists such as George Homans, whose aspiration to construct a science of human society he shared. If, in addition, such a social anthropologist can make connections with archaeologists like Gordon Childe and cultural historians of the calibre of Peter Burke, he is well qualified to transcend the conventional boundaries of his discipline—to lead the way in revising dominant European narratives, through comparative investigations of the social relations of Africa, Eurasia and the entire planet.

CHRIS HANN
Max Planck Institute for Social Anthropology, Halle;
Corpus Christi College, Cambridge

Note: Goody was my PhD supervisor in Cambridge between 1975 and 1979. Everyone seemed to call him Jack, so I did too, from the beginning. He retired in the year that I was appointed to the staff of the Department and I was not particularly close to him personally; but we kept in touch over the years and he gave the keynote lecture at the first conference in the permanent buildings of the Max Planck Institute for Social Anthropology in December 2001. When he visited again in 2004 he delivered a more personal talk about the development of his thinking. I have a transcription and hope to publish it in due course, together with a collection of the Goody Lectures which we have organised in Halle every year since 2011: http://www.eth.mpg.de/3789573/Goody_Lectures.

Since his passing I have been made aware of the existence of a large number of boxes of field notes and research papers deposited at St John's College, Cambridge. The Special Collections Librarian will welcome enquiries. I have not probed into unpublished materials for this memoir. I thank Peter Brown, former Secretary of the British Academy, for supplying practical guidelines and a copy of a CV prepared by Goody himself. A tidier bibliography running to 2004 is provided at the end of D. R. Olson and M. Cole (eds.), *Technology, Literacy, and the Evolution of Society* (Mahwah, NJ, 2006), pp. 325–42. The most complete bibliography, maintained by Susan Mansfield until 2015, can be consulted at St John's College.

Jack Goody looked back on his life and work quite frequently. He paints a particularly harmonious picture of the Cambridge social anthropology department in its heyday in 'Towards a room with a view: a personal account of contributions to local knowledge, theory, and research in fieldwork and comparative studies', *Annual Review of Anthropology*, 20 (1991), 1–23. Some personal detail can also be gleaned from his foray into disciplinary history (which includes wistful restatements of his philosophy of anthropology as a cumulative science, composed at a time when this was singularly unfashionable): J. Goody, *The Expansive Moment. Anthropology in Britain and Africa, 1918–1970* (Cambridge, 1995).

Jack would be the first to appreciate that elements of orality have intruded throughout this text. Numerous friends have helped me, either in person, or through informal communications in the latest digital media, or both. Special thanks to Ray Abrahams, Keith Hart, Gilbert Lewis and Alan Macfarlane for sharing their perceptions of a teacher and colleague; to Martine Segalen for the reception in France; and to Peter Burke, one of Jack's closest intellectual confidants from the 1980s onwards, who shares his determination to combat excessive specialisation in the humanities and social sciences, and to reunite these realms.. I also wish to thank Jeremy Goody (Lokamitra), Esther Newcomb Goody, Mary Goody, Rachel Goody and Juliet Mitchell. The more information I received from family members, the clearer it became that, to cite the words of Ludwig Wittgenstein in a quite different context, 'whereof one cannot speak, thereof one should be silent'.

FRANK HORACE HAHN

Frank Horace Hahn
1925–2013

FRANK HAHN HAD A TRANSFORMATIVE IMPACT on British economics wherever he went, building on his love of, and competence in, mathematics and greatly influenced by his numerous American colleagues. He was at the heart of the development of General Equilibrium theory, which he criticised for its inability to include money. As a mathematical economist he was aware of the power of maximisation to deliver testable propositions about competitive equilibrium, but he was also sceptical about competitive equilibrium as a useful description of any actual economy. Later he was to attack what he termed Lucasian macroeconomists (Robert Lucas and his followers) for assuming that economies were in competitive equilibrium. His published works live on along with his huge impact on the profession. He brought together and worked with the best economists of his generation, nurtured and launched his students and colleagues, and, crucially, introduced the modern American rigorous theoretical economic approach to the more literary-minded and even anti-mathematical English style that had been prevalent since Marshall.

Hahn was a leader—he held the highest offices in the profession as President of the Econometric Society (in 1968), was elected to the British Academy (in 1975), and was a transformative President of the Royal Economic Society (1986–9)—but he engaged intensely with everyone and anyone willing to talk economics, whether the undergraduates that he invited weekly to his house, or his colleagues in the faculty common room at coffee and tea time, at faculty seminars and when visiting. He was hugely supportive of his friends and students, and to quote Solow on Hahn's 1956 visit to Massachusetts Institute of Technology (MIT),

Biographical Memoirs of Fellows of the British Academy, XVI, 485–525. © The British Academy 2017.
Posted 14 November 2017. © The British Academy 2017.

'I cannot remember whether it was literally love at first sight. By the end of that year, however, a lifelong friendship had come into being' (Solow, 1992, 3). That was a sentiment echoed by many other visiting economists, who duly arrived as Overseas Fellows at Churchill College in Cambridge in response to invitations from Hahn after he joined the college as a founding fellow in 1960, many of whom were subsequently to be awarded the Nobel Prize.

He could be abrupt, combative and impatient with what he considered to be intellectually mediocre; he was often politically incorrect and sometimes dismissive of those with whom he disagreed: worse, he was sometimes impatient with the administrative staff for not intuiting exactly what he wanted. He was always fiercely intellectual, and his first question on seeing a colleague might be 'What new theorems have you proved?'. He recounted how when invited to give a lecture at Berkeley in 1959 he reminded them that 'America is the only country that went from barbarism to decadence without civilization in between.' Apparently that went down a treat and he was offered a position in their economics department.

Life and career

Frank Horace Hahn was born in Berlin on 26 April 1925, the younger of two sons, to Arnold Hahn, German-speaking, and Maria Hahn, Czech-speaking, with roots in the Jewish community. The family were Central European intellectuals. Hahn would delight in reminding one that he was a mitteleuropäisches Jew (who toyed with the idea of becoming a Catholic when a young student at Oxford, and later would hanker for the life of a Trollopian rural dean).[1] He would exaggerate his accent—'wee Breeteesh' —and stated most emphatically that 'England made me'.

His father was a chemist, but became a rather well-known literary figure, author of a book of sonnets, writing a weekly column for *Simplicissimus*, a satirical magazine founded in 1896, as well as popular science books and novels. Hahn described him as 'formidably learned' and his mother as 'beautiful and rather pleasure-loving'. His father was clearly a disciplinarian, not allowing Frank any dessert until he had equalled his older brother in solving problems. His upbringing gave him a

---

[1] I was with Hahn at a conference at Varenna, Lake Como, in June 1967 at the outbreak of the Six-Day War, and Hahn was all for offering his services to Israel—the war was over too soon for this to take effect.

'voracious appetite for reading and intellectual speculation', which he retained throughout his life.

The family left Berlin for Prague in 1931, where he and his elder brother, Peter (born 1923), were sent to English schools but also learned Czech. At the relatively late date of 1938 they wisely left permanently for England, first for London and then Oxford. His father continued to publish, perhaps remarkably for wartime London, in German (Hahn, A., 1943), while Hahn was sent at the age of 13 to board at Bournemouth Grammar School, for which he retained an abiding fondness. Like his brother Peter, who went to University College of Swansea in 1941 but enlisted in the RAF after a year, Frank went to Oxford to read mathematics, and also enlisted in the RAF after a year's study in 1943.

Frank's father had suggested that he study economics at university, but his real love was always pure mathematics, although he recognised early that he was unlikely to make a good enough mathematician to justify continuing. It is hardly surprising that Hahn is always described as a mathematical economist and admitted that as an economist he might 'lack some of the attributes of an economist that Keynes thought necessary' with a 'weak interest in the practical end of the subject'.

While serving in the RAF (as a navigator latterly hunting for U-boats) he started reading economics books, and notably Hicks's *Value and Capital*, at the suggestion of his father's friend Michal Kalecki. Kalecki was a distinguished Polish economist, hired by the Oxford Institute of Statistics in 1940, who established close links with the Cambridge 'post-Keynesians' around Richard Kahn and Joan Robinson. Kalecki's approach to macroeconomics based on imperfectly competitive firms should have been as influential with that group as it was with Hahn. *Value and Capital* had a lasting impact on the young Hahn, leading to a sustained interest for the rest of his life with General Equilibrium theory. Hicks stressed, and Hahn was persuaded, of the critical importance of the micro-foundations of macroeconomics. Later, in the preface to their joint book, Hahn and Solow (1995, vii) explained what this meant: '... we both regarded ourselves as neoclassical economists in the sense that we required theories of the economy to be firmly based on the rationality of agents and on decentralized modes of economic communication among them. Indeed, it was this general approach that led us to the view that the new macroeconomists were claiming much more than could be deduced from fundamental neoclassical principles.' Kalecki clearly had a major impact, as Hahn took his advice that it would be easy to read for a London external degree in economics while in the forces, which he did, graduating in 1945.

While his brother Peter decided to return to Prague after the war (and remained there until escaping with his family, a suitcase and £500 at the end of the Prague Spring in 1968), Frank went to the London School of Economics (LSE) to pursue a PhD at the tender age of 20. Hahn wrote that his time at the LSE was 'fortunate in many ways. I met my wife (also an economist) whose intelligence exceeds mine by an order of magnitude and whose good sense has been invaluable' (Szenberg, 1992, 162). The story is that he met Dorothy Salter and proposed to her the following day, marrying in 1946 at the age of 21—an excellent example of his rapid perception followed by decisive action.

The LSE was an international hothouse of economists. Lionel Robbins, Nicky Kaldor, Ronald Coase, Arthur Lewis and Friedrich Hayek were active in the seminars that Hahn attended. His initial PhD supervisor for the first three months was Kaldor, but Hahn only had two supervisions from him before moving to Robbins. His thesis, 'The share of wages in national income', was completed in 1951. Kaldor was later to write 'According to the preface of Ricardo's *Principles*, the discovery of the laws which regulate distributive shares is the "principal problem in Political Economy"' (Kaldor, 1955, 83; distributive shares are the shares of wages and profits in national income). In 1950 Hahn published a condensed version of part of the thesis as the short article 'The share of wages in the trade cycle' in the *Economic Journal*, followed by Hahn (1951), which has the same title as the thesis but is essentially just chapter 3.

The thesis was eventually published in full (Hahn, 1972) and illuminatingly discussed by Solow (1992, 3), who argues that 'Hahn has an excellent claim to be the originator of the "macroeconomic theory of distribution", to have been—dare I say it? a sort of proto-Kaldor.' In the Preface to the published thesis Hahn first disarmingly notes that 'To publish unchanged a thesis written over twenty years ago is a dubious enterprise and certainly requires an explanation.' He also notes in the first sentence that 'Professor Kaldor recalls a conversation with me about 1947 in which he expressed the view that "the best approach to distribution theory is macro-economic"' (Hahn, 1972, 1). The reason for finally publishing his thesis was that it was 'largely concerned with an exploration of the consequences for the distribution of income of a postulated difference in the savings propensities out of wages and profits. This avenue of exploration has been much discussed in recent years …' (i.e. in the 1950s Cambridge discussions about growth and distribution), but Hahn argued that long-run theory was 'basically uninteresting' and that he was concerned with 'the study of disequilibrium, which I took to be the "normal" state of a capitalist economy.'

Kaldor, who had moved from the LSE to Cambridge and was probably instrumental in persuading Hahn to come to Cambridge in 1960, later wrote extensively on the importance of differences in savings out of wages and profits in determining the long-run share of wages in growth models (Kaldor, 1956, 1957). Hahn surveyed these models in the masterful work with Robin Matthews 'The theory of economic growth: a survey' (hereafter the *Growth Survey*, Hahn and Matthews, 1964) but without mentioning any connection with his own earlier work at that time.

In 1948, Hahn left for a teaching post in Birmingham University where he met, and found irresistible, Terence Gorman, who had 'by far the best and clearest mind I had yet come across' (Szenberg, 1992, 162). They remained lifelong friends, surprisingly different in manner but equally devoted to the application of mathematics to understanding and illuminating claims in economics. They both decided to accept professorships at the LSE in 1967, Gorman moving from a chair in Oxford while Hahn moved from Cambridge.

Birmingham under Gilbert Walker was one of the first departments to take mathematical economics seriously, and although small (it still had only seven staff in 1962) had in addition Alan Walters (later Hahn's *bête noire* as a monetarist and advisor to Prime Minister Thatcher), Michael Beesley, David Rowan and Esra Bennathan (who both remained lifelong friends). While at Birmingham, Hahn supervised Maurice McManus' PhD, another distinguished mathematical economist.

In 1956 Hahn took a sabbatical at MIT, which was hugely influential, both in creating strong links to the leading American economists of the day, particularly Bob Solow and Paul Samuelson, and in reassuring him of the validity of the mathematical approach to economic theory. Hicks in *Value and Capital* relegated mathematical arguments to the appendix, rather as Marshall used mathematics to clarify his thinking, before putting the argument into words and relegating any essential mathematics to footnotes. The same was even more the case with Keynes, who consciously eschewed mathematics in his economics writings (opening himself to the criticism that he was as a result imprecise and failed to clinch arguments). This was despite graduating as the twelfth-best undergraduate mathematician at Cambridge in 1905 and starting his research on probability, producing an early draft of his *Treatise on Probability* in 1908.

Much of this very British approach to economics was the feeling that the 'real world' was too complex and chaotic to capture in a simple model, and, as Keynes is claimed (after his death) to have said, 'It is better to be roughly right than precisely wrong.'[2] Hahn, always a mathematician at heart, had read Hicks and his contemporaries, but was hugely influenced by Samuelson's (1947) *Foundations of Economic Analysis*, which he cites in the first chapter of his thesis. Nevertheless, the thesis shows its origins in the literary style of his British contemporaries, in contrast to the more carefully axiomatic approach of the later Hahn. (Although he was sometimes willing to write what he would describe as 'blah blah' articles that reflected on debates in a more literary style.) Given the opacity of some of Hahn's mathematical arguments these were often a useful supplement to understanding the central points he was trying to make, and in some articles (e.g. Hahn, 1966) he would write 'some comments' at the end, in which he explained what was really going on behind the mathematical opacity.

The insight that so appealed to any mathematician encountering the *Foundations* was the revelation that maximising behaviour (firms maximising profits, or consumers maximising their utility) and the dynamic stability of market equilibria could generate powerful and testable propositions, the mark of a proper science. Later Hahn, enunciating his philosophy, stated that the claim of economics to be a science is premature and pretentious, but defended economics as useful and important. 'It provides grammatical arguments and methods for summarizing economic data. ... a powerful aid to thought in providing clear limits to understanding, and can demonstrate genuine nonsense' (Szenberg, 1992, 163).

Terence Gorman further convinced him of the power of mathematics and was later to demonstrate that by employing maximisation to derive utility and profit as functions of competitive prices rather than quantities. That immediately made them directly applicable to observable market data and hence testable. Solow, reflecting on that first visit of Hahn to MIT, observes that 'By 1956, Hahn was already recognizably the economic theorist the world knows now' (Solow, 1984, 3). Hahn also met Ken Arrow, with whom he started a lifelong collaboration that resulted in arguably his definitive legacy—*General Competitive Analysis* (Arrow and Hahn, 1971), started when Arrow was visiting Cambridge in 1963–4.

Hahn was elected Reader in Mathematical Economics at Birmingham in 1958. In 1959 he visited the University of California at Berkeley where

---

[2] The correct attribution is to Carveth Read in *Logic, Deductive and Inductive* (1898, p. 351): 'It is better to be vaguely right than exactly wrong', https://en.wikiquote.org/wiki/John_Maynard_Keynes (accessed 3 July 2017).

Kaldor was also visiting (as was Aubrey Silberston, also on leave from Cambridge, and Donald Winch, another lifelong friend). By all accounts Kaldor, by then at Cambridge, urged Hahn to come to Cambridge in 1960 to a lectureship, but it was Richard Kahn, perhaps surprisingly given his suspicion of mathematical economics,[3] who secured Hahn's appointment.

Churchill College was founded in 1960 as the national memorial to Sir Winston Churchill. In March 1960 the master of the embryonic college, Sir John Cockcroft, considered Hahn for a fellowship while he was still on sabbatical at Berkeley. It is fascinating to read some of the references solicited as part of that very careful scrutiny for the new college. Hicks, whose book had been the strongest influence on Hahn's early interest in economics, wrote rather disarmingly that 'he really is a good man and should go far'. Paul Samuelson, who had met him on his visit to MIT in 1956, wrote that he has the 'priceless ingredient (in our profession!) of enthusiasm'; In contrast with some coming from mathematics he has an 'excellent "feel" for economically important aspects of a problem'. Kaldor, writing from Berkeley, was even more fulsome: 'an economic theorist of considerable ingenuity and subtlety' with 'exceptional intellectual ability' and 'scrupulous intellectual honesty' who 'gives his help unstintingly and generously to all who need it in their own intellectual problems'.

As Hahn's lectureship started on 1 October 1960, Cockcroft wrote in April 1960 to offer Hahn a fellowship from the same date. Hahn thus became a founding fellow, although as Churchill had no buildings he was hosted at Kaldor's college, King's, for a short period. He also became Director of Studies in Economics, responsible for admitting and arranging the teaching of economics undergraduates, a task that I took over from him when he left in 1966.

Hahn's arrival in Cambridge was like a refreshing blast for those wishing to drag Cambridge out of its disputatious and backward-looking controversies. Keynes had died in 1946, exhausted by wartime financial negotiations. Sir Dennis Robertson, a close collaborator of Keynes in the early development of *The General Theory*, had been cast out by Keynes and his circle for criticising some of Keynes's arguments. The bitter feuding of the 1930s continued after Robertson had retired and Keynes had died, carried on by Keynes's acolytes, Richard Kahn and Joan Robinson. Kahn had been responsible for bringing Hahn to Cambridge to continue the faculty's standing as a world-class economics faculty, despite his

---

[3] Kahn studied mathematics in his first year as an undergraduate, physics in his second year, but Finals of the Economics Tripos in his third year.

scepticism and even hostility to mathematical economics. Joan, however, was a fierce opponent of neoclassical economics, a position she maintained long after her retirement. Austin Robinson, husband of Joan, was a professor (as was Kahn, but not at that time), and both he and Joan had worked closely with Keynes in the 1930s. Austin and the Canadian economist Donald Moggridge were chiefly responsible for editing the thirty volumes of Keynes's *Collected Writings*.

Austin Robinson had been the prime mover behind the creation of a new faculty building, completed in 1961 and named after him on his ninetieth birthday in 1987. Harcourt's obituary describes him as '… the unsung hero of Cambridge economics. Through selfless service, often as secretary, sometimes as chairman of the Faculty Board of Economics and Politics, before and after the Second World War, Robinson, more than anyone else, enabled the various opposing factions of the faculty to coexist, and its intellectual life thereby to thrive.'[4] His peace-making was not always successful, and Austin and Joan could not have been more different, seeming distant from each other even when both in the faculty coffee room.

The Faculty of Economics and Politics (as it then was) already had an impressive set of academics when Hahn arrived. James Meade, who had spent a postgraduate year in Cambridge in 1930–1 working with Kahn on the development of Keynes's *General Theory*, had moved from a chair at the LSE in 1957 to become the Professor of Political Economy (the sole chair before the war and always the senior chair) and was later to win the Nobel Prize. Joan Robinson made his life a misery, to the point that he took early retirement to continue writing his books.

Richard Stone (Nobel Prize winner in 1984) had worked with James Meade for the wartime British Government and became the first Director of the Cambridge Department of Applied Economics (DAE, that Keynes had proposed before the war) from 1945 to 1955. Under Stone, the DAE became a leading centre of economic theory and statistical methodology. With postwar funding from the USA, the DAE attracted some of the world's leading econometricians, including James Durbin and Geoffrey Watson. Stone's Directorship had been brought to an end by Kahn and Robinson, who blocked his reappointment as Director. The University elected him to the newly secured P. D. Leake Chair of Finance and Accounting, which Stone, to the dismay of the sponsoring firm, interpreted

---

[4] At http://www.independent.co.uk/news/people/obituary-sir-austin-robinson-1489686.html (accessed 3 July 2017).

as Social and National Accounting. The Faculty Board ensured that the DAE was entrusted to, in its view, a safer pair of hands in Brian Reddaway, Director from 1955 to 1980, a commonsense economist sceptical of abstract theory.

Nevertheless, Stone, at the suggestion of Alan Brown, bundled up his various projects on consumer demand, input–output and national accounts into the *Growth Project*, separately funded (by the UK Social Science Research Council) but located in the DAE,[5] taking full advantage of the right, at that time, of professors not to have to lecture. Charles Feinstein (later Chichele Professor of Economic History at Oxford), joined the DAE in 1958 to work on National Income and Expenditure, and later Stone recruited Angus Deaton (Noble Laureate) and Mervyn King (later Governor of the Bank of England) to work on the *Growth Project*.

Michael Farrell had joined the DAE in 1949 to work with Stone and was subsequently appointed to a lectureship and later to a Readership in the faculty. Farrell, an editor of the *Review of Economic Studies* and fellow of the Econometric Society, developed empirical methods of identifying the efficient production frontier, and was the first economist to point out that under certain aggregation conditions, non-convexities need not rule out the existence of competitive general equilibrium. Farrell was therefore very much at home in Hahn's world of mathematical economics and the two much admired each other. One measure of the pettiness and vindictiveness of Kahn and Robinson is that when Kahn took over Keynes's Monday seminar, known as the 'secret' seminar,[6] Farrell, with some other prominent faculty like Malcolm Fisher and Ron Henderson, supporters of Robertson, were excluded. Meade and Hahn were invited to the 'secret' seminar, although Meade then withdrew.

Several other members of the faculty should be mentioned to demonstrate its pre-eminence and schizophrenia in 1960. David Champernowne had been at Cambridge as an undergraduate in the 1930s and was appointed a lecturer in statistics in 1938. In 1940 he was drafted into Churchill's wartime Government statistical department. In 1944 he was instrumental with Keynes in setting up the Department of Applied

---

[5] Until the Faculty closed it down (and took all its funds) the DAE housed the staff employed on all externally funded research projects. Reddaway had secured an excellent financial settlement when he became Director that enabled it to operate as an autonomous and self-sustaining budget holder.

[6] So-called to give the misleading impression that those specifically not invited would not know that they had been excluded.

Economics in Cambridge, but after the war he moved to Oxford to become Director of the Institute of Statistics from 1945 to 1948, and professor of statistics from 1948 to 1959. He apparently missed being in Cambridge and was willing to accept the more junior post of Reader there in 1959, which he held until he became Professor of Economics and Statistics in 1970.

Nicky Kaldor has already been mentioned, and was perfectly happy talking to both sides of the great divide in the faculty, frequently earning the wrath of Joan Robinson for his heretical views (such as the tendency of capitalist economies towards full employment). He later collaborated with Jim Mirrlees who helped with the mathematics of his growth model. Kaldor was a larger than life figure (as was Hahn), hugely engaging and a brilliantly perceptive economist, frequently remarking that the world was not linear—and his sideways profile certainly was not. Like Hahn, he was supremely self-confident, outspoken and could be hostile in seminars. Joan Robinson had '(in Shove's view) a very poor understanding of what neoclassical economics said about a lot of theoretical problems' (Harcourt, 1995) but was anxious to discuss economics with Hahn. On hearing this, Kaldor rang Hahn and said 'Don't you dare talk to that woman! She will steal my ideas from you.' Kaldor was concerned on this occasion about his theory of distribution and growth. According to Harcourt, Joan Robinson and Kaldor 'were "at it" with Joan Robinson trying to mend fences, Nicky being impossible, and Kahn stirring the waters whenever peace looked like breaking out'.[7]

Robin Matthews (who had graduated in PPE from Oxford) had been at Cambridge since 1949. As the author of the highly regarded 1954 *A Study in Trade Cycle History*, he was less in the neo-Keynesian firing line, and followed that up with the influential book on *The Trade Cycle* (Matthews, 1958). He was to join forces with Hahn to write the Hahn–Matthews *Growth Survey* (Hahn and Matthews, 1964) but left Cambridge in 1965 to become the Drummond Professor of Political Economy at Oxford from 1965 to 1975. Dick Goodwin, who had been a Rhodes Scholar in the 1930s, and described himself as 'a lifelong but wayward Marxist' (Desai and Ormerod, 1998), had arrived in Cambridge after being forced out of Harvard (where he had taught since 1942) by McCarthyism. Goodwin had also published two articles on the trade cycle (Goodwin, 1953, 1955), worrying, as had Harrod in his original article, about how the short-term rate of growth determined by investment could

---

[7] Email of 23 August 2016.

bear any relationship to the long-run rate of growth determined by technology and population growth. Goodwin, as a well-trained American economist, was quite comfortable with sophisticated mathematics, and later constructed a very elegant predator–prey differential equation model of the trade cycle (Goodwin, 1967).

Luigi Pasinetti had been a student of Piero Sraffa and Richard Kahn in the 1950s and returned to Cambridge (and King's College) at the behest of Kahn in 1962. He followed Kaldor in studying the impact of different savings propensities on the distribution of income, but in this case distinguishing the savings behaviour of workers (who might receive profits) and capitalists who received profits (Pasinetti, 1962). That model was also reviewed in the Hahn–Matthews *Growth Survey*.

Cambridge in 1960 when Hahn arrived therefore had a distinguished but factious faculty, although Ken Binmore, in his obituary in *The Times* (3 February 2013) and writing from the distance of the LSE, gave a rather more downbeat assessment: 'In the time of such Cambridge luminaries as Marshall and Keynes, British economists led the world, but the mantle of leadership had passed to America by the 1950s, and Cambridge had become an ineffectual talking shop. However, a new generation of young economists led by Frank Hahn kept the United Kingdom in the running by abandoning the literary style that had been the norm since Adam Smith.'

Christopher Bliss, who read economics from 1959 to 1962, in correspondence before Hahn died, wrote:

> Frank Hahn came to Cambridge in 1960, when I was a second-year undergraduate. The important point to appreciate concerning the Cambridge Economics of that time is that it suffered greatly from the mess that Keynes (who died 14 years earlier) had left behind him. Despite his unquestionable greatness, Keynes could be an arrogant and intolerant person. Once his ideas had settled he often had no time for anyone who ventured to disagree with him. This affected in particular Sir Denis Robertson, who had been his chum, but who refused to be born again into the new Keynesian faith, although he pursued a revised macroeconomics of his own. The aftermath of all this was a sharp and fractious division in the Faculty between the 'neo-Keynesians' (notably Kahn and Joan Robinson) and the 'Neoclassicals' (in particular James Meade).[8] Like the religious divisions of Sixteenth-Century Europe, this mainly proved to be unproductive, with different parties talking past each other, although it did sometimes spin off new ideas and good work. Broadly one can say that the 'Keynesian' stream was backward-looking and sterile. The 'Neoclassical' stream on the other hand, for all its faults, and they were several, was dynamic and creative;

---

[8] Meade was a lifelong Keynesian, and not simply a 'neoclassical' economist.

part of a world-wide research programme involving mathematical economics, game theory and econometrics. The arrival of Frank Hahn into this fetid atmosphere was like a breath of fresh air, and the same could be said of Amartya Sen's influence. Both these men refused to sign on to one side or the other in the holy war of Cambridge Economics. Yet they both communicated vigorously with all parties, and they were evidently too strong to be ignored.[9]

Later, in another communication, Bliss wrote of Hahn: 'His impact was huge. Like John Nash he had a beautiful mind, and his energy was massive. Aside from conducting his own research, he engaged with anyone who cared to talk to him. He was not intimidated either by distinction or by aggression from Joan Robinson.'[10] Later on Hahn and the growing number of young Turks that he attracted were to set up the Churchill seminar as a rival to the 'secret seminar', which they outcompeted in attracting attendees, until Kahn dissolved the seminar in 1969.

However, in the early 1960s the 'secret seminar' was still in full swing, with Hahn very much in attendance. Harcourt recalls that in November 1963 Ken Arrow, visiting Cambridge and Churchill College, read from the proofs of his classic 1963 paper 'Uncertainty and the welfare economics of medical care', while the following February Bob Solow, who was also visiting Cambridge (and gave the Marshall Lectures on 'Effective Demand and Capital Theory'), commented on a draft of the Hahn–Matthews *Growth Survey*.

I arrived at Trinity College to read for Part II of Mathematics Tripos in 1961, and, after taking Finals in 1963, and unclear what to do with my third year, met with Jim Mirrlees at the suggestion of a fellow Scot and my Director of Studies, Keith Moffatt. Mirrlees had no difficulty in persuading me to read for Part II of the Economics Tripos (1963–5). My first encounter with Hahn was in 1964, attending his lectures on general equilibrium. They were quite brilliant, not only for setting out the elegant and powerful theory but also for pointing out its limitations—its inability to account for the role of money, and hence for the problems that afflict real-life economies, such as unemployment.

Monjit Chatterji recalls a similar experience of Hahn: 'His Lectures were exhaustively demanding. Frank himself made no bones about it. His cyclostyled lecture notes with hand drawn diagrams (without the benefit of a French curve) were a real *tour de force*.' Chatterji cites from Hahn's handout: 'The lectures (and notes) are intended to serve a small minority

---

[9] Email, 2013.
[10] Memorandum from Christopher Bliss, August 2016.

of those reading Economics. They are not required for examinations. Moreover there are many successful practical economists everywhere who are quite innocent of the matters to be discussed so that the lectures are not required to ensure comfort in later life. There are also many people who regard this kind of careful and abstract approach as not worthwhile and they are just as often respected academically as those who hold the opposite view. So the lectures are not required for academic respectability.' And again '… if you do not like "difficult lectures" these are not for you' (Chatterji, 2013).

No undergraduate could be unaware of the seething disagreements within the faculty. Joan Robinson was lecturing as though their school (the post-Keynesians) had refuted neoclassical economics, while Hahn and others were providing convincing arguments (to at least the majority of students) that this was far from the case. Later, as a final-year student, I was slightly shocked to hear Hahn crowing that he had just delivered the final nail in the coffin of capitalism, perhaps referring to his paper on 'Equilibrium dynamics with heterogeneous capital goods' (Hahn, 1966). Hahn was always quite clear about important distinctions such as that between the efficiency of competitive equilibrium and its distributional justice, and between equilibrium as a concept and its likelihood of describing an economy at any moment. In contrast, the Kahn–Robinson clique (and many of their circle) considered that undermining neoclassical economics was essential to remove what they saw as its justification for the existence of profits in a capitalist society.

We were all convinced that economics was of the utmost significance, so passionate were the arguments we were exposed to. It helped that Keynes was viewed as the economist who had provided the tools to enable governments to avoid the Great Depression, and that numerous faculty members were for ever rushing off to advise the Government of the day. Reddaway (then Director of the DAE and the inventor of war-time points rationing) convinced us to become familiar with the *Blue Book* of National Accounts (and other statistical publications) and that we should be able to ground our arguments using such statistical evidence in language that an intelligent, but non-economist, civil servant could understand.

Tony Atkinson, who graduated from Churchill College in economics in 1966, recalls that he first met Hahn as his Director of Studies. His initial greeting was characteristically off-putting: 'are you as stupid as you look?' Later, after an initial year's supervision with Jan Graaff (another Churchill Overseas Fellow invited by Hahn), Atkinson faced Hahn's 'idiosyncratic— and sometimes counter-productive—style of teaching: 'Surely', he would say of my essay, '"you can do better than Professor X", the aforementioned X having recently published an article on the topic in a leading journal. I like to think that we got on well, perhaps because I did not take him too seriously, or perhaps because I took him seriously when he meant to be.'[11]

Churchill College's founder Winston Churchill had a vision of the college as an MIT for Britain and the statutes require that 70 per cent of its students are in sciences, engineering and mathematics. At its foundation, the college received a generous endowment to invite distinguished American academics (later extended to all nationalities). Following Churchill's vision, Hahn thought that Economics could play a similar role in a science- and engineering-oriented college as it did in MIT. He took delight in persuading a steady stream of future Nobel laureates and other almost equally distinguished economists to visit the college for between one and three terms.

The first buildings in the college were the Sheppard Flats, named for the architect of the whole college, wonderfully located in a cluster surrounded by formal gardens and trees, looking down over the playing fields to the college buildings proper, and these were provided to the Overseas Fellows. In short order, Arrow, Diamond, Uzawa, Radner, Solow, Maskin, Debreu and Scarf arrived to stay in the Sheppard Flats and visit the faculty. Joe Stiglitz was visiting from MIT in 1965 (and indeed spent a tumultuous few weeks nominally as Joan Robinson's student, before moving to Hahn) and was rapidly elected to the Tapp Research Fellowship at Gonville and Caius College, Cambridge (1966–70, although he was Assistant Professor of Economics at MIT, 1966–7, before moving to Yale).

The faculty was also recruiting young economists. Jim Mirrlees was the first. Mirrlees had taken his PhD in 1964 with a thesis on 'Optimum planning for a dynamic economy' (supervised by Richard Stone) and was appointed to the faculty in 1963. Although Hahn had recruited me to replace him as the economics teaching fellow at Churchill College starting in 1966, I spent my first year after graduation (1965–6) as an Overseas Development Institute Nuffield Fellow in the Treasury of the Tanzanian Government. I was invited while there to apply for an assistant lectureship in the faculty, and was appointed without even an interview, so powerful was Hahn's influence at that time. Christopher Bliss, who had been an undergraduate and then PhD student at Cambridge, gained his PhD in

---

[11] Atkinson's talk at Hahn's memorial event.

1966 on capital–labour substitution and economic growth, and was appointed to a lectureship also in 1966. A year later Tony Atkinson was appointed (also a year after graduating—those were the days) and we shared an office, before he and Bliss were both appointed professors at Essex University. Partha Dasgupta had also switched from Mathematics to Economics and was being supervised for the PhD under Mirrlees, winning a Research Fellowship at Trinity Hall in 1968.

I was a seriously undereducated economist, at that time without any graduate experience. Hahn immediately saw that I needed some further education and arranged with his friend Herb Scarf to invite me for a sabbatical term at the Cowles Foundation in 1969, where Joe Stiglitz was now an Associate Professor. Joe ran an informal small seminar that provided the bulk of my exposure to research in economics, while sharing an office with Atkinson provided further stimulation.

Hahn was offered a chair at the LSE in 1966 at the same time as his close friend, Terence Gorman, making the offer irresistible. The college then elected him to a Title E Fellowship (E for Extraordinary, which certainly fitted Hahn perfectly). He continued to live in Cambridge (in the house in Adams Road that he purchased from Matthews when he moved to Oxford), and continued to engage with the young Turks in the faculty, at the rival Monday seminar held in Churchill College and at his house, where he hospitably entertained with Dorothy. (Dorothy was teaching economics at Newnham College as well a holding the very responsible position of Bursar, and came to my rescue by looking after first-year students when I took up my fellowship as a totally inexperienced supervisor.)

Hahn arrived at the LSE in 1967 like a whirlwind, just as he had at Cambridge. Richard Jackman (taught by both Hahn and myself at Churchill) wrote in the LSE's obituary:

> According to the folklore LSE Economics was in decline and the then Convener, Ely Devons, was advised by his junior colleagues that the situation could be saved only by the appointment of world class (as we would now say) scholars. It is alleged that each of those recruited (Frank Hahn, Terence Gorman, Harry Johnson and Alan Walters) agreed to come only in the belief that the other three had already accepted. Though not long at LSE (he returned to Cambridge in 1972), the years he spent here were amongst the most momentous in the history of the Department. Hahn and the other newly appointed professors set about imposing serious academic standards with traumatic consequences. Several

junior lecturers were denied tenure on the grounds, which seemed extraordinary at the time, that they hadn't published anything.[12]

Dasgupta's (2013) obituary for the Royal Economic Society echoed these comments: 'They (Hahn, Gorman and Sargan) re-structured the graduate programme into its modern form, persuaded the other Professors to call a moratorium on appointments to Lectureships until a suitable cohort had been trained (David Hendry and Stephen Nickell were among the first of the new batch of Lecturers there), and organized the establishment of Chairs so as to attract Amartya Sen and Michio Morishima.' Desai remarks that 'He even on occasion came to the Econometrics Workshop which Denis Sargan ran.' Desai also recounts a wonderful occasion at the Association of University Teachers of Economics (AUTE) meeting in Aberystwyth in April 1972: 'As we all trooped into a large hall completely packed, Frank came on stage and began "Although you see a small Hungarian (sic[13]) Jew before you, let me tell you that I am John the Baptist. I have come to tell you about what is coming." Having got our attention, he went on to give a memorable lecture about what was passionately occupying him at that time. This was the collective effort by several young theorists and himself to integrate money into Walrasian General Equilibrium theory. He told us about the young French theorists Jean Michel Grandmont, Jean Pascal Benassy, Roger Guesnerie et al. He got us all engaged in what he told us was an absolutely central problem of economics.'

Meanwhile, back in Cambridge, the disputes and disagreements in the faculty were going from bad to worse, hardly providing an attractive place to stay. Mirrlees had moved to a chair in Oxford in 1969, shortly followed in 1971 by his former student, Partha Dasgupta, who moved to the LSE. Bliss left for a chair in Essex in 1971, as did Atkinson. Geoffrey Heal, an undergraduate student of Hahn with Atkinson in Churchill, and later a PhD student there, was appointed Assistant Lecturer in 1969 but left for a chair at Essex in 1973, following Atkinson and Bliss. Later the faculty was to fail to appoint Angus Deaton (a subsequent Nobel Laureate who left the DAE for a chair at Bristol in 1976 before emigrating to the USA), just as they failed to promote Oliver Hart (another future Nobel Laureate), despite support from Hahn, and lost him first to the LSE and then to MIT.

---

[12] At http://www.lse.ac.uk/economics/newsEventsSeminars/files/EconomicsReview20122013.pdf.
[13] Hahn described his father as an Austro-Hungarian with a bust of Franz-Joszef on his desk, but Frank was born in Germany.

Aubrey Silberston had been Chairman of the Faculty Board and found it a challenging time to be running the Faculty, for despite his diplomatic skills the factions continued to fight. The Kahn–Robinson axis fought for control of the Faculty Board in order to appoint the Appointments Committee and make nominations to professorial electoral boards, thereby controlling appointments to the Faculty. 1968–9 saw the students in economics and sociology playing a leading part in their version of the student revolution, and the faculty left was now divided between the Maoists and the anti-Maoists (this was a period in which Joan Robinson was impressed with the Chinese approach to economic development).

The Appointments Committee started making doubtful appointments that sometimes seemed based more on whether the candidate signed up to the Kahn–Robinson line than whether they were potentially outstanding. Kaldor manoeuvred the Electoral Board to appoint Robert Neild as Joan Robinson's replacement when she retired from her professorship in order to keep Hahn out, even though Kaldor and Hahn lived in Adams Road and continued to see each other. Silberston (Faculty Chairman) had a terrific row with Kaldor over Neild's appointment, because by then Kaldor had become anti-mathematical and also anti-Hahn. Apparently Neild's appointment in preference to Hahn caused so much outrage that when Richard Kahn retired eighteen months later, Hahn was elected to Kahn's chair in Economics in 1972, and to a professorial fellowship at Churchill.

Hahn's inaugural lecture, given in February 1973, was entitled 'On the notion of equilibrium in economics' and followed hot on the heels of *General Competitive Analysis* (Arrow and Hahn, 1972), begun when Arrow had been visiting Hahn at Cambridge in 1962–3. In it he also responds sharply to Kaldor's (1972) 'On the irrelevance of equilibrium economics', criticising him for his incorrect view of Debreu's classic (1959) *The Theory of Value*. In the same year Hahn was to publish another critique, this time of Kornai's book *Anti-equilibrium* (Hahn, 1973b), so Hahn returned to Cambridge in combative mood.

The Cambridge faculty, in contrast to the LSE that Hahn left, was neither a happy nor intellectually vibrant environment in 1972. Dasgupta observed that 'Hahn faced an insular and worse-than-mediocre Faculty, displaying nevertheless an academic self-confidence unsurpassed anywhere I have seen. ... Unable to modernize the Faculty (the best deal he was able to reach with those wielding political power in the Faculty Board was to have one Lectureship appointment of his choice for every three), Hahn made a move that displayed for a second time his gifts as an academic visionary and administrator. He obtained, what would be impossible today, a loosely specified research grant for studying risk and incentives from the then Economic and Social Research Council.'[14]

Hahn's intellectual energy knew no bounds and he used this remarkably successful research programme to redress some of the shortcomings of General Equilibrium theory—its lack of a theory of unemployment, money and market adjustments. The so-call *Risk Project* attracted an amazingly impressive group of young researchers such as Eric Maskin, David Kreps, Oliver Hart, Mark Machina, Lou Makowski, Douglas Gale, Ben Lockwood, Jonathan Thomas, Paolo Gottardi, David Canning, Bob Evans, Paul Seabright, Luca Anderlini, Costas Gatsios and David Kelsey, as well as many members of the Faculty, such as myself. Most of the researchers funded under this project went on to distinguished academic careers, many in the United States; Paul Seabright moved from Churchill College to Toulouse in France. Some fortunately stayed in Britain (where those who left Cambridge all became professors).

Hahn's weekly internal *Risk* seminars were typical of his idiosyncratic but effective research style. They became known as 'Quaker' meetings, as they had no formal agenda but let the spirit move participants to speak—if they were quick enough to seize the chalk. Newly minted post-docs could hold forth before visiting Nobel laureates, rapidly gaining insights, experience and confidence that stood them in good stead later on. These Quakers were intensely productive, producing a steady stream of green discussion papers that in those pre-pdf times were posted around the world, signalling the vigour of the Hahn enterprise.

The 1970s were turbulent times politically, with the high inflation following the oil shocks of 1973, strikes and labour unrest culminating in the 'winter of discontent' of 1978–9 (curiously echoing the title of Hahn, 1973b). In 1979 the country elected Margaret Thatcher's Conservative Government to replace a failing Labour Government. Hahn was much incensed by the monetarist advice his former colleague, Alan Walters, had been providing the Government. In the view of Milton Friedman, much lauded by Sir Keith Joseph and other Conservatives, high inflation was simply due to an excessive expansion of the money supply. This is where the great value of the Cambridge faculty coffee room showed its worth. The faculty (and the DAE) met for coffee every day in term time, and argued vigorously not just over theory (these were disputatious academics,

[14] See http://www.res.org.uk/view/article3Apr13Correspondence.html (accessed 3 July 2017).

after all) but also about policy (many of the faculty were active policy advisors and commentators).

Perhaps surprisingly, given their prior history, Hahn and Neild (who had pre-empted Hahn's earlier return) criticised monetarist doctrine in an article in *The Times* (25 February 1980) 'Monetarism: why Mrs Thatcher should beware'.[15] Friedman responded aggressively, claiming that reducing monetary growth 'may increase unemployment temporarily, to be rewarded by a much sharper reduction in unemployment later' (*The Times*, 3 March 1980). Unemployment had risen from 7 per cent in 1980 to 10 per cent in 1981. Geoffrey Howe, Chancellor of the Exchequer, delivered the Budget on 10 March 1981, after which Hahn and Neild sat down in the coffee room and drew up a response, circulated it and secured the signatures of 364 economist academics (including themselves) to a letter published in *The Times* on 29 March 1981, stating that:

a) There is no basis in economic theory or supporting evidence for the Government's belief that by deflating demand they will bring inflation permanently under control and thereby induce a recovery in output and employment;
b) present policies will deepen the depression, erode the industrial base of our economy and threaten its social and political stability;
c) there are alternative policies; and
d) the time has come to reject monetarist policies and consider urgently which alternative offers the best hope of sustained economic recovery.

By 1984 unemployment reached 12 per cent and remained above 10 per cent until the end of 1987, accompanied by a rapid fall in inflation from 18 per cent in 1980 to 5 per cent in 1984. There was much discussion about these policies (the Thatcher revolution also set in motion subsequent waves of privatisation and rolling back the frontiers of the state). Neild's measured assessment written in 2012 was that 'When inflation struck in Britain the necessary response was (a) a short hard dose of deflation and (b) a radical reform of the trades unions. A hard-headed Keynesian analysis, or common sense, would have led to that conclusion. But before 1979 Labour and Conservative governments jibbed at such harsh policies, and so did the great majority of economists of whom I was one. Much as I abhor the social philosophy of Mrs Thatcher (and her

---

[15] *The Times*, 25 February 1980, p. 19. I am indebted to Robert Neild's note 'The 1981 budget and the letter by 364 economists', 23 July 2012.

follower, Mr Blair) I now give her credit for having introduced these two controversial policies that were necessary to check inflation—though I deplore the fact that monetarism so blinded the government that it pressed home deflation too hard and too long' (Neild, 2012).

Peter Clarke, then writing his *The Keynesian Revolution in the Making*, remembers discussing with Hahn that Keynesians would agree that deflationary policies (a slump) would reduce inflation, along with the economic activity that generated it. Howe's 1981 budget, though deflationary, acted mainly through fiscal policy, and the monetary targeting was thereafter more a political charade to cover this shift in policy.

Hahn spent many of his summers visiting his close colleague, Kenneth Arrow, at Stanford, which annually gathered an impressive range of visitors to the Institute for Mathematical Studies in the Social Sciences (IMSSS). In 1992 his colleagues presented him with the suitably weighty Festschrift on his retirement from Cambridge (Dasgupta et al., 1992). Of course, Hahn could not retire from active economics, and promptly took a post in Siena, and he and Dorothy (whose Italian was considerably better than Frank's) moved, living in a modest flat within the city walls, very supportive of their local Contrada (Giraffa). He would invite his colleagues for stimulating conferences in the glorious Certosa outside the city walls in a monastery on a Tuscan hill—a wholly suitable place for Quakers to meet, though with the gastronomic delights to tempt a pope. As Hahn says in his autobiographical notes (Szenberg, 1992, 160), mentioning a Borgia pope (Leo X), 'God has given us the papacy, now let us enjoy it'—very much the spirit in which he and Dorothy entertained colleagues and students at seminars at his Cambridge house, as well as the dinner parties for visitors and friends. I have vivid memories as a guest of Secondo Tarditi with the Hahns at the Palio in Siena on one such visit to the Hahns.

In his obituary, Dasgupta (2013) paid tribute to the closeness of their marriage: '... over the nearly five decades that I knew him it has always seemed to me that without Dorothy there would be no Frank. She was the practical and emotional centre of his life; she had a professional career, but it was her support at home that enabled him to spend his days thinking, reading, scribbling (his words), conversing, and listening to music and to others. He loved his garden at 16 Adams Road, but beyond cutting the odd flower head, I don't believe he did any gardening himself. I cannot remember an occasion when on arriving at his home for tea or a glass of wine I didn't find him reading.'

If there is one theme that runs through Hahn's life, it was to attract the right people and move decisively to support them. He was also intensely loyal to the college right from its foundation to the last days of his life, indeed he was sitting next to me at dinner in college when he was taken ill at the end of his life (he died on 29 January 2013). He believed passionately in the merits of the Cambridge supervision system and the Socratic Method—which his Quaker seminars and the Churchill seminars exemplified. He brought outstanding teaching fellows to Churchill— Oliver Hart, Roger Witcomb, Margaret Bray, Jayasri Dutta and others.

He was delighted when first Douglas Gale and then David Kelsey became Junior Research Fellows (both moved quickly to become professors), and subsequently Daniel Sgroi joined Churchill first as a Junior Research Fellow before becoming a teaching fellow. Junior Research Fellows in economics are relatively rare in Cambridge, partly because in the past the natural career path normally involved a lectureship fairly soon after the PhD, partly because economists are so much more critical of each other than those in other subjects, whose students invariably walk on water. But Hahn appreciated that time to pursue research without the pressures that a full-time faculty appointment requires could be of immense value for an economist at the start of his or her career. The *Risk Project* supported many such, often in partnership with Churchill where they supervised— and the combination of young and enthusiastic researchers rubbing shoulders with their seniors at Quaker meetings and then passing on that enthusiasm to undergraduates at Churchill in turn prompted many of them to pursue glittering academic careers.

In that spirit Hahn strongly supported the College's proposal to create the Hahn Fellowship in Economics—and became its overwhelmingly most generous donor. It is a fitting memorial to his contributions to the profession, his college and Cambridge friends.

Works

The early years

Hahn was greatly influenced by Hicks's (1939) *Value and Capital* and even more by Samuelson's (1947) *Foundations of Economic Analysis*. Paul Romer, in his blog,[16] gives a clear sense of the significance of 'the

---

[16] See https://paulromer.net/what-went-wrong-in-macro-historical-details/ (accessed 3 July 2017).

Samuelson program', starting from the observation that from 1890 to 1940 'economists avoided the use even of calculus and spent 50 years mired in the confusion spawned by the talky, market-by-market, supply-and-demand-ish approach to economic analysis codified in 1890 in Alfred Marshall's *Principles of Economics*. Samuelson saw that recovery for economics would require both the precision of mathematics and a commitment to models that could handle more than two variables at the same time.' Samuelson himself later wrote that 'Shortly after 1930 economics burst out into new life. At least four revolutions erupted: the monopolistic competition revolution, the Keynesian macro revolution, the mathematicization revolution, and the econometric inference revolution' (Medema and Waterman, 2014, 26).

One relevant example that demonstrated the power of general equilibrium over simple market-by-market analysis was to take just two industries with constant returns to scale in capital and labour and therefore perfectly horizontal Marshallian supply curves with apparently constant prices independent of demand. Stolper and Samuelson (1941) showed that imposing an economy-wide constraint on the amounts of labour and capital gave a smooth production possibility frontier that showed that prices would vary with the pattern of demand—familiar enough in the Edgeworth tradition but lacking in the atheoretical Marshallian approach. Not surprisingly, Hahn saw the importance of rigorous proofs, requiring mathematics, a general equilibrium approach and the significance of the Keynesian revolution, which still lacked a rigorous foundation.

Harrod (1939), a strong supporter of the Keynesian revolution, was to influence Hahn's approach to economic stability, and whether there was any reason in the longer run for an economy to be able to sustain full-employment growth. Hahn's PhD thesis 'The share of wages in national income' demonstrates his early commitment to the application of micro-economic theory to understanding macro-economic phenomena, consistent with his first supervisor Kaldor's advice that 'the best approach to distribution theory is macro-economic'.

Keynesian macroeconomics calls for a general equilibrium approach in the loose sense that agents in different sectors (consumers, investors, banks, not to mention the rest of the world through trade and capital flows) interact to determine the level of output, employment, prices and the rate of interest. Keynes and his followers were also concerned with equilibrium, and whether in particular an equilibrium with unemployment could persist (that is, was stable) without a strong tendency to return to full employment. However, the theory of general equilibrium in the narrower sense (GE for short) of a full specification of agents, endowments, preferences and production possibilities interacting through markets was seriously incomplete in 1945. This was despite 'a long and fairly imposing line of economists from Adam Smith to the present who have sought to show that a decentralized economy motivated by self-interest and guided by price signals could be compatible with a coherent disposition of economic resources that could be regarded, in a well-defined sense, as superior to a large class of alternative dispositions. ... it is important to know not only whether it *is* true, but also whether it *could* be true' (Arrow and Hahn, 1971, vi–vii).

Hahn (1977) later commented on the relationship between Keynesian economics and GE, noting that GE theorists 'have been unable to deliver one half at least of the required story: how does general equilibrium come to be established? Closely related to this lacuna is the question of what signals are perceived and transmitted in a decentralised economy and how. The importance of Keynesian economics to the general equilibrium theorist is two-fold. It seems to be addressed to these kinds of questions and it is plainly in need of proper theoretical foundations.'

Given this background, it is not surprising that Hahn began to develop a proper general equilibrium model with Keynesian features as early as the time of his doctoral thesis. Later, he, with many of his mathematical economic contemporaries, would gradually develop a fully rigorous theory of general competitive equilibrium. This would require a study of stability and, crucially, whether it was possible to include money in the theory of general competitive equilibrium.

In his PhD thesis Hahn embeds a risk-averse imperfectly competitive firm with some power to influence prices in a one-good general equilibrium model of the whole economy. His interest goes beyond the Keynesian problem of the determination of output and employment to investigate what happens to the share of wages and profits in total output, building a rigorous model of the short-run evolution of the economy from an initial starting point. The first chapter notes a number of problems with the classical production function approach, specifically that it conflicts 'with what we now know about the role of money in the system'. He notes that 'much of modern trade cycle theory is based on the assumption that such (a dynamic general) equilibrium is in fact unstable, so that ... a "comparative dynamic equilibrium" approach to distribution may be impossible', and that if 'the assumption of perfect competition is dropped ... the production function approach is useless'.

Solow (1992) stresses the novelty of both considering imperfect competition in a general equilibrium model and allowing firms to be risk averse, developments that became more familiar considerably later. The third novel element was to allow the supply of savings to depend on the distribution of income, as Hahn argued that workers would save less than firms (or their owners). This last element was much used later by Kaldor and other Cambridge post-Keynesian economists such as Pasinetti, often to argue against the idea that wages and profits were returns to labour and capital, and therefore ethically defensible. Kaldor (1956) summarises Kalecki's theory as 'capitalists earn what they spend, and workers spend what they earn', which suggests that profits are not earned and therefore not ethically defensible.

Hahn (1972), in the preface to his (belatedly) published thesis, reacts to the muddle in which he finds the debate. On one side 'neoclassical practitioners have not been able to resist the temptation to make the theory yield simple answers to sociologically motivated questions' such as the distribution of income. In contrast, the other side has 'criticised it on logical grounds where, as it happens, it is particularly robust. To make matters worse the controversy has been overlaid by ideological clap-trap: the neoclassical theorist is said to be justifying the *status quo* while his opponent is the harbinger of progress.'

In his collected works (Hahn, 1984b, 1–2) Hahn set out very clearly what he meant by a neoclassical economist:

1. 'I am a reductionist in that I attempt to locate explanations in the actions of individual agents.
2. In theorising about the agent I look for some axioms of rationality.
3. I hold that some notion of equilibrium is required and that the study of equilibrium is useful.'

Hahn goes on to comment on the first point that while he has no problem with the idea of class, any theory of class interest would on his view need to be grounded in the interests of individual members. The notion of equilibrium is of course central to GE theory, but far wider than that. The Hahn–Matthews *Growth Survey* discusses the confusions of interpretation and the dubious nature of such political-economic claims at considerable length.

The final building block in the PhD model is the demand for investment, which looks like an accelerator function of national income. Together these relations give rise to an equilibrium in which the supply of savings that depends on the share of wages in total income is equal to the demand for investment, which is an increasing function of the profit margin. Firms will be happy when they can sell what they produce (in this imperfectly competitive world in which they cannot sell any amount at an externally set price), and in turn demand, income, wages and profits are such that supply and demand are balanced. Given this model it is possible to explore how its elements (output, the share of wages, the level of employment, etc.) respond to various shocks or parameter changes—very much part of the Samuelson programme.

Solow's celebratory essay on Hahn's PhD commends its delivery of a complete short-run macro-model, but goes on to say 'I resist the 1972 Hahn's rejection of loosely aggregative economics, and I would defend the approach of the younger Hahn against his maturer self' (Solow, 1992, 16). Earlier, Solow remarks that his own belief is that 'economics, as an applied science, is about approximations, not theorems. So I have a deep interest in the aggregative use of microeconomic ideas.' It says much for their mutual respect and friendship that such apparently disparate views of the subject did not prevent them collaborating together on a major book (Hahn and Solow, 1995).

Money and general equilibrium

During the first part of his academic career, Hahn was still formulating his response to the Keynesian revolution, and specifically whether Keynes's claims could be true and, if so, under what assumptions. His first paper after those of his PhD was a critique of Patinkin's attempt to include money in a general equilibrium model (Hahn, 1952, 1960a), arguing that it 'failed to model the essential intertemporal aspect of money' (Hahn, 1985, 2). The disputes of this period are reflected in his paper on the rate of interest (Hahn, 1955), which revisited the old Keynes–Robertson dispute over Loanable Funds (LF) vs Liquidity Preference (LP) as 'determining' the rate of interest. Hahn dismisses this confusion as one of determining the period chosen for consideration. The LF theory differs from the LP theory 'only in so far as it is concerned with the value of the rate of interest at any one moment of time during the income period'.

Clearly this was a hotly disputed area, and Hahn acknowledges prior interactions with Joan Robinson, Harrod, Patinkin and Harry Johnson. It resulted in the 1962 IEA conference 'The theory of interest and money' to examine developments since Keynes's *General Theory of Employment, Interest and Money*. In the preface to the conference volume Hahn notes that 'all essential points of interest may be lost if we construct models of a monetary economy in which price uncertainty and market imperfections have been assumed away' (Brechling and Hahn, 1965). The concept of equilibrium becomes problematic in the face of differing expectations, and strengths of belief in the absence of a complete set of futures markets. The main contribution of the conference was not any new theory but the clearing away of various obscurities. Hahn was clearly somewhat disappointed that a successful integration of real and monetary forces failed to emerge, leaving growth theory in an unsatisfactory state. The role of money in satisfactory equilibrium models was to engage Hahn for the rest of his career (Hahn, 1965, 1971, 1973, 1975).

In 1968 Jerome Stein secured NSF funds for a 'Conference on money and economic growth' at Brown University, subsequently published in the then new *Journal of Money, Credit and Banking* in 1969. It was intended to discuss 'the basic questions (that) concern the extent to which financial policies and institutional arrangements can affect the time profiles and steady-state values of the capital–labor ratio (or capital intensity) $k(t)$, the real wage $w(t)$ and the rent $r(t)$ per unit of capital' (Stein, 1969).

Hahn's (1969) paper starts 'Economic theory still lacks a "Monetary Debreu".' Hahn constructs a simple neoclassical growth model with money to see whether, given active government intervention, 'mediation by money must restrict the accumulation choices of an economy. The answer is no, and so, in a proper sense, for a rational society, money is neutral' (Hahn, 1969, 180). On the other hand, the government is required to be active (taxing, transferring and investing) to ensure a desirable outcome (or dynamic evolution).

It should be hardly surprising that there is a problem in providing a motive for holding non-interest bearing money in a competitive general equilibrium model which, in its properly articulated form, has a set of well-defined, homogeneous products, whose prices are already known at every date in the future (and, in the extension to deal with risk, prices in each state of nature). As there are no transaction costs, contracts (to borrow) can be costlessly enforced, and as agents cannot influence prices, they can draw up their lifetime work, asset accumulation and consumption plan when they reach the age of competence. There would be no need for money either as a means of exchange or as a store of value.

Hahn (1975a) sets out his views on the subject in a non-technical way, pointing out all the difficulties involved in the path along which others such as Patinkin and Clower had set out. They start with the axiom that only money buys goods, and then consider sequence economies in which agents hold money from one period to the next. In such economies agents must form expectations about future prices. Even supposing that these price expectations are correct, there are problems in establishing the existence of a short-period equilibrium. The article is typical of Hahn's approach to the subject, setting out clearly the gaps in the theory and the unsatisfactory nature of the current state of understanding, before concluding that we are still far from a satisfactory theory.

In their definitive summary of GE theory, Arrow and Hahn (1971) turn, in their concluding chapter 13,[17] to the Keynesian Model and the relation 'of certain features of this model to what has gone before' (i.e. GE theory). Money and the lack of futures markets, with the implication that expectations are important, immediately introduces the idea of bankruptcy, and that, as they put it, 'may make it impossible to guarantee the continuity properties of the various functions and correspondences and this is bad for existence proofs' (Arrow and Hahn, 1971, 354).

One of their key questions is whether Keynes discovered 'features of an economy that ... make it impossible to establish the existence of a temporary equilibrium' (Arrow and Hahn, 1971, 354) in which all markets including the labour market clear and the prices of labour and money are non-zero. While they are not claiming to be able to establish any general non-existence results they are able to construct an example in which there exists no temporary equilibrium, thus vindicating a central Keynesian proposition.

This leads to a discussion of what might happen out of equilibrium, when a temporary equilibrium does not exist. After quoting Keynes on how money wages might respond to unemployment (and what might then happen to real wages) they note that it is hard to relate the kinds of adjustment processes they have considered and 'the kind of forces that Keynes thought to be important. This is partly due to the fact that he was quite imprecise in these matters, but *largely because a precise formulation would be extremely complex*' (Arrow and Hahn, 1971, 367, emphasis added). Their conclusion is 'that the Keynesian revolution cannot be understood if proper account is not taken of the powerful influence exerted by the future and past on the present and by the large modifications that must be introduced into both value theory and stability analysis, if the requisite futures markets are missing' (Arrow and Hahn, 1971, 369).

Hahn's final remarks on GE were presented after he retired from Cambridge and took up a post at the University of Siena in 1992, where

---

[17] Chapter 12, section 6, almost at the end of the book, is the first time that money is mentioned in any significant way.

he engaged actively in the annual summer schools organised at the Certosa near that wonderful city. The XII Workshop of 1999 took as its topic 'General equilibrium: problems, prospects, alternatives', and led to the conference volume (Petri and Hahn, 2003). Much of the conference was taken up with raking over the old capital controversies on the 1960s that Italy and Siena had kept alive, set out at some length in Petri's co-introduction to that volume.[18] Hahn's rejoinder in his co-introduction remarks that the most strident critics of GE are the neo-Ricardians, but he has 'never found it easy to see their objections ...'. Hahn's own contribution (Hahn, 2003) summarises some of the problems with the Arrow–Debreu form of GE and approaches that have been taken to address them. He admits that there remains no satisfactory economy-wide theory that takes account of these problems, concluding that instead of looking for micro-foundations for macroeconomics (where Hahn started his career) perhaps what is needed is a macro-foundation for microeconomics. When agents need to form expectations about the future, macro-variables such as the rate of inflation, the level of unemployment and others are likely to influence these expectations and hence their resulting actions.

General equilibrium and stability

Samuelson (1941) had already drawn attention to the limited nature of nineteenth-century Walrasian competitive theory, noting that stability is central to any equilibrium theory, for unless there are forces that tend to drive an economy towards an equilibrium, then such a state would not likely persist. Conversely, if the economy is driven towards equilibrium, then it may be legitimate to make predictions about where the economy will move if some parameter changes (e.g. the productivity of labour in some sector) by examining the new equilibrium defined by the changed parameter.

Hahn was therefore concerned with establishing the stability of general equilibrium, as evidenced by a rapid series of papers on the subject (Hahn, 1960b, 1961, 1962a, 1962b). Starting with Hicks (1939), Arrow and Debreu (1954) and Debreu (1957), rigorous foundations for the static theory of GE were laid down, specifically establishing conditions under

---

[18] Kirman in his contribution remarks that 'taking part in a meeting on general equilibrium in Siena is very much like taking part in an intellectual Palio' (Kirman, 2003, 468). Il Palio is an ancient and particularly brutal, no-holds barred horse race held in the Piazza del Campo in Siena.

which a competitive equilibrium exists (relatively weak), that it is unique (where local uniqueness is generally the case, but global uniqueness requires strong assumptions) and its optimality—the relationship between competitive equilibrium and its efficiency.

A competitive equilibrium can be shown to be Pareto efficient given a complete set of markets, all agents have full information about all prices, and there are no transactions costs and no one is satiated. Pareto efficiency means there is no other feasible allocation of goods in which no one is worse off and at least one person is better off. The second welfare theorem makes the more significant claim that with the additional assumption of convexity (i.e. no economies of scale) any feasible Pareto-efficient allocation can be decentralised as a competitive equilibrium with lump-sum transfers. While competitive equilibria have no claim to fairness or social equity, given some social preference function that allows one to rank alternative allocations among households, the social optimum can be supported by a competitive price system, with the massive proviso that transfers can be arranged in a way that does not affect choices. The force of a lump-sum transfer is that they must not depend on any observable action, such as earning income or spending money, and thus requires the Benevolent Dictator to see into the hearts and minds of all agents.

Clearly such lump-sum transfers are quite impractical, but the modern theory of public economics has been concerned with finding the best feasible outcome, subject to the information available to the tax authorities and the incentives that agents face when confronted with taxes. Diamond and Mirrlees (1971a, 1971b) in their theory of optimal indirect taxes (on goods and services) showed that allocations on the second-best Pareto Frontier satisfy aggregate efficiency and can be achieved in a decentralised setting under the usual assumptions, even taking account of the limited information of the tax authorities.

Following the rigorous static part of GE, Arrow et al. (1958, 1959) set out to establish conditions for the stability of competitive equilibria (CE), firmly retaining the Walrasian concept of *tâtonnement* in which an auctioneer would call out prices for every good, receive information back as to demands and supply at each price, and then adjust prices until supply is at least as great as demand in every market (and if strictly greater, the price has fallen to zero). The crucial assumption is that no exchanges would take place until the process had found a set of equilibrium prices for every good, under which they were able to find conditions ensuring that the CE was stable.

Something like this process on a much simpler scale happens in the European day-ahead electricity auction, to which all those wishing to offer to supply or bid to demand electricity for a given hour next day submit an offer or demand schedule, and the intersection of the aggregate demand and supply will set the price (this is a simplified story). In this auction market only one price (that of electricity in the hour) is to be determined and the prices of all other goods are assumed to remain unchanged (or have already been contracted, such as the gas and coal for generation).

Hahn and Negishi (1962), following these papers of Arrow et al., abandoned the Walrasian assumption that no trade takes place before a complete set of equilibrium prices is determined, and allowed trade to take place even if some markets were not in equilibrium. In this model of a pure trading economy (i.e. without production) prices are still 'called' (presumably by an auctioneer) and at those prices trading continues until there is never an individual with any unsold good on hand when that good is in excess demand nor with an unpurchased good when that good is in excess supply.

Whereas Hicks had approached the question of stability using classical differential equation theory (examining the Jacobian of responses of demands to price changes) Hahn and Negishi picked up the newly rediscovered Second Method of Lyapunov, originally published in Russian in 1892 as *The General Problem of Stability of Motion*. Operations researchers anxious to develop algorithms for guiding missiles enthusiastically plundered this Russian gem (and that of Pontryagin, whose 1956 article laid out principles of optimal control), making this powerful technique generally accessible (although Hahn and Negishi reference a 1956 article by Wolfgang Hahn in German). Hicks's method only establishes local stability—that is, the system will converge to the equilibrium providing it starts sufficiently close to that equilibrium. The Lyapunov method, in contrast, establishes global stability, starting from any initial condition.

The crucial step in the proof, which is all but hidden by some heavyweight and pretty obscure mathematics, is that each step in the price adjustment process is one in which agents become disappointed, so their expected utility decreases. Sellers, when they cannot find buyers, have to accept lower prices, while buyers, if they cannot find sellers, have to face increasing prices. Expected utility therefore decreases but is bounded below hence, by the Lyapunov argument, converges to the competitive equilibrium.

This article is justifiably considered a seminal contribution, as it shows that under reasonable conditions the model trading economy will tend towards an equilibrium under weaker conditions than those required for the stability of a Walrasian equilibrium (with no out-of-equilibrium trading). This model still assumed an auctioneer to ensure that at any moment everyone faces the same price for a good (even if it is not an equilibrium price), as otherwise there would need to be agents who changed prices. Giving an agent the power to change prices in response to perceived demand immediately introduces imperfect competition, raising the next question of whether such market power would ultimately vanish at the final CE—a question Franklin Fisher devoted fifteen years of his life pursuing (Fisher, 2011). But the Hahn–Negishi approach was a critical step in moving away from the Walrasian *tâtonnement* and modelling sequential trading in markets.[19]

In the subsequent development in Arrow–Hahn (1971, chapter 13) this non-*tâtonnement* process is extended to allow the use of money to mediate exchange, building on Clower (1965). The paper with Negishi was also important in sparking further research to generalise the results by the brilliant mathematician, Smale, and in encouraging Fisher to extend the model to include production. A rather pessimistic assessment of the stability of GE is provided by Kirman (2003, 473), who counts the failure to establish any tendency towards equilibrium as the most striking failure of GE theory, while 'the (Arrow–Debreu) model is intact but now looks almost irrelevant to the understanding of real economic phenomena' (Kirman, 2003, 483).

Growth theory

The *Growth Survey* (Hahn and Matthews, 1964) is an excellent example of bringing the approach that clarified GE theory to the simple but dynamic models of growth that had been sparked by the early work of Harrod (1939) and its neoclassical responses of Solow (1956) and Swan (1956). The *Growth Survey* came when growth theory was evolving rapidly and needed clarifying, which the *Growth Survey* achieved magnificently. Harrod (1939) and Domar (1946) introduced growth theory to the

---

[19] Later there was considerable interest in the stability properties of Agent-based models, that allow different agents to interact in a sequence of production and trading dates, but such developments took place both later and with different objectives in mind. Newbery and Greve (2015, Appendix B) gives a brief summary of some of these developments.

English-speaking audience, although von Neumann (1938) had already published a highly sophisticated multi-sector model of growth in German, but that was not available until translated by Morgenstern (von Neumann, 1946, which Hahn covers extensively in the *Growth Survey* and reprints in Hahn, 1971, with Champernowne's 1946 note).

Growth theory concerns itself with the prospect of steady growth, an important shift from earlier concerns with 'long-period' equilibrium that was presumably considered as static. Harrod was much concerned with both the existence of steady-state growth with full employment (a dynamic counterpart to Keynesian concerns) and with the 'knife-edge' instability of steady growth paths. Stability in growth theory has two dimensions. The first, *equilibrium dynamics*, asks whether equilibrium non-steady state paths converge to steady-state growth. The second, *disequilibrium dynamics*, asks whether, if the economy is disturbed and hence departs from equilibrium, agents react to restore equilibrium. The latter requires additional specifications of out-of-equilibrium behaviour, a subject that Hahn accepts as a necessary evil, but is concerned that it can so easily become arbitrary. It leads to trade-cycle theory and, with that, a need to reconcile growth and fluctuations.

Harrod's existence problem arises because the natural rate of growth, n, determined by the growth of the labour force at full employment, and the warranted rate of growth, determined by the ratio of the savings share, s, to the capital–output ratio, v, or $g_w = s/v$, are unlikely to be equal given the assumption that all three variables are given and independently determined. The *Growth Survey* therefore considers models that differ in which of these can be variable and adjust to the required relationship, $n = s/v$. Hahn in his thesis noted that the average savings rate could depend on the distribution of income, and hence changes in that distribution could allow the necessary change in the average s. The neoclassical models of Solow and Swan assume that capital and labour can be substituted to allow v to adjust. Hahn–Matthews accept that Harrod did not rule out a flexible v, but that the Keynesian approach saw difficulties in reaching short-run full employment equilibrium, which Harrod extended to the longer run, and which others like Kaldor picked up.

Hahn (1960) was already concerned with the stability of growth paths in simpler models, and specifically whether they were stable and how money might be included in a simple Solow-type model. In these models producers can make mistakes and investment is not necessarily equal to full employment savings, while money plays a role and can influence investment decisions. Even though capital and labour can be smoothly substituted (a neoclassical production function) Harrod's knife-edge stability remains problematic.

After discussing one-good, one-sector models in which capital is like corn, capable of investment and consumption, the *Growth Survey* considers two-sector models where capital is physically different from consumption and needs a price in terms of consumption. This creates a mini-general equilibrium model in which there can be multiple equilibria and, even more exciting, discontinuities with capital accumulation in which multiple equilibria collapse to a single equilibrium, possibly with massive redistributions of income (assuming full employment could ever be maintained).

The final part, largely written by Hahn, considers multi-sector linear models in which there are many different types of capital good, and hence the concept of a single capital aggregate is no longer simple (but nor is it needed to derive rates of profit in equilibrium). The section considers an extension of the dynamic input–output model with a single non-produced factor of production (labour), many goods in which there is a large number of different processes to produce each good. Provided the system is productive, the set of competitive prices is independent of the pattern of demand—the dynamic (non-) substitution theorem.[20] This had been noted in the static context by Samuelson (1951) and was made much of by Sraffa (1960). In the *Growth Survey* Sraffa's model is somewhat dismissively treated on a par with similar 'Leontief–Samuelson–Sraffa' multi-sector models.

Hahn followed this final line of questioning in another of his most influential papers on 'Equilibrium dynamics with heterogeneous capital goods' (Hahn, 1966). This is a simple stripped-down model to demonstrate the instability of growth models that have more than one type of capital good, even if there is only one consumer good. Agents have to decide what kind of capital to invest in, and given competitive markets they will seek those with the highest rate of return, including capital gains. In equilibrium as all types of capital are needed all must earn the same rate of return, but even when agents start with a set of initial expectations, the economy may pursue a variety of equilibrium paths. The problem remains even if there are only two types of capital when, even if a single equilibrium path is found, there are many initial conditions for which such equilibrium paths do not approach the balanced growth path.

This article was written when Hahn had returned to Cambridge amid the so-called Cambridge capital controversy, sometimes called 'the two

---

[20] Mirrlees (1969) gives a proof of the most general formulation.

Cambridges debate' as economists at Cambridge MIT (Solow, Samuelson and Stiglitz) were also participants. That debate, which need not detain us here, in one sense revolved around whether one could attach any meaning to an aggregate capital concept, convenient in the original single sector growth models, and what might be the relationship, if any, between 'the' rate of profit and 'the' quantity of capital. Of course, in the full Arrow–Debreu model there is a complete set of intertemporal prices for all goods, and Bliss argues 'that capital theory should be liberated from the concept of the rate of interest, meaning by that one rate… Instead, we will find the concept of inter-temporal prices to be fundamental and will see that working with the rate of interest is a clumsy groping for that concept' (Bliss, 1975, 10).

Hahn's 1966 paper certainly chimes nicely with Bliss's comment that 'It has always seemed to me to be supremely ironic that in the war between the post-Keynesians and the Neoclassical school the major damage to orthodox theory came from the latter.' After he retired from Cambridge in 1992, Hahn moved to the economics department at the University of Siena, a hotbed of neo-Ricardian economics. Hahn (1982c) had earlier written on the neo-Ricardians (specifically on Sraffa, 1960) and states on the first page 'I … show that there is no correct neo-Ricardian proposition which is not contained in the set of propositions which can be generated by orthodoxy. I shall therefore conclude that the neo-Ricardian attack via logic is easily beaten off' (Hahn, 1982c, 353). Hahn concludes that marginal productivity concerns an economy in full neoclassical equilibrium: 'But on the manner in which such an equilibrium is supposed to come about, neoclassical theory is highly unsatisfactory. Sraffa's work shows that certain simplified routes are very risky and not free from logical difficulties. The remarkable fact is that neither he nor the Sraffians have made anything of this' (Hahn, 1982c, 373).

The Cambridge *Risk* Project: 1976–94

In his Presidential address to the Econometric Society in 1968 Hahn expressed concern about the performance of the 'invisible hand', in other words with the idea that a general competitive equilibrium could be established by any plausible market process (Hahn, 1970). While recognising the achievements of GE theory in the previous twenty years, Hahn considered it somewhat scandalous that so much effort was devoted to 'refining the analyses of economic states which they give no reason to suppose will ever, or have ever, come about. Equilibrium economics, because of its well-known welfare economics implication, is easily convertible into an apologia for existing economic arrangements and it is frequently so converted' (Hahn, 1970, 1).

The last remark on welfare economics is illuminating, and goes some way to explaining his views in *Reflections* (Szenberg and Ramrattan, 2004) that he was rather repelled by utilitarianism ('mechanical morality'), and so was uninterested in welfare economics: 'Nevertheless, I often find myself on the utilitarian side.' He concludes in his presidential address that he is assailed by 'Doubts' that GE can deliver: 'The most intellectually exciting question of our subject remains: is it true that the pursuit of private interest produces not chaos but coherence, and if so, how is it done?' (Hahn, 1970, 12).

That thought germinated in a proposal to the Economic and Social Research Council, the UK social science funding body, for the project 'Information, risk and quantity signals in economics', which would bring together academics within the Cambridge Economics Faculty, younger PhDs, post-docs and visitors to address the serious incompleteness of Walrasian theory. This *Risk* project was funded and extended for three-year periods until 1994, two years after Hahn's formal retirement from Cambridge in 1992, by which time it had published 199 working papers, most of which emerged as published articles. Hahn (1989, 1) summarises its aim as 'to move beyond the Walrasian paradigm without abandoning the commitment to lucid and rigorous thinking'.

The incompleteness of this Walrasian theory resided partly in the implausibility of agents taking prices as given when firms were often large and clearly could act strategically, which required the rapidly developing field of game theory for its analysis.[21] At a more fundamental level, Arrow–Debreu GE assumed market completeness, but evidently markets were seriously incomplete, with missing futures and Arrow security markets. When trading has to take place in their absence, agents need to trade on the basis of expectations and in response to signals which provide some but incomplete information about opportunities and prospects. That in turn raises questions about how agents learn about their environment,

---

[21] Hahn was interested in what Game Theory had to offer, but not in actively working in the area. Chapter 8 of Arrow and Hahn (1971) is devoted to the core of the economy, a game-theoretic concept that picks up from Edgeworth's bargaining approach to equilibrium, and shows that under certain conditions the core converges on the Walrasian equilibrium. Hahn clearly found this an attractive way of reconciling the Edgeworth and Walrasian approaches to GE, but was always somewhat repelled by the multiplicity of possible equilibria that game theory could support with no obvious way of selecting any one single 'solution'.

and what role prices play in aggregating, revealing and transmitting information.

The importance of incomplete and asymmetric information for market functioning was recognised by Akerlof (1970) and Stiglitz and Rothschild (1976)—for which Akerlof and Stiglitz with Spence won the 2001 Nobel Prize—so the *Risk* project was very much in at the start of the resulting revolution in economics, with implications for incentive compatibility, and for the necessity of other institutional arrangements (contracts, standards, monitoring, accreditation, guarantees, etc.) to address the missing markets and missing information (Newbery, 1989). Hahn, in the introduction, had to admit that 'neither we, nor, as far as I know, anyone else has managed to integrate the new insights into a comprehensive theory of the economy in the manner of Walrasian theory'.

The *Risk* project may have failed to deliver that comprehensive theory, but it did produce a remarkable amount of good and useful insights, adding to the sum total of knowledge and, equally important, stimulating a whole generation of economists to think deeply about hard problems, to learn from the brightest and best that Hahn gathered around, and to be stimulated by his probing questions and continued engagement with these hard problems. By forcing theorists to recognise the inadequacies of the only really well-articulated theory of an economy, it encouraged the development of theories to address some of these inadequacies, although in a partial, rather than general equilibrium setting. The theory of the firm, of modern public finance, of insurance and health markets have all been enriched by theorists tackling these hard problems.

Hahn's retirement was marked with a weighty Festschrift (Dasgupta et al., 1992), notable for containing twenty-seven contributions from a galaxy of the talents that Hahn had gathered around himself during his career including, among many, Solow, Atkinson, Hart, Maskin, Stiglitz, Arrow, Aumann, Radner, Diamond, Mirrlees, Gorman and Samuelson, as well as many other active participants in the *Risk* project. The book had three thematic parts—on the Microeconomic Foundations of Macroeconomics, Information and the Theory of Games, and Equilibrium with Missing Markets, with a final Miscellany, but it would take us too far afield to discuss their contributions.

Frank Hahn started his career at a critical moment for British economics, after the monopolistic competition revolution and the Keynesian macro-revolution, but not yet impacted by the other two revolutions sweeping the USA, noted by Samuelson—the mathematicisation revolution and the econometric inference revolution. Hahn led successive generations of economists to adopt 'the rigorous analysis made possible by the mathematical modelling introduced by American economists like Arrow, Samuelson and Solow. Hahn and his emulators thereby created an intellectual culture in British economic theory that remains dominant to this day' (Binmore, 2013). His published legacy is substantial and important; the stimulus he imparted to his students, colleagues and the profession is equally impressive.

DAVID NEWBERY
Fellow of the Academy

Note: I am indebted to conversations, interviews and correspondence with a large number of Hahn's friends and colleagues, but particularly to Kenneth Arrow, Tony Atkinson, Christopher Bliss, Monojit Chatterji, Partha Dasgupta, Peter Diamond, Dorothy Hahn, Geoff Harcourt and his many friends who came and made tributes at his memorial. I have drawn on his personal contribution in Szenberg (1992) as well as many obituaries.

References

Akerlof, G. A. (1970) 'The market for "lemons": quality uncertainty and the market mechanism', *Quarterly Journal of Economics*, 84, 488–500.
Arrow, K. J. (1962) 'The economic implications of learning by doing', *Review of Economic Studies*, 39, 155–73.
Arrow, K. J. and Debreu, G. (1954) 'Existence of equilibrium for a competitive economy', *Econometrica*, 22, 265–90.
Arrow, K., Block, J. and Hurwicz, L. (1958) 'On the stability of the competitive equilibrium, II', *Econometrica*, 27, 82–109.
Arrow, K. J. and Hurwicz, L. (1958) 'On the stability of the competitive equilibrium, I', *Econometrica*, 26, 522–52.
Arrow, K. J. and Hahn, F. H. (1971) *General Competitive Analysis* (San Francisco, CA).
Arrow, K. J. and Hahn F. H. (1999) 'Notes on sequence economies, transaction costs and uncertainty', *Journal of Economic Theory*, 86, 201–18.
Binmore, K. (2013) 'Obituary', *The Times*, 3 February 2013.
Bliss, C. J. (1975) *Capital Theory and the Distribution of Income* (Amsterdam).
Chatterji, M. (2013) Frank Hahn—Economist, Thinker and Teacher Extraordinaire. Memorial address at Churchill College, 29 September 2013
Clower, R. W. (1965) 'The Keynesian counter-revolution: a theoretical appraisal', in F. H. Hahn and F. P. R. Brechling (eds.), *The Theory of Interest Rates: Proceedings of a Conference held by the International Economic Association* (London), pp. 103–25.
Dasgupta, P. (2013) 'Obituary', *Royal Economic Society Newsletter*, April.

Dasgupta, P., Gale, D., Hart, O. and Maskin, E. (eds.) (1992) *Economic Analysis of Markets and Games: Essays in Honor of Frank Hahn* (Cambridge, MA).
Debreu, G. (1959) *The Theory of Value: an Axiomatic Analysis of Economic Equilibrium* (New Haven, CT).
Debreu, G. (1962) 'New concepts and techniques for equilibrium analysis', *International Economic Review*, 3, 257–73.
Desai, M. and Ormerod, P. (1998) 'Richard Goodwin: a short appreciation', *The Economic Journal*, 108, 1431–5.
Diamond, P. and Mirrlees, J. (1971a) 'Optimal taxation and public production I: production efficiency', *American Economic Review*, 61, 8–27.
Diamond, P. and Mirrlees, J. (1971b) 'Optimal taxation and public production II: tax rules', *American economic Review*, 261–78.
Domar, E. D. (1946) 'Capital expansion, rate of growth and employment,' *Econometrica*, 14, 137–57.
Fisher, F. M. (2011) 'The stability of general equilibrium—what do we know and why is it important?', in P. Bridel (ed.), *General Equilibrium Analysis* (London and New York), pp. 34–45.
Friedman, B. and Hahn, F. H. (eds.) (1990) *Handbook of Monetary Economics, I—II* (Amsterdam).
Goodwin, R. M. (1953) 'The problem of trend and cycle', *Yorkshire Bulletin of Economic and Social Research*, 5, 89–97.
Goodwin, R. M. (1955) 'A model of cyclical growth', in E. Lundberg (ed.), *The Business Cycle in the Post-war World, Proceedings of International Economic Association Conference* (London, 1955), pp. 203–21.
Goodwin, R. M. (1967) 'A growth cycle', in C. H. Feinstein (ed.), *Socialism, Capitalism and Economic Growth* (Cambridge), pp. 54–8.
Hahn, A. (1943) *Das Volk Messias (Sonnets in Favour of the Jews)* (London).
Hahn, F. H. (1952) 'The general equilibrium theory of money: a comment', *Review of Economic Studies*, 19, 179–85.
Hahn, F. H. (1955) 'The rate of interest and general equilibrium analysis', *The Economic Journal*, 65, 52–66
Hahn, F. H. (1958) 'Gross substitutes and the dynamic stability of general equilibrium', *Econometrica*, 26, 169–70.
Hahn, F. H. (1960a) 'The Patinkin controversy', *Review of Economic Studies*, 28, 37–43.
Hahn, F. H. (1960b) 'The stability of growth equilibrium', *Quarterly Journal of Economics*, 74, 206–26.
Hahn, F. H. (1961) 'Money, dynamic stability and growth', *Metroeconomica*, 13, 57–76.
Hahn, F. H. (1962a) 'A stable adjustment process for a competitive economy', *Review of Economic Studies*, 29, 62–5.
Hahn, F. H. (1962b) 'On the stability of a pure exchange equilibrium', *International Economic Review*, 62, 206–13.
Hahn, F. H. (1962c) 'The stability of the Cournot oligopoly solution', *Review of Economic Studies*, 29, 329–31.
Hahn, F. H. (1963) 'On the disequilibrium behaviour of a multi-sectoral growth model', *The Economic Journal*, 73, 442–57.

Hahn, F. H. (1965) 'On some problems of proving the existence of an equilibrium in a monetary economy', in F. H. Hahn and F. P. R. Brechling (eds.), *The Theory of Interest Rates: Proceedings of a Conference Held by the International Economic Association* (London), pp. 126–35.

Hahn, F. H. (1966) 'Equilibrium dynamics with heterogeneous capital goods', *Quarterly Journal of Economics*, 80, 633–45.

Hahn, F. H. (1968) 'On warranted growth paths', *Review of Economic Studies*, 35, 175–84.

Hahn, F. H. (1969) 'On money and growth, 1969', *Journal of Money, Credit and Banking, Conference on Money and Economic Growth*, 1, 172–87.

Hahn, F. H. (1970) 'Some adjustment problems', *Econometrica*, 38, 1–17 (Presidential Address)

Hahn, F. H. (1971) 'Equilibrium with transaction costs', *Econometrica*, 39, 417–39.

Hahn, F. H. (ed.) (1971) *Readings in the Theory of Growth* (London).

Hahn, F. H. (1973a) *On the Notion of Equilibrium in Economics: an Inaugural Lecture* (Cambridge).

Hahn, F. H. (1973b) 'The winter of our discontent', *Economica*, 40, 322–30.

Hahn, F. H. (1973c) 'On some equilibrium growth paths', in J. A. Mirrlees and N. H. Stern (eds.), *Models of Economic Growth* (London), pp. 193–206.

Hahn, F. H. (1973d) 'On transaction costs, inessential sequence economies and money', *Review of Economic Studies*, 40, 449–61.

Hahn, F. H. (1975a) 'Money and general equilibrium', *Indian Economic Journal*, 23, 109–22.

Hahn, F. H. (1975b). 'Revival of political economy: the wrong issues and the wrong arguments', *The Economic Record*, 51, 360–4.

Hahn, F. H. (1977) 'Keynesian economics and general equilibrium theory: reflections on some current debates', in G. C. Harcourt (ed.), *Microeconomic Foundations of Macroeconomics* (London), pp. 25–40.

Hahn, F. H. (1980) 'Monetarism and economic theory', *Economica*, 47, 1–17.

Hahn, F. H. (1981) 'General equilibrium theory', in D. Bell and I. Kristol (eds.), *Crisis in Economic Theory* (New York), pp. 123–38.

Hahn, F. H. (1983) *Money and Inflation* (Cambridge, MA).

Hahn, F. H. (1982b) 'Reflections on the invisible hand', *Lloyd's Bank Review*.

Hahn, F. H. (1982c) 'The neo-Ricardians', *Cambridge Journal of Economics*, 6, 353–74.

Hahn, F. H. (1982d) 'Stability', in K. J. Arrow and M. D. Intriligator (eds.), *Handbook of Mathematical Economics* (Amsterdam), pp. 745–93.

Hahn, F. H. (1984a) 'Why I am not a monetarist', in F. H. Hahn (ed.), *Equilibrium and Macroeconomics* (Cambridge, MA), pp. 307–26.

Hahn, F. H. (ed.) (1984b) *Equilibrium and Macroeconomics* (Cambridge, MA).

Hahn, F. H. (1985a) 'In praise of economic theory', in F. H. Hahn (ed.), *Money, Growth and Stability* (Oxford), pp. 10–28 (The Jevons Lecture).

Hahn, F. H. (ed.) (1985b) *Money, Growth and Stability* (Oxford).

Hahn, F. H. (ed.) (1989) *The Economics of Missing Markets, Information, and Games* (Oxford).

Hahn, F. H. (1989) 'Robinson-Hahn love-hate relationship; an interview', in G. R. Feiwel (ed.), *Joan Robinson and Modern Economic Theory* (London), pp. 85–91.

Hahn, F. H. (1990) 'Liquidity', in B. Friedman and F. H. Hahn (eds.), *Handbook of Monetary Economics, I—II* (Amsterdam), pp. 63–80.

Hahn, F. H. (1999) 'A remark on incomplete market equilibrium', in G. Chichilnisky (ed.), *Markets, Information and Uncertainty: Essays in Economic Theory in Honour of Kenneth J. Arrow* (Cambridge), pp. 67–71.

Hahn, F. H. and Brechling, F. (eds.) (1965) *The Theory of Interest Rates: Proceedings of a Conference Held by the International Economic Association* (London).

Hahn, F. H. and Matthews, R. C. O. (1964) 'The theory of economic growth: a survey', *The Economic Journal*, 74, 779–902.

Hahn, F. H. and Negishi, T. (1962) 'A theorem on non-tâtonnement stability', *Econometrica*, 30, 463–9.

Hahn, F. H. and Solow, R. M. (1995) *Critical Essay on Modern Macroeconomic Theory* (Cambridge, MA).

Harcourt, G. and King, J. (1995) 'Talking about Joan Robinson: Geoff Harcourt in conversation with John King', *Review of Social Economy*, 53, 31–64.

Harrod, R. F. (1939) 'An essay in dynamic theory', *The Economic Journal*, 49, 14–33.

Harrod, R. F. (1948) *Towards a Dynamic Economics* (London).

Harrod, R. F. (1950) *The Trade Cycle* (Oxford).

Hicks, J. R. (1939) *Value and Capital: an Inquiry into Some Fundamental Principles of Economic Theory* (Oxford).

Kaldor, N. (1956) 'Alternative theories of distribution', *Review of Economic Studies*, 23, 83–100.

Kaldor, N. (1957) 'A model of economic growth', *The Economic Journal*, 67, 591–624.

Kaldor, N. (1972) 'On the irrelevance of equilibrium economics', *The Economic Journal*, 82, 1237–55.

Keynes, J. M. (1936) *The General Theory of Employment, Interest and Money* (London).

Kirman, A. (2003) 'General equilibrium: problems, prospects, alternatives—an attempt at synthesis', in F. Petri and F. H. Hahn (eds.), *General Equilibrium: Problems and Prospects* (London), pp. 468–85.

Kornai, J. (1971) *Anti-equilibrium: on Economic Systems Theory and the Tasks of Research* (Amsterdam).

Medema, S. G. and Waterman, A. M. C. (eds.) (2014) *Paul Samuelson on the History of Economic Analysis: Selected Essays* (Cambridge).

Mirrlees, J. A. (1969) 'The dynamic nonsubstitution theorem', *The Review of Economic Studies*, 36, 67–76.

Mirrlees, J. A. (1971) 'An exploration in the theory of optimum income taxation', *The Review of Economic Studies*, 38, 175–208.

Neild, R. (2012) The 1981 Budget and the Letter by 364 Economists, mimeo (Cambridge).

von Neumann, J. (1938) 'Über ein ökononomisches Gleichungsystem und eine Verallgemeinerung des Brouwerschen Fixpunktsatzes', in K. Menger (ed.), *Ergebnisse eines Mathematische Seminars* (Vienna), pp. 73–83.

von Neumann, J. (1945) 'A model of general equilibrium', *The Review of Economic Studies*, 13, 1–9.

Newbery, D. M. (1989) 'Missing markets: consequences and remedies', in F. H. Hahn (ed.), *Economics of Missing Markets, Information, and Games* (Oxford), pp. 211–42.

Newbery, D. M. and Greve, T. (2015) 'The robustness of industrial commodity oligopoly pricing strategies'. *EPRG 1522* at http://www.eprg.group.cam.ac.uk/wp-content/uploads/2015/12/1522-PDF.pdf (accessed 4 July 2017).
Panayi, P. (1996) *Germans in Britain since 1500* (London).
Pasinetti, L. L. (1962) 'Rate of profit and income distribution in relation to the rate of economic growth', *The Review of Economic Studies*, 29, 267–79.
Petri, F. and Hahn, F. H. (eds.) (2003) *General Equilibrium: Problems and Prospects* (London).
Samuelson, P. A. (1941) 'The stability of equilibrium: comparative statics and dynamics', *Econometrica*, 9, 97–120.
Samuelson, P. A. (1947) *Foundations of Economic Analysis* (Cambridge, MA).
Solow, R. M. (1956) 'A contribution to the theory of economic growth', *Quarterly Journal of Economics*, 70, 65–94.
Solow, R. M. (1992) 'Hahn on the share of wages in national income', in P. Dasgupta, D. Gale, O. Hart and E. Maskin (eds.), *Economic Analysis of Markets and Games: Essays in Honor of Frank Hahn* (Cambridge, MA), pp. 3–18.
Sraffa, P. (1960) *Production of Commodities by Means of Commodities: Prelude to a Critique of Economic Theory* (Cambridge).
Stein, J. L. (1969) 'Conference on money and economic growth: introduction', *Journal of Money, Credit and Banking*, 1, 131–7.
Stiglitz, J. E. and Rothschild, M. (1976) 'Equilibrium in competitive insurance markets: an essay on the economics of imperfect information', *Quarterly Journal of Economics*, 90, 629–49.
Stolper, W. F. and Samuelson, P. A. (1941) 'Protection and real wages', *The Review of Economic Studies*, 9, 58–73.
Swan, T. W. (1956) 'Economic growth and capital accumulation', *The Economic Record*, 32, 334–61.
Szenberg, M. (ed.) (1992) *Eminent Economists: their Life Philosophies* (Cambridge).
Szenberg, M. and Ramrattan, L. (eds.) (2004) *Reflections of Eminent Economists* (Cheltenham).

ASA BRIGGS © *National Portrait Gallery, London*

Asa Briggs
1921–2016

Keighley

ASA BRIGGS WAS BORN ON 7 May 1921 in Keighley, Yorkshire. He received the unusual name, Asa, in memory of his mother's younger brother of the same name who died just before he was born. A biblical name, it originated in the Nonconformist, Congregationalist faith of his mother and her family.[1] His father, William, was a skilled engineer who had worked for Vickers naval yard in Barrow-in-Furness, but in Asa's early years he ran a greengrocer's shop established and previously run successfully by his wife, Jane's, father, once a small farmer, driven off the land as agriculture declined. The family, including Asa's sister, Emma, lived upstairs and Jane, and Asa as a young boy, helped in the shop. William was a reluctant shopkeeper, less successful than his father-in-law, driven to it by the depression which hit northern manufacturing from late 1920 and the desire to keep it in the family. As the depression deepened in the 1930s the shop failed and he returned to work as an engineer in a local textile engineering plant.

Briggs recalled Keighley as a small, smoky, industrial town, hard hit by the depression but relieved by the presence of moorlands nearby and Haworth, Brönte country. The family lived in a working-class district and he had a 'happy childhood, despite money worries... [but]... with no sense of economic security or prosperity'.[2] 'We were not straight working class

---
[1] A. Briggs, *Special Relationships. People and Places* (Barnsley, 2012), p. 19.
[2] Asa Briggs interviewed by Jose Harris, 'Interviews with Historians', Institute of Historical

but very near to it,' he said later.³ His father was a skilled pianist and his mother sang in her chapel choir: the family really did sing together around the piano.⁴ It was different from Margaret Thatcher's experience around the same time (she was born in 1925) as a shopkeeper's daughter in the relative security of Grantham. Like her, he gained from his family a strong commitment to hard work and self-help, but not of a narrowly individualistic kind; he grew up with a belief in 'society' and a commitment to helping others. He recalled the environment with affection but no romanticisation of working-class community. Rather, his early life shaped his later commitment to realistic reconstruction of the history of working-class lives and the influence upon them of economic change such as the interwar depression.

Another influence upon his later interests was his grandfather, William's father, also a former engineer, a foreman in Barrow. When Asa was young he took him to 'every abbey and castle and small town in Yorkshire',⁵ firing his interest in history and also another life-long interest in science and technology. An older boy he knew nearby was Denis Healey, future Labour Minister, also son of an engineer of humble origins, later head of a technical college, though he and Asa attended different schools. Asa became active in the vigorous Labour Party culture in Keighley. Even as a boy he was in demand as a speaker for the local Co-operative Socialist Guild and the Workers' Educational Association (WEA), which he came to know well. This was not due to family influence. He believed his father voted Conservative until 1945, and they had vigorous, stimulating arguments, while his mother was a lifelong Liberal.⁶ His parents also differed in their religious beliefs, his father an Anglican, mother Congregationalist. He was brought up Congregationalist, becoming Anglican at Cambridge. He was not actively religious but faith mattered to him in History and throughout his own life.⁷

Research, University of London; http://store.london.ac.uk/product-catalogue/school-of-advanced-study-publications/institute-of-historical-research/interviews-with-historians/interviews-with-historians (accessed 15 June 2017).
³ T. Dalyell, obituary, 'Lord Briggs: historian and public servant who was an authority on the Victorian era and a pioneer of adult education', *The Independent*, 16 March 2016.
⁴ G. Smith, 'Asa Briggs: a personal profile', in D. Fraser (ed.), *Cities, Class and Communication: Essays in Honour of Asa Briggs* (London, 1990), p. 11. Smith was a journalist and novelist, a student of Briggs at Worcester, who kept in touch.
⁵ D. Snowman, 'Asa Briggs', *History Today*, 49 (November 1999), 22–4.
⁶ Harris, interview.
⁷ Ibid.; Smith, 'Asa Briggs', p. 15.

Cambridge

He attended a local elementary school. Aged ten he won a competition in a local newspaper for an essay on the League of Nations.[8] He won a scholarship and a free place at Keighley Grammar School where he did well, without appearing to work unduly hard. His sister said later, 'he had lots of friends and the house was always full of people.... He would do his homework and then be off for the evening.'[9] Briggs believed the cleverest boy at his school was not himself but a butcher's son who left to join the family business.[10] His father had also attended a grammar school. His parents did not expect him to go to university but, unlike some other low-income parents, created no obstacles when his headmaster encouraged him to read History at Sidney Sussex College, Cambridge, as he had done. Briggs thought he was better at Chemistry than History at school and might have opted to read sciences,[11] but Physics was badly taught and he chose History, while retaining a lifelong interest in the sciences. He was interviewed at Cambridge at the early age of sixteen in 1937. The History fellow who interviewed him said, presciently: 'Briggs, you are only a baby, but there is going to be a war and I would like you to take your degree before you go into uniform.'[12]

Remarkably, he took two, parallel, degrees, graduating in 1941 with starred Double Firsts in Parts 1 and 2 of the History Tripos from Cambridge and a First in Economics from the London School of Economics (LSE), displaying the prodigious capacity for multi-tasking and successful hard work which distinguished the rest of his career. He kept his LSE studies secret from his Cambridge tutors. LSE was evacuated to Cambridge at the time, enabling him to develop the belief rooted in his background in the need to understand economic change to analyse historical change. Acquiring the necessary skills created his lifelong commitment to interdisciplinarity and scepticism about rigid academic boundaries. At LSE he was taught by economic historians Eileen Power and Michael Postan and by Harold Laski, at Cambridge by Herbert Butterfield (also at Keighley Grammar School some years before) and two historians

[8] Ibid., p. 11.
[9] Ibid., pp. 10–11.
[10] T. Hunt, 'Asa Briggs: the last Victorian improver', BBC Radio 4 broadcast, 7 January 2017, www.open.edu/openlearn/tv-radio-events/radio/asa-briggs-the-last-Victorian-improver (accessed 15 June 2017).
[11] Harris interview.
[12] P. Lay, 'Asa Briggs: a very open intelligence', *History Today*, 61 (January 2011), 60, based on an interview.

of political thought, Ernest Barker and Michael Oakeshott. He seems not to have been active in left-wing politics at Cambridge but was involved in student campaigns to reform curricula and teaching methods, to change how History was conceived of and taught, another lifelong commitment.[13] He made a little money writing for magazines. He expressed no sense of being wrenched from his roots by higher education, remaining close to his family and early environment, proud of it and building upon it rather than rejecting it.

In his second year at Cambridge, the Physics Fellow at Sidney Sussex suggested he might join the research in progress into radar, becoming a scientist for the duration of the war. He visited C. P. Snow, who controlled university science appointments. He said long after 'I thought he was the ugliest man I had ever seen, but he was terribly nice and he told me I was exactly the kind of person they wanted.'[14] Snow said he should inform him when he was called up for conscription (due on his 21st birthday in 1942) and he would get him deferred from armed service to work on radar. When he graduated in 1941 he was offered a graduate fellowship in Economics at LSE which he delayed until after the war, then turned down because he was offered an Oxford Fellowship. He returned home to Keighley to teach part-time at his old school until he received his call-up papers, then contacted Snow. He replied that radar was now successfully operating and historians were no longer needed to retrain as scientists to bring it about. Briggs joined the Royal Corps of Signals, did initial training at Catterick Camp in North Yorkshire, and was then transferred to Trowbridge in Wiltshire where he trained as an interceptionist, learning high-speed Morse Code.

Bletchley

A friend and contemporary at Sidney Sussex was Howard Smith, later British Ambassador to Moscow then head of MI5. At the outbreak of war Smith was recruited to work at the code-breaking establishment at Bletchley by Gordon Welchman, who devised operations there. Smith recommended Briggs to Welchman and in 1942 he was transferred to the Intelligence Corps and recruited to Hut 6, run by Welchman, the hub of

---

[13] J. McIlroy, 'Asa Briggs and the emergence of Labour History', *Labour History Review*, 77 (2012), 214.
[14] Lay, 'Asa Briggs: a very open intelligence'.

the Bletchley operation, working with Alan Turing, among others, 'whom we all deferred to because he was a genius', Briggs said later.[15] He was promoted to become the youngest warrant officer in the British army, helped to crack the Enigma code and worked on enemy signals from the Mediterranean, then the successful duping of the Germans into believing the D-Day landings would take place elsewhere than Normandy. He enjoyed Bletchley, appreciating its egalitarian atmosphere and the company, describing it as his 'second university',[16] making friends easily, as ever. Among other colleagues and friends was Roy Jenkins, another future Labour Minister. Like others at Bletchley, Briggs told no one, even his wife, of their activities, crucial as they were to winning the war, until the official secrets ban was lifted in the 1970s. He wrote about his experiences much later in his life.[17]

Oxford

While still at Bletchley he was offered a research fellowship at Peterhouse, Cambridge, then a full fellowship in politics and economics at Worcester College, Oxford. He turned down the LSE studentship and accepted the Worcester fellowship. He was also invited to contest a safe Labour seat in Yorkshire in the coming election. 'This put me in a quandary', he wrote later, because he felt pressure both from his local MP and from Hugh Dalton, soon to be Labour Chancellor of the Exchequer, whom he had met during the war and who was keen to encourage bright young graduates to enter politics. Further invitations followed but, in retrospect, he was sure he made the right choice; 'I would have found it difficult to accept the discipline of a political party.' In the election campaign he worked for Roy Jenkins in unwinnable Solihull.[18]

He gained speedy release from the services to take up the fellowship. Soon after, he and his former tutor at Sidney Sussex, later Master of the College, David Thomson, joined a group reporting on post-war international relations which visited occupied Germany.[19] An outcome was Briggs' first, co-authored, book, with Thomson and Ernest Meyer,

---

[15] To a future obituarist: Nigel Jones, 'Asa Briggs obituary', *Guardian*, 15 March 2016.
[16] Hunt, 'Asa Briggs: the last Victorian improver'.
[17] A. Briggs, *Secret Days: Code-Breaking in Bletchley Park* (Barnsley, 2011).
[18] Ibid., pp. 144–6.
[19] M. Taylor, 'Introduction: Asa Briggs and public life in Britain since 1945', in M. Taylor (ed.), *The Age of Asa, Lord Briggs, Public Life and History in Britain since 1945* (London, 2014), p. 4.

Patterns of Peacemaking (London, 1945), which sought to place current events in historical context. He always believed politicians gave too little attention to history when considering contemporary issues.[20] Also after the war he was among the young historians summoned by Winston Churchill as 'consultant readers' to fact-check and proof-read his *History of the English Speaking Peoples*. Briggs was quite critical—accusing Churchill of being too Marxist in his interpretation of the American constitution.[21]

At Worcester he initially taught most courses on the PPE degree, after speedily teaching himself Philosophy. With Hugh Clegg, fellow in industrial relations at Nuffield College, and Henry Pelling, History Fellow at The Queen's College, he taught 'Labour Movements since 1815'. They were among those, much influenced by G. D. H. Cole, Chichele Professor of Social and Political Theory at Oxford, a long-time supporter of the Labour Party, the Fabian Society and the Co-operative Movement, seeking to develop a non-Marxist labour history, challenging the growing influence of the Communist Party History Group. They aimed to bring it into university syllabuses, building on the earlier work of J. L. and Barbara Hammond, Sidney and Beatrice Webb and others outside the universities. Briggs became concerned that the approach of Pelling, Clegg and other Oxford colleagues was too narrowly institutional. He developed an optional History course, 'British Social and Economic History since 1760', aiming to place working-class history within this broader context and extend the Oxford syllabus beyond its focus on high politics and the ruling elite, breaking down the 'cages' within which he believed academic subjects were confined. In 1950 Cole had him appointed Reader in Recent Social and Economic History. He also taught on the Oxford Diploma in Economics and Political Science, taken mainly by trade unionists studying at Ruskin College, next door to Worcester in Walton Street. Another lasting commitment was enabling working people to extend the education of which they had too often been deprived earlier in life, a fate he was intensely grateful to have avoided. He wanted Oxford to contribute to social reform through educating adults. Hence he was also active again in the WEA, in which Cole was prominent along with other Oxford academics. Briggs became its Deputy-President (1954–8), and President (1958–67).

---

[20] Snowman, 'Asa Briggs'.
[21] Ibid.

For similar reasons, he believed History should be widely accessible, and accessibly written, not confined to narrow academic circles and journals. He was involved from the start with *History Today*, the monthly magazine with similar objectives founded in 1950 by Brendan Bracken, Churchill's close associate and wartime Minister of Information. Briggs published an article about Peel and Cobden in an early issue, becoming the longest-serving member of its Advisory Board and a regular book reviewer. In 1948 he published, with Harry Bancroft and Eric Treacy, *One Hundred Years: the Parish of Keighley, 1848–1948* (Keighley) a homage to his home town, locally published for local readers. He had a major influence on the development of local, non-metropolitan, history and the history of northern England, making it academically respectable as well as locally accessible.

His major opportunity to write accessibly about Victorian society, urban development and locality came when he was commissioned to write an official history of Birmingham. This originated in his admiration for Joseph Chamberlain who, as mayor, transformed Victorian Birmingham. His *History of Birmingham: Borough and City, 1865–1938* (Oxford, 1952) was an early stimulus to the emergence of urban history as a strand of historical scholarship and to reviving appreciation of Victorian culture, architecture and artefacts. In the 1950s 'Victoriana' was still widely disparaged and Victorian buildings destroyed, culminating in the demolition in 1961 of the entrance to London's Euston Station, the Great Arch, constructed in 1837, while the grand building of St Pancras Station nearby was threatened.

Briggs continued his mission to educate the British about the Victorians in 1954 when he published *Victorian People. A Reassessment of Persons and Themes, 1851–67* (London, 1965), describing the period as 'one of the least studied and least understood chapters in English history',[22] a lacuna he steadily filled. He illuminated the period by presenting men who made a distinctive contribution to Victorian politics and culture including 'Samuel Smiles and the Gospel of Work', trade unionist Robert Applegarth, Thomas Hughes for his representation of public schools in *Tom Brown's Schooldays*, Trollope and Disraeli. He was conscious of including no women, many years before Women's Liberation made an issue of this, aware that many women 'reacted against the formality and superficiality of subordinate status' and played important roles in Victorian community life, but that they could not progress further in a

---

[22] Briggs, *Victorian People*, p. 9.

'community devoted to getting on, and limited at its edges by masculine codes of inherited authority'. A rare exception was Florence Nightingale, but she had recently been well represented in Cecil Woodham-Smith's biography which he saw no reason to summarise.[23] The insightful, carefully researched essays stimulated interest and research in the period. The book was written for a wide audience, without academic footnotes but with suggestions for further reading. This offended some academic critics but Briggs was unrepentant, believing footnotes alienated many readers.[24] It remains in print and in twenty-first-century format as an e-book.

Briggs published increasingly prolifically, especially reviews, in the national press as well as in academic journals, always reaching out to wide, non-academic audiences, a pattern he long continued. In 1952, apart from the *History of Birmingham*, he published three academic articles and eighteen book reviews in academic and more popular places; in 1953, one academic article and sixteen reviews and occasional short newspaper articles; in 1954 *Victorian People*, four short articles and twelve reviews. So his output continued, only slowing in the early 2000s, in his eighties.[25] His industry, as ever, was impressive: half an hour before his wedding in 1955, awaiting the bride, he sat in a church ante-room typing a review for the *New Statesman*.[26] Tam Dalyell, former Labour MP, another friend, commented in an obituary 'It is doubtful whether Briggs ever spent a truly idle moment in his life.'[27] In 1954 he also produced a report for UNESCO, *Workers Education for International Understanding: a Study Sponsored by the International Federation of Workers' Educational Associations* (Paris) another product of his commitment to workers' education, the first of several reports on current issues for national and international bodies.

In 1950 his efforts to educate Britain about the Victorians included an article about Sir Robert Peel in what was then the *Manchester Guardian*. He remained a regular contributor and reviewer, as it transformed into the *Guardian*, until 1990. From 1952 he also reviewed regularly for the *New Statesman* until the mid–1960s and for the influential weekly journal on social issues, *New Society*, throughout its life from 1962 to 1988. Until the 1990s he also contributed occasional reviews and short articles to the

---

[23] Ibid., p. 21.
[24] Fraser, *Cities, Class and Communication*, p. 8.
[25] For a thirty-eight-page list of Briggs' publications, see *Bibliography of Works by Asa Briggs*, a web supplement to Taylor, *The Age of Asa*, www.history.ac.uk/makinghistory/historians/briggs. asa.html (accessed 15 June 2017). Despite its length, there are a few omissions.
[26] Smith, 'Asa Briggs', p. 10.
[27] Dalyell, obituary.

Financial Times, Observer, still more occasionally the *New Scientist, Times* and *Listener*. Not always about History: in 1956 he reviewed Anthony Crosland's revisionist *The Future of Socialism* for the *Observer*, finding it too optimistic and parochial.[28] A. J. P. Taylor, also teaching at Oxford at the time, thought him an outstanding lecturer and recommended him to the BBC. He broadcast regularly thereafter. He was certainly a popular lecturer: he wrote later, 'My early morning lectures in Worcester College were overcrowded.'[29]

Among his students at Worcester was Rupert Murdoch, future media magnate, then a member of the Oxford University Labour Club. In 1952 they made a camping tour of the Middle East, with Harry Pitt, another fellow of Worcester, and George Masterman, another Australian undergraduate, in Murdoch's father's car which they collected in Istanbul after visiting Athens. They travelled through Turkey, Syria, Jordan, Arab Jerusalem (they were not allowed into the Israeli section), Lebanon and Egypt, often sleeping in the open, not always welcomed by local people, returning home by ship from Port Said. Briggs and Murdoch kept in irregular touch for the rest of his life: Murdoch attended his seventieth birthday in Oxford and sent a handwritten note on his ninetieth.[30]

Briggs came to love travelling and pursued it as vigorously as his other enthusiasms. He 'believed in learning through travelling',[31] saying in later life 'I've always been a traveller and I want desperately to keep in contact with the non-European world.'[32] He gave 'travelling' as his sole recreation in his *Who's Who* entry from its first appearance in 1956.[33] He visited Gibraltar in 1946, arranged by the Army Education Corps to lecture to British troops, travelled to occupied Germany several times, in 1948 lecturing at the University of Münster, as he did at Oxford, 'on the problems of and opportunities of a "welfare state"', later visiting other German and Belgian cities, then Paris for the first of many times.[34] In 1950 he took a summer holiday in Venice with two more of his Worcester students who, due to war service, were, like Murdoch, only slightly younger than himself. In 1951 he travelled to Africa, to Accra on the initiative of the Director of Extramural Studies at Oxford who arranged for him to write six articles

---

[28] A. Briggs, 'Socialism and society', *Observer*, 30 September 1956.
[29] Briggs, *Special Relationships*, p. 170.
[30] Ibid., pp. 184–7.
[31] Ibid., p. 184.
[32] Smith, 'Asa Briggs', p. 19.
[33] Briggs, *Special Relationships*, p. 163.
[34] Ibid., p. 170.

on the political situation in what would soon be Ghana (then the Gold Coast) for a periodical *West Africa*. He met Kwame Nkrumah, later leader of independent Ghana, who had just won the country's first general election.[35] In 1952 he was invited by the Army Education Corps to visit Malaya, since 1948 in a 'state of emergency', divided by a Communist-led rebellion against British rule. He went with soldiers on night patrols and lectured to them on life in Britain, again meeting future leaders of independent Malaya, then making short visits to Singapore and Hong Kong.[36] He spent 1953–4 at the Institute for Advanced Study at Princeton.

In 1955 he married Susan Banwell, a graduate student in History at St Anne's College, Oxford. They had two sons and two daughters and fourteen grandchildren—Briggs was prolific in all respects—and a long, happy relationship.

Leeds

Also in 1955 he was invited to take the Chair of Modern History at Leeds University. He returned enthusiastically to his home county, to a Victorian City. He was also frustrated by the conservatism of the Oxford History curriculum and the difficulty of changing it. Leeds was not more obviously progressive, but he became, stated an obituary by a former colleague,

> a formative influence ... he oversaw the complete modernization of the curriculum. Under his influence the chronological reach of teaching here was extended from c. 1850 to post-1945; and its geographical reach was dramatically expanded beyond Western Europe to include the USA, Russia and Asia. Other innovations included introducing seminar-based courses, addressing colleagues by their first name (instead of surname alone) and dispensing with wearing academic gowns when teaching...[37]

A former student remembered him as 'always open and approachable and remembered people and their personal details despite being so busy', while conveying enthusiasm for historical research.[38] A later Vice-Chancellor at Leeds, former Conservative Minister Sir Edward Boyle, said

---

[35] Ibid., pp. 176–9.
[36] Ibid., pp. 182–3.
[37] University of Leeds School of History, 'In Memory of Asa Briggs (1921–2016)', 16 March 2016. leeds.ac.uk/arts/news/article/4476/in_memory_of_Asa_Briggs_1921–2016 (accessed 15 June 2017).
[38] Fraser, *Cities, Class and Communication*, p. 4.

that he 'galvanized the department',[39] though at Leeds also change was never easy. The University was reluctant to make new appointments and a senior colleague expressed doubts about the viability of recent history: 'we know where we are with a book on the seventeenth century [but] the criteria of work on history that is almost contemporary have not yet been established',[40] not an uncommon reaction among conventional historians. Briggs introduced courses on modern Russia, USA and Asia by teaching them himself, often barely ahead of the students in his reading.[41] He expanded postgraduate research and tried, with limited success, to develop collaboration in teaching and research with other departments.

At Leeds he also continued to build labour history. One colleague in History, Donald Read, worked on early nineteenth-century radicalism and Chartism and members of the Economics department studied the past and present of industrial relations. Leeds had a very active extra-mural department which promoted labour history while it declined elsewhere. Through involvement in the local WEA, Briggs made contact with colleagues there including E. P. Thompson and J. F. C. Harrison, a Cambridge contemporary of Briggs, another scholarship boy, both future respected historians. With Briggs they formed the core of a Leeds Labour History Group, united by the desire to stimulate 'history from below' and its inclusion in scholarly history. Academic interest in labour history grew in the second half of the 1950s against a background of growing Labour Party membership, despite its divisions and electoral failures, the crisis in the Communist Party over Hungary and Khrushchev's denunciation of Stalin in 1956, the formation of the Campaign for Nuclear Disarmament in 1958, and the growth of social criticism and protest in Britain and elsewhere. As Labour historian John McIlroy has commented, the growing numbers of labour historians were 'disparate, sometimes antagonistic, undeniably disputatious',[42] perhaps due to this divisive context. One area of expansion since the war had been the Communist Party History Group (CPHG), founded in 1946, involving historians of future distinction including Christopher Hill, E. J. Hobsbawm, E. P. and Dorothy Thompson. It dissolved in 1956 when the Thompsons and others left the party, while Hobsbawm, among others, did not. Despite his belief that the economy had a major influence on social and political change, Briggs was never a

[39] Dalyell, obituary.
[40] M. Chase, 'Back to Yorkshire: "Asia" Briggs at Leeds, 1955–1961', in Taylor, *The Age of Asa*, p. 220.
[41] Ibid., p. 217.
[42] McIlroy, 'Emergence of Labour History', 226.

Marxist. Indeed he criticised the CPHG for sometimes over-simplifying and taking the narrow view of history he resisted in all its forms, in particular focusing on the working-classes disconnected from the wider context in which they lived and worked. This was evident in his review of a collection of their essays, *Democracy and the Labour Movement* (London, 1954), edited by John Saville, then lecturer in economic history at Hull University.[43] In 1952 E. P. Thompson, Hobsbawm and Hill were among the founders, with some non-Marxists, of the academic journal *Past and Present*, committed to challenging conventional approaches to History. Briggs thought its approach still too narrow, though he always supported it. He issued a challenge in an early issue, with an article 'Middle-class consciousness in English politics, 1780–1846',[44] a solitary complement to the burgeoning studies of working-class consciousness in the period, exploring influential strands of middle-class thinking, progressive and otherwise, which he felt were neglected or caricatured in Marxist analyses of class relations in the period, pointing out that 'the story of Chartism is an important episode in the story of middle-class as well as working-class consciousness'.[45] He stressed what divided as well as what held together the middle classes, believing that another weakness of Marxist analysis was prioritising class unity. Characteristically, he did not launch a polemical assault upon those with whom he disagreed. At the time intense conflicts were all too common, notably that raging through the later 1950s and early 1960s between historians of the left, including Hobsbawm, who argued that industrialisation caused deterioration in British living standards, and those, including R. M. Hartwell in Oxford, who discerned improvement.[46] Briggs resisted such tensions at this and other times and sought co-operation where possible.

He increasingly appreciated the work of Hobsbawm and Thompson as it developed, and they his. His openness and tolerance of different perspectives helped him build cooperation and collaboration to build a multi-faceted labour history. This was promoted though his editorship of *Chartist Studies* (London, 1959) which drew together historians of different political views (though Edward Thompson delivered his contribution too late and too long) to examine Chartism in previously unexplored

---

[43] A. Briggs, 'Marxists', *Manchester Guardian*, 22 February 1955.
[44] A. Briggs, 'Middle-class consciousness in English politics, 1780–1846', *Past and Present*, 9 (April 1956), 65–74.
[45] Ibid., 71.
[46] E. J. Hobsbawm, 'The standard of living debate: a postscript', in E. J. Hobsbawm (ed.), *Labouring Men* (London, 1964), pp. 120–5.

areas of Great Britain, stimulating further research. Hobsbawm praised it as 'The most important contribution to the study of this remarkable movement made in the past forty years.'[47] Next he co-edited *Essays in Labour History* (London, 1960) with John Saville. This was prepared as a festschrift for G. D. H. Cole, but became a memorial when he died in 1959. It represented the current, expanding, state of labour history, especially of the nineteenth century, from different perspectives, with more Marxist contributors than to *Chartist Studies*, aimed at non-academic as well as academic audiences. Both books were widely reviewed in the national press as well as in academic journals and had wide sales; *Chartist Studies* went through twelve editions between 1954 and 1973.[48]

Contributors to the volumes and their associates in Leeds and elsewhere, including former members of the CPHG, created the Society for the Study of Labour History (SSLH), launched at a conference in London in 1960, initiated by the Leeds group, with Briggs as its first chair. Unusually for an academic conference this was reported in the *Guardian*, as it now was.[49] Briggs was crucial to the society's foundation and success,

> in a situation where there were differences and quarrels about historiography and politics, he was a unifying figure. A bridge between Marxists and non-Marxists, the extra-mural fringe and the internal academy, social history and institutional approaches, he proved indispensable to the Society's success.[50]

SSLH flourished, recruiting amateur and professional historians, and still continues. At Leeds he not only connected with Labour historically, he was good friends with Hugh Gaitskell, Labour Party leader from 1955 until his sudden death in 1963, MP for Leeds South, a former academic at University College London. They met in Oxford when Gaitskell's stepson was a student at Worcester. In Leeds Briggs found that 'Gaitskell took a great interest in me and made me several offers of public jobs' (which he appears to have refused), though 'I preferred Bevan (leader of the left-wing Labour faction opposed to Gaitskell) to him'.[51]

He also lectured to servicemen at Catterick Camp on industrial history and technical development and on courses for National Health Service administrators.[52] Pursuing his commitment to local history, in 1956 he organised an interdisciplinary group at Leeds to study 'problems of North

---

[47] Review in *New Statesman*, 31 October 1959, 594–5.
[48] McIlroy 'Emergence of Labour History', 228, n. 73.
[49] *Guardian*, 28 May 1960, 'Professor Briggs Chairman of Labour Society'.
[50] McIlroy, 'Emergence of Labour History', 229.
[51] Briggs, *Special Relationships*, 133.
[52] Chase, 'Back to Yorkshire', p. 213.

of England history' which led in 1966 to the launch of the journal *Northern History*, the first regional history journal. He was an editorial adviser from its inception until his death.[53] He chaired the Standing Conference for the Study of Local History (1969–76), and the British Association for Local History (1984–6). His broad conception of History emerged also in 1956 with another commissioned, centenary, history, of Liverpool-based Lewis's department store, exploring a business enterprise established in Victorian times to provide for working- as well as middle-class people.[54]

Then he was commissioned in 1957 by the BBC to write its history. He had no idea how long it would take (almost forty years), but was eager to start while many of its veterans were still alive, especially the first Director-General, John Reith, a difficult man who was resistant until Briggs, characteristically, won his friendship and complete co-operation.[55] The first volume of five, covering 1922–7, appeared in 1961,[56] the last in 1995.[57] He had research assistance for the massive project. The volumes have been criticised by historians as too factual and pedestrian—his writing was always stronger on factual details than analysis and debate—but they did much to stimulate the emergence of media history, which hardly existed when he started, and media historians have been more enthusiastic. Jean Seaton, who succeeded him as historian of the BBC, described his work as

> part of a very significant and necessary retelling of the narrative of the BBC back to the people charged to carry it forward…[which]…established the nature of the institution and the importance of the key values…[of]…impartial, public service broadcasting … all set in the larger framework of social history.[58]

Valuably for future researchers, he persuaded the BBC to establish an archive at Caversham near Reading and from 1976 chaired the committee which developed and oversaw the collection.[59]

Briggs further affirmed his broad approach to history and extended knowledge and understanding of the nineteenth century by publishing *The Age of Improvement, 1783–1867* (London, 1959) which went further

---

[53] Ibid., p. 215; Editors, 'Asa Briggs and *Northern History*', *Northern History*, 53 (2016), 157–60.
[54] A. Briggs, *Friends of the People: the Centenary History of Lewis's* (London, 1956).
[55] Briggs, *Special Relationships*, p. 96.
[56] A. Briggs, *The History of Broadcasting in the United Kingdom*, vol. 1: *The Birth of Broadcasting* (Oxford, 1961).
[57] A. Briggs, *The History of Broadcasting in the United Kingdom*, vol. 5: *Competition* (Oxford, 1995).
[58] J. Seaton, 'Asa and the epochs: the BBC, the historian, the institution and the archive', in Taylor, *The Age of Asa*, p. 186.
[59] Briggs, *Special Relationships*, pp. 94–9.

than previous work in integrating economic, social, political and labour history, the title expressing his belief that British industrialisation brought progress. It was widely praised and read. By 2000 it had gone through eighty-four editions around the world. From 1959 to 1967 he was also a member of the University Grants Committee, which advised the government on the distribution of funding to British universities, from which he learned much about universities.

He still travelled, undertaking lecture tours and conferences for the British Council in India and Ceylon in 1957 and in Poland in 1959. In 1960 he spent six months as Visiting Professor at the Australian National University, Canberra. He studied Sydney and Melbourne as Victorian cities, building up to a chapter in his book, *Victorian Cities* (London, 1963).[60] He made contacts in the Australian WEA and influenced the formation of the Australian Labour History Society, modelled on SSLH and long successful.[61] Also in the early 1960s he paid the first of several visits to China, during Mao Tse Tung's Cultural Revolution, of which he was enthusiastically uncritical, probably protected from its worst features. It was also an opportunity to amass a collection of Chinese ceramics of which he was proud. He later accepted that Mao had 'probably' been a monster.[62]

In 1961 he published an assessment of the work of the influential, Yorkshire-born and based poverty researcher and social reformer Seebohm Rowntree.[63] This was requested by the Rowntree Trust, supported by the Rowntree family. Briggs refused to write a full biography, preferring to focus on the work, including Rowntree's highly successful business life, which Briggs found instructive. The study informed Briggs' writings on the history of the welfare state.[64]

---

[60] 'Melbourne, a Victorian community overseas', in A. Briggs, *Victorian Cities* (Harmondsworth, 1968), pp. 277–310.
[61] F. Bongiorno, 'Australian Labour History: contexts, trends and influences', *Labour History* (Australia), 100 (2011), 1–15; F. Bongiorno 'Asa Briggs and the remaking of Australian historiography', in Taylor (ed.), *Age of Asa*, pp. 90–107.
[62] Jones, obituary.
[63] Asa Briggs, *Social Thought and Social Action: a Study of the Work of Seebohm Rowntree, 1871–1954* (London, 1961).
[64] Briggs, *Special Relationships*, pp. 134–5; initially, A. Briggs, 'The welfare state in historical perspective', *Archives Européennes de Sociologie*, 2 (1961), 221–58. For further contributions see Taylor, *Bibliography of Works*.

Sussex

Also in 1961 Briggs moved to the new University of Sussex as it prepared to open. Sussex was one of eight new universities opened between 1961 and 1967. Government-funded university expansion was recommended by the 1963 Robbins Report on Higher Education, on the grounds that, with only 4 per cent of eighteen–nineteen-year-olds entering university, Britain was lagging behind international competitors, harming the economy. The Conservative government which established the committee and Harold Wilson's Labour government which succeeded it in 1964 accepted the recommendation. A local university had long been an aspiration in Brighton and by 1961 sufficient endowments had accumulated to enable its opening before Robbins reported. As a member of the UGC, Briggs was well aware of these developments. In the late 1950s, as planning for the new university was under way, he was approached by Lord (John) Fulton, designated Vice-Chancellor, to join Sussex as a pro-Vice-Chancellor and Professor of History. Fulton wanted to create a university that was 'new' in all respects and sought a distinguished scholar to lead academic development who was willing to explore new approaches. It was the opportunity Briggs wanted. In 1961, before starting at Sussex, with the UGC he visited York, where another new university was planned. He was invited to become York's Vice-Chancellor, but he had accepted Sussex and it was too late to agree to stay in his home county.

At Sussex he took charge of academic affairs, constructing what was for Britain an innovative system of teaching and learning. He and his family lived on the site on the downs near Brighton as the university was built and, with colleagues, he was responsible also for planning its construction. It was an opportunity to dismantle academic boundaries and establish interdisciplinarity, 'drawing a new map of learning', as he put it, enthusiastically supported by the university's founders.[65] Staff and students were placed in interdisciplinary Schools rather than departments. Students majored in their 'core' subject, while spending half their time studying other disciplines within their School. Briggs became Dean of the School of Social Studies and in the early years taught Sociology, which he had studied at LSE, as well as History. The method of teaching he introduced, again unusually, gave more prominence to seminars, Oxbridge-style tutorials and essays than lectures. He introduced innovative uses of

---

[65] A. Briggs, 'Drawing a new map of learning', in D. Daiches (ed.), *The Idea of a New University: an Experiment in Sussex* (London, 1964), pp. 60–80

technology into teaching, language labs, closed-circuit TV for classroom observation and teacher training, to record and play back lectures and display teaching materials.[66] True to his long-term interest in the natural sciences he encouraged their development at Sussex, including in 1966 establishing the Science Policy Research Unit (SPRU) for interdisciplinary research 'to contribute... to the advancement of knowledge of the highly complex social process of research, invention, development, innovation and the diffusion of innovation and thereby to a deeper understanding of policy for science and technology'.[67]

He also encouraged the formation of the interdisciplinary Institute for Development Studies which became highly influential in an emerging field to which he was deeply committed and long remained involved with it. He remained a member of the UGC, requiring often time-consuming committees and visits to universities, but in 1967 when he became Vice-Chancellor of Sussex was required to resign. He coped with a still-massive workload through skilled delegation, but even he recognised limits. He gradually withdrew from active involvement in SSLH, stepping down as chair in 1964, becoming its first President until 1970. He was Vice-Chancellor until 1976, through the period of student revolt. That this was calmer at Sussex than at, particularly, Essex and LSE was attributed to Briggs' handling. Characteristically, he listened to students and tried to work closely with them as individuals, including during demonstrations. He told Tam Dalyell he owed his skill at dealing with them to his study of Chartism.[68] He hoped that the creation of new universities including Sussex would widen the narrow social access to UK universities, democratising higher education. There was high demand for places at Sussex, but it attracted a higher proportion of students from independent schools than other universities outside Oxbridge, partly because it became an attractive symbol of the 'swinging sixties', promoted by media images of fashionable female students. It did attract more women than the 10 per cent at Cambridge, 15 per cent at Oxford and 25 per cent average of other UK universities: 50 per cent in 1962, though the percentage fell as the sciences expanded, by 1966–7 to 36.4, marginally above Warwick and Lancaster and below the other new universities.[69]

---

[66] D. Weinbren, 'Asa Briggs and new maps of learning', *Open Learn* (Buckingham: Open University) www.open.edu/openlearn (accessed 15 June 2017).
[67] A. Briggs, *Loose Ends and Extras* (Barnsley, 2014), p. 75.
[68] Dalyell, obituary.
[69] C. Dyhouse, *Students: a Gendered History* (London, 2006), p. 102.

As Vice-Chancellor, Briggs brought the Mass Observation archive to Sussex. This exceptional social research organisation, founded in 1937, from 1949 became a market research institution. One of its founders, anthropologist Tom Harrisson, took control of its pre-1949 material but never had time to sort or catalogue it and it languished at his home until his friend Briggs suggested in 1967 he bring it to Sussex, where he became a professor. It was gradually catalogued and opened to researchers and took on a new life researching attitudes to contemporary issues.[70] Briggs also brought to Sussex other invaluable archives including those of Virginia Woolf, whose country home at Charleston was not far away, and Rudyard Kipling, once a resident of nearby Rottingdean. He also worked to establish the Gardner Arts Centre which opened on the campus in 1968, providing a venue for touring theatre companies, music, exhibitions and other activities. He believed it was essential for students to have contact with the arts.

Briggs admired Harold Wilson, Prime Minister from 1964 to 1970. An achievement of this government was the foundation of the Open University (OU), an idea floated by Wilson to the Labour Party conference in 1963, then handed to Jennie Lee, Minister for the Arts from 1964, to make reality. Briggs, in his own words, 'became one of the most active members of an energetic organizing committee set up in 1967'.[71] Originally called the University of the Air, it was intended significantly to widen access to university-level education by enabling part-time students to learn from lectures on TV, supplemented by printed materials, local seminars and telephone calls with tutors plus intensive summer schools. It appealed to Briggs' enthusiasm for wide access, technology and new approaches to lifelong learning but attracted criticism from more conventional academics, civil servants and others for potentially debasing higher education. He 'was delighted to be given the vitally important task of chairing the curriculum sub-committee' for the Open University as it was now called. It opened in 1970. Briggs gave a TV lecture course in its early days, 'Leeds. A study in civic pride', using film and music to supplement the words, as encouraged by the OU.[72] At his death, the OU created an Asa Briggs Chair of History and PhD studentship to commemorate his contribution. Furthering adult education, at Sussex he organised day release courses for

---

[70] T. Jeffery, *Mass Observation: a Short History* (Mass Observation Occasional Paper No. 10, University of Sussex Library, 1999).
[71] Briggs, *Special Relationships*, p. 125.
[72] Weinbren, 'New maps'; D. Weinbren, 'Asa Briggs and the opening up of the Open University', in Taylor (ed.), *The Age of Asa*, pp. 248–66.

shop stewards, weekend schools for GPs and seminars for magistrates' clerks. He established public lectures, giving the first himself on the 1870 Education Act.[73]

In 1969 he was invited by Richard Crossman, Secretary of State for Health, to chair a committee on the nursing profession. He refused a request by Harold Wilson in 1967 to chair a Commission on Prices and Incomes, because, thought Tam Dalyell, 'being asked to please Barbara Castle on the one hand and Frank Cousins on the other was mission impossible'.[74] The future of nursing was less politically explosive and in 1972 the committee recommended improved pay and conditions and overhaul of the currently rather disorganised and regionally disparate nurse training. Briggs saw this as one more facet of adult education and recommended it should be directed by a central body, outside NHS institutions, where the students would be 'in true learning situation and not just junior employees in the nursing service'.[75] Edward Heath's Conservative government was now in power and little happened until another Labour government introduced the Nurses, Midwives and Health Visitors Act, 1979, which established a Central Council responsible for regulating nurse training and maintaining standards, leading among other changes to degree-level training for nurses.

Alongside his university and public roles Briggs continued to research and publish. Research on the history of the BBC continued, with assistants generally experienced at working in the BBC contributing valuably to the work;[76] the second volume appeared in 1965,[77] the third in 1970.[78] In 1975 he was awarded the Marconi Medal by the Aspen Institute in Colorado for his work on the history of communications, with a financial prize that enabled him to fund further assistance. This work too won the opprobrium of more conventional historians who thought it a waste of his time and talents. Briggs 'was and am sure that they were wrong. It is impossible to understand the political, social and cultural history of the United Kingdom, or indeed of any country, without examining the

---

[73] Smith, 'Asa Briggs', p. 17.
[74] Dalyell, obituary.
[75] Smith, p. 17.
[76] Briggs, *Special Relationships*, pp. 101–5.
[77] A. Briggs, *The History of Broadcasting in the United Kingdom*, vol. 2: *The Golden Age of Wireless* (Oxford, 1965).
[78] A. Briggs, *The History of Broadcasting in the United Kingdom*, vol. 3: *The War of Words* (Oxford, 1970).

evolution and influence of what has come to be called its media system, with newspapers long preceding broadcasting.'[79]

In 1962 he edited a collection of William Morris's writings and designs for Penguin and *They Saw it Happen: an Anthology of Eyewitness Accounts of Events in British History, 1897–1940* (Oxford).[80] Most importantly in 1963 *Victorian Cities* appeared, probably his most effective and influential promotion of the culture, architecture and achievements of the Victorians, highly regarded by academics and accessible to a wider audience. He assisted a revival of appreciation of Victorian culture. St Pancras Station was saved following a campaign led by John Betjeman, strongly supported by Briggs. Wilson's government ended several decades of demolition of Victorian 'slums' and replacement by high-rise flats by subsidising owner-occupiers and councils to renovate what were increasingly recognised as durable and attractive homes.

Shorter books, pamphlets, articles and reviews in academic journals and the national press continued to pour forth, including in 1972 the only book co-edited with his wife.[81] It was said that he regularly wrote a review on the train from Brighton to London, then worked on the BBC history between a committee and dinner and reviewed another book on the way home.[82] And he kept travelling abroad. In 1966 and 1972 he was Visiting Professor at the University of Chicago, 'which I regarded as my second university', where he was regarded as a sociologist as much as a historian and was much influenced by ongoing work in urban sociology.[83] He travelled to conferences in Cyprus, Mexico, Yugoslavia, the USA and elsewhere.[84] In 1970 he refused to become rector of the international postgraduate college of the European Community (as it then was), the European University Institute in Florence, then being planned to promote European cultural exchange, which opened in 1976.[85]

---

[79] Briggs, *Special Relationships*, p. 103.
[80] A. Briggs (ed.), *William Morris: Selected Writings and Designs* (London, 1962).
[81] A. Briggs and S. Briggs (eds.), *Cap and Bell: Punch's Chronicle of English History in the Making, 1841–61* (London, 1972).
[82] Smith, 'Asa Briggs', p. 14.
[83] Briggs, *Special Relationships*, p. 12.
[84] Ibid., p. 103.
[85] Taylor, *The Age of Asa*, p. 12.

Return to Oxford

In 1976 he left Sussex and returned to Worcester, as Provost, until retirement in 1991. He told Sussex he would leave in 1976 when he had completed ten years as Vice-Chancellor. He was proud of Sussex but by 1975 felt 'I had become very institutionalized and I thought that was intolerable ... Nobody thought I'd go.'[86] He had no plans for the future and was surprised to receive an invitation from Worcester. He said later, 'I never expected to come back ... I've never regretted coming back; but I like to know what is going on at Sussex.'[87]

Also in 1976 he was appointed a life peer: Baron Briggs of Lewes, East Sussex, where he lived. He refused the Labour whip and always sat on the cross-benches. He told James Callaghan, who had just succeeded Wilson as Labour Prime Minister, that he would not have time to attend the Lords very often,[88] and it was not prominent in his busy life. He remained deeply interested in politics but did not make his maiden speech until 1979, on the Bill finally implementing his 1972 proposals on the nursing profession.[89] He spoke just ten more times before his death.[90]

He wanted, again, to reform Oxford and break down disciplinary barriers but found it as conservative as before. He wrote later:

> while I was happy to be back in a college that I loved, I often felt more frustrated once there than I had ever been at Sussex. The Fellows of the College had changed far less than I had...I was never asked by any Fellow...what my Sussex years had been like except for how I had dealt with radical students...there were too many college committees and not enough of a sense of individual initiative.[91]

But if he could not transform the formal academic structures he could achieve change by other means: Oxford historian, Jose Harris, later praised 'Asa Briggs, who for many years fostered conviviality and argument among Oxford historians of modern Britain. With Asa's retirement conviviality declined, but the legacy of argument fortunately remains.'[92] He played little part in university politics, throwing himself into the life of his college, where he could wield some influence, saying 'I'm not a

---

[86] Smith, 'Asa Briggs', p. 18.
[87] Ibid.
[88] Lay, 'Asa Briggs: a very open intelligence'.
[89] *Hansard*, House of Lords Debates, 19 February, 1979, vol. 398, cols 1660–4.
[90] Taylor, *The Age of Asa*, p. 15, n. 15.
[91] Briggs, *Loose Ends and Extras*, p. 57.
[92] J. Harris (ed.), *Civil Society in British History* (Oxford, 2003), p. i.

university politician, I'm a very collegey person.'[93] As at Sussex, he worked hard to develop the natural and applied sciences in a college which had very few scientists in the 1950s. Fellowships in science and engineering increased. In 1978 Worcester became co-educational along with other colleges, following the Sex Discrimination Act, 1975. He had no obligation to teach but supervised research students. He worked particularly hard and successfully at fundraising, since Worcester was not a rich college by Oxford standards. And he believed 'a college should be a place where people enjoy their three or four years';[94] sociable as ever, he and his wife opened the Provost's Lodgings to entertain undergraduates and others.

He carried on broadcasting and writing, pouring out reviews and articles for academic and national publications as tirelessly as ever, and books individually and co-written, individually and co-edited. Those that made the greatest impact were the fourth volume of the History of the BBC, published in 1979,[95] and the third of his Victorian Trilogy, *Victorian Things* (London, 1988 and 1990). He later called this his favourite book, but it was criticised by some academics as just a list of nineteenth century bric-à-brac with little analysis, 'an idiosyncratic and apparently unorderly selection of interesting facts and anecdotes [which] perhaps indicated too clearly the limitations of Briggs' historical method'.[96] Victorian objects were now much more widely appreciated and less in need of promotion, and many younger academics in particular were impatient with Briggs' empiricism, but the book has also been hailed as sparking historians' interest in material culture and consumption.[97] In 1977 he and John Saville co-edited another volume of *Essays in Labour History, 1918–39* (London). Later, *A Social History of England* (London, 1983 and 1985) ranged 'from the Stone Age to Mrs Thatcher' in 340 pages. It aimed to popularise the interest in social history which was now highly developed among historians by describing as many facets as possible of everyday life. The Social History Society had been successfully launched in 1976 by Harold Perkin, Professor of Social History at Lancaster, and Briggs was its President from the beginning until his death.[98] The book probably had a wider

---

[93] Smith, 'Asa Briggs', p. 19.
[94] Ibid., p. 21.
[95] A. Briggs, *The History of Broadcasting in UK*, vol. 4: *Sound and Vision* (Oxford, 1979).
[96] M. Hewitt 'Asa Briggs 1921–', in K. Boyd (ed.), *Encyclopaedia of Historians and Historical Writing*, vol. 1: *A–L* (London and Chicago, IL, 1999) p. 125.
[97] R. McWilliam 'Asa Briggs (1921–2016)', British Association for Victorian Studies Obituary. www.bavs.ac.uk/uploads/media/Asa_Briggs_tribute.pdf (accessed 15 June 2017).
[98] When I was honoured to succeed him.

popular than academic impact. In 1983 he delivered a TV series *The Karl Marx Legacy* on another figure in Victorian history, published with John Dekker and John Mair as *Marx in London: an Illustrated Guide* (London, 1983).

He wrote more commissioned histories: *Marks and Spencer, 1884–1984: a Centenary History of Marks and Spencer: the Originators of Penny Bazaars* (London, 1984), followed by the history of Victoria Wine.[99] Also in 1984 he published a, less handsomely-funded, centenary history of a different institution, *Toynbee Hall: the First Hundred Years* (with Anne Macartney, London), celebrating the centenary of the first settlement house and its ongoing struggle against the persisting, shifting social problems of East London and elsewhere, extending his long-term interest in the history of social welfare. In the same year he edited another collection of the writings and designs of William Morris;[100] he was an early member, then President, of the William Morris Society (1978–91). In 1991 came a commissioned history of the Leverhulme Trust, established in 1925 with the legacy and at the behest of another Victorian entrepreneur, William Lever.[101] Briggs remained fascinated by institutions created by Victorians and their subsequent development.

Of course he was tirelessly active outside Oxford, causing, as at Leeds and Sussex, some resentment among colleagues, though there is no sign of his neglecting college duties. Some activities were more time-consuming than others. He and his wife loved music and he was, from 1966 to 1991, a trustee of Glyndebourne, also of the Brighton Pavilion (1975–2008), a Governor of the British Film Institute (1970–7), Vice-Chair of the UN University in Tokyo (1974–80), requiring visits to Japan, and Trustee of the London-based charity, the International Broadcasting Institute (1968–87), which fostered broadcasting as an educational medium. He chaired the Paris-based Council of the European Institute for Education (1975–90) and was active in the politics of European higher education. In 1975 he chaired the Educational Panel of European Architectural Heritage Year, then persuaded the Department of the Environment to continue its mission. He chaired the resulting Heritage Education Group (1976–86), bringing him into close contact with schools, architects and planners. He also chaired the Civic Trust (1976–86).

---

[99] A. Briggs, *Wine for Sale: Victoria Wine and the Liquor Trade, 1860–1984* (London, 1985).
[100] Briggs, *William Morris*.
[101] A. Briggs, *The Story of the Leverhulme Trust: for Purposes of Research and Education* (London, 1991).

While Provost he took on yet more external roles. In 1987 the Commonwealth Heads of Government established an expert group to encourage the development and sharing of open learning and distance education practice, resources and technologies across Commonwealth countries, to extend high quality education to remote regions and people with limited or no face-to-face learning opportunities. Briggs was a member of the group which published a report in 1987,[102] leading to the establishment in 1989 of the Vancouver-based Commonwealth of Learning, which is still active, and the creation of distance learning operations in all member countries. It matched Briggs' commitment to adult education and belief that education is vital for economic development. He was active in the organisation until 1993, requiring more travels. He became a Fellow of the British Academy in 1980,[103] President of the Victorian Society in 1983, of the Ephemera Society in 1984, the Brontë Society, 1989–96, from 1986 Vice-President of the Historical Association, which gave him a Lifetime Achievement award in 2010, followed by the Archives and Records Association in 2012. He joined the Advisory Board for Redundant Churches (1983–9). In 1987, with Paul Thompson of Essex University, who for over a decade had led the development of oral history as a method of historical investigation especially of the lives of working people, he established the National Life Stories Collection at the British Library. It aimed 'to record first-hand experiences of as wide a cross-section of present-day society as possible', as it continues invaluably to do, including fifteen hours of Briggs himself interviewed by Thompson.[104] In 1991 he gave the Ford lectures on 'Culture and Communication in Victorian England'. They were much praised but never published, perhaps because he had too many other commitments despite the fact that he formally retired from Worcester in 1991, aged seventy.

---

[102] *Towards a Commonwealth of Learning: a Proposal to Create the University of the Commonwealth for Cooperation in Distance Education.* Report of the Expert Group on Commonwealth Cooperation in Distance Education and Open Learning (London, Commonwealth Secretariat, 1987).

[103] At age 59 he was somewhat older at his election than his contemporaries, who were elected, on average, at age 55 in 1980.

[104] www.bl.uk/projects/national-life-stories (accessed 15 June 2017).

Lewes

He returned to live in Lewes. He did not retire from historical and other work, saying from the outset 'I shall travel and go on teaching and examining and writing. I shall be glad to be free of committees and free of the business of raising money. But we want to remain in a community where there are 18 to 21-year-olds. With them every year is a new year; you never get entirely old.'[105] He carried on many of his national and international roles, as we have seen, travelled for pleasure with his wife and continued to pour out his accustomed range of writings. He said around this time 'A day without writing is for me an inadequate day'; his writing day began at 6 am.[106] In 1991 he published the history of the Leverhulme Trust and his third volume of collected essays, following volumes 1 and 2 in 1985.[107] In 1994 he published another commissioned history, of a premier French wine-producing dynasty *Haut-Brion: an Illustrious Lineage* (London, 1994): he always loved good wine. In 1995 Volume 5 of his history of broadcasting appeared.[108] This became the final volume, not by his choice and much to his regret. John Birt, Director-General of the BBC, was under government pressure to make drastic cuts, and the History was one of the victims,[109] though after his death the BBC organised a memorial service and commissioned Tristram Hunt to make a commemorative radio programme.[110] In 1995 also he published *The Channel Islands: Occupation and Liberation, 1940–45* (London). In 1996 he co-edited with broadcaster Daniel Snowman *Fins de Siècle: How Centuries End, 1400–2000* (London), in which historians discussed experiences and attitudes at the end of each century since the fourteenth, as the millennium approached. In 1997 he produced with Patricia Clavin, then a lecturer at Keele, the successful survey *Modern Europe, 1979–1989* (London), and edited the collected works of his lifetime hero Samuel Smiles (London). In 1998 *Chartism* (Stroud), a popular 128-page summary, was less well received by specialists. In 2000 came *Go For It: Working for Victory on the Home Front* (London), commissioned by the Imperial War Museum to accompany a

---

[105] Smith, 'Asa Briggs', p. 21.
[106] Ibid., p. 20.
[107] A. Briggs, *The Collected Essays of Asa Briggs*, vol. 1: *Words, Numbers Places, People* (Brighton, 1985); vol. 2: *Images, Problems, Standpoints, Forecasts* (Brighton, 1985); vol. 3: *Serious Pursuits: Communications and Education* (London, 1991).
[108] Briggs, *The History of Broadcasting in the United Kingdom*, vol. 5: *Competition*.
[109] Seaton, 'Asa and the Epochs', pp. 203–4.
[110] Hunt, 'Asa Briggs: the last Victorian improver'.

major exhibition on the theme and the unveiling of a war memorial in Coventry Cathedral. In 2001 came a biography of *Michael Young: Social Entrepreneur* (London), a biography of a friend whose energy, including in promoting adult education and citizen rights, equalled his own, including creating the Consumers' Association, the National Extension College and the University of the Third Age. In the same year *A Social History of the Media: from Gutenberg to the Internet* (Oxford), co-written with Peter Burke, a former historian colleague at Sussex now at Cambridge, aimed, successfully, 'to show the relevance of the past to the present by bringing history into media studies and the media into history'.[111] It was an innovative, influential text which went through several editions, translated into Arabic, Chinese, Italian, Polish, Portuguese, Romanian, Spanish and Turkish.[112]

Briggs' output slowed a little in his eighties, until in 2005 came the commissioned *History of the Royal College of Physicians of London*, vol. 4: *1948–83* (Oxford) exploring the impact of the National Health Service, which won him an Honorary Fellowship of the Royal College. In 2008, a last commissioned work was another product of his interest in the history of successful businesses with Victorian roots, *A History of Longman and Their Books, 1724–1990: Longevity in Publishing* (London), on which he had worked, intermittently, from the early 1970s when Longmans first approached him. In 1992 he gave the Ellen McArthur lectures at Cambridge, 'Commerce and Culture: the Publishing Business in Britain', which focussed on Longman's history, including its extensive early involvement in colonial and foreign markets. He was strongly interested in books as media of communication, past and present, and at Worcester (1983–91) organised influential, convivial, interdisciplinary seminars on the history of the book, which helped establish it as a field of study and supported the publication of many books in the field including Briggs' own.[113] It also led to the establishment of the Archive of British Publishing and Printing at Reading University, the main UK archive for the records of publishing firms.[114] The Longmans book was regarded as a 'significant contribution to publishing history',[115] 'an astute and attractive history'.[116]

---

[111] 2nd edition (Cambridge), 2005, p. viii.
[112] Taylor, *The Age of Asa*, p. 36.
[113] J. Raven, 'From Worcester to Longman: devising the history of the book', in Taylor, *The Age of Asa*, pp. 267–78.
[114] Ibid., p. 271.
[115] Ibid., p. 267.
[116] Ibid., p. 279.

He published three more books before his death, all memoirs, and very little else: *Secret Days* in 2011 at last revealed details of his wartime work. Although knowledge of Bletchley code-breaking had been public since the 1970s, he believed 'there are still some secrets left' and many misconceptions requiring correction.[117] *Special Relationships: People and Places* (Barnsley, 2012) and *Loose Ends and Extras* (Barnsley, 2014) both ranged widely over his friendships, contacts and activities. They were unconventionally, informally, written, published in Yorkshire by the relatively obscure Frontline Books of Barnsley and not widely noticed. But even death did not halt the output: a final publication came in April 2016. He had written, but not published, poetry since the age of 13 and *The Complete Poems of Asa Briggs: Far Beyond the Pennine Way* (Brighton, 2016) contained one hundred poems, with an introduction discussing his ideas about poetry and how and why he had written it over the years. He had always been interested in the relationship between literature, history and society. To the end (he died on 15 March 2016), his range of interests and energy in pursuing them never ceased to surprise and impress.

He was survived by his wife, children and grandchildren as well as his massive output of publications.

PAT THANE
Fellow of the Academy

---

[117] Briggs, *Secret Days*, pp. 1–2.